Labor Imperfectus

Trends in Classics – Supplementary Volumes

Edited by
Franco Montanari and Antonios Rengakos

Associate Editors
Stavros Frangoulidis · Fausto Montana · Lara Pagani
Serena Perrone · Evina Sistakou · Christos Tsagalis

Scientific Committee
Alberto Bernabé · Margarethe Billerbeck
Claude Calame · Kathleen Coleman · Jonas Grethlein
Philip R. Hardie · Stephen J. Harrison · Stephen Hinds
Richard Hunter · Giuseppe Mastromarco
Gregory Nagy · Theodore D. Papanghelis
Giusto Picone · Alessandro Schiesaro
Tim Whitmarsh · Bernhard Zimmermann

Volume 157

Labor Imperfectus

Unfinished, Incomplete, Partial Texts
in Classical Antiquity

Edited by
Jacqueline Fabre-Serris, Marco Formisano
and Stavros Frangoulidis

DE GRUYTER

ISBN 978-3-11-221554-8
e-ISBN (PDF) 978-3-11-134094-4
e-ISBN (EPUB) 978-3-11-134101-9
ISSN 1868-4785

Library of Congress Control Number: 2023946886

Bibliographic information published by the Deutsche Nationalbibliothek
The Deutsche Nationalbibliothek lists this publication in the Deutsche Nationalbibliografie; detailed bibliographic data are available on the internet at http://dnb.dnb.de.

© 2025 Walter de Gruyter GmbH, Berlin/Boston
This volume is text- and page-identical with the hardback published in 2024.
Editorial Office: Alessia Ferreccio and Katerina Zianna
Logo: Christopher Schneider, Laufen
Printing and binding: CPI books GmbH, Leck

www.degruyter.com

Preface

The present collection brings together 20 papers, all of which were presented (either in person or remotely) at the 15th *Trends in Classics* conference on "*Labor Imperfectus*: Unfinished, Incomplete, Partial Texts in Classical Antiquity", held in Thessaloniki, June 27–29, 2022. The event was jointly hosted by the Faculté des Humanités, Département des Langues et Cultures Antiques, University of Lille; the Department of Literary Studies and GIKS, Ghent University; and the Department of Classics at the Aristotle University of Thessaloniki.

The idea of this conference arose in a conversation between Jacqueline Fabre-Serris and Marco Formisano on the occasion of the 13th *Trends in Classics* conference in Thessaloniki, devoted to the topic of "Intended Ambiguity" and organized by our colleagues Martin Vöhler, Therese Fuhrer and Stavros Frangoulidis in May 2019. This conversation focused on the unfinishedness of Claudian's *De raptu Proserpinae*, the poem discussed by Marco Formisano at the 2019 conference. The title of the 15th *Trends in Classics* conference, *Labor Imperfectus*, is a quotation from Claudian's poem (1.271), a text not only incomplete probably because of Claudian's death, but also constantly thematizing unfinishedness both in its language and in its content.

Due to the wide variety of incomplete, unfinished or fragmentary texts and approaches addressed at the conference and in the volume, editorial standardization has paid attention to bringing the various styles displayed by the manuscripts in line with the *Trends in Classics* style-sheet. Beyond this, contributors were free to use either UK or US spelling as well as reference and punctuation conventions as they preferred. Several contributors to the volume refer to websites; the editors have checked all addresses and found they were accessible at the time of publication.

We are most grateful to all in person and remote speakers, for having agreed to speak at the conference and having produced an extraordinary series of compelling chapters that, as we hope, will represent an important contribution to one of the most fascinating but also complex aspects of ancient Greek and Latin textuality.

We would also like to thank all speakers, panel chairs and audience members for a stimulating conference, which gave much food for thought and generated lively responses. Much of the conference's success was also due to the assistance of past and present graduate and undergraduate students under the conscientious leadership of Dr. Danae Christidou and Dr. Dimitra Karamitsou.

We gratefully acknowledge the generous funding we received from our conference sponsors: the City of Thessaloniki and its mayor, the Honorable Constantine Zervas; the Aristotle University Research Committee and its chair, Professor

Efstratios Stylianidis, Vice Rector for Research and Lifelong Learning; the Aikaterini Laskaridis Foundation and University Studio Press.

We would like to thank the Welfare Foundation for Social and Cultural Affairs (KIKPE), and above all its Vice Chair, Mr. Manos Dimitrakopoulos, not only for assistance in organizing the *Labor Imperfectus* event in particular, but also for generously sponsoring the *Trends in Classics* Conference Series from 2012 onwards. Through this fruitful collaboration, the Foundation has forged a unique relationship with the long-term research activity of *Trends in Classics*, held annually in Thessaloniki.

The Aristotle University Research Dissemination Center (KEDEA) and its PR Office Director, Mr. Dimitrios Katsouras, deserve our gratitude for hosting the event and offering invaluable assistance throughout.

Many thanks are also due to Mr. George Roussos, IT System Administrator at the Office of Technological Support for Academic Activities, for offering his computer expertise and for providing tutorials whenever needed.

We are indebted to Prof. Craig Williams for his generosity in reading parts of the present volume and offering language and style editing. We would also like to thank Dr. Stephanie Winder and Dr. Maria Leventi for providing their assistance with proof-reading, and Dr. Leventi for undertaking the unenviable task of indexing the volume.

At De Gruyter we were privileged to work with Dr. Serena Pirrotta, Editorial Director of Classical Studies and Philosophy, and Dr. Carlo Vessella, Acquisitions Editor. We thank them both for their advice and meticulous editorial work at every stage of the production process.

Last but not least, we are indebted to both Franco Montanari and Antonios Rengakos, General Editors of *Trends in Classics*, for their unflagging interest and assistance, as well as their keenness to see the present collection of papers included in the *Trends in Classics* Supplementary volumes series.

Jacqueline Fabre-Serris
Marco Formisano
Stavros Frangoulidis

Contents

Preface —— V
List of Figures —— XI

Jacqueline Fabre-Serris and Marco Formisano
Introduction —— 1

Part I: Facing Unfinishedness

Evina Sistakou
From the Authorial to the Editorial *tour de force*: How to Read Callimachus' *Aetia* and *Hecale* —— 21

Myrto Garani
How to Walk Along a Pioneer's Fragmentary Track: Theophrastus' *Meteorological* Studies —— 41

Craig Williams
Fragments of Roman Sexuality in Petronius' *Satyricon* —— 59

Part II: Questioning (In)Completeness

Richard Hunter
The "Alexandrian End" of the *Odyssey* —— 89

John F. Miller
Reconsidering Closure in Ovid's *Fasti* —— 115

Philip Hardie
Statius' *Achilleid*: How to Break off a *carmen perpetuum* —— 127

Laura Jansen
***Literatura Incompleta*: Borges' Antiquity between World and Universe** —— 143

Part III: Constitutive Unfinishedness

Rosa Rita Marchese
Sed redeo ad formulam (*Off.* 3.20): Completeness and Imperfection in Cicero's *De officiis* —— 165

Fabio Tutrone
Relativizing Unfinishedness: Lucretian Textuality and Epicurean Therapy —— 189

Sylvie Thorel
The Fragment as a Form: A Reading of *Fragments d'un discours amoureux* by Barthes —— 211

Paolo Felice Sacchi
Arrhythmic Historiography, Lost Letters and Broken Meanings: Fulgentius's *De aetatibus mundi et hominis* —— 225

Marco Formisano
"This City Will Always Pursue You": The Impossible End of Rutilius Namatianus' Return —— 241

Part IV: Reading Unfinishedness

David Konstan
Finishing *Iphigenia in Aulis* —— 261

Stavros Frangoulidis
Seneca's *Phoenissae*: In Search of an Ending —— 275

Jacqueline Fabre-Serris
How to Read Hyginus' *Fabulae*? Theories and Practices —— 289

Giulia Sissa
The Rest was not Perfected: Platonic Endings and their Modern Echoes —— 311

Francesca Cadel
War as a Permanent Civil War: The "Unfinished" History in Pasolini's *Petrolio* —— 331

Part V: Searching for Completion

Andrew Zissos
The Missing Conclusion to Valerius Flaccus' *Argonautica* —— 353

Bettina Reitz-Joosse
Speaking Silences: The Incompleteness of Tacitus' *Annals* and Gustav Freytag's *Die verlorene Handschrift* —— 383

Stéphanie Dord-Crouslé
Putting an Unfinished Novel Back into Motion: A Digital Tool to Create Possible "Second Volumes" of *Bouvard et Pécuchet* —— 405

List of Contributors —— 419
General Index —— 423
Index of Passages —— 427

List of Figures

Fig. 1: Sample page of Latin text in Müller 2009. —— 82
Fig. 2: Sample page of a translation (Sullivan 2011). —— 83
Fig. 3: Sample page of Latin text in Schmeling 2020. —— 84
Fig. 4: Page from ninth-century MS B, containing compressed text of Petr. *Sat.* 7.1 – 17.6 (Richardson 1993, pl. 1). —— 85
Fig. 5: Page from the Quartilla episode in Müller 2009. —— 86
Fig. 6: Plato's allegory of the cave by Jan Saenredam, according to Cornelis van Haarlem, 1604, Albertina, Vienna. ——329

Jacqueline Fabre-Serris and Marco Formisano
Introduction

1 *Labor imperfectus*: searching for the endless

In the first book of *De raptu Proserpinae*, the mythological epic composed by Claudian at the end of the fourth century, the goddess Ceres hides her daughter Proserpina in Sicily while she is traveling to Phrygia in order to attend Cybele's rites. While the girl is in the palace adding the last touches to a tapestry which significantly depicts the birth of the cosmos, she interrupts her work because of the sudden arrival of Venus, Diana and Pallas:

> *coeperat et vitreis summo iam margine texti*
> *Oceanum sinuare vadis; sed cardine verso*
> *cernit adesse deas imperfectumque laborem*
> *deserit*
>
> 1.269–272

> "She had even now begun to curl the Ocean with its glassy waves round the very edge of the weaving; but the door-hinge turned and she saw that the goddesses had arrived and left her work unfinished…"[1]

Like the cosmos depicted in Proserpina's tapestry, Claudian's epic is itself incomplete. Although readers will be familiar with this ancient myth especially through the Homeric *Hymn to Demeter* and Ovid's *Metamorphoses* (5.385–571), Claudian's poem, which presumably included at least a fourth book, abruptly ends in the midst of book 3, when Ceres is desperately searching for her daughter while one of Scylla's dogs is barking (*latrat* is the last word, 3.448). It is interesting to notice that within the narrative there is a specific attempt to complete Proserpina's tapestry. This takes place in book 3 while Ceres enters the deserted hall where her daughter had earlier been waiting, and views a peculiar scene:

> *divinus perit ille labor, spatiumque relictum*
> *audax sacrilego supplebat aranea textu*
>
> 3.157–158

> That wonderful task of the goddess had gone to waste, and the bold spider was completing the gap left behind with her sacrilegious web.

---

[1] All translation from Gruzelier 1993.

Proserpina's *labor imperfectus* is destined to remain so. The spider's bold attempt to bring it to a completion is nothing but a sacrilegious act.

Labor imperfectus is the title of this volume not only because it suggests incompleteness and unfinishedness. It also refers to the conceptual situation presented by Claudian's poem: its very unfinishedness — whatever its cause might have been, the death of its author or the impossibility of bringing it to an end for other reasons — unintentionally reflects the aesthetics of a poem which continuously, not only in the case of Proserpina's tapestry, thematizes brokenness and interruption. Claudian's poem felicitously invites readers to conceptualize unfinishedness of both content and form as a hermeneutic key to the narrative of the *raptus* itself, which comes in the middle of the central book of the extant poem (Book 2) and as an act of violence against the *virgo* Proserpina represents an interruption par excellence.

These considerations have important consequences for interpretation. The first is that the figure of the author, and his supposed intentions, are subordinated to the incomplete form of the text or, to put it more precisely, the author function is — to say the least — problematized. While it was almost certainly not Claudian's intention to leave his epic unfinished, it is equally true that precisely its incompleteness perfectly fits both the narrative (Proserpina's unfinished tapestry and the *raptus* itself, among other aspects) and the form. In other words, if Claudian were a post-modern author, we would not spend time speculating why he did not finish his work or what the complete text might have looked like. This leads us to a second consequence: from which perspective do modern readers approach an incomplete ancient poem? Must they necessarily take an historically critical approach to Claudian's *non-finito*, seeking to reconstruct the circumstances and possible motivation for the interruption, or can they embrace its incompleteness as a fortunate coincidence which paradoxically allows a re-evaluation of the aesthetic unity of the text? There is yet another fascinating implication deriving from the unfinished status of this or any text. The author and the reader find themselves on the same level: both somehow lose control over the work. On the one hand, incompleteness is in most cases not the author's conscious decision; it is the result either of his or her sudden death or of an accident in transmission, both factors inherently highlighting the text's independence. On the other hand, readers are confronted with material difficulties such as fragmentariness and/or the lack of an unrecoverable end, and this not only makes any interpretation unstable — as every interpretation should be — but also reduces the hermeneutic work to a set of assumptions that can never be firmly asserted. In other words, could Claudian's sacrilegious spider serve as an allegory of the philologist's attempts to speculate about the complete form of texts that have been, for whatever reason, transmitted incomplete, fragmentary and/or unfinished?[2]

2 Incompleteness and absence

It is perhaps not a coincidence that in recent years there has been a distinct interest in ancient forms of incompleteness and unfinishedness. In particular two collections of papers deserve brief mention. In 2019, art historian Massimiliano Papini edited a volume bearing the title *Opus imperfectum. Monumenti e testi incompiuti del mondo greco e romano*, which presents a wide range of discussions about the aesthetic implications of various forms of incompleteness both in Greek and Roman material artifacts and in texts. Papini observes that, though a discourse of incompleteness and unfinishedness existed in pre- and early modern cultures, it is in the 20th century that their conceptualization fully emerges due to the turn away from regular and closed forms, along with philosophical discussions that privilege in various ways endlessness and interminability. Papini emphasizes that a taste for the *non-finito* in visual arts and literature did not really exist earlier, implying that ancient artists and authors did not conceptualize or consciously apply this exquisitely modern aesthetic category in their works[3]. The volume contains many inspiring points for reflection upon forms of unfinishedness and incompleteness in the ancient world. In general, the art historical and archaeological discussions by Papini and others in the volume are fundamentally oriented to material or personal reasons that may have caused incompleteness, while the literary discussions consider the dialectic "completed / unfinished" as a motif or as a subject for debate (for example: the striving for formal perfection makes a work definitive and able to resist the passing of time, but Hellenistic taste imposes a continuous process of refinement that can never really be completed).[4] In short, the volume considers how monuments and texts bear traces of the dialectic relationship between what can be considered finished and complete and what remains incomplete, even when the works are in fact finished.

The other volume that conceptualizes forms of incompleteness is *Unspoken Rome. Absence in Latin Literature and Its Reception*, published in 2021. Tom Geue

---

[2] Readers of this volume might wonder why none of its chapters specifically discusses Claudian's unfinished epic. Besides the discussion in this *Introduction*, one of the editors has treated *De raptu Proserpinae's* incompleteness in other publications (Formisano 2018 and 2020).
[3] Papini 2020 X and XIII.
[4] See for instance Cucchiarelli 2020, 261.

and Elena Giusti open their Introduction with a powerful assertion: "Classicists are nothing if not experts on absence."[5] Indeed, classical philology is traditionally a discipline which by definition tries to fill lacunae of all sorts — form, content, and context — that are always unrecoverable. While Papini and his colleagues are interested in the "dialettica compiuto/incompiuto" in classical art and literature, *Unspoken Rome* considers Latin texts in their specificity as Roman artifacts imbued in political discourses on the one hand and in the relationship with Greek language and literature on the other. The volume considers how "gaps in our knowledge of both texts and contexts" produce a "process of contestation and renewal of 'meaning' — an incessant transformation of textual presence into absence, into presence-as-illusion, into further absence-becoming-presence."[6] The scholarly agenda underlying the vision of this volume is to make textual absences in Latin literature "active producers of meaning rather than empty vessels waiting to be filled by speculation."[7] The editors and the contributors have a distinct focus on textual silences indicating both sensible political issues or aesthetic reflections. In other words, while this volume discusses "absence as writing/writing as absence," its focus is not on the specific status of ancient unfinished or fragmentary texts and the kind of hermeneutic responses they generate, but rather on the kinds of unfinishedness or fragmentariness used by authors to realize their particular aesthetic and/or political goals.

3 Our *labor imperfectus*

Our volume focuses on unfinishedness and incompleteness as a feature that is central to ancient Greek and Roman literature arguably more than to any other period in the history of Western literature. In many cases the manuscript tradition, most often because of a physically damaged or anthologized or excerpted archetype, results in texts which are for us irreparably mutilated at the beginning, in the middle, and/or at the end. Other texts are unfinished in the sense that their authors, for whatever reasons, did not complete or fully revise or polish them before publication. Finally, there are a number of texts which implicitly or explicitly thematize their own substantive "unfinishedness."

---

5 Geue, Giusti 2021, 1.
6 Geue, Giusti 2021, 1–2.
7 Geue, Giusti 2021, 3.

Although classicists are deeply familiar with this situation, and perhaps precisely because of its centrality, they do not always reflect on its possible implications for our interpretation or for the reception of the texts which we study. This large question provides the opportunity to bring together specialists in ancient Greek and Roman and other Western literatures, working on texts belonging to different genres: epic, tragedy, elegy and other poetic genres, mythographic texts, rhetorical texts, philosophical treatises, and the novel. The methodologies used are as varied as the type of incomplete, unfinished or fragmentary texts to which they are applied. Reading a text by questioning its current unfinishedness or incompleteness, or the textual signs suggesting an unfinished or incomplete state, has led the contributors to examine, in their specificity, the relations between author, reader and text as required by the verbal, generic and aesthetic features of each work. Crucial questions concern how and to what extent the very fact that many ancient texts we read *are* unfinished or incomplete has influenced and still influences their aesthetic perception and interpretation, but also how various editorial arrangements of texts in fragments or in *corpora* influence the reconstruction of closure. Another question explored by this volume is whether classicists approach their incomplete texts in a different way from scholars of modern and contemporary literatures. While the latter in most cases know why a certain text is incomplete, and thus they are generally not confronted with problems in material transmission, classicists almost never know exactly *why* their texts have been handed down in a fragmentary status or unfinished. A guiding critical goal of this volume is to compare *differences*: comparing different kinds of fragmentariness and incompleteness can give us a key to understanding and discussing the aesthetical and hermeneutical implications of this feature. Moreover, considering an incomplete, unfinished or fragmentary text is also always a matter of reception much more than in the case of a finished work, precisely because in order to make sense of the incompleteness, readers often need to detach themselves from a reconstruction of authorial intentions, or at least to relativize them.

Unlike many previous projects, this volume's primary focus is not on unfinishedness itself as a concept or an aesthetic criterion. Rather, in perhaps more pragmatic fashion, it gathers discussions of texts which for a variety of reasons are or have been transmitted to us incomplete. We negotiated with the contributors which text they would discuss, but of course we were unable to include treatments of many other incomplete texts. Indeed, our selection could arguably have been expanded almost *ad libitum*, beyond the reasonable limits imposed by the series and its publisher. In this sense, this volume performs incompleteness, itself being a *labor imperfectus*.

The twenty papers collected in this volume are organized into the following five thematic sections, which are only meant to provide a preliminary orientation. These sections are by no means intended to be parameters for reading through the collection; those, arguably few, who read the volume in its entirety are invited to find their own ways.

3.1 Facing unfinishedness

The transmission of ancient literature has a long and complicated history in which, from its beginning in the Middle Ages and the Renaissance, editors have played, and are still playing, a major role. Most authors did not leave their texts unfinished, but, due to their fragmentary transmission some of them are now perceived as unfinished or incomplete. Each editor takes an active part in the transmission process, but in the case of fragmentary texts this part is so important that the editing work has decisive effects on the way the author's work is read and interpreted. Since surviving fragments are differently collected and ordered by successive editors, as modern readers we are confronted with highly mediated texts which for centuries functioned as a space of editorial experimentation, even though all editors intended to provide access to original writings.

In his library brought with him from Constantinople, Michael Choniates kept a full copy of each of Callimachus' most celebrated poems, the *Aetia* and the *Hecale*. He was the last reader of a complete copy of these poems. It was not until the first half of the 20th century, when another scholar, Rudolf Pfeiffer, reconstructed the 'unfinished' Callimachus by collecting and organizing hundreds of smaller and larger pieces of his verses in coherent poetic sequences, which in turn were incorporated into the oeuvre of Callimachus. Many editors after him have dedicated their skills and labor to the same aim in the last century. In her chapter, Evina Sistakou explores "how to read" the two poems of Callimachus by taking into account three underlying premises: a) the text of the poems is a palimpsest reflecting the views of all scholars, commentators and editors throughout the centuries, b) the reader must differentiate between factual evidence, subjective views and hypotheses surrounding the poems, c) the poems are unfinished both because they have come down to us in fragmentary state and because they are structurally fragmented and consist of partial narratives. Combining historical evidence on textual transmission and editorial practice with aesthetics, Sistakou first outlines the problems associated with the 'unfinishedness' of both poems and the editorial solutions given to them, then uses two metaphors, those of the jigsaw puzzle and of the fragmented body, to explain the differences between them in the context of their genre, and eventually suggest reading strategies for these poems.

The following chapter revisits the problems involved in what can be called "modern reception" of Theophrastus' meteorological studies and in particular his Μεταρσιολογικά, a treatise preserved only in fragmentary Syriac and Arabic translations. In 1992, Hans Daiber published the Arabic translation of a Syriac translation plausibly written by the Nestorian Ibn al-Khammār (10th century), while taking into account the editions of the other Syriac-Arabic texts. Myrto Garani argues that, given the fact that the original Theophrastean target text is rendered from ancient Greek into Syriac, then again into Arabic, and finally into English and since the majority of scholars rely exclusively on Daiber's authority and translation, what we study as Theophrastus' meteorological treatise is the final textual product of a multi-layered process of translation and cultural transference. Garani explores the tension caused by this textual scarcity vis-à-vis a presumed significant impact: Theophrastus' meteorological ideas would have been extremely influential in the history of the field. To appreciate this influence, scholars build on presumed intertextual relationships of Theophrastus' passages with previous poets, Homer and Aristophanes, and a posterior poet, Lucretius, described as Theophrastus' ancient reader who perceives these intertextual hints and the latter's corresponding mediating role and responds to them accordingly.

In his chapter, Craig Williams focuses on a famous 'incomplete text', Petronius' *Satyricon*, as an exemplary illustration of the challenges and the rewards of reading *any* fragmentary text. The *Satyricon* we have today is the result of generations of scholarly work of stitching together pieces of the text from a variety of sources, ranging from medieval manuscripts to a body of handwritten and printed editions of the surviving portions of the *Satyricon* done by French humanists in the second half of the sixteenth century. Each editor and translator creates and recreates the text anew each time. As observed by some scholars, not only has the *Satyricon* come to us perforated with holes and tears, but it also seems to have been "undertaken with the deliberate intention of defeating the expectations of an audience accustomed to an organizing literary form".[8] In this paper, Williams examines the episode in the brothel (7–8) and another episode from the early portions of today's *Satyricon* — Encolpius' now highly fragmented narrative of a gathering hosted by Quartilla (16–26) — by way of illustrating how readers over the centuries have had sometimes significantly different encounters with Petronius' text and, through it, with the language and imagery of gender and sexuality in Latin literature. As his discussion of these two exemplary episodes shows,

---

8 Rimell 2002, 2–3; quotation from Zeitlin 1971, 635, both quoted by Williams.

what we might think is evidence for a certain feature of ancient sexual discourses might not be, for not only do we sometimes find the same textual details cited in support of different conclusions, but there is also no single text of our partial *Satyricon* shared by all readers today.

3.2 Questioning (in)completeness

In some cases incompleteness is not an objective reality, as in the case of the *Satyricon*, but a possibility that is considered and a question that is asked when reading texts, whether finished or unfinished. This type of questioning originates in Antiquity itself and reflects the importance of the role played by readers in the reception of a text.

In his chapter, focused on the *Odyssey*, a poem that hangs over all modern discussions of closure in ancient literature, Richard Hunter considers, first, some of the implications for ancient and modern criticism of the fact that Aristophanes of Byzantium and Aristarchus placed the τέλος (ending) or πέρας (limit) of the *Odyssey* at 23.296. The second part of his paper considers ancient citations of the verse, and the role it played in ancient appreciations of the *Odyssey*. In his third part, Hunter suggests that Virgil knew, and wanted readers to remember, that *Od.* 23.296 was in some sense the τέλος of Homer's song and narrative. He argues that in his description of the first sexual union between Dido and Aeneas, Virgil is alluding both to the happy reunion of Odysseus and Penelope as well to the illicit love-making of Ares and Aphrodite. By stressing upon the love-making of Dido and Aeneas as a beginning (4.169–170), not as the 'end' which lawful and proper love-making should be, Virgil has thus used but also inverted the 'Alexandrian' end of the *Odyssey*.

While Hunter shows how, in the *Odyssey*, a moment of closure was identified (or speculated) by readers who were such influential literary critics that their assumption was reused by a later poet, John Miller examines the case of Ovid's *Fasti*, described by its author as unfinished due to an external cause: his exile (Ov. *Trist.* 2.549–552). Later, the *Fasti* was in fact published as a truncated calendar, with a dedication to Germanicus Caesar rather than to Augustus[9] and other conspicuous revisions during exile. Miller points out that Ovid's statement that his poem is incomplete is challenged by his own contradictory narrative practices. Within his poem Ovid refers ahead to festivals that would have occurred in the missing months of his calendar-poem, but, on the other hand, book 6 is

---

[9] *Fasti* 2.3–17, addressed to Augustus, is commonly taken to be the work's original proem.

crammed with closural features which seem designed to bring the whole work, and not just the month of June, to a resounding close. In his paper Miller draws attention to the varied interplay between closure and open-endedness at the end of individual books of the *Fasti*. He offers a very detailed examination of Book 5 in particular: noting that its conclusion might be a vestige of the work's *actual* incompleteness — *rupit opus*, as Ovid described to Augustus his exile's effect (*Tr.* 2.552) — he shows how the miscellany closing Book 5 as we have it does gesture towards closure in several respects. The dynamic between open-endedness and closure in Ovid's calendar-poem, as described by Miller, suggests that the author of the *Fasti* was aware of the special situation created by his exile: his poem devoted to the twelve months of the year was suddenly stopped, but in fact later continued and reworked while remaining incomplete.

The third chapter focuses on Statius' *Achilleid*, a narrative poem that after a book and a bit breaks off and is generally regarded as incomplete. Like Miller, Philip Hardie supports the idea that the author is involved in the issue of the finiteness or (un)finiteness of his book. Even among incomplete epics, the *Achilleid* is unusual in breaking off at a point near the beginning of a book, and it is usually assumed that death prevented Statius from writing the epic through to completion. Hardie wonders whether we might consider "the book and a bit, within its own limits, a well-wrought urn". He refers to Peter Heslin, who he believes has made the most convincing case that "the *Achilleid* is a coherent and polished piece of work".[10] To further support the proposition that what we have at the end of the text is a well-formed point of provisional closure to the epic, Hardie examines in detail the last lines of the *Achilleid*. He argues that these lines are marked by signals both of closure and of the promise of continuation, reinforced by intertextuality with Statius' *Thebaid*. Furthermore, the fragment of book 2 itself displays evidence of ring composition.

Jorge Luis Borges (1899–1986) is renowned as the modern author who has cast the most innovative light on the matter of classical unfinishedness. Laura Jansen examines how continuously Borges urges his readers to conceive of literature, classical and modern, as a phenomenon which is always in the making, and never fully accessible. Yet, for him, the impossibility of knowing literature "whole" should not be regarded as a source of frustration or anxiety. Instead, Borges proposes a therapeutic form of reading, between knowing and not knowing, which Jansen characterises as "imperfect". She explores this motif in three key examples from Borges' oeuvre. First, she examines the endless, errant trajectories that the figure of Julius Caesar takes from Shakespeare and Quevedo, back

---

10 Heslin 2005, 57: the key discussions come at 62–70; 62–65 "Coherence and design".

to Roman antiquity and forth to Argentine modernist gauchesque literature. Then she takes as another case study the notion of Babel, explored through the figure of the vast library, as an imaginary realm where lost classical texts, such as the lost Tacitean *Histories* and *Annals* of Caligula, Vespasian, Titus and Domitian, are stored in complete yet inaccessible form. Jansen shows how Borges does also explore other Babel-like spaces in which complete visions of the classics, or a recreative version of those visions, are possible. This is the case of the allusive Elysium in "To a Minor Poet of the Greek Anthology," from *The Maker* (1960). The final theme that Jansen explores is the influence of Heraclitus and his flowing river that are central to Borges' conception of the classical as an imperfect form, as well as to his thinking about how antiquity circulates across traditions as an unfinished event.

3.3 Constitutive unfinishedness

The papers in the third section consider texts in which unfinishedness must be examined in relation to the topic, the argumentative tradition, the writing practices, or formal constraints chosen by the author.

Rosa Marchese shows that in Cicero's *De officiis* the tension between completeness and incompleteness, perfection and imperfection is constitutive. She argues that imperfection is set as the epistemological horizon of this treatise, because to deal with *officia* is precisely to make a choice of a theoretical nature that challenges the concept of completeness at its roots. This epistemological choice has consequences on the imperfect/unfinished morphology of the text itself. Cicero's intention to achieve definitional exactitude is continually frustrated by contents that tend, conversely, towards dilution and dispersion. Focusing on the notion of *decorum*, Marchese demonstrates how its treatment allows us to identify an unresolved tension between the search for definition and its failure, between completeness and incompleteness, between the finite and the unfinished, which belongs to the deep structure of this text. She also highlights how the third book of the *De officiis*, traditionally considered the most "imperfect", fully expresses the conflict between the aspiration to complete a void, to find a *formula* that can be readily used, and the stationing in the unfinished.

Over the past few centuries, scholars have often regarded Lucretius' *De Rerum Natura* as a fascinating example of artistic *non-finito*, mirroring the untimely death of a solitary genius. Fabio Tutrone argues that a careful reassessment of the 'degree of completeness' of Lucretius' text should be based on a thorough understanding of the special features of Roman didactic poetry and Epicurean therapeutic pedagogy as culturally situated discourses of self-formation. He focuses on two emblematic issues — recursive argumentation and thematic adaptability — which are crucial for determining whether the *De Rerum Natura* was left unfinished by its author. Tutrone shows that neither the practice of recursive argumentation, with the studied repetition of crucial lines in different books, nor the gradual modification of thematic priorities over the course of Lucretius' poem can be taken as evidence of unfinishedness as neither is a culturally neutral mode of rhetorical expression. In fact, both verbal repetition and thematic adaptability have substantially different implications in the intellectual world of Roman and Epicurean didacticism than in our modern literary sensibility. Since the ancient tradition of didactic poetry into which Lucretius taps concentrates on the development and the negotiation of a fictional relationship between poet/teacher and reader/student, Lucretius expects his reader to participate in the process of textual construction and to integrate the teachings of *De Rerum Natura* by finding other arguments on his own.

Instead of being the result of an accident of material transmission, Roland Barthes' *Fragments d'un discours amoureux* is a text conceived by its author in the form of a series of fragments supposed to be excerpted from an inaccessible preexisting whole: 'a discourse of love'. Barthes extensively commented on his text, and Sylvie Thorel examines in detail how he explains his project and offers keys to reading these series of fragments. For example, the pronoun 'I' must be taken as not personal, but theoretical, and the present tense is chosen not for its temporal value but for its aspectual and quasi-gnomic value. However, in this modern text, like in ancient texts, the question arises of how to read the remaining fragments of an unknown whole. Thorel highlights the hidden tensions between the reading pact that Barthes proposed to the reader, and its application to the text, and suggests another way of interpreting the 'discourse of love', underlying the edited fragments. Drawing on the fact that Barthes repeatedly refers to Goethe's *Werther*, Thorel suggests that, although obscured because of the fragment's form, it is possible to trace a novel, 'autobiographically inspired', in which Barthes has somewhat dismembered Goethe's famous novel in relation to his grief at the death of his mother and his love for a man, Roland Havas. This attractive interpretation gives the last word to the text, which can be read, beyond the fragmentary form chosen, also as "the form of a strongly constrained novel".

The text examined by Paolo Felice Sacchi is a noteworthy example of literature produced according to serial procedures and formal restrictions that the author imposed on himself. The *De aetatibus* aims at telling universal history by making the epochs of the world and the different ages of human life run in parallel, but also by adding a more remarkable restriction: these multiple stories will be narrated in twenty-three chapters, one for each letter of the Latin alphabet, letters that will be progressively absent from the related chapter itself: letter *a* is going to be missing in the first chapter, *b* in the second one, *c* in the third one and so on. Contrary to what is declared by the author in the prologue, though, the narrative does not exhaust the whole alphabet, stopping suddenly at chapter 14 (letter O). Sacchi reflects on the structure of a work in which the excess of constraints that seem to doom it to "closure" ends up producing, instead, an unstable textual object whose boundaries are indistinct. He examines in detail whether, and how, the program is, or not, fulfilled. In doing so, he investigates the friction between closed and open structures, finite series (alphabet, Christian salvation history, human life) and infinite series (time). In his third part, he relates Fulgentius's treatment of time to his allegorical technique. Comparing it to Fulgentius' practice in the *Mythologiae* and *Expositio Virgilianae continentiae*, Sacchi shows the limits of his ambitious scopes, which were: to provide allegorical mechanisms universally applicable to the entire corpus of "pagan" myths, and to establish a system of correspondences between macrocosm, microcosm and writing.

Marco Formisano observes that late antiquity, as a period marked by a tension between the ancient past as object of desire and the full consciousness of the irretrievability of that past, offers many unfinished texts. He suggests that this unfinishedness, far from representing only a simple accident due to material transmission or biographical reasons, must guide our interpretation as a hermeneutic criterion. Formisano offers, as an example of this critical approach, new views on Rutilius Namatianus' *De reditu suo*, in which the poet relates his departure from Rome and part of his journey to return home in Gaul. This poem not only is incomplete, and not only thematizes fragmentariness and interruption both through language and narrative: through its topic, the journey towards a *lost* home, it represents per se the impossibility of any completion since the Odyssean paradigm. Rutilius Namatianus' "return" home is paradoxically presented through the language, style and meter (the elegiac couplet) of exile. Describing an 'impossible' return, continually deferred and even erased (by the announcement of an eventual return to the City after the return to Gallia), the text includes verbal, narrative and aesthetic elements (like the motif of ruins and the description of rising waters) that reflect its (accidental) unfinishedness.

3.4 Reading unfinishedness

The papers in the fourth section offer examples of how modern scholars can read ancient texts clearly identified as not finished. David Konstan examines Euripides' *Iphigenia in Aulis*, deemed by scholars to have been mutilated both by the excision of passages in the original version and by their replacement by later interpolations. He observes that the play is notable for the numerous occasions in which leading characters change their minds. Each new plan is taken to suggest a potential plot line that is cut off by successive obstacles. The play thus constantly invites the audience to imagine alternative scripts and narrative possibilities. Konstan points out that the repression or blocking of alternative narratives is characteristic of ideology in general, which nevertheless cannot eliminate all traces of other visions and the scripts that authorize them. Euripides' *Iphigenia in Aulis* makes manifest the ideological labor of the text, as it brings to the surface programs that are not allowed to advance, and cannot be seamlessly assimilated to a single overarching unity. Finally, Konstan argues that the exceptional disjointedness of the *Iphigenia in Aulis* may in turn reflect Euripides' response to the extraordinary tensions of the time, as the defeat of Athens in the Peloponnesian War seemed ever more imminent, and the motives of those who prolonged it ever more suspicious. Athenians must have wondered, for example, what would have happened had Athens not sent the fleet to Sicily but had respected instead the Peace of Nicias, among other possible paths not taken.

Seneca's *Phoenissae* exhibits several features that have led the majority of scholars to suggest we have an incomplete work, either because Seneca did not finish it or because of losses during textual transmission. Stavros Frangoulidis proposes a reading of the play's closure, based on the examination of various clues inserted by the author for the use of the spectators. He argues that the problem of how to find the right ending is foregrounded from the very beginning and the play dramatizes a search for closure and its resignification as the plot unfolds. His chapter focuses on how Oedipus' debate about the right way to end his life as a punishment sets up a meta-theatrical contest between his master narrative of total destruction and the other characters' vain attempts to force him (either in person or symbolically) into a reconciliatory role. These characters oppose Oedipus' plot and try to direct it to their own endings. Through this series of interrupted trajectories, the plot advances towards its tragic resolution. The dramatic deadlock in Thebes parallels the meta-theatrical stand-off in the play with a series of debates involving characters with an objective opposed to that of Oedipus who try to forestall the forward movement of his single vision.

The following chapter of this section focuses on a text unanimously considered unfinished: Hyginus' *Fabulae*. The text of Hyginus 'as we have it today' results from the editing work of a Renaissance scholar, based on a single damaged manuscript, in which an 'original text' was/is impossible to identify due to successive interpolations and deletions, all anonymous and difficult to identify. How to read this version of the text as we have it now? Jacqueline Fabre-Serris argues that two approaches can be applied to this 'unfinished text', depending on the answers given to two questions: What is a mythographer? What is his project? The first approach is based on the idea that the mythographer is a compiler who intended to provide a variety of information, deemed useful for a better knowledge of mythology in general. It consists of comparing the current text to all the texts and figurative documents transmitted to us in order to try to identify its sources. The second approach, which includes the first, but as a preliminary step to appreciate what the mythographer has selected from the mythological tradition and what he has changed or invented, is based on the idea that 'the first author' wrote his text as poets do, that is, by creating personal reconfigurations of myths. It consists of applying the methods of structural analysis to the various *fabulae*, and can be justified by the similarity between this modern tool of analysis used by the reader (to deconstruct these narratives) and the ancient technique used by the first author, Hyginus (to construct them), when he wrote his summaries and put them together in a narrative cycle. This second approach is supported by a detailed analysis of *fabulae* 66–75, a cycle centred on the Theban myth.

Giulia Sissa's chapter takes its inspiration from Francis Bacon's response to Plato's incomplete *Critias*, whose Latin title is *Atlanticus*. Bacon's *New Atlantis* (1626) ends, or fails to end, or even refuses to end with the equally famous, maddening, bracketed sentence: "[the rest was not perfected]". Sissa argues that, if we want to understand the significance of this double textual "imperfection" — ancient (in the *Critias*) and modern (in the *New Atlantis*) —, we must concentrate on three moments in Bacon's "work unfinished": the identification of Plato's Atlantis as Great Atlantis, namely America; the replacement of an earthquake with a deluge, so that, unlike old Atlantis, New Atlantis is not engulfed in mud; and the experimental re-writing of Plato's allegory of the cave in the *Republic*.

In the last chapter of this section, Francesca Cadel focuses on a novel, *Petrolio*, which was not finished when its author, Pier Paolo Pasolini, was murdered in 1975, and published only in 1992. This surviving text is fragmentary: (sub)divided not into chapters but into notes. The book is announced as the critical edition of an unpublished work, which would be a reconstruction based on a comparison of four or five manuscripts. Here too there is a presupposed, but inaccessible whole. The book in preparation incorporates texts not written by the author/editor, such as letters from friends, and includes many different genres (from autobiography to essay) and media (from film documentary to radio and tv interviews). The current fragmentary form is intended to reflect the uninterrupted flux of events which have taken place in the social and political history of post-war Italy. More precisely, the novel depicts, in loosely connected fragments of stories and allegorical tales, the dual personality of a man named Carlo, his rise to power and his possible complicity with the Fascists and the mafia. The fragmentary and unfinished form of *Petrolio* cannot be attributed only to Pasolini's accidental death, but is clearly theorized by its author as the most appropriate for his initial project. A consequence of this choice is the active role attributed to the reader, who is often addressed by the author: advancing through the work, he could resolve the incompleteness of what Pasolini called "a modern *Satyricon*".

3.5 Searching for completion

Unfinished texts challenge the interest and ingenuity of readers so that they may be tempted to respond to incompleteness and try to fill in the gaps by applying philological methods or daring a more creative approach through personal rewriting. The *Argonautica* of Valerius Flaccus breaks off after line 467 of the eighth book. The question of how the completed poem might have concluded entails three separate but related issues: (i) how much of the poem is missing? (ii) at what point in the myth of Jason and Medea would it have concluded? (iii) which additional episodes would have been included? In his chapter Andrew Zissos aims to survey the full spectrum of scholarly theories and to establish a set of analytical principles for assessing their plausibility. Valerius Flaccus has a chief narrative model in the *Argonautica* of the Hellenistic poet Apollonius Rhodius, and a chief poetic model in Virgil's *Aeneid*. Zissos highlights two strategic devices used by the Flavian poet to signal his elimination of episodes from Apollonius' later narrative: 'episodic foreclosures' (e.g. when Venus assumes the form of Medea's aunt Circe and pays her 'niece' a visit in Colchis, which implies the elimination of the Apollonian episode in which Jason and Medea visit Circe on her island off the coast of Italy) and 'preemptive reallocations' of Apollonian elements that also argue strongly against an Apollonian replay on Valerius' part (e.g. the new use of the cloak that Hypsipyle gives Jason during the Argonauts' sojourn on Lemnos). Zissos employs intratextual and intertextual arguments in support of the following hypotheses: that the eighth was to be Valerius' final book, that less than 400 verses remained to complete the poem, and that it would have concluded with the Turnus-like death of Absyrtus on the island of Peuce.

The incompleteness of Tacitus' historical works, the *Annals* and the *Histories*, has also sparked the imagination of his readers for centuries. The lost sections of the *Annals*, on which Bettina Reitz-Joosse focuses in her chapter, appear to have been dramatic highpoints of the narrative: the stand-off between Sejanus and Tiberius, the entire reign of the notorious Caligula, Nero's death. She proposes to reflect on the incompleteness of Tacitus' *Annals* through the lens of a 19th century German novel by Gustav Freytag (1816–1895), entitled *Die verlorene Handschrift* ("The Lost Manuscript"). In this novel published in 1864, a Latin professor, Felix

Werner, comes across clues about the existence of a manuscript which appears to contain the entire *Annals* and *Histories*. His search will lead him to a text that results from a forgery due to a certain Magister Knips. Werner will find only the covers of the precious manuscript, thrown away and lost forever. Reitz-Joosse first shows how the characters in Freytag's novel model a range of different responses to Tacitean incompleteness. *Die verlorene Handschrift* challenges us to reflect on these responses and to question the characters' — and our own — motives for wishing to fill in Tacitus' gaps. In the second part of her chapter, Reitz-Joosse argues that the novel in its entirety proposes a different way of responding to the incompleteness of the Tacitean works: to understand and embrace *silence*, including the silence produced by the lost sections, as an essential characteristic and as an integral and meaningful feature of Tacitus' work. Freytag's novel itself performs a constructive response to Tacitus' silences: it treats them as the inviting pauses of an interlocutor who falls silent to allow us to speak.

As Gustave Flaubert (1821–1880) feared, death interrupted the writing process of *Bouvard et Pécuchet*. Stéphanie Dord-Crouslé in her chapter wonders whether this is the only reason for the novel's unfinishedness. Or does this incompletion express the structural impossibility of completing an encyclopedic novel that was to include, in its unwritten second volume, something like the totality of the world's discourses? When Flaubert suddenly died, it was certain that the book was to have two volumes. In the first volume, the only thing missing is the final scene of the tenth chapter. The second volume, although Flaubert stated in January 1880 that it was three-quarters done, exists only as an outline and as a collection of gathered documents. Without denying the value of an approach to this novel as precursor of our modernity, the Bouvard project (https://www.dossiers-flaubert.fr) wanted to consider its incompletion as essentially undergone and situational. Although the printed editions of the "second volume" have considerable merit, they suffer from unavoidable bias insofar as they have to make selections and classification choices from the documentary materials gathered by Flaubert, while at the time of the author's death, these materials were only a work in progress. By using digital media, it started again from the same documentary materials, and gave new life to the specific composition process of the second volume, based on an arrangement of textual fragments. It indeed allows the emergence of a plurality of possible "second volumes", which, far from remedying the effective incompleteness of the work, takes account of it and makes the mobility of its fragments a constitutive dimension of this unfinished work.

Antiquity is a period that is difficult to define in its historical limits. As a cultural moment, its reception never seems to end. The process began in Antiquity itself in the various forms of cultural transfer in the Mediterranean area, then from

Greece and Rome to subsequent Western culture. Already in Greece and Rome, this reception had taken the form of continual re-editions and rewritings of all sorts of texts: poetry, prose, history, philosophy, sciences. While it seems that there will be no end to the survival of ancient literature, fragmentariness is a central feature both of that literature and its ongoing reception. We have only partial access to ancient textuality itself, and many surviving texts have been handed down to us unfinished and incomplete. What emerges from the papers collected in our volume is that this feature of ancient texts has had a strong impact on interpretation of both ancient and later literatures, particularly in our times, when tensions between the fragmentary and the whole continue to be explored in various ways that actively involve readers in acts of interpretation.

Bibliography

Formisano, Marco (2018), "Fragments, Allegory, and Anachronicity: Walter Benjamin and Claudian", in: S. Schottenius Cullhed/M. Malm (eds.), *Reading Late Antiquity*, Heidelberg, 33–50.

Formisano, Marco (2020), "*Legens*. Ambiguity, Syllepsis and Allegory in Claudian's *De raptu Proserpinae*", in: M. Vöhler/T. Fuhrer/S. Frangoulidis (eds.), *Strategies of Ambiguity in Ancient Literature*, Berlin/Boston, 219–233.

Gruzelier, Claire (ed.) (1993), *Claudian's* De raptu Proserpinae, Oxford.

Papini, Massimiliano (ed.) (2020), Opus imperfectum. *Monumenti e testi incompiuti del mondo greco e romano*, Roma.

Cucchiarelli, Andrea (2020), "Monumenti più forti del fuoco. Incompiuto, immortalità e potere nella poesia augustea", in: M. Papini (ed.), Opus imperfectum. *Monumenti e testi incompiuti del mondo greco e romano*, Roma, 261–276.

Geue, Tom/Giusti, Elena (eds.) (2021), *Unspoken Rome. Absence in Latin Literature and Its Reception*, Cambridge.

Heslin, Peter (2005), *The Transvestite Achilles. Gender and Genre in Statius' Achilleid*, Cambridge.

Rimell, Victoria (2002), *Petronius and the Anatomy of Fiction*, Cambridge.

Zeitlin, Froma (1971), "Petronius as Paradox: Anarchy and Artistic Integrity", *Transactions of the American Philological Association* 102, 632–684.

Part I: **Facing Unfinishedness**

Evina Sistakou
From the Authorial to the Editorial *tour de force*: How to Read Callimachus' *Aetia* and *Hecale*

Abstract: Callimachus did not leave his poems unfinished, but they are perceived as "unfinished" due to their fragmentary transmission. Michael Choniates was the last reader of the complete *Aetia* and *Hecale* in the 13th century. Since then, editors and commentators — among which Rudolf Pfeiffer holds a prominent place — have developed numerous hypotheses in the quest for the lost original. Hence, the modern reader is faced with a highly mediated text which for centuries functioned as a space for editorial experimentation. Combining historical evidence on textual transmission and editorial practice with aesthetics and reception, the paper, first, outlines the problems associated with the "unfinishedness" of Callimachus' poems and the editorial solutions given to them, second, employs two metaphors, that of the jigsaw puzzle for the *Aetia* and the fragmented body for the *Hecale*, to explain their compositional differences, and, finally, suggests various interpretive strategies for aspiring readers of these major Hellenistic poems.

> Still speaking in a low voice, the stranger said, "It can't be, but it *is*. The number of pages in this book is no more or less than infinite. None is the first page, none the last. I don't know why they're numbered in this arbitrary way. Perhaps to suggest that the terms of an infinite series admit any number."
>
> Jorge Luis Borges, *The Book of Sand* (1977)
> (transl. N.Th. di Giovanni)

1 Introduction: the "unfinished" Callimachus

Two scholars are key to understanding the fortunes of the "unfinished" Callimachus across the centuries. The first is Michael Choniates (1138–1222), the archbishop of Athens, who defended the city against the Franks during the siege of 1205. His personal library, which he brought with him from Constantinople and was probably housed in the Acropolis, included a full copy of each of Callimachus' most celebrated poems, the *Aetia* and the *Hecale*. Although the greatest part of this library was destroyed by the Crusaders, the copies of Callimachus' poems were transferred by Choniates to the island of Ceos and kept there until his death. Nothing else is known about these books beyond this point, yet scholars assume that Choniates was the last reader of Callimachus' *Aetia* and *Hecale* in their entirety.[1] This accident in the textual transmission defined the reception of the Cyrenaean poet for centuries, since his two most significant poems were thereafter perceived as a heap of scattered and obscure fragments. It was not until the first half of the 20th century that another scholar, Rudolf Pfeiffer, reconstructed the "unfinished" Callimachus by collecting and organizing hundreds of smaller and larger pieces of his verses into coherent poetic sequences, which in turn were incorporated into the oeuvre of Callimachus. Pfeiffer's philological endeavor resulted in the publication of the monumental edition of Callimachus' *Fragmenta* (Oxford 1949). Though Callimachus remains essentially "unfinished", it is thanks to the inventive imagination of Rudolf Pfeiffer that his major works, the *Aetia* and the *Hecale*, can be conjured up once more in the mind of modern readers.

Callimachus as author did not leave his poems unfinished or without the necessary authorial and/or editorial revision. On the contrary, he meticulously arranged and polished his works before circulation. Callimachus was among those who introduced the concept of the "poetry book", which then became a trend in the Hellenistic period.[2] The *Aetia*, whose four books were framed by a prologue (fr. 1 Pf./H.) and an epilogue (fr. 112 Pf./H.), which are considered now to be later additions to the work, testifies to this fact. Likewise, Callimachus was so certain of the "final" arrangement of his edition that he even announced his next work, the *Iambi* or a prose treatise, with the last phrase of the *Aetia* Epilogue (fr. 112.9 Pf./H. αὐτὰρ ἐγὼ Μουσέων πεζὸν [ἔ]πειμι νομόν "I, however, will go to the foot-pasture of the Muses").[3] Moreover, a 6th century epigram reflects the fact that all Callimachean works constituted a standard corpus throughout antiquity and for the most part of the Byzantine era (T 23 Pf.). So, it is reasonable to assume that the Fourth Crusade marks a turning point in Callimachean textual history,

---

[1] That Michael Choniates read the original Callimachus was first argued by Richard Reitzenstein in 1898. Choniates is considered not only the last (Hollis 2009, 37–40) but also the most creative reader of Callimachus; see Pontani 2011, 114–117 and Kennedy 2016.
[2] The term "poetry book" was coined by Kathryn Gutzwiller to denote the corpus of Theocritus' *Idylls* and Posidippus' epigram collection. The author as sophisticated editor is a common trend among modernist poets too, see Bornstein 1991, 1–16.
[3] Pfeiffer 1949–1953, 2.xxxvi maintains that Callimachus not only published his poems individually but also arranged them in the right order in a second edition; apparently, Callimachus edited the *Aetia* twice during his lifetime, cf. Harder 2012, 1.2–12.

which should be divided into the era B(efore) C(honiates), when the two signature poems of Callimachus were known as a whole, and the one A(fter) C(honiates), which introduced the concept of the "unfinished" Callimachus.

As unfortunate as this accident may seem — who would not want to read the *Aetia* and the *Hecale* in their entirety today and who knows whether such a reading would have dramatically changed Hellenistic scholarship — it also poses an opportunity to explore questions about the notions of authorial and editorial intention, reception and reader response. It is well known that Roland Barthes in an influential 1968 essay declared "the death of the author". By deconstructing the idea of the Author-God, the powerful creator who conveys his message through a fixed text, and thus removing the author from the text and rendering writing a recurrent act to be performed by each reader, Barthes has liberated textual interpretation from the concept of authorial intention. In his study *S/Z* (1970) and in *The Pleasure of the Text* (1973), Barthes makes a distinction between texts based on the kind of reading they involve: a *texte lisible* ("readerly or readable text") requires only passive reading, whereas a *texte scriptible* ("writerly or writable text") is one for which reading is an active process that produces infinite meanings; this distinction establishes the divide between classical and modernist conceptions of literature and its criticism. Seen from this Barthean angle, the *Aetia* and the *Hecale* constitute modernist texts, eternally rewritten by the reader in the present, and therefore Callimachus' original work reflecting his authorial intention is of secondary importance.

Callimachus' poetic corpus provides an excellent case of a text that has been actively re-created in the process of its transmission. More than 23 centuries of scholarship have re-read and, in a Barthean sense, re-written, this corpus and especially the much-discussed *Aetia* and *Hecale* with different intentions. Various categories of master readers have left their traces on both poems: post-Hellenistic philologists, including Theon, Epaphroditus and Salustius, who provided commentaries to shed light on their obscure details; the anonymous scholars who summarized these poems in the surviving *Diegeses*; the Roman and later Greek and Byzantine authors who creatively responded to both Callimachean poems; the authors who incorporated single verses or phrases into their own works as quotations; the numerous Byzantine lexicographers and grammarians who excerpted the poems outside their literary context.[4] While all

---

[4] That Callimachus is the Hellenistic author who survived mainly through quotations in the works of other authors is forcefully argued by Pontani 2011. For the sources of the *Aetia* divided into three categories, namely the testimonia, the book fragments and the papyrus fragments, see Harder 2011.

these readers had access to the complete Callimachean corpus from which they drew their readings, after Choniates the process was reversed. Against the backdrop of a fragmented text a new category of master readers emerged, namely the editors.

The editing of Callimachus' major works may be called "intentionalist" in the sense that his editors aspire to reconstruct the lost original that has been obscured by the various readings of these works through the centuries.[5] An array of scholars from the 19th century onwards, like Hecker who published the *Commentationes Callimacheae* in 1842, A.F. Naeke, the first editor of *Hecale* in 1845, and Otto Schneider who first published Callimachus' fragments in 1873, and primarily Rudolf Pfeiffer, Adrian Hollis, and Annette Harder, as well as Hugh Lloyd-Jones and Peter Parsons who compiled the *Supplementum Hellenisticum*, have dedicated their skills and labor to this aim in the last century.[6] But they have not limited themselves to the reconstruction of the "original" text to ensure the historical accuracy of their edition. They have gone much further by developing innumerable, and, at times, quite bold hypotheses in the quest for the authoritative Callimachean text. While scholars are grateful for the herculean task they have undertaken, since without their adherence to authorial intention and authenticity Callimachus' works would still be a heap of textual scraps, nevertheless, contemporary reception is mediated by their choices and assumptions about the constitution of Callimachus' poetic corpus.[7]

With these thoughts as a starting point, the question I explore in the present paper is "how to read Callimachus' *Aetia* and *Hecale*", two major Hellenistic poems that are in a state of textual flux. Some underlying premises that should be taken into account are the following: a) the text of the poems is a palimpsest reflecting the views of all scholars, commentators and editors throughout the centuries; b) the reader must differentiate between factual evidence, subjective views and hypotheses surrounding the poems; c) the poems are "unfinished" both because they have come down to us in a fragmentary state and because

---

[5] The theory and standards of intentionalist editing are especially associated with G. Thomas Tanselle (Tanselle 1990 and, for a recent theoretical overview, 1995), who follows the principles introduced by Fredson Bowers (in his 1959 book *Textual and Literary Criticism*, Cambridge). On the theoretical background of editing as an interpretative tool of modernist texts, see Bornstein 1991.

[6] In fact, Callimachus was rediscovered in the modern era in the 16th century by Henricus Stephanus who first collected his fragments: for the fascinating story of reconstructing Callimachus especially through the papyri from the 16th up to the 20th century, see Lehnus 2011.

[7] A recent collection of papers on the reconstruction of the Greek past through the editing of fragments is Derda/Hilder/Kwapisz 2017.

they are structurally fragmented and consist of partial narratives. Combining historical evidence on textual transmission and editorial practice with aesthetics, I first outline the problems associated with the "unfinishedness" of both poems and the editorial solutions given to them, then use two metaphors, that of the jigsaw puzzle and the fragmented body respectively, to explain the differences between them in the context of their genre, and finally suggest reading strategies for these two poems. The broader question is to what extent and by what standards is a reader allowed to "finish" Callimachus' poems — a question that is worth pursuing but must remain open-ended.

2 The *Aetia* as a jigsaw puzzle

The *Aetia* is a catalogue poem, which Callimachus edited twice during his lifetime: the first edition comprised Books 1–2 framed as a dialogue of the poet with the Muses, and the second Books 3–4, which consisted of individual, unconnected elegies; to the final edition a prologue and an epilogue were added.[8] According to the calculations of Annette Harder, the authoritative editor of the *Aetia* in the 21st century, the poem must have comprised about 5000 lines (with estimations varying between 4000 and 6000), from which we have today about 1200 lines, that is, less than one quarter of the original.[9] But there are also other aspects of the textual transmission that mark the *Aetia* as an essentially unfinished poem. From the ca. 40 narrative sections (*fabulae*) identified by Pfeiffer, a number increased by the more recent survey of Harder to 58,[10] apparently only four, i.e. one tenth or far less of the known narrative sections, are almost complete in the sense that we know their beginning, ending and approximate length.[11] These are by no means the longest surviving fragments: fr. 75 Pf./H. from the aition of "Acontius and Cydippe" comprises 77 lines of continuous narrative including also the closing lines; "The Victory of Berenice" (frs. 54–60j H.) has now been reconstructed from its opening lines followed by longer and smaller

---

8 Harder 2012, 1.2–12.
9 On the estimated size of the *Aetia*, see Harder 2012, 1.12–15.
10 See the titles in Latin added by Pfeiffer 1949–1953, 1.1–160; for the updated list of the aitia, to which prologue, epilogue and dream are added, with titles in English, see Harder 2012, 2.1025–1026.
11 Harder 2012, 1.63 n.199 maintains that these are the ritual at Zancle (fr. 43 Pf./H.), the tomb of Simonides (fr. 64 Pf./H.), the Argive springs (frs. 65–66 Pf./H.) and the statue of Apollo at Delos (fr. 114 Pf./H.).

narrative sections; from the aitiological elegy "The Lock of Berenice" (frs. 110–110f Pf./H.) we have a great part of the original lines and its almost literal "translation" by Catullus (*Carm.* 66). Luckily, we also have the ancient summaries, the *Diegeses*, of almost every aition in Books 3–4, which also provide the incipit for each aition. From a different angle, unfinishedness in the *Aetia* is omnipresent in the text of the poem, owing to the poor state of the papyrological transmission on the one hand, and to the extreme selectivity of ancient authors, philologists and anthologists on the other, who merely quote words and, only in exceptional cases, complete verses, from which the lacunae of the transmitted text are supplemented. We may visualize it as a shattered whole, a text torn to shreds and pieces, a poem that is unfinished both on a macro- and a microscale.

Faced with a text of multiple challenges, the editors of the *Aetia* are bound to be intentionalists. Among them, Rudolf Pfeiffer marks a turning point in the history of the *Aetia* text, since his editorial decision-making has dominated our perception of the poem as an artistic work.[12] It is worth asking, then, which principles he applied to "finish" Callimachus' text. Due to the limitations of space, I shall only refer to the most striking cases of his editorial interventions, arranging them in order from those based on evidence to those that suggest more creative methods:

1) Merging of different textual sources (by combining papyrus fragments with book fragments)
2) Allocation of the fragments to the four books of the *Aetia* (with an additional section comprising the *fragmenta incerti libri*)
3) Ordering of the fragments and/or narrative sections (*fabulae*) within each book (according to the papyrological sources and testimonia)
4) Numbering of the fragments (including not only quotations of the actual text but also testimonia, scholia and other indirect sources that supplement the missing text)
5) Grouping of the fragments into narrative sections (mainly fact-based and partly conjectural)
6) Identification of the narrative sections and tagging with descriptive titles (all titles in Latin are coined by the editor)

---

[12] However, Pfeiffer modestly concludes his *praefatio* to Callimachus' edition as follows (Pfeiffer 1949–1953, 2.vii): "*Studiorum Callimacheorum nihil nisi initia offero; ad ulteriora pervestiganda eruditis magna patet area*" ("my contribution to Callimachean studies is just a beginning; a great field is open for scholars to investigate further").

7) Use of subliteral material such as the summaries (*Diegeses*) (for the reconstruction of the contents of each narrative section and its arrangement within each book)
8) Juxtaposition of the text with secondary sources that help supplement the original (such as the ancient scholia and the Catullan poem/translation of the original)
9) Quotation of evidence before and after the *Aetia* (model texts and imitations/variations by later authors)
10) Integration of the editor's conjectures and interpretations into the commentary printed below the text (marked as uncertain by the frequent use of expressions such as *ut videtur, nihil adhuc constat, si recte, fortasse* etc.)

As may be deduced from the above list, resourceful editing is of the essence, especially in a highly unfinished text like the *Aetia*. Because of the restrictions in reconstructing the Callimachean text *per se*, Pfeiffer utilized all sources available to produce a multilayered paratext around the core poem and hence reimagine how the *Aetia* might have looked in antiquity. The wealth of paratextual material surrounding the remains of the original text in Pfeiffer's *Aetia* has obvious implications for the perception of the reader.[13] Pfeiffer not only gives voice to the authorial intentions of Callimachus, as these may be detected in the transmitted text, but moreover he urges the reader to review the text through his eyes and filter it through his philological consciousness. Six decades later, in 2012, Annette Harder re-edited and commented on the text of the *Aetia*, and partially corrected some of Pfeiffer's editorial choices.

The way Pfeiffer meticulously fills in the gaps in the textual transmission and combines the fragments of the *Aetia* to make them interlock in accordance with the greater plan of the poem resembles the process of piecing together a jigsaw puzzle. It is not difficult to visualize this poem as a puzzle: the papyri provide various frames that must be filled in with smaller papyrological or otherwise transmitted fragments, whereas the printed text in the Oxford edition clearly resembles an unfinished puzzle with many missing pieces. But, unlike other ancient texts surviving in fragments, the *Aetia* has the logic of the puzzle incorporated into the design of the poem as well. Books 1–2 are framed by a

---

13 According to Genette 2009, 2, the paratext is a "threshold to interpretation", "a zone between text and off-text, a zone not only of transition but also of *transaction:* a privileged place of a pragmatics and a strategy, of an influence on the public, an influence that — whether well or poorly understood and achieved — is at the service of a better reception for the text and a more pertinent reading of it".

dream narrative, where the poet converses with the Muses, within which numerous aitiological narratives are nested; there are several threads connecting these narratives both with the dream frame and with each other. Conversely, Books 3–4 have neither a unifying frame nor internal connections between the aitia; the aitiological narratives form individual elegies, akin to any sequence of poems edited in a book collection. It is not known why Callimachus chose to edit the two parts of the *Aetia* differently, but this editorial design probably reflects the intention of the old-aged poet.[14] Callimachus adopted and evolved the Hesiodic catalogue form as a means to freely increase and decrease the number of narrative sections/elegies to be included in the final edition, thus suggesting infinite compositional possibilities. Beyond the macrostructure, unfinishedness is also evident in the microstructuring of each aition: narratives are fragmentary, elliptical, without openings or definite closures, partial narrations of aitiological stories. From a generic viewpoint, the *Aetia* defies unity of genre conventions, uniformity of time and place, linear ordering and wholeness.[15] Thus, it may be characterized, in Umberto Eco's terminology, as an "open text", a "work in progress" that must be finalised by the creative mind of the reader.[16]

So, if we accept that Callimachus conceptualized the *Aetia* as a mind game for readers, one that should be solved and completed through the challenges posed to them, how should today's readers approach it? The *Aetia* prompts the reader to fill in its hermeneutic gaps in two directions: first, the one associated with the missing or misplaced textual evidence (where the input of the editor is of utmost importance), and, second, the one stemming from the author's compositional strategies (in which case the editor's paratextual interventions are normative and may even be misleading). A telling example of the latter case are the descriptive titles added by the editors, beginning with Rudolf Pfeiffer who

---

14 For the two different techniques of composition adopted by Callimachus in the *Aetia*, Massimilla 2011 is essential, another 21st century editor of the poem who has also provided an exhaustive commentary (cf. Massimilla 1996 and 2010).
15 The compositional complexities of the *Aetia* have been extensively studied: Harder 2004 and 2012, 1.51–56 (narrative technique), Morrison 2007, 178–199 (narrators and narratives), Hunter 2005 (compositional form of the catalogue), Harder 1998 (generic games), Sistakou 2009a, 394–401 (fragmented narrative), 2019 (postmodern narration) and 2021 (postmodern ambiguity).
16 These terms, put forward by Umberto Eco (*Opera aperta*, 1962 and *The Role of the Reader*, 1984) pertain to the idea that the avant-garde work needs the contribution of the perceiver (reader, viewer or performer) to be completed.

coined them as a help for the reader.¹⁷ Although these titles are indeed useful, since they codify the contents of each narrative section and have become a reference tool for studying the *Aetia*, they nevertheless give the false impression that this is a standardized poetic collection. And if this is partly true in Books 3–4, the division of Books 1–2 into individualized elegies, as suggested by the titles, overlooks the fact that due to the frame the poetic collection should be read as a continuum.¹⁸

That the aitia were not intended to be read separately is suggested by the fact that there are multiple aitia in the first two books. "The Return of the Argonauts and the Ritual at Anaphe" (frs. 7c–21d Pf./H.) and "The Sacrifice at Lindos" (22–23c Pf./H.) are united by the introductory question (fr. 7c, 1–2 H.), Κῶς δέ, θεαί, ·[···] μὲν ἀνὴρ Ἀναφαῖος ἐπ' αἰσ[χροῖς/ ἡ δ' ἐπὶ δυ[σφήμοις] Λίνδος ἄγει θυσίην ("And why, goddesses, does a man at Anaphe sacrifice with insults and Lindos with shameful words ..." transl. A. Harder), whereas the Lindian aition was directly joined to the subsequent one, "Thiodamas of Dryopia" (frs. 24–25d Pf./H.), as implied by the scholion (Sch. Call. *Aet.* on fr. 23, 8–10). Similar cases of a double aition are the story behind the Theodaisia and the plant *styrax*, which connect Haliartus of Boeotia with Crete (entitled "Haliartus", fr. 43b–c H.) and the human sacrifices performed by king Busiris of Egypt and the tyrant Phalaris of Acragas (entitled "Busiris and Phalaris", frs. 44–47 Pf./H.).¹⁹ The editorial habit of labelling these narrative sections through titles not only defines them as individual elegies (which they are not), but it also highlights a specific thematic aspect in them, whether it is the myth, the aition, the protagonists or the geographical place (which can be misleading).²⁰

Editorial interventions that influence the readers' perception may easily be multiplied and include those pertaining to the arrangement of the books, the ordering of the aitia and the estimation of their length.²¹ Master readers from the

---

17 Pfeiffer 1949–1953, 2.xxxiv *"titulos in usu lectorum ipse finxi"* ("I have made up the titles for the readers' use").
18 Cf. Harder 2012, 1.3, who notes that "Books 1–2 were not modified in the second edition, probably rightly, because the narrative framework of the dialogue with the Muses would make these books into a unity which might be disturbed by taking away or adding elements".
19 These cases indicate that the questions addressed to the Muses were part of the narrative and that the framework, consisting of the setting on the Helicon and the scene of the banquet, was "flexible", see Massimilla 2011, 47–49.
20 Titles are used to designate a work, indicate its content or attract the reader; for an overview of the functions and semantics of titles in literature, see Genette 1988.
21 Massimilla 2011 classifies the editorial problems of the *Aetia* and the possible solutions to them.

past, like the anonymous author of the *Diegeses*, can also misdirect the contemporary readers of the *Aetia*. For example, the summary accompanying "The Lock of Berenice" is one of the shortest *Diegeses*: "He says that Conon turned the lock of Berenice into a constellation, which she promised to dedicate to the gods when he came home from the war in Syria" (transl. A. Harder). Thanks to the papyrological remains and the translation of Catullus, we now know that this elegy was of medium to long length, comprising almost 100 lines. Moreover, we are aware that the most striking feature of this elegy was not the emphasis on court politics, but the first-person discourse of the animated object, i.e. the speaking lock, and its romantic undertones.[22] Broadly speaking, this means that the assumptions about the length and narrative technique of lost aitia stemming from the *Diegeses* are questionable. Even the arrangement of the aitia in Books 3–4, which follows the order of the corresponding *Diegeses* in the papyrus, does not necessarily date back to Callimachus' edition, but may reflect later reconstructions.[23]

The problems inherent in the textual transmission and the paratextual material are only a part of the puzzle. As an experimental work, the *Aetia* consists of twists, riddles and mind games inviting the reader to engage intellectually with them. Reading the *Aetia* is like competing against an opponent, who is incorporated into this dynamic text; the master of the game is "Callimachus", the fictional *persona* of the poet, and his narrators.[24] The game logic of the poem is evident already in the child imagery of the Prologue,[25] whereas the strategy of unfinishedness is built into the opening declaration (fr. 1.3–6 Pf./H.):

εἴνεκε]ν οὐχ ἓν ἄεισμα διηνεκὲς ἢ βασιλ[η
......]ας ἐν πολλαῖς ἤνυσα χιλιάσιν
ἢ····]·ους ἥρωας, ἔπος δ' ἐπὶ τυτθὸν ἑλ[ίσσω
παῖς ἅτ]ε, τῶν δ' ἐτέων ἡ δεκὰς οὐκ ὀλίγη.

---

22 An example of a prose version of the story, which overlooks the element of fantasy in the elegy, is provided by the constellation aition narrated by Hyginus (*Astr.* 2.24). On the aesthetics of Callimachus' elegy, see the analysis by Gutzwiller 1992.
23 Massimilla 2011, 59 warns against the reliability of this source: "We get the impression that the very nature of the aitia of Books 3 and 4, disconnected as they are each from the next and lacking any narrative links, has exposed them to instability in the order of their transmission. Therefore, we cannot be sure that the order of the elegies, as witness the *Diegeses* (or other papyri also), always reflects Callimachus' intention".
24 For "Callimachus" denoting the fictional *persona* of the poet as projected in the *Aetia*, see Morrison 2007, 182–195.
25 For the programmatic function of the metaphor of the child and the poem as game, see Acosta-Hughes/Stephens 2001, Ambühl 2007 and Cozzoli 2011.

…because I did not complete one single continuous song (on the glory of?) kings…in many thousands of lines or on…heroes, but turn around words a little in my mind like a child, although the decades of my years are not few. (Transl. A. Harder)

Reader-response theory is key to understanding the compositional strategies of the *Aetia*. The lack of "classical" narrative devices, the ever-changing styles, the poem's generic hybridity and hypertextuality invite the reader to interact with the text and fill in its gaps, as the reader-response theorist Wolfgang Iser would put it, by recourse to his/her erudition and imagination.[26] Moreover, today's readers belong to an "interpretive community",[27] as Stanley Fish would call it, which approaches the *Aetia* under specific premises, such as the *de facto* recognition of Callimachus as a "neoteric" and "experimental" poet, and the application of analytical tools such as narratology and genre studies. From a wider perspective, the interpretive skills of 21st century readers have evolved within the context of contemporary culture, where the notion of fragmentariness and game aesthetic prevail.[28] As a consequence, the *Aetia* readers today, building on the foundation of the painstaking research of the poem's editors and commentators, need to be active and reflexive, and open to the challenges posed by this unique work. Indeed, the *Aetia* provides a fractured look on myth and history by constantly shifting the focus to different temporal and spatial centers. It destabilizes continuous storytelling, either by resorting to complex narratives in Books 1–2 or by introducing thematic discontinuity in Books 3–4. By constantly confusing the generic expectations and redirecting the narrative spotlight from stories to lore to metapoetry and vice versa, "Callimachus" invites the reader to play with his text and finish it in his/her own idiosyncratic way.

---

26 Cf. Iser's theory on what he calls "the act of reading", a process during which the reader completes the gaps inherent in the literary text (Iser 1978, esp. IV. Interaction Between Text and Reader, 160–231).
27 According to Stanley Fish, an "interpretive community" is a group of readers who deploy a common set of interpretive strategies to read a text; therefore, "meaning" is not inherent in the text but is created by the different interpretive communities (Fish 1976).
28 Two cultural trends may be relevant here: the rise of fragmented fiction (see Guignery/Drąg 2019) and the emergence of the so-called puzzle films (see Buckland 2009), both of which provide a "cognitive playground" for those perceiving these works (on the cognitive attractiveness of the latter see Kiss/Willemsen 2018).

3 The fragmented body of the *Hecale*

Most of the conditions that render the *Aetia* an unfinished text also apply to the *Hecale*: almost a dozen poorly preserved papyri with the additional source of the wooden Vienna Tablet from the 4th–5th century, and the scattered fragments extracted from the *Suda* and other Byzantine etymological lexica amount to a severely damaged text. The *Hecale*, regularly characterized as *the* paradigm of the Hellenistic epyllion, is of unknown length, estimated to somewhere between 1000 and 1700 lines. The editors are not even certain how many verses have fully and partially survived; the updated estimate of Adrian Hollis is 125 (plus 8 from the uncertain fragments) for the former, 254 (plus 18 from the uncertain fragments) for the latter.[29] The reconstruction of this epyllion poses different problems as compared to those of the *Aetia*, since, in addition to the dispute over the interrelation of fragments, little is known about their position in the overall narrative design of the *Hecale*.

The *Hecale* invites the synthesis of intentionalist and creative editing, a fact that its numerous editors recognized early on.[30] Rudolf Pfeiffer explains his editorial strategy in his lengthy introduction to the *Hecale*; his main interventions may be summarized as follows:[31]

1) Combination of different textual sources (book fragments, especially those stemming from the *Suda* and other Byzantine lexica, are checked against the papyrological fragments)
2) Arrangement of the key fragments (those which, in Pfeiffer's opinion, can be more safely positioned in the narrative sequence)[32] according to the ancient testimonia on the poem, i.e. the lengthy *Diegesis* and Plutarch's *Theseus* (frs. 230–264 Pf. *ad ordinem narrationis*)
3) Arrangement of the rest of the fragments according to their alphabetical ordering in the lexicographical sources (frs. 265–377 Pf. *secundum fontium ordinem alphabeticum*)

---

[29] For the theories regarding the length of the *Hecale* from Naeke to Pfeiffer, Hutchinson and Hollis, see Hollis 2009, Appendix II, 337–340.
[30] The reconstruction of the *Hecale* and the other fragmentary works of Callimachus in the "After Choniates" era dates to Politian in 1489: for the story of editions from Politian to the nineteenth century, see Pfeiffer 1949–1953, 2.xliii–l.
[31] Pfeiffer 1949–1953, 1.226–229.
[32] Pfeiffer 1949–1953, 1.229 states that "*in priore igitur parte ea collegi quae satis certae sedis mihi videntur*" ("in the first part I have assembled those fragments that, in my view, had a fairly fixed place [i.e. in the poem]").

4) Numbering of the fragments (in continuous numbering within the volume of Callimachus' fragments)
5) Critical examination of the hypotheses put forward by previous editors (especially Naeke and Hecker) regarding mainly the position of the fragments within the narrative design of the poem
6) Contextualization of the fragments in the ancient testimonia (conjectural linking of the fragments with the plot of the *Hecale*)
7) Quotation of evidence before and after the *Hecale* (model texts and imitations/variations by later authors)
8) Incorporation of the editor's conjectures and interpretations into the commentary printed below the text (especially those concerning the alphabetically ordered fragments)[33]

Pfeiffer concludes that, despite meticulous editing, the *Hecale* cannot be adequately reconstructed.[34] About four decades later, Adrian Hollis challenged this claim by editing Callimachus' epyllion anew. Although the discovery of new papyrological fragments, without which no substantial advancement in the *Hecale* text *per se* should be expected, is still the *desideratum* of the editors,[35] Hollis has enhanced our perception of the *Hecale* by contextualizing, relocating and reediting the known fragments on the one hand, and by shedding light on the style and compositional design of the poem on the other. Moreover, Hollis has enriched the text by adding numerous fragments of uncertain attribution, which Pfeiffer was more reluctant to incorporate into his edition of the *Hecale*.[36] As an editor, Hollis, like Pfeiffer, carefully establishes the confines between fact

---

[33] Pfeiffer 1949–1953, 1.229 notes that "*in parte posteriore cetera fragmenta (265–377) ad ordinem alphabeticum fontium redacta sunt, sed indicavi, si certo carminis loco cum aliqua veritatis similitudine tribui posse videbantur*" ("in the second part I have placed the remaining fragments (265–377) according to the alphabetical order of their sources, at the same time indicating which of them can be attributed, fairly plausibly, to a specific part of the poem").

[34] Pfeiffer 1949–1953, 1.229: "*Diegesis est argumentum breve carminis epici; neque illius neque novarum Hecalae papyrorum ope ipsum carmen 'restitui' potest*" ("the *Diegesis* is a short summary of the epic poem; neither this nor the new papyrological fragments can help us restore the poem itself").

[35] As Hollis 2009, viii admits in the Preface (to the first edition of 1990), "for substantial progress, we need new papyri of *Hecale* itself; as well as Egypt, perhaps one day Herculaneum will reveal its secrets". Hollis counterbalances the lack of such evidence in his 2009 second edition by gleaning information from the Byzantine sources (both the lexicographical collections and the authors from Nonnus to Michael Choniates who had imitated the *Hecale*).

[36] Some of these additions can be found in Appendices I "Some Other Fragments" and V "Ten Poetic Citations in *Suidas*" of the Hollis edition (Hollis 2009, 333–336 and 358–361).

and speculation (for example when he makes a clear division between the *Fragmenta Hecalae* and the *Fragmenta Incerta*), but is more bold than his predecessor in suggesting new solutions to the old textual and interpretational problems of the poem.[37]

But to recreate the *Hecale* relying only on textual transmission is not sufficient; editors and readers must resort to other strategies to reconstruct the lost original. Unlike the *Aetia*, which is rather fluid in its structure, the *Hecale* follows a more fixed design. Thus, if we were able to reveal its underlying compositional plan, then we could adequately address the key problems stemming from its unfinished state. In other words, we must reimagine the *Hecale* moving from its core, i.e., its narrative layout, towards its periphery, by arranging the surviving fragments into clusters and then supplementing the missing parts based on plausible hypotheses. In this sense, the *Hecale* is not visualized as a puzzle whose parts can be rearranged within a fixed frame, but rather as a fragmented body whose relationship with its lost or damaged parts can only be established through philological speculation and, hence, each rearrangement of these parts (the "members") within the poem (the "body") dramatically changes its design and composition.[38] The image also suggests the concept of wholeness and organic unity, and their rescinding, in the *Hecale*, which is quite different from the discontinuity and interchangeability of the parts constituting the *Aetia*.[39]

To reinforce the metaphor of the "fragmented body", one has first to address the questions surrounding the composition of the *Hecale*. According to the ancient scholia, Callimachus wrote this epyllion as a response to his literary opponents and their ironic claims that he was incapable of composing a "long or grand (in scale or tone)" poem (Sch. in Call. *Hymn*. 2.106). Although we are not sure whether this comment reflects the thoughts of Callimachus himself or the ones projected posthumously on his work by his later readers, and despite

---

[37] This is illustrated e.g. by the grouping of the *extra ordinem narrationis* fragments not in alphabetical order, as Pfeiffer did, but according to their subject-matter (Hollis 2009, 48 and 269).
[38] The "text-as-body" metaphor was introduced by Plato who envisaged discourse (λόγος) as a body with head and feet properly attached to it (*Phaedr.* 264c), whereas Aristotle paralleled the plot to a living body in regard to its magnitude (μέγεθος, *Poet.* 1451a3–6).
[39] Both metaphors, that of the puzzle and the fragmented body, should be viewed against the background of Aristotelian "wholeness" (*Poet.* 1451a.31–34): τὸν μῦθον, ἐπεὶ πράξεως μίμησίς ἐστι, μιᾶς τε εἶναι καὶ ταύτης ὅλης, καὶ τὰ μέρη συνεστάναι τῶν πραγμάτων οὕτως ὥστε μετατιθεμένου τινὸς μέρους ἢ ἀφαιρουμένου διαφέρεσθαι καὶ κινεῖσθαι τὸ ὅλον ("the plot, since it is a representation of action, ought to represent a single action and a whole one at that; and its parts ought to be constructed so that, when some part is transposed or removed, the whole is disrupted and disturbed" transl. R. Janko).

the ambiguity of the term μέγα ποίημα, it appears that the *Hecale* was conceived both as a tribute to traditional epic narrative and an attempt to renew epic.[40] This dual generic identity of the *Hecale*, its quality of being epic and not epic at the same time, poses numerous challenges to editors and readers.[41]

Taking the paratextual material of the *Diegesis* and Plutarch's *Theseus* 12 and 14 (after Philochorus, probably one of Callimachus' sources) as a starting point, one can roughly outline the contents of the *Hecale* (its *fabula*), glean limited information about the arrangement of the events (its *story*) and detect only occasional hints of its verbal representation (its *text*).[42] The *Hecale*, narrating one of Theseus' labors, the capturing of the Marathon bull, is based on a linear plot, comprising the journey of Theseus from Troezen to Athens until the events directly following his successful taming of the bull. However, the ancient testimonia and the surviving fragments suggest that Callimachus, rather than focusing on the young hero and his feat, turned the spotlight on the obscure old woman Hecale and her encounter with Theseus during a stormy night. In Aristotle's terms, this work has (or strongly suggests) a plot that *could be* self-contained and organic, but, in effect, steers the attention towards a peripheral episode, a "snapshot", i.e. the hospitality offered by Hecale.[43]

But, while *Hecale*'s *fabula* is simple and its larger thematic framework of Theseus' adventure complies with traditional epic, its plot- and timeline are distorted. The epyllion starts neither from the beginning of Theseus' itinerary from Troezen in linear progression nor *in medias res* from a critical stage of the hero's adventure, such as the tempest, but zooms in on Hecale in her Attic abode and then briefly refers to her legendary hospitality (frs. 230–231 Pf.= 1–2 H.). This is an assumption adopted both by Pfeiffer and Hollis who, with a dose of philological speculation, combine the incipit provided by the *Diegesis* with other

---

[40] For a well-argued analysis of the ancient scholion and the generic qualities of the *Hecale* within the tradition of short hexameter poetry, see Gutzwiller 2012.

[41] The generic "paradox" inherent in the *Hecale*, i.e. that it is a grand and short epic at the same time, is best summarized by Gutzwiller 2012, 232–233: "The term μέγα ποίημα would suggest, to those familiar with third-century poetic theory, the contradiction of labelling 'grand' a poetic unit designed to highlight refinement of word choice and arrangement. It was a huge challenge to maintain the verbal perfection demanded of the technically proficient poet in a longer composition with a tightly structured plot, fully developed characters, and complex dialogue, but this was what Callimachus undertook to do in writing the *Hecale*".

[42] These narratological categories were introduced by Bal 1985; other theorists have adopted different views by distinguishing e.g. between *fabula* (story)-*sjuzhet* (plot) (Shklovsky) and *story-narrative* (Genette).

[43] For this understanding of the epyllion which focuses on a "snapshot", thus causing a major retardation of the central heroic "praxis", see Sistakou 2009b, esp. 298–306.

textual evidence and testimonia.⁴⁴ It is also argued by both editors that immediately after this very short introduction (comprising no more than three lines) there followed the episode about Theseus and Medea in Athens (fr. 232 Pf.=3–7 H.), in which first the recognition scene between Theseus and Aigeus (frs. 235–236 Pf.=9–11 H.) took place and then a flashback to the Troezenian childhood of the hero (frs. 12–15 H.) was embedded. Editors also assumed that after this point the plot developed in a linear sequence of events: the departure of Theseus for Marathon, the tempest, the hero's sheltering in Hecale's hut, the extensive hospitality scene, the fight with the Marathonian bull, the return of the hero, Hecale's funeral and the constitution of the aitia in her honour.⁴⁵ There are, however, at least three additional "digressions" to be found in this narrative sequence, i.e. the flashback to Hecale's past and the retrospective narrations of the heroic feats of Theseus in Corinth, which were almost certainly embedded in the dinner scene, the enigmatic dialogue between two birds on Attic antiquities and an obscure ἀγγελία, which, according to the Vienna tablet, was placed somewhere after the feat of Theseus but without any clear thematic link to it.⁴⁶

Since editors have given their hypothetical answers to the question of *Hecale*'s composition, at which point in the procedure of "finishing" the poem does the reader come into play? The first step to be taken is to distance oneself from *Hecale*'s plot layout both as suggested by the *Diegesis* and implemented by the editors. Indeed, the former may be utterly misleading, as numerous cases of dissonance between the *Diegeses* and the surviving fragments in the *Aetia* clearly demonstrate,⁴⁷ whereas the latter involves the danger of accepting the edited Pfeiffer/Hollis text as the definitive text, the one that best captures Callimachus' authorial intention. Readers should be alerted to the fact that the narrative of the *Hecale* was only partially "linear" (an impression falsely reproduced by the editing of the fragments "*ad ordinem narrationis*"), since Callimachus often resorts to flashbacks, "story within a story" and "nested loops" narrative techniques as also to learned digressions geographically or thematically clustered.

---

44 Pfeiffer 1949–1953, 1.229 maintains that "*carmen (sine 'prooemio') ab Hecalae domicilio nunc constat*" ("it is now agreed that the poem began (without a proem) from Hecale's abode") and Hollis 1997 boldly supplements the poem's opening based on a paraphrasis of the lines by Choniates.
45 For a hypothetical reconstruction of the plot and hence the arrangement of the fragments, see Pfeiffer 1949–1953, 1.229 and Hollis 2009, 46–48.
46 On the editorial and compositional problems arising from these digressions, see Hollis 2009, 175–177 and 224–233.
47 That *Hecale*'s narrative outline given by the *Diegesis* should not be confused with its actual plot- and timeline is stressed by Hollis 2009, 46–47.

The "fragmented body" metaphor may be useful to readers as a reminder that different arrangements of the individual parts not only disfigure the reconstructed body but result in different bodies. In other words, deciding the ordering of the episodes, scenes and digressions and determining the temporal patterns that drive the plot in the *Hecale* create various versions of the poem which correspond to diverse poetic strategies on the writing of epic. A simple example: where should the aitiological climax of the *Hecale* be located? A widely accepted answer is after the events of Hecale's funeral, which, according to the *Diegesis* and editorial consensus, took place in linear sequence towards the end of the poem.⁴⁸ It should be emphasized, though, that this is just one possibility. Given that the honours established after Hecale's death were thematically linked to the theme of hospitality (a recurrent *Leitmotiv* found also at the beginning and in the middle of the poem), it is possible that the poem's double, or triple, aition — the naming of the Attic deme, the building of a τέμενος in honour of Ἑκάλειος Ζεύς and the constitution of the annual Ἑκάλεια δεῖπνα — was placed after the opening lines or embedded in digressions while the main plot unfolded. The first is an intriguing possibility, since there is a visible gap between the opening lines on Hecale (which might also have included aitiology in the form of etymology)⁴⁹ and the dramatic leap to the Theseus-Medea plot. The latter case is amply evidenced by other aitiological narratives of Callimachus, such as the aition of the "Sicilian cities" and "Acontius and Cydippe" from the *Aetia*.⁵⁰

A reader specializing in Callimachus might observe that the random interchange between plot and aitiological lore is an essential feature of the *Aetia* — so why not of the *Hecale* as well? A genre-oriented reader might review the design of the *Hecale* through the lens of epic narration by considering the innovations found in other Hellenistic epyllia and the narratological features of aitiological poetry; thus, the "nonlinear" and "multilinear" directions of *Hecale*'s narration would come into view. A reader interested in reception might attempt to reconstruct the lost *Hecale* through its later, Latin, Greek and Byzantine, imitations, by assuming that the safest way to approach Callimachus' epyllion

---

48 See Hollis 2009, 263–269.
49 Whether the opening lines also referred to the name "Hecale" and its etymology, is open to speculation: see Pfeiffer 1949–1953, 1 on fr. 230 *"fortasse nominis Hecalae veriloquium cum his versibus coniunctum erat"* ("perhaps the etymology of the name 'Hecale' was connected to these verses"). Hollis 2009, 139 is more sceptical when he states that "etymologizing of names is certainly typical of Hellenistic poets ... but I am not wholly convinced that Callimachus is likely to have played with Hecale's name at this stage of the poem".
50 For Callimachus' strategy of deconstructing the stories he tells in the *Aetia*, which I have termed "denarrating the narratable", see Sistakou 2019.

would be to resort to the *Diegesis*, Plutarch and Choniates. And yet a reader trained in formalism and aesthetics might argue for the uniqueness of *Hecale*'s style, which renders any attempt at reconstruction impossible, since Callimachus is notorious for the unexpected twists and turns of his poetry. By reading diversely and dynamically, each "interpretive community" would thus create its own version of *Hecale* and ideally produce "multiple texts" in place of a definitive one.[51]

4 Conclusion: "unfinishedness" and reader response

As can be inferred from the preceding analysis, the contemporary reader of the two "unfinished" Callimachean poems, the *Aetia* and *Hecale*, is faced with a highly mediated text that for centuries has been seen as a space for editorial experimentation. Commentators and scholars have ventured not only to establish the authoritative text but also to re-write Callimachus' fragmentary poems as closely to the lost original as possible. Moreover, in addition to the questioning of editorial interventions there is another challenge posed by Callimachus' poetics, namely, fragmentariness as a structural and narrative device. In essence, both the *Aetia* and the *Hecale* experiment with the generic conventions of elegiac and epic storytelling by challenging the idea of wholeness, comprehensiveness and linearity. Thus, the "unfinished" poems of Callimachus are paradoxically also a result of an aesthetic choice, which renders them difficult to reconstruct and allows for various readings.

This conclusion leads us back to Roland Barthes' argument, which challenged the authority of a single authentic text and instead asserted the reader as a defining factor of its understanding. The author may be the producer, the "scriptor" of the text, and, in the case of Callimachus, his editors function as interpreters of the poet's assumed intentions, but the reader is called to re-create the poems actively and individually. By thus destabilizing the concept of

---

[51] The textual critic Donald Reiman has introduced the notion of "versioning", an editorial practice according to which a text should be offered to readers in its various versions and not filtered through "eclectic editing"; he thus places emphasis on editing as a progressive, cumulative, and communal procedure (Reiman 1987, 167–180). "Versioning" would prove illuminating in the case of Callimachus in reflecting the experimental and progressive nature of works like the *Aetia* and the *Hecale*.

the authorial and editorial intentions, readers of the *Aetia* and the *Hecale* generate multiple texts which reflect their theoretical and aesthetic expectations as well as their cultural biases. New papyrological discoveries or different interpretations of existing textual evidence could easily overturn such hypothetical readings. Until then, the "unfinishedness" of Callimachus' poems, reinforced by the poet's penchant for fragmentariness, will remain a source of fascination for generations of sophisticated readers to come.[52]

Bibliography

Acosta-Hughes, Benjamin/Stephens, Susan A. (2001), "*Aetia* fr. 1.5: I Told my Story like a Child", *ZPE* 136, 214–216.

Ambühl, Annemarie (2007), "Children as Poets – Poets as Children? Romantic Constructions of Childhood and Hellenistic Poetry", in: Ada Cohen/Jeremy B. Rutter (eds.), *Constructions of Childhood in Ancient Greece and Italy*, Princeton, 373–383.

Bal, Mieke (1985), *Narratology. Introduction to the Theory of Narrative*, Toronto.

Bornstein, George (1991), *Representing Modernist Texts. Editing as Interpretation*, Ann Arbor.

Buckland, Warren (2009), *Puzzle Films: Complex Storytelling in Contemporary Cinema*, Oxford.

Cozzoli, Adele-Teresa (2011), "The Poet as a Child", in: Benjamin Acosta-Hughes/Luigi Lehnus/Susan Stephens (eds.), *Brill's Companion to Callimachus*, Leiden/Boston, 407–428.

Derda, Tomasz/Hilder, Jennifer/Kwapisz, Jan (eds.) (2017), *Fragments, Holes, and Wholes. Reconstructing the Ancient World in Theory and Practice*, Warsaw.

Fish, Stanley E. (1976), "Interpreting the 'Variorum'", *Critical Inquiry* 2, 465–485.

Genette, Gérard (1988), "Structure and Functions of the Title in Literature", *Critical Inquiry* 14, 692–720.

Genette, Gérard (2009) [1997], *Paratexts. Thresholds of Interpretation*, trans. by Jane E. Lewin/foreword by Richard Macksey, Cambridge.

Guignery, Vanessa/Drąg, Wojciech (eds.) (2019), *The Poetics of Fragmentation in Contemporary British and American Fiction*, Wilmington, Delaware.

Gutzwiller, Kathryn (1992), "Callimachus' *Lock of Berenice*: Fantasy, Romance, and Propaganda", *AJPh* 113, 359–385.

Gutzwiller, Kathryn (2012), "The *Hecale* and Hellenistic Conceptions of Short Hexameter Narratives", in: Manuel Baumbach/Silvio Bär (eds.), *Brill's Companion to Greek and Latin 'Epyllion' and Its Reception*, Leiden, 221–244.

Harder, Annette (1998), "Generic Games in Callimachus' *Aetia*", in: Annette Harder/Gerry C. Wakker/Remco F. Regtuit (eds.), *Genre in Hellenistic Poetry*, Groningen, 95–113.

---

[52] On the fascination of reconstructing "an imaginary whole" in literature and art, see Most 2009, who observes that if we had to choose between the fragment and the original, real whole we would perhaps choose the fragment "because the hypothetical whole we can imagine on its basis can come to seem far more deeply satisfying to us, because we ourselves have helped to create it" (p. 19).

Harder, Annette (2004), "Narrator, Narratees and Narrative in Callimachus", in: Irene J.F. de Jong/René Nünlist/Angus Bowie (eds.), *Narrators, Narratees and Narratives in Ancient Greek Literature*, Leiden/Boston, 63–81.

Harder, Annette (2011), "Callimachus as Fragment", in: Benjamin Acosta-Hughes/Luigi Lehnus/Susan Stephens (eds.), *Brill's Companion to Callimachus*, Leiden/Boston, 63–80.

Harder, Annette (2012), *Callimachus: Aetia*, Vols. 1–2, Oxford.

Hollis, Adrian S. (1997), "The Beginning of Callimachus' *Hecale*", *ZPE* 115, 55–56.

Hollis, Adrian S. (2009), *Callimachus* Hecale, Oxford.

Hunter, Richard (2005), "The Hesiodic *Catalogue* and Hellenistic Poetry", in: Richard Hunter (ed.), *The Hesiodic Catalogue of Women*, Cambridge, 239–265.

Iser, Wolfgang (1978), *The Act of Reading: A Theory of Aesthetic Response*, London.

Kennedy, Scott (2016), "Callimachus in a Later Context: Michael Choniates", *Eikasmos* 27, 291–312.

Kiss, Miklós/Willemsen, Steven (2018), "Wallowing in Dissonance: The Attractiveness of Impossible Puzzle Films", in: Ian Christie/Annie van den Oever (eds.), *Stories: Screen Narrative in the Digital Era*, Amsterdam, 55–84.

Lehnus, Luigi (2011), "Callimachus Rediscovered in Papyri", in: Benjamin Acosta-Hughes/Luigi Lehnus/Susan Stephens (eds.), *Brill's Companion to Callimachus*, Leiden/Boston, 23–38.

Massimilla, Giulio (1996), *Aitia: Libri primo e secondo*, Pisa/Rome.

Massimilla, Giulio (2010), *Aitia: Libro terzo e quarto*, Pisa/Rome.

Massimilla, Giulio (2011), "The *Aetia* through Papyri", in: Benjamin Acosta-Hughes/Luigi Lehnus/Susan Stephens (eds.), *Brill's Companion to Callimachus*, Leiden/Boston, 39–62.

Morrison, Andrew D. (2007), *The Narrator in Archaic Greek and Hellenistic Poetry*, Cambridge.

Most, Glenn W. (2009), "On Fragments", in: William Tronzo (ed.), *The Fragment: An Incomplete History*, Los Angeles, 9–22.

Pfeiffer, Rudolf (1949–1953), *Callimachus*, Vols. 1–2, Oxford.

Pontani, Filippomaria (2011), "Callimachus Cited", in: Benjamin Acosta-Hughes/Luigi Lehnus/Susan Stephens (eds.), *Brill's Companion to Callimachus*, Leiden/Boston, 93–117.

Reiman, Donald H. (1987), *Romantic Texts and Contexts*, Columbia, Missouri.

Sistakou, Evina (2009a), "Fragments of an Imaginary Past: Strategies of Mythical Narration in Apollonius' *Argonautica* and Callimachus' *Aitia*", *RFIC* 137, 380–401.

Sistakou, Evina (2009b), "'Snapshots' of Myth: The Notion of Time in Hellenistic Epyllion", in: Jonas Grethlein/Antonios Rengakos (eds.), *Narratology and Interpretation: The Content of the Form in Ancient Texts*, Berlin.

Sistakou, Evina (2019), "Denarrating the Narratable in the *Aetia*: A Postmodern Take on Callimachean Aesthetics", in: Jacqueline J.H. Klooster/Annette Harder/Remco F. Regtuit/Gerry C. Wakker (eds.), *Callimachus Revisited. New Perspectives in Callimachean Scholarship*, Leuven, 329–350.

Sistakou, Evina (2021), "Borges in Alexandria? Modes of Ambiguity in Hellenistic Poetry", in: Martin Vöhler/Therese Fuhrer/Stavros Frangoulidis (eds.), *Strategies of Ambiguity in Ancient Literature*, Berlin/Boston, 101–121.

Tanselle, Thomas (1990), *Textual Criticism and Scholarly Editing*, Charlottesville, Virginia.

Tanselle, Thomas (1995), "The Varieties of Scholarly Editing", in: David C. Greetham (ed.), *Scholarly Editing: A Guide to Research*, New York, 9–32.

Myrto Garani
How to Walk Along a Pioneer's Fragmentary Track: Theophrastus' *Meteorological* Studies

Abstract: The paper revisits the problems involved in what can be called the "modern reception" of Theophrastus' meteorological studies and in particular his Μεταρσιολογικά, a treatise which is preserved only in fragmentary Syriac and Arabic translations. It explores the tension caused by two contradictory scholarly criteria, i.e. textual scarcity versus presumed significant impact. It argues that, given the fact that the original Theophrastean source text is rendered from ancient Greek into Syriac, then again into Arabic, and finally into English, what we study as Theophrastus' meteorological treatise is the final textual product of a multi-layered process of translation and cultural transference. Within this framework, it discusses various factors which define our reconstruction of Theophrastus' scientific and literary portrait. Particular emphasis is placed upon his intertextual relationship with Homer, Aristophanes and Lucretius.

1 Introduction

I owe my acquaintance with Theophrastus' meteorological studies to my research on Lucretius' *DRN* Book 6. There is a scholarly consensus that, while Lucretius explains the physical causes of various dreadful atmospheric and subterranean phenomena by recourse to analogical images and multiple explanations in order to liberate his pupil, Memmius, from the fear of gods and death, he looks back — indirectly via Epicurus or even directly — to Theophrastus' meteorological treatise, the so-called Μεταρσιολογικά. From this work Lucretius draws not only specific explanations but also hermeneutic principles and specific metaphorical vehicles. Still, given the fact that all we know about Theophrastus' meteorological account must be drawn from 10th century Syriac-Arabic fragmentary translations, it is not difficult to realize that something is missing from our crystallized image of Theophrastus, Aristotle's colleague and successor as head of the Lyceum, as a pioneer meteorologist.

I would like to thank Jacqueline Fabre-Serris, Marco Formisano and Stavros Frangoulidis for their invitation to the conference and their hard work afterwards. Han Baltussen and Sophia Papaioannou read an earlier version of my paper and offered invaluable encouragement and insightful comments, for which I am more than grateful.

To make things worse, contrary to the scantiness and the idiosyncratic nature of our sources — an issue to which I will come back below in more detail — a quick look at relevant scholarship readily points to a striking paradox: despite the fact that today we have only very limited and fragmentary access to Theophrastus' original meteorological studies, scholars unanimously agree that Theophrastus' meteorological ideas were extremely influential in the history of the field.[1]

The focus of the present volume provides me with the opportunity to revisit the framework of what can be called the *modern reception* of Theophrastus' meteorological studies, and explore the tension caused by these two contradictory statements, i.e. *textual scarcity* versus presumed *significant impact*. Along these lines, I will consider the ways in which our restricted access to Theophrastus' meteorological writings affects our grasp of his ideas and consequently the assessment of his role in the history of the field. To do so, it is necessary to shift the focus of our inquiry from the specific information about Theophrastus' natural studies that we can glean from subsequent writers to the theoretical implications and parameters entailed by the fact that such a pivotal text, despite its great impact, is lost in its original and can be recovered only from secondary sources. As we will see, the drawing of our *own* picture of Theophrastus is dictated by both *ancient* and *modern* reception, the latter being different from what I will refer to as "*our* reception"; both ancient and modern processes will be shown to function as a *distorting lens* when it comes to *our* perceiving of Theophrastus' identity.

It was Aristotle, Theophrastus' teacher, who wrote the first extant treatise entitled Μετεωρολογικά (from the Greek word μετέωρα, referring to "things in the sky"), in order to offer naturalistic explanations of meteorological phenomena and thus reject the role of the traditional gods. Aristotle claims that the term μετεωρολογία had already been used by "all our predecessors" (*Mete.* 338a26 ὃ πάντες οἱ πρότεροι μετεωρολογίαν ἐκάλουν). His treatise is part of the larger project of studying nature and natural motion (*Physics, On Heavens, On Generation and Corruption*). Since Aristotle claims that meteorological phenomena are caused by the motions in the celestial region and in turn affect living beings on

---

[1] Daiber 1992, 292–293: "Theophrastus' *Meteorology* has influenced later authors till the 6th century A.D. Traces can be found already in Epicurus, then in Strato of Lampsacus; the compiler of the Aristotelian *Problemata physica*; the author of *De mundo*; the Stoics, above all Posidonius; Lucretius; Nicolaus Damascenus; Seneca; Arius Didymus; Vitruvius; Pliny; Plutarch; Flavius Arrianus (2nd c. A.D); Alexander of Aphrodisias; Ammianus Marcellinus; Galen; Adamantius; Proclus; Philoponus; Olympiodorus".

earth, he attributes to the meteorological processes an intermediating role. Aristotle defines the topic of his enquiry as "everything which happens naturally, but with a regularity less than that of the primary element of bodies, in the region which borders most nearly on the movements of the stars" (*Mete.* 338b20–22 ταῦτα δ' ἐστὶν ὅσα συμβαίνει κατὰ φύσιν μέν, ἀτακτοτέραν μέντοι τῆς τοῦ πρώτου στοιχείου τῶν σωμάτων, περὶ τὸν γειτνιῶντα μάλιστα τόπον τῇ φορᾷ τῇ τῶν ἄστρων). Μετεωρολογικά sought to explain weather phenomena, such as wind, rain, thunder, lightning (now classified as atmospheric), as well as comets and earthquakes (now regarded as astronomical or seismological, respectively).

In the history of meteorological studies, Theophrastus is the second philosopher to whom a treatise devoted exclusively to this topic is ascribed. Diogenes Laertius (V.44) refers to a treatise consisting of two books (Μεταρσιολογικῶν α' β'), part of Theophrastus' Περὶ Φυσικῶν. Plutarch mentions a fourth book (*Quaest. Graec.* 292C). Speaking in more general terms about Theophrastus' meteorological studies, Robert Sharples claims that "we are relatively well informed from *direct* sources" [my emphasis].[2] However, as I am going to argue, this statement can be proved to be rather misleading. Let me first briefly review our main evidence. Of the relevant works, only Theophrastus' treatises *On Winds* and *On Fire* are preserved in their original Greek.[3] The treatise *On Waters*, also listed in Diogenes Laertius, is now lost. A summary of Theophrastus' meteorological treatise, most likely incomplete, can be recovered from Proclus' *Commentary on* Plato's *Timaeus* (*In Platonis Timaeum* 35A = ii p. 121.3 Diehl = Theophr. 159 FHS&G). Last but not least, almost half of our meteorological testimonia are derived from Aristotle's ancient commentators.[4]

---

[2] Sharples 1998a, 144.
[3] See the recent edition by Mayhew 2017. See also Coutant and Eichenlaub 1975.
[4] Theophrastus frs. 186a–194 (FHS&G 1992, 356–365): 186A: Alexander of Aphrodisias, *On Aristotle's* Meteorology 2.4 361a22–b1 (CAG vol. 3.2 p. 93.26–94.2 Hayduck), 186B: Olympiodorus, *On Aristotle's* Meteorology 1.13 349a12–b1 (CAG vol. 12.2 p. 97.5–17 Stüve), 187: Alexander of Aphrodisias, *On Aristotle's* Meteorology 2.6 364b14–17 (CAG vol. 3.2 p. 112.26–34 Hayduck), 188: Alexander of Aphrodisias, *On Aristotle's* Meteorology 2.6 363b24–5 (CAG vol. 3.2 p. 108.30–3 Hayduck). For ancient philosophical commentary see Baltussen 2016 and 2018. For meteorology and commentary tradition in Byzantium, see Telelis 2019.

2 The oriental tradition in translation

Scholars usually focus their attention on three texts of the so-called oriental tradition: 1) a fragmentary Syriac translation of Theophrastus' work — or, according to some scholars, of a Hellenistic compilation of the original Theophrastean work which was adapted into an Aristotelian framework — probably by the Nestorian Job of Edessa (dated to the beginning of the 9th cent., ed. Drossaart Lulofs 1955, Wagner/Steinmetz 1964),[5] 2) an incomplete Arabic paraphrasis of the Syriac translation by the Nestorian Bar Bahlūl (10th cent., ed. Bergsträsser, 1918) and 3) an independent — complete or abridged — Arabic *translation* of the Syriac translation plausibly by the Nestorian Ibn al-Khammār (10th cent.). This Arabic translation, manuscripts of which have been discovered in various places in India, was published in 1992 by Hans Daiber; in his edition, Daiber has taken into account the editions of the other Syriac-Arabic texts.[6] Similar meteorological material was plausibly replicated in Theophrastus' doxographical work, *Φυσικαί Δόξαι* (*Physical Opinions*), in which his goal was different, i.e. to compile a sort of encyclopaedia.[7]

Scholars agree that al-Khammār's text faithfully reproduces Theophrastus' *ideas*. Daiber remarks that, "As the Arabo-Syriac apparatus shows, the Arabic translation by Ibn al-Khammār can be regarded as the best substitute for the Greek text and its Syriac translation".[8] Along these lines, there is a general scholarly agreement that the original Theophrastean work was neither an excerpt from a Theophrastean doxographical work nor a combination of doxography and theoretical discussions.[9] If we were to draw any conclusions from the evidence at our disposal, we could claim that we are dealing with a draft for lectures, in which Theophrastus expounds his *own* meteorological doctrines by means of illustrative examples. Nevertheless, we should bear in mind that a significant degree of uncertainty remains. To quote Ian Kidd, "It still seems to

---

[5] We do not know whether the Syriac translator shortened his Greek original himself or used a Greek text which is a summary of the original.
[6] Daiber 1992. See now Daiber's revised edition of the Arabic translation 2021. See also Taub 2003, 115–124. For Theophrastus' presence in the Arabic tradition, see Daiber 1985 and Gutas 1985. For the Syriac fragments of Theophrastean meteorology see Takahashi 2002. For the Aristotelian meteorology in Syriac, see Takahashi 2004. For the reception of Aristotle's meteorology in the Arab world, see Lettinck 1999 and 2015.
[7] Sedley 1998, 182 who believes that in *DRN* 6 Lucretius looks back to Theophrastus' *Physical Opinions*.
[8] Daiber 1992, 219.
[9] Daiber 1992, 285. For the opposite view, see Bergsträsser 1918.

me an open question as to what extent the evidence may be a collection or how diluted, composite, garbled, epitomised or faithful a survival it is of an ultimate Theophrastean original".[10]

In his *Metarsiologica*, Theophrastus discusses the causes of the phenomena in the following order: thunder, lightning, thunder occurring without lightning, lightning without thunder, the reasons why lightning precedes thunder, thunderbolts, clouds, different kinds of rain, snow, hail, dew, hoar frost, different winds, the halo around the moon and earthquakes. Unlike Aristotle, Theophrastus seems to exclude discussion of the Milky Way, comets, and shooting stars.

One can easily realize the idiosyncratic nature of the text that Daiber has handed down to us. Given the fact that the original Theophrastean source text is rendered from ancient Greek into Syriac, then again into Arabic, and finally into English, what *we* study as Theophrastus' meteorological treatise is the final *textual product* of a *multi-layered* process of *translation* and *cultural transference*. We do not even know whether we are dealing with a fragment of the original work or with a testimony of its immediate Hellenistic or Syriac reception, in case the Syriac translator used a summary of the original Greek text made either by someone else or even by *himself*. We should also bear in mind that the majority of scholars who study Theophrastus' meteorology — and certainly I am not the exception to this rule — do not have the required language skills and thus no direct access to the Syriac or Arabic transcribed text — not to mention the manuscripts themselves — and so they are bound to rely *exclusively* on Daiber's authority and his translation.[11]

Ibn al-Khammār gives us elsewhere a general idea of *his* own method of translation: "The translator who wants to convey the meaning [of the author whom he translates] must understand the language from which he translates so that he can think in it like a native speaker of the language, and he must know how to use the language from which he translates and the language into which he translates".[12]

---

[10] Kidd 1992, 294.

[11] A further complicating factor is the arguments that were recently raised by Bakker 2016 against the authenticity of the Theophrastean origin of the Arabic text or at least part of it (i.e. the so-called theological excursus). Bakker (2016, 153) went so far as to claim that "It is possible, however, that the Syriac meteorology is a compendium of some sort, derived for the most part from Epicurus' meteorology, but supplemented and 'corrected' on the basis of other, possibly Peripatetic or even specifically Theophrastean theories." See also discussion in Van Raalte 2003.

[12] Daiber (1992, 220) quotes Ibn al-Khammār's statement from a critical note on Athanasius of Balad's Syriac translation of Aristotle's *Sophistici Elenchi*.

2.1 Translation as an interpretative intervention

When it comes to the translation of Theophrastus' meteorology, Ibn al-Khammār assimilates it into his own *cultural* and *religious* context. In a way similar to Lucretius' practice of providing Roman examples for didactic purposes,[13] when Ibn al-Khammār translates Theophrastus' description of the impact of lightning upon metals, such as gold or silver, he refers to *dinars* (*Metars.* 6.86–91).[14] Ibn al-Khammār also inserts references to the Christian God (*Metars.* 14.17: "might and exalted is He"; 14.28–29: "There is no indication of passing away in the case of God and any indication of being like an angel").[15]

Daiber points to at least two cases of al-Khammār's *mistranslations* from Syriac into Arabic, characterized as *Syriacisms*, which may have an impact on *our* interpretation of Theophrastus. In both cases, Daiber identifies Syriac words that bear double meanings, and claims that al-Khammār chooses the wrong one of the two meanings and thus ends up with the wrong translation. In *Metars.* 7.3, when Theophrastus discusses the formation of clouds and gives as a possible cause the transformation of air into water (due to the accumulation of air), al-Khammār translates the latter phrase as "*nature* of water" instead of "*watery substance*". In *Metars.* 6.81, when Theophrastus explains why thunderbolts reach the high places and not the low ones before they are dissolved, al-Khammār has Theophrastus point analogically to the image of *clay* which would behave in a similar manner. Daiber remarks that this illustration would not be an effective one since, due to its mineral ingredients, clay could not become dissipated. In order to make the image more scientifically accurate, Daiber opts for *earth*, a word that he spots in the still unpublished *Hexaemeron* by the Nestorian Moses Bar Kepha (c. 813–903). In this Syriac work of the 9th cent., we can also find extensive excerpts of Theophrastus' *Meteorology*, which unfortunately are not

---

13 See discussion in Garani (2007, 58–61) about the Presocratic socio-political imagery which is assimilated into the Roman context (e.g. the use of phrases such as *foedera naturai* "the laws of nature" and *alte terminus haerens* "deep-set boundary mark").
14 *Metars.* 6.86–91 "When, moreover, someone demands that we give the reason why the thunderbolt, when it falls upon a purse with *dinars*, does not affect the purse but affects and melts the *dinars*, we can give (this) answer. The purse is porous, so that it gives the thunderbolt a way to penetrate. But because the *dinars* are dense and do not give (the thunderbolt) a passage, the result is that the violent thunderbolt comes to a standstill at them. For this reason it has no influence upon the purse, but affects and melts the *dinars*." (Translation by Daiber). Cf. also the reference to the desert which plausibly is added in *Metars.* 2.6, in which Theophrastus explains lightning caused by friction by reference to the rubbing of wood.
15 Strohmaier 1968, 131–132.

always literal translations, but paraphrases with added information from other sources and his own observations.[16] However, we should perhaps be more cautious and refrain from correcting what we actually read in al-Khammār's Arabic version, since otherwise we rather rely on our preconception of what ideally would be for Theophrastus an elucidating scientific explanation, a preconception which is formed due to our knowledge of his other writings. And such a correction may be indicative of the way that we, as modern readers, impose *our* expectations upon Theophrastus' scientific value.

There is one striking case in which we can identify the Arabic and modern translators' embarrassment when it comes to dealing with a particularly obscure phenomenon, that of *prester* (13.43–44). According to Aristotle (*Mete.* 371a15–18), *prester* is the name given to a hot or rarefied wind that is drawn down from the clouds and because of its conflagration, the neighboring air catches fire and becomes coloured. Aristotle derives its name from πίμπρημι ("I burn")/πρήθω ("I blow up"). In the treatise *On Fire* (*De igne* 1.8–9), Theophrastus views the *prester*, like Aristotle before him, as a fiery whirlwind, closely related to the thunderbolt. By contrast, in his *Metarsiologica* Theophrastus argues that *prester* is of windy nature; along these lines, he changes the standard doxographical order of the topics and places the discussion of *prester* under the heading of winds.[17] The modern translator (Daiber) suppresses the fact that the Greek word is not translated either in the Syriac original (since apparently no Syriac word could be found), or in the Arabic texts and this is the practice that he himself follows. At this point it should not go unobserved that in his translation of Bar Bahlūl's Arabic paraphrasis (§ 52), Bergsträsser also has the Greek word, but he gives a translation in German too.[18] Still, in order to shed light upon the inexplicable phenomenon, Daiber seems to have turned to Lucretius' corresponding account about *prester* (*DRN* 6.423–435):

---

[16] Gottschalk (1965, 761) finds an analogy with Strato fr. 73 Wehrli "water falling from a height falls as a continuous stream from some distance but then breaks up into drops."

[17] In Theophrastus' *On Winds* 53, the term πρηστήρ is used to describe a waterspout. The origin of *presteres* is attributed to the *conflict* of contrary winds. See Mayhew 2017, 321–324. In the opening section of his *On Fire* (*De igne* 1.4–11), Theophrastus states that most fire is generated "with force as it were" and goes on to give as an example the concentration and compression (and so friction) of air in clouds, which forcibly produce "*presters* and lightning bolts". For more on *prester* in Lucretius and his predecessors see Garani (2022).

[18] Bergsträsser 1918, 23.

> *Quod superest, facilest ex his cognoscere rebus,*
> ***presteras Graii quos ab re nominitarunt,***
> *in mare qua missi ueniant ratione superne.* 425
> *nam fit ut interdum tamquam **demissa columna***
> *in mare de caelo descendat, quam freta circum*
> *feruescunt grauiter spirantibus incita flabris,*
> *et quaecumque in eo tum sint deprensa tumultu*
> *nauigia in summum ueniant uexata periclum.* 430
> *Hoc fit ubi interdum non quit uis incita uenti*
> *rumpere quam coepit nubem, sed deprimit, ut sit*
> *in mare de caelo **tamquam demissa columna**,*
> *paulatim, quasi quid pugno bracchique superne*
> *coniectu trudatur et extendatur in undas;* 435

"To pass on, it is easy from these thoughts to understand in what way *those things which the Greeks call from their nature presteres* come down from above into the sea. For it happens at times that a *kind of column* let down from the sky comes down into the sea, around which the waters boil stirred up by the heavy blast of the winds; and if any ships are caught in that tumult, they are tossed about and come into great peril. This happens when at times the force of the wind stirred up is unable to burst the cloud which it attempts to burst, but depresses it so that it is *like a column* let down from the sky into the sea, little by little, as though something were being pushed and stretched out towards the waves by a fist and the thrust of an arm from above." (Transl. by Rouse, revised by Smith)

In this Epicurean context, the Greek word πρηστήρ is again not translated, but transliterated, a rare case indeed in the Epicurean poem (*DRN* 6.424).[19] What is even more remarkable, in his effort to illuminate the phenomenon Lucretius compares it to a pillar (*DRN* 6.426, 433 *tamquam demissa columna* "a kind of column let down"). It seems, therefore, that under the influence of the Lucretian metaphorical image Daiber adapts what he reads in the Arabic translation and refers to Theophrastus' *prester* as being "similar to an airy pillar". In other words, the modern translator *imposes* on Theophrastus' reader his own interpretation of the phenomenon, taking it for granted that afterwards Lucretius also embraced it. The projection of Lucretius' text backwards in order to edit Theophrastus' fragmentary text reminds us of the similar practice to which Usener (1887), Epicurus' editor, resorted in connection with the corresponding passage about *prester* in Epicurus' *Letter to Pythocles* (*Ep. Pyth.* 104). In that context, we read the adverb στυλοειδῶς, which also bears metaphorical connotations of a column-like phenomenon; this textual emendation is probably based

---

19 Sedley 1998, 48–49.

on Lucretius' account.[20] Despite this interpretative intervention in silence, Daiber himself omitted as *interpolation* Ibn al-Khammār's clarification regarding the contradictory behaviour of a certain kind of wind, when the latter writes "However, we believe that the clouds are drawn by the wind which pushes away the ships" (*Metars.* 13.37–38).

2.2 Poetic intertext lost in translation

On a different front, while scholars strive to evaluate the *philosophical* and *scientific* status of Theophrastus within the meteorological tradition on the basis of the Syriac-Arabic tradition, I think that due to the atypical textual nature of the *Metarsiologica* they downgrade the impact of Theophrastus' possible engagement with intertexts from the previous poetic tradition. There are at least two such striking cases to which I would like to draw our attention.

Among the seven causes of thunder that Theophrastus puts forward, he suggests that this happens when fire falls into a humid cloud and then is extinguished. To explain this phenomenon, he uses the analogy of the tempering of iron: when a blacksmith throws iron into water, a great noise is produced (*Metars.* 1.9–11). In his account of the causes of lightning he resorts to the same image of the blacksmith, this time though to demonstrate how the thin part of the cloud is ignited, when fire is extinguished in a humid cloud (*Metars.* 2.10–12):

> *Metars.* 1.9–11 "The third case: When *fire* falls into a humid cloud and then is extinguished. We can observe something similar amongst us: When an ironsmith throws glowing iron into water, a great noise is the result."

> *Metars.* 2.10–12 "The third case: When *fire* is extinguished in a humid cloud, the thin (part) of (the cloud) is ignited. We can observe something similar amongst us: When the ironsmith (pl) submerges glowing iron in water, fire is caused by that." (Transl. by Daiber)

We should point to a seemingly slight intervention by Daiber; we do not have any indication why we should not keep the plural of ironsmiths in the image of a workshop, which in fact could make the illustration a more general one.[21]

It is generally agreed that Theophrastus may draw his explanations along with the illustrations by means of which he builds his analogies from the

---

20 Verde/De Sanctis 2022, 119.
21 See also the plural used in Bar Bahlūl's paraphrasis (§ 11), as we can see from Bergsträsser's German translation (1918, 15).

Presocratic tradition.[22] Aëtius ascribes an analogy similar to what is read in Theophrastus to Archelaus, with regard to the cause of thunder, lightning and relevant phenomena. Archelaus appeals to common experience and more precisely to "what happens to red-hot stones, when they are plunged into cold water" [D16 Laks/Most (DK60 A16) = Aët. 3.3.5 (Stob.)] under the heading περὶ βροντῶν ἀστραπῶν κεραυνῶν πρηστήρων τε καὶ τυφώνων "On thunders, lightnings, thunderbolts, *presters* and typhoons":

> Ἀρχέλαος ταὐτὸ λέγει παρατιθεὶς τὸ *τῶν διαπύρων λίθων καθιεμένων εἰς ψυχρὸν ὕδωρ πάθος*.
>
> Archelaus says the same thing [scil. as Anaxagoras about thunder, lightning, etc.], comparing them to what happens to *red-hot stones* when they are plunged into *cold water*. (Transl. by Laks and Most).

Still, Archelaus' analogical image is that of *fiery stones*, not of iron. Scholars generally believe that in his own explanation Theophrastus looks back intertextually to the *Homeric* image of the sound heard when a blacksmith immerses an axe or an adze in cold water (*Od.* 9.391–393):[23]

> ὡς δ' ὅτ' ἀνὴρ χαλκεὺς πέλεκυν μέγαν ἠὲ σκέπαρνον
> εἰν ὕδατι ψυχρῷ βάπτῃ μεγάλα ἰάχοντα
> φαρμάσσων· τὸ γὰρ αὖτε σιδήρου γε κράτος ἐστίν·
>
> [The Cyclops' eye hissed round the olive stake] in the same way that
> an axe or adze hisses when a smith plunges it into cold water to quench
> and strengthen the iron.
>
> (Transl. by E.V. Rieu, revised by D.C.H. Rieu in
> consultation with P.V. Jones)

In the original context, the image was used to describe the noise made by the glowing stake that Odysseus and his men twist into Polyphemus' eye. In his turn, Theophrastus has been identified as the intermediary ring in the intertextual chain that leads from Homer to Lucretius' corresponding explanation about thunder (*DRN* 6.145–149):[24]

---

[22] Daiber 1992, 287–288.
[23] Daiber 1992, 288. Cf. Quintilian's testimony that Theophrastus valued the reading of poets for the orators (Quint. *Institutio oratoria* 10.1.27 = 707 FHS&G).
[24] Garani 2007, 130–133.

> *Fit quoque, ubi e nubi in nubem vis incidit ardens*
> *fulminis: haec multo si forte umore recepit*   146
> *ignem, continuo magno clamore trucidat,*
> *ut calidis candens ferrum e fornacibus olim*
> *stridit, ubi in gelidum propter demersimus imbrem.*

"Thunder occurs also when the burning force of lightning falls from a cloud upon a cloud: if this cloud chance to be soaked with water when it receives the fire, it makes a great noise in destroying it at once, just as white-hot iron from the hot furnace often hisses when we have dipped it into cold water nearby." (Transl. by Rouse, revised by Smith 1992)

In a way similar to Theophrastus but now resuming the literary device of the Homeric simile, Lucretius also describes what happens when lightning falls from a cloud onto a water-laden cloud and the hissing sound of thunder is produced; he also compares thunder to the similar sound heard when a red-hot iron from a hot furnace is plunged into a vessel full of water. This very analogical image is replicated in later natural philosophical contexts — such as Seneca and Pliny — in association with the explanations of thunder.[25] The possibility that Theophrastus was plausibly the first to transplant this specific Homeric image into his meteorological context has not yet been adequately evaluated.

Regarding the explanation of thunder and lightning as a result of the collision and splitting up of clouds by means of the image of a bladder, Daiber points to a parallel in Aristophanes' *Clouds*. Socrates explains how a thunderbolt is caused due to dry wind which gets trapped in the clouds by appealing to what happens to a bladder (*Nu.* 403–407):[26]

> Στ.   οὐκ οἶδ᾽· ἀτὰρ εὖ σὺ λέγειν φαίνει. τί γάρ ἐστιν δῆθ᾽ ὁ κεραυνός;
> Σω.   ὅταν εἰς ταύτας (sc. τὰς νεφέλας) ἄνεμος ξηρὸς μετεωρισθεὶς κατακλῃσθῇ,
>   ἔνδοθεν αὐτὰς <u>ὥσπερ κύστιν</u> φυσᾷ, κἄπειθ᾽ ὑπ᾽ ἀνάγκης
>   ῥήξας αὐτὰς ἔξω φέρεται σοβαρὸς διὰ τὴν πυκνότητα,
>   ὑπὸ τοῦ ῥοίβδου καὶ τῆς ῥύμης αὐτὸς ἑαυτὸν κατακαίων.

Strepsiades: I don't know; but you seem to have a good argument. Very well, what is the thunderbolt, then?

---

25 Cf. Sen. *Nat. Quaest.* 2.27 "Some people think that fiery breath moving through cold and moisture generates the noise. For red-hot iron is not silent either when it is plunged in liquid: if a glowing lump is lowered into water it is extinguished with loud noise." Pliny *N.H.* 2.112 "when fires of stars fall into the cloud a hissing steam is produced, just as when a red-hot iron is plunged into water." cf. Lucilius 291 M. *primum fulgit, uti caldum e furnacibu' ferrum* "First it glares like hot iron from the furnaces.").
26 Daiber 1992, 288.

> Socrates: When a dry wind rises skyward and gets locked up in these Clouds, it blows them up from within like a bladder, and then by natural compulsion it bursts them and is borne out in a whoosh by dint of compression, burning itself up with the friction and velocity. (Transl. by Henderson)

Although we cannot identify any specific Presocratic theory behind the Aristophanic explanation, scholars call attention to the fact that it was Anaxagoras who used the bladder (*Nu.* 405 κύστιν) as a model in an experiment in order to prove that air is a material body (D60 Laks & Most < DK59 A68) = Aristotle *Physics* 4.6, 213a22–27):

> οἱ μὲν οὖν δεικνύναι πειρώμενοι ὅτι οὐκ ἔστιν, οὐχ ὃ βούλονται λέγειν οἱ ἄνθρωποι κενόν, τοῦτ' ἐξελέγχουσιν [...], ὥσπερ Ἀναξαγόρας καὶ οἱ τοῦτον τὸν τρόπον ἐλέγχοντες. ἐπιδεικνύουσι γὰρ ὅτι ἔστι τι ὁ ἀήρ, *στρεβλοῦντες τοὺς ἀσκοὺς* καὶ δεικνύντες ὡς ἰσχυρὸς ὁ ἀήρ, καὶ ἐναπολαμβάνοντες ἐν ταῖς κλεψύδραις.

> Those people who try to prove that it [i.e. the void] does not exist do not refute what men mean by 'void' [...]; this is the case of Anaxagoras and of those people who refute in this way. For they demonstrate that air is something by *twisting wineskins*, showing that air is strong, and by enclosing it in clepsydras. (Transl. by Laks & Most)

In turn, Theophrastus repeatedly opts for the *bladder* as an ideal image in his description of the texture and the physical behaviour of clouds (*Metars.* 6.29–41, 6.63–67).[27]

> The thunderbolt emerges from the cloud, in which the fire (29) is hidden, when the cloud is cut through — as from a bladder (30) or a skin the air restrained in them begins to emerge when they are trodden underfoot and burst. [...] When the thunderbolt reaches us, it happens as a result of two causes: (37) because the bottom of the cloud is split or because some storms or winds (38) have beaten it on top. We can observe something similar amongst us: When an arrow (39) hits a shield, it returns with great violence. And in addition: when a blown up skin is split (40) from the bottom, the air which is restrained in it emerges suddenly and (goes) (41) downwards because of that splitting.
> [...] (63) When the clouds are extended by the wind which is produced (64) in their interior, the result is that they are split not from above in (65) the dense places, but from below in the rarefied places. (66) We can observe something similar amongst us: When a bladder which is not regular (67) in its parts is filled with air, those parts of it are split which are weaker. (Translation by Daiber)

What is even more significant, Theophrastus engages closely with this particular comic intertext in an additional tangible way. In *Metars.* 6.67–81, Theophrastus

---

[27] Lucretius points to the noise produced when a small bladder containing air is split open if inflated (*DRN* 6.121–131).

offers naturalistic explanations for the fact that thunderbolts are more frequent in spring and high places. Then follows a theological excursus in which Theophrastus claims that such phenomena are *not* the work of God, since it would be absurd to assume that "God spares the sinners and punishes the righteous" (*Metars.* 14.14–29):

> (14) Neither the thunderbolt (pl.) nor anything that has been mentioned has its origin in God. For it is (15) not correct (to say) that God should be the cause of disorder in the world; nay (He is) the cause (16) of its arrangement and order. And that is why we ascribe its arrangement and order to God (17) {mighty and exalted is he!} and the disorder of the world to the nature of the world. And moreover: (18) if thunderbolts originate in God, why do they mostly occur (19) during spring or in high places, but not (20) during winter or summer or in low places? In addition: why do thunderbolts fall on uninhabited mountains, on (22) seas, on trees and on irrational living beings? God (23) is not angry with those! Further, more astonishing would be the fact that *thunderbolts* (24) *can strike the best people and those who fear God,* (25) *but not those who act unjustly and propagate evil*. It is thus not right to (26) say <about> hurricanes that they come from God; (we may) only (say the following) about something that happens to us (27) to our harm or that diminishes divine power: It happens (28) without any order. Consequently there is no indication of passing away in the case of God and any (29) indication of being like an angel (= godlike) is to be removed from us. (Transl. by Daiber)

In this context, scholars acknowledge Theophrastus' distinction between "arrangement", "order" ascribed to God and "disorder" ascribed to nature and discuss Theophrastus' critique of the Aristotelian teleological principle, which is, however, not totally denied.[28] A thorough discussion of Theophrastus' teleological ideas and their potential divergence from Aristotle lies outside the scope of this paper. Mansfeld persuasively claims that in his remarks Theophrastus seems to be specifically resuming Socrates' similar point in Aristophanes' *Nubes* 398–402, when Socrates wonders how it is possible that Zeus spares the perjurers but strikes his own temples and the promontory of Sunium and blasts high oaks.[29]

> Σωκράτης
> καὶ πῶς ὦ μῶρε σὺ καὶ Κρονίων ὄζων καὶ βεκκεσέληνε,
> εἴπερ βάλλει τοὺς ἐπιόρκους, δῆτ' οὐχὶ Σίμων' ἐνέπρησεν
> οὐδὲ Κλεώνυμον οὐδὲ Θέωρον; καίτοι σφόδρα γ' εἴσ' ἐπίορκοι·
> ἀλλὰ τὸν αὑτοῦ γε **νεὼν** βάλλει καὶ Σούνιον ἄκρον Ἀθηνέων
> καὶ τὰς δρῦς τὰς μεγάλας· τί μαθών; οὐ γὰρ δὴ δρῦς γ' ἐπιορκεῖ.

---

[28] Lennox 1985; 2001, 259–279.
[29] Mansfeld 1992, 320–321.

> (Socrates) How's that, you moron redolent of the Cronia, you mooncalf! If he really strikes perjurers, then why hasn't he burned up Simon or Cleonymus or Theorus, since they're paramount perjurers? On the other hand, he strikes his own temple, and Sunium headland of Athens, and the great oaks. What's his point? An oak tree certainly doesn't perjure itself! (Transl. by Dover)

This passage precedes the verses that we have just discussed in association with the thunderbolt and bladder, in which Socrates refers to necessity (*Nu.* 404 ὑπ' ἀνάγκης). Both Aristophanes' Socrates and Theophrastus argue that there is *no divine causation* due to wrong human behaviour or intentionality involved in the meteorological phenomena. Theophrastus inverts the comic undermining of Socrates' natural explanation and instead validates it as the proposed philosophical truth that he himself has been able to unveil. Therefore, his Aristophanic allusion is a clear case of opposition *in imitando*. The Theophrastean argument is resumed and elaborated in Epicurean terms by Lucretius in a corresponding theological excursus (*DRN* 6.387–422); in this passage — the thorough discussion of which falls beyond the scope of this paper — we can easily identify a double allusion to both Aristophanes and Theophrastus.[30]

We have so far briefly discussed two cases in which Theophrastus engages with the previous poetic tradition (Homer and Aristophanes), in order to explicate and communicate his own meteorological ideas. In both cases, Lucretius emerges as Theophrastus' ancient reader who perceives these intertextual hints and the latter's corresponding mediating role and replies to them accordingly. As a consequence, in his practice of embracing poetic intertexts in his philosophical discourse on nature, Theophrastus becomes a forerunner of Lucretius' *DRN* and then of Seneca in his prose treatise *Naturales Quaestiones*.

At this point, since we do not have the original Theophrastean text, we can only speculate whether Theophrastus' intertextual allusions have any special bearing regarding the literary aspirations in his treatise. Whatever the case may be, we should bear in mind that, since Theophrastus' ancient readers — including Epicurus and possibly Lucretius — had access to the original Greek text, they had an advantage over us, so as to better appreciate Theophrastus' *literary* credentials.[31]

---

[30] Sedley 1998, 180–181 regarding the exclusion of direct divine causation from the sublunary world. For comparison with Lucretius, see also Mansfeld 1992, 326–327.

[31] See above [footnote 24] Theophrastus' views regarding the value of reading poets for the orators that he expounded in his now lost treatise *On Style*, as we can recover it from Quintilian's *Institutio oratoria* (10.1.27 = Theophrastus 707 FHS&G). See also Theophrastus' theory of "apologetic metaphor" (Cicero's *verecunda tralatio* in *Fam.* 16.17.1). Cf. Theophrastus 698A

Given the mutilated state in which Theophrastus' meteorological studies have been handed down to us, so far I have tried to explore certain factors — not all of them of equal importance — which define our reconstruction of his scientific and literary portrait. When we study Daiber's English translation of Theophrastus' Arabic *Metarsiologica*, we should take into account various theoretical issues related to the process of translation, such as our absolute incapability of retrieving the first and second stages of the textual transmission (i.e. the Syriac-Arabic fragmented or abridged texts), as well as the translator's interferences.

Bibliography

Bakker, Frederik (2016), *Epicurean Meteorology: Sources, Method, Scope and Organization*, Leiden/Boston.

Baltussen, Han (2016), "Philosophers, Exegetes, Scholars: The Ancient Philosophical Commentary from Plato to Simplicius", in: Christina S. Kraus/Christopher Stray (eds.), *Classical Commentaries: Explorations in a Scholarly Genre*, Oxford, 173–194.

Baltussen, Han (2018), "Philosophical Commentary", in: Scott McGill/Edward J. Watts (eds.), *A Companion to Late Antique Literature*, Malden MA, 297–311.

Bergsträsser, Gotthelf (1918), *Neue meteorologische Fragmente des Theophrast, arabisch und deutsch*, Heidelberg.

Coutant, Victor/Val L. Eichenlaub (1975), *Theophrastus: De Ventis*. Edited with Introduction, Translation and Commentary, Notre Dame.

Daiber, Hans (1985), "A Survey of Theophrastean Texts and Ideas in Arabic", in: William Wall Fortenbaugh/Pamela M. Huby/Anthony A. Long (eds.), *Theophrastus of Eresus: On his Life and Work*, RUSCH 2, New Brunswick NJ/Oxford, 103–114.

Daiber, Hans (1992), "The Meteorology of Theophrastus in Syriac and Arabic Translation", in: William Wall Fortenbaugh/Dimitri Gutas (eds.), *Theophrastus: His Psychological, Doxographical, and Scientific Writings*, RUSCH 5, New Brunswick NJ/London, 166–293. Now in: Daiber, Hans (2021), *From the Greeks to the Arabs and Beyond*, Vol. 1: *Graeco-Syriaca and Arabica* in collaboration with Helga Daiber, Leiden/Boston, 308–418.

Dover, Kenneth J. (1968), *Aristophanes: Clouds*. Edited with Introduction and Commentary, Oxford, rpr. 1970.

Drossaart, Lulofs/Hendrik Joan (1955), "The Syriac Translation of Theophrastus' Meteorology", in: *Autour d'Aristote: Recueil d'études de philosophie ancienne et médiévale offert à Monseigneur A. Mansion*, Bibliothèque philosophique de Louvain 16, Louvain, 433–449.

Fortenbaugh, William Wall (ed.) (2005), *Theophrastus of Eresus: Sources for his Life, Writings, Thought and Influence.* Vol. 8: *Sources on Rhetoric and Poetics* (Texts 666–713), Leiden/Boston.

FHS&G (= Philodemus *On Rhetoric* 4, P.Herc. 1007 /1673 col. 13, BT vol. 1 p. 173.13–23 Sudhaus), 689B FHS&G (= Cicero *Ad familiares* 16.17.1), 690 FHS&G (pseudo-Longinus *On the Sublime* 32.3) with Fortenbaugh 2005, 286–292.

Fortenbaugh, William Wall/Pamela M. Huby/Anthony A. Long (eds.) (1985), *Theophrastus of Eresus: On his Life and Work*, RUSCH 2, New Brunswick NJ.
Garani, Myrto (2007), *Empedocles Redivivus: Poetry and Analogy in Lucretius*, London/New York.
Garani, Myrto (2022), "Lucretius on *Prester* (*DRN* vi 423-450)", *Maia* 74, 497–506.
Gottschalk, Hans B. (1965), "Review of *Der syrische Auszug der Meteorologie des Theophrast*, by E. Wagner & P. Steinmetz", *Gnomon* 37, 758–762.
Gottschalk, Hans B. (1998), "Theophrastus and the Peripatos", in: Johannes M. van Ophuijsen/Marlein van Raalte (eds.), *Theophrastus: Reappraising the Sources*, RUSCH 7, New Brunswick NJ, 281–298.
Gutas, Dimitri (1985), "The Life, Works, and Sayings of Theophrastus in the Arabic Tradition", in: William Wall Fortenbaugh/Pamela M. Huby/Anthony A. Long (eds.), *Theophrastus of Eresus: On his Life and Work*, RUSCH 2, New Brunswick NJ/Oxford, 63–102.
Henderson, Jeffrey (ed., trans.) (1998), *Aristophanes, Clouds, Wasps, Peace*, Loeb Classical Library, Cambridge MA.
Kidd, Ian Gray (1992), "Theophrastus' *Meteorology*, Aristotle, and Posidonius", in: William Wall Fortenbaugh/Dimitri Gutas (eds.), *Theophrastus: His Psychological, Doxographical and Scientific Writings*, RUSCH 5, New Brunswick NJ/London, 294–306.
Lennox, James G. (1985), "Theophrastus on the Limits of Teleology", in: William Wall Fortenbaugh/Pamela M. Huby/Anthony A. Long (eds.), *Theophrastus of Eresus: On his Life and Work*, RUSCH 2, New Brunswick NJ/Oxford, 143–163.
Lennox, James G. (2001), *Aristotle's Philosophy of Biology: Studies in the Origins of Life Science*, Cambridge Studies in Philosophy and Biology, New York.
Lettinck, Paul (1999), *Aristotle's Meteorology and its Reception in the Arab World, with an Edition and Translation of Ibn Suwār's Treatise on Meteorological Phenomena and Ibn Bājja's Commentary on the Meteorology*, Aristoteles Semitico-Latinus 10, Leiden/Boston/Köln.
Lettinck, Paul (2015), "Aristotle's 'Physical' Works and the Arabic Tradition", in: Ahmed Alwishah/Josh Hayes (eds.), *Aristotle and the Arabic Tradition*, Cambridge, 105–120.
Mansfeld, Jaap (1992), "A Theophrastean Excursus on God and Nature and its Aftermath in Hellenistic Thought", *Phronesis* 37, 314–335.
Mayhew, Robert (2017), *Theophrastus of Eresus*: On Winds, Leiden.
Rieu, E.V. (trans.) (1991), *Homer, Odyssey*, revised by D. C. H. Rieu in consultation with P.V. Jones, London.
Rouse, W.H.D. (trans.) (1924), *Lucretius: On the Nature of Things*, revised by Martin F. Smith, Loeb Classical Library, Cambridge MA.
Sedley, David Neil (1998), *Lucretius and the Transformation of Greek Wisdom*, Cambridge.
Sharples, Robert W. (1998a), *Theophrastus of Eresus: Sources for his Life, Writings, Thought and Influence* — Commentary Volume 3.1: Sources on Physics (Texts 137–233), with contributions on the Arabic material by Dimitri Gutas, *Philosophia Antiqua* 79, Leiden/Boston/Köln.
Sharples, Robert W. (1998b), "Theophrastus as Philosopher and Aristotelian", in: Johannes M. van Ophuijsen/Marlein van Raalte (eds.), *Theophrastus: Reappraising the Sources*, RUSCH 7, New Brunswick NJ, 267–280.
Steinmetz, Peter (1964), *Die Physik des Theophrastos von Eresos*, Palingenesia 1, Bad Homburg/Berlin/Zürich.

Strohmaier, Gotthard (1968), "Zweites Kapitel: Die griechischen Götter in einer christlich-arabischen Übersetzung. Zum Traumbuch des Artemidor in der Version des Hunain ibn Is-ḥāk", in: Franz Altheim/Ruth Stiehl (eds.), *Weitere Neufunde — Nordafrika bis zur Einwanderung der Wandalen — Dū Nuwās. Die Araber in der Alten Welt* V/1, Berlin/Boston, 127–162.

Takahashi, Hidemi (2002), "Syriac Fragments of Theophrastean Meteorology and Mineralogy. Fragments in the Syriac Version of Nicolaus Damascenus, Compendium of Aristotelian Philosophy, and Accompanying Scholia", in: William Wall Fortenbaugh/Georg Wöhrle (eds.), *On the Opuscula of Theophrastus*: Akten der 3. Tagung der Karl-und-Gertrud-Abel-Stiftung vom 19-23 Juli 1999 in Trier, Stuttgart, 189–224.

Takahashi, Hidemi (2004), *Aristotelian Meteorology in Syriac. Barhebraeus, Butyrum sapientiae, Books on Mineralogy and Meteorology*, Aristoteles Semitico-Latinus 15, Leiden/Boston.

Taub, Liba Chaia (2003), *Ancient Meteorology*, London/New York.

Telelis, Ioannis (2019), "Meteorology and Physics in Byzantium", in: Stavros Lazaris (ed.), *A Companion to Byzantine Science*, Leiden/Boston, 177–201.

Usener, Hermann (1887), *Epicurea*, Leizpig.

van Ophuijsen, Johannes M./Marlein van Raalte (eds.) (1998), *Theophrastus: Reappraising the Sources*, RUSCH 8, New Brunswick NJ.

van Raalte, Marlein (2003), "God and the Nature of the World: The 'Theological Excursus' in Theophrastus' "Meteorology"", *Mnemosyne* 56, 306–342.

Verde, Francesco (2022), *Epicuro, Epistola a Pitocle*: In collaborazione con Mauro Tulli, Dino De Sanctis, Francesca G. Masi, *Diotima: Studies in Greek Philology* 7, Baden-Baden.

Wagner, Ewald/Peter Steinmetz (1964), *Der syrische Auszug der Meteorologie des Theophrast*, Wiesbaden.

Craig Williams
Fragments of Roman Sexuality in Petronius' *Satyricon*

Abstract: Reading Petronius' *Satyricon* is an experience of the incomplete and the unknown. Not only do modern editions and translations consist of stitched-together segments representing some unknown but small portion of the original whole, but they bear frequent marks of lacunae, not all of them universally accepted. In this article, I focus on two episodes from the surviving portions of this text (7–8, 16–26) to illustrate implications for our understandings of gender and sexuality in Latin literature, an area in which the *Satyricon* has long played a prominent role. We find the same textual details cited in support of quite different conclusions; readers over the centuries have had sometimes significantly different texts in front of them; and the practices of editors and translators have sometimes increased the effects of the uncertain and the open. Reading Petronius provides an exemplary illustration of the possibilities and limitations of reading not only fragmentary texts, but ancient texts in general.

1 Introduction

Readers of Petronius' *Satyricon* are frequently introduced to an incomplete text and prepared to engage with the regrettable, the ambivalent, or even the mysterious. The title page of the standard Latin text (Müller 2009) reads PETRONII ARBITRI SATYRICON RELIQVIAE, *Remains of the Satyrica of Petronius Arbiter*; the "Note on the Text and Translation" in Sullivan's Penguin translation opens with the remark that "the surviving text of Petronius is regrettably fragmented and mutilated"; Walsh's preface to his translation in the Oxford World's Classics series begins by observing that "few readers of Petronius can be spared the feelings of ambivalence which have dogged the reception of the *Satyricon* for close on two thousand years"; and the introduction to Schmeling's Loeb edition starts off by noting that "author and work are both surrounded by mysteries".[1]

---

[1] Sullivan 2011, xxxi; Walsh 2017, vii; Schmeling 2020, 3. This editorial practice has a long history: consider the title pages of Burman 1743 (*Petronii Arbitri Satyricon quae supersunt*) and Bücheler 1862 (*Petronii Arbitri Satirarum reliquiae*; the page preceding the body of the text introduces *Petronii Arbitri Satirarum* excerpta *ex libris XV et XVI*) and the *incipit* of the fifteenth-century manuscript A (*Petronii Arbitri Satyri fragmenta ex libro quinto decimo et sexto decimo*).

https://doi.org/10.1515/9783111340944-004

The most basic of questions about this text remain unanswered: who wrote it, when, and under what title? There is widespread but not universal consensus that its author was the Petronius whose memorable suicide in 66 CE is narrated by Tacitus (*Ann.* 16.17–19), but certainty is impossible. There is no consensus on the praenomen and cognomen either of Tacitus' Petronius or of our text's author, and scholarly practice varies on whether or not to identify the author as "Petronius Arbiter", making a cognomen out of Tacitus' reference to the Neronian Petronius as *elegantiae arbiter* (Tac. *Ann.* 16.18), or simply as "Petronius". As for the title, the widely used form *Satyricon* is generally explained as a Greek genitive plural (*Satyricōn libri*), in which case the grammatically correct title is *Satyrica*, a neuter plural analogous to *Georgica* or *Astronomica*. Yet editions and translations continue to oscillate, sometimes even internally, between *Satyrica* and *Satyricon*, the latter implying a substantivization of the genitive plural as a title in its own right, unparalleled but sanctioned by generations of use.[2] The root itself is variously spelled and interpreted. It might refer to *satyroi*, the hybrid beings of Greek myth and art, in which case the title is metaphorical in a way unusual for ancient texts, since the narrative takes place in a realistic contemporary setting where no satyrs are to be found; or it might be alluding to the Latin literary genre *satura* or *satira*, a mixed "medley" which Quintilian famously describes as entirely Roman, more precisely to what Quintilian calls "that other, earlier kind of *satura*" (*alterum illud prius saturae genus*), a mixture of prose and verse initiated by Varro (Quint. *Inst.* 10.1.93–95); and it is intriguing to find Encolpius telling of an aphrodisiac drink prepared from a plant called *satyrion* (8.4, 21.1).[3] However spelled, the title probably suggests all of the above – the mythic and the contemporary, the Greek and the Roman, poetry and prose, and a common thread of the erotic – by punning associations, but definitive answers to the questions of who the author was, what his *tria nomina* were, how the title of this text should be spelled and what it denotes or suggests, remain unattainable.

---

[2] While the title page of Müller 2009 reads SATYRICON RELIQVIAE, hence giving *Satyrica* as the title, the first page of its Latin text is headed PETRONII ARBITRI SATYRICON. The Latin text in Schmeling 2020 bears the heading PETRONII SATYRICA and the introduction uses the form *Satyrica* throughout, but the English translation is headed SATYRICON.

[3] For the aphrodisiac effects of the plant *satyrion* see Plin. *N.H.* 26.96, 28.119. There have been further variations on the title. Ernout 1950 and Sage/Gilleland 1983 print the title as *Satiricon*, while Bücheler's influential editions used first the plural *Satirae* (1862) and then the singular *Satura* (1904). In yet a further variation, the incipit in the fifteenth-century manuscript A reads *Petronii Arbitri Satyri fragmenta ex libro quinto decimo et sexto decimo*.

Readers' encounters with the text itself are inevitably marked by further uncertainties. Whether they have in front of them a critical edition of the Latin text or one of many translations, readers encounter ellipses, asterisks, angle brackets, square brackets, obeloi, and other signs of incompletion and doubt on nearly every page outside of the *cena Trimalchionis* (Fig. 1, typical page of a Latin edition; Fig. 2, typical page of a translation). And, not least because of back-references to scenes not found in the text they are reading, attentive readers will quickly realize that these fragments come from a significantly larger, now-lost whole. But how much larger? On the basis of a handful of indications in testimonia and manuscripts, scholars now generally agree that today's *Satyricon* consists of excerpts from Books 14–16, but there is no consensus on how many books the original text had: guesses have included sixteen, twenty, and twenty-four, but no one really knows.

Readers who delve more deeply will learn a less immediately obvious but equally important fact. *No single surviving manuscript or manuscript family contains all of the text that is printed in today's editions and translations.* Today's *Satyricon* has been stitched together from a variety of sources, ranging from medieval manuscripts, the earliest of which, B, dates to the ninth century, to handwritten and printed editions by French humanists of the second half of the sixteenth century. Michael Hadrianides' 1669 edition was the first to contain all of the segments of text found in today's editions and translations; before then, generations of readers were reading even more fragmented texts of the *Satyricon* than ours is today, and, as we will see, they sometimes read significantly different texts from ours.

In this article, I focus on two episodes from the opening portion of the surviving text in order to suggest some implications of the incompleteness of the *Satyricon* for understandings of gender and sexuality in Latin literature, an area in which this text has long played a prominent role. I will also show how the practices of editors and translators have sometimes intensified the effects of the incomplete, uncertain, and open. Throughout, my focus is on experiences of reading. Petronius' *Satyricon* is in Barthes' terms a *texte scriptible* or "writerly text" to an especially high degree, and it provides an exemplary illustration of the possibilities and limitations of reading not only fragmentary texts, but ancient texts in general.

2 Basic interpretive uncertainties

Our *Satyricon* consists of pieces of a framing autodiegetic narrative by Encolpius, who is clearly speaking some time after the events he narrates. But how much later, to whom, and in which circumstances did he narrate? We cannot know. What we do know is that Encolpius sometimes comments ironically on characters in his narrative, including his earlier self, but an endlessly debatable question raised by Gian Biagio Conte in *L'autore nascosto* is this: Is the "hidden author" Petronius in turn ironically commenting on Encolpius, whether as character, as narrator, or both? And if so, since for us Encolpius' narrative comes with no frame, on what basis can we claim to perceive when and how this ironic commentary is occurring?

Whether cited for its confirmation of patterns found elsewhere or highlighted as idiosyncratic or unique, the *Satyricon* plays an important role in the study of gender and sexuality in Greek and Roman literature. What, then, of Encolpius' on-off, non-monogamous but obviously committed relationship with Giton? Through all the ups and downs, rivalries and triangles, this relationship is central to Encolpius' narrative as we have it from beginning to end; but was this true of the full text written by Petronius and read by earlier generations of readers? Was Giton already a part of Encolpius' life at his narrative's opening, or did Encolpius introduce him along the way, and if so, how far along the narrative did he do this?[4] Did he at some point tell of how they finally separated? In short, how central was Encolpius' relationship with Giton to his *entire* narrative?

The question has important implications. It has been claimed, for example, that, by placing a male couple at its center, Petronius' text is responding to and perhaps parodying the five Greek novels which survive intact (by Achilles Tatius, Xenophon of Ephesus, Longus, Chariton, and Heliodorus) for, while pederastic desire certainly features in their narrative and cultural landscapes, all five have male-female couples at their center. Yet even the surviving portion of the *Satyricon* undermines a simplistic contrast between Petronius' text as centering on a "homosexual" couple (or triad, or triads) and the Greek novels as celebrating

---

[4] Encolpius refers to his relationship with Giton as having a long history and Ascyltos' arrival on the scene as not being particularly recent: cf. 10.7, *iam dudum enim amoliri cupiebam custodem molestissimum ut veterem cum Gitone meo rationem reducerem* ("for a while now I was trying to get rid of this annoying chaperone [Ascyltos] and return to my old ways with dear Giton"), 80.6, *ego qui vetustissimam consuetudinem putabam in sanguinis pignus transisse* ("I thought my long-standing relationship [with Giton] had turned into a bond of blood"). But Encolpius as narrator notoriously overstates and exaggerates.

"heterosexual" love, and of course we cannot know the full range of erotic configurations found in Petronius' whole text.[5] An attempt to hypothesize a contrast on this point is further undermined by a second-century CE papyrus from Oxyrhynchus containing fragments of a Greek text alternating between prose and verse. Featuring a character named Iolaos along with someone apparently pretending to be a γάλλος or castrated priest of the Mother Goddess, and someone (perhaps Iolaos, perhaps not) insulted as a κίναιδος, the text seems to tell of an elaborate ruse to give a man sexual access to a woman. The preliminary publication of the fragment by Peter Parsons in 1971 bore the title "A Greek *Satyricon*?"[6] and the question mark is suggestive. What would the relationships between the *Satyricon* and Greek prose fictions look like if we had more of each?

3 The mechanics of fragmentation: not all lacunae are alike

Today's incomplete *Satyricon* has been stitched together from sources usually divided into four classes (*O*, *Φ*, *L*, and *H*), none of which contains everything readers see in modern editions, assembled in an agreed-upon order and divided into sections numbered 1–141. Appendices to modern editions present a set of further fragments from other sources, under subtly but significantly different titles, such as *Fragmenta sparsim tradita* (Müller 2009), *Fragments, Testimonies, Poems* (Walsh 2017), *The Fragments and the Poems* (Sullivan 2011), or *Fragmenta / Fragments* (Schmeling 2020), and these are numbered according to varying systems. Throughout, readers encounter a text marked not only by the usual signs of editorial additions <abc> or deletions [abc] but also, in some editions, by vertical dividers | signalling which portions of the text are found in which of the manuscript classes and — most strikingly of all — frequent ellipses and as-

---

[5] Schmeling 2020, 10–11: "The ideal Greek novels with their pair of heterosexual protagonists falling in love, being separated, and then seeking legitimate marriage, are far away in sentiment from the *Satyrica*, with its triad of homosexual protagonists, wealthy freedmen, unsuccessful poets, and a narrator who relates in detail the specifics of his impotence." Yet Encolpius, Giton, and Ascyltos cannot easily be described as "homosexual" (all of them enthusiastically engage in sexual relations with women as well as men) and they are "protagonists" only in the first part of the surviving text: Ascyltos disappears after section 98, after which a new triad (Encolpius, Giton, Eumolpus) begins to form.
[6] Subsequent texts and translations include Parsons 1974, Merkelbach 1973, Reardon 1989, Stephens/Winkler 1995.

terisks marking lacunae (see Fig. 1 for a sample page from Müller 2009, and Fig. 3 for a sample page from Schmeling 2020).

Here an important distinction is worth emphasizing, especially because it will not be obvious to all readers. Ellipses (in Müller ... and in Schmeling < ... >) mark places where editors suggest that something has dropped out *within* the segments of continuous text handed down in one or more of the four manuscript classes; these suggestions are open to debate, and editors themselves sometimes change their minds.[7] By contrast, asterisks (in Müller *, in Schmeling <* * *>) mark discontinuities *between* those segments of continuous text which are handed down in one or more of the manuscript classes. These asterisks are generally reproduced without debate, and indeed they seem to rest on more solid ground. Schmeling explains that, whereas ellipses mark "lacunae suggested by editors of the Latin text", asterisks indicate "lacunae based on the authority of the manuscripts" (Schmeling 2020, 49), and Müller's Latin preface explains that ellipses indicate "gaps not attested by the authority of any texts" (*lacunae nulla librorum auctoritate testatae*) while asterisks mark "gaps which texts similarly indicate by means of one or more asterisks" (*lacunas, quas similiter libri asteriscis singulis pluribusve significant,* Müller 2009, li).

A closer look, however, shows that the "manuscripts" and "texts" (*libri*) which are the authority for the asterisks are specifically those of class *L*, which is different from the other three classes in a crucial way. Schmeling summarizes:

> None is a true medieval MS. Two are printed editions, the others are secondary sources, collations of manuscripts, edition prototypes; written between 1565 and 1587, but for reasons of necessity assigned the status of manuscripts ... Only in *L* are found the indications <* * *> of lacunae.[8]

The discontinuities indicated by asterisks in *L* are (almost) universally accepted,[9] and usually for good reasons: breaks in syntax, the absence of connectives typical

---

[7] Müller's Latin preface to his 1995 fourth edition, reprinted in the 2009 *editio iterata correctior*, includes self-criticism of his first edition from 1961: it was "too hastily" done (*nimis festinata*) and he "handled many things incorrectly" (*multa a me non recte administrata*), in particular by being overzealous in identifying interpolations and in his excessive use of obeloi.

[8] Schmeling 2020, 40. Müller's Latin term for the texts of class *L* (*libri*) contrasts with the standard term he uses for manuscripts from the other three classes: *codices*, in other words those which Schmeling calls "true medieval manuscripts." See Richardson 1993 for discussion of the *L* class and their historical and cultural contexts.

[9] Van Thiel 1971 shows that modern editions, including Müller's, do not reproduce the asterisks in *L* with complete consistency. He also observes that there are two different kinds of asterisks in *L* (those with six rays, indicating gaps, and those with five rays, referring readers to

of Encolpius' narrative style, shifts in scene too abrupt even for a text in the *tyche* tradition, and back-references to intervening scenes now lost. But in an under-cited study from 1971, Helmut van Thiel reminds us that the archetype of the *L* class (which he calls Λ, professing agnosticism as to its date) was "a secondary collection of various collections of Petronian excerpts", and he further observes that not all of the asterisks necessarily mark gaps between discontinuous segments; some seem to indicate the beginnings or endings of poems or speeches. Van Thiel reasonably concludes that the *L* class might contain errors of omission or commission in its indications of gaps and that its sequencing of segments need not be correct in every case, and he offers a tentative scheme for rearranging the surviving segments.[10] Whether or not one finds all of his suggestions persuasive, van Thiel's resistance to unquestioningly accepting the authority of the asterisks in the *L* class is just as valid as scholars' readiness to debate the decisions made by modern editors flagged by ellipses. In sum: not all lacunae in this text are alike, and some might not even be lacunae at all.

4 Reading experiences of continuity and discontinuity

Some have linked the fragmentation of the "text" of the *Satyricon* in the technical sense of the term with distinctive features of this "text" in the broader sense, i.e. a woven artifice of language. Citing Froma Zeitlin's seminal 1971 article "Petronius as Paradox: Anarchy and Artistic Integrity", Victoria Rimell writes:

> Not only has the *Satyricon* come to us perforated with (possible) holes and tears, or even shrunk down to a fraction of its original size, but it also seems to have been "undertaken with the deliberate intention of defeating the expectations of an audience accustomed to an organizing literary form."[11]

Indeed, today's fragmented *Satyricon* is marked by tensions between continuity and discontinuity which we have every reason to believe characterized the whole text, from the episodic structure (some translations visually break up the

---

a marginal note) and that one of the first printed editions (Pithou 1577) sometimes conflates the two (van Thiel 1971, 68).
10 van Thiel 1971, 7 ("eine sekundäre Sammlung verschiedener Sammlungen von Petronexzerpten"), 76–78.
11 Rimell 2002, 2–3; quotation from Zeitlin 1971, 635.

text into episodes with their own titles and sometimes numbers), to the twists and turns in the *tyche* tradition of ancient prose fictions, to the unexpected shifts from prose to poetry and back again and sudden changes in register within the prose narrative, most famously in the speeches of the inebriated freedmen during the banquet hosted by Trimalchio.

Readers over the centuries have had yet other experiences of continuity and discontinuity, and these have differed from each other depending on the text that readers have had before them. The anthologies of the φ class, for example, present discontinuous quotations which create a significantly different reading experience both from the exemplar(s) from which they were selected and from the modern text. Catherine Connors summarizes:

> Someone used the creation of discontinuity to implement a moralizing discourse. Like many pagan texts, the *Satyricon* is mined for its worthwhile and instructive nuggets, and these are duplicated and transmitted to subsequent readers. What is ironic and humorous in the *Satyricon* becomes a tame commonplace when isolated in an anthology. Excuses which the characters make to get themselves out of tight situations become slogans to live by, and verse sentiments which were ironically undercut by their prose frames become tidy assertions about the nature of fortune or love. (Connors 1998, 9)

Rather like Rimell's alignment of "holes and tears" with Zeitlin's perception of a text which defeats expectations of a single "organizing literary form", Connors argues that the compiler of the archetype of φ "was not being false to the dynamics of the *Satyricon*", for "the discontinuities which he created correspond to the discontinuities that were already deployed for artistic effect within the text" (ibid.). Manuscripts of the O class, by contrast, conceal the fact that they are giving their readers stitched-together segments.[12] Thus, if the explicit *discontinuity* of the text in the φ anthologies creates a *Satyricon* significantly different from the one we now know, the seeming *continuity* of the text in manuscripts of the O class does the same thing, but with different effects.

This feature of the O class has repercussions for the study of gender and sexuality in Latin literature and its reception over the centuries, not least because it has been claimed that the now-lost archetype of this class omitted "scenes of homosexuality" or "more obscene pederastic passages".[13] Yet, as the

---

[12] Cf. Schmeling 2020, 31: "The excerptor chose sections for preservation and then carefully resewed them so that no one should recognize that they were pieces from a much larger whole — except for the readers who much later would have access to the other classes of manuscripts."

[13] Schmeling 2020, 31, describing O as "severely excerpted fragments, which delicately avoid scenes of homosexuality"; Müller 2009, xi, noting that the L class includes "certain more obscene

comparative suggests, this scribal censorship of scenes telling of sexual desire and acts between males was neither consistent nor absolute. To cite just one example, O manuscripts give their readers an episode toward the very beginning in which an unnamed "gentleman" picks up Ascyltos on the street, takes him to a brothel, and offers him money for sex (8.3 in today's text), and when Ascyltos resists, the gentleman responds with a verbal threat of rape: "If you are Lucretia, you've found a Tarquin" (9.5).

Attentive readers familiar with today's *Satyricon* may be surprised at this brief summary, for in today's text the allusion to the rape of Lucretia comes in a later scene, made not by the unnamed gentleman attempting to have his way with Ascyltos in a brothel, but by Ascyltos himself, as reported by Giton when he tells Encolpius of Ascyltos' attempt to rape him. In what follows, I focus on this episode (7–8) and another from the opening portions of today's *Satyricon* — Encolpius' narrative of a gathering hosted by Quartilla (16–26) — by way of illustrating how readers over the centuries have had sometimes significantly different encounters with the language and imagery of gender and sexuality in Latin literature.

5 Encolpius, Ascyltos, and the "gentleman" in the brothel (7–8)

For readers of O manuscripts, Encolpius tells of how he asked an old woman he met on the street for directions to his lodging, whereupon she takes him to a brothel, where he meets Ascyltos, who reveals that he had been brought there by a "gentleman" (*paterfamilias*). So far, so familiar to readers of today's *Satyricon*. But readers of the O manuscripts then find the following passage (see Fig. 4 for a page from the ninth-century manuscript B; my transcription below modernizes punctuation and capitalization).

> *per anfractus deinde obscurissimos egressus in hunc locum me perduxit prolatoque peculio coepit rogare stuprum. iam ille mihi iniecerat manum, et nisi valentior fuissem dedissem poenas. cum ego proclamarem, gladium strinxit, et si Lucretia es, inquit, Tarquinium invenisti.*
>   *quid faciunt leges ubi sola pecunia regnat,*
>   *aut ubi paupertas vincere nuda potest?*
>   *ipsi qui cynica traducunt tempora cera*

---

pederastic passages modestly omitted by the O epitomator" (*obsceniora et paederastica quaedam capita ab epitomatore O pudenter omissa*).

> *nonnumquam nummis verba solent emere.*
> *ergo iudicium nihil est nisi publica merces*
> *atque eques in causa qui sedet empta probat.*
> sed ut primum beneficio Gytonis praeparata nos implevimus cena, hostium non satis audaci strepitu exsonuit impulsum.

> And then going through pitch-dark winding streets, he brought me to this place, took out his cash and asked me for indecent sex. Now he laid a hand on me, and had I not been stronger, I would have paid the price! As I was shouting out, he drew his sword and said: "If you are Lucretia, you've found a Tarquin".
> > What use are laws when money alone rules,
> > Or where can bare poverty win?
> > Even those who scorn the times with Cynics' wax tablets
> > Sometimes purchase words with cash.
> > So a courtroom is nothing but merchandise on public sale,
> > And the knight sitting in judgment makes purchased decisions.
> But once we had sated ourselves with a dinner prepared thanks to Giton's kindness, there was a knock on the door, not especially bold.

Ascyltos thus tells of how this unnamed man verbally feminized him as a latter-day Lucretia while attempting to rape him. In view of the absence of quotation marks in manuscripts, it is unclear whether the subsequent poem is still in the voice of Ascyltos or rather in that of the narrator Encolpius, but in any case it reads as a comment on the attempted sexual assault, reflecting on the futility for poor people of recourse to the law. With the next sentence, clearly in Encolpius' narrative voice, we read a scene of domestic tranquility enjoyed by Ascyltos, Giton, and Encolpius until they are interrupted by a knock on the door, ushering in the next episode with the introduction of Quartilla's slave woman.

Although they give no clue of this to their readers, the O manuscripts present as continuous text a sequence of segments which are found in four different passages in today's text (7.1–3, 9.5, 14.2, 17.6). Below is Müller's text of these segments, separated by intervening text marked (...).

> 7.3–4 "*per anfractus deinde obscurissimos egressus in hunc locum me perduxit prolatoque peculio coepit rogare stuprum. iam pro cella meretrix assem exegerat, iam ille mihi iniecerat manum, et nisi valentior fuissem dedissem poenas*" ... *adeo ubique omnes mihi videbantur satyrion bibisse.*[14]

---

[14] Müller 2009 and Schmeling 2020 print an ellipsis between *dedissem poenas* and *adeo ubique*, thereby signaling that the lacuna is a modern scholar's suggestion. Yet Müller's own apparatus attributes the indication of this lacuna to Pierre Pithou's printed editions of 1577 and

(...)
9.5 "*cum ego proclamarem, gladium strinxit, et 'si Lucretia es,' inquit, 'Tarquinium invenisti.'*"
(...)
14.2
quid faciunt leges ubi sola pecunia regnat,
   aut ubi paupertas vincere nulla potest?
ipsi qui Cynica traducunt tempora pera
   nonnumquam nummis vendere verba solent.
ergo iudicium nihil est nisi publica merces
   atque eques in causa qui sedet empta probat.
(...)
17.6 *sed ut primum beneficio Gitonis praeparata nos implevimus cena, ostium [non] satis audaci strepitu exsonuit impulsum.*

7.3–5 "And then going through pitch-dark winding streets, he brought me to this place, took out his cash and asked me for indecent sex. Now a female prostitute exacted payment of one *as* for a chamber, and now he laid a hand on me; had I not been stronger, I would have paid the price!" ... Really, it seemed to me that everyone in the place had drunk an aphrodisiac.
(...)
9.5 "As I was shouting out, he drew his sword and said: 'If you are Lucretia, you've found a Tarquin'".
(...)
14.2
What use are laws when money alone rules,
Or poverty can never win?
Even those who scorn the times while holding a Cynic's pouch
Sometimes sell their words for cash.
So a courtroom is nothing but merchandise on public sale,
And the knight sitting in judgment makes purchased decisions.
(...)
17.6 But once we had sated ourselves with a dinner prepared thanks to Giton's kindness, there was quite a bold knock on the door.

Three significant points emerge from a comparison.[15] First: thanks to a clause missing from *O* (*iam pro cella meretrix assem exegerat*), readers of today's *Satyricon* are given a valuable glimpse into the history of brothels which, as far as I

1587, which belong to the *L* class. Hence most translations more accurately print asterisks here rather than an ellipsis.

15 Like all other modern editions, Müller's prints emendations and a deletion in 14.2 and 17.6 on the basis of other manuscript classes or scholarly conjectures (*nuda > nulla, cera > pera, emere > vendere, non satis > satis*). These have little effect on the gendered or sexual dynamics of the scene.

know, no other text surviving from antiquity gives us: the possibility that customers might pay a small fee (here, one *as*) for use of a chamber with a partner whom they brought there for the purpose, making the payment to one of the brothel's workers.[16] Second: the poem about the futility of poor people appealing to the law appears in yet another episode — a scene at a marketplace (12–15) — where it is prompted not by an attempted sexual assault but by competing claims on a stolen cloak. And third: as we have seen, for today's readers the allusion to Lucretia is made not by the unnamed gentleman in the brothel to Ascyltos, but in a later episode by Ascyltos himself as he tries to have his way with Giton. More precisely, Giton reports Ascyltos' actions and words to Encolpius, prompting one of several fights between Encolpius and Ascyltos (9.6–10.3) leading to Encolpius' proposal, accepted by Ascyltos, that the time has come for the two to separate (10.4–7). Readers of O thus saw things that readers of today's text do not (an explicitly gendered dimension to Ascyltos' encounter with the unnamed gentleman, and a poem reflecting on the lack of legal recourse for poor victims of sexual assault) but they could not see an important detail available today: the possibility of room rentals in a brothel. And whereas readers of O observed Encolpius, Giton, and Ascyltos enjoying a scene of domesticity, today's readers are treated to dramatic tensions *within* that triangle.

Yet another kind of experience awaits readers of François Nodot's 1694 Latin-French bilingual edition of the *Satyricon* and its later translations into German and English. Allegedly on the basis of a Latin manuscript discovered in Belgrade in 1688, Nodot's text fills all gaps within and between surviving segments, with further supplements (too) conveniently extending only a few sentences before and after the surviving text. Nodot's readers are insistently reminded of the hitherto fragmentary nature of Petronius' text: the 1694 edition introduces a "complete work" (*ouvrage complet*), the title page of a 1707 edition of the Latin text alone proclaims that it is "now at last whole" (*nunc demum integrum*), and both editions visually distinguish the new additions from the previously existing text by alternations between italic and roman type. Although the supplements were quickly dismissed as a fake, Nodot's *Satyricon* has

---

16 Ascyltos calls her a *meretrix*, "prostitute" (Weeber 2018: "eine Hure"; Aragosti 1995: "una delle prostitute"), but some translations (Walsh 2017, Schmeling 2020) give her the specific role of "the madam", and Sullivan 2011 translates "the woman", seemingly referring to the one who had brought Encolpius to this place. McGinn cites this passage (with, however, a distinct note of uncertainty) as sole textual evidence for "assignation-houses": "We also know that brothels functioned in part as assignation-houses. This is securely attested, *I believe*, by the incident recounted by Petronius, where a prostitute charges the companion of Ascyltos for the use of a room" (McGinn 2004, 217, emphasis added).

been read by generations and is still worth a read. By imagining what the original whole *might* have looked like, this "complete" *Satyricon* puts into sharper focus what we do and do not have, prompting us to ponder some of the possibilities raised by our broken-up text.[17]

Below is Nodot's Latin text of sections 7 and 8 in modern editions, with additions from the alleged Belgrade manuscript marked in bold, followed by my own translation.

> "*per anfractus deinde obscurissimos egressus, in hunc locum me perduxit, prolatoque peculio coepit rogare stuprum. jam pro cella meretrix assem exegerat, jam ille mihi injecerat manum et nisi valentior fuissem, poenas dedissem.*" **dum sortem suam mihi narrat Ascyltos, ipse paterfamilias comitatus muliere haud inculta supervenit, et respiciens ad Ascylton rogavit ut domum intraret, certiorem faciens nil timendum; sed cum patiens esse nolet, saltem agens foret. aliunde mulier urgebat consensum ut secum venirem. subsequimur ergo et conducti inter titulos aspicimus complures utriusque sexus ludentes in cellis;** *adeo ubique omnes mihi videbantur satyrion bibisse.* **ut conspicimur, nos cynaedica petulantia allicere conati sunt, statimque unus alte succinctus invadit Ascylton et super eum grabato prostratum molere conatus est. succurro statim patienti** *et junctis viribus molestum contempsimus.*

"And then going through pitch-dark winding streets, he brought me to this place, took out his cash and asked me for indecent sex. Now a female prostitute exacted payment of one *as* for a room, and now he laid a hand on me; had I not been stronger, I would have paid the price!" **While Ascyltos was telling me what had befallen him, the gentleman himself came up, accompanied by a lovely woman. Looking at Ascyltos, he asked him to enter the building with him, assuring him that he had nothing to fear; since Ascyltos did not wish to be passive, he could be active at any rate. On the other side the woman was urging me to agree to go in with her. And so we followed them in, and there amongst the inscriptions we saw quite a few people of each sex fooling around in the rooms**; really, it seemed to me that all of them in the place had drunk aphrodisiac. **Once we were noticed, they attempted to lure us in with cinaedic boldness, and right away one of them, his tunic hitched high, pounced on Ascyltos, threw him down on to a bed, and tried to grind away on top of him. Right away I came to his aid in his suffering** and we joined forces and defied the troublesome man.

Whereas in today's *Satyricon* Ascyltos describes his encounter with this unnamed gentleman suggestively but vaguely — at most, his phrase *prolato peculio*

---

[17] Discussions of Nodot's Petronius include Stolz 1987 and Stucchi 2010. See Hübner 1987 for Wilhelm Heinse's German translation, published in 1773 and reprinted in 1925. W.C. Firebaugh's "complete and unexpurgated" English translation of Nodot's text was published in 1922 "for private circulation only"; a 1927 adaptation censored numerous details, sometimes but not always flagging its actions by means of ellipses.

("took out his cash") might be a double-entendre hinting at the man's penis[18] — Nodot's text is more explicit. After the initial rejection, the gentleman reveals himself to be versatile, assuring Ascyltos that "since he did not wish to be passive, he could be active at any rate" (*cum patiens esse nollet, saltem agens foret*).[19] Soon thereafter, we read of people in the brothel accosting Encolpius and Ascyltos "with cinaedic boldness" (*cinaedica petulantia*). Whatever the phrase might suggest and however it might be translated,[20] in view of Encolpius' remark that he saw "quite a few people of both sexes fooling around in the rooms", this "cinaedic boldness" would seem to characterize both men and women. This Petronian passage — if it were one — would thus add to our repertoire of attestations of the noun *cinaedus* and related forms, words which have a long history of being translated or glossed in ways which refer specifically to men: clinical but inaccurate phrases like "passive male homosexual", the noun "sodomite" (inappropriately religious or legalistic in tone and a semantic mismatch with *cinaedus*), terms such as "catamite" (opaque to many modern readers), or insults like "pansy" or "faggot" (misleading in their imputation of homosexuality *per se*).

For readers of Nodot's Petronius, one of the men in this mixed-sex group throws Ascyltos on to a bed and attempts to "grind away" on top of him (*super eum ... molere conatus est*). Encolpius' remark *succurro patienti* ("I came to his aid in his suffering"), coming so soon after a phrase distinguishing between sexual roles called *patiens* and *agens*, hints that Ascyltos was "suffering" attempts at penetration by this man.[21] Nodot's text thus illustrates a narrative technique of pairing with variation characteristic of the *Satyricon*. For when he later tells of sexual acts which a *cinaedus* performed or attempted on Ascyltos and himself during the evening with Quartilla, Encolpius again uses the imagery

---

18 See Schmeling/Setaioli 2011 *ad loc.* and Adams 1982, 43.
19 The euphemisms in Nodot's French ("puis qu'il n'étoit pas d'humeur à souffrir ses caresses, il vouloit au moins lui procurer d'autres plaisirs") and Heinse's German ("und wann er nichts mit sich wollte anfangen lassen, so sollte er wenigstens selbst was anfangen") obscure the reference to penetrative role. Firebaugh 1922 is as direct as the Latin ("since he was unwilling to take the passive part, he should have the active"), but the 1927 adaptation omits the clause entirely, adding a suggestive ellipsis ("assuring him that there was nothing to fear ...").
20 Nodot 1694 "faisant à nos jeux mille postures lascives"; Heinse 1773 "mit buhlerischer Frechheit"; Firebaugh 1922 "with paederastic wantonness" (1927 adaptation: "with vulgar wantonness").
21 Nodot's French ("mais je le secourus") and Heinse's German ("ich sprang ihm zu Hülfe") avoid translating *patienti* entirely; Firebaugh 1922 and 1927 both translate "I succored the sufferer immediately."

of "grinding on top" (23.5 *super inguina mea diu multumque frustra moluit*). Nodot's text invites its readers to imagine the men in both episodes — the first acting with *cinaedica petulantia*, the second explicitly called a *cinaedus* — attempting to penetrate their male partners. As we will see next, however, the question of who is trying to penetrate whom in the second of these episodes has received more than one answer.

6 Chez Quartilla (16–26)

Encolpius' narrative of a gathering hosted by Quartilla (16–26) is fragmented to an unusually high degree even for this text, perhaps because it tells of an unusually high degree of sexual variety even for this text — the scene features swapping partners, light bondage, the use of an aphrodisiac, and the staged deflowering of the approximately seven-year-old Pannychis by Giton — and thus may have provoked a higher degree of scribal censorship (see Fig. 5 for a sample page from Müller 2009).[22] At one point Encolpius tells of a man whom he calls a *cinaedus* (text from Müller 2009, followed by my translation).

> 21.2–3 *ultimo cinaedus supervenit myrtea subornatus gausapa cinguloque succinctus ... modo extortis nos clunibus cecidit, modo basiis olidissimis inquinavit, donec Quartilla ballaenaceam tenens virgam alteque succincta iussit infelicibus dari missionem*
>
> *
>
> *uterque nostrum religiosissimis iuravit verbis inter duos periturum esse tam horribile secretum*
>
> *
>
> Finally a *cinaedus* came up, decked out in shaggy myrtle-colored clothing and wearing a ... belt. First he banged us with twisted buttocks, then he befouled us with stinking kisses, until Quartilla, holding a whale-bone rod and with tunic hitched up high, ordered a reprieve for us in our misfortune.
>
> *
>
> We both swore a most sacred oath that so dreadful a secret would die with the two of us.
>
> *

---

22 Translators and commentators differ in their understanding of where this episode takes place, how long it lasts, and what Quartilla's role is. Did this all occur in one night, or over the course of two or three? Was it in Quartilla's home, rented quarters, or a brothel (whether the same one as in the earlier scene or not)? Is she the "hostess" of an "orgy", or the "priestess of Priapus" overseeing rites in the god's honor?

The ellipsis after *succinctus* in Müller's Latin text can easily be taken to hint that Encolpius originally told of further, even more scandalous doings, a tantalizing possibility. Yet readers who consult Müller's apparatus will see that this lacuna was first hypothesized by Bücheler in his 1862 edition, and not because of any indication in any manuscript, but simply because of his impressions that "Petronius had added a reference to the color of the belt" worn by the *cinaedus* and furthermore that "there is a gap in the syntax" (*colorem quoque cinguli addiderat Petronius. hiat praeterea constructio orationis*). In my translation above I have located the ellipsis accordingly ("and wearing a ... belt" rather than "and wearing a belt ..."), but translations which print an ellipsis at the *end* of the clause suggest that something more than a color word may be missing — perhaps something salacious, which is, after all, one function of ellipses in modern texts.

> Zuletzt kam noch eine Tunte hinzu, herausgeputzt mit einem myrtenfarbigen Wollumhang und mit einem Gürtel umwunden ... bald bumste er uns mit seinen auseinandergezogenen Arschbacken, bald besudelte er uns mit besonders eklig stinkenden Küssen. (Holzberg 2013)

> Da ultimo sopraggiunse un cinedo, con indosso una veste color mirto ed ai fianchi una cintura < ... > un po' ci strusciò addosso il suo sedere sculettante, un po' ci imbrattò il viso dandoci dei baci fetidissimi. (Aragosti 1995)

> Am Ende kam eine Mannshure daher, mit einem pelzgefütterten Plaid in Myrtenfarbe drapiert und einen Gurt um die Hüften ... Bald berammelte er uns unter Verrenkungen seines Hintern, bald schmierte er uns widerlich stinkenden Küsse ins Gesicht. (Müller/Ehlers 2004)

> Pour nous achever, survint un danseur équivoque, vêtu d'une robe vert-myrte et retroussé jusqu'à la ceinture ... Tantôt il nous laboura de ses fesses qu'il tortillait, tantôt il nous souilla de ses baisers immondes. (Ernout 1950)

Readers of other translations, however, find no indication that there might even be something missing here. Some translations tacitly accept Bücheler's suggestion and insert a color word describing the belt.

> At the end a catamite appeared on the scene, dressed in a myrtle green cloak and hitched up with a cherry colored belt, who first pulled our buttocks apart and beat his way in, then befouled us with the stinkiest kisses. (Schmeling 2020)

> Finally, up came a male prostitute, dressed in myrtle-green shaggy felt, which was tucked up under a cherry-red belt. He pulled the cheeks of our bottoms apart and banged us, then he slobbered vile, greasy kisses on us. (Sullivan 2011)[23]

Others simply ignore Bücheler's hypothesis of a lacuna and translate the text as found in the manuscripts.

> Eventually a catamite appeared on the scene, dressed in a cloak of myrtle green hitched up with a belt. First he wrenched our buttocks apart and forced his way in, and then besmirched us with the foulest of stinking kisses. (Walsh 2017)

> Am Ende kam noch ein schwuler Kerl dazu; er trug einen myrtenfarbenen, hoch geschürzten Umhang. Bald zog er uns die Hinterbacken auseinander und stieß hinein, bald besudelte er uns mit übel stinkenden Küssen. (Weeber 2018)

> Endlich kam noch ein Buhltänzer dazu mit einem Myrthenfarbnen Mäntelchen geputzt und hoch aufgegürtet. Bald trieb er unsere Schenkel von einander und wollte den Jupiter machen, und bald besudelte er uns mit dem eckelhafttesten Gezünzle. (Heinse 1773)

Translations differ even more significantly in how they render Encolpius' description of what the *cinaedus* did to Ascyltos and himself: *extortis nos clunibus cecidit*, "he banged us, buttocks twisted apart." The detail has important implications for the range of sexual roles and acts attributed to *cinaedi* in Latin texts. Readers of many translations find this *cinaedus* forcefully spreading Encolpius' and Ascyltos' buttocks as he "banged" or "poked" them, or "beat his way in" or "thrust in."[24] This indeed seems the most obvious way of understanding Encolpius' phrase, in view of attested uses of *caedere* ("bang, strike, hit") to signify the act of sexual penetrating another person.[25] In this case, Encolpius is narrating a memorable scene indeed. Across surviving Latin texts, the noun *cinaedus* suggests a range of behaviors and styles marked as unmanly such as suggestive dance performances, a voice or gait that could be described as "soft" (*mollis*), a soft and sensuous style that could be coded as womanly, or taking

---

23 The translators' choice of color is evidently inspired by 28.8: *ostiarius prasinatus cerasino succinctus cingulo*, "the door-keeper dressed in green cinched with a cherry-red belt."
24 Schmeling 2020: "first pulled our buttocks apart and beat his way in"; Weeber 2018: "bald zog er uns die Hinterbacken auseinander und stieß hinein"; Walsh 2017: "first he wrenched our buttocks apart and forced his way in"; Sullivan 2011: "he pulled the cheeks of our bottoms apart and banged us"; Heseltine/Warmington 1969: "almost dislocated our buttocks with his poking."
25 Adams 1982, 145–146.

pleasure in being sexually penetrated.²⁶ On this reading of Petronius' text, however, we see a *cinaedus* who not only penetrates two men, but does so quite aggressively. Even more strikingly, a male narrator tells of how *he himself* had been anally penetrated, something almost unparalleled in Latin texts surviving from antiquity.²⁷

This understanding of Encolpius' words leads us down a winding path lined by glimpses at *cinaedi* who are (perhaps) described as sexually penetrating others. A decontextualized quotation by Plutarch of the Greek philosopher Arcesilaus, translated into Latin by Aulus Gellius, voices the view that "it makes no difference whether a man is a *cinaedus* in his front parts or behind."²⁸ A one-line fragment from Lucilius drawing on stereotypes of gender nonconformity speaks of "beardless men-women, bearded adulterer-*cinaedi*" (fr. 1058 Marx, *imberbi androgyni, barbati moechocinaedi*). A graffito from Pompeii insults a man named Vesbinus as a *cinaedus*, but, like many of the graffiti scratched on walls two thousand years ago and in many cases barely legible today, the text has been interpreted variously, sometimes by the same scholars, including myself. I earlier understood it to be proclaiming that the *cinaedus* Vesbinus "fucked Vitalius in the ass", thus insulting both men, but I now incline to seeing the imagined configuration the other way around, the message being that Vitalio (not Vitalius) fucked the *cinaedus* Vesbinus: still an insult of Vesbinus, but not necessarily of Vitalio, who is cast in the normatively masculine sexual role.²⁹

For readers of other translations of the *Satyricon*, however, such questions are not even raised. For them, Encolpius is not telling of how the *cinaedus* penetrated Encolpius and Ascyltos, but rather of how he sat astride them, spreading

---

26 See most recently Sapsford 2022. In Williams 2015 I attempt to illustrate a polysemy network of the lexeme *cinaed-*. Sullivan's translation of *cinaedus* as "male prostitute" is an unusual choice and probably misleading.
27 For potential parallels see Williams 2010a, 216–218, 294.
28 Plut. *Quaest. conviv.* 705E ὅθεν Ἀρκεσίλαος οὐδὲν ἔφη διαφέρειν τοῖς ὄπισθεν εἶναι κίναιδον ἢ τοῖς ἔμπροσθεν; Plut. *De tuend. san.* 126A μηδὲν διαφέρειν ὄπισθέν τινα ἢ ἔμπροσθεν εἶναι κίναιδον; Aul. Gell. 3.5: *nihil interest quibus membris cinaedi sitis, posterioribus an prioribus*.
29 CIL 4.2319b with add p. 216 (written on a streetside façade): *Vesbinus cinedus Vtialio* [sic] *pedicavit*. In Williams 1999 I took *Vtialio* to be *Vitalio(m)*, understanding both the archaic spelling *-om* and omission of the final nasal: "Vesbinus the *cinaedus* fucked Vitalius." But in Williams 2010a, like Varone 1994 and Sapsford 2022, I understood "Vesbinus is a *cinaedus*; Vitalio fucked him" (with an implied *eum* as object of *pedicavit*); both the nomen *Vitalius* and the cognomen *Vitalio* are attested elsewhere, but only the cognomen *Vitalio* has so far been found in Pompeiian graffiti. (Varone introduces a probably needless complication by speculating that *Vesbinus cinaedus* might be nominative for vocative, with *te* rather than *eum* as implicit object of the verb: "Vesbinus, you *cinaedus*, Vitalio fucked you.")

his own buttocks and "banging", "belaboring", or "ramming" his partners with his vigorous motions.[30] To be sure, this is not an immediately obvious interpretation, above all because it would require an unparalleled sense of *caedere*, but also because the verb *extorquere* may more readily suggest the act of violently twisting apart someone else's buttocks than spreading one's own. Yet precisely this consideration has been cited in support of this interpretation. Edward Courtney sees Encolpius' *cecidit* as a characteristically Petronian "reversal" of common linguistic usage, and Tom Sapsford uses scare quotes to signal an unusual use of *caedere* ("'banged' us with his buttocks wrenched apart"), evoking contemporary Anglophone gay discourse to explain: "To use modern gay vernacular, an example of power-bottoming, where the penetrated partner's actions are so aggressive that he becomes the dominant actor in the sexual scenario."[31]

Readers of these translations see a further example of the narrative technique of pairing with repetition and variation characteristic of this text, for Encolpius soon thereafter tells of how a *cinaedus* — opinions differ as to whether this is the same man as in the earlier scene — attempted to engage in sexual encounters first with Encolpius himself ("he ground away on top of my groin, for quite a while but in vain", *super inguina mea diu multumque frustra moluit*, 23.4) and then with Ascyltos (whom he "pounded with his buttocks and kisses" as he sat astride him, *clunibus eum basiisque distrivit*, 24.4). These translations enable their readers to see continuities between *clunibus* in 21.2 and 24.4 (in both cases referring to the "buttocks" of the *cinaedus*) and between *cecidit* in 21.2, *moluit* in 23.4, and *distrivit* in 24.4 ("banged", "ground," and "pounded", all referring to his forceful actions as he rode astride his partners). But what if this second encounter (23–24) were not in our *Satyricon*? Would scholars and translators have even raised this interpretive possibility?[32]

---

30 Ernout 1950: "tantôt il nous laboura de ses fesses qu'il tortillait"; Müller and Ehlers 2004: "bald berammelte er uns unter Verrenkungen seines Hintern"; Aragosti 1995: "un po' ci strusciò addosso il suo sedere sculettante"; Courtney 2001, 68: "he beloboured us with his grinding buttocks"; Holzberg 2013: "bald bumste er uns mit seinen auseinandergezogenen Arschbacken"; Firebaugh 1922; "he nearly gored us to death with his writhing buttocks" (1927 adaptation: "he nearly gored us to death with his writhing").
31 Courtney 2001, 68; Sapsford 2022, 139.
32 Further options were proposed by scholars cited in Burman 1743, who were more open to radical emendations than modern editors tend to be. For example: rather than being "twisted apart" (*extortis*), the buttocks — whosoever they were — were perhaps "exposed" (*extectis*) or "bared" (*exertis*) or "worn down" (*extritis*), or maybe the *cinaedus* "banged" Ascyltos and Encolpius using "his entire buttocks" (*ex totis*). In Nodot 1694, Encolpius does not tell of a sexual act at all: the *cinaedus* struck Encolpius and Ascyltos with his buttocks while perform-

Finally, what of Quartilla herself, her tunic hitched up high and "holding a whalebone rod" (21.2, *ballaenaceam tenens virgam*)? Elsewhere I have interpreted these details as casting her in the role of masculine director of a scene which performs gender in a variety of ways.[33] But what exactly might this object be, and why might she be holding it? In their editions, Nodot and Burman take their cue from the phrase *dari missionem* ("that a reprieve be given"), suggesting that the object is or resembles the staff used by trainers of gladiators and athletes as a sign of their authority, and Burman also cites some possible emendations of *ballaenaceam* which take us down various byways of speculation, featuring a poisoned rod, a Celtic god, and riding crops of a kind used by female equestrians in eighteenth-century France and Holland.[34] Nearly all recent translations keep the manuscripts' reference to whalebone, but vary subtly but significantly in how they describe the object (*virgam*) and Quartilla's action (*tenens*): in English translations, for example, she is "carrying a whalebone rod" (Sullivan 2011), "wielding a whalebone ferula" (Walsh 2017), or "carrying a whalebone staff" (Schmeling 2020), but "carrying" is different from "wielding", and a "rod" is not quite the same as a "staff". Schmeling/Setaioli 2011 bring out an implication, adding a further English noun into the mix: "It is a whalebone *wand*, presumably a phallic symbol, as we might expect from a priestess of Priapus."[35] Yet the question of the precise design and function of this "wand" or "rod" or "staff" remains unanswered. And might it be something more than a symbol? Might it be, for example, a dildo? In that case, we would once again have an example of Petronian pairing with repetition and variation, for Encolpius later narrates a scene in which, in an attempt to cure his impotence, Oenothea anally penetrated him with a leather dildo lubricated with olive oil and sprinkled with crushed pepper and nettle seed (138.1).[36]

---

ing a vigorous dance ("lequel faisant mille contortions avec le corps, nous donnoit en dansant, tantôt des coups de son derriere, et tantôt nous infectoit de salles baisers").
33 Williams 2010b.
34 Burman 1743: "alii *belluatam*. alii *venenatam*. quid si *balenatam*, e balenae setis confectam, quales in Gallia et Batavia gestari solent a nobilibus foeminis equo vectis. *Venenatam*, φαρμακώδη. Noricis *Belenus* deus."
35 Schmeling/Setaioli 2011 *ad loc.* (emphasis added). Uniquely among modern translators, Holzberg 2013 emends *ballaenaceam* to *gallinaceam*, giving his readers a Quartilla who holds a marjoram branch. Holzberg explains in a note, without citing sources, that the herb was used as an aphrodisiac.
36 I owe the suggestion that this *virga* might be a dildo to Ashley Weed, who in a University of Illinois seminar paper from 2021 interpreted Quartilla as a *tribas*.

This possibility brings us back to the asterisks printed in texts and translations circulating today.

> 21.2–3 *modo extortis nos clunibus cecidit, modo basiis olidissimis inquinavit, donec Quartilla ballaenaceam tenens virgam alteque succincta iussit infelicibus dari missionem*
>
> *
>
> *uterque nostrum religiosissimis iuravit verbis inter duos periturum esse tam horribile secretum*
>
> First he banged us with twisted buttocks, then he befouled us with stinking kisses, until Quartilla, holding a whale-bone rod and with tunic hitched up high, ordered a reprieve for us in our misfortune
>
> *
>
> We both swore a most sacred oath that so dreadful a secret would die with us.

As we have seen, these asterisks first appeared in the sixteenth-century editions of the *L* class, and van Thiel has reminded us that we are not bound to accept their authority on every point. If those editions erroneously mark a gap here, the *tam horribile secretum* which Encolpius and Ascyltos swore to keep seems to be precisely that which they had just experienced with the *cinaedus* — whatever exactly that was — and this would be further reason to understand the phrase *extortis nos clunibus cecidit* as signifying that he had anally penetrated them.

On the other hand, if this asterisk correctly marks a gap, how much text is missing and what might have intervened? Did Encolpius go into further detail about what the *cinaedus* did to Ascyltos and himself, or did he move on to another encounter with someone else? This "dreadful secret" might thus be something now lost to us, and it might be one of the "other people's secrets" that Ascyltos had been warned against interfering in (20.3, *alienis intervenire secretis*), or else something in which Quartilla herself was involved. After all, she herself had earlier melodramatically begged them not to "betray secrets of so many years which barely a thousand people know of" (17.9, *neve traducere velitis tot annorum secreta, quae vix mille homines noverunt*).[37] Did Quartilla do something to Encolpius and/or Ascyltos in the intervening portion of narrative? If her "whalebone rod" was a dildo, did she use it with them? In that case we would have a unique scene in Latin literature: that of a woman anally penetrating men

---

[37] Here too different readers read different texts. Müller 2009 prints Nisbet's emendation of the manuscripts' *mille* to *tres*, thereby removing the ironic joke (Schmeling/Setaioli 2011 *ad loc.*: "Quartilla is surely bragging that hers is an exclusive cult, entrance into which is limited to the one thousand who have had sex with her").

with a dildo in a scene of sexual hijinks after those same men had been penetrated by a *cinaedus*. Then again, we might not.[38]

7 Concluding remarks

The *Satyricon* is an outstanding case study in the rewards, challenges, and limitations not only of reading incomplete texts, but also of inquiry into the language and imagery of gender and sexuality in ancient literature. We find the same textual details cited in support of quite different conclusions; readers over the centuries have had sometimes significantly different texts in front of them; and the practices of editors and translators have not infrequently increased the effects of the uncertain and the open. Raising more questions than it can answer, Petronius' fragmented and endlessly stimulating text invites scholars, translators, and readers to humility, reminding us on every page that we have access to only a small portion of the vast range of ancient Greek and Latin textuality, about whose full variety we can freely speculate and productively imagine, but which we can never hope to know in its entirety.

Bibliography

Adams, J.N. (1982), *The Latin Sexual Vocabulary*, Baltimore.
Aragosti, Andrea (trans.) (1995), *Petronio: Satyricon*, Milan.
Bücheler, Franz (ed.) (1862), *Petronii Arbitri Satirarum reliquiae*, Leipzig.
Bücheler, Franz (ed.) (1904), *Petronii Saturae et Liber Priapeorum*, Berlin.
Burman, Pieter (ed.) (1743), *Titi Petronii Arbitri Satyricon quae supersunt*, Amsterdam.
Connors, Catherine (1998), *Petronius the Poet*, Cambridge.
Conte, Gian Biagio (1997), *L'autore nascosto. Un'interpretazione del Satyricon*, Bologna.
Courtney, Edward (2001), *A Companion to Petronius*, Oxford.
Ernout, Alfred (trans.) (1950), *Pétrone: Le Satiricon*, Paris.
Firebaugh, W.C. (trans.) (1922), *The Satyricon of Petronius Arbiter*, New York.
Firebaugh, W.C. (trans.) (1927), *The Satyricon of Petronius Arbiter, adapted from the translation of W.C. Firebaugh*, New York.
Heinse, Wilhelm (trans.) (1773), *Begebenheiten des Enkolp*, Rome.
Heseltine, Michael (trans.)/Warmington, E.H. (rev.) (1969), *Petronius: Satyricon*, Cambridge MA.

---

[38] For women penetrating male partners, though not explicitly said to use a dildo, see Mart. 7.67, Sen. *Epist.* 95.21, and, at least on my interpretation of the poem, Phdr. 4.16 (with Williams 2010a, 233–239).

Hübner, Wolfgang (1987), *Die Petronübersetzung Wilhelm Heinses*, Frankfurt.
Holzberg, Niklas (trans.) (2013), *Petronius: Satyrische Geschichten*, Berlin.
McGinn, Thomas (2004), *The Economy of Prostitution in the Roman World*, Ann Arbor.
Merkelbach, Reinhold (1973), "Fragment eines satirischen Romans: Aufforderung zur Beichte", *Zeitschrift für Papyrologie und Epigraphik* 11, 81–100.
Müller, Konrad (ed.) (2009), *Petronii Arbitri Satyricon Reliquiae*, Berlin.
Müller, Konrad/Ehlers, Wilhelm (trans.) (2004), *Petronius: Schelmenszenen*, Zurich.
Nodot, François (ed.) (1694), *La Satyre de Petrone, traduite en François avec le texte latin, suivant le nouveau manuscrit trouvé à Bellegrade en 1688. Ouvrage complet*, Cologne.
Nodot, François (ed.) (1707), *Titi Petronii Arbitri equitis Romani Satyricon cum fragmentis Albae Graecae recuperatis anno 1688. Nunc demum integrum*, London.
Parsons, Peter (1971), "A Greek *Satyricon*?", *Bulletin of the Institute of Classical Studies* 18, 53–68.
Parsons, Peter (1974), "Narrative about Iolaos", *Oxyrhynchus Papyri* 42, 34–41.
Reardon, B.P. (ed.) (1989), *Collected Ancient Greek Novels*, Berkeley.
Richardson, Wade (1993), *Reading and Variant in Petronius*, Toronto.
Rimell, Victoria (2002), *Petronius and the Anatomy of Fiction*, Cambridge.
Sage, Evan/Gilleland, Brady (eds.) (1983), *Petronius: The Satiricon*, Irvington.
Sapsford, Tom (2022), *Performing the Kinaidos*, Oxford.
Schmeling, Gareth/Setaioli, Aldo (eds.) (2011), *A Commentary on the Satyrica of Petronius*, Oxford.
Schmeling, Gareth (ed. and trans.) (2020), *Petronius: Satyricon*, Cambridge MA.
Stephens, Susan/Winkler, John (eds.) (1995), *Ancient Greek Novels: The Fragments*, Princeton.
Stolz, Walter (1987), *Petrons Satyricon und François Nodot*, Mainz.
Stucchi, Silvia (2010), *Osservazioni sulla ricezione di Petronio nella Francia del XVII secolo*, Rome.
Sullivan, J.P. (trans.) (2011), *Petronius: The Satyricon*, London.
van Thiel, Helmut (1971), *Petronius: Überlieferung und Rekonstruktion*, Leiden.
Varone, Antonio (1994), *Erotica Pompeiana. Iscrizioni d'amore sui muri di Pompei*, Rome.
Walsh, P.G. (trans.) (2017), *Petronius: The Satyricon*, Oxford.
Weeber, Karl-Wilhelm (trans.) (2018), *Petronius Arbiter: Satyrica*, Stuttgart.
Williams, Craig (1999), *Roman Homosexuality: Ideologies of Masculinity in Classical Antiquity*, Oxford.
Williams, Craig (2010a), *Roman Homosexuality*, Oxford.
Williams, Craig (2010b), "*Cessamus mimum componere?* Performances of Gender in Petronius' Satyricon", in: Formisano, Marco/Fuhrer, Therese (eds.), *Gender-Inszenierungen in der antiken Literatur*, Trier, 25–44.
Williams, Craig (2015), "The Language of Gender: Lexical Semantics and the Latin Vocabulary of Unmanly Men", in: Masterson, Mark/Rabinowitz, Nancy/Robson, James (eds.), *Sex in Antiquity*, London, 461–481.
Zeitlin, Froma (1971), "Petronius as Paradox: Anarchy and Artistic Integrity", *Transactions of the American Philological Association* 102, 632–684.

Figures

inquit 'quae mihi acciderunt'. 'quid novi?' inquam *LO*
2 ego. at ille deficiens 'cum errarem' inquit 'per totam
civitatem nec invenirem quo loco stabulum reliquis-
sem, accessit ad me pater familiae et ducem se itineris
3 humanissime promisit. per anfractus deinde obscuris-
simos egressus in hunc locum me perduxit prolatoque
4 peculio coepit rogare stuprum. | iam pro cella meretrix *L*
assem exegerat, | iam ille mihi iniecerat manum, et nisi *LO*
valentior fuissem, dedissem poenas' . . .
| adeo ubique omnes mihi videbantur satyrion bi- *L*
bisse

*

iunctis viribus molestum contempsimus

*

9 quasi per caliginem vidi Gitona in crepidine semitae
stantem et in eundem locum me conieci . . .
2 cum quaererem numquid nobis in prandium frater
parasset, consedit puer super lectum et manantes la-
3 crimas pollice extersit. perturbatus ego habitu fratris
quid accidisset quaesivi. at ille tarde quidem et invitus,
sed postquam precibus etiam iracundiam miscui,
4 'tuus' inquit 'iste frater seu comes paulo ante in con-
ductum accucurrit coepitque mihi velle pudorem ex-
5 torquere. | cum ego proclamarem, gladium strinxit et *LO*
"si Lucretia es" inquit "Tarquinium invenisti".'

L (= *ldmrtp*), *O* (= *BRP*) 9 *Lac. ind. Pithoeus* 14 *Lac. ind. Hadrianides* 17 extersit *Fr. Pithoeus*: expressit | ego *lp*[2]: ergo *ceteri* 19 etiam *l*: et *ceteri*

6

Fig. 1: Sample page of Latin text in Müller 2009.

16   THE SATYRICON

the maid clapped her hands and said: 'I did put it down near you, young man. But have you drunk all that medicine by yourself?' 'Really?' said Quartilla. 'Has Encolpius drunk all the aphrodisiac there was?'

Her sides shook with her charming laughter.

In the end even Giton joined in the joke, particularly when the little girl threw her arms round his neck and kissed him an incredible number of times without any struggle.

21. In our desperation we wanted to shout for help, but there was no one to come to our aid. Besides, whenever I wanted to call for assistance from outside, Psyche stuck a hairpin into my cheeks. Meanwhile the girl was stifling Ascyltus with a cosmetic brush which she had soaked in aphrodisiac.

Finally, up came a male prostitute, dressed in myrtle-green shaggy felt, which was tucked up under a cherry-red belt. He pulled the cheeks of our bottoms apart and banged us, then he slobbered vile, greasy kisses on us, until Quartilla, carrying a whalebone rod, with her skirts up round her, ordered an end to our torments.

Both of us swore a solemn oath that such a dreadful secret would die with us.

Some training attendants came in, who rubbed us with the appropriate oil and made us feel better. Somehow or other we threw off our weariness, put on dinner clothes again and were taken into the next room. There were three couches ready and every other refinement of gracious living magnificently laid out. We took our places as we were told, and beginning with some wonderful hors d'oeuvres we were then practically swimming in Falernian wine. After helping ourselves to a long series of dishes, we were beginning to fall asleep, when Quartilla said, 'Do you actually intend to go to sleep when you know the whole night has to be a vigil in honour of our guardian Priapus?'

Fig. 2: Sample page of a translation (Sullivan 2011).

PETRONIUS

5   ab eadem anicula esse deductum. | itaque ut ridens eum
     consalutavi, quid in loco tam deformi faceret quaesivi.
     8. sudorem ille manibus detersit et "si scires" inquit "quae mihi
2   acciderunt." "quid novi?" inquam ego. | at ille deficiens "cum
     errarem" inquit "per totam civitatem nec invenirem quo loco
     stabulum reliquissem, accessit ad me pater familiae et ducem se
3   itineris humanissime promisit. | per anfractus deinde
     obscurissimos egressus in hunc locum me perduxit prolatoque
4   peculio coepit rogare stuprum. | ^{L}iam pro cella meretrix assem
     exegerat, ^{OL}iam ille mihi iniecerat manum, et nisi valentior
     fuissem, dedissem poenas." ⟨. . .⟩ ^{L}adeo ubique omnes mihi
     videbantur satyrion bibisse.
                    ⟨***⟩

     iunctis viribus molestum contempsimus
                    ⟨***⟩

         9. quasi per caliginem vidi Gitona in crepidine semitae stantem
2   et in eundem locum me conieci. ⟨. . .⟩ | cum quaererem numquid
     nobis in prandium frater parasset, consedit puer super lectum et
3   manantes lacrimas pollice extersit.[31] | perturbatus ego habitu
     fratris quid accidisset quaesivi. at ille tarde quidem et invitus, sed
4   postquam precibus etiam iracundiam miscui, | "tuus" inquit "iste
     frater seu comes paulo ante in conductum accucurrit coepitque
5   mihi velle pudorem extorquere. | ^{OL}cum ego

Fig. 3: Sample page of Latin text in Schmeling 2020.

Fig. 4: Page from ninth-century MS B, containing compressed text of Petr. *Sat.* 7.1 – 17.6 (Richardson 1993, pl. 1).

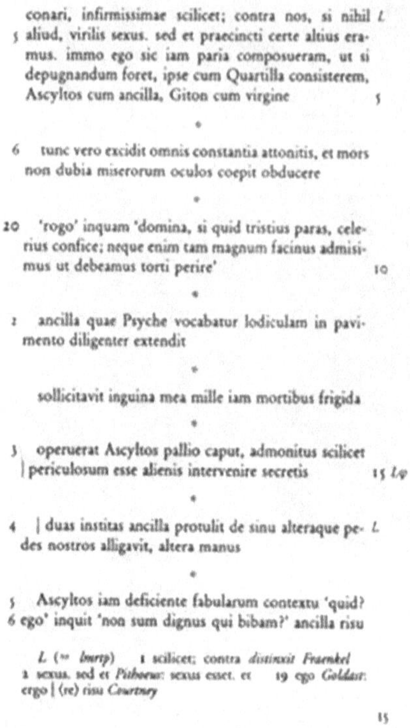

conari, infirmissimae scilicet; contra nos, si nihil *L.*
aliud, virilis sexus. sed et praecincti certe altius era-
mus. immo ego sic iam paria composueram, ut si
depugnandum foret, ipse cum Quartilla consisterem,
Ascyltos cum ancilla, Giton cum virgine   5

6   tunc vero excidit omnis constantia attonitis, et mors
    non dubia miserorum oculos coepit obducere

20 'rogo' inquam 'domina, si quid tristius paras, cele-
    rius confice; neque enim tam magnum facinus admisi-
    mus ut debeamus torti perire'   10

2   ancilla quae Psyche vocabatur lodiculam in pavi-
    mento diligenter extendit

    sollicitavit inguina mea mille iam mortibus frigida

3   operuerat Ascyltos pallio caput, admonitus scilicet
    | periculosum esse alienis intervenire secretis   15 *Lφ*

4 | duas institas ancilla protulit de sinu alteraque pe-   *L*
    des nostros alligavit, altera manus

5   Ascyltos iam deficiente fabularum contextu 'quid?
6   ego' inquit 'non sum dignus qui bibam?' ancilla risu

    L (= *lmrtp*)   1 scilicet; contra *distinxit Fraenkel*
    2 sexus. sed et *Pithoeus*: sexus esset. et   19 ego *Goldast*:
    ergo | (re) risu *Courtney*

                    15

Fig. 5: Page from the Quartilla episode in Müller 2009.

Part II: **Questioning (In)Completeness**

Richard Hunter
The "Alexandrian End" of the *Odyssey*

Abstract: This paper considers, first, some of the implications for ancient and modern criticism of the fact that Aristophanes of Byzantium and Aristarchus placed the τέλος ('end') or πέρας ('limit') of the *Odyssey* at 23.296. The second part of the paper considers ancient citations of the verse, the role it played in ancient appreciations of the *Odyssey*, and, in the final section, an allusion to the Alexandrian "end" in Virgil.

1 The Alexandrian end

The *Odyssey* hangs over all modern discussions of closure in ancient literature, but our familiarity with the issues can make us forget (or take for granted) the extent to which the question of closure is thematised in the *Odyssey* itself, both through Teiresias' prophecy to Odysseus in the Underworld and through Odysseus' report of it to Penelope after the recognition:[1]

> ὦ γύναι, οὐ γάρ πω πάντων ἐπὶ πείρατ' ἀέθλων
> ἤλθομεν, ἀλλ' ἔτ' ὄπισθεν ἀμέτρητος πόνος ἔσται,
> πολλὸς καὶ χαλεπός, τὸν ἐμὲ χρὴ πάντα τελέσσαι.
> > Homer, *Odyssey* 23.248–250

> My wife, we have not yet come to the limit of all our challenges, but there remains in front of me measureless labour, large and difficult, and I must complete it in full.

> οὐδὲ γὰρ αὐτὸς
> χαίρω, ἐπεὶ μάλα πολλὰ βροτῶν ἐπὶ ἄστε' ἄνωγεν
> ἐλθεῖν, ἐν χείρεσσιν ἔχοντ' εὐῆρες ἐρετμόν,
> εἰς ὅ κε τοὺς ἀφίκωμαι, οἳ οὐκ ἴσασι θάλασσαν
> ἀνέρες οὐδέ θ' ἅλεσσι μεμιγμένον εἶδαρ ἔδουσιν ...
> > Homer, *Odyssey* 23.266–270

I am grateful to participants in the Thessaloniki conference of June 2022 for their helpfully sceptical reactions and to an audience at the Venice International University and to Rebecca Laemmle and Cédric Scheidegger Laemmle for their comments on earlier versions. As usual, I have not sought to remove every trace of this paper's origin in an oral presentation.

1 On these verses cf., e.g., Purves 2006, 4–6; Loney 2019, 207–208.

> I myself find no pleasure in it, since he told me to visit very many cities of men, carrying in my hands a balanced oar, until I come to men who do not know the sea and do not eat their food seasoned with salt ...

Odysseus' translation of Teiresias' words into an echo of the poem's proem (23.267–268 ~ 1.1–3) plays with the idea that the loop of the *Odyssey* may never close.[2] If, then, Homer persistently invites us to look to and for the *telos*,[3] we can hardly be surprised if Aristophanes of Byzantium and Aristarchus took up the challenge.

In this paper I will sidestep the big question which looms here for us, but not for the Alexandrian grammarians, namely "What sort of an end ought we to be looking for in a (? predominantly) oral poem?",[4] but before turning to the "Alexandrian end" I want to make one further observation which will, I hope, not be thought flippant. One issue which hangs over many questions of "the end" and "the unfinished" in literature is "the death of the author", here meant in a quite literal sense. It has always struck me as curious that, if there was in antiquity any dissatisfaction with the end of the *Odyssey*, it seems never to have been suggested that Homer left it unfinished at death. This may have something to do with the fact that, however full a biography (or biographies) of Homer antiquity might construct, he always remained, and was always felt to be, a very different kind of "historical person" than a Euripides or a Virgil or a Lucan. What perhaps comes closest to such a suggestion about the *Odyssey* in antiquity is the famous discussion in Longinus, *On the Sublime* 9.11–15.[5] Here the *Odyssey* is, as it is elsewhere (though not universally) in the ancient critical tradition,[6] the work of the poet's old age (γῆρας), and some of what Longinus has to say makes Homer sound very old indeed (λῆρος, "nonsense", *Subl.* 9.14); Longinus gestures towards the famously long-lived Nestor as another of Homer's self-portraits. Nevertheless, Longinus has nothing to say about what we call Books 23 and 24, the "latest" reference in *On the Sublime* being to the ἀπίθανα, "implausibilities", in the episode of the slaughter of the suitors (*Subl.* 9.14).[7] I am

---

2 Cf. also Tsagalis 2008, 71.
3 For the *Odyssey*'s own concern with narrative "endings" cf. the very different concerns of Peradotto 1990, chap. 4, Purves 2010, chapter 2 and Hauser 2020; Loney 2019, chapter 6 offers an interesting account of the end of our *Odyssey* in terms of a divine closure upon the otherwise open-endedness of revenge, and Grethlein 2017, chapter 7 provides sensitive readings of the poem's multiple "ends".
4 Cf., e.g., Foley 1999, 158–167; Fowler 2000, 256–257; Kelly 2007; Bakker 2020.
5 Cf. Falkner 1995, chap. 1; Hunter 2018, 186–193; Halliwell 2022, 171–178.
6 Cf., e.g., Bühler 1964, 44–47 for the evidence.
7 Cf. further below p. 98 n. 33.

not of course suggesting that Aristophanes of Byzantium and Aristarchus did indeed entertain the idea that Homer died just after composing 23.296, although the thought of his expiry just as Odysseus and Penelope reclaim the marital bed has a certain romantic appeal.

That Homer's death is indeed relevant to the end of the *Odyssey* was in fact suggested by J.B. Bury a century ago,[8] with the added twist that Homer had conveyed to a pupil (or a son? – cf. perhaps Euripides' *Iphigeneia in Aulis*) how he intended to complete the poem, with the result that the end of the poem is not-Homeric, but also not entirely not-Homeric.[9] Some tradition of this state of affairs will ultimately have reached Alexandria, just as Stephanie West too held that the Alexandrians knew of some anecdotal tradition about 23.296, perhaps parallel to the famous ancient report about the *Doloneia*.[10] Christiane Sourvinou-Inwood expanded such views to the speculation that "the Homeric *Odyssey* had had a different ending [i.e. after 23.296], which was replaced by the present Continuation, which incorporated material both from the original *Odyssey* ending and from elsewhere", that "elsewhere" being "a different epic which had preceded the *Odyssey*, in which the Nekyia had been situated at the end of the poem".[11] Why any of this is important (in the context of this volume) is that "the end of the *Odyssey*", quite apart from the problem of the "Alexandrian end", forces us to confront the limitations of criticism and of ourselves as critics as brutally as does any ancient text. If the *Odyssey* was indeed *labor imperfectus*, how would we tell?

The principal evidence for the Alexandrian τέλος or πέρας are the laconic scholia on *Odyssey* 23:

(296) ἀσπάσιοι λέκτροιο] ἀσπαστῶς καὶ ἐπιθυμητικῶς ὑπεμνήσθησαν τοῦ πάλαι τῆς συνουσίας νόμου. Ἀριστοφάνης δὲ καὶ Ἀρίσταρχος πέρας τῆς Ὀδυσσείας τοῦτο ποιοῦνται. M.V. Vind. 133.

---

8 Bury 1922.
9 There is a strange echo perhaps of Bury's view in Rutherford 2013, 101 who describes the final scene of the poem as "almost ... a rough sketch which was awaiting further elaboration" (a view frequently expressed, cf., e.g., Mackail 1936, 6). So too, there are remarkable echoes (not made explicit) of both ancient and modern scholarship (notably Bury) in Stephanie West's view of the poet of the *Odyssey* as "an elderly singer" suffering "increasing infirmity" whose "grand design" was completed by one or more "pupils" who were able, at least initially, to "check with [the] master" (S. West 2018, 67–68).
10 S. West 1989, 120.
11 Sourvinou-Inwood 1995, 98, 101; that the *nekuia* of Book 11 was "originally" at the end of the poem is of course a very familiar critical position. Kay 1957 suggests that the "continuation" actually begins with 23.300, although 23.296 was indeed the "Alexandrian end".

ἀσπάσιοι λέκτροιο παλαιοῦ θεσμὸν ἵκοντο] τοῦτο τέλος τῆς Ὀδυσσείας φησὶν Ἀρίσταρχος καὶ Ἀριστοφάνης. H.M.Q.

(310–343) οὐ καλῶς ἠθέτησεν Ἀρίσταρχος τοὺς τρεῖς καὶ τριά-
κοντα· ῥητορικὴν γὰρ πεποίηκεν ἀνακεφαλαίωσιν καὶ ἐπιτομὴν τῆς
Ὀδυσσείας. Q.V.

Scholia on Odyssey 23 (Dindorf)

296 With pleasure and desire did they renew their old custom of intercourse. Aristophanes and Aristarchus make this the πέρας ('limit') of the *Odyssey*. M.V. Vind. 133. "Gratefully they came to the custom of their bed of old". Aristarchus and Aristophanes say that this is the τέλος ('end') of the *Odyssey*. H.M.Q.

310–43 Aristarchus was mistaken to athetize the following thirty-three verses, for [Homer] has composed a rhetorical recapitulation and epitome of the *Odyssey*. Q.V.

These brief notices are of course deeply frustrating, but at the very least they do not, I think, immediately suggest that the Alexandrian scholars simply denied Homeric authorship to, "athetised" if you like, everything which followed 23.296;[12] if that is what they meant, this is, I think, not how we would have expected that to be reported. Eustathius does, however, say this very clearly (*Hom.* 1948.42–1949.2 = II 308.22–35 Stallbaum), drawing, as Hartmut Erbse pretty conclusively demonstrated,[13] on no more knowledge than we have.[14] Of course, the scholia on the later books of the *Odyssey* are, on the whole, brief and jejune, and no weight can be placed upon their wording as a thread leading directly back to Hellenistic Alexandria, but — for what it is worth — the scholia more immediately suggest that a line is being drawn under the *Odyssey* and that, as a consequence, what follows (to which the scholia in fact make no reference) must therefore belong to another poem, which may or may not be by Homer. Some have indeed toyed with the idea that this is what the scholia do mean: what follows the reunion of Odysseus and Penelope may be being assigned to another poem from the epic cycle.[15]

---

[12] The scholia on v.296 are traced back ultimately to Aristonicus (with some later additions) by Carnuth 1869, 162.
[13] Erbse 1972, 167–168. For discussions before Erbse see, e.g., von der Mühll, *RE* Suppl. 7.763, Van der Valk 1964, 2601; Petzl 1969, 44–46.
[14] περατοῦσι τὴν Ὀδύσσειαν, τὰ ἐφεξῆς ἕως τέλους τοῦ βιβλίου νοθεύοντες, "they make this the limit of the *Odyssey*, considering what follows until the end of the work as spurious".
[15] Cf. above p. 91 and, e.g., Merkelbach 1969, 143–144; Dawe 1993, 823. The condemnation of everything after 23.296 in Page 1955, chapter 5, proved very influential in the Anglophone world.

The wording of the scholia would, however, also suit the alternative view, namely that "end" here is being used in the sense of "conclusion, point to which the narrative has been leading" rather than "end-point" in a strictly literal sense. That this is what the scholia do mean is probably as close to a current *communis opinio* as we are likely to get, particularly since the major discussion by Hartmut Erbse.[16] The principal objection (above all others) to the strictest form of the "textual" interpretation of the scholia has always been, of course, the two long atheteseis by Aristarchus which follow, of 23.310–343 ("the recapitulation") and 24.1–204 (the "second *nekuia*"); many have found it very difficult to believe in athetesis of parts of a text which had already been declared wholly spurious, even taking account of the possibility of multiple Aristarchan commentaries and works on Homer.[17] Certainly, the athetesis of the "recapitulation" follows a familiar Aristarchan pattern: if the verses are removed, there will be no trace that they were ever there — and no one (I think) would ever have missed them. Eustathius observed, and obviously approved, the contrast in length between the four verses devoted to Penelope's narration (23.302–305) and the many more given to Odysseus' account (*Hom.* 1949.3–11 = II 308.35–39 Stallbaum), but perhaps others (including Aristarchus?) felt that the like-minded (ὁμόφρων) couple would be better represented by equal airtime.[18] The athetesis of the second *nekuia* is, despite its much greater length, a rather similar case: who would ever have thought something was missing? If the "Erbse view" of the "Alexandrian end" is correct, then Aristarchus (at least) presumably considered 24.205–548 as the final book of the poem, and that does not seem inherently implausible.[19]

---

[16] Erbse 1972, 167–177. Heubeck's note on 23.297 offers helpful discussion and an extensive summary and bibliography of contributions.

[17] For the arguments and bibliography cf. Schironi 2018, 35–45. Some "softer" versions of the textual interpretation of what Aristophanes and Aristarchus noted about 23.296 as "the end of the *Odyssey*" (cf. above p. 91) would, on the other hand, be quite compatible with Aristarchan athetesis of parts of what followed.

[18] Danek 1998, 460–461 observes that the difference must be connected to Amphimedon's recapitulation of events on Ithaca during the second *nekuia* of Book 24.

[19] Stephanie West observes that if Aristophanes or Aristarchus were responsible for the division of the poems into twenty-four books (cf. [Plut.] *Hom.* 2.4), then we might have expected 23.297–24.548 to form the last book, cf. S. West 1988, 40 n. 19. The belief that the Alexandrians considered 23.296 to be "the end" in some literal sense of the *Odyssey* has in fact often been used as an argument that Homeric book-divisions cannot be owed to them, as otherwise 23.296 would surely have been the end of a book. The argument was always a fragile one, and must of course be abandoned totally if "end" is to be understood differently.

For Eustathius (*Hom.* 1949.15–18 = II 308.43–46 Stallbaum), Odysseus' ἀνακεφαλαίωσις was, after the temporal fireworks of the first half of the *Odyssey*, a bravura rhetorical display of a very different kind of κατὰ τάξιν ("in serial order") narration,[20] beginning from the κατὰ φύσιν τῆς Ὀδυσσείας ἀρχή ("natural beginning of the *Odyssey*"), i.e. the Kikones who are named both in the first verse of the *apologoi* proper and in the first verse of the summary (9.39 ~ 23.310).[21] Whether or not there is here (and in the corresponding scholium on vv. 310–343) some resonance of Ὀδύσσεια in the sense of "story of Odysseus", rather than Homer's *Odyssey*, may be debated; that Eustathius was (at some level) aware of the possibility of some conflict between the two would seem suggested by his remark that perhaps the Alexandrians did not mean that this was the conclusion of "the book/poem (βιβλίον) of the *Odyssey*", but only of the καίρια ("important parts") of the *Odyssey*. Nevertheless, it is very clear that vv. 310–341 are indeed, as vv. 306–307 might be thought to foreshadow, a summary of Odysseus' *nostos*, "the story of Odysseus", not of Homer's *Odyssey*.[22] Moreover, the narrator himself has precisely prepared us for what follows by telling us of two separate "epic" narrations, Penelope's "story of Penelope" (23.302–305) and Odysseus' adventures (23.306–307); both of them belong to the poem called Ὀδύσσεια, but only one to "the story of Odysseus" (there was much of "the story of Penelope" which Odysseus did not know). Odysseus' summary finishes with what is related in the early part of Book 13; those who wish to place a (perhaps *the*) major division of the poem at 13.87–92 can find support for this position in Odysseus' summary in Book 23. Homer excuses the "premature" end of the

---

20 This may, of course, have been one of Aristarchus' objections to it; for him, such narrative was characteristic of οἱ νεώτεροι, cf., e.g., the bT-scholia on *Iliad* 2.494–877. For a kind of neo-Eustathian appreciation of the recapitulation cf. Goldhill 1991, 49; Danek 1998, 460–461 (though neither make any reference to Eustathius). Another approach in antiquity to the recapitulation was to see it as a masterful demonstration of how to reduce a very long narrative to a brief summary, cf. [Plut.], *De Homero* 174. In the background of such an approach stands Arist. *Rhet.* 3.1417a13–14, where the Ἀλκίνου ἀπόλογος ("tale to Alcinous") told to Penelope "in sixty verses" is (apparently) an example of an appropriately rapid (and summarising) narrative. There are textual and interpretative difficulties here — it is unclear whether "sixty" is the correct text (i.e. *Od.* 23.264–284 and 310–341) and Gomperz's suggestion of a lacuna before παράδειγμα (see Kassel's apparatus) seems attractive — but the point seems to be that the recapitulation omits everything that might bring οἶκτος or δείνωσις: it is the very plainest of narrations.
21 For bibliography of modern discussion of the recapitulation cf. Oswald 1993, 106–117; Heubeck on 23.310–343.
22 The (partial, in both senses) narrative of Amphimedon's ghost at *Od.* 24.120–190 is very largely a retelling of the second half of the *Odyssey* and, as such, must also be seen against the "recapitulation"; both are indeed experimental narrative modes.

summary, if that is what it is, as the point at which the hero fell asleep (23.342–343), thus echoing the famous sleep he enjoyed on board the Phaeacian ship and then on Ithaca (13.79–92);[23] the narrator's framing closure echoes Odysseus' return to Ithaca, just as the "recapitulation" itself replays (basically) Books 9–12. Nevertheless, although the narrator seems only to foreshadow at 23.306–307 a summary of "the story of Odysseus", not of the *Odyssey*, one might think that there is some apparent tension between Homer's introductory frame, in which it is said that Penelope did not fall asleep "until Odysseus had narrated everything" (πάρος καταλέξαι ἅπαντα) and the pointed manner in which the narrator identifies the Phaeacian gifts and carriage home as the δεύτατον ... ἔπος, "last word", before sleep overcame Odysseus himself, as though there was more he might have said. It is not just the framing poem, but the "recapitulation and epitome of the *Odyssey*/story of Odysseus" (schol. 23.310–343) which offers a problematised ending, a *telos* which is not all it seems.

The relation between Ὀδύσσεια as "the *Odyssey*" and "the story of Odysseus" is delicate and difficult, and much of the difficulty we feel was presumably felt in antiquity also. When Aristotle singles out Homer's *Odyssey* in comparison with poems entitled *Herakleis* or *Theseis*, or perhaps even someone else's *Odyssey*,[24] as a poem with a unitary μῦθος, i.e. one with a beginning, middle and end, a unitary πρᾶξις (*Poet*. 1451a15–29), he is not merely defending the importance and superiority of Homeric epic, but also in part responding to, or perhaps rather putting as brave a face as he can on, critical issues which are already adumbrated in the poem itself. The critical agenda was in some ways already set by Homer. We may think it "realistic"[25] that Odysseus tells Penelope his adventures on their first night back in bed together, but the extended recapitulation of vv. 310–341 does indeed impose some kind of narrative closure, while also lessening the gap between *Odyssey* and "story of Odysseus". The scholiast who described these verses as "a rhetorical recapitulation and epitome of the *Odyssey*" (cf. above) almost certainly did mean "the *Odyssey*", not "the story of Odysseus' adventures on the way home from Troy", although, as the scholiast will presumably have known very well, the verses are anything but a recapitulation of the *Odyssey*.[26] It is difficult, however, to blame the scholiast; Homer has already opened the door to such equivocations.

---

23 Cf. Di Benedetto on *Od*. 23.310–341.
24 Cf. Else 1957, 298 n.11 on Ὀδύσσειαν at *Poet*. 1451a24.
25 Cf., e.g., de Jong 2001, 562.
26 Eustathius (*Hom*. 1948.56 = II 308.28 Stallbaum) adds the grace-note "... an epitome of the whole, so to speak (ὡς εἰπεῖν), *Odyssey*", which just calls even more attention to the issue.

The scholia on 23.310–343 make it clear (γάρ) that the description of the verses as "a rhetorical recapitulation and epitome of the *Odyssey*" is a defence against Aristarchus' athetesis. Behind this very abbreviated report must lie the idea, which will have been very familiar to rhetorically trained scholiasts, that a recapitulation is entirely in place at the end of a long work. That the τέλος of a speech should be devoted to recapitulation (ἐπάνοδος), in which the listeners are summarily (ἐν κεφαλαίῳ) reminded of what has been said, is claimed to be "agreed by all" at Plato, *Phaedrus* 267d3–6,[27] and in fact is the assumption which already lies behind the conclusion of Gorgias' *Palamedes*;[28] Aristotle observes that a speech does not need an ἐπίλογος ("epilogue") if the facts are "easy to remember" (*Rhet.* 3.1414b6).[29] Thus the scholiastic defence of the recapitulation, despite the fact that it rejects the "Alexandrian end", in fact very likely takes off from an assumption that we have indeed reached the τέλος "of the *Odyssey*", perhaps "final part" rather than (literal) "end"; whether or not this can shed light on how Aristophanes and Aristarchus used the term (if they did) may be debated. Secondly, there is in fact another sense in which the summary and the summary of the summary (23.306–307) are a kind of *Odyssey*, not just "the story of Odysseus". It may be tendentious to claim that vv. 306–307 echo the proem of the poem (so I will not do that), but what is clear is that, like both the poem itself (cf. 1.2) and Odysseus' *apologoi* (cf. 9.38–39), the summary is very distinctly "after Troy"; it may be "realistic" that Odysseus does not treat Penelope to a post-coital *Iliad*, but the silence is here a loud one. As often, Eustathius' gloss suggests his sharp critical instincts: after citing vv. 306–307 almost verbatim, he adds "... [*all that he himself suffered*] after the departure from Troy; of what happened at Troy there is absolutely no word at all (οὐδεὶς οὐδόλως ... λόγος, *Hom.* 1949.12 = II 308.40 Stallbaum)". It is not, of course, true that there is "absolutely no word at all" of events at Troy in the *Odyssey* and in the *apologoi*, but the simple and powerful idea that the *Odyssey* comes "after Troy",

---

27 The *Phaedrus* itself has a (very memorable) recapitulation (278b–c), just before its "end", as (in part) an element of Plato's shaping of the work as a novel kind of rhetorical performance.
28 "To give a brief reminder of what has been said at length makes sense if the judges are worthless, but there is no point even considering that the first of Greeks among the very first of Greeks neither pay attention nor remember what has been said" *Palamedes* 37). I have wondered whether this conclusion, like the opening of the argument (*Palamedes* 4, cf. Hunter 2018, 126), is, not just a reference to rhetorical theory about the parts of a speech, but also another of Palamedes' hits at the Homeric Odysseus, in this case at the recapitulation of the *Odyssey*.
29 For the later evidence in rhetorical writers about a closing recapitulation cf. Lausberg 1960, 237–238.

or as Longinus (*Subl.* 9.12) put it, is an ἐπίλογος to the *Iliad*, is reinforced by the silence of the recapitulation.

Aristotle had another go at "the *Odyssey* problem" in a famous passage which has become central to this discussion:

> ἐν μὲν οὖν τοῖς δράμασιν τὰ ἐπεισόδια σύντομα, ἡ δ' ἐποποιία τούτοις μηκύνεται. τῆς γὰρ Ὀδυσσείας οὐ μακρὸς ὁ λόγος ἐστίν· ἀποδημοῦντός τινος ἔτη πολλὰ καὶ παραφυλαττομένου ὑπὸ τοῦ Ποσειδῶνος καὶ μόνου ὄντος, ἔτι δὲ τῶν οἴκοι οὕτως ἐχόντων ὥστε τὰ χρήματα ὑπὸ μνηστήρων ἀναλίσκεσθαι καὶ τὸν υἱὸν ἐπιβουλεύεσθαι, αὐτὸς δὲ ἀφικνεῖται χειμασθείς, καὶ ἀναγνωρίσας τινὰς ἐπιθέμενος αὐτὸς μὲν ἐσώθη τοὺς δ' ἐχθροὺς διέφθειρε. τὸ μὲν οὖν ἴδιον τοῦτο, τὰ δ' ἄλλα ἐπεισόδια.
>
> Aristotle, *Poetics* 1455b16–23

> Now, in plays the episodes are concise, but epic gains length from them. The *Odyssey*'s story is not long: a man is away from home many years; he is watched by Poseidon, and isolated; moreover, affairs at home are such that his property is consumed by suitors, and his son conspired against; but he returns after shipwreck, allows some people to recognise him, and launches an attack which brings his own survival and his enemies' destruction. That is the essential core; the rest is episodes. (trans. Halliwell)

Aristotle's "brief *logos*" of the *Odyssey* seems to include, or at least gesture to, both the "Penelopiad", of which we get a glimpse at *Od.* 23.302–305, and (at a pinch) perhaps also the "Telemachy"; the basic narrative structure to which Aristotle is pointing is clear, though perhaps only an excess of generosity of spirit[30] can here save any "Aristotelian unity" for the poem. It is very obvious why Aristotle chose the *Odyssey*, rather than the *Iliad*, to illustrate the distinction between τὸ ἴδιον of an epic and the "episodes",[31] but in doing so he lays very bare one of the central narratological issues of the poem and one very much at the heart of the debate about "the Alexandrian end".

---

30 For such generosity cf., e.g., Else 1957, 512–514.

31 The "summary" of the plot of the *Iliad* at [Plut.] *Hom.* 1.7, which moves almost directly from Book 1 to Patroclus' request to Achilles in Book 16, presumably derives from an educational context (cf. Plut. *Mor.* 14e with Hunter/Russell 2011, 72), but may go back eventually to a descendant of Aristotle's summary of the *Odyssey*. At *Od.* 2.174–176 Halitherses claims that, when the Greeks set out for Troy, he had prophesied that "having suffered many misfortunes and lost all his comrades, Odysseus would return home in the twentieth year, unrecognizable by everyone"; Eustathius (*Hom.* 1440.16–18 = I 90.38–40 Stallbaum) describes this as a σύνοψις of the *Odyssey* (as does S. West on *Od.* 2.174–176) "in less than three whole verses". The Aristotelian distinction between τὸ ἴδιον and the "episodes" is, in Eustathius, a distinction between what is ἐν καιρῷ and the rest; Eustathius' view here of what is ἐν καιρῷ in the *Odyssey* is even sparer than Aristotle's. On 2.174–176 cf. de Jong 2001, 55; M. West 2014, 157 sees "an *ad hoc* invention ... modelled on Calchas' prophecy in [*Iliad* 2].301–30".

Hartmut Erbse saw in the scholia reporting that "Alexandrian end", as others had before him, a descendant of this Aristotelian-peripatetic teaching; the importance of such teaching to Alexandrian γραμματική has been recently re-emphasised by Francesca Schironi.³² In the *Poetics*, Aristotle uses τέλος both to mean "the end" in a quite literal sense, whether of a literary work or a historical event, and also as "end in view, purpose"; in the latter sense the term may be applied to the "purpose" of the whole τέχνη of poetry, as at 1460b24–7, or of an individual set of events, as at 1459a26–8. Erbse suggested that what Aristophanes and Aristarchus had in mind was indeed the Aristotelian *logos* of the *Odyssey* (cf. above), the "conclusion" (τέλος, πέρας) of which is the "destruction of Odysseus' enemies", by which is presumably meant the suitors, rather than their fathers and relations in Book 24.³³ When in Book 24 events in the town are resumed, Ὄσσα reports precisely μνηστήρων στυγερὸν θάνατον καὶ κῆρ(α), "the grim death and fate of the suitors" 24.413 (cf. further below), as though that had been some kind of "climax". Aristotle does not in fact use the term τέλος in connection with the λόγος of the *Odyssey*, but there seems no reason why the term might not have been used in connection with the Aristotelian summary. Erbse, like others before him, was able to adduce another observation of Eustathius, namely that the killing of the suitors was the σκοπιμώτατον τέλος, "most intended conclusion", of the poem (*Hom.* 1393.55–58 = I 23.22–24 Stallbaum) for which everything else from the beginning had been preparing, and once the suitors had been killed "the poet brings the work to an end".³⁴ Erbse had, of course, to suggest that Aristophanes tinkered with the Aristotelian *logos* by extending it to include the happy couple's reunion in bed, rather than placing "the end" at the killing of the suitors, but that might be thought a mere detail (or it might not).

---

32 Cf. Schironi 2009, 2018: Index s.vv. Aristotle, Peripatetic.
33 For what it is worth, when at *Subl.* 9.14 Longinus singles out unfortunate examples of λῆρος from the *Odyssey*, he lists them, though he does not say this, in order of appearance in the poem, and the final case is the ἀπίθανα in the episode of the killing of the suitors. More striking is the fact that all of the examples come from the *apologoi* of Books 9–12, except for the killing of the suitors; was this last, perhaps surprising, example brought in as the "conclusion" of the *Odyssey*, to suggest (somewhat deceptively) that the phenomenon with which Longinus is concerned occurs throughout the poem? There is, I think, no reference in *On the Sublime* to anything which occurs after the killing of the suitors. It may also be relevant that, whereas the killing of the suitors has quite a strong iconographic presence in the classical period (cf. *LIMC* s.v. Mnesteres II), there really is very little trace of anything from the part of the *Odyssey* after the recognition of Odysseus and Penelope.
34 Cf. Erbse 1972, 172 n. 17, 175.

It is often objected that we have no real evidence that Aristophanes, let alone Aristarchus, would have been interested in such "literary" matters, but the argument lacks conviction; we just do not know enough about the range of their interests. Martin West, accepting Erbse's explanation, suggested that Aristophanes "made the point in his oral teaching, which was then reported by Aristarchus in his commentary. It would have occasioned a diple in the margin of the text, the meaning of which would have been explained by Aristonicus. His lapidary formulation gave rise to different interpretations in later antiquity".[35] We can hardly rule such a speculation, or indeed several others, out of court. There is, however, evidence that the grammatical tradition made capital out of the semantic range of "beginning" and "end". Dionysius of Halicarnassus, no stranger to Alexandrian traditions of γραμματική, plays with the two senses of τέλος at *Letter to Pompey* 3.3, where he describes Herodotus' declaration of purpose at the opening of the *Histories* as καὶ ἀρχὴ καὶ τέλος ... τῆς ἱστορίας;[36] equivocations and "puns" on ἀρχή were certainly well established in the rhetorical tradition (cf. Arist. *Rhet.* 3.1412b4–10, citing Isocrates, *Philippus* 61, *On the Peace* 101). Perhaps Aristophanes and/or Aristarchus too exploited the semantic range of τέλος to make a smart point about *Od.* 23.296, and it is this which lies behind all the critical anxiety — *hinc illae lacrimae*; when at *Rhet.* 3.1415a21–23 Aristotle himself observes that the most crucial aspect of a proem (προοίμιον) is that it should make clear τὸ τέλος οὗ ἕνεκα ὁ λόγος, "the end at which the speech aims", we do not seem very far from a significant word-play. Unfortunately, the Odyssean scholia are, as already observed, very far indeed from whatever was originally recorded, and any trace of Aristophanes' wit has long since disappeared.

2 Citations of the Alexandrian end

A curiosity of the "Alexandrian end" is its apparent isolation. If Aristophanes and Aristarchus really saw something important happening at 23.296, why do we not hear more about it? How arcane a piece of grammatical lore was it? When in the introduction to the *Homeric Problems* "Heraclitus" notes that the only πέρας for our concern with Homer is the end of life itself (1.7), is he alluding to and wittily revising the grammarians' search for the πέρας/τέλος of the

---

35 M.L. West 2017, 41.
36 Cf. Fowler 2000, 266.

poems themselves? Ὅμηρος *sine fine*? Why we apparently hear so little of the "Alexandrian end" is just one more question about the "end of the *Odyssey*" which can nag away at you, if you let it. One possible way to try to assuage that itch may be to look at the indirect tradition of the "end", and that is what I shall do in this second section, by looking briefly at the six ancient citations of 23.296 known to me, in roughly chronological order.[37] An obvious, but important, preliminary word of caution is necessary. No ancient reader of the *Odyssey* needed Aristophanes of Byzantium or Aristarchus (or anyone else) to tell them that 23.296 marked a τέλος of some kind, and in considering citations of this verse in ancient literature we must always bear that in mind. This would always have been a significant moment of the poem, regardless of what a couple of pedantic grammarians had to say about it, and we must therefore set the bar quite high if we are looking for echoes of "the Alexandrian end" (narrowly defined) in the literature which survives to us. Moreover, intertextual allusion takes many more forms than verbatim citation, and I will return at the end to a case where verbatim citation would have been impossible. The search for allusions to 23.296 other than citation would, however, greatly increase the area of uncertainty and so I limit myself here in the present context to verbatim citation.

One possible allusion which cannot, however, go unremarked is the final verse of Apollonius' *Argonautica*.[38] Whatever view one takes of the relationship between *Arg.* 4.1781 and *Od.* 23.296 and however much Apollonius foreshadows the grim subsequent history of Jason and Medea, he has left us in no doubt at all where his poem ends (4.1773–1781), and that in itself is certainly in part a reaction to the problems posed by the endings of archaic epic, notably the *Odyssey*, whether or not there is a specific allusion to 23.296. For Apollonius and his heroes the *labor* is *perfectus*.

A second preliminary consideration. It is well known that the second half of the *Odyssey* was the least cited, and apparently least read, part of the Homeric poems in antiquity, whether we are judging from citations in subsequent authors or what survives on papyri, both higher-end "literary" papyri and what look like school exercises. On 16/7/22 the *LDAB* recorded 16 ancient texts containing some part of *Odyssey* 23, of which two contained v. 296; one of these two

---

[37] Drago 2021 briefly considers two (Chariton, Aristaenetus) of the six cases, in order to establish that the "Alexandrian end" functioned "da archetipo della consolidate struttura romanzesca "separazione-avventure-ricomposizione""; cf. also Bianchi 2017.
[38] Hunter 2015, 320; cf. now Drago 2021, 202–204.

is *P.Ryl.Gr.* I 53, which was originally a codex text of the complete poem.³⁹ These figures are of course not to be pressed too hard, but it is still worth reflecting upon the fact that the only citation or evocation of *Odyssey* 23 in the Lucianic corpus is of vv. 314–315 (from the "Recapitulation") in the *Philopatris* (chap. 14), which is, I think, universally agreed to be a work of the tenth century. Should we be surprised that a Lucian found no occasion to cite the "Alexandrian end" of the *Odyssey*?⁴⁰ I do not know the answer to that question — or, rather, I can think of more than one answer — but I do think that such considerations lead in relevant directions; the "Alexandrian end", whatever it was, made only very moderate ripples in the pond of ancient educational and literary culture. To what extent this is true of Alexandrian γραμματική more generally is a large and important question, but not one that can be pursued here.

Here again, there are general considerations which must be borne in mind. Verses which have a generalising or moralising tenor tend, of course, to be cited more freely than those which are closely bound to a particular context. We might think that the end of our *Iliad* is movingly and memorably low-key, but a glance at Martin West's edition will show how sparse is the indirect tradition for those verses. The final verse (24.804) is cited three times (for three different reasons) in the grammatical tradition, and it perhaps owes that prominence to its final position, but surviving "literary citations" of the final ten verses are perhaps restricted to v. 797, which is echoed as early as Sophocles' *Ajax*.⁴¹ As for the *Odyssey*, West's edition records only sparse citations in the grammatical tradition from 24.472 (Athena's intervention to Zeus) onwards, with two verses of Eudocia's cento being the only "literary" citations; there is no indirect tradition at all for the final twelve verses of the poem. Such statistics are, of course, not to be pressed, and a thorough TLG search might perhaps reveal fresh riches, but it seems very unlikely that the general picture would be much changed. Modern "literary critics" have often (at least in spirit) averted their eyes from the end of our *Odyssey*, and it may seem also not to have made much of an impression in antiquity. Citation — to repeat — is, however, not necessarily a reliable index of familiarity.

---

39 The other is an unpublished Oxyrhynchos papyrus (542 in West's list) containing 23.288–300 (*non uidi*). On 16/7/22 the *Leuven Database of Ancient Books* listed 23 texts containing all or parts of *Odyssey* 24, the vast majority from Oxyrhynchos; this is not out of line with the numbers for the second half more generally (the lowest are Books 16 (17), 20 (16) and 23 (16)).
40 Lucian is, in fact, a very marked case of the general discrepancy in level of ancient quotation between the first and second halves of the *Odyssey* and between the *Odyssey* and the *Iliad*, as a glance at the lists in Householder 1941 and Macleod's OCT will confirm.
41 *Ajax* 1165, 1403; Philostratus, *VA* 4.11.3 also (explicitly) recalls that verse.

The earliest surviving quotation of *Od.* 23.296 is a brief notice in Stobaeus 3.5.43 (περὶ σωφροσύνης, "On sober-mindedness") that the peripatetic Hermippos "the Callimachean" reported Demetrius of Phaleron as having said that Homer composed *Od.* 23.296 εἰς σωφροσύνην.[42] It is certainly intriguing that such a major figure appears to have singled out this verse, and Franco Montanari suggested that it was Demetrius, not, as Erbse had it, Aristophanes of Byzantium, who initiated the slight readjustment of the "Aristotelian τέλος" of the poem from the killing of the suitors to the reunion of Odysseus and Penelope, an ending more perhaps in tune with the "romantic" narratives favoured in, for example, Menander.[43] I will return to Demetrius' (for us contextless) observation, but — to anticipate — let me briefly draw attention to an observation of Eustathius in the *Preface* to the *Parekbolai* ("Observations") on the *Odyssey* which has perhaps been overshadowed by the more familiar claim some pages later (cf. above) that it is the killing of the suitors which is the σκοπιμώτατον τέλος of the poem. In the *Preface*, we find a somewhat different claim:

> σωφροσύνη δὲ τῆς ποιήσεως ταύτης ὁ κεφαλαιωδέστατος σκοπός, καὶ φιλανδρίαν δὲ παιδεύει ἔννομον τὸ βιβλίον τοῦτο, προθέμενον τὴν Πηνελόπην εἰς ἀμφοτέρων ἀρχέτυπον.
>
> Eustathius, *Preface to the Odyssey*
> 1380.2–3 = I 2.31 Stallbaum

> *Sōphrosynē* is the principal aim of this poem, and this book [i.e. the *Odyssey*] teaches lawful love of one's husband; Penelope is presented as a model for both of these things.

Penelope as a model of both σωφροσύνη ("sober-mindedness/chastity") and φιλανδρία ("husband-love") had been commonplace long before Eustathius,[44] and it is likely enough that the foregrounding of σωφροσύνη in evaluations of the *Odyssey* was common in Byzantine schoolrooms; a moralising reading of the *Odyssey* and its hero certainly has very deep roots in antiquity,[45] and it would be very easy to see Homer himself, through the ghost of Agamemnon, as advertising the *Odyssey* as a "praise of Penelope":[46]

---

[42] Hermippos fr. 92W² = Demetrius fr. 145 Fortenbaugh-Schütrumpf.
[43] Montanari 2000, 403–406 (~ 2012, 345–347).
[44] Cf., e.g., Julian, *Or.* 3.127c–128d, [Plut.] *Hom.* 2.185, Hillgruber 1999, 386. The two virtues frequently travel together in praise of (and epitaphs for) women, cf. Laemmle 2019.
[45] For some discussion and bibliography cf. Hunter 2014, 32–36. [Plut.] *Hom.* 2.4 characterises the *Odyssey* as a presentation of ψυχῆς γενναιότης, "nobility of spirit", as the *Iliad* was of ἀνδρεία σώματος, "bodily courage".
[46] Cf. Heubeck on 24.197–198, "the poet is well aware of the worth of his own achievement: his own κλέος ["fame"] will be immortal alongside the κλέος of Penelope".

> τῷ οἱ κλέος οὔ ποτ' ὀλεῖται
> ἧς ἀρετῆς, τεύξουσι δ' ἐπιχθονίοισιν ἀοιδὴν
> ἀθάνατοι χαρίεσσαν ἐχέφρονι Πηνελοπείῃ.
>
> Homer, *Odyssey* 24.196–198

Therefore, the fame (*kleos*) of her virtue will never fade, and the immortals will fashion a lovely song for mortals in honour of wise Penelope.

An anonymous epigram of uncertain date (*AP* 9.522) describes the *Odyssey* as Ὀδυσσείης ... τὸ σῶφρον/γράμμα, "the chaste poem which is the *Odyssey*", and that poem is presumably in touch with the same streams of moralising criticism. In the *Praefatio in Homerum* of "Isaac Porphyrogenitus"[47] it is the σωφροσύνη of Odysseus himself, who resists the seductive Calypso because of his "memory of his own wise and chaste (σώφρων) wife", which is set before us as a model (*Praef.* 41–42). Moreover, and to this too we shall return, Isaac also sets out how the poem makes clear the folly of adultery and illicit desire through the story of Agamemnon, Clytemnestra and Orestes; in other words the *Odyssey* puts both faithful marital love and its opposite centre-stage.[48] The folly of adultery is a lesson which the exegetical scholia see also at the heart of Demodocus' "Song of Ares and Aphrodite" (cf. further below), and something like this perhaps lurks behind [Plutarch], *De Homero* 2.185 where Penelope reveals "the σωφροσύνη and φιλανδρία of a wife" and Odysseus "a husband's desire (πόθος) *for his own wife*"; the possessive αὐτοῦ is probably doing serious work there. However commonplace such praise of Odysseus and Penelope may be, there is no real parallel (I think) to Eustathius' claim that "σωφροσύνη is the principal aim (σκοπός)" of the *Odyssey*, and — to anticipate again — we may wonder whether this has anything to do with Demetrius of Phaleron and the "Alexandrian end" of the poem. σκοπός is not exactly the same as τέλος, and elsewhere Eustathius uses σκοπός to mean something almost like "subject-matter",[49] and the two Eustathian σκοποί of the poem (σωφροσύνη and the killing of the suitors) can certainly be reconciled, but does Eustathius at 1380.2–3 reflect, however dimly, ancient critical lore?

---

[47] On the identity of the author and the probable date of this treatise cf. Kindstrand 1979, 13–18; Kindstrand makes the author a younger contemporary of Eustathius. Cf. also Pontani 2005, 161–163.

[48] Isaac does, however, seem to make the killing of the suitors the actual τέρμα of the poem, cf. 48.

[49] Cf. 1382.24 where ἄνδρα μοι ἔννεπε, "tell me of the man", foreshadows the σκοπός of the poem, just as μῆνιν ἄειδε Ἀχιλλέως, "sing of the wrath of Achilles", does for the *Iliad*.

After Demetrius, we must wait until the first century BCE, when, in *On the Good King according to Homer* (col. 20.33–34 Dorandi), Philodemus cites λέκτροιο παλαιοῦ θεσμόν, "custom of the bed of old", alongside φιλοτησίαν τέρψιν, "pleasure in love-making", which is not quite a Homeric phrase, but may evoke *Od.* 5.227 τερπέσθην φιλότητι, "they took their pleasure in love-making", of the final love-making of Calypso and Odysseus. The detailed context cannot be reconstructed, but Oswyn Murray's description of it as "a digression, attacking the illegitimate use of certain Homeric passages to justify sexual licence" seems unlikely to be far wrong.[50] Such a use of *Od.* 23.296, a verse celebrating the renewal of full marital union, would indeed be "illegitimate", and it is at least worth bearing in mind the possibility that the Homeric phrase was cited precisely as a model for the decency (? σωφροσύνη) with which Homer presented such matters. Fortunately, the next citation is fully preserved.

The final book of Chariton's *Callirhoe* (? first century CE) replays the pattern of *Odyssey* 23–24.[51] Chaereas and Callirhoe are reunited early in the book (8.1.8–10), Φήμη spreads the news of the reunion (8.1.11),[52] the happy couple spend the night telling each other of their adventures (8.1.14–17),[53] and then, "when they had had enough of tears and narratives, they embraced each other, ἀσπάσιοι λέκτροιο παλαιοῦ θεσμὸν ἵκοντο ("gladly did they come to the custom of the bed of old")"; the rest of the book is devoted to tidying up some important loose ends, the return to Syracuse, the public recapitulation of the events of the novel (8.7.3–8.8.11)[54] and Callirhoe's final reconciliation with Aphrodite. Given the Homeric *mimesis* of the whole novel, the reunion of Odysseus and Penelope was the very obvious model here, and we can hardly conclude from the citation of *Od.* 23.296 that Chariton was using some known grammatical lore about that verse.[55] The verse comes, as in our text of the *Odyssey*, towards the end of the work, but not at the very end. What is, however, worthy of note, as we move on to other citations

---

50 Murray 1965, 167, cf. Asmis 1991, 37, "Philodemus seems to ... defend Homer against the charge ... of corrupting his listeners by his frank depictions of sexual behavior".
51 Unsurprisingly, something similar happens at the end of Xenophon of Ephesos (5.13–15), the other extant novel in which the lovers who are reunited at the end are already married to each other.
52 Cf. below pp. 107–110; on Φήμη in Chariton more generally cf. Tilg 2010, chap. 7.
53 Callirhoe's embarrassed silence about events at Miletus and Chaereas' jealousy (8.1.15) may replay the fact that Odysseus says nothing about Nausicaa in his recapitulation to Penelope.
54 The "recapitulation" in *Odyssey* 23 is the ultimate ancestor of the recapitulation in Book 8 of Chariton's *Callirhoe*, but the latter is much more extensive and detailed.
55 For Chariton's familiarity with the Homeric critical tradition as well as with Homer cf. Hunter 2018, 134–135.

of 23.296, is that the happy reunion of 8.1.17, including the citation of the "Alexandrian end", is presumably what Chariton means at 8.1.4 when he promises his readers that this last book of the novel will contain ἔρωτες δίκαιοι <καὶ> νόμιμοι γάμοι, "justly reciprocal love and lawful marriage". This is presumably not too far from the σωφροσύνη which Demetrius of Phaleron found in the verse.

Probably the next citation in sequence comes in the *De musica* of Aristides Quintilianus, a treatise of perhaps the third century CE, but certainly containing much material drawn from sources earlier than that. Chapter 9 of the second book is a discussion of some of Homer's virtues and extraordinary effects of sound in the context of education through music and poetry. At one point Aristides creates a three-tiered system of how Homer controls our responses in the matter of sex:

> καὶ μὴν ἐπὶ ταὐτοῦ πράγματος τὰ μὲν περὶ Ἄρεα καὶ Ἀφροδίτην διὰ τραχέων ὀνομάτων ἀφηγεῖται, τὸ "ἐμίγησαν" καὶ τὸ "λάθρη" καὶ τὸ "ᾔσχυνε" λέγων [*Od.* 8.268–269], ὧν τὸ μὲν τὸν ἐξ ἡδονῆς μιασμόν, τὸ δὲ τὸ ἐπίψογον τῆς πράξεως, τὸ δὲ τὴν αἰσχρὰν ἀδικίαν ἐμφαίνει· ἐπὶ δὲ τοῦ Ὀδυσσέως σεμνοῖς ῥήμασι κοσμεῖ τὸν λόγον· τὴν γὰρ ἐν δίκῃ καὶ νόμιμον πρᾶξιν ἐνέφηνεν, εἰπών
>
> > ἀσπάσιοι λέκτροιο παλαιοῦ θεσμὸν ἵκοντο. [*Od.* 23.296]
>
> ἐπὶ δέ γε τῆς οὔτε μεμπτῆς κατὰ νόμον οὔτε ἐπαινουμένης ὁμιλίας συμπλοκῇ τῆς τῶν σημαινομένων ἐναντιότητος πεποίηται τὴν μεσότητα, εἰπών
>
> > μήποτε τῆς εὐνῆς ἐπιβήμεναι ἠδὲ μιγῆναι,
> > ἣ θέμις ἀνθρώπων πέλει, ἀνδρῶν ἠδὲ γυναικῶν. [*Il.* 9.133–134]
>
> Aristides Quintilianus 2.9, pp. 70.20–71.5 Winnington-Ingram

> Indeed, on the same subject, he relates with harsh words things about Ares and Aphrodite, saying: "they lay together" and "secretly" and "he fouled"; of which the first reveals the crime born of pleasure, the second the blameworthiness of the action, and the third the shameful offence. But in the case of Odysseus, he adorns the phrase with dignified expressions, for he reveals the right and lawful action, saying, "gladly they renewed the rites of their bed of old". By contrast, on an association neither contemptible under the law nor commendable, by a combination of the contrariety of the things signified, he composed a middle state, saying, "that I never entered her bed and never lay with her as is natural for human people between men and women". [trans. T.J. Mathiesen]

The whole chapter is full of interest, but in the present context the two most striking aspects of Aristides' discussion are the contrast he draws between the reunion of Odysseus and Penelope at 23.296 and the adulterous love making of the two gods in Demodocus' "Song of Ares and Aphrodite" and the description of the former scene as τὴν γὰρ ἐν δίκῃ καὶ νόμιμον πρᾶξιν, "an action which is just and lawful"; somewhat later Aristides will describe Ares' actions as παρανόμως (2.10, p. 75.5 Winnington-Ingram). A moralising and paideutic reading of Demodocus' song was of course common in antiquity — the scholia represent the bard as "chastening" (σωφρονίζων) the pleasure-loving Phaeacians (Schol. Od. 8.267) and a few pages later Aristides himself takes such a didactic view of the Song,[56] but the similarity here to Chariton's phrase in 8.1.4 (cf. above), and indeed to Eustathius' praise of Penelope's φιλανδρία ἔννομος, "lawful husband-love",[57] leaps to the eye and raises the immediate question of whether both Chariton and Aristides reflect an already standard critical judgement about this passage of the Odyssey. How far back does such a characterisation of the "Alexandrian end" of the Odyssey go, and how far back may we trace the contrast between the two scenes of love-making in Odyssey 8 and 23?

The final two examples are also anything but chronologically fixed, and the first might be very late indeed. A scholium on Sophocles, Ajax 492 contrasts how two women (Tecmessa in the Ajax and Hera at Il. 15.39) chastely appeal to their husbands through their shared marriage-bed, whereas the wording of Od. 23.296, with its emphasis on pleasure, is appropriate for Odysseus, as the poet "makes clear the mutual goodwill of those who come together in the expectation of procreation" (τὴν εὔνοιαν δηλῶν τῶν οὕτω συνιόντων ἐπιμονῇ παιδοποιίας). The Odyssean verse, in other words, is particularly appropriate for the "equal" relationship of Odysseus and Penelope. It would be very nice to know something of the sources for this scholium, but at the very least we can say that it is this verse which is chosen to illustrate a paradigm of married life. Whether or not the scholiast (or his source) knew it as a verse with a particular scholarly heritage, we cannot say.

My final example is one of the erotic letters of Aristaenetus which are usually dated c. 500 CE, but the chronology is (again) very uncertain. In Epistle 1.12 a young man praises his girlfriend's charms and explains that his experience proves wrong the old wisdom of "out of sight, out of mind". While he was away, he never forgot her, indeed his desire was even stronger, and when he returned, "some love poet doing a Homer (ἐρωτικὸς ποιητὴς καθομηρίζων)" might say of the couple ἀσπάσιοι λέκτροιο παλαιοῦ θεσμὸν ἵκοντο ("gladly did they come to

---

[56] 2.10, p. 74.25–28, 75.5–6 Winnington-Ingram. In 2.17, p. 88.9–89.4 Winnington-Ingram Aristides offers an allegorical interpretation of the Song as concerned with the nature of soul.
[57] At Hom. 567.28 Eustathius refers to Aphrodite's ψεκτὴ φιλανδρία, where the noun must mean "fondness for men", cf. Pontani 2000, 39; Laemmle 2019; Penelope and Aphrodite are thus also contrasted in the kind of φιλανδρία which they embody.

the custom of the bed of old");⁵⁸ that is the end of the letter. The young man himself is here clearly "doing an Odysseus (if not a Homer)", with his beloved as Penelope, and I think it is hard to deny that if *Od.* 23.296 were known to be a τέλος of a particular kind, then this would add an extra point to the young man's "Odyssey". It is perhaps relevant that before reaching the happy conclusion the young man plays with ideas of ἀρχή and τέλος:

> οὔκουν τῶν ἀφροδισίων, ὡς ἔφη τις, εἰς τὸ τῆς ἡδονῆς τέλος ὁδός ἐστιν μία. ἀναφρόδιτοι γὰρ αἱ δυσειδεῖς γυναῖκες, καὶ ἡδονῆς ἐν ἐκείναις οὐκ ἀρχὴν οὐ τέλος εὕροι τις ἄν.
> Aristaenetus 1.12.24–26 Mazal⁵⁹

> The path of love-making which leads to the perfection (*telos*) of pleasure is not, then, as someone has said, single. It is ugly women who are without Aphrodite's charms, and in them one could find neither the beginning nor the end (*telos*) of pleasure.

Od. 23.296 does indeed describe τὸ τῆς ἡδονῆς τέλος, as the young man puts it, and it is the τέλος of his letter; was it also known to be the τέλος of his principal literary model?

The picture to be gleaned from the indirect tradition is perhaps not as informative as we would like, and it may seem unsurprising that *Od.* 23.296 was a "classic" verse to describe the proper and "decent" sexual relations of a man and wife, but there are, I think, enough hints to make us suspect a rather richer critical tradition surrounding this verse than is revealed by the two famous scholia. Be that as it may, we shall see in the next section that both the point and the position of the verse were exploited in at least one ancient text to very powerful effect.

3 An end and a beginning in Virgil's *Aeneid*

The love-making of Ares and Aphrodite and of Odysseus and Penelope share another narrative structure. The adultery of Book 8 is immediately revealed by a messenger to the god most affected by it:

> αὐτὰρ ὁ φορμίζων ἀνεβάλλετο καλὸν ἀείδειν
> ἀμφ' Ἄρεος φιλότητος ἐϋστεφάνου τ' Ἀφροδίτης,
> ὡς τὰ πρῶτ' ἐμίγησαν ἐν Ἡφαίστοιο δόμοισι

---

58 Drago 2021, 206 follows Bianchi 2017 in identifying this ἐρωτικὸς ποιητής as Chariton.
59 With the idea of ὁδός, "path", here cf. Longus, *D&C* 3.18.4.

> λάθρῃ· πολλὰ δὲ δῶκε, λέχος δ' ᾔσχυνε καὶ εὐνὴν
> Ἡφαίστοιο ἄνακτος. ἄφαρ δέ οἱ ἄγγελος ἦλθεν   270
> Ἥλιος, ὅ σφ' ἐνόησε μιγαζομένους φιλότητι.
>
> Homer, *Odyssey* 8.266–271

> But he started to play on his lyre and to sing beautifully about the love-making of Ares and fair-crowned Aphrodite, how they first made love secretly in the house of Hephaestus. He gave many gifts, and disgraced the marriage and bed of the lord Hephaestus. Straightaway a messenger went to him, Helios, who had seen them mingling in love-making.

In books 23 and 24 this structure is obscured but essentially similar. After the night of love and story-telling, Odysseus goes off to the countryside where much of the next book is set, other than the "Second *Nekuia*". When events in the town are resumed, it is precisely with a messenger bearing the news of what has happened:[60]

> Ὄσσα δ' ἄρ' ἄγγελος ὦκα κατὰ πτόλιν ᾤχετο πάντῃ
> μνηστήρων στυγερὸν θάνατον καὶ κῆρ' ἐνέπουσα.
> οἱ δ' ἄρ' ὁμῶς ἀΐοντες ἐφοίτων ἄλλοθεν ἄλλος   415
> μυχμῷ τε στοναχῇ τε δόμων προπάροιθ' Ὀδυσῆος,
>
> Homer, *Odyssey* 24.413–416

> Rumour went swiftly carrying all over the town the message of the miserable death and fate of the suitors. All alike when they heard it gathered in front of Odysseus' house, with groans and lamentations.

The pattern is, no doubt, common enough – we have already seen one such similar instance in Chariton (8.1.11, above p. 104) – but there can hardly be any doubt about the most famous case in ancient literature:

> *speluncam Dido dux et Troianus eandem*   165
> *deueniunt. prima et Tellus et pronuba Iuno*
> *dant signum; fulsere ignes et conscius aether*
> *conubiis summoque ululaurunt uertice Nymphae.*
> *ille dies primus leti primusque malorum*
> *causa fuit; neque enim specie famaue mouetur*   170
> *nec iam furtiuum Dido meditatur amorem:*
> *coniugium uocat, hoc praetexit nomine culpam.*
> *extemplo Libyae magnas it Fama per urbes,*
> *Fama, malum qua non aliud uelocius ullum ...*
>
> Virgil, *Aeneid* 4.165–174

---

60 Cf. above p. 104. On this passage cf. Hardie 2012, 64–66.

> To the same cave come Dido and the Trojan leader. First-born Earth and Juno, guardian of weddings, give the sign; fires and the aether, witness to the wedding, blazed forth, and on the mountain-top the Nymphs uttered a scream. That day, the first of death and the first of troubles, was the origin; no longer is Dido moved by appearance or report, and no longer does she contemplate a secret love-affair. She calls it marriage, and by this name covers over her fault. Straightaway, Report goes through the great cities of Libya, Report, swifter than any other evil ... [61]

The principal Greek model for Dido and Aeneas' tryst in the cave has always (and rightly) been seen as the cave-wedding of Medea and Jason in the fourth book of Apollonius' *Argonautica*,[62] a wedding followed by a νημερτὴς βάξις spread abroad by Hera (vv. 1184–1185), although many other scenes, including Odysseus' final night in Calypso's cave, have made a contribution.

One of those other scenes seems indeed to have been the opening of Demodocus' "Song of Ares and Aphrodite", which reports the subject of that song as the gods' first (τὰ πρῶτα)[63] and secret (λάθρη) love-making; this is one model for the *furtiuus amor* of Dido's story. The love-making in the cave was indeed the "first" for Dido and Aeneas, but it was also the *dies primus leti primusque malorum*, "the first day of death and the first of troubles"; Virgil has taken the simple Homeric temporal expression and done something much more powerful with it. The moral indignation of Aristides Quintilianus at the Homeric story of adultery, which he labels τὴν αἰσχρὰν ἀδικίαν, "disgraceful wrongdoing", (p. 70.24–25 Winnington-Ingram), is then compressed into the pregnant Virgilian *culpam*, "guilt" (cf. also 194 *turpique cupidine captos*, "held captive by shameful desire", ~ τὸν ἐξ ἡδονῆς μιασμόν, "the disgrace caused by pleasure", in Aristides, p. 70.23–24 Winnington-Ingram); Virgil has thus painted the love-making of Dido and Aeneas in the colours of the most notoriously "immoral" episode in the Homeric poems, one which he had used elsewhere in his epic in a very different way.[64] As we have seen, one contrasting ancient paradigm of δίκαιοι καὶ νόμιμοι γάμοι, "just and lawful marriage", Virgil's *coniugium*, the misleading title which Dido apparently claims, was the happy reunion of Odysseus and Penelope, and this, at least later, was explicitly opposed to the illicit love-making of Ares and Aphrodite. Perhaps then Virgil has run the two Homeric scenes together, so that Dido can claim a "replay" of Odysseus and Penelope (*coniugium*), when really it

---

61 These verses are notoriously difficult to translate, and the translation offered here is not intended to support any argument about the passage.
62 Cf., e.g., Heinze 1915, 131; Pease on *Aen.* 4.166; Cairns 1989, 47–49; Nelis 2001, 148–152.
63 On the meaning of this phrase cf. further Hunter 2012, 102.
64 *Aen.* 1.742–746 (the song of Iopas), cf., e.g., Hardie 1986, 61–63.

is of "Ares and Aphrodite" (*furtiuus amor*, "secretive love"), and the imposition of a narrative τέλος, when it is really the ἀρχὴ κακῶν, "the beginning of troubles". The cosmic fires of the Virgilian scene might replay not just the torches of the wedding of Jason and Medea, but also the torches, evocative (like the preparation of the bed) of a wedding-scene, which accompany Odysseus and Penelope to bed (*Od.* 23.290–294), with *pronuba Iuno*, "Juno who watches over weddings", as a rather grander version of Εὐρυνόμη θαλαμηπόλος, "Eurynome the chamber-attendant" (*Od.* 23.293). It might even be worth wondering whether Virgil's description also takes the notion that *Odyssey* 23.296 is a τέλος in a new direction by having the love-making of Aeneas and Dido accompanied by phenomena often associated with a cultic rite (τέλος).

This might seem rather a lot to hang on *coniugium*, and the Virgilian verses, especially vv. 171–172, are notoriously problematic,[65] but another consideration might be helpful. We have already seen how Virgil powerfully re-uses the Homeric τὰ πρῶτα from the beginning (ἀρχή) of Demodocus' song. If he had known (how could he not have known?) and wanted us to remember that *Od.* 23.296 was in some sense the τέλος of Homer's song and narrative, then this would be another opposition between Homer's song and that of his textual reflection, Demodocus,[66] and one that gave further point to Virgil's stress upon the love-making of Dido and Aeneas as a beginning (4.169–170), not as the "end" which lawful and proper love-making should be. Virgil has thus used and inverted the "Alexandrian" end of the *Odyssey*. More importantly, the tension between two kinds of sexual union which vv. 171–172 seem to construct may be seen as either a foreshadowing of the Byzantine (and earlier?) reading of the *Odyssey* to which I have already pointed and/or a reflection of critical discussion of the poem already familiar to Virgil. At this very Odyssean moment of the *Aeneid*, as Aeneas disappears into a cave with his Calypso, Dido threatens to derail the Latin *Odyssey*, as Calypso (and indeed, in a quite different way, Nausicaa) had threatened to derail the Greek, by appropriating Homer's narrative arc, which had led unmistakably to the lawful marital *telos* of 23.296, for the competing narrative of *furtiuus amor*.

---

[65] Casali 2018 offers full discussion and bibliography.
[66] For Demodocus as a "self-portrait" of Homer cf., e.g., Schol. *Od.* 8.63b, f1 Pontani, Hardie 1986, 53–55; Graziosi 2002, 138–142.

Bibliography

Asmis, Elizabeth (1991), "Philodemus's Poetic Theory and 'On the Good King according to Homer'", *Classical Antiquity* 10, 1–45.
Bakker, Egbert (2020), "How to End the *Odyssey*", *Trends in Classics* 12, 48–68.
Bianchi, Nuncio (2017), "'Ἐρωτικὸς ποιητής. Aristeneto lettore di Caritone", *Futuro Classico* 3, 143–167.
Bühler, Winfried (1964), *Beiträge zur Erklärung der Schrift vom Erhabenen*, Göttingen.
Bury, John (1922), "The End of the *Odyssey*", *Journal of Hellenic Studies* 42, 1–15.
Cairns, Francis (1989), *Virgil's Augustan Epic*, Cambridge.
Carnuth, Otto (1896), *Aristonici περὶ σημείων Ὀδυσσείας reliquiae emendatiores*, Leipzig.
Casali, Sergio (2018), "Dido's *furtiuus amor* (Virgil, *Aeneid* 4.171–2)", in: Peter Knox/Hayden Pelliccia/Alexander Sens (eds.), *They Keep It All Hid. Augustan Poetry, its Antecedents and Reception*, Berlin, 41–49.
Danek, Georg (1998), *Epos und Zitat. Studien zu den Quellen der Odyssee*, Vienna.
Dawe, Roger (1993), *The Odyssey. Translation and Analysis*, Lewes, Sussex.
Drago, Anna Tiziana (2021), "*Lieti obbedirono alla legge dell'antico talamo*: episodi di memoria odissiaca in età ellenistica e tardoantica", in: R.J. Gallé Cejudo/M.S. Ortiz de Landaluce (eds.), *Studia Hellenistica Gaditana* II, Lecce, 199–208.
De Jong, Irene (2001), *A Narratological Commentary on the Odyssey*, Cambridge.
Else, Gerald (1957), *Aristotle's Poetics. The Argument*, Cambridge MA.
Erbse, Hartmut (1972), *Beiträge zum Verständnis der Odyssee*, Berlin.
Falkner, Thomas (1995), *The Poetics of Old Age in Epic, Lyric, and Tragedy*, Norman OK.
Foley, John (1999), *Homer's Traditional Art*, University Park PA.
Fowler, Don (2000), *Roman Constructions. Readings in Postmodern Latin*, Oxford.
Goldhill, Simon (1991), *The Poet's Voice*, Cambridge.
Graziosi, Barbara (2002), *Inventing Homer. The Early Reception of Epic*, Cambridge.
Grethlein, Jonas (2017), *Die Odyssee. Homer und die Kunst des Erzählens*, Munich.
Halliwell, Stephen (2022), *Pseudo-Longinus, On the Sublime*, Oxford.
Hardie, Philip (1986), *Virgil's Aeneid: Cosmos and Imperium*, Oxford.
Hardie, Philip (2012), *Rumour and Renown. Representations of Fama in Western Literature*, Cambridge.
Hauser, Emily (2020), "Putting an End to Song: Penelope, Odysseus, and the Teleologies of the *Odyssey*", *Helios* 47, 39–69.
Heinze, Richard (1915), *Virgils epische Technik*, 3rd ed., Leipzig.
Hillgruber, Michael (1999), *Die pseudoplutarchische Schrift De Homero*, Teil 2, Stuttgart/Leipzig.
Householder, Fred (1941), *Literary Quotation and Allusion in Lucian*, Dissertation Columbia.
Hunter, Richard (2012), "The Songs of Demodocus: Compression and Extension in Greek Narrative Poetry", in: Silvio Bär/Manuel Baumbach (eds.), *Brill's Companion to Greek and Latin "Epyllion" and Its Reception*, Leiden, 83–109.
Hunter, Richard (2014), "Horace's other *Ars Poetica*: *Epistles* 1.2 and Ancient Homeric Criticism", *Materiali e Discussioni* 72, 19–41.
Hunter, Richard (2015), *Apollonius of Rhodes, Argonautica IV*, Cambridge.
Hunter, Richard (2018), *The Measure of Homer*, Cambridge.

Hunter, Richard and Russell, Donald (2011), *Plutarch, How to Study Poetry (De audiendis poetis)*, Cambridge.
Kay, F.L. (1957), "Aristarchus' "τέλος", *Odyssey* xxiii.296", *Classical Review* 7, 106.
Kelly, Adrian (2007), "How to End an Orally-derived Poem", *Transactions of the American Philological Association* 137, 371–402.
Kindstrand, Jan Frederik (1979), *Isaac Porphyrogenitus, Praefatio in Homerum*, Uppsala.
Laemmle, Rebecca (2019), "Atalante *philandros*: Teasing out Satyric Innuendo (Sophocles, fr. 1111 Radt = Hermogenes, *On Ideas* 2.5)", *Classical Quarterly* 69, 846–857.
Lausberg, Heinrich (1960), *Handbuch der literarischen Rhetorik*, Munich.
Loney, Alexander (2019), *The Ethics of Revenge and the Meanings of the Odyssey*, Oxford.
Mackail, John (1936), "The Epilogue of the *Odyssey*", in: Cyril Bailey (ed.), *Greek Poetry and Life*, Oxford, 1–13.
Merkelbach, Reinhold (1969), *Untersuchungen zur Odyssee*, 2nd ed., Munich.
Montanari, Franco (2000), "Demetrius of Phalerum on Literature", in: William Fortenbaugh/Eckart Schütrumpf (eds.), *Demetrius of Phalerum. Text, Translation and Discussion*, New Brunswick NJ, 391–411.
Montanari, Franco (2012), "The Peripatos on Literature. Interpretation, Use and Abuse", in: Andrea Martano/Elisabetta Matelli/David Mirhady (eds.), *Praxiphanes of Mytilene and Chamaeleon of Heraclea*, New Brunswick NJ, 339–358.
Murray, Oswyn (1965), "Philodemus *On the Good King according to Homer*", *Journal of Roman Studies* 55, 161–182.
Nelis, Damien (2001), *Vergil's Aeneid and the Argonautica of Apollonius Rhodius*, Leeds.
Oswald, Renate (1993), *Das Ende der Odyssee*, Graz.
Page, Denys (1955), *The Homeric Odyssey*, Oxford.
Peradotto, John (1990), *Man in the Middle Voice*, Princeton.
Petzl, Georg (1969), *Antike Diskussionen über die beiden Nekyiai*, Meisenheim am Glan.
Pontani, Filippomaria (2000), "Il proemio al *Commento all'Odissea* di Eustazio di Tessalonica", *Bollettino dei Classici* 21, 5–58.
Pontani, Filippomaria (2005), *Sguardi su Ulisse. La tradizione esegetica greca all'Odissea*, Rome.
Purves, Alex (2006), "Unmarked Space: Odysseus and the Inland Journey", *Arethusa* 39, 1–20.
Purves, Alex (2010), *Space and Time in Ancient Greek Narrative*, Cambridge.
Rengakos, Antonios (1993), *Der Homertext und die hellenistischen Dichter*, Stuttgart.
Rutherford, Richard (2013), *Homer*, 2nd ed., Cambridge.
Schironi, Francesca (2009), "Theory into Practice: Aristotelian Principles in Aristarchean Philology", *Classical Philology* 104, 279–316.
Schironi, Francesca (2018), *The Best of the Grammarians. Aristarchus of Samothrace on the Iliad*, Ann Arbor.
Sourvinou-Inwood, Christiane (1995), *"Reading" Greek Death, to the End of the Classical Period*, Oxford.
Tilg, Stefan (2010), *Chariton of Aphrodisias and the Invention of the Greek Love Novel*, Oxford.
Tsagalis, Christos (2008), *The Oral Palimpsest*, Washington DC.
Van der Valk, Marchinus (1964), *Researches on the Text and Scholia of the Iliad*, Part 2, Leiden.
West, Martin (2014), *The Making of the Odyssey*, Oxford.

West, Martin (2017), "Aristophanes of Byzantium's Text of Homer", *Classical Philology* 112, 20–44.
West, Stephanie (1988), "The transmission of the Text", in: Alfred Heubeck/Stephanie West/J.B. Hainsworth (eds.), *A Commentary on Homer's Odyssey*, Vol. I, Oxford, 33–48.
West, Stephanie (1989), "Laertes Revisited", *Proceedings of the Cambridge Philological Society* 35, 113–143.
West, Stephanie (2018), "Odysseus' Eclectic Itinerary", in: Simon Hornblower/Giulia Biffis (eds.), *The Returning Hero: Nostoi and Traditions of Mediterranean Settlement*, Oxford, 65–82.

John F. Miller
Reconsidering Closure in Ovid's *Fasti*

Abstract: This chapter explores the dynamic between open-endedness and closure in Ovid's calendar-poem, *Fasti*, both in the work as a whole and especially at the end of individual books. Among the book-ends, that of Book 5 stands out as in some respects unique, but is shown to come to an artful close via retrospective references, dense metapoetic phrasing, and the evocation of the experience of standing before a calendar on public display.

1 Introduction

Near the end of his lengthy epistle to Augustus from Tomis, Ovid says that he wrote twelve books of his *Fasti*, two groups of six, but that his unfortunate lot as an exile interrupted the work (2.549–552):

> sex ego Fastorum scripsi totidemque libellos,
>   cumque suo finem mense volumen habet,
> idque tuo nuper scriptum sub nomine, Caesar,
>   et tibi sacratum sors mea rupit opus.
>
> I have written six and as many books of *Fasti*: each book ends with its month. This poem was recently written under your name, Caesar, but my lot has broken off the work dedicated to you.

He used the same phrase *rupit opus* to characterize the state of the *Metamorphoses* in the previous book of *Tristia*.[1] Even allowing for the fact that he is speaking of unpublished works, the perfect tenses *scripsi ... scriptum* here suggest that the *Fasti* was substantially complete, a calendar-poem, with, as we would expect, one book for each month of the year. On the other hand, *rupit opus*, his exile has left the work incomplete, which of course is the state in which we have the *Fasti* today — a six-book calendar-poem, January through June. Both claims in *Tristia* 2 aimed to appeal to the emperor who had relegated him,[2] to whom he has dedicated the *Fasti* — note his repetition of that fact: the full poetic calendar that he

---

[1] *Tristia* 1.7.14–15 *carmina mutatas hominum dicentia formas, / infelix domini quod fuga rupit opus.*
[2] See the judicious discussion of Ingleheart on *Tr.* 2.549–552.

has composed will bring glory to Augustus (*tuo ... scriptum sub nomine, Caesar; tibi sacratum ... opus*), if only a more lenient treatment repaired the rupture and allowed the work to be polished and see the light of day.

Ovid's unhappy lot never did change but the *Fasti* was eventually published as a truncated calendar, with a dedication to Germanicus Caesar rather than to Augustus[3] and other conspicuous revisions during exile. What we have is a poem that is both incomplete and complete. Its incompleteness is evident not only from its lack of half the year, which a neo-Latin poet in the seventeenth century attempted to set right by substituting his version of July through December.[4] Moreover, within the poem Ovid refers ahead to festivals that would have occurred in the missing months of his calendar-poem: in Book 3, when recounting the rescue of the exposed infants Romulus and Remus, he apostrophizes the boy's rustic helpers, Larentia and Faustulus, with a promise to honor them on the Larentalia in December (3.57–58 *vester honos veniet, cum Larentalia dicam: / acceptus geniis illa December habet*, "Your tribute will come when I speak of the Larentalia. December, pleasing to genial spirits, has that feast"); likewise in March, Ovid's divine interlocutor Mars tells the poet that Consus will tell him the story of the Rape of the Sabines when he celebrates that divinity's feast, which recurred in August and December (3.199–200 *"festa parat Conso. Consus tibi cetera dicet, / illa facta die dum sua sacra canet"*, "He [Romulus] prepares a feast for Consus, who will tell you the rest of what happened on that day, when he sings of his rites to you."). When digressing from the traditional feast day of the Lares Praestites on the Kalends of May to comment on the separate cult of Lares Compitales coopted by Augustus, Ovid catches himself and points ahead to August, the proper time to treat the new imperial *sacra* (5.147–148 *quo feror? Augustus mensis mihi carminis huius / ius dabit*, "Where am I headed? The month of August will give me the right to sing about this."). On the other hand, the end of what was published as Ovid's massive calendrical fragment is crammed with closural features which seem designed to bring the whole work, and not just the month of June, to a resounding close. In introducing his entry for June 30 on the Temple of Hercules Musarum which was restored by L. Marcius Philippus (6.797–812), Ovid asks the Muses to add *summa*, a conclusion, to his *coepta*, to what he has begun (6.798 *Pierides, coeptis addite summa meis*). Alessandro Barchiesi and others have explored the dense network of

---

[3] *Fasti* 2.3–18, addressed to Augustus, is commonly taken to be the work's original proem.
[4] Claude-Barthélemy Morisot, *P. Ovidii Nasonis Fastorum libri duodecim, quorum sex posteriores a Claudio Bartholomeo Morisoto Divionensi substituti sunt* (Dijon 1649). On Morisot's *Fasti*, see recently Xinyue 2018.

programmatic allusions in this section to the endings of poetic collections by Horace, Propertius, and Ovid himself.[5] Clio's encomium of a member of the imperial family strikes a closural note. And underlying the occasion is a subtextual reminder of the shrine's original foundation by M. Fulvius Nobilior, who famously set up there annotated sacral *fasti*, an important precursor to Ovid's poetic calendar.[6] The effect of all this is aptly summarized by Stephen Heyworth: "The poet wants us to regard the poem as both finished and unfinished, written in Rome and written in Tomi, composed both before exile and years later, after the death of Augustus".[7] In other words, completeness in the *Fasti* is not just an issue of composition — its stages and when and why Ovid broke off the initial project — but lies at the core of the poem's deconstructive aesthetic, of the dialectic between continuity and discontinuity at the heart of Ovid's play with the calendar. At the most basic level, while Ovid's overlapping calendrical schemata of Roman festivals and astronomical events imbue his almanac with capacious potential for commemorating most days of the year, we are never sure which stellar or sacral events he will include, or omit, and his treatment ranges between a single couplet and hundreds of verses. Many day-entries resemble self-contained epigrams or elegies except for the nearly always explicitly stated temporal link with the previous entry, so that readers experience throughout what Don Fowler in his fundamental paper on closure called a tension between text and supertext.[8]

---

5 See especially Barchiesi 1997A, 203–207; 1997B, 266–271 and Newlands 1995, 211–221, who stresses the problematic nature of the poem's closure. The allusions in question are Hor. *Od.* 4.15.1–2 *Phoebus ... increpuit lyra*; Prop. 4.11 (praise of Cornelia); Ov. *Am.* 3.15.17 *increpuit ... Lyaeus*. Hercules' gesture at the very close, 6.812 *adnuit Alcides*, also seems to refer back to Ovid's address to Germanicus in the proem, 1.15 *adnue conanti*. Kaesser 2013 considers whether closing the calendar-poem at the end of Book 6 is "deceptive".
6 This is not to deny that memory of the original dedication of the temple by Fulvius here could suggest its Augustan erasure as well as a more celebratory absent presence. On Fulvius' temple and calendar, see recently Rüpke 2006 and Walther 2016, 208–245, both of whom explore the role of Ennius. On the broader impact of Philippus' rededicated monument, including on Latin poetry, see Heslin 2015.
7 Heyworth 2018, 124. See further Heyworth 2019, 11–12.
8 See Fowler 1989, 82–88; also Fowler 2013. On sections as epigrams or elegies see, for instance, Miller 2002, 183–184 (critiquing Braun 1981), and more recently Hutchinson 2008, 105.

2 Book ends

The present paper focuses attention on the varied interplay between closure and open-endedness at the end of individual books of the *Fasti*. I just noted some of the ways that the finale of Book 6 brings the whole poem to an effective conclusion. At the same time, that section on the last day of June draws attention to the premature end of Ovid's calendar by referencing the following month (6.797): *tempus Iuleis cras est natale Kalendis*, "tomorrow is the birthday of the Kalends of July." But July never comes, and readers are no doubt struck that Ovid stops just as the imperial stamp on the contemporary calendar would be most conspicuous, at the month relabeled in recent years after the deified Julius Caesar, to be followed in turn by the month taking its name from Augustus. A different kind of closural game is staged in Book 2, as Francesca Martelli has shown.[9] Near the start of the book, Ovid asserts that in the old Roman year February was the last month, only later moved adjacent to January, and that in the ancient configuration the feast of Terminus marked the end (or limit, the *finis*) of the festivals of the year, and of course also of the month: *tu quoque sacrorum, Termine, finis eras*. Ovid's February, however, does not conclude with the Terminalia on the 23rd, which he duly celebrates, but continues with two more *sacra* that follow in the month's regular sequence of rituals, the Regifugium on the 24th, to which he devotes hundreds of verses (2.685–852), and the Equirria of February 27 (2.857–862). Thus does Ovid frustrate the expectation that he created earlier about the month's ending, which Martelli suggests is inspired by the legacy of the now obsolete intercalary month periodically inserted after the Terminalia.

Ovid does draw February to an emphatic close, but at the same time looks ahead to the following month (2.857–864):

> *Iamque duae restant noctes de mense secundo,*
>   *Marsque citos iunctis curribus urget equos;*
> *ex vero positum permansit Equirria nomen,*
>   *quae deus in campo prospicit ipse suo.*
> *iure venis, Gradive: locum tua tempora poscunt,*
>   *signatusque tuo nomine mensis adest.*
> *venimus in portum libro cum mense peracto.*
>   *naviget hinc alia iam mihi linter aqua.*

---

[9] Martelli 2013, 139–144.

> And now two nights remain from the second month, and Mars urges his swift horses on after yoking his chariot. The Equirria — the truthfully assigned name has endured — is what the god himself sees in his field. You come rightfully, Gradivus. Your time demands its place, and the month marked by your name is at hand. We have come into port now that the book has been completed along with the month. Let my boat now sail from here in other waters.

The final festival commemorated, the Equirria, he notes, occurs when two nights of the second month remain, that is, on the 27th. The god honored at the feast, Mars, who here both urges on the horses pulling his chariot and watches the equestrian games in his eponymous Campus Martius, arrives with double appropriateness (2.861 *iure venis*); for the month that bears his name is at hand. The book's final couplet likewise has the sense of open-ended closure.[10] The month and the book together come to an end (2.863 *libro cum mense peracto*); the poet has reached the harbor, suggesting the end of his journey through February. But he points to continuation of the nautical voyage in the "other waters" of March.

The last distich of Book 1 marks the concurrent close of month and book with similar language (1.724–725):

> *Sed iam prima mei pars est exacta laboris,*
>   *cumque suo finem mense libellus habet.*

> The first part of my work has been completed (*est exacta*); book and month coincide in their ending (*finem*).

The pentameter, moreover, echoes Ovid's characterization of the whole poem's book structure in *Tristia* 2 (550 *cumque suo finem mense volumen habet*); one summoning to mind that intertextuality here could see the poet making good on his promise, even if he will not realize the plan of twelve such books, as stated there. Right before this we find encomiastic celebration of the Ara Pacis's anniversary on January 30 (1.709–722), which effects strong thematic closure after the accents on peace throughout Book 1.[11] January's final entry also pointedly embodies the programmatic declaration in the proem that Caesar's wars belong to other poets, while Ovid will instead sing of Caesar's *altars* (1.13–14 *Caesaris arma canant alii: nos Caesaris aras / et quoscumque sacris addidit ille dies*) — here a particularly prominent Augustan *ara*. The phrasing that opens the section is also noteworthy in this regard (1.709): *ipsum nos carmen deduxit Pacis ad*

---

10 For the term, see Nagle 1983.
11 See 1.67–68, 285–288, 697–704. On this theme in Book 1, see recently Krasser 2008.

aram, "the poem itself has led us to the Altar of Peace." *Carmen deduxit* makes another programmatic gesture as appropriate to a conclusion as to a proem, by allusively affirming the work's place in the Hellenistic tradition of *carmen deductum*, "finely spun song".[12] The wording also suggests that the Altar's anniversary is the book's destination or *telos*, as the *carmen* has now moved *down* (*deduxit*; cf. *OLD* 5) the row of days in January as if visualized on a marble calendar on view in a public space.[13] Ovid notes that this will be the second day from the month's end (1.710 *haec erit a mensis fine secunda dies*), but with such overdetermined closure here we hardly expect anything for January 31.[14]

Likewise, when Ovid wraps up Book 4 with the Augustan anniversary on April 28 — of the new shrine for Vesta in the emperor's house on the Palatine — the sense of an ending cancels any anticipation of notices for the month's two remaining days, for which Columella records the rising and falling of constellations in the manner of Ovid throughout the *Fasti* (4. 943–954):[15]

> *Cum Phrygis Assaraci Tithonia fratre relicto*
>   *sustulit immenso ter iubar orbe suum,*
> *mille venit variis florum dea nexa coronis;*
>   *scaena ioci morem liberioris habet.*
> *exit et in Maias sacrum Florale Kalendas:*
>   *tunc repetam, nunc me grandius urget opus.*
> *aufer, Vesta, diem: cognati Vesta recepta est*
>   *limine; sic iusti constituere patres.*
> *Phoebus habet partem: Vestae pars altera cessit:*
>   *quod superest illis, tertius ipse tenet.*
> *state Palatinae laurus, praetextaque quercu*
>   *stet domus: aeternos tres habet una deos.*

---

12 Cf. Virg. *Ecl.* 6.3–5 *Cum canerem reges et proelia, Cynthius aurem / vellit, et admonuit: "pastorem, Tityre, pinguis / pascere oportet ovis, deductum dicere carmen,"* referring to Call. *Ait.* fr. 1.21–24; Ov. *Met.* 1.4 *ad mea perpetuum deducite tempora carmen* with Barchiesi 2005 *ad loc.* On the metaliterary resonance here, see Hinds 1987, 20. On allusive interplay between endings and beginnings see Zetzel 1983, 261.
13 One can see the reconstructed configuration today in the fragments of the *Fasti Praenestini* as displayed in the Palazzo Massimo in Rome; cf. Degrassi 1963, 116 and Tab. XXXVI.
14 The astronomical and meteorological phenomena for the day may anyway have been thought to be not particularly promising. Colum. 11.2.5 notes that on Jan. 31 the sequential setting of several constellations over the previous days causes a storm or gives indications thereof; confirmed by the fifth-century codex-calendar of Polemius Silvius.
15 Columella 11.2.37 *Tertio Kal. Maias mane Capra exoritur, Austrinus dies, interdum pluviae. Pridie Kal. Maias Canis se vespere celat; tempestatem significat.*

> When the wife of Tithonus has left the brother of Phrygian Assaracus, and thrice lifted up her radiance in the boundless world, a goddess comes decked with multicolored garlands of a thousand flowers; the stage enjoys the custom of freer play. The festival of Flora extends also to the Kalends of May; then I will return to that subject, now a grander work urges me on. Take away the day, Vesta. Vesta has been welcomed on the threshold of her kinsman: so have the just fathers decided. Phoebus has part, another part has been granted to Vesta. What is left over from them he himself holds as a third. O laurels of the Palatine, endure in your place, and may the house wreathed with oak endure. One house holds three eternal deities.

As with the Ara Pacis in January, he seals the day and the whole book with a prayer for the imperial house (4.953–954; cf. 1.721–722 *utque domus, quae praestat eam, cum Pace perennet / ad pia propensos vota rogate deos*, "Ask the gods, well disposed to pious prayers, that the house which guarantees her may last for many years with Peace"). The end of Book 4 is not stated outright, but the poet points ahead to the following month in acknowledging that Vesta's new feast shares April 28 with the traditional festival of Flora, which extends into May (4.947 *exit ... in Maias ... Kalendas*). In deference to what he calls the *grandius opus* of the Augustan *sacra*, Ovid postpones treatment of the merry Floralia to the following month in a kind of *recusatio*.[16] In terms of poetic closure, the section serves as a hinge between April and May.

Ovid commemorates another Augustan memorial on the penultimate day of March, the occasion in 10 BCE of the Princeps erecting statues of Salus, Concordia, and Pax, not recorded in extant calendars but reported by Dio, to whose list of divinities Ovid adds Janus (3.879–882):[17]

> *Inde quater pastor saturos ubi clauserit haedos,*
>   *canuerint herbae rore recente quater,*
> *Ianus adorandus cumque hoc Concordia mitis*
>   *et Romana Salus Araque Pacis erit.*

> When four times from then the shepherd has penned his well-fed goats, and the grass has whitened four times with fresh dew, it will be time to worship Janus and with him gentle Concord and Roman Safety and the Altar of Peace.

---

16 See Miller 2018.
17 Dio 54.35.2 ἐπειδή τε ἀργύριον αὖθις ἐς εἰκόνας αὐτοῦ καὶ ἐκείνη καὶ ὁ δῆμος συνεσήνεγκαν, ἑαυτοῦ μὲν οὐδεμίαν, Ὑγιείας δὲ δημοσίας καὶ προσέτι καὶ Ὁμονοίας Εἰρήνης τε ἔστησεν, "When both the senate and the people again contributed money for statues of him, he set up statues not of himself, but of Salus Publica, Concordia, and Pax".

To designate the progress of time with the picturesque image of a shepherd corraling his goats at day's end (3.879) strikes a closural note hinting that the book of March is concluding.[18] Complementing that touch is the retrospective phrasing of what Dio says was Pax's *statue* as the *Ara* Pacis, the imperial monument that Ovid celebrates at the end of January. While these two couplets might thus make for an effective close to Ovid's March, an additional distich more definitively punctuates the whole book (3.883–884):

> *Luna regit menses: huius quoque tempora mensis*
> *finit Aventino Luna colenda iugo.*

Just as the moon, and the moon goddess, determine the course of the months (*Luna regit menses*), the worship of Luna on the Aventine — that is, commemoration of her temple's foundation on March 31 — also ends the times of this month, that is, the days and their various festal and stellar events. Here Ovid marks the month's limit with the language of finality (*finit*), just as he does Books 1 (724) and 2 (863). The word *tempora* evokes the programmatic opening of the whole poem (1.1 *Tempora cum causis* …). Thus the last two calendrical entries in March, each nearly a self-contained epigram, work in tandem closurally by pointing backwards as they signal the end of both the month and the book.

3 Book 5

Quite unlike the other books, finally, is the close of Ovid's May, a cascade of very brief notices of festivals and stellar events in seven couplets for the seven days May 21 to 27 (5.721–734):

Ad Ianum redeat, qui quaerit Agonia quid sint:	21 May
quae tamen in fastis hoc quoque tempus habent.	
Nocte sequente diem canis Erigoneius exit:	22 May
est alio signi reddita causa loco.	
Proxima Volcani lux est, Tubilustria dicunt:	23 May
lustrantur purae, quas facit ille, tubae.	
Quattuor inde notis locus est, quibus ordine lectis	24 May
vel mos sacrorum vel fuga regis inest.	
Nec te praetereo, populi Fortuna potentis	25 May
publica, cui templum luce sequente datum est.	
hanc ubi dives aquis acceperit Amphitrite,	

---

18 See Heyworth 2019 *ad loc.*

> *grata Iovi fulvae rostra videbis avis.*
> *Auferet ex oculis veniens aurora Booten,*   26 May
>   *continuaque die sidus Hyantis erit.*   27 May

Let him who asks what the Agonia are return to Janus; yet that feast has this time too in the calendar. On the night that follows the day the dog of Erigone rises; the reason for the constellation has been given in another place. The next day belongs to Vulcan: they call it the Tubilustria. The trumpets he makes are cleansed and rendered pure. Next there is a place with four marks, in which are signified, when read in order, either the custom of the rituals or the flight of the king. And I do not pass you by, Public Fortune of the powerful people, to whom a temple was granted on the following day. When Amphitrite, wealthy in waters, has received this day, you will see the tawny bird's beak that pleases Jupiter. The coming dawn will take Bootes from sight, and on the succeeding day the star of Hyas will be present.

This is such an unusual conclusion to a book that we may wonder if it is a vestige of the work's *actual* incompleteness — *rupit opus*, as Ovid described to Augustus his exile's effect (*Tr.* 2.552). First comes, in verse 721, a cross-reference to the Agonia also in January, where the rare lack of temporal linkage with the previous day may signal inauguration of a new movement beyond the couplet.[19] Then fleeting mentions of the Dog Star, the Tubilustria, the feast abbreviated QRCF, the anniversary of Fortuna Publica, and the three constellations Aquila, Bootes, and the Hyades. We find a similar procedure in Book 3, where Ovid rounds off March with three short entries (3.877–884) — one distich on the solstice, two on the divine statues dedicated by Augustus, and one on Aventine Luna. But there the quick series ends by explicitly indicating the month's end (3.883 *Luna ... finit*), as in the two previous books. Elsewhere, as we have seen, Ovid at the book's close looks to the coming month, which is also lacking here. In May he breaks off on the 27th, four days from the end instead of one or two days early as in the other books. One of those days, May 29, would have furnished the opportunity to celebrate an imperial anniversary, that of Honos and Virtus known from the 4th century Fasti of Philocalus which Dio tells us was reoriented by Augustus.[20] Such a conclusion to May would have matched the Ara Pacis Augustae climaxing January and the new feast of Palatine Vesta end-

---

[19] Such temporal connectors are lacking at the start of three major feasts, Floralia (5.183), the feast of Mercury (5.663), and Vestalia (6.249). Movement to the next day (or two days later?) is only implicit at 6.785 (*rediens*); the dates of the Parentalia whose treatment starts at 2.533 are specified only at the close of the section at 2.567–570.

[20] Fasti Filocali on May 29 *Ludi. Honos et Virtus*. Dio 54.18.2 (for 17 BC) τήν τε τῆς Τιμῆς καὶ τῆς Ἀρετῆς πανήγυριν ἐς τὰς νῦν ἡμέρας μετέστησε, "He (Augustus) transferred the festival of Honos and Virtus to its present dates ..." See Rich 1990, 194.

ing April. On the basis of such evidence, Stephen Heyworth in a forthcoming discussion suggests that Book 5 of the *Fasti* is incomplete, whether here truncated by the poet himself as with the year's last six months, or with part of the ending sequence otherwise lost.[21]

That said, the miscellany closing Book 5 as we have it does gesture towards closure in several respects. The final verse's reference to the rising Hyades as the *sidus Hyantis*, "the constellation of Hyas," recalls precisely the star-myth as told near the book's start of the stellified nymphs named for their slain brother Hyas (5.182 [on May 2] *nomina fecit Hyas*). So, ring-composition of a sort. More strikingly, the movement looks back to the poem's four previous books. For the Agonia on the 21st Ovid refers us to the same feast day on January 9 (5.721; cf. 1.317–318 *Quattuor adde dies ductos ex ordine Nonis, / Ianus Agonali luce piandus erit* ... "Add to the Nones four days taken in succession. Janus will have to be appeased on the Agonal day ..."); he reminds us that the Dog-star emerging on the 22nd he has already mentioned *alio ... loco* (5.724), namely on the Robigalia of April 25;[22] next is the Tubilustria of the 23rd, which he noted on the same day in March;[23] the puzzlingly abbreviated feast QRCF immediately follows the Tubilustria both here and in March (though that is not recorded in Book 3), but one of Ovid's explanations for the festival's name (5.728 *fuga regis*) recalls instead his presentation of the Regifugium on February 24, which he introduces with the very same phrase at 2.685 *nunc mihi dicenda est regis fuga* "Now I must speak of the flight of the king." Carole Newlands sees in this cluster of retrospective references "a sign of the winding down of the first part of the poem",[24] but that effect is particularly appropriate at the end of the book. Compare the similar, albeit fleeting, cross-reference that we noted above from the penultimate entry in March to the Ara Pacis at the end of Ovid's January. Just as

---

21 Others see here a sign that "Ovid is running out of material" (Geue 2014, 121); cf. Fantham 1983, 211, who finds that Ovid faced a "decline in quality and variety of material over the last two months".

22 4.939–942 "*est Canis, Icarium dicunt, quo sidere moto / tosta sitit tellus praecipiturque seges: / pro cane sidereo canis hic imponitur arae, / et quare fiat nil nisi nomen habet.*" The flamen Quirinalis there explains to Ovid that a dog is sacrificed on the Robigalia to ward off the ill effects of the Dog Star, rather than, as the retrospective reference suggests (5.724 *signi ... causa*), that an aition for the constellation is offered.

23 3.849–850 *Summa dies e quinque* [= Mar. 23] *tubas lustrare canoras / admonet et forti sacrificare deo*. Ovid highlights the different divinities honored at the two occurrences of the feast, Vulcan in May but Mars in March. Some follow the variant reading *deae*, who would be Minerva, just featured at the Quinquatrus, but two calendars note March 23 as *feriae Marti* (Degrassi 1963, 429) and the descriptor *forti* suits him well.

24 Newlands 1995, 209–210.

in that case, but more extensively here, three of the backward allusions align closely with the actual day in the earlier month, Dog-star on May 22 with Robigalia on April 25, Tubilustria on May 23 looking to the same on March 23, and *fuga regis* explaining the feast of May 24 in terms of the Regifugium on February 24. As with *deduxit* at 1.709 to introduce the progress of his poem to the Ara Pacis on January 30, Ovid seems to be evoking the visual experience of beholding a calendar on public display: the reader of the poem is invited to imagine standing before the column of May in a painted or inscribed *fasti* and repeatedly looking to the left at more or less the same axis of sight.[25] In verse 727 Ovid even speaks of *reading* the calendrical notice for March 24 (*notis ... lectis*), as if on site, and just above at the movement's start, *in fastis* (5.722) refers in the first instance to an actual calendar, not just to Ovid's poetic version thereof. All this has programmatic force, suitable to a book's conclusion, as do the echoes of key terms of the whole work's premise at this closing section's start. Compare the sequence *tempus ... signi ... causa* in the first two couplets (5.721–724) with the first two couplets of the entire *Fasti*: <u>*tempora*</u> cum <u>*causis*</u> Latium digesta per annum / lapsaque sub terras ortaque <u>*signa*</u> canam, "I will sing of times along with their causes arranged throughout the Latin year, and the constellations sunk beneath the earth and risen." The rapid run of diurnal *tempora* that ends Book 5 consists of four Roman festal notices and four astronomical notices, the two main foci of the calendar as Ovid constructs it. That fact adds to the other closural pointers the sense that Ovid's calendar-poem is represented here in concentrated form, and that this unique book-ending, which does not explicitly declare the month's end or momentously mark it with an Augustan finale, is, after all, a mise-en-abyme of Ovid's *Fasti*.

Bibliography

Barchiesi, Alessandro (1997), "Endgames: Ovid's *Metamorphoses* 15 and *Fasti* 6", in: Deborah H. Roberts/Francis M. Dunn/Don Fowler (eds.), *Classical Closure. Reading the End in Greek and Latin Literature*, Princeton, 181–208.
Barchiesi, Alessandro (1997b), *The Poet and the Prince. Ovid and Augustan Discourse*, Berkeley.

---

25 The intratextuality, in other words, mirrors the experience of calendrical tables in this instance. That the cross-references are not all exact corresponds to the fact that such Roman technologies seem not to have been designed for precise comparison. See the discussion of Riggsby 2019, 74–75; and 55–57 on calendrical *fasti*.

Braun, Ludwig (1981), "Kompositionskunst in Ovid's 'Fasti'", *Aufstieg und Niedergang der römischen Welt* 2.31.4, 2344–2383.
Degrassi, Attilio (1963), *Inscriptiones Italiae*, 13.2. Fasti Anni Numani et Iuliani, Rome.
Fantham, Elaine (1983), "Sexual Comedy in Ovid's *Fasti*: Sources and Motivation", *Harvard Studies in Classical Philology* 87, 185–216.
Fowler, Don (1989), "First Thoughts on Closure: Problems and Prospects", *MD* 22, 75–122.
Fowler, Don (2013), "Second Thoughts on Closure", in: Deborah H. Roberts/Francis M. Dunn/Don Fowler (eds.), *Classical Closure: Reading the End in Greek and Latin Literature*, Princeton, 3–22.
Geue, Tom (2014), "*Festina lente*: Progress and Delay in Ovid's *Fasti*", *Ramus* 39, 104–129.
Heslin, Peter (2015), *The Museum of Augustus. The Temple of Apollo in Pompeii, the Portico of Philippus in Rome, and Latin Poetry*, Los Angeles.
Heyworth, Stephen (2018), "Editing and Interpreting Ovid's *Fasti*. Text, Date, Form", in: Luis Rivero/Maria Consuelo Álvarez/Rosa Maria Iglesias/Juan A. Estévez (eds.), *Viuam! Estudios sobre la obra de Ovidio — Studies on Ovid's Poetry*, Huelva–Murcia (Huelva Classical Monographs 1), 111–126.
Heyworth, Stephen (2019), *Ovid Fasti Book III*, Cambridge.
Hinds, Stephen (1987), *The Metamorphosis of Persephone. Ovid and the Self-conscious Muse*, Cambridge.
Hutchinson, Gregory O. (2008), *Talking Books: Readings in Hellenistic and Roman Books of Poetry*, Oxford.
Kaesser, Christian (2013), "False Closure and Deception", in: Farouk Grewing/Benjamin Acosta-Hughes/Alexander Kirichenko (eds.), *The Door Ajar: False Closure in Greek and Roman Literature and Art*, Heidelberg, 29–42.
Krasser, Helmut (2008), "*Ianus victor* — Ein Leitmotiv im ersten Fastenbuch Ovids", in: Helmut Krasser/Dennis Pausch/Ivana Petrovic (eds.), *Triplici invectus triumpho. Der römische Triumph in augusteischer Zeit*, Stuttgart, 225–284.
Martelli, Francesca (2013), *Ovid's Revisions. The Editor as Author*, Cambridge.
Miller, John F. (2002), "The *Fasti*: Style, Structure, and Time", in: Barbara Weiden Boyd (ed.), *Brill's Companion to Ovid*, Leiden/Boston/Cologne, 167–196.
Miller, John F. (2018), "Flora, Ovid, and Augustus", in: Lucia Athanassaki/Christopher Nappa/Athanassios Vergados (eds.), *Gods and Mortals in Greek and Latin Poetry. Studies in Honor of Jenny Strauss Clay*, Rethymnon, 343–357.
Nagle, Betty Rose (1983), "Open-ended Closure in *Aeneid* 2", *CW* 76, 257–263.
Newlands, Carole (1995), *Playing with Time. Ovid and the Fasti*, Ithaca NY.
Rich, John W. (1990), *Cassius Dio. The Augustan Settlement (Roman History 53–55.9)*, Warminster.
Riggsby, Andrew M. (2019), *Mosaics of Knowledge: Representing Information in the Roman World*, Oxford.
Rüpke, Jörg (2006), "Ennius's *Fasti* in Fulvius's Temple: Greek Rationality and Roman Tradition", *Arethusa* 39, 489–512.
Xinyue, Bobby (2018), "Augustus in Morisot's 'Book 8' of the *Fasti*", in: Penelope J. Goodman (ed.), *Afterlives of Augustus, AD 14–2014*, Cambridge, 198–218.
Walther, Andre (2016), *M. Fulvius Nobilior. Politik und Kultur in der Zeit der Mittleren Republik*, Heidelberg.
Zetzel, James E.G. (1983), "Catullus, Ennius, and the Poetics of Allusion", *ICS* 8, 251–266.

Philip Hardie
Statius' *Achilleid*: How to Break off a *carmen perpetuum*

Abstract: At a book and a bit, Statius' *Achilleid* has barely got underway before it breaks off. This paper provides further arguments for the thesis, most fully articulated by Peter Heslin, that the ending of the *Achilleid* is not an abrupt break, the result of the author's death or incapacity, or of an accident of transmission, but that it shows signs of being a carefully calculated provisional ending. The last two lines of book 2 are marked by signals both of closure and of the promise of continuation, reinforced by intertextuality with Statius' *Thebaid*. Furthermore, the fragment of book 2 itself displays evidence of ring composition.

1 Epics unfinished, ancient and early modern

Long epic narrative poems are more likely than shorter literary productions to be prone to incompletion, whether through the death of their authors in the course of the long process of writing, or through the failure of the heroic impetus required to carry them through to completion. In antiquity, incompleteness would appear to be a problem that bedevils the surviving Latin epics more than it does Greek epics. Leaving the Homeric epics aside, Apollonius of Rhodes' *Argonautica* is polished to a high degree of completion. And in late antiquity, the 48 books of Nonnus' *Dionysiaca* are a monumental example of an epic on the grandest scale brought to its conclusion.

The first hexameter epic in Latin, Ennius' *Annals*, survives only in fragments; the fragmentary and the incomplete are clearly distinct, if related. The *Annals* are also incomplete, in a sense, however, not dependent on the continued existence and energy of their author, but on the incompleteness of historical time. An epic on the history of Rome can never be "complete" until the destruction of Rome, or the end of time itself. This fact is registered in the addition by Ennius, late in life, of a further three books, on the wars of the 180s and 170s, to the original, and complete in its own terms, edition in fifteen books. The incompleteness of history is a problem for the teleology of Virgil's legendary and historical epic, a problem thrown in Virgil's face, a little unfairly I think, by W.H. Auden in his poem "Secondary epic". But the incompletion of the *Aeneid* is primarily of another kind, that recorded in the Suetonian-Donatan *Vita*'s account that Virgil would have taken another three years to give the *Aeneid* the *summa manus*, and in the story that on his deathbed he tried to have the poem burned, so inaugurating a recurrent 'myth' of the epic poet's despair as to the completability of his work.

Turning to post-Virgilian epic, Lucan's *Bellum Civile* breaks off in midcourse, we assume because of the sudden breaking off of the poet's life, but nevertheless at a point in the narrative that may reveal a conscious calculation.[1] The incomplete state of Valerius Flaccus' *Argonautica* is more widely considered to be the result of authorial death or failure, rather than an accident of transmission.[2] Silius Italicus' *Punica* appears to be complete, although the unusual number of books, seventeen, has raised eyebrows, and some think that the poem was left lacking its final revision at Silius' death.

Two post-Virgilian epics stamp their completion with an epilogue or envoi. *Iamque opus exegi* ("Now I have completed a work ...") begins the Epilogue to Ovid's *Metamorphoses*, and a threefold use of *iam* in the envoi to Statius' *Thebaid* signals the post-completion beginning of the poem on its journey into the future on a path of fame, and as a book canonized through being read in schools. Yet the composition of an epilogue need not preclude later revisions or additions to a poem, and it is not impossible that Ovid continued to revise the *Metamorphoses* in exile. In *Tristia* 1.7, in a re-enactment of the Virgilian myth of the poet on his deathbed, Ovid claims that when he went into exile, the *Metamorphoses* lacked the *summa manus* and *ultima lima*, and that he actually succeeded in burning — a copy of, at least — the *Metamorphoses*. *Tristia* 1.7 ends with a material supplementation of the poem, in the form of a mournful prologue of six lines to be prefaced to the poem itself (which, unsurprisingly, have not been transmitted with the text of the *Metamorphoses*).[3] This is an example of the editorial "revisionism" that marks Ovid's compositional persona from the time of the prologue to the *Amores* which announces that we have in our hands a three-book version boiled down from an original five books.[4] There is also an incompleteness of reading, as well as of composition: even if such episodes as that of Actaeon had been completed in their present form before Ovid's exile, this and similar tales of transformation and sparagmos will reveal a fuller — more complete? — meaning only to the readers of Ovid's exile poetry.

Coming finally to the last of the surviving post-Virgilian epic poems of the early empire, Statius' *Achilleid* is very obviously incomplete, breaking off a short

---

[1] See Masters 1992, 216–259; Tracy 2011.
[2] See Zissos 2008, pp. xxvi–xxviii; Zissos in this volume.
[3] See Hinds 1985.
[4] See Martelli 2013.

way into the second book at line 167. This imbalance of incompletion may have had its effect on the transmission of the poem. O.A.W. Dilke notes: "Early editors, following the worse MSS, began the second book at this line [1.675]; the scribes had perhaps wished to divide the first from the incomplete second book more equally".[5]

For other examples of epics that break off at an early point in their course, one can look to the early modern period. Of the *Franciade* by Pierre Ronsard (1524–1585), planned as the national French epic, on the model of the *Aeneid*, and taking as its subject the legendary Trojan origins of the French nation, only four books of a projected 24 were completed, published in 1572. The St Bartholomew's Day Massacre of that year, and the death of Ronsard's royal dedicatee, Charles IX, in 1574 may have discouraged him from continuing. Looking to England in the following century, Abraham Cowley (1618–1667) completed only four books, of a projected twelve, of a highly Virgilianizing biblical epic on the life of David, the *Davideis*. Among other things, the *Davideis* was an important precursor of Milton's *Paradise Lost*, an epic that was brought to a triumphant conclusion, despite the adversity under which Milton lived after the Restoration of the monarchy in 1660, finally in the twelve-book edition of 1674, an expansion of the 1667 ten-book edition. Abraham Cowley is also the author of another incomplete epic on contemporary history, *The Civil War*, which the staunchly Royalist Cowley abandoned after it became clear that the war was going very badly for Charles I.

2 The *Achilleid*

Even among incomplete epics, the *Achilleid* is unusual in breaking off at a point near the beginning of a book. It is usually assumed that death prevented Statius from writing the epic through to completion, but that leaves open the question of just how fragmentary is what we have. Are we to imagine that at line 167 of book 2 Statius was overcome by death, and laid down his stylus, in the way that Petrarch imagines that Virgil was overcome as he penned the last line of the *Aeneid, uitaque cum gemitu fugit indignata sub umbras* ("and with a groan, his life fled indignant down to the shades"): "Virgil, you were too accurate a prophet of your own fate; for as you spoke these words, your life too deserted you, also fleeing indignant, if I am not mistaken", Petrarch writes in the margin of

---

5 Dilke 1954, 128.

his copy of the works of Virgil. Or is the book and a bit, within its own limits, a well wrought urn? Does the end of the *Achilleid*, as we have it, give us any clues as to how it might have continued? And, more generally, what might we speculate about Statius' handling of the rest of the life of Achilles from the book and a bit as a whole?

Much recent criticism of the *Achilleid* has been concerned to bring out the very Ovidian qualities of the Scyros episode, as opposed to the more Virgilian *Thebaid*. Less has been said on the *Achilleid* as a very unVirgilian *carmen perpetuum*, a "continuous song" on the life of the greatest of Greek heroes. Statius' wish is to *ire per omnem ... heroa* ("go through the whole story of the hero") (1.4–5), as neither Homer nor Virgil do, and *tota iuuenem deducere Troia* ("lead the youth through the whole tale of Troy") (1.7), where *deducere* alludes to Ovid's use of the verb at *Met.* 1.4 *in mea perpetuum deducite tempora carmen* ("bring down a continuous song to my own times"). Statius is no doubt alert to the paradoxical division in the meanings of the Ovidian *deducere*, both "extend" in a long, unCallimachean, poem, and "finely spin" a Callimachean poem.[6] The temporal span of Achilles' brief life is a mere fraction of the Ovidian span from the beginning of the world *ad mea tempora* (although it is possible that the *Achilleid* might have continued to Achilles' afterlife on the Isles of the Blessed), but a completed *Achilleid* is likely to have mirrored the generic pluralism of the *Metamorphoses*, combining erotic and romantic episodes of intrigue and deception, such as the Scyros episode, with hyper-epic episodes of warfare and slaughter, of a kind that are exemplified on a large scale in the *Metamorphoses*, for example in book 12, framed by Achilles' duel with Cycnus and the death of Achilles, brought about by Neptune's mindful anger at the fate of his son Cycnus. So the *Achilleid* could have continued on Ovidian tracks, without confining itself to the particular Ovidianisms manifested in the Scyros episode.

---

6 Statius also alludes to the Ovidian prologue in Phorbas' description of the contingent of troops from Helicon, *Theb.* 7.285–289 "*patriis concentibus audis | exultare gregem, quales, cum pallida cedit | bruma, renidentem* **deducunt** *Strymona cycni. | ite alacres, numquam uestri morientur honores, | bellaque perpetuo memorabunt* **carmine** *Musae*" ("you hear your people exult in the songs of their fatherland, such as those that swans sing in praise of smiling Strymon, when pale winter gives way. Go boldly, your praises shall never die, and the Muses will recount your wars in unending songs"): see Smolenaars 1994 on 7.287, 288 f.

3 Provisional closure

I turn to the issue of how easily an epic poet can temporarily, and deliberately, suspend the course of his poem. In the *Achilleid*, Statius chooses to write an epic constructed along the lines of an Ovidian *perpetuum carmen* rather than of an organically unified Virgilian plot, an epic consisting of a succession of episodes given cohesion by thematic and aesthetic principles other than an Aristotelian beginning, middle and end. Such an epic, it might be thought, is one that could more easily be brought to a provisional point of closure. Conversely, it might be said that the suspension of the forward movement of a juggernaut set on telling everything from the very beginning to the very end is more obtrusive than might be the suspension of an epic plot of more limited temporal scope. There is another point to be made about suspending the action of an epic on a hero who is possessed of demonic energy, and finds it hard to know when to stop. On the other hand, Achilles' career is notoriously interrupted by suspensions. The whole of the Scyros episode is itself a suspension of Achilles' hyper-heroic trajectory. At the beginning of the *Iliad*, Achilles' furious impulse to strike Agamemnon is checked by Athena, and he subsequently suspends his own heroic career for the greater part of the *Iliad*.

Peter Heslin, building on comments by Ralph Johnson, has made the most convincing case of which I am aware that "The *Achilleid* is a coherent and polished piece of work".[7] By line 167 of book 2, Statius has resolved the two narrative strands of (a) Thetis' attempt to prevent Achilles from joining the Greek expedition against Troy, and (b) Ulysses' mission to bring Achilles to Aulis. This extends to a near numerical symmetry of the alternating sections of these two strands, A — B — A — B (of 396 — 163 — 400 — 167 lines). Heslin points to the ring composition whereby our *Achilleid* opens with reference to Achilles' father, 1.1 *Magnanimum Aeaciden*, and ends with his mother, in the last word of the last line, 167 *mater*. Heslin rebuts what Dilke claims as detailed verbal evidence of incompletion.[8] He further suggests that the *Achilleid* was the model for another epic left deliberately incomplete, Claudian's *De raptu Proserpinae*, incomplete like the tapestry that Proserpina abandons when Venus, Diana, and Pallas arrive to lure the virgin out of her house, 1.271–272 *imperfectumque laborem / deserit* ("she abandons the unfinished work"). Heslin concludes that the *Achilleid* as we have it was put out into the world as a "prospectus", "designed to

---

[7] Heslin 2005, 57: the key discussions come at 62–70; 62–65 "Coherence and design".
[8] Dilke 1954, 7.

whet the taste of the public for a new epic and to offer his patrons a sample of what they would be underwriting",[9] and also provoking more questions than answers, a tease.

4 *Achilleid* 2.166–167

I want now to turn the microscope on the last lines of the *Achilleid*, and to offer more support for the proposition that what we have is a well formed point of provisional closure to the epic, without venturing to speculate further on what audience or readership Statius may be targeting. The speech of Achilles that concludes the *Achilleid* (2.96–167) is delivered in answer to Diomedes' request for an account of his earliest years. Achilles begins at the point when he was first taken into the care of the centaur Chiron on mount Pelion, and catalogues a relentlessly tough upbringing, nurtured not on milk but on the flesh of lions and the marrow of wolves, and constantly exposed to the harshness of wild beasts and wild nature. Achilles is trained to swiftness of foot by racing against Lapith horses and against Chiron himself, and prepared for war by hunting the fiercest of wild beasts, and by extreme forms of athleticism, the climax of which, he remembers (143), was to face the full force of the river Sperchios in spate by standing midstream against the boulders and trees carried down by the raging water. Achilles remembers an event in his childhood, but for poet and reader this is a literary memory of the Iliadic episode for which it is both a preparation and a foreshadowing: Achilles' fight with the river Scamander. After this hyper-hard-primitivist syllabus, Achilles concludes with a more normal list of activities and subjects in the education of Achilles (154–165): traditional athletics, discus throwing, wrestling and boxing, music, herbal medicine, and finally the precepts of the justice by which Chiron administered laws to the peoples of Pelion, and pacified his own people, the centaurs, 165 *suos solitus pacare biformes* ("accustomed to tame his own two-shaped people"). This last is not a lesson that Achilles seems to have learned very well. Or has he perhaps learned the lesson too well, with the result that an over-developed sense of justice will lead to his disastrous quarrel with Agamemnon?

Achilles breaks off in the last two lines of his speech, and of the *Achilleid*, 2.166–167:

---

9 Heslin 2005, 85–86.

> hactenus annorum, comites, elementa meorum
> et memini et meminisse iuuat: scit cetera mater.

So far, comrades, I remember the training of my early years and joy in the memory. My mother knows the rest.[10]

Almost every word of these two lines appears well chosen. *annorum ... elementa meorum* forms a ring with the terms of Diomedes' opening request at 2.86–91, beginning "*quin ritusque tuos elementaque primae indolis ... edis?*" ("Nay ... why not tell of your ways, the rudiments of earliest nature?"). Closure, then, to this particular exchange.

et memini et meminisse iuuat draws attention to the role of memory in all epic narrating, appropriately enough at the end, however provisional, of an epic, and, more specifically, is a memory of a famous line of Virgil, *Aen.* 1.203 *forsan et haec olim meminisse iuuabit*. Aeneas there opines that in future there may be pleasure even in remembering the Trojans' terrifying experiences on their sea journey, in contrast to other, unspecified, experiences whose memory might be more obviously pleasurable. In Achilles' words the emphasis is on the repeated *et*: this early school of hard knocks (whose memory for one less tough than Achilles might not be so pleasurable) I *both* remember, *and* take pleasure in remembering; the rest I do not enjoy remembering. This is a convenient way of avoiding repetition of what the reader has been told at length in book 1: *scit cetera lector*. Dilke's comment is heavy-handed: "This ending to Achilles' narrative seems somewhat inappropriate, since Ulysses and Diomede would hardly be helped by being referred to Thetis; perhaps Achilles is preferring to keep silence about his stay in Scyros, for which his mother was responsible".[11] Indeed. Nor can Heslin be right in suggesting that *cetera* must refer to the question, never answered in *Achilleid*, of how Achilles came to live with Chiron in the first place.[12] *cetera* is naturally taken of the sequel, not the prequel, to what has just been narrated. It is immaterial that Achilles has already refused to discuss the topic of his arrival in Scyros at 2.43–45, "*longum resides exponere causas / maternumque nefas; hoc excusabitur ense / Scyros et indecores, fatorum crimina, cultus*" ("it would take too long to set out the causes of my tarrying and my mother's crime. By this sword shall Scyros and the unseemly habit be excused, reproach of destiny"). That was addressed to Ulysses, and this to Diomedes. There Achilles uses the excuse of the tedious length of time such a narrative

---

10 Translations of Statius are from the Loeb (Shackleton Bailey).
11 Dilke 1954 *ad loc.*
12 Heslin 2005, 63 n. 21.

would take, and expresses rather his own eagerness to hear of the causes of the Trojan War; here he avoids the topic by referring to another authority, albeit one to whom Diomedes has no immediate access.

cetera also signals that Achilles' ending looks to a continuation, that this is not the end of the story, albeit deceptively for Statius' reader, who has already been told the rest of the story to date: Achilles' analeptic narrative joins seamlessly to the moment when Thetis first catches sight of her son on Pelion (1.158 ff.), following Chiron's aposiopesis, 158 *"sed taceo"* ("but I keep quiet"). Ulysses also falls silent once reassured, at the beginning of the sea-journey to Troy, that Achilles' enthusiasm for battle will not be deflected by his love for the wife that he has left behind on Scyros: 2.85 *tacuit contentus Ulixes* ("Ulysses was content, and fell silent"). An extradiegetic silence soon falls, on the text itself, after Achilles' last words at 2.167, but the reader knows that there is more to follow in this famous story, as Ulysses is made certain of Achilles' determination to proceed to Troy by his reaction to the suggestion that another Paris might attempt a rape of Deidamia (2.81–83).

However, given the knowledge of the future that this mother has, through the prophecy that Achilles would either have a glorious, but short, life, or a long, but inglorious, life at home (*Iliad* 9.410–417), *scit cetera mater* ("my mother knows the rest") may, ironically, have a meaning that Achilles does not intend. She knows something of "the rest", if not, at this point, the exact course that the future will take.[13] This imperfect knowledge of the future might also mirror that of the reader, who knows the rest of Achilles' story (including his choice to stay at Troy and die young), but not exactly how it will play out in this retelling of it.

scit cetera mater also calls to mind a famous Ovidian example of truncated narrative, the "erotic aposiopesis" of *Amores* 1.5.25 *cetera quis nescit? lassi requieuimus ambo* ("Who does not know the rest? We both rested, exhausted"). If that line hovers in the background, then *cetera quis nescit?* is apposite for the reader, in two ways: both in the immediate context — all readers of *Achilleid* 1–2 know the rest of the story up to the present point in legendary time, and in fact know rather more than Achilles, having had access to information relating to

---

13 There is no indication that Statius' Achilles knows, at this point, that he is doomed to die young, or to live a long inglorious life. It is perhaps an unintended irony that Statius' justification in the proem for daring to rival Homer, 1.3–4 *quamquam acta uiri multum inclita cantu | Maeonio (sed plura uacant)* ("although the hero's deeds are highly celebrated in Maeonian song (but more remain untold)") could also be appended to what we have of the *Achilleid*: *plura uacant*, or *plura desunt* ("more is lacking") indeed.

Thetis' thoughts and actions to which Achilles does not have access, including, for example, his conveyance while sleeping from Pelion to Scyros; and, in the wider context, who does not know, in general outline at least, the whole story about Achilles, *omnis heros* (1.4–5)? And I am also tempted to wonder whether famous lines from the prologue to Virgil's third *Georgic* are not also in the mix, for readers both of *Amores* 1.5 and of the *Achilleid*: *Geo.* 3.3–5 cetera *quae uacuas tenuissent carmine mentes, | omnia iam uulgata:* quis aut Eurysthea durum | aut inlaudati nescit Busiridis aras? ("All the other themes which might have charmed with song idle minds are too well known: who does not know of harsh Eurystheus, or the altars of loathsome Busiris?").[14] If we do remember the Virgilian lines, Achilles, who already in Homer is a singer of epic poetry (*Iliad* 9.186–189), now for a moment plays the part of a Callimachean poet. The result of the premature truncation of the *Achilleid* leaves us with something the size of a rather large epyllion, rather than a full-scale Homeric epic.

5 "Thus far ..."

If *cetera* marks a point of provisional closure, but to be continued, the same is true of the adverb *hactenus*: thus far in Achilles' account of his life to date, and thus far in the narrative of the *Achilleid*. *hactenus memini* ("thus far I remember"): thus far in my recounting of epic *memoria*. *hactenus* is used by Statius elsewhere six times, at a point of provisional closure or transition. I list four of the occurrences:

> *Silv.* 4 praef., *hunc tamen librum tu, Marcelle, defendes, si uidetur,* hactenus; *sin minus, reprehendemur. uale.* ("In spite of everything you, Marcellus, will defend this book, if you see fit, up to this point; if not we shall stand rebuked. Farewell.")[15]

> *Silv.* 5.1.135–136 hactenus *alma chelys. tempus nunc ponere frondes, | Phoebe, tuas maestaque comam damnare cupresso.* ("Thus far the kindly lyre. Now it is time to lay aside your leaves, Phoebus, and doom my hair with sad cypress.")

> *Theb.* 3.96–98 *sed ducis infandi rabidae non* hactenus *irae | stare queunt; uetat igne rapi, pacemque sepulcri | impius ignaris nequiquam manibus arcet.* ("But the wild wrath of the

---

14 *cetera* and *nescit* or *scit* do not in fact occur very frequently in near juxtaposition.
15 The meaning, and function, of *hactenus* here are disputed. I adopt the text, and translation, of Coleman 1988.

infamous ruler cannot halt there; he forbids funeral fire and impiously, but in vain, denies the peace of the tomb to the unwitting ghost.")

Eteocles' excessive epic anger is unable to reach even a temporary point of stasis.

> *Theb.* 10.827–828 *hactenus arma, tubae, ferrumque et uulnera: sed nunc / comminus astrigeros Capaneus tollendus in axis.* ("Thus far of arms, trumpets, of steel and wounds. But now Capaneus must be raised aloft into the starry vault, to fight at close quarters.")

hactenus both for the character Capaneus, who now moves on to a different level of fighting, and for the poet Statius, who now raises his epic strains to a new sublimity.

The remaining Statian example of *hactenus* comes shortly after a character in the *Thebaid*, Parthenopaeus, in many ways a mirror to Achilles, albeit a failed Achilles,[16] ends a speech with an abruptness comparable to the ending of Achilles' final speech in the *Achilleid*,[17] *Theb.* 9.788–800:

> *iamdudum hunc contra stimulis grauioribus ardet*
> *trux Atalantiades; necdum ille quierat, et infit:*
> *"sera etiam in Thebas, quarum hic exercitus, arma*　　790
> *profero; quisnam adeo puer, ut bellare recuset*
> *talibus? Arcadiae stirpem et fera semina gentis,*
> *non Thebana uides: non me sub nocte silenti*
> *Thyias Echionio genetrix famulata Lyaeo*
> *edidit, haud umquam deformes uertice mitras*　　795
> *induimus turpemque manu iactauimus hastam.*
> *protinus astrictos didici reptare per amnes*
> *horrendasque domos magnarum intrare ferarum*
> *et - quid plura loquar? ferrum mea semper et arcus*
> *mater habet, uestri feriunt caua tympana patres."*　　800

Against him Atalanta's fierce son long burns, heavily stung. The other had not yet finished when he begins: "Even too late I bring my weapons against Thebes if this is her army. Who is so much a boy that he would refuse to fight the likes of these? You see before you Arcadia's stock, seed of warlike race, not Theban. Me did no Thyiad mother, servant to Echionian Lyaeus, bring forth in the silent night, I never put unsightly turbans on my head or brandished a shameful spear. Straightway I learned to crawl over frozen rivers and enter the dread homes of great beasts; and (why say more?) my mother ever has steel and bow about her, your fathers strike hollow drums."

---

[16] On reworkings of material in the *Thebaid* in the *Achilleid*, see Parkes 2008, 386–387 on Achilles as another Parthenopaeus.
[17] The comparison is made by Dilke 1954 on *Achill.* 2.167.

Here the two-line break-off comes just after Parthenopaeus has boasted of an upbringing in the wilderness very like that of Achilles on Pelion. By contrast, Parthenopaeus' mother is the source of his pride in his weapons, the reverse of the relationship between Achilles and Thetis. Line 800 is framed by *mater* and *patres*, as the *Achilleid* as a whole is framed by Achilles' father and mother. The word *hactenus* follows a few lines later, in the plea of Diana, disguised as Dorceus, at 9.811–814 *huius tum uultu dea dissimulata profatur: | "hactenus Ogygias satis infestasse cateruas, | Parthenopaee, satis; miserae iam parce parenti, | parce deis, quicumque fauent."* ("By his countenance then disguised, the goddess speaks: 'Enough thus far to have harried the Ogygian troops, Parthenopaeus, enough! Now spare your unhappy mother, spare the gods, whosoever of them wish you well.'") For Parthenopaeus, soon to die, *hactenus* will indeed mark a terminus, the end of a story, not so for Achilles.

The abruptness of Achilles' conclusion to his narrative is mirrored by the abruptness of Statius' (provisional) ending to his epic, and leads to further thoughts of Achilles as a figure for the poet. We already know from the *Iliad* that Achilles sings epic songs, and we learn from the *Achilleid* that he does so already as a boy, taught of course by Chiron: 1.188–194; 188–189 *canit ille libens immania laudum | semina ...* ("Willingly he sings mighty seeds of glory"), a song ending with the wedding of his own parents, 193–194 *maternos in fine toros superisque grauatum | Pelion: hic uicto risit Thetis anxia uultu* ("finally his mother's marriage bed and Pelion weighed down by the High Ones. Here Thetis' anxious countenance yielded in a smile") — the point in time of his own conception. He has thus already sung the prequel to his narrative of his childhood in book 2, and the prequel to the epic poet Statius' *Achilleid*.

6 The cohesion of book 2 of the *Achilleid*

I now look more narrowly still at the cohesion of the fragment of book 2 when viewed from the point of its prematurely closing lines, perhaps no more than a fifth in to what might have been its full length. The book begins conventionally enough with a dawn, and with a contrast, 1–11:

> *Exuit implicitum tenebris umentibus orbem*
> *Oceano prolata dies, genitorque coruscae*
> *lucis adhuc hebetem uicina nocte leuabat*
> *et nondum excusso rorantem lampada ponto.*
> *et iam punicea nudatum pectora palla*   5
> *insignemque ipsis, quae prima inuaserat, armis*

> *Aeaciden - quippe aura uocat cognataque suadent*
> *aequora - prospectant cuncti iuuenemque ducemque*
> *nil ausi meminisse pauent; sic omnia uisu*
> *mutatus rediit, ceu numquam Scyria passus* 10
> *litora Peliacoque rates escendat ab antro.*

Dawn rising from Ocean frees the world from its envelope of dank shadows and the father of flashing light raises his torch still dull from neighbouring night and dewy with sea not yet shaken off. And now all look to Aeacides, as with breast stripped of purple cloak he shines with the arms on which he had first seized (for the breeze summons and the kindred seas persuade); they fear him as warrior and captain, not daring to remember anything. So he returned all changed to view, as though he had never endured Scyros' shores and were embarking from Pelion's cavern.

The contrast is between the natural world, where dawn seems reluctant to get out of bed (adhuc *hebetem ... lampada*, nondum[18] *excusso ... ponto*), and the human hero, who appears already (*et iam*) shining in his new armour like some heavenly body, having stripped off the dark woman's robe (*palla*) that had veiled his true nature, and eager to be getting his martial epic under way. There is a momentary threat to that impetuous *uirtus*, when Achilles looks back at Deidamia, herself watching her departing husband from a tower on Scyros, 29–30 *occultus sub corde renascitur ardor / datque locum uirtus* ("Fire hidden in his heart is reborn and valour yields place"). *uirtus* is put back in place when, in justification of mounting a war against Troy to recover a stolen wife, Ulysses asks Achilles how he would feel if someone were to commit a rape of Deidamia. Achilles' instant reaction is to reach for his sword, 84–85 *illius ad capulum rediit manus*[19] *ac simul ingens / impulit ora rubor; tacuit contentus Ulixes* ("The other's hand went to his swordhilt and a deep flush struck his face. Ulysses was content and said no more"). The conflicting motivations of love and war have been brought into alignment, for the time being, and we can now finally move on from the Scyrian episode.

Ulysses' question to Achilles comes at the end of the first of two sections of analeptic narrative in book 2. Firstly, Ulysses narrates the *tanti* primordia belli

---

[18] For *nondum* metapoetically introducing a dawn at the beginning of a book of the *Thebaid*, cf. 12.1–2 *Nondum cuncta polo uigil inclinauerat astra / ortus* ("Not yet had the wakeful dawn sent all the stars sinking from the sky"); on which see Hardie 1997, 153.
[19] Cf. *Iliad* 1.190–191 Achilles debates whether to draw his sword and kill Agamemnon. Restrained by Athena, Achilles does not draw his sword against an enemy immediately present; the consequence will be his withdrawal from the war effort. Statius' Achilles reaches for his sword-hilt, but does not draw the sword, since the enemy is only imagined in the future; but the consequence is his wholehearted commitment to the war effort.

("the beginnings of so great a war") (47). Secondly, in response to Diomedes' request, Achilles narrates elementa *primae indolis* ("the first training of your talent") (87–88). Statius draws attention to the fact that, so far, his epic has hardly progressed much beyond first beginnings. One can place this beside Statius' report on his work in progress on the *Achilleid*, at *Silvae* 4.7.21–24, to Vibius Maximus:

> *torpor est nostris sine te Camenis,*
> *tardius sueto uenit ipse Thymbrae*
> *rector et **primis** meus ecce **metis***
>   *haeret Achilles.*

My Muses are sluggish without you, the lord of Thymbra himself comes more slowly than usual, and, look, my Achilles is stuck at the first turn.

In the figurative chariot-race that is the composition of the *Achilleid*, swift-footed Achilles has stalled (or crashed) at the first turning-post. This is one of the external pieces of evidence adduced by Heslin in support of his claim that the *Achilleid* in its present form was put out as a "prospectus" for potential patrons, such as Vibius Maximus.[20]

A striking ring is also drawn between the final line and the opening lines of book 2. Achilles distinguishes what he likes to remember and what he does not, *et memini et meminisse iuuat*. Those who, at the beginning of the book, gaze in awe at the transformed Achilles, 8–9 *iuuenemque ducemque* / nil ausi meminisse pauent ("they fear him as warrior and captain, not daring to remember anything"). What they don't dare to remember, much less relate, is the *cetera* which the mother knows. Book 2 is thus framed by allusion to the topos of the effect emotions have on epic memory, and hence on the objectivity of the epic narrator.[21] Statius perhaps has particularly in mind the large-scale deployment of this topos in Ovid, *Metamorphoses* 12.536ff., when Tlepolemus wonders at Nestor's silence on Hercules' part in the battle of Lapiths and Centaurs. Nestor replies, 542–548:

---

20 Heslin 2005, 60–61.
21 For the opposite, a positive emotional spur to narrate, here met with a show of modest resistance, cf. *Achill.* 2.94-95 *quem pigeat sua facta loqui? tamen ille modeste / incohat, ambiguuus paulum propiorque coacto* ("Who would find it hard to tell of his own deeds? Yet he begins modestly, somewhat uncertain and more like one compelled").

> *quid me meminisse malorum*
> *cogis et obductos annis rescindere luctus*
> *inque tuum genitorem odium offensasque fateri?*
> *ille quidem maiora fide (di!) gessit et orbem*
> *inpleuit meritis, quod mallem posse negare;*
> *sed neque Deiphobum nec Pulydamanta nec ipsum*
> *Hectora laudamus - quis enim laudauerit hostem?*

Why do you force me to remember wrongs, to reopen a grief that was buried by the lapse of years, and to rehearse the injuries that make me hate your father? He has done deeds beyond belief, Heaven knows! and filled the earth with well-earned praise, which I would gladly deny him if I could. But neither Deïphobus nor Polydamas nor even Hector do we praise; for who cares to praise his enemy?

Nestor ends his speech 575–576 '*nec tamen ulterius quam fortia facta silendo / ulciscor fratres; solida est mihi gratia tecum*' ("Yet for my brothers I seek no other vengeance than to ignore his mighty deeds. Between me and you there is unbroken amity").[22] How much more of this kind of distorted or occluded narrative might have found its way into the continuation of the *Achilleid*? Might this have been one of the ways in which Statius renewed the old stories? One large-scale example of epic memory subjected to selection and deformation is the *Armorum iudicium* in *Metamorphoses* 13 — suggesting to Statius other ways of developing an Ovidian *Achilleid*?

As it is, we will never know. If, with Heslin, we posit that Statius consciously chose the point of provisional closure at which our texts of the *Achilleid* end, then we might conclude ourselves that it was by a very Ovidian *fortia facta silendo*.

7 Statian *mora*

If that is one way of thematising the silence that falls at the end of an epic prematurely broken off, but to be continued, another way might be to see the break as marking a very Statian kind of *mora* ("delay"). At *Silvae* 4.7.24, the verb used of the suspension of the *Achilleid* at the "first turning-post" (*primis metis*) is *haeret* ("is checked"). That is the verb found in a Ciceronian use of the same charioteering metaphor (and possibly a source for Statius' metaphor), *pro Caelio* 75 *in hoc flexu quasi aetatis ... fama adulescentis paululum haesit ad metas notitia noua mulieris* ("At what may be called the turning-point of his age the youth's

---

22 See Zumwalt 1977, 216–217.

reputation was for a while checked at the turning-post through his recent acquaintance with this lady").[23] It is also the verb used by Ulysses at the moment when Achilles is about to unmask himself, at the sight of the weapons brought to Scyros by Ulysses and Diomedes, *Achill.* 1.866–874:

> tunc acer Ulixes
> admotus lateri summissa uoce: "**Quid haeres?**
> scimus' ait, 'tu semiferi Chironis alumnus,
> tu caeli pelagique nepos, te Dorica classis,
> te tua suspensis exspectat Graecia signis,   870
> ipsaque iam dubiis nutant tibi Pergama muris.
> **heia, abrumpe moras!**[24] sine perfida palleat Ide,
> et iuuet haec audire patrem, pudeatque dolosam
> sic pro te timuisse Thetin."

Then keen Ulysses approached him and speaking softly: "Why do you hesitate?" he says. "We know. You are half-beast Chiron's fosterling, grandson of sea and sky. The Dorian fleet attends you, your Greece expects you with flying standards and Pergamus herself nods to you with walls already tottering. Up now, no more delay! Let treacherous Ide turn pale, let your father rejoice to hear the news and wily Thetis be ashamed to have so feared for you."

A few lines later Lycomedes realises that he cannot resist Achilles' request to be joined in marriage to his daughter, secretly impregnated by Achilles, and cannot further delay Achilles' departure for war, 1.912–916:

> ille, etsi carae comperta iniuria natae
> et Thetidis mandata mouent prodique uidetur
> depositum tam grande deae, tamen obuius ire
> tot metuit fatis **Argiuaque bella morari;**
> fac uelit: ipsam illic matrem spreuisset Achilles.

Moved though he was by the discovery of his daughter's wrong and by Thetis' charge, though feeling that the goddess' grand trust is betrayed, he fears to oppose so many destinies and delay the Argive war. Suppose he so desired, Achilles would have spurned even his mother in this.

For the 167 lines of book 2, the ship bearing Achilles to Troy is making rapid progress, as also is the ship of Achillean martial epic, bar the momentary wob-

---

[23] The parallel is noted by Coleman 1988 on *Silv.* 4.7.23–24.
[24] Cf. Virg. *Geo.* 3.42–43 *en age segnis / rumpe moras: uocat ingenti clamore Cithaeron* ("come, break off sluggish delay: Cithaeron calls with a great shout"); *Aen.* 4.569 *heia age, rumpe moras* ("come, break off delay"); 9.13 *rumpe moras omnis* ("break off all delay").

ble when Achilles looks back at Deidamia (2.27–30: see above). The reader knows that there are further *morae* ahead, the ten years of the war before Troy is captured, and the delay in the tenth year caused by the wrathful Achilles' withdrawal from the battlefield in the *Iliad*. Those are *morae* in the tradition; novel, and unexpected, is the *mora* that arises before ever Achilles' ship reaches Troy, when its course comes to an abrupt halt — in the event, never to continue.

Bibliography

Barchiesi, Alessandro (2021), "*Rege sub uno*: On the Politics of Statius' *Achilleid*", in: C.W. Marshall (ed.), *Latin Poetry and its Reception: Essays for Susanna Braund*, London, 56–74.
Coleman, Kathleen M. (1988), *Statius Silvae IV*. Edited with an English translation and commentary, Oxford.
Dilke, Oswald A.W. (1954), *Statius Achilleid*. Edited with introduction, apparatus criticus and notes, Cambridge.
Hardie, Philip (1997), "Closure in Latin Epic", in: D.H. Roberts/F.M. Dunn/D. Fowler (eds.), *Classical Closure. Reading the End in Greek and Latin Literature*, Princeton, 139–162.
Heslin, Peter J. (2005), *The Transvestite Achilles. Gender and Genre in Statius' Achilleid*, Cambridge.
Hinds, Stephen (1985), "Booking the Return Trip: Ovid and *Tristia* 1", *PCPS* 31, 13–32.
Martelli, Francesca K.A. (2013), *Ovid's Revisions. The Editor as Author*, Cambridge.
Masters, James (1992), *Poetry and Civil War in Lucan's Bellum Civile*, Cambridge.
Parkes, Ruth (2008), "The Return of the Seven: Allusion to the *Thebaid* in Statius' *Achilleid*", *AJP* 129, 381–402.
Smolenaars, Johannes J.L. (1994), *Statius Thebaid VII. A Commentary*, Leiden/New York/Köln.
Tracy, Jonathan (2011), "Internal Evidence for the Completeness of the *Bellum Civile*", in: P. Asso (ed.), *Brill's companion to Lucan*, Leiden/Boston, 34–53.
Zissos, Andrew (2008), *Valerius Flaccus Argonautica. Book 1. A Commentary*, Oxford.
Zumwalt, Nancy (1977), "*Fama subversa*: Theme and Structure in Ovid *Metamorphoses* 12", *CSCA* 10, 209–222.

Laura Jansen
Literatura Incompleta: Borges' Antiquity between World and Universe

Abstract: Both an erudite scholar and a master of the imagination, Borges casts innovative light on classical unfinishedness. In his writings, he urges us to regard literature as a phenomenon which is always in the making, never fully accessible. For Borges, not knowing literature "whole" is not a source of frustration; instead, he proposes a therapy of reading in the "imperfect," somewhere between knowing and not knowing. This essay explores this process in three examples of Borges' oeuvre: the endless, errant trajectories that Julius Caesar takes from Shakespeare and Quevedo, back to ancient Rome and forth to the Argentine gauchesque; Babel as an imaginary realm where lost classical texts are stored in complete yet inaccessible form; Hellenic "absences" dwelling in an Elysium-like geography, where unknown ancient authors can be recuperated somehow. Heraclitus' flowing river underscores Borges' imperfect approach to reading the classical, as well as our own reading of Borges' antiquity.

Marked by brevity, fragmentation, and bifurcating form, the oeuvre of Jorge Luis Borges (Buenos Aires, 1899–Geneva, 1986) casts imaginative light on the matter of literary unfinishedness. In his writings, classical antiquity plays an intriguing part in the subject, and this essay aims to explore how it does so and to what effects. My first point of discussion draws attention to Borges' "imperfect reading" of literature, ancient and modern, an approach he cultivates from childhood onwards and could be seen to foreshadow the sense of the unlimited one finds in complex networks such as the World Wide Web, invented three years after Borges' death. The core of the essay then probes inflections of classical unfinishedness in three case studies: i. the endless, errant trajectories that the figure of Julius Caesar takes from Shakespeare and Quevedo, back to Roman antiquity and forth to Argentine modernist gauchesque literature; ii. the notion of Babel, explored through the figure of the vast library, as an imaginary realm where lost classical texts are stored in complete yet inaccessible form; iii. the narratives of Hellenic "absences" (i.e. fragmentary, lost, and/or forgotten voices and texts) dwelling in an Elysium-like geography, where unknown ancient authors can be recuperated somehow. These three examples (of which there are more[1]) speak powerfully to a twentieth-century approach to antiquity in which the classical is mobilised to substantiate deeper and often oblique literary histories, whose totality is technically irrecoverable yet creatively recalled. In Borges' thinking, the figure of Heraclitus and his flowing river is a key point for how the classical circulates across traditions, and how this mode of circulation discloses novel ways to account for authors, texts and ideas as unfinished phenomena. Towards the end of the essay, I consider Borges in a network of (near) contemporary authors who may be viewed as conforming to a tradition of unfinishedness. I then conclude by turning my attention to the reader, asking what it means for us to look back on antiquity in the manner of Borges.

1 Imperfect reading and the network of classical unfinishedness in Borges

In his 2013 lecture series for TV Pública, Argentine author Ricardo Piglia (Buenos Aires, 1941–2017), renowned for his knowledge of Borges, delves into the question of Borges' mode of reading literature. In contrast with Kafka, who read single books intensively, Piglia notes that Borges read texts extensively, fragmentarily, and often simultaneously. It was also a practice he had cultivated since early childhood in his family home library, situated in the affluent Buenos Aires neighbourhood of Palermo. That library afforded him a rich, varied collection of national and world literatures in Spanish and English, which the young Borges encountered with great curiosity. Its stacks included some of the ancient Greco-Roman canonical authors in translation, especially Homer and Virgil, as well as reference works, his favourite being the *Encyclopaedia Britannica*, whose entries he read in a deliberately random and experimental manner.[2] Borges' taste for expansive, varied reading continued in adulthood when he was first a librarian and eventually director of the Mariano Moreno National Library in Buenos Aires. It was in great part during the long hours spent in this library that he deepened his interests in Norse, Japanese, Persian, Chinese, Arabic, American, English, French, and Rioplatense[3] literature and philosophy, as he

---

[1] See Jansen 2018. For Borges' "subterranean" translation of Homer and Virgil see García Jurado and Salazar Morales 2014.
[2] Carricaburo 2011, 461–473.
[3] The term "Rioplatense" refers to the region around the basin of the Río de la Plata, which includes Uruguay and Borges' Buenos Aires, as well as to the Spanish language spoken in the area.

wrote his famous *A History of Eternity* (1936), *Ficciones* (1944), *The Aleph* (1949), *Dreamtigers* (1960), and *The Book of Sand* (1975), to name a few.[4] In his final years, and in between world travel and university lecturing, others read to the nearly blind Borges in a similar fashion. One reader was the teenaged Alberto Manguel (Buenos Aires, 1948–), author of the monumental *A History of Reading* (1996) and *The Library at Night* (2006). In *With Borges* (2006), an extended essay on his sessions reading to Borges in the 1970s, Manguel offers rich illustrations of Borges' reading habits and preferences. It was common for Manguel to read him passages from different works in a single session, and for Borges to make unexpected connections between them that could become the impetus of new stories for him.[5]

As Piglia points out, Borges' inclination was to move from book to book erratically in a single day. He often tackled passages rather than chapters, and he did so through a philosophy of reading that one could call "imperfect." Namely, he was not particularly motivated by teleological procedures or a need for closure *per se*, whether of an entire book or of a narrative. Instead, imperfect reading paved the way for his conception of literature as an infinite body, whose dissemination and connectivity extend to all forms of knowledge, in a manner not dissimilar to French philosopher Edgar Morin's paradigm of *la pensée complexe*, which posits that all knowledge necessarily operates in a dialogic network of ideas which superimposes rational and imaginary elements.[6] Borges understood that network of textual unfinishedness to be compounded by two subtly intertwined spheres: world and universe, broadly equivalent to our tangible and metaphysical domains. Crucially for my discussion, his engagement with Mediterranean antiquity is intrinsic to this intellectual and artistic position. In his writings, ancient Greco-Roman texts, authors, and ideas are recast in this context as ever-unfinished, imperfect and/or incomplete phenomena endlessly moving across dimensions of Borges' modernist *imaginaire*.

Indeed, the notion of a finite text is highly deceptive for Borges. Many of his famous *Ficciones*, or short stories of an essayistic kind, thematise this idea one way or another. One can cite "The Garden of Forking Paths" (1941) or "Pascal's Sphere" (1951), in which Borges implicitly represents literature as a phenomenon whose identity is never fully graspable or even knowable. In "The Immortal"

---

[4] I give the dates of publications in the original Spanish, while citing the English translations from *Collected Fictions* (*CF*) 1998, *Selected Non-Fictions* (*SNF*) 1999a, and *Selected Poems* (*SP*) 1999b.
[5] Manguel 2006, 5–14.
[6] Morin 2005, 1–10, in which the author presents the concept and its scope.

(1949), he parallels the motif of infinite literature with a bizarre biography of Homer, or an "idea" of Homer, that unfolds a labyrinthine narrative and spatio-temporal network that link the supposedly blind Homer, whoever he was, to the blind Borges himself.[7] Here, versions of the author of the *Iliad* and *Odyssey* proliferate across giddy and often multi-dimensional spaces and temporalities well beyond the poles of the archaic, classical, and modern worlds; at points in this story, one can capture fragments of Homer in dreams, mirages, or perplexing realms nearly outside of the reader's time. And, of course, there is also the case of Borges' famous "The Library of Babel" (1941). In this five-page story in Spanish, the librarians, dwelling in single hexagons (roughly equivalent to the scale of personal or national libraries), are aware of a "Total Book," a text that contains knowledge of all there is to know, within and beyond our human access. Yet, no matter how hard they try, or how many books they consult about its location and contents, the librarians recurrently fail to find it. Borges aligns this total text with "The Library," a universe representing all branches of knowledge and existing in "eternity", a concept which Borges defines as the sum of the three tenses: past, present, and future.[8] It is in this literally out-of-this-world, out-of-time Library that, in theory, one would experience the otherwise impossible idea of the complete or finished text. I say "impossible" because our human narratives necessitate a temporal design which would be of no use in comprehending Babel's insurmountable and eternal "finished-ness", and "in theory" because, as we shall see, the eternal library can also be subject to unfinishedness. All we seem to have to help us grasp the idea of Babel is the power of metaphor, a conveying medium which Borges applies with great mastery in his story about the unattainable search for the total network of literature.

At a key point of his first lecture, Piglia draws on the implications of this network in Borges' famous narrative, commenting on the striking similarities between "The Library of Babel", published by Borges in 1941, and our grasp of the World Wide Web, invented 48 years later in 1989:

---

[7] Jansen 2018, 52–74 and Porter 2004, 324–343 and 2021.
[8] See Borges *SNF* 1999, 124. For a discussion of Borges, Heraclitus and time, see Jansen 2018, 30–40 and the bibliography included there.

> This is why Borges is truly contemporary. Because we all have that feeling when we browse the web, don't we, that the web has no limits, no borders, just like Babel, in which one does not even know where points begin and end. Borges most aptly conveys *the sense of the unfinished text*: the idea that there is always something left to read, even if this is lost or unknown, and that this very part which remains unread determines what and how we actually read.
>
> "Borges, por Piglia" (22/08/2013)
> (my translation and emphasis)

It is worth pondering over these remarks, broadly in terms of Borges' imperfect reading habits outlined above, and specifically with regard to Piglia's point that, for Borges, the text's unfinishedness determines how we read and produce literature in at least three interrelated ways: 1. with the knowledge that the unfinished text circulates in a network whose spatio-temporal beginning and end points we don't know; 2. that this network includes, but often conceals, a total body of literature; and 3. that the intuition that there exists a limitless, timeless space where literature stands "complete" can bring about a tension in our philosophies of reading. Is textual finishedness, or "wholeness", whichever kind we are after (an accurate interpretation of words in a poem; the reconstruction of a lost work or fragments of it; the origins of a given source), ever realistically possible or no more than an illusion? What are we after, and why, when we pursue an impulse to complete the *labor imperfectus*, either structurally or interpretatively? And, if we accept Borges' proposition that all we have is unfinishedness, how else might we approach our reading practice and regard for the notion of human literature?

For the remainder of this essay, I want to bring these larger questions to bear as I discuss some key examples from Borges' oeuvre that disclose his far-reaching poetics of classical unfinishedness. "Far-reaching" because of the sweeping narrative scope of the theme of unfinishedness in his writings, but also for the spectacular part the Greco-Roman classics (or Borges' take on them) play in this narrative. The body of my discussion will explore inflections of unfinishedness in his engagement with the figures of Julius Caesar, Tacitus, and an unnamed poet of the *Greek Anthology*. As stated above, crucial to his vision of the classical as imperfect literature is Borges' intimate dialogue with Heraclitus of Ephesus and his river metaphor, a theme that informs his presentation of the ancient Greco-Roman tradition as an ongoing collection of movements circulating across world and universe.

2 The endless trajectories of Julius Caesar

Unfinishedness informs the very logic of Borges' disclosure of antiquity, especially when one bears in mind the permeable, kaleidoscopic, and highly encyclopaedic character of his literary system. Take his experimentations with the figure of Julius Caesar and his last words to Brutus — "et tu, Brute?" — as they appear in Shakespeare's play (1599) and later in Spanish Baroque writer Francisco de Quevedo's *Vida de Marco Bruto* (1644). The line tends to circulate as a version in deeply anachronic ways across Borges' work, and always with a sense of broad connectivity with human literature and knowledge. I will mention just two examples. First, the phrase is fleetingly recalled by a character called "Funes, the Memorious" (1962), an early-20th century Uruguayan of humble origins with a prodigious ability to memorise everything he reads, including Caesar's line, while being cognitively unable to process such data. Here, Caesar's words form part of Funes' "endless" catalogue of readings, which is so vast that it could be regarded as a "world" version of "The Total Book" of Babel. Second, versions of the line also feature frequently in obscure stories about mirrors, labyrinths, and dreams in the collection *The Maker* (1960), in what Francisco García Jurado brilliantly identifies as Borges' subterranean classicism.[9] In each case, Borges invites readers to appreciate Caesar's utterance, not as rooted in Shakespeare or Quevedo, nor even in the events that led to Caesar's assassination in Rome, but as an aesthetic event in which a classical object is subject to potentially infinite circulation and dissemination. Here, the aesthetic point rests in its effect, namely the transient character of Caesar's incessant trajectories, as well as the capacity of the classicising reference for never-ending variation. All we have is the version, a claim Borges himself makes regarding the nature of Homeric translations ("The Homeric Versions," 1932).

A case in point is "The Plot" (1981), in which Caesar's phrase speaks powerfully to the transferability of the classics and/or classically-inclined narratives, well beyond Shakespeare's Elizabethan England and Quevedo's Castillian nobility. The piece surprises the reader with an unexpected, syncretic point of contact between ancient Rome and 19th-century rural Buenos Aires, where gauchos lived:

---

[9] Garcia/Salazar Morales 2014, 111–112.

> To make his horror complete, Caesar, pressed to the foot of a statue by the impatient daggers of his friends, discovers among the blades and faces the face of Marcus Julius Brutus, his protegé, perhaps his son, and ceasing to defend himself he exclaims: 'You too, my son!' Shakespeare and Quevedo revive the pathetic cry.
> Fate enjoys repetitions, variations, symmetries. Nineteen centuries later, in the south of the province of Buenos Aires, a gaucho is attacked by other gauchos. As he falls, he recognizes the face of one of his godsons and says to him with mild reproach and slow surprise (these words must be heard, not read): '¡Pero che!' He dies, and he doesn't know that he's dying in order to repeat a scene.
>
> "The Plot" (1981, CF, 157)

"The Plot" tends to be discussed in relation to Borges' poetics of translation and (self-) repetition.[10] Yet, for me, the fortuity that is said to frame "repetitions, variations, [and] symmetries" of one same scene in markedly unconnected traditions is paradigmatic of Borges' *ad infinitum* poetics of reading the classical not as a source of originality (an idea that would come close to something "integral" or "total" in our world), but as a highly combinable linguistic utterance partaking of a network whose totality is no more than imaginable to us. For what would Caesar's line look or read like in the totality of a Babel? Such a mode of reception would be cognitively beyond our reading capabilities.

Borges does nevertheless attempt to represent this kind of totality in his experimental writings, with great mastery and vision. Take, for instance, the remarkably expansive, driven-towards-perfect-form trajectory of the dagger that kills Caesar in "In Memoriam J.F.K." (1963), a text of only 217 words in Spanish:

> This bullet is an old one.
> In 1897, it was fired at the president of Uruguay by a young man from Montevideo, Avelino Arredondo, who had spent long weeks without seeing anyone so that the world might know that he acted alone. Thirty years earlier, Lincoln had been murdered by that same ball, by the criminal or magical hand of an actor transformed by the words of Shakespeare into Marcus Brutus, Caesar's murderer. In the mid-seventeenth century, vengeance had employed it for the assassination of Sweden's Gustavus Adolphus in the midst of the public hecatomb of battle.
> In earlier times, the bullet had been other things, because Pythagorean metempsychosis is not reserved for humankind alone. It was the silken cord given to viziers in the East, the rifles and bayonets that cut down the defenders of the Alamo, the triangular blade that slit a queen's throat, the wood of the Cross and the dark nails that pierced the flesh of the Redeemer, the poison kept by the Carthaginian chief in an iron ring on his finger, the serene goblet that Socrates drank down one evening.

---

10 Manguel 2012.

> In the dawn of time it was the stone that Cain hurled at Abel, and in the future it shall be many things that we cannot even imagine today, but that will be able to put an end to men and their wondrous, fragile life.
>
> "In Memoriam, J.F.K." (1963, *CF*, 326)

Pythagoras' metempsychosis organises the entire philosophy that edifies this miniature World History. In addition to its performance in tragic drama, the bullet that kills Kennedy embodies all the weapons employed in the assassinations and suicides recorded in human history. Borges' catalogue includes the classics: the dagger that killed Caesar and the venom that assisted Socrates and Hannibal to their deaths, as well as multiple other characters at recognisable points over the centuries. Yet, the bullet's trajectory also takes the reader into Deep Time, and towards a temporality that nearly blurs the boundaries of the "before" of Cain and Abel and the "afterwards" of human time and existence. Put differently, the bullet spans a world which includes the pre- and post-human. This is a heavily abbreviated Deep History that reveals as much as it occludes the killings that have happened, will happen, might happen, and will never happen. The piece further tracks the course of a bullet that, paradoxically, is at once all bullets and no single bullet, since "all" it can be is an object in constant transmigration. The bullet thus effectively gestures towards its own condition of unfinishedness: it will never stop its trajectory of killing in the human and deep histories of our world.

3 Tacitus in eternal Babel

Borges' thematization of classical unfinishedness becomes even more substantive in the Escher-like narratives of "The Library of Babel", introduced above.[11] Take, for instance, a climactic, highly focalised passage in this story, in which the Borgesian narrator mentions Tacitus, as he attempts to catalogue the entire contents of the Eternal Library in a totalising drive which emerges as even more intense than that featured in "In Memoriam J.F.K.":

> The Library is 'total' — perfect, complete, and whole ... its bookshelves contain all ... all that is able to be expressed, in every language. All — the detailed history of the future, the autobiographies of archangels, the faithful catalogue of the Library, thousands and thousands of false catalogues, the proof of the falsity of those catalogues, the proof of the falsity of the true catalogue, the Gnostic gospel of Basilides, the commentary upon that gospel,

---

[11] Lapidot 1991, 607–615.

the commentary on the commentary on that gospel, the true story of your death, the translation of every book in every language, the interpolations of every book in all books, the treatise Bede could have written (but did not) on the mythology of the Saxon people, the lost books of Tacitus.

"The Library of Babel" (1944, *CF*, 115)

Borges' focalisation of Tacitus' lost books at the close of Babel's universal catalogue of literatures and histories is not insignificant to the student of Tacitus: it would be here where one ideally could read Tacitus "whole", since Babel includes the lost *Histories* and *Annals* of Caligula, Vespasian, Titus and Domitian, works that have been the object of much scholarly reconstruction and speculation.[12] This form of unfinishedness, however, is not without tension or paradox. For, while the stacks of Babel contain Tacitus in complete form, no human being would be able to read, let alone relate to this material in a dimension whose narratives operate outside of human temporality and modes of cognition. Babel, then, as the quintessential symbol of "la literatura completa", ultimately emerges as a deeply frustrating reality for us, if all we are after is the attainment of perfect(ed) reading. The library is "solitary", utters the Borgesian narrator at one point, suggesting that its *raison d'être* is to stand alone, untouched by our expectation that it fulfils its own core purpose, which is to offer readers "literature uncut."

Tacitus re-emerges as a highly abbreviated classical reference elsewhere in Borges' fictional pieces, most prominently in "The Garden of Forking Paths" (1941), one of Borges' most labyrinthine stories, in which the main character, called Tsun, gets on a train to the south-west of England. As Tsun looks for a seat in the empty train, he spots a young passenger "fervently" reading *The Annals* ("There was almost no one ... I walked through the cars ... I recall ... a young man fervently reading Tacitus' *Annals*", *CF* 121). Such levels of abbreviation speak powerfully about Borges' understanding of Tacitus' writings as literature that operates imperfectly between world and universe, sometimes affording a high visibility in our reading, and sometimes being eclipsed by fate and/or loss. Borges' creative response to this phenomenon is to represent and read Tacitus as the imperfect/incomplete text *par excellence*. In other words, Tacitus as a *labor imperfectus* circulates in a network that spans world and universe *without end*.

There is arguably a therapeutic dimension to this approach. It opens our reading to psychoanalytical inspection, questioning the more persistent, and

---

[12] For the history of the transmission of Tacitus, see Martin 2010, 241–252. For the fragmentary character of Tacitus' *Histories* and *Annals*, see Benario 2012, 101–122.

often reductive, modes of plotting the classics and their contested tradition through closural procedures. What drives our desire to get hold of Tacitus' *œuvre complète*? Surely, an understanding of his writings that would more fully substantiate our working hypotheses. Yet, Borges would think of this drive to completion as a fallacy, since there would always be further Tacitean connections to be revealed or reimagined in the vast, insurmountable network that Borges presents. Deferral (of interpretation, completion, *telos*) thus becomes the rhythmical logic of the network that joins the Tacitus we hold in our hands to the silent author dwelling in Babel. One can slightly adjust Piglia's remarks to apply to Borges' Tacitus: "the idea that there is always some Tacitus left to read, even if this is lost or unknown, and that this very part which remains unread determines what and how we actually read". Borges' poetics of unfinishedness thus unfolds an all-encompassing paradigm for reading the extant and lost Tacitus imperfectly, while prompting his own readers to rethink the way we read partially occluded, unknown or lost literatures and why.

4 Visions of eternal unfinishedness: Hellenic absences

While Babel works as a metaphor for the total literature that we, frustratingly, cannot ever fully recover or reconstruct, Borges does explore other Babel-like spaces in which visions of the classics complete, or a recreative version of those visions, are possible. This is the case of the allusive Elysium that is the landscape of Borges' "To a Minor Poet of the Greek Anthology", from *The Maker* (1960):

> Where now is the memory
> Of the days that were yours on earth, and wove Joy with
> Sorrow; and made a universe that was your own?
> The river of years has lost them
> From its numbered current; you are a word in an index.   5
> To others the gods gave glory that has no end:
> Inscriptions, names on coins, monuments,
> Conscientious historians;
> All that we know of you, eclipsed friend,
> Is that you heard the nightingale one evening.   10
> Among the asphodels of the Shadow, your shade, in its vanity,
> Must consider the gods ungenerous.
> But the days are a web of small troubles,
> And is there a greater blessing

Than to be the ash of which oblivion is made?	15
Above other heads the gods kindled	
The inexorable light of glory, which peers	
Into the secret parts and discovers each separate fault;	
Glory, that at last shrivels the rose it reveres;	
They were more considerate with you, brother.	20
In the rapt evening that will never become night	
You listen without end to Theocritus' nightingale.	

"To a Minor Poet of the Greek Anthology"
(1964, SP, 167)

The piece is significantly informed by Borges' poetics of classical absences, namely texts from the Greco-Roman past that have been forgotten and/or now are lost to us.[13] Within this theme, the poem draws attention to two contrasting modalities of recalling classical memory, which embed ideas of how unfinishedness operates across the physical and the imaginal. One of these relates to (hegemonic) traditions that elevate the surviving classics to long-lasting, even "never-ending" ("no end", 6) monumentality, as objects of high-impact symbolic and material value (7–8). By contrast, the other modality plots the classical according to a framework of "history from loss", through which narratives of occlusion ("eclipsed friend", 9) and forgetfulness (*passim*) accentuate the loss.[14] The latter is Borges' strategy in this poem. He innovatively appeals to the index in (his copy of?) the *Anthologia Palatina* and transforms it into a site of absence, which functions mnemotechnically as the point from which he recreates the afterlife of the minor poet, a lover of Theocritus' songs (22). Borges situates this intricate narrative in Elysium (or Oblivion, 15), a classicising landscape seemingly eternal like Babel, but also subject to a form of cyclical endlessness; the minor poet inhabits a realm in which time does not pass or, more precisely, exists indefinitely as an unchanging form ("evening ... never becomes night", 21), while he listens to Theocritus "without end" (22). Similarly, there is "no end" to the hegemonic glory attributed to the surviving classics (6; 19) within a world rhythmically organised by years (implied in 4–5). In other words, the poem presents the motif of unfinishedness as a concept marked by tension and paradox — especially when it comes to "eternal" localities — that is supposed to overcome the idea of the end. Even in eternal spaces like Elysium, literature continues to exist in a network of unfinishedness which cannot be disentangled; the ceaseless repetitions of a Groundhog Day in Elysium or Babel, if you will.

---

13 Jansen 2022, 178–203.
14 Greenwood 2023, 15–21.

A similar inflection of eternal unfinishedness can be found in a stanza from Borges' "Ars Poetica" (1960), describing the moment Odysseus casts his eyes upon Ithaca on his much-sought return. The lines roughly point to the returning hero's self-revelation in *Odyssey* Book 22, although Borges focuses on Ithaca as a symbol of poetic art. Here, Odysseus' island becomes a vision of endless eternity within the mythical landscape of the ancient Mediterranean world:

> [...]
> They tell how Ulysses, glutted with wonders,
> Wept with love to descry his Ithaca
> Humble and green. Art is that *Ithaca*
> *Of green eternity*, not of wonders.
>
> "Ars Poetica", *The Maker* (1960, *SP*, 137)

Much like the minor poet of the *Anthologia Palatina*, Odysseus finds himself removed from the heroic-world action. He now inhabits a space where certain activities, like the contemplation of the greenness of the Ithacan land, enter the universal network of Borges' unfinished classics. Borges would continue to recreate such visions of "eternal unfinishedness" in his readings of Buenos Aires and Geneva, two cities whose classical literariness he plots in his late biographical writings.[15]

5 Ever-flowing texts and readers: Borges' Heraclitus

> [Art] is also like an endless river
> That passes and remains, a mirror for one same
> Inconstant Heraclitus, who is the same
> And another, like an endless river.
>
> "Ars Poetica", *The Maker* (1960, *SP*, 137)

The last stanza of "Ars Poetica" links the question of eternal unfinishedness with my final theme: the influence of Heraclitus in Borges' poetics of reading "imperfectly"; that is, as a flowing phenomenon operating in a network with no clear beginning or end, as Piglia remarks. Borges frequently refers to Heraclitus when invoking the inexorability of change, and he repeatedly cites the natural philosopher's comparison of time to a flowing river, into which no-one can step

---

[15] Jansen 2018, 14–19.

twice because the river is constantly changing. In the lines cited above, the river of Heraclitus becomes a, if not *the* paradigm for reading literature in the imperfect — or, perhaps more to the point, reading literature as an imperfect notion. In fact, the reference to Heraclitus becomes a recurrent aphorism in Borges; he repeatedly affirms that, when it comes to our literature — including the classics — all we have, our *totality of things*, is *versions* which flow inconstantly vis-à-vis the cyclical permanence of his imaginary Babel.

In a short but telling paragraph in *Seven Nights* (1977), Borges relates these Heraclitean notions to the fluid interaction of books and readers:

> When we open [a book], when the book surrenders itself to its reader, the aesthetic event occurs. And even for the same reader the same book changes, for we change; we are the river of Heraclitus, who said that the man of yesterday is not the man of today, who will not be the man of tomorrow. We change incessantly, and each reading of a book, each rereading, each memory of that rereading, reinvents the text. The text too is the changing river of Heraclitus.
>
> *Seven Nights* ([1977]1984, 76)

Like Heraclitus' river, neither reader nor text can ever be the same in the flux of time. We have observed this idea in Borges' Julius Caesar, mediated by Shakespeare and Quevedo, whose ever-changing utterance turns out to be "an aesthetic event" stressing process over original sources. Similarly, the prospect of seeing Tacitus or the minor poet from the *Anthologia Palatina* "whole" is cyclically deferred in the eternal unfinishedness of spaces like Babel and Elysium, respectively. In these examples, Borges' sense of antiquity fundamentally — and repeatedly — adheres to Heraclitus' dictum. One could delve even further than I have here. Take, for instance, the case of Borges' Homer in "The Immortal" (1947), mentioned earlier, in which the author(s?) of the *Iliad* and *Odyssey* only exists as an entity that roams non-stop, back and forth, across real and imaginary worlds, or "Some Versions of Homer" (1932), in which the same figure becomes what readers make of him through the centuries, to the extent that it seems impossible to determine what we mean by 'Homer'.

6 Borges and the tradition of unfinishedness

There is a curious interactive map online that charts global networks of authors and their readerships.[16] One can enter just about any name, from Confucius and Dante to V.S. Naipaul and Toni Morrison, and the map will reconfigure data to reveal which other authors readers of these authors have read and liked. (The data can often disclose overlapping connections which one may not easily think of or notice when browsing titles in the library or a bookshop.) And if one clicks on any of these related authors, the network will then expand farther and farther, highlighting a system of associations that begins to resemble the universe of Babel. In the case of Borges, the network of authors, as well as their related networks, is vast, with the map showcasing the extent of his global impact, even as his authorship is linked to writers of a markedly different profile. If one converts Borges' literary map into a list, this becomes significantly long. I cite below just a few names in a random order that speak to my own curiosity and interests: Homer; Virgil; Statius; Dante; Dostoevsky; Tolstoy; Kafka; Marcel Proust; Virginia Woolf; Silvina Ocampo; Emily Dickinson; Albert Camus; Pablo Neruda; H.P. Lovecraft; St.- John Perse; Salman Rushdie; Derek Walcott; Vladimir Nabokov; Aimé Césaire; Italo Calvino; Édouard Glissant; Umberto Eco; Haruki Murakami; Don DeLillo; Ricardo Piglia; Roberto Bolaño; César Aira; Beatriz Sarlo; Alan Pauls; *et cetera*.

In my last sentence, I wrote "*et cetera*" (rather than the conventional "etc." or "and so forth") because, as I typed the list on my page, my mind began to turn to Umberto Eco and his famous *The Infinity of Lists* (2009), in which he associates Borges' interest in lists with a "poetics of everything included" and of "etcetera." In this book, produced by the Louvre Museum, Eco tracks a history of the Western art catalogue, from antiquity, through the Renaissance, to modernity. The book includes a series of "tables" that follow, for instance, images of Aphrodite/Venus, from pre-archaic and classical images all the way to iconic photographs of Monica Bellucci. It is a pity that the English edition features the word "infinity" in the title, rather than "vertigo". The title of the Italian original is *La Vertigine della Lista* (2009), which gives more precision to what Eco means about the potential effects of the list: how they can go on and on, to the point one begins to feel their *vertigine* — that is, their giddiness, even light-headedness, as we also find in Borges' catalogue in "The Library of Babel" (cited above). In that passage, though, Borges does not end with an "etc." Instead, he uses

---

[16] See https://www.literature-map.com/jorge+luis+borges [accessed on 12/08/2023].

deliberate focalisation, as well as inserting a sense of suspense: "... the lost books of Tacitus," a phrase that arguably leaves the reader of his own vertiginous catalogue in a state of shock. Back to *La Vertigine della Lista*, Eco begins with Homer's "Catalogue of Ships" in *Iliad* 2.494–759, while, also crucially, engaging with Borges' own encyclopaedism. Eco's passage is eloquent when it comes to the mind-blowing feeling one experiences in following Borges's own seemingly infinite lists:

> If anyone were to read my novels he would see that they abound with lists [...] the model list par excellence: the catalogue of ships in Homer's *Iliad*, from which this book takes its cue [...] already in Homer it seems that there is a swing between a poetics of "everything included" and a poetics of "etcetera.' While this was already clear to me, I had never set myself the task of making a meticulous record of the infinite cases in which the history of literature [...] offers examples of lists, even though Borges [...] come[s] to my mind straight away. The result of [his] hunt was prodigious, enough to make your head spin.
>
> Umberto Eco, *The Infinity of Lists* (2009, 7)

Italo Calvino (Santiago de Las Vegas, 1923–Siena 1985), another self-confessed admirer of Borges,[17] also showcases narratives that have strong points of contact with Borges' presentation of the *labor imperfectus*, vast networks, and infinite catalogues. Take, for instance, his *Invisible Cities*, published in 1972. With Marco Polo as the internal narrator, Calvino charts the imaginary geographies and complex temporalities of fifty-five urbanities, many of which echo classical names (e.g. Chloe, Eudoxia, Phyllis, Berenice, Octavia, Pyrrha, Penthesilea), and all of which allude to the city of Venice in the thirteenth century. The novel presents Venice as ultimately *imperfect* — a "multiverse" city in the making that can be found in ancient Troy and Carthage or in a city in the future somewhere off the shores of California, whose form is yet to be known:

> Marco Polo leafs through the pages [of the emperor's atlas]; he recognizes Jericho, Ur, Carthage, he points to the landing at the mouth of the Scamander where the Achaean ships waited for ten years to take the besiegers back on board, until the horse nailed together by Ulysses was dragged by windlasses through the Scaean gates. But speaking of Troy, he happened to give the city the form of Constantinople and foresee the siege which Mohammed would lay for long months until, astute as Ulysses, he had his ships drawn at night up the streams from Bosporus to the Golden Horn, skirting Pera and Galata. And from the mixture of those two cities a third emerged, which might be called San Francisco and which spans the Golden Gate and the bay with long, light bridges and sends open trams climbing its steep streets ... The atlas has these qualities: it reveals the form of cities that do not yet have a form or a name ... The catalogue of forms is endless: until every

---

17 Calvino 2009, 238.

> shape has found its city, new cities will continue to be born. When the forms exhaust their variety and come apart, the end of cities begins. In the last pages of the atlas there is an outpouring of networks without beginning or end, cities in the shape of Los Angeles ... without shape.
>
> Italo Calvino, Invisible Cities (1997, 125–26)

To be sure, Calvino's antiquity is not the same as Borges'. His concern with the classical, as outlined in his *Six Memos for the Next Millennium* (1985), is with its value and viability as a literature worth preserving (or not) in the future.[18] Yet, in "Multiplicity," the fifth essay in this collection, Calvino recognises the profound impact that the Argentine author's paradigm of unfinishedness has on his intellectual and artistic thought:

> The reasons for my fondness of Borges don't end there [i.e. in Calvino's discussion of multiplicity in Borges]. I'll try to list the most important: because every text of his contains a model of the universe or of an attribute of the universe: the infinite, the innumerable, time that is eternal or simultaneous or cyclical.
>
> Italo Calvino, "Multiplicity",
Six Memos for the Next Millennium (2016, 119)

Even in the case of writers such as César Aira (Argentina, 1949), whose career and politics emerge in sharp contrast with Borges',[19] one can trace a declension of unfinishedness that is substantially Borgesian. In an interview with the *New Yorker* in 2017, Aira looks back at his oeuvre with increasing recognition of the part that Borges plays in his thought, admitting that it can be understood as an "infinite footnote to Borges".[20] In fact, it is hard not to recall Borges in Aira's story "The Infinite". In this autobiographical narrative, two boys from the quiet town of Pringles in the south of Buenos Aires, come up with a game that consists of beating one another by listing greater and greater numbers: ("tres, cien, ciento uno, ciento uno, coma cero uno [...] cuatro millones, medio trillón..." 53). Towards the end of the story, as the boys realise that the ever-increasing figures are making the game unmanageable, they switch to the word "infinity," which they believe can overcome the problems of enumeration (for, what is larger than infinity?). Yet, this presents an even greater challenge for them, as the language of infinity turns into a "trabalenguas" (a "tongue-twister" 60). Their list also

---

18 Jansen 2023.
19 For Aira's shifting position regarding his place in the tradition of Borges in Argentina, see Geraghty 2020, 130–138. For Borges' political thought, see Salinas 2010, 299–324.
20 Graedon 2017.

recalls the vertiginous poetics of "et cetera" that Eco finds in Homer and Borges (B1 and B2 for the two boys in dialogue are my own addition to the text):

> B1–Dos infinitos.
> B2–Doscientos treinta millones de infinitos.
> B1–Siete quintillones de infinitos.
> B2–Siete billones de quintillones de infinitos.
> B1–Cien mil billones de billones de trillones de quintillones de infinitos. [...]
> B2–Infinito de infinitos.
> B1–Diez billones de infinitos de infinitos.
> B2–Ocho mil billones de trillones de cuatrillones de quintillones de infinitos de infinitos. [...]
> B1–Infinito de infinitos de infinitos de infinitos de infinitos de infinitos de infinitos de infinitos de infinitos de infinitos de infinitos de infinitos.
>
> César Aira, "El infinito", El cerebro musical
(2005, 59–60)

And so on, back and forth, in Aira's Borgesian story of *the* imperfect game *par excellence*.

7 Epilogue: we, readers, should also be imperfect

One may question, even feel frustrated by, Borges' take on antiquity and its tradition as an unfinished, imperfect, ever-changing cultural phenomenon. And one may even posit that his classical presences are no more than fleeting events that barely touch everyday reality and/or tangible concerns. There is no doubt that Borges is not a thinker like Marx or Foucault (or any other writer who delves into antiquity to advance philosophies that attempt to warn us about hidden forms of oppression and/or structures that perpetuate injustice). Borges' contribution lies elsewhere. His strategies of reading antiquity "in the imperfect", as I argue in this essay, become relevant, indeed *tangible*, if we pause momentarily to consider our impulses as readers and interpreters of the classical past, beyond the often-guarded confines of our disciplinary practices and concerns.

As we strive to obtain the fullest accounts of antiquity possible, a simple fact stands true for us: the distant past will remain mostly buried or ruined, even lost, and our findings will only ever amount to a partial haul. It remains true that no matter how many lines we manage to restore or interpolate, how much material we find under the ground or scattered amongst ruins, or what new evidence we uncover, our knowledge of that past will always be transmitted to us in parts. Unless past and present were unprecedentedly to unite in a single moment and place (and Borges has much to say about the matter),[21] responses to lacunae will probably continue to be a matter of scholarly conjecture, fragments of material culture will likely retain their fractured shape, and lost books may well remain lost. An inquisitive scholar himself, Borges understood well the thrill and frustrations of attempting to know past cultures "whole," and his writings on antiquity urge us to rethink this persistent feature in our approach. For, Borges would argue, if we were to recover that past in its entirety, we would certainly feel the pleasure of its full disclosure: but would that mean that we have quenched our desire to know — more, and more, and more? A psychoanalytical view may suggest that our insistence on seeking antiquity as a perfect form entails something of a pathology that the French term *la douleur exquise*: that bittersweet pain of realising, with certainty, that there are marked limits to our ability to obtain something complete, while simultaneously attempting to prevail over those very limits in the hope of succeeding anyway. On the one hand, the pursuit of antiquity as *douleur exquise* points to a challenging realisation: we may not be after the end product but rather the *frisson* of the quest. On the other hand, however, the thrill of the quest powerfully suggests, as Borges' philosophy does, that what we are after can perhaps be found somewhere in between: in between the experience of not knowing and getting to know, and in-between the moments and spaces in which we position ourselves to contemplate the past.

Both challenging visions of the classical as a finished form and re-conceptualising its identity as an imperfect idea, Borges subtly rewrites antiquity and its literary histories. He alerts us to the limits and frustrations that arise from a totalising drive for possession of the classical past. His response is at once abstract and tangible. Borges relocates Homer, Caesar, Tacitus, or a minor Hellenic poet between world and universe, without attempting to retell their full stories, stories that we can only partially know. He instead recalls them "imperfectly," even as that sense of imperfection is also subject to tensions, deferrals, and giddiness, as I have tried to show here. His is a twentieth-century model of cognition which, in its refusal to see antiquity in perfect form, directs our attention to our choices as readers. We don't always have to read for the whole: we can read in between, fragmentarily, accepting the partial disclosures, silences, and losses that the past presents to us, without wanting to bridge the gap between knowing and not knowing. We can read antiquity imperfectly. We can be *imperfect* readers. And that is fine too.

---

21 See n. 8.

Bibliography

Aira, César (2005), *El cerebro musical*, Buenos Aires.
Benario, Herbert (2012), "The Annals", in: Victoria Emma Pagán (ed.), *A Companion to Tacitus*, Malden MA/Oxford, 101–122.
Borges, Jorge Luis (1998), *Collected Fictions*, translated by A. Hurley, New York.
Borges, Jorge Luis (1999a), *Selected Non-Fictions*, edited by E. Weinberger, New York.
Borges, Jorge Luis (1999b), *Selected Poems*, edited by A. Coleman, New York.
Borges, Jorge Luis (2009), *Seven Nights*, New York.
Carricaburo, Norma (2011), "Los enciclopedistas y el enciclopedismo de Jorge Luis Borges", in: Magdalena Cámpora/Javien Roberto González (eds.), *Borges – Francia*, Buenos Aires, 461–473.
Calvino, Italo (1996), *Six Memos for the Next Millennium*, London.
Calvino, Italo (1997), *Invisible Cities*, London.
Calvino, Italo (2009), *Why Read the Classics?*, London.
García Jurado, Francisco/Salazar Morales, Roberto (2014), *La traducción y sus palimpsestos: Borges, Homero y Virgilio*, Madrid.
García Martin, Elena (2005), "The Dangers of Abstraction in Borges's 'The Immortal'", *Variaciones Borges* 20, 87–100.
Geraghty, Niall (2020), "Argentine Responses: César Aira and Ricardo Piglia", in: Robin Fiddian (ed.), *Jorge Luis Borges in Context*, Cambridge, 130–138.
Graedon, Alena (2017), "César Aira's Infinite Footnote to Borges", *The New Yorker*, January 17.
Greenwood, Emily (2023), "The Poetics of Loss and the Pragmatics of Failure in Thucydides' History", in: Marnie Hughes-Warrington/Daniel Woolf (eds.), *History from Loss: A Global Introduction to Histories Written from Defeat, Colonization, Exile, and Imprisonment*, London, 15–21.
Jansen, Laura (2018), *Borges' Classics: Global Encounters with the Graeco-Roman Past*, Cambridge.
Jansen, Laura (2022), "Classical Absences (1896–2017)", *Classical Receptions Journal* 14.2, 178–203.
Jansen, Laura (2023), "Lightness and the Future of Antiquity in Six Memos for the Next Millennium", *California Italian Studies* 12.2.
Lapidot, Ema (1991), "Borges y Escher: artistas contemporáneos", *Revista Iberoamericana* LVII, 155–156, 607–615.
Manguel, Alberto (1997), *A History of Reading*, London.
Manguel, Alberto (2006), *With Borges*, London.
Manguel, Alberto (2012), "Translating Borges", Biblioasis International Translations Blog, http://biblioasistranslation.blogspot.com/2012/04/alberto-manguel-translating-borges.html [accessed on 12/08/2023].
Martin, Ronald (2010), "From Manuscript to Print", in: Anthony John Woodman (ed.), *The Cambridge Companion to Tacitus*, Cambridge, 241–252.
Morin, Edgar (2005), *Introduction à la pensée complexe*, Paris.
Piglia, Ricardo (2013), "Clase 3: "La biblioteca y el lector en Borges", *Borges por Piglia*, www.tvpublica.com.ar/programa/borges-por-piglia [accessed on 12/08/2023].
Porter, James (2004), "Homer: The History of an Idea", in: Robert Fowler (ed.), *The Cambridge Companion to Homer*, Cambridge, 324–343.

Porter, James (2021), *Homer: The Very Idea*, Chicago.
Salinas, Alejandra (2010), "Political Philosophy in Borges: Fallibility, Liberal Anarchism, and Civic Ethics", *The Review of Politics* 72.2, 299–324.

Part III: **Constitutive Unfinishedness**

Rosa Rita Marchese
Sed redeo ad formulam (*Off.* 3.20): Completeness and Imperfection in Cicero's *De officiis*

Abstract: In this paper I try to show that in Cicero's *De officiis* the tension between completeness and incompleteness, perfection and imperfection is constitutive. As we shall see, imperfection is set as the epistemological horizon of the treatise, because to deal with *officia* is precisely to make a choice of a theoretical nature that challenges the concept of completeness at its roots. This epistemological choice has consequences in terms of the morphology of the work. The intention to achieve definitional exactitude is structurally disregarded, frustrated by contents that tend, conversely, towards dilution and dispersion. In this perspective, the third book of the *De officiis*, traditionally considered the most "imperfect", fully expresses the conflict between the aspiration to complete a void, to find a *formula* that can be readily used, and the staying in the unfinished.

> There is the type of work that, in the attempt to contain everything possible, does not manage to take on a form, to create outlines for itself, and so remains incomplete by its very nature.
>
> Italo Calvino, *Six memos for the next millennium*, 1988

1 Beyond the editorial question

Cicero's *De officiis* is not an incomplete work, mutilated or wounded by the events of its transmission. On the contrary, it has enjoyed an unbroken and extensive direct tradition, as well as an indirect tradition deriving from its early circulation as a school text, e.g. through Nonius' *Doctrinal compendium* (*De compendiosa doctrina*).[1] But as editors and scholars of the *De officiis* are well

---

I wish to thank Marco Formisano, Jacqueline Fabre-Serris and Stavros Frangoulidis for their *labor perfectus* as organizers of the Conference and editors of this book. I am deeply grateful to Craig Williams for improving, with his suggestions, the English version of this paper.

1 Fedeli 1974, 133–134.

aware, the convergence of a large number of codices and a process of ancient contamination has resulted in a state of the text that is nonetheless problematic.[2] And despite the programmatic statements of Cicero, who claims for himself a professional competence in the areas of clarity and precision ("And if, when I have devoted the best part of my life to oratory, I then claim for myself what is proper to an orator, that I speak suitably, clearly and elegantly, I seem to have some right to lay such a claim" *Off.* 1.2),[3] the work presents a design that escapes from its frame, to make a first analogy to the field of the figurative arts, which, as we shall see, will have wide importance in Cicero's treatise.

One certain fact, then, is that the text of the *De officiis* appears layered, dense, and complex; and given that, compared with the common standards of Latin authors, a singularly short space of time elapsed between the months in which Cicero testifies to working on the treatise and his death,[4] it is easy to conclude that the *De officiis* was not the subject of a final revision by its author. According to ancient conventions, therefore, it is an unfinished text.[5] Indeed, Cicero's last work appears to be marked by repetition, by the echoing of many passages, entire periods, and single words that may present themselves to a sequential reading as laborious. Many of these widespread redundancies have been interpreted as author variants, the outcome of Cicero's troubled writing process and multiple redactions that, in the absence of a final revision, entered the textual tradition as the inexhaustible activity of scribes continued.[6] On the other hand, it is precisely a consideration of scribal activity that has given rise to the contrary view, namely that the marginal annotations that entered the text did not come from Cicero's hand, but from copyists eager to clarify and explain obscure points.[7] The editorial non-finiteness of *De officiis* has also generated interpretations aimed at identifying explanations for its differences from the author's stylistic habits in other philosophical and rhetorical texts. For example,

---

2 On these topics, see Fedeli 2000, a review of Winterbottom's critical edition, but also Fedeli 1965a and 1973.
3 *Quod est oratoris proprium, apte distincte ornate dicere, quoniam in eo studio aetatem consumpsi, si id mihi adsumo, videor id meo iure quodam modo vindicare.* The translation of the *De officiis* is, here and throughout, by Margaret Atkins, in Griffin/Atkins 2006[12].
4 Testard 1965, 7–21; Dorandi 2007, 83–101; Pecere 2010, 101–192.
5 So Atzert 1971[5], v; Winterbottom 1994, xii.
6 In general terms, see Dorandi 2007, 123–139.
7 Fedeli 1973, 387; 2000, 593–599; Winterbottom 1994, xi–xii. Brüser 1949 and Thomas 1971 are still valuable resources for scholars.

the speed of execution,[8] the magnitude of the stakes (primarily, the need to give space to the intergenerational communication of values in crisis),[9] the simultaneous engagement on several levels,[10] the density of the arguments combined with a failure to control complex philosophical issues[11] are just some of the explanations, not all benevolent,[12] that have been offered to explain a difficult text.[13]

The reading I present here invites us instead to go beyond the editorial question.[14] I will try to show that (in)completeness and (im)perfection are thematised within the *De officiis*, that the tension between completeness and incompleteness, perfection and imperfection is constitutive and conditions its entire communicative programme, at "the content and relationship levels of communication".[15] Taking this perspective can perhaps help illuminate the ambivalences that have conditioned the interpretation of this text over time.[16] As we shall see, imperfection is set as the epistemological horizon of the treatise, because to deal with "duties" (*officia*), to take them on as a philosophical object, is precisely to make a choice of a theoretical nature that challenges the concept of completeness at its roots, and comes to terms with imperfection. This epistemological choice has consequences in terms of the morphology of the work. The intention to achieve definitional exactitude, conceptual and expressive clarity, declared in 1.2, is structurally disregarded, frustrated by contents that tend, conversely, towards dilution and dispersion. We witness the loss of

---

8 So Testard 1965, and later, among others, Narducci 1989, 111. Bringmann 1971 is still useful on the works of Cicero's maturity.
9 Gabba 1979; Picone 2019², xxix–xxxvi.
10 Regarding the coeval attack against Antony in the *Philippics*, see van der Blom 2003; Stone 2008; Marchese 2014, 88–98.
11 Testard 1965, 25–49, who also supports the "caractère improvisé de cet ouvrage" (14).
12 The history of malevolent judgements on Cicero is well outlined in Narducci 2004, 241–388, and summarised in Narducci 2005, 3–8. See also Kumaniecki 1972, 7–25; more recently Altman 2015; Begemann 2015.
13 Testard 1965, 96; Narducci 1989, 111–112.
14 For a more in-depth look at Cicero's editorial practices, I refer to Gurd 2007; more generally see Gurd 2012, in which a very interesting position is expressed regarding the ways in which Cicero, also in the editorial sphere, valorises the non-finite: "Because what was not yet perfect could be discussed and therefore serve as the site of communal dialogue" (5; but see the whole of chapter 3 of the book).
15 "Any communication implies a commitment and thereby defines the relationship", Watzlawick/Helmick Beavin/Jackson 2011 (1967), 32.
16 Long 1995, 213; Appiah 1997; 2006; Rigotti 2019, 61–71; Marchese 2019; Nussbaum 2019 (2020, 17–20).

form (*forma*), suspended between the author's quest for precision and the indeterminacy in which the reader remains a prisoner. In this perspective, the third book of the *De officiis*, traditionally considered the most "imperfect" in its fragmented concepts and its casuistry,[17] fully expresses the profound tension between the aspiration to complete a void, to find a "rule" (*formula*) that can be readily applied, and the staying in the unfinished.

2 Imperfection as a theme: the epistemological choice of the *De officiis*

To consider how imperfection presents itself as the epistemological horizon of the treatise, it will be useful to read *Off.* 1.7, where Cicero proposes his definition of what *officium* is, while also defining the boundaries and conceptual features of the subject of the treatise:

> *Omnis de officio duplex est quaestio. Unum genus est quod pertinet ad finem bonorum, alterum quod positum est in praeceptis, quibus in omnes partes usus vitae conformari possit. Superioris generis huiusmodi sunt exempla, omniane officia perfecta sint, num quod officium aliud alio maius sit, et quae sunt generis eiusdem. Quorum autem officiorum praecepta traduntur, ea quamquam pertinent ad finem bonorum, tamen minus id apparet, quia magis ad institutionem vitae communis spectare videntur; de quibus est nobis his libris explicandum.*

> The whole debate about duty is twofold. One kind of question relates to the end of good things; the other depends upon advice by which one ought to be fortified for all areas of life. The following are examples of the former: are all duties 'complete'? Is one duty more important than another? And other questions of that type. The duties for which advice has been offered do indeed relate to the end of the good things, but here it is less obvious, because they appear rather to have in view instruction for a life that is shared. It is these that I must expound in these books.

These books do not deal with "complete duties" (*officia perfecta*), which contribute to the attainment of the highest good, but with those *officia* which can be taught through a series of prescriptive indications, and which, while aiming at the highest good, have less of an appearance of doing so, from the point of view of theoretical structure, because, as Cicero makes clear, their purpose is to

---

[17] Mirroring Cicero's inability to defuse the illusory nature of appearances according to Lotito 1981, 124. About *officia* and casuistry, also in the third book of the *De officiis*, see Irwin 2014.

provide foundations for the life of all.[18] The *De officiis* focuses on the variety that characterises human sociality and the institutions that govern it, a variety that is structurally open and imperfect, as we shall see in a moment. In 1.8 there appears a more precise division (*divisio*), one which places *perfectum officium* beyond the perimeter of the treatise, which will instead focus on "shared duty" (*commune officium*), that is, the one which provides rules for inter-subjective exchange and interaction:

> Atque etiam alia divisio est officii. Nam et medium quoddam officium dicitur et perfectum. Perfectum officium rectum, opinor, vocemus, quoniam Graeci κατόρθωμα, hoc autem commune officium ‹καθῆκον› vocant. Atque ea sic definiunt, ut rectum quod sit, id officium perfectum esse definiant; medium autem officium id esse dicunt quod cur factum sit ratio probabilis reddi possit.

> There is also another division to be made concerning duty. For a duty can be called either 'middle' or 'complete'. 'Complete' duty we may, I think, label 'right' as the Greeks call it *katorthoma*; while the duty that is shared they call *kathekon*. They give their definitions in such a way as to define complete duty as what is right; while middle duty, they say, is that for which a persuasive reason can be given as to why it has been done.

In this sense, as an action embedded in the social sphere, the *officium* Cicero will discuss falls within the domain of the "middle" (*medium*), that which lies between two extremes. What remains outside this horizon? Certainly spontaneous and improvised action, but also perfect action: on a conceptual level, the moral action on which Cicero's reflection will develop in the *De officiis* lies, literally, "on this side" of perfection.[19] A very clear choice is expressed here, on the epistemological level.

Cicero's work therefore starts again from the point where the exposition entrusted to Cato the Younger in the third book of the *De finibus* ended, in which he reiterated precisely the epistemological boundaries pertaining to *officia*: "actions to do" that are configured as consistent with the pursuit of "honourable conduct" (*honestum*), even though they are themselves neutral actions, i.e. neither good nor contrary to good in themselves.[20] These *officia media* are to be connected to the *principia naturae*, i.e. natural motives that are not themselves the good, a quality which intervenes only later. Such actions may in fact become perfect, but they are not yet so. Human beings make calculations regarding

---

18 In more general terms, Moreau 1983.
19 Griffin 2011, 313–314.
20 About Stoic moral reflection in the *De finibus* I refer to Bénatouïl 2016; Ioppolo 2016 for Cicero's critique in the fourth book of the work.

these actions, based on the criterion of the preservation of their own nature, a calculation "common" to all men, offering themselves as initial movements in a process that can lead to the realisation of the true good, which arises later: *consequens enim est et post oritur* ("is an outgrowth of these, a later development", *Fin.* 3.22).

Consistent with these assumptions, therefore, the *De officiis* contains concrete indications for the everyday conduct of any individual:

> *Nulla enim vitae pars neque publicis neque privatis neque forensibus neque domesticis in rebus, neque si tecum agas quid neque si cum altero contrahas, vacare officio potest, in eoque et colendo sita vitae est honestas omnis et neglegendo turpitudo.*
>
> *Off.* 1.4

> For no part of life, neither public affairs not private, neither in the forum nor at home, neither when acting on your own nor in dealings with another, can be free from duty. Everything that is honourable in a life depends upon its cultivation, and everything dishonourable upon its neglect.

In the *officia media* restored as subjects for a fully moral reflection, Cicero identifies the most appropriate tools for entering the warmth and variety of common life, because no part of life can be without reference to the action "that must be done". Average actions thus can be fully enhanced in an existential horizon that takes human imperfection into account:

> *Quoniam autem vivitur non cum perfectis hominibus planeque sapientibus, sed cum iis, in quibus praeclare agitur si sunt simulacra virtutis, etiam hoc intellegendum puto, neminem omnino esse neglegendum, in quo aliqua significatio virtutis appareat [...].*
>
> *Off.* 1.46

> Since we do not live with men who are perfect and clearly wise, but with those who are doing splendidly if they have in them mere images of virtue, I think that we must understand this too: no one should be wholly neglected if any indication of virtue appears in him [...].

In 1.46 Cicero describes sociality as that which arises between individuals who are not *perfecti*. Let us remember that it is not the perfection of the act performed in itself that is at the centre of the *De officiis*, but the average or neutral action, which everyone can find themselves choosing to perform insofar as it lies at the crossroads of interactions between people in a shared life (*commune*), and this can be reasonably accounted for, within the limits of the calculations that are within everyone's reach. In the *De officiis*, therefore, Cicero consciously undertakes the task of directing the imperfect conduct of ordinary people into learnable, teachable, verifiable paths. In this sense, therefore, the subject matter is intrinsically, epistemologically, imperfection, that is, action which is not yet *perfecta*, not yet fully completed, but which needs to be framed in negotiations, in mediations and in the exercise of self-control. This is a field in itself variable, changeable, and subject to dispersion, which not by chance jeopardises conceptual exactitude and terminological precision in the description of the system of the four virtues from the exercise of which the *honestum* springs.

3 The morphology of text: the influence of content on form

The most conspicuous consequence of the choice of the *commune*, the *medium*, and the *non perfectum* as epistemological content can be found in the imperfect/unfinished morphology of the text itself. The treatment of the fourth virtue,[21] "seemliness" (*decorum*), offers us an exemplary case study. Let us start with the definition:

> *Sequitur ut de una reliqua parte honestatis dicendum sit, in qua verecundia et quasi quidam ornatus vitae, temperantia et modestia omnisque sedatio perturbationum animi et rerum modus cernitur. Hoc loco continetur id, quod dici Latine decorum potest, Graece enim* πρέπον *dicitur* [*decorum*].
>
> Off. 1.93

> Next we must discuss the one remaining element of honourableness. Under this appear a sense of shame and what one might call the ordered beauty of a life, restraint and modesty, a calming of all the agitations of the spirit, and due measure in all things. Under this heading is included what in Latin may be called *decorum* (seemliness); the Greek for it is *prepon*.

The last part of *honestas* is described in 1.93 with six different expressions: "sense of shame", "beauty of a life", "restraint", "modesty", "calming of all the agitations", "measure" (*verecundia, quasi quidam ornatus vitae, temperantia, modestia, sedatio perturbationum, rerum modus*), words or periphrases which suggest the effort and fatigue of making a conceptual approximation to the same object, one which would seem to be patently obvious. The *decorum* "can be seen" (*cernitur*), it can be separated by the gaze from its background, yet it resists unambiguous and clear-cut naming. Faced with the multiple implications of *decorum*, which seems to be a value in itself but also a regulator of the

---

21 Narducci 1989, 141–150; Schofield 2012.

other virtues,[22] terminological exactitude shatters, it is unable to separate the concepts it expresses. Indeed, Cicero recognises that the *forma* of *decorum* is arrived at by intuition and not by explanation, since it cannot be separated from the *forma* of *honestum*[23] ("[...] for what is seemly is honourable, and what is honourable is seemly. It is easier to grasp than to explain what the difference is between 'honourable' and 'seemly'", 1.94).[24] Abstraction, which has led to the display of a singular, albeit dispersive, mastery of terminology, must account for the variety of *res* it describes. Hence, exactitude conspires against clarity, causing indeterminacy. To illuminate for the reader the *forma* of the *decorum*, the virtuosic game of definitions is not enough, and a simile is immediately introduced:

> *Ut venustas et pulchritudo corporis secerni non potest a valetudine, sic hoc de quo loquimur decorum totum illud quidem est cum virtute confusum, sed mente et cogitatione distinguitur. 96. Est autem eius descriptio duplex; nam et generale quoddam decorum intellegimus, quod in omni honestate versatur, et aliud huic subiectum, quod pertinet ad singulas partes honestatis.*
>
> *Off.* 1.95–96

> Just as bodily loveliness and beauty cannot be separated from healthiness, similarly the seemliness that we are discussing is indeed completely blended with virtue, but is distinguished by thought and reflection. 96. But furthermore this has two senses: first, we understand a seemliness of a general kind, involved with honourable behaviour as a whole, and secondly, something subordinate to this, which relates to an individual element of what is honourable.

There are ultimately two ways to conceptualise *decorum*: firstly, through a process of abstraction; then through its framing in terms of things, and thus bringing attention back to the *officia* pertinent to each individual virtue. The exemplarity of the fourth virtue as a case study for interpreting the influence of imperfect content on imperfect expressive form in the *De officiis* could not appear clearer: the effort at precision and classification finds its limit in the epistemological imperfection of the object represented. The non-finiteness, the structural incompleteness of the *officia* compel a duplicity, both expressive and argumentative, that militates against the brilliance of the writing. In the final analysis, conceptual clarity is achieved not by reasoning, nor the dusty classification of

---

[22] Marchese 2016, 51–80; 2019, 62–64.
[23] We can see here, according to Lotito 1981, "lo stesso imbarazzo ciceroniano nel definirne la specificità rispetto ad altri valori".
[24] *Nam et quod decet honestum est et quod honestum est decet. Qualis autem differentia sit honesti et decori, facilius intellegi quam explanari potest.*

vocabulary, but by an image, the simile with the human body in which beauty and good health are seen together and can only be distinguished in the abstract. This is an effective way of intuiting the dual function of *decorum*: on the one hand "conceptual beauty", and on the other the basis of every other virtuous action which is present in the accurate execution of all the *officia* already discussed. Cicero first attempts to restore this duplicity by drawing on his linguistic creativity, imprinting a strong terminological pressure on the concept, and then arriving at a simplification that resolves the *decorum* into the *honestum*. We thus detect a profound tension between the terminological vacuum that Cicero tries to fill by coining numerous definitions (*definitiones*), and a structurally unattainable exactness in the description of the imperfect actions of which human existence is composed. In the field opened by this tension, the impossible quest for *exactitude*[25] that permeates the *De officiis* is consummated.

4 In search of a *formula*: the third book, perfect closure of a treatise without conclusion

This consideration of *decorum* has allowed us to identify an unresolved tension between the search for definition and its failure, between completeness and incompleteness, between the finite and the unfinished, which belongs to the deep structure of this text, in relation to a virtue, specifically the fourth, which more than any other permeates *officia*, that is, the kind of "imperfect" daily conduct which can direct human beings from the natural propensity towards goodness to the authentic realisation of the *honestum*. This subterranean impulse emerges to the surface at a specific moment in the text,[26] in the third book where Cicero explicitly declares that he seeks to complete the unfinished treatment by Panaetius:[27]

> *Panaetius igitur, qui sine controversia de officiis accuratissime disputavit quemque nos correctione quadam adhibita potissimum secuti sumus, tribus generibus propositis in quibus deliberare homines et consultare de officio solerent, uno cum dubitarent honestumne id esset de quo ageretur an turpe, altero utilene esset an inutile, tertio, si id, quod speciem haberet*

---

25 The notion explored by Calvino 1988, 55–80.
26 Dyck 1996, 488 reveals all the difficulties of the *divisio*.
27 While claiming to proceed without the support of external sources (*Hanc igitur partem relictam explebimus nullis adminiculis*, *Off*. 3.34): "The major problem posed by Book 3 is the evaluation of this unique claim", Dyck 1996, 483.

honesti, pugnaret cum eo, quod utile videretur, quomodo ea discerni oporteret, de duobus generibus primis tribus libris explicavit, de tertio autem genere deinceps se scripsit dicturum nec exsolvit id quod promiserat. 8. Quod eo magis miror, quia scriptum a discipulo eius Posidonio est, triginta annis vixisse Panaetium posteaquam illos libros edidisset.

Off. 3.7–8

Now Panaetius indisputably discussed the question of duties with extreme precision, and I have followed him in particular, though applying some amendments. He proposed three headings under which men are accustomed to deliberate upon and discuss the matter of duties: the first, when they doubt whether the course in question is honourable or dishonourable: the second, whether it is beneficial or harmful; and the third, if that which has the appearance of honourableness conflicts with that which seems beneficial, how one should decide between them. He gave an exposition of two of these topics in his first three books; but though he wrote that he was going to discuss the third in its turn, he did not, however, fulfil his promise. 8. I am all the more surprised by this because his pupil Posidonius wrote that Panaetius lived for thirty years after he had produced those books.

The threefold *divisio* remained unfinished; Panaetius did not find the time in the thirty years that followed the publication of his treatise on the καθῆκον (the "common duty") to return to the subject; nor did Posidonius, who limited himself to cursory allusions to a field that he recognised as the most deserving of attention in the whole range of philosophy.[28] In the concluding book of *De officiis*, then, a central impulse towards the constitution of the treatise is projected on the text's surface: the need to complete what is missing, to give full completion to a matter perceived as conceptually important but still in need of consideration and investigation. Once again, the tension between this profound, deep-rooted movement toward completion/accomplishment, and the marked stylistic and formal imperfection of which the text bears the signs, offers itself as an attractive hermeneutic option, a decisive line of force to be reckoned with.[29]

---

28 Griffin/Atkins 2006[12], xxv; Dyck 1996, 23–24 discusses Panaetius' incompleteness relying on Striker 1991, 47.
29 I refer to the contributions in Papini *et al.* 2019, starting with Papini 2019b, with a detailed bibliography on the subject.

4.1 Completing the unfinished: Apelles' perfection and Panaetius' incompleteness

The goal of completing Panaetius is an operation which has given rise to harsh evaluations of Cicero.[30] Although he appears quite aware of the risks of this undertaking, he does not shy away from taking it on as indispensable, not being satisfied with a review of authoritative opinions. Why indeed should the treatment promised by Panaetius, but not completed, remain unfinished?

> Nam qui e divisione tripertita duas partes absolverit, huic necesse est restare tertiam. Praeterea in extremo libro tertio de hac parte pollicetur se deinceps esse dicturum. 10. Accedit eodem testis locuples Posidonius, qui etiam scribit in quadam epistula P. Rutilium Rufum dicere solere, qui Panaetium audierat, ut nemo pictor esset inventus qui in Coa Venere eam partem quam Apelles inchoatam reliquisset absolveret (oris enim pulchritudo reliqui corporis imitandi spem auferebat), sic ea, quae Panaetius praetermisisset [et non perfecisset] propter eorum quae perfecisset praestantiam neminem persecutum.
>
> Off. 3.9–10

> For if someone has completed two parts of a work divided into three, then necessarily the third remains to be done. Besides, in his third and final book he promises that he will go on to speak of this part in its turn. 10. Posidonius comes forward as a reliable witness to the same point; for he also wrote, in a letter, that Publius Rutilius Rufus, who was a pupil of Panaetius, was accustomed to say that just as no painter could be found who would complete the part of 'Venus of Cos' that Apelles had only begun, and then left (for the beauty of the face dispelled any hope of representing the rest of the body) so no one had attempted the part that Panaetius had overlooked, and not finished, because of the excellence of the part that he finished.

In the opinion of Rutilius Rufus, consul in 105 BCE and also an *auditor* of Panaetius, it was *praestantia*, i.e. conceptual fullness or superiority that discouraged anyone else from *persequi*, from continuing and completing what the philosopher had left out. It was the formal perfection of the parts composed by Panaetius that acted as a deterrent. In this sense, to reinforce his argument, Rutilius had compared[31] Panaetius' unfinished work to the painting of Venus of Cos that Apelles had left unfinished; no painter had dared to complete (*absolveret*)

---

30 In general, on the relationship with Panaetius, see at least Labowsky 1934; Pohlenz 1934 (1971); 1955 (1967). More recently Lefèvre 2001; see also Griffin 2011, 321 f.
31 On the deep, ancient interferences between literature and the visual arts, see Berndt 2014; on the non-finite between art and literature Lulli 2019, 237–238.

Apelles' work by painting a body which could attain the perfection of her face.[32] Similarly, according to the illustrious Roman politician, no one could have brought to full completion (*perficere*) Panaetius' work without at the same time showing his own inferiority. Is the simile introduced by Rutilius Rufus, who seems to superimpose the competitive pupil/master model on the aesthetic model of pictorial perfection, legitimate?

Later, Pliny would explain how the fame that accompanied Apelles' unfinished Venus depended precisely on the conditions that left it unfinished:[33]

> *Illud vero perquam rarum ac memoria dignum est, suprema opera artificum inperfectasque tabulas, sicut Irim Aristidis, Tyndaridas Nicomachi, Mediam Timomachi et quam diximus Venerem Apellis, in maiore admiratione esse quam perfecta, quippe in iis liniamenta reliqua ipsaeque cogitationes artificum spectantur, atque in lenocinio commendationis dolor est manus, cum id ageret, exstinctae.*
>
> HN 35.145

> It is also a very unusual and memorable fact that the last works of artists and their unfinished pictures such as the Iris of Aristides, the Tyndareus' Children of Nicomachus, the Medea of Timomachus and the Aphrodite of Apelles which we have mentioned, are more admired than those which they finished, because in them are seen the preliminary drawings left visible and the artists' actual thoughts, and in the midst of approval's beguilement we feel regret that the artist's hand while engaged in the work was removed by death. (Translated by H. Rackham)

Apelles' painting, like the three other works by well-known painters mentioned here, had been interrupted due to the artist's death, and it was therefore presented as the aesthetic and emotional bearer "of the final touch", we might say, of the author. This fact, says Pliny, makes the unfinished works of painters perfect "in the midst of approval's beguilement" (*in lenocinio commendationis*), in the judgement of the public seduced by the detection, in the work of farewell, of the culminating moment of their art. What determined the renown of Apelles'

---

32 The use of Apelles' art, his Venus and his aesthetic reflections, to think about (in)completeness and (im)perfection also returns elsewhere in Cicero's writing: *Fam.* 1.9.15, where the Venus of Cos is compared to the incompleteness of the political rescue action against it; *Att.* 2.21.4 (the artist's bitterness at the deformed work; but could refer to the Venus "rising from the sea"); *Or.* 73 (the difficulty of painters in identifying what is sufficient to define a work); *Brut.* 71 (on the artistic perfection of Apelles, Aetius, Nicomachus and Protogenes). See Papini 2019a, 5–6.

33 Papini 2017 on the imperfect/incomplete in Pliny the Elder, particularly in the prefatory epistle. See also Faedo 2019, 165: "Incompiuto e incompleto sono condizioni distinte che rimandano a un intero da cui si differenziano per l'origine [...]. Il non compimento di un'opera dipende strettamente dall'autore e dalle sue vicende; l'incompletezza è invece determinata dalle vicende dell'opera stessa in precedenza considerata finita".

last Venus was precisely the incompleteness that consecrated the extreme expressive point of arrival of the artist caught in death, and in this sense, although unfinished, the work could be considered perfect: the last will manifested and expressed by the artist could not be replaced. This fact had prevented the completion of the work, but its surviving part represented perfection in common judgement, all the more so since in this painting Apelles had manifested his intention to surpass himself, i.e. to compete with his other Venus, known as "rising from the sea" (*anadyomene*). A few chapters earlier (35.92) Pliny had specified the details of this peculiar condition of Apelles' last painting ("Apelles had also begun on another Aphrodite at Cos, which was to surpass even his famous earlier one; but death grudged him the work when only partly finished, nor could anybody be found to carry on the task, in conformity with the outlines of the sketches prepared", trans. by H. Rackham).[34]

Pliny's considerations now allow us to return to Cicero's text.[35] Was the similarity established by Rutilius between Apelles' Venus and Panaetius' incomplete work persuasive to Cicero himself? Evidently not. He explicitly declared his astonishment that, even though Panaetius lived for thirty more years after the publication of the books Περί τοῦ καθήκοντος ("On duties"), he had not kept his promise. Rutilius Rufus has therefore inappropriately superimposed the competitive master/pupil model on that of the perfection of unfinished works of painters, because, in the case of the philosopher, it was not the formal perfection "of the final touch" that could be a deterrent to its completion. Unknown reasons, and not the end of his life, prevented Panaetius from dealing with that point. Cicero thus appears entirely justified in taking on the task of "completing the unfinished", particularly in the third book of the *De officiis*, which thus assumes a doubly conclusive status: with respect to the *De officiis* itself and with respect to Panaetius' project. With what results?

4.2 The need for a *formula*

Meanwhile, the reader's attention is shifted back to the subject matter, in order to reiterate the epistemological framework of the *De officiis*. Panaetius intended to identify a criterion for selecting the correct conduct in the case of a conflict

---

34 *Apelles inchoaverat et aliam Venerem Coi, superaturus etiam illam suam priorem. Invidit mors peracta parte, nec qui succederet operi ad praescripta liniamenta inventus est.* On this text Papini 2019b, xiv; Faedo 2019, 165.
35 Also debated in Papini 2017, 46–47.

between *utile* and *honestum*; according to Cicero, he was not wrong in doing so (*de iudicio Panaetii dubitari non potest*, "one can, therefore, have no doubt about Panaetius' decision", 3.11). The Stoics, following Socratic teaching, held that *utilitas* and *honestas*, i.e. utility and morally honourable behaviour, are by nature one and the same thing, and thus not separable; hence, the realisation of the highest good is living conformably to nature (*convenienter naturae vivere*, 3.13). But when it comes to discussing *officia*, one must turn one's gaze away from the behaviour of the *sapiens* to the wide range of *non sapientes*, i.e. those in an epistemologically and ethically imperfect condition:

> *Atque illud quidem honestum quod proprie vereque dicitur, id in sapientibus est solis neque a virtute divelli umquam potest. In iis autem, in quibus sapientia perfecta non est, ipsum illud quidem perfectum honestum nullo modo, similitudines honesti esse possunt.*
>
> *Off.* 3.13

> And what is more, the honourableness that is properly and truly so called is found in wise men only, and can never be severed from virtue. In those whose wisdom is not complete, this honourableness, complete as it is, cannot exist at all; however, semblances of the honourable can exist.

All of them, Cicero has already made clear, calculate the *officia communia* and *media*, and for them the path to goodness progresses *per similitudines*: ordinary human beings see similarities between certain actions they can perform and the highest good towards which they aim, but which they do not yet possess. The *De officiis* is intended to provide rules for "middle" actions, as the Stoics call them:

> *Haec enim officia, de quibus his libris disputamus, media Stoici appellant; ea communia sunt et late patent, quae et ingenii bonitate multi adsequuntur et progressione discendi. Illud autem officium quod rectum idem appellant perfectum atque absolutum est et, ut idem dicunt, omnes numeros habet, nec praeter sapientem cadere in quemquam potest. 15. Cum autem aliquid actum est, in quo media officia compareant, id cumulate videtur esse perfectum, propterea quod vulgus quid absit a perfecto, non fere intellegit; quatenus autem intellegit, nihil putat praetermissum. Quod idem in poematis, in picturis usu venit in aliisque compluribus, ut delectentur imperiti laudentque ea quae laudanda non sint, ob eam, credo, causam, quod insit in his aliquid probi quod capiat ignaros, qui idem quid in unaquaque re vitii sit nequeant iudicare. Itaque cum sunt docti a peritis, desistunt facile sententia.*
>
> *Off.* 3.14–15

> The duties that I discuss in these books are those that the Stoics call 'middle'. They are shared, and widely accessible. Many achieve them by the goodness of their intellectual talent, and by their progress in learning. But the duty that the same men call 'right' is complete and unconditional and, as they say, 'fulfils all the numbers'; and it cannot belong to anyone except the wise man. 15. However, when some action is performed where

middle duties are in evidence, it is seen abundantly 'complete', that is because ordinary people cannot really understand how it falls short of being complete. In so far as they do understand it, they think that nothing has been overlooked. The same thing tends to happened with poems, pictures and many other things, by which inexperienced people are delighted, praising them when they ought not to be praised; the reason, as I believe, is that there is some worth in them that attracts the ignorant, but they are unable to judge what faults each may have. Therefore, when they are taught by experienced people, they readily abandon their view.

When such *officia* come into play, the actions "seem" complete, because ordinary people are short-sighted and to that extent think nothing is missing. The analogy with the artistic assessments of those without specific skills is very effective. Ordinary people believe that there is always something good in a work they observe, enough to make it, in their eyes, free of shortcomings. But when they have received a relevant education, which makes them competent with respect to the forms they observe, they realise that what they thought was good and perfect, only partially makes sense, and that previously, as uneducated people (*ignari*), they were unable to identify what was really missing in order for the work to be complete. The enjoyment of artworks is once again an effective paradigm for exploring the complexity of the theme addressed by Cicero. Art is able to strike the imagination and interest of all, but the ability to appreciate its true value belongs only to those who possess a technical education. The same principle applies to moral conduct, and explains the difference between the perfect action of the wise and the average or imperfect action of ordinary people. From the point of view adopted here, however, the distinction does not operate as a ranking of merits: there is much to be valued even among "imperfect" behaviours, and *officia* as average actions allow for the expression and manifestation of positive talents, and of those principles naturally aimed at the good with which every human being is endowed. Among those cited by Cicero as expressing this propensity, some were revered names from the history of the Roman Republic, such as Gaius Fabricius Luscinius, an example of rectitude in warfare and in negotiations with Pyrrhus, or public men whose prudence earned them the appellation *sapientes*, such as Marcus Porcius Cato and Gaius Laelius (3.16: "Not even Marcus Cato and Gaius Laelius were in fact wise, although they were called and considered wise, nor the famous seven. Rather, because of their repeated practice of middle duties, they exhibited a kind of likeness to and appearance of wise men").[36] Cicero emphasises

---

36 *Nemo enim horum sic sapiens ut sapientem volumus intellegi, nec ii qui sapientes habiti et nominati, M. Cato et C. Laelius, sapientes fuerunt, ne illi quidem septem, sed ex mediorum officiorum frequentia similitudinem quandam gerebant speciemque sapientium.*

that such recognition is proof that there is a sphere of "common" moral behaviour that "common" sense can reach and comprehend, in which men who deserve the consideration of wise (*sapientes*), even though not perfect, stand out. It is thus for the imperfect men who live in this "common" sphere that it seems especially important to provide guidance. Panaetius' intention to extend his discussion to the conflict between *utile* and *honestum* was intended to dispel doubts as to the real nature of certain circumstances which call ordinary people to make a choice:

> *Itaque existimo Panaetium, cum dixerit homines solere in hac comparatione dubitare, hoc ipsum sensisse quod dixerit, solere modo, non etiam oportere. [...] Quid ergo est quod nonnumquam dubitationem adferre soleat considerandumque videatur? Credo, si quando dubitatio accidit quale sit id de quo consideretur.*
>
> *Off.* 3.18

> Therefore I am of the opinion that when Panaetius said that men were accustomed to hesitate about a comparison, he meant only what he said: 'were accustomed to' and not also 'were right to'. [...] What is it, then, that sometimes tends to raise a doubt and seems to need consideration? Such occasions arise, I believe, whenever there is doubt over the nature of the action that one is considering.

Given, therefore, that ordinary people are not *sapientes*, it is necessary for things to be stripped of their deceptive nature and be clearly placed within eligible or non-eligible spheres of action. Within the sphere of common and imperfect morality, criteria of conformity must be identified in order to adopt behaviour appropriate to the real nature of the action under consideration. It is necessary to constitute a *formula* — an expression of conformity, as the legal context from which the word originates suggests:[37]

> *Itaque, ut sine ullo errore diiudicare possimus, si quando cum illo, quod honestum intellegimus, pugnare id videbitur, quod appellamus utile, formula quaedam constituenda est; quam si sequemur in comparatione rerum, ab officio numquam recedemus.*
>
> *Off.* 3.19

> Therefore in order that we may pronounce judgment without error, if ever that which we call beneficial seems to conflict with that which we understand to be honourable, a rule of procedure must be established. If we follow this when comparing courses, we shall never fall away from duty.

In a trial, the judge was called upon to bring together the differing assertions of the two parties and of himself, stitching together contradictory assertions and

---

[37] Atkins in Griffin/Atkins 2006[12], 107 n. 3; Griffin 2011, 313–314.

arguments in multiple utterances in order to achieve a well-controlled combination, memorable and repeatable.[38] Likewise, through the process of combining those actions which to ordinary people seem moral but harmful, or immoral but useful, one can achieve a stable and univocal harmonisation of all the specific, multiple, and different situations one must navigate in the performance of *officium*. The nature of the *formula* that will be outlined in the course of Cicero's third book will provide a needed reconciliation, an epistemological crutch for the accomplishment of *officia*. It will not be needed at the level of perfect actions, where the knowledge of a full coincidence between *utile* and *honestum* makes it superfluous for the *sapientes*, but rather, it will be necessary for the average, common, imperfect actions of imperfect people – precisely the *officia* of which Cicero speaks in his treatise.

To the definition of the *formula*, however, Cicero himself finds it difficult to return (3.20: *Sed redeo ad formulam*, "But I return to my rule of procedure") because it is difficult, except at the cost of much repetition and casuistic redundancy, to determine the full range of conduct according to a unifying criterion which would apply the principle of justice:[39]

> *Detrahere igitur alteri aliquid et hominem hominis incommodo suum commodum augere magis est contra naturam quam mors, quam paupertas, quam dolor, quam cetera, quae possunt aut corpori accidere aut rebus externis. Nam principio tollit convictum humanum et societatem.*
>
> *Off.* 3.21

> Now then, for one man to take something from another and to increase his own advantage at the cost of another's disadvantage is more contrary to nature than death, than poverty, than pain and than anything else that may happen to his body or external possessions. In the first place, it destroys the common life and fellowship of men.

In the *formula* which states that one should not cause harm to others in order to obtain one's own advantage, we find the golden rule for the realisation of justice[40] already outlined in 1.20–22, its difficulties recognised:[41] do no harm unless

---

38 Bettini 2022, 106–110: "Sappiamo infatti che la *formula* consisteva in un enunciato o serie di enunciati che, nella fase *in iure* del processo, venivano concordati tra il magistrato e le parti", 106.
39 On the limits of the application of this *formula* Schofield 2021, 196; Dyck 1996, 524–525 also notes its redundancy in the argumentative structure of the third book.
40 It is no coincidence that in 3.28 *iustitia* is defined as "mistress and queen of virtues" (*domina et regina virtutum*); Atkins 1990.
41 In 1.30 Cicero noted the difficulty of exercising justice in a balance between protecting oneself and the affairs of other men (*Est enim difficilis cura rerum alienarum*, "it is not an easy matter to be really concerned with other people's affairs"); see Marchese 2019, 60–65.

having been wronged; allow people to use common possessions for the common interests, private property for their own; remember to benefit others.[42] The *formula* is, in a way, the syncopated and distilled representation of the moral and perfect nature of correct behaviour,[43] and it is cast in the conflictual world of imperfection, where personal gain obscures the view of the good:

> Atque etiam, si hoc natura praescribit, ut homo homini, quicumque sit, ob eam ipsam causam quod is homo sit, consultum velit, necesse est secundum eandem naturam omnium utilitatem esse communem. Quod si ita est, una continemur omnes et eadem lege naturae, idque ipsum si ita est, certe violare alterum naturae lege prohibemur. Verum autem primum, verum igitur extremum.
>
> *Off.* 3.27

> Furthermore, if nature prescribes that one man should want to consider the interests of another, whoever he may be, for the very reason that he is a man, it is necessary, according to the same nature, that what is beneficial to all is something common. If that is so, then we are all constrained by one and the same law of nature; and if that also is true, then we are certainly forbidden by the law of nature from acting violently against another person. The first claim in indeed true; therefore the last is true.

The kind of intervention that Cicero is ready to carry out is therefore expressed in an architectural simile.[44] The work was begun and unfinished by Panaetius, and is now almost complete, as if the author was finally ready to place the *fastigium*, the capstone, on top of the construction:

> Eiusmodi igitur credo res Panaetium persecuturum fuisse, nisi aliqui casus aut occupatio eius consilium peremisset. Ad quas ipsas consultationes ex superioribus libris satis multa praecepta sunt, quibus perspici possit, quid sit propter turpitudinem fugiendum, quid sit quod idcirco fugiendum non sit quod omnino turpe non sit. Sed quoniam operi inchoato, prope tamen absoluto, tamquam fastigium imponimus, ut geometrae solent non omnia docere, sed postulare ut quaedam sibi concedantur, quo facilius quae volunt explicent, sic ego a te postulo, mi Cicero, ut mihi concedas, si potes, nihil praeter id quod honestum sit propter

---

[42] *Sed iustitiae primum munus est, ut ne cui quis noceat, nisi lacessitus iniuria, deinde ut communibus pro communibus utatur, privatis ut suis*, 1.20; [...] *ad usum hominum omnia creari, homines autem hominum causa esse generatos, ut ipsi inter se aliis alii prodesse possent*, 1.22).

[43] "[...] the notion, already implicit in the discussion of justice in Book I (21, 42 *Fin.*), that it is contrary to nature to secure a benefit for oneself at someone else's expense", Griffin/Atkins 2006[12], xxv. See also Schofield 2021, 215–216.

[44] An analogy that allows us to recover the interpretative suggestions about unfinished buildings in Papini 2019c.

se esse expetendum. 34. [...] *Hanc igitur partem relictam explebimus nullis adminiculis, sed, ut dicitur, Marte nostro. Neque enim quicquam est de hac parte post Panaetium explicatum, quod quidem mihi probaretur, de iis quae in manus meas venerint.*

Off. 3.33–34

I believe therefore that Panaetius would have pursued questions of this kind had not some mischance or other preoccupation spoiled his plan. There is in the preceding books plenty of advice concerning these very problems, which may enable one to see what should be avoided because it is dishonourable, and what need not be avoided because it is not at all dishonourable. But now we are placing the capstone, as it were, on work that is unfinished and yet almost complete. Therefore, just as geometers do not usually teach everything, but demand that certain things are granted them so that they may more easily explain what they want, in the same way, I demand to you, my dear Cicero, grant me, if you are able, that nothing except the honourable ought to be sought on its own account. 34. [...] The part that he left, therefore, I shall complete without any auxiliaries, but, as the saying goes, fighting my own battle. For there is no treatment of this question since Panaetius, at any rate such that meets with my approval, in the writings that have come into my hands.

Fastigium imponere is a technical expression that developed, in this context, a deep symbolic meaning:[45] to give the final touch, the completing detail, to a building. Architecturally, the capstone completed temples as well as elegant palaces. As the highest point, the apex of a structure, the *fastigium* would metaphorically become the main point of a narrative.[46] It is the point that can be seen from afar, that stands out in a complex, confused, blurred background. The *fastigium* toward which Cicero is striving is the maximum of completeness he can reach; it is the postulate from which everything can be derived, exactly as geometers (*geometrae*) do, who do not explain point by point, who do not give reasons for every single thing, but who describe the principle from which the rest derives. Let us not be distracted by the geometrical simile; Cicero is not talking about mathematical calculations, but about an enunciation capable of putting together the instances of life and those of *forma*: indeed, a *formula* capable of organising the multiplicity, the disorder of life itself within the sphere of "what is right to do".

---

[45] TLL s.v. *fastigium*, 6.1.320.13–83; Ernout-Meillet, s.v.: "en architecture 'toit' en pente et formant pointe au sommet, par opposition aux toits plats".
[46] Thus, in Verg. *Aen.* 1.342, Venus tells Aeneas "the chief point" (*summa* [...] *fastigia rerum*) of Dido's story.

5 To conclude: accepting imperfection as a constitutive unfinishedness

Fulfil the unfinished, complete the imperfect. The last book of the *De officiis* seeks to offer a general rule whenever a contradiction between *honestum* and *utile* seems to arise. It is the kind of life, the one of appearances, that constrains and conditions human beings' choices; finding a *formula* seems necessary because of its general capacity to order the unfinished disorder of life. The third book "concludes" in the imperfect way in which life develops, with a commitment to identifying instruments capable of saving the common life of an agonising city.[47] But the high price to pay, accepting imperfection as a given, is precisely the loss of *forma*: the work has the flavour of the "unfinished" regardless of its editorial status; it is incomplete and imperfect, it cannot "conclude" from a literary point of view.[48] The text does not obey the intentions of its author, who is now unable to imprint his own tidy concluding form on the writing, and in this process, the imperfection and variety of the real allow the regularity of a *formula* to emerge, one which has the capacity of bringing together discordant perspectives, but which cannot freeze or paralyse the warm movements of life.

Bibliography

Altman, William H.F. (2015), "Cicero and the Fourth Triumvirate: Gruen, Syme, and Strasburger", in: William H.F. Altman (ed.), *Brill's Companion to the Reception of Cicero*, Leiden, 215–246.
Appiah, Kwame A. (1997), "Cosmopolitan Patriots", *Critical Inquiry*, 23.3, 617–639.
Appiah, Kwame A. (2006), *Cosmopolitism. Ethics in a World of Strangers*, New York/London.
Atkins, E. Margaret (1990), "*Domina et regina virtutum*: Justice and *Societas* in *De officiis*", *Phronesis*, XXXV, 258–289.
Atzert, C. (ed.) (1971), *Scripta quae manserunt omnia, XLVIII: De officiis, De virtutibus*, Leipzig.

---

[47] As Levy 1989, 12 significantly noted: "Ces problèmes ont certes leur importance, mais il est quelque chose de plus essentiel, nous semble-t-il: l'enracinement de l'œuvre philosophique dans l'expérience vécue".

[48] In its most problematic distancing from the usual closure strategies of ancient literary works. From the extensive bibliography on these topics I choose the seminal Fowler 1989; the essays in Roberts/Dunn/Fowler 1997; Dolfi 2015, in particular Biagini 19–52. The scholarly debate, as Fowler's studies explicitly show, owes much to Smith 1968 and his interpretative line on the notion of poetic closure.

Begemann, Elisabeth (2015), "Damaged Go(o)ds: Cicero's Theological Triad in the Wake of German Historicism", in: William H.F. Altman (ed.), *Brill's Companion to the Reception of Cicero*, Leiden, 248–280.

Bénatouïl, Thomas (2016), "Structure, Standards and Stoic Moral Progress in *De finibus* 4", in: Julia Annas/Gábor Betegh (eds.), *Cicero's* De finibus: *Philosophical Approaches*, Cambridge, 198–220.

Berndt, Frauke (2014), "Literarische Bildlichkeit und Rhetorik", in: Claudia Benthien/Brigitte Weingart (eds.), *Handbuch Literatur & Visuelle Kultur*, Berlin/München/Boston, 48–67.

Bettini, Maurizio (2022), *Roma, città della parola*, Torino.

Biagini, Enza (2015), "Non finito e teorie dell'incompiutezza", in: Anna Dolfi (ed.), *Non finito, opera interrotta e modernità*, Firenze, 19–52.

Bringmann, Klaus (1971), *Untersuchungen zum späten Cicero*, Göttingen.

Brüser, W.J. (1949), *Der Textzustand von Ciceros Büchern* De Officiis, diss. Köln.

Calvino, Italo (1988), *Six Memos for the Next Millennium*, Cambridge, MA. [Calvino, Italo (1988), *Lezioni americane. Sei proposte per il prossimo millennio*, Milano].

Dolfi, Anna (ed.) (2015), *Non finito, opera interrotta e modernità*, Firenze.

Dorandi, Tiziano (2007), *Nell'officina dei classici: come lavoravano gli autori antichi*, Roma.

Dyck, Andrew R. (ed.) (1996), *A Commentary on Cicero,* De officiis, Ann Arbor MI.

Faedo, Lucia (2019), "L'incompiuto, l'incompleto e i *liniamenta reliqua*: sguardi sull'arte antica tra XV e XVIII secolo", in: Massimiliano Papini (ed.), Opus imperfectum. *Monumenti e testi incompiuti del mondo greco e romano, Scienze dell'antichità* 25.3, 165–178.

Fedeli, Paolo (ed.) (1965), *Opera omnia quae exstant: De officiis libri tres.* Milano.

Fedeli, Paolo (1965a), "Studi sulla tradizione manoscritta del *De officiis* di Cicerone", *Annali della Facoltà di Lettere e Filosofia/Università degli Studi di Bari* X, 43–79.

Fedeli, Paolo (1973), "Il *De officiis* di Cicerone. Problemi e atteggiamenti della critica moderna, I,4", in: Hildegard Temporini-Vitzthum (ed.), *Aufstieg und Niedergang der römischen Welt.Geschichte und Kultur Roms im Spiegel der neueren Forschung. Joseph Vogt zu seinem 75. Geburtstag gewidmet, I: Von den Anfängen Roms bis zum Ausgang der Republik*, 4 [Philosophie und Wissenschaft, Künste], Berlin, 357–427.

Fedeli, Paolo (1974), "Nota critica al *de officiis*", in: Leonardo Ferrero/Nevio Zorzetti (eds.), *Marco Tullio Cicerone, Opere politiche e filosofiche*, I, Torino, 133–153.

Fedeli, Paolo (2000), "Review of *M. Tulli Ciceronis De officiis. Recognovit brevique adnotatione critica instruxit*, by M. Winterbottom", *Gnomon* 72.7, 593–599.

Fowler, Don P. (1989), "First Thoughts on Closure. Problems and Prospects", *Materiali e Discussioni per l'Analisi dei Testi Classici* XXII, 75–122.

Gabba, Emilio (1979), "Per un'interpretazione politica del *De officiis* di Cicerone", *Atti della Accademia Nazionale dei Lincei, Classe di Scienze morali, storiche e filologiche. Rendiconti* XXXIV, 117–141.

Griffin, Miriam T./Atkins, E. Margaret (eds.) (2002[12]), *Cicero, On Duties*, Cambridge.

Griffin, Miriam (2011), "The Politics of Virtue: Three Puzzles in Cicero's *De Officiis*", in: Ben Morison/Katerina Ierodiakonou (eds.), *Episteme*, Essays in Honour of Jonathan Barnes, Oxford, 310–328.

Gurd, Sean Alexander (2007), "Cicero and Editorial Revision", *Classical Antiquity* 26.1, 49–80.

Gurd, Sean Alexander (2012), *Work in Progress: Literary Revision as Social Performance in Ancient Rome*, Oxford/New York.

Kumaniecki, Kazimierz F. (1972), *Cicerone e la crisi della repubblica romana*, Roma.

Ioppolo, Anna Maria (2016), "*Sententia explosa*: Criticism of Stoic Ethics in *De finibus* 4", in: Julia Annas/Gábor Betegh (eds.), *Cicero's* De finibus: *Philosophical Approaches*, Cambridge, 167–197.
Irwin, Terence H. (2014), "«Officia» and Casuistry: Some Episodes", *Philosophie Antique* 14, 111–128.
Labowsky, L. (1934), *Der Begriff des PREPON in der Ethik des Panaitios. Mit Analysen von Cicero De off. I 93–149 und Horaz Ars poetica*, Heidelberg.
Lefèvre, Eckard (2001), *Panaitios' und Ciceros Pflichtenlehre: vom philosophischen Traktat zum politischen Lehrbuch*, Stuttgart.
Lévy, Carlos (1989), "Le *de officiis* dans l'oeuvre philosophique de Cicéron", *Vita Latina* 116, 11–16.
Long, Anthony A. (1995), "Cicero's Politics in the *De officiis*", in: André Laks/Malcolm Schofield (eds.), *Justice and Generosity: Studies in Hellenistic Social and Political Philosophy: Proceedings of the Sixth Symposium Hellenisticum*, Cambridge/New York, 213–240.
Lotito, Gianfranco (1981), "Modelli etici e base economica nelle opere filosofiche di Cicerone", in: Andrea Giardina/Aldo Schiavone (eds.), *Società romana e produzione schiavistica, III: Modelli etici, diritto e trasformazioni sociali*, Bari, 79–126.
Lulli, Laura (2019), "L'immagine del non-finito: riflessioni sull'incompiutezza da Platone al trattato *Sul sublime*", in: Massimiliano Papini (ed.), Opus imperfectum. *Monumenti e testi incompiuti del mondo greco e romano, Scienze dell'antichità* 25.3, 237–247.
Marchese, Rosa Rita (2014), "Speech and Silence in Cicero's Final Days", *The Classical Journal* 110.1, 77–98.
Marchese, Rosa Rita (2016), *Uno sguardo che vede: l'idea di rispetto in Cicerone e in Seneca*, Palermo.
Marchese, Rosa Rita (2019), "Non nuocere, aiutare, non offendere. Rileggere il *De officiis* di Cicerone nel conflitto tra prossimi e lontani", *Classico Contemporaneo* 5, 52–71.
Moreau, Joseph (1983), "La place des *officia* dans l'éthique stoïcienne", *Revue de Philosophie Ancienne* I, 99–112.
Narducci, Emanuele (1989), *Modelli etici e società. Un'idea di Cicerone*, Pisa.
Narducci, Emanuele (2004), *Cicerone e i suoi interpreti*, Pisa.
Narducci, Emanuele (2005), *Introduzione a Cicerone*, Roma/Bari.
Nussbaum, Martha Craven (2004), "Duties of Justice, Duties of Material Aid: Cicero's Problematic Legacy", in: Steven K. Strange/Jack Zupko (eds.), *Stoicism: Traditions and Transformations*, Cambridge/New York, 214–249.
Nussbaum, Martha Craven (2019), *The Cosmopolitan Tradition: A Noble but Flawed Ideal*, Cambridge MA/London. [Nussbaum, Martha Craven (2020), *La tradizione cosmopolita. Un ideale nobile ma imperfetto*, tr. it. Milano].
Papini, Massimiliano (2017), "Firmare un'opera come se fosse l'ultima: l'imperfetto e l'incompiuto in Plinio il Vecchio", *Bollettino della Commissione Archeologica Comunale di Roma* 118, 39–54.
Papini, Massimiliano (ed.) (2019), *Opus imperfectum. Monumenti e testi incompiuti del mondo greco e romano, Scienze dell'antichità* 25.3.
Papini, Massimiliano (2019a), "*Pendono interrotte le opere*". *Antichi monumenti incompiuti nel mondo greco*, Roma.
Papini, Massimiliano (2019b), "L'incompiuto nel mondo antico tra archeologia e letteratura: un'introduzione", in: Massimiliano Papini (ed.), Opus imperfectum. *Monumenti e testi incompiuti del mondo greco e romano, Scienze dell'antichità* 25.3, IX–XXVI.

Papini, Massimiliano (2019c), "Non lavorato, non rifinito, non scanalato, non levigato: edifici incompiuti nel mondo greco", in: Massimiliano Papini (ed.), Opus imperfectum. *Monumenti e testi incompiuti del mondo greco e romano, Scienze dell'antichità* 25.3, 1–15.

Picone, Giusto (2019²), "Di generazione in generazione: *mores, memoria, munera* nel *de officiis* di Cicerone", in: Giusto Picone/Rosa Rita Marchese (eds.), *Marco Tullio Cicerone,* De officiis. *Quel che è giusto fare,* Torino, IX–XXXVI.

Pohlenz, Max (1934), *Antikes Führertum. Cicero De officiis und das Lebensideal des Panaitios,* Leipzig. [Pohlenz, Max (1971), *L'ideale di vita attiva secondo Panezio nel De officiis di Cicerone,* tr. it. Brescia].

Pohlenz, Max (1934–1936), "Cicero *de officiis* III", in: *Nachrichten von der Gesellschaft der Wissenschaften zu Göttingen, Philosophisch-Historische Klasse,* 1–40.

Pohlenz, Max (1955), *Die Stoa. Geschichte einer geistigen Bewegung, II: Erläuterungen,* Göttingen. [Pohlenz, Max (1967), *La Stoa. Storia di un movimento spirituale,* tr. it. Firenze].

Rawson, Elizabeth (1985), *Intellectual Life in the Late Roman Republic,* London.

Rigotti, Francesca (2019), *Migranti per caso. Una vita da expat,* Milano.

Roberts, Deborah H./Dunn, Francis M./Fowler, Don P. (eds.) (1997), *Classical Closure: Reading the End in Greek and Latin literature,* Princeton.

Schofield, Malcolm (2012), "The Fourth Virtue", in: Walter Nicgorski (ed.), *Cicero's Practical Philosophy,* Notre Dame, Ind., 43–57.

Schofield, Malcolm (2021), *Cicero: Political Philosophy,* Oxford.

Smith Herrnstein, Barbara (1968), *Poetic Closure. A Study of How Poems End,* Chicago.

Striker, Gisela (1991), "Following Nature: A Study in Stoic Ethics", *Oxford Studies in Ancient Philosophy* IX, 1–73.

Stone, A. M. (2008), "Greek Ethics and Roman Statesmen: De *officiis* and the *Philippics*", in: Tom Stevenson/Marcus Wilson (eds.), *Cicero's "Philippics": History, Rhetoric and Ideology,* Auckland, 214–239.

Testard, Maurice (ed.) (1965), *Les devoirs. Introduction. Livre I,* Paris.

Thomas, K.B. (1971), *Textkritische Untersuchungen zu Ciceros Schrift De officiis,* Münster.

Van der Blom, Henriette (2003), "*Officium* and *res publica*: Cicero's Political Role after the Ides of March", *Classica et Mediaevalia* 54, 287–320.

Watzlawick, Paul/Beavin, Janet Helmick/Don D. Jackson (2011), *Pragmatics of Human Communication. A Study of Interactional Patterns, Pathologies and Paradoxes,* New York.

Winterbottom, Michael (1993), "The Transmission of Cicero's *De officiis*", *Classical Quarterly* 43, 215–242.

Winterbottom, Michael (ed.) (1994), *De officiis,* Scriptorum Classicorum Bibliotheca Oxoniensis, New York.

Winterbottom, Michael (2017), "The Pleasures of Editing", *Revue d'Histoire des Textes* N. S. 12, 393–413.

Fabio Tutrone
Relativizing Unfinishedness: Lucretian Textuality and Epicurean Therapy

Abstract: Over the past few centuries, scholars have often regarded Lucretius' *DRN* as a fascinating example of artistic *non-finito*, mirroring the untimely death of a solitary genius. The present chapter reassesses the literary, philological, and historical evidence supporting this classical view, arguing that a careful reassessment of the 'degree of completeness' of Lucretius' text should be based on a thorough understanding of the special features of Roman didactic poetry and Epicurean therapeutic pedagogy as culturally situated discourses of self-formation. The chapter makes clear that neither the practice of recursive argumentation, with the studied repetition of crucial lines in different books, nor the gradual modification of thematic priorities over the course of Lucretius' poem can be taken as evidence of unfinishedness as neither is a culturally neutral mode of rhetorical expression. On the contrary, both verbal repetition and thematic adaptability have substantially different implications in the intellectual world of Roman and Epicurean didacticism than in our modern literary sensibility.

1 Polynesian prologue: Lucretius and the *non-finito*

Let me start this chapter from the light green coasts of Polynesia. When in the Easter of 1722 the first European sighted what became known as Easter Island, with its giant statues made up of compacted volcanic ash, a vigorous debate arose among Western observers about the state and the meaning of the island's artistic heritage. Some of Easter Island's statues — the so-called *moai* — stood on impressive platforms but faced inland rather than out to sea. Other statues lay scattered across the island — broken or abandoned — and some partially complete *moai* near a quarry faced the sea. To the Western eye imbued with the mystic sensibility of Michelangelo, this may have looked like a remarkable (and bizarre) example of *non-finito*.[1] Yet three centuries of archaeological investigations have made clear that things can look quite different if one looks at the

---

[1] On the early modern idea of *non-finito* and its roots in ancient aesthetics, see Bomford 2015 and Baum/Bayer/Wagstaff 2016.

moai from the cultural perspective of the Easter Island natives. For instance, as two specialists in Polynesian archaeology have pointed out, one should not expect that the finished *moai* — which represent dead chiefs and ancestors — were anything comparable to the colossal monuments watching over the harbors of classical antiquity: "that the *moai* were religious images explains why the vast majority face inland, watching over their descendants day after day. With their backs to the sea, the *moai* had not been carved as sentries, warding off potential intruders, as with the Colossus of Rhodes".[2]

As a rule, establishing whether an artifact — be it a statue or a literary text — is complete in its creator's intentions requires the adoption of a *native* outlook on the artifact itself. The very concepts of finishedness, completeness, and perfection — which are not mutually interchangeable — heavily depend on culturally relative and socially embedded assumptions, which, in turn, are transformed within the idiosyncratic universe of authorial discourses. In the present paper, I shall argue that, when assessing the aesthetic and material condition of an ancient text, close attention should be paid to the historical and intellectual variables that practically determine the construction, use, and reception of each text. Indeed, what is complete in a given context — for a certain purpose or a certain audience — can appear utterly incomplete if seen through different cultural lenses. I shall focus on one of the most controversial cases of supposedly unfinished work in the history of classical literature — Lucretius' poem *On the Nature of Things* (*De Rerum Natura*, hereafter *DRN*) — in an attempt to show that a careful reassessment of the "degree of completeness" of Lucretius' text should be based on a thorough understanding of the special features of Roman didactic poetry and Epicurean therapeutic pedagogy as culturally situated discourses of self-formation. Just like Polynesian statues, Lucretius' arguments can appear more or less "complete" depending on whether one regards them from the standpoint of the modern classicistic aesthetic — whose ideal of perfection still exerts its influence on classical scholarship[3] — or from the internal vantage point of Lucretius' milieu.

Paradoxically enough, the aura of unfinishedness surrounding Lucretius' poem has powerfully contributed to its successful *Nachleben*. The *DRN* provides

---

[2] Hunt/Lipo 2011, 2. For an overview of the scholarly debate over the history, environment, and interpretation of the *moai*, see also Bahn/Flenley 2011 and Rull/Stevenson 2022.

[3] On the long-standing impact of the ancient and early modern notions of classical perfection on the history of scholarship, see Porter 2006. As Porter observes (18), "at the end of the road we find the term *classical* and *classicism* and a series of attempts to claim and to purify their meaning. But the attempts are never definitive — the central concepts and their referents are at no point uniformly agreed upon".

compelling evidence for the veracity of Pliny the Elder's remark — which is one of the inspiring influences of the early modern taste for the *non-finito* — that "the last works of artists (*suprema opera artificum*) and their unfinished pictures (*in<p>erfectasque tabulas*) are more admired than those which they finished (*perfecta*)". In fact, according to Pliny, the audience of unfinished works has the impression of seeing "the sketches left visible and the artists' actual thoughts (*liniamenta reliqua ipsaeque cogitationes artificum*), and in the midst of approval's beguilement (*in lenocinio commendationis*) we feel regret that the artist's hand while engaged in the work was removed by death (*dolor est manus, cum id ageret, exstinctae*)".[4] No other work by Lucretius survives or is known to have been written (and finished). But ever since the Renaissance the imagination of Lucretius' readers has been bewitched by the perilous interaction between biographical speculation and textual criticism — by the melancholic image of a brilliant Epicurean hand removed by early death.[5] Dubious pieces of anecdotal information — such as Lucretius' poisoning, madness, and suicide[6] — have been used to explain the most tantalizingly complex problems of the textual tradition of *DRN*, sometimes at the risk of creating a sort of short-circuit effect. Is the poem incomplete because of Lucretius' untimely death? Or is the state of Lucretius' Carolingian manuscripts the only apparent evidence for Jerome's extremely controversial account of the poet's life?

A good starting point may be to divorce philology from biography — which is nothing new for those classical scholars who have been contemplating the "death of the author" for several decades.[7] Yet dismissing biographical criticism

---

[4] Plin. *HN* 35.145. On Pliny's role in the development of a modern aesthetics of the *non-finito*, see Baum/Bayer/Wagstaff 2016, 13–14, and Bayer 2016, 18–21, who notes that Pliny's passage was "already flagged by Petrarch about 1350 in the marginalia of his own manuscript", and that Pliny's questions "were then interpreted by artists and authors in the Renaissance and Baroque periods". Cf. also Maleuvre 2019, 57–61, and Hamilton/Pearson 2021, exploring the "aesthetics of imperfection" in music and the arts.
[5] On the Renaissance biographies of Lucretius and their importance for the construction of the modern "myth of Lucretius", see Palmer 2014, 101–191. For a caustic criticism of the enduring scholarly tendency to fill the gaps in Lucretius' *vitae*, see Holford-Strevens 2002.
[6] I refer, of course, to the much-debated account of Lucretius' folly and death in Jerome (*Chron. s.a.Abr.* 1923 = *Ol.* 171.3 = 94 BC). For a reassessment of this and the other (scanty) sources about Lucretius' biography, see Canfora 1993.
[7] There is no need to restate the enormous influence of Roland Barthes' theory about *la mort de l'auteur*, according to which "literature is that neuter, that composite, that oblique into which every subject escapes, the trap where all identity is lost, beginning with the very identity of the body that writes" (cf. Barthes 1977, 142). For a new approach to the same issue, see Gallop 2011.

cannot mean turning one's back on cultural history and comparative critique, for textual criticism is blind without history and literary theory. It is more than possible that — as David Butterfield pointed out summing up a century of Lucretian philology — the *DRN* "was almost, but not entirely, completed", an assumption based on the belief that "the unfinished state and improbable order of several arguments [...] cannot be satisfactorily explained by textual corruption".[8] However, when one starts to analyze in detail the evidence supporting this assumption, one is inevitably transported into the realm of cultural and historical relativity, for according to Butterfield himself the bulk of the evidence comes from "the survival of dual passages" and "the unfulfilled claim at 5.155 that Lucretius would discuss the nature of the gods *largo sermone*".[9] Indeed, neither the practice of recursive argumentation nor the gradual modification of thematic priorities is a culturally neutral mode of rhetorical expression. On the contrary, they have substantially different implications in the intellectual world of Roman and Epicurean didacticism than in our modern literary sensibility.

In what follows, I will focus on these two emblematic issues — recursive argumentation and thematic adaptability — which are crucial for determining whether the *DRN* was left unfinished by its author. I will try to show that in both cases cross-cultural comparison can bring to light a set of distinctive features of Lucretius' poem that attest to its original understanding as a cognitive tool for healing and spiritual awakening. Whatever the vicissitudes of its manuscript tradition, the *DRN* was not conceived of by its author (and by its ancient audience) as a model of aesthetic perfection in any modern sense. Rather, formal beauty and the notions of order and disorder — balance and imbalance — were seen by Lucretius as subordinate to the purpose of persuading, instructing, and *saving* the reader's soul.[10] Even from the narrower point of view of Lucretius' literary culture, abstract ideals of discipline, purity, and completeness remain inapplicable insofar as the aesthetic of *DRN* is closer to the epic exuberance of

---

8 Butterfield 2013, 2. Cf., e.g., Volk 2002, 82 n. 41: "there are signs that point to the fact that the poem was left unfinished [...] and it is reasonable to entertain the notion that the end of the poem, especially, might still have been modified by the author". See also below, n. 30.
9 Butterfield 2013, 2 n. 7.
10 Epicurean texts often recall that moral — not metaphysical — "salvation" (σωτηρία) is the ultimate goal of Epicurus' teachings, and that fellow philosophers ideally tend to "be saved by one other" (δι' ἀλλήλων σῴζεσθαι): see, e.g., Philod. *Lib. Dic.* frs. 4.9; 34.5; 36.1–2; 40.8; 78.6–7; col. 6b.10–11 Olivieri; *PHerc.* 346 (the so-called "Trattato etico epicureo" edited by Capasso 1982), fr. 3 IVb.7; IV.24–28; VII.24; Diog. Oen. frs. 2.5.14; 72.3.13; 116.6–8 Smith. Cf. Capasso 1987, 28–34, and Clay 1998, 238–242.

Empedocles and Ennius than to classicist grace.¹¹ If Rembrandt was right in claiming that a complete work is that in which "the master's intentions have been realized",¹² a rigorous assessment of the "degree of perfection" of Lucretius' work should begin by establishing whether — and how — Lucretius has managed to devise a poetically vigorous strategy of ethical salvation.

2 Recursive argumentation: Lucretius' spiritual exercises

In the Epicurean tradition to which Lucretius remains faithful, saving oneself and one's audience is not just a matter of linear argumentation and propositional logic. The good Epicurean teacher knows that the supreme goal of moral perfection can hardly be achieved by explaining Epicurus' doctrine once and for all. Indeed, most of the pedagogic efforts of Epicurean instructors — from the time of Epicurus to that of Lucretius and Philodemus — are directed towards the transmission of a set of *psychagogic* techniques, which are meant to produce a gradual transformation of consciousness. The studies of Pierre Hadot and Michel Foucault, among others, have made it clear that such techniques were understood by ancient teachers and practitioners as "spiritual exercises" in a distinctly moral — i.e., non-metaphysical and pre-Christian — sense.¹³ As Epicurus himself explains in his *Letter to Menoeceus*, the problem is not just *believing* (νομίζειν), but rather *accustoming oneself to believe* (συνεθίζειν ἐν τῷ νομίζειν),¹⁴

---

11 On the enormous influence of Empedocles and Ennius on Lucretius' poem, see Garani 2007 and Nethercut 2021, respectively.
12 According to Arnold Houbraken's 1718 biography of Rembrandt, this was Rembrandt's reply to the question why he was "so quick to change and move on to other things", leaving "many things only half finished" (cf. Bayer 2006, 29). To many classical scholars, Rembrandt's statement will seem to be inevitably connected with the thorny issue of authorial intention, which has been recently revisited by Farrell 2017. As Farrell (242) admits, "the airless textualism of the mid-twentieth century has long dispersed, and historical inquiry has again become the primary concern of literary scholars". Certainly, historical inquiry and cultural contextualization are my primary concerns in the present essay.
13 See especially Foucault 1986, 2005, and Hadot 1995, 2002. On Epicurean psychagogy, which intends to act on both an individual and a collective moral dimension, see Gigante 1983, 62–67, and Glad 1995.
14 Cf. Epic. *Ep. Men.* 124: "accustom yourself to believe that death is nothing to us" (συνέθιζε δὲ ἐν τῷ νομίζειν μηδὲν πρὸς ἡμᾶς εἶναι τὸν θάνατον). Translations from the works of Epicurus are taken or adapted from Yonge 1853.

and the acquisition of this familiarity with Epicurean wisdom requires that the student exercises himself day and night, often with the support of a community of like-minded friends.[15] Memory and repetition become the pillars of a system of spiritual exercises, individual and communal, which are the real historical basis of the Epicurean tradition of epitomes, maxims, and *florilegia* — a tradition started by Epicurus himself, according to whom "we must give preference to former knowledge and lay up in our memory those principles on which we may rest in order to arrive at an exact perception of things and at a certain knowledge of particular objects".[16]

As Voula Tsouna points out, "Epicurus' insistence on repetition and practice indicates that the relevant trains of thought become increasingly faster to the point of building quasi-automatic moral reflexes"[17] — which, however, does not mean that Epicurus "discovers the unconscious", as Martha Nussbaum controversially contends.[18] Following his master's advice, "Lucretius clearly believes that such techniques help us not just learn, but internalize the teachings of the poem".[19] In fact, in the initial stages of his scientific catechism, Lucretius (2.581–585) explains that it is advisable (*convenit*) to keep the truth of

---

15 In *Ep. Men.* 135, Epicurus gives the following recommendation: "exercise yourself in these and kindred precepts day and night, both by yourself and with him who is like to you (ταῦτα οὖν καὶ τὰ τούτοις συγγενῆ μελέτα πρὸς σεαυτὸν ἡμέρας καὶ νυκτὸς <καὶ> πρὸς τὸν ὅμοιον σεαυτῷ); then never, either in waking or in dream, will you be disturbed, but will live as a god among people (καὶ οὐδέποτε οὔθ' ὕπαρ οὔτ' ὄναρ διαταραχθήσῃ, ζήσῃ δὲ ὡς θεὸς ἐν ἀνθρώποις)". On the Epicurean emphasis on both self-cultivation and communal life as methods of self-divinization, see Clay 1998, Erler 1993, and Tutrone 2021.
16 Epic. *Ep. Hdt.* 36: βαδιστέον μὲν οὖν καὶ ἐπ' ἐκεῖνα συνεχῶς, ἐν <δὲ> τῇ μνήμῃ τὸ τοσοῦτο ποιητέον, ἀφ' οὗ ἥ τε κυριωτάτη ἐπιβολὴ ἐπὶ τὰ πράγματα ἔσται καὶ δὴ καὶ τὸ κατὰ μέρος ἀκρίβωμα πᾶν ἐξευρήσεται. Cf. also *Ep. Pyth.* 84–85. There is even evidence that Epicurus' precepts on memorization led to interpretive conflicts among his later followers. For instance, in *De elect.* 11.7–20, Philodemus refutes a rival Epicurean position according to which repetition and memorization "can *replace* arguments and achieve *alone* the patient's healing" (Tsouna 2009, 255, author's emphasis).
17 Tsouna 2009, 255–258.
18 Nussbaum 1994, 133 (criticized by Tsouna 2009, 258). For a sharp distinction between the modern idea of the unconscious and the principles of Epicurus' rational therapy, see Gladman/Mitsis 1997. According to Leigh 2020, 32: "perhaps the Epicureans thought that the affective components of *pathē* and desires take time to undergo change, or that repetition promotes associations among impressions that lead to the right action, or that memorization of central principles itself causes them to be causally efficacious in belief formation. Or perhaps repetition and accustoming oneself to what is true is necessary, somehow, to counter opposing fears and desires".
19 Tsouna 2009, 258.

atomic laws under seal (*obsignatum habere*) and to "retain it in the depository of one's memory" (*memori mandatum mente tenere*). With this cultural background in mind, it becomes methodologically incorrect to apply to Lucretius (and to the Epicurean tradition) the modern view that repetition is a sign of aesthetic imperfection or textual corruption.[20] Rather, one should recognize that Lucretius successfully combines the characteristically epic taste for formulaic diction, mnemonic devices, and the repetition of typical scenes[21] with the rhetorical devices of Epicurean pedagogy, among which the practice of recursive argumentation is paramount. However, given the overwhelming influence of the Romantic ideas of originality, creativity, and innovation on the history of Western literature, it is no surprise that many modern critics have proved reluctant to regard the repetition of entire lines and sections in *DRN* as part of a well-thought-out strategy of persuasion, meditation, and interiorization — a reluctance which has ultimately resulted in the perpetuation of anti-historical and, so to speak, *ethnocentric* readings of *DRN*.

A simple example can suffice to show that, far from providing evidence of the poem's unfinishedness, the recurrence of the same lines in different places makes a fundamental contribution to the development of Lucretius' didactic project. In Book 1 (112–135), Lucretius famously introduces the main subject of his poem, its literary novelty, and its purpose of converting an illustrious Roman dedicatee, Gaius Memmius. Readers are told that in order to avoid groundless fears it is of central importance to understand the nature of the soul, of which earlier poets like Ennius have allegedly offered a misleading description. In the same context (1.136–145), the *DRN* is presented as a pioneering therapeutic effort to overcome the limits of the Latin language in the name of Lucretius' friendship with Memmius — whose mind will be enlightened "to see right to the heart of hidden things" (*res quibus occultas penitus convisere possis*). This early reference to the "rhetoric of light", which lies at the heart of the poem's

---

[20] An analogous claim was made by Clay 1998, 55–62, with regard to the recurrence of the same maxims in different Epicurean writers. As Clay (57) observes, "the discovery of Epicurean texts which became known only after Usener had published his *Epicurea* in 1887 holds a lesson for the philologist who considers the 'enucleation' and 'individuation' of ancient texts as his only task. Many of his philological dilemmas arise out of his failure to consider the kernel in its husk and the individual in its community".

[21] On the persisting influence of these epic techniques on ancient didactic poetry, see the case studies discussed in Atherton 1998, Gale 2004a, and Canevaro/O'Rourke 2019.

conception,[22] is followed by three lines that reappear in the very same order in Books 2, 3, and 6 (1.146–148 = 2.59–61 = 3.91–93 = 6.39–41):

> *hunc igitur terrorem animi tenebrasque necessest*
> *non radii solis neque lucida tela diei*
> *discutiant, sed naturae species ratioque.*

> This terrifying darkness that enshrouds the mind must be dispelled not by the sun's rays and the dazzling darts of day, but by the rational understanding of natural phenomena.[23]

Since the rational understanding of natural phenomena is the kernel of the Epicurean recipe for a fearless and happy life, it should be no wonder that the same inspiring triptych of verses is used to build a kind of *meditative crescendo* throughout the poem. As Alessandro Schiesaro observes, "the didactic narrator repeats words and concepts because they are fundamental tenets of his theories, and the reader repeats their reading because this is the only way he can come to master the lesson".[24] More precisely, what the poet creates is a gradually ascending *Ringkomposition*, for Lucretius' strategy of recursive argumentation has its starting and ending point in the charismatic teaching of Epicurus and is in fact intended to inculcate in the reader's mind the salvific truth that Epicurus is the only light in the darkness of human ignorance. Just as the above-cited passage of Book 1 is preceded by a first enthusiastic eulogy of Epicurus, who is said to have defeated the dark tyranny of religion (1.62–83), the fourth and last occurrence of our triptych comes in Book 6 immediately after Lucretius' concluding praise of Athens and Epicurus (6.1–34). In the proem to Book 6, Lucretius sums up the central belief underlying his poem — the belief that Epicurus "purged people's minds with words of truth and laid down limits to desire and fear" (*veridicis igitur purgavit pectora dictis/ et finem statuit cuppedinis atque timoris*, 6.24–25) by elucidating the nature of the supreme good and the

---

[22] As Volk 2002, 93, points out, "the various instances of the light-dark metaphor combine to convey a positive image of the speaker's poem that is associated with light (a force with positive connotations) throughout: both the light of Epicurean reason that casts out the darkness of the human mind and the light of clear diction that illuminates even the most obscure teachings of philosophy". It is just a step from here to the early modern rhetoric of the Enlightenment: see Baker 2007.

[23] Here and elsewhere, I use the translation of Smith 2001 (slightly modified).

[24] Schiesaro 1994, 103, who shows that "from the microtextual level of repeated sounds, to formulae, passages and themes, Lucretius' poem presents its reader with a strong sense of repetition and continuity, as a series of material bodies whose components constantly rearrange themselves in cyclical fashion without ever being reduced *in nihilum*" (100).

sources of moral evil. Between Lucretius' first and last eulogy of Epicurus two other occurrences of our meditative triptych serve to signal the gradual introduction of the *content* of Epicurus' diagnosis: whereas in Book 2 (37–54) we are taught that wealth, luxury, and power are not conducive to happiness, in Book 3 (32–86) we learn about the causal connection between such desires, their apparent insatiability, and the fear of death. As David Konstan has shown, Lucretius' ultimate purpose is to demonstrate that "not only does the irrational fear of death induce limitless desires, but that, in turn, such desires are at least in part responsible for the anxieties that human beings have in regard to death".[25] Step by step, the reader-student is led to achieve, and meditate upon, what in Book 6 is praised as the crowning gift of Epicurean wisdom: the rational understanding of, and liberation from, the real causes of pain.

Significantly, in all our four passages except the first, Lucretius' meditative triptych is preceded by another four verses that explicitly introduce the image of humans — of the writer *and* the reader — into the above-cited picture of light and dark (2.55–58 = 3.87–90 = 6.35–38):

> *Nam vel uti pueri trepidant atque omnia caecis*
> *in tenebris metuunt, sic nos in luce timemus*
> *interdum, nihilo quae sunt metuenda magis quam*
> *quae pueri in tenebris pavitant finguntque futura.*

> For, just as children tremble and fear everything in blinding darkness, so we even in daylight sometimes dread things that are no more terrible than the imaginary dangers that cause children to quake in the dark.

Again, Lucretius' repetition has a profound didactic function. The reader-student — who is urged to sympathize with the teacher by the use of the first person plural — is cyclically reminded of his original condition of ignorance and fear, which Epicurus' physical-*cum*-moral teaching has the potential to dispel. By restating the symbolic contrast between light and darkness, childish trepidation and rational composure, at crucial stages in his didactic explanation, the poet intends to move, reassure, and educate his audience. To quote Epicurus' *Letter to Herodotus*, he intends to make his discourse (λόγος) more powerful (δυνατός) insofar as "these truths being stored in a practitioner's memory will be a constant assistance to him" (αὐτὰ ταῦτα ἐν μνήμῃ τιθέμενα συνεχῶς βοηθήσει).[26]

---

25 Konstan 2008, XI.
26 Cf. Epic. *Ep. Hdt.* 83.

What is more, Lucretius' taste for repetition relies on a fundamental principle of Epicurean poetics — which is discussed in both Philodemus' *On Poems* and Lucretius' own verses — the so-called "impossibility of metathesis", according to which if one transposes the same elements (words or letters) to a different context, or if one arranges them in a slightly different order, the transposition (μετάθεσις) affects the basic meaning of the elements themselves, insofar as "subject, *res*, and style, *verba* and *versus*, are inseparable functions one of the other".[27] In a perceptive article, Stratis Kyriakidis has shown that one of the most well-known cases of apparent repetition in Lucretius' poem — the re-use of the so-called "apology" of Book 1 as a proem to Book 4 (1.926–950 = 4.1–25) — reflects precisely Lucretius' awareness of the semantic shift (and the didactic potential) implied in the poetic process of metathesis. In fact, not only does Lucretius significantly alter the context of his statement by excluding from Book 4 the introductory remarks on poetic inspiration that featured in Book 1 (921–925), but he also shifts the focus of his conclusion from atomic theory (*qua constet compta figura*, 1.950) to the moral usefulness of Epicurean philosophy (*ac persentis utilitatem*, 4.25), thus substantially transforming the meaning and purpose of his words.[28] Admittedly, if dual passages — *qua* textual equivalents of verbal repetition and mental memorization — are signs of imperfection, Lucretius' imperfection is deliberately modelled after that of Epicurus and other Epicureans. But there is excellent reason to believe that *our* philological method needs to be perfected in order to get closer to Epicurus' and Lucretius' cultural universe.

---

27 Armstrong 1995, 227, who compares the second half of Philodemus' *Tractatus Tertius* (*PHerc.* 1676) with Lucretius' famous "atomology" in Book 1 (cf. Friedländer 1941, Snyder 1980) and convincingly argues that "the outlines of a fully stated Epicurean-atomistic theory of poetry, worked out in cold prose by Philodemus as in poetry by Lucretius, are before us".

28 As Kyriakidis 2006, 610, observes, these changes "highlight the difference in function between the two passages and enhance the Lucretian view of intransferability of things as the latter appears in the Latin poet's work. Many, if not all, of the cases considered as repetitions in the *DRN* may perhaps owe their presence in the Lucretian work on similar grounds to the ones discussed here". Another possible example is the slight formal difference between 2.177–181 and 5.195–199 mentioned below (cf. n. 51), which is the product of two different contexts and stages of conceptual development.

3 From unfinishedness to infinity: Thematic adaptability, poetic simultaneity, and palingenesis

An analogous approach should be used to understand more deeply the transformation of Lucretius' didactic approach and priorities over the course of his poem. Lucretius' failure to fulfil his promise of discussing "with ample argument" (*largo sermone*) the nature of the gods[29] has often been considered indicative of the fact that the text of *DRN* transmitted to us does not include all the materials that the poet wished to include.[30] But does this suffice to conclude that the poem as a whole, with its carefully developed structural plan,[31] is unfinished?

On the basis of Jerome's biographical note,[32] it has been surmised that Lucretius failed to apply his *ultima manus*, his finishing touch, to the work. Although this hypothesis is not implausible, it is hard to claim that the internal

---

29 Cf. Lucr. 5.155.
30 Already Masson 1884, 168 n. 3, speculated that "Lucretius, had he lived, would have concluded his poem with a description of the Epicurean Gods and their heaven" (cf., e.g., Bignone 1945, 318–322, with further conjectures). In more recent times, Sedley 1998, 148–157, has interpreted several passages in Books 4 and 5 as signs of incomplete revision, but his approach (which tries to revive the "genetic" method of *Quellenforschung*) has been criticized by O'Hara 2007, 69–76, who, following Farrell 1994, 82–89, has called attention to the pointed and intended ambiguity of *DRN*, which does not always match the modern (arbitrary) expectations about a work's "consistency". In the words of O'Hara 2007, 76, "as at the start of the *DRN*, where scholars have wanted to remove the statement of Epicurean principles that seems to clash with the Hymn to Venus, and in later books that Sedley faults for not matching up with his version of their prologues, we do not in Lucretius' history of mankind need to emend or distort the text, if the poet is using techniques used throughout Greek and Roman literature". Techniques used in the history of Epicurean literature – I would add – should be given especially careful attention.
31 As recalled by Kazantzidis 2021, 37–38, such careful studies as those by Fowler 1995, Kyriakidis 2004, and Farrell 2007, have demonstrated that the architecture of *DRN* is thoughtfully designed by its author: "Lucretius' six-book epic falls as neatly into three distinct parts (1–2 + 3–4 + 5–6) as it can be divided into two halves (1–3 + 4–6). According to the first division, the poem makes a start with an investigation into the basic constituents of the universe (1–2), moves on to examine the material nature of the soul (3–4) and expands on the natural world and its wonders (5–6). The second model, which suggests a structural arrangement that is simultaneously conceived with and in effect complements the first, is based in its turn on a transition from the basic principles of atomism (1–3) to its ethical and psychological implications (4–6)".
32 See above, n. 6.

evidence of the poem provides incontrovertible support for it, since, for instance, the textual lacunae in the poem may have arisen at different stages in the history of the manuscript tradition,[33] and the history of Western literature provides several examples of apparently (or even undoubtedly) finished works that do not fulfil all the promises of their authors. Here it may suffice to quote just a few eloquent examples.

As for philosophical literature *sensu stricto*, Plato's aporetic dialogues provide especially relevant insights. In the conclusion of Plato's *Philebus*, for instance, Protarchus proclaims that what Socrates has said is perfectly true (ἀληθέστατα), but when Socrates asks if he can leave the scene, Protarchus replies — and concludes — as follows: "there is still a little left (σμικρὸν ἔτι τὸ λοιπόν), Socrates. I am sure you will not give up before we do, and I will remind you of what remains (τὰ λειπόμενα)".[34] Yet, to the best of my knowledge, scholars have never claimed that this finale is evidence of textual incompleteness. Rather, a detailed study of Plato's conclusion has shown that "the end that is not an end matches the beginning that was not a beginning, when the dialogue began with a conversation represented as already ongoing".[35] The Lucretian reader can be reminded of the fact that when Venus sets off the grandiose cycle of cosmic nature in the first proem, the Epicurean gods are already there — and will never go.

Even those ancient texts that purport to bring their readers face-to-face with the highest truths do not share the modern ideas of authorship, textualization, and publication. This has been most strikingly demonstrated in Matthew Larsen's study of the early Christian tradition of the gospels. As Larsen points out, "a first- or second-century reader of the texts we now call the Gospel according to Matthew and the Gospel according to Mark would not have thought of them as two separate books by two different authors", with distinct beginnings and ends, but "as the same open-ended, unfinished, and living work: the gospel — textualized".[36] Ancient discourses of truth and wisdom make the most of the reader's active participation in the process of textual construction —

---

[33] Lacunae and interpolations are among the main subjects of the long-standing debate about the poem's tenuous textual transmission: see, e.g., Deufert 1996 and Butterfield 2013.
[34] Pl. *Phlb.* 67b. Trans. Fowler 1925.
[35] Harte 2019, 267, who thinks "this unfinished quality less a cue to look for questions unanswered than a signal of the contrast between Socrates, who will never run from a discussion, and Philebus". Cf. also Gosling 1975, 228, according to whom "the inconsistencies are less than they can seem, so that Plato could well have thought there were none".
[36] Larsen 2018, 4, who, for the sake of comparison, provides a useful overview of Greek and Roman "unfinished and less authored texts" — from Plato and Cicero to Plutarch, Galen, and the so-called *hypomnemata* tradition (11–77).

which is *ipso facto* a process of knowledge creation — and in fact Lucretius expects that his addressee will integrate the teachings of *DRN* by finding other arguments by himself.[37]

Not surprisingly, the assumption that a work strewn with unfulfilled promises is necessarily unfinished is not supported by modern literature either. To cite only one representative work of the later epic tradition, Ludovico Ariosto's poem *Orlando Furioso* — one of the great masterpieces of the European Renaissance — contains several themes and characters that are mentioned at some point, arouse in the reader the expectation that they will be dealt with in more depth, but never come back to the fore. Yet we know for certain that Ariosto did finish his work. More precisely, he finished it three times as he lived to publish three different editions of his labyrinthic chivalric poem — in 1516, 1521, and 1532.[38] Lucretius may not have been as digressive as Ariosto or as other modern narrators, such as Ivan Nyukhin, the protagonist of Chekhov's one-act play *On the Harmful Effects of Tobacco*, who at the insistence of his wife proposes to give a lecture on smoking, but never gets to the topic.[39] Still, modern critics should concede that Lucretius' transient promise of focusing in detail on divine nature cannot count as definitive evidence of unfinishedness.

On the textual critical front, we should be humble enough to admit that it is impossible to know with absolute certainty which lacunae go back to Lucretius' day and which are the product of scribal errors and material damages. Sometimes we tend to forget that the history of the transmission of an ancient text does not start with the archetype — which is not the *autograph* and is itself an elusive presence — a fact that sets objective limits to the attempts of classical scholars to determine when and if omissions are the author's responsibility.[40]

---

[37] Cf. Lucr. 1.398–409; 6.527–534. For a discussion of this aspect of Lucretius' didactic technique, see Tutrone 2020. Indeed, if seen with the eyes of the ancients, Greek and Roman didactic poetry offers fertile ground for an application of the so-called reader-response theory and the transactional theories of reading: see Schiesaro/Mitsis/Clay 1993 for several case studies; on the special situation of Lucretius, see the (methodologically different) analyses by Mitsis 1993, Conte 1994, 1–34, Gale 2004b, and Taylor 2020.

[38] On Ariosto's three editions and the related textual problems, see Dorigatti 2018, 19–21. Scholars of Renaissance literature are prepared to admit that "Ariosto's chessboard is ultimately unable, or unwilling, to *contain* the romance's exuberant diversity — or better, it is not truly *designed* to contain it" (Cavallaro 2016, 153, author's emphasis).

[39] For a comprehensive analysis of this and other one-act and full-length plays by Chekhov, see Gottlieb 2000.

[40] In this respect, the work of the editors and critics of classical texts will always differ from that of scholars of modern literature. In classical philology, "there is always a gap between the desire to reach *ad fontes* and its possible fulfilment. Scholars bridge this gap with varying

Certainly, it would be naïve to think that Lucretius' gradual adjustment of his precepts, methods, and style — a strategy that includes the marginalization of previously dominant themes and the progressive emergence of more nuanced distinctions — provides evidence of the poem's unfinished state. Whereas unity and uniformity are often at the center of the aesthetic preoccupations of later writers, the ancient tradition of didactic poetry into which Lucretius taps concentrates on the development and the negotiation of a fictional relationship between poet/teacher and reader/student — a relationship which, by definition, goes through different phases depending on the reader's cognitive and moral progress. This is what Katharina Volk has aptly called the "teacher-student constellation" of ancient didactic poetry, which is typically accompanied by the illusion of "poetic simultaneity" — "the illusion that the poem is only coming into being at it evolves before the reader's eyes, that the poet/persona is composing it 'as we watch'".[41] Step by step, the poet adjusts his approach to the very same themes in order to make his argument more suitable and compelling. A brief overview of Lucretius' changing descriptions of his addressee's relationship to religious worship may suffice to clarify this point.

Shortly after his first eulogy of Epicurus in Book 1, Lucretius presents Iphigenia's sacrifice in Aulis as a typical case of the nefarious consequences of religious beliefs for human life. At this initial stage, the reader/student — who, as a neophyte, identifies himself with the dedicatee Gaius Memmius but is subtly led to sympathize with the teacher[42] — is told that he will probably abandon Lucretius' course in Epicurean philosophy because of the emotional appeal of "fablemongers" (*vates*) — the "prophets/seers/poets" whom, as Philip Hardie points out, Lucretius is trying to replace (1.102–106):[43]

> *Tutemet a nobis iam quovis tempore vatum*
> *terriloquis victus dictis desciscere quaeres.*
> *quippe etenim quam multa tibi iam fingere possunt*
> *somnia, quae vitae rationes vertere possint*
> *fortunasque tuas omnis turbare timore!*

---

levels of the rhetoric of certainty, and varying markers of the closeness of the 'almost, if not quite'. But the gap always remains" (Goldhill 2021, 47).
41 Volk 2002, 13; see also 39–40.
42 On the strategy of "didactic coercion" resulting from this deliberate intratextual shift, see Mitsis 1993.
43 See Hardie 1986, 17–22, according to whom Lucretius "adopts for himself, as purveyor of the *true*, Epicurean, piety, the Empedoclean stance of the prophet-poet".

> One day you yourself, terrorized by the fearsome pronouncements of the fable-mongers, will attempt to defect from us. Consider how numerous are the fantasies they can invent, capable of confounding your calculated plan of life and clouding all your fortunes with fear.

Modern readers may be surprised by this prophecy of betrayal, which is made unequivocal by the use of the future indicative (*quaeres*). Not only is religious discourse blamed indiscriminately for its misleading messages, but the student's capacity to resist such messages is overtly underrated. By contrast, at the end of his didactic journey in Book 6, Lucretius — who in Book 5 (1161–1240) has already unveiled the physical basis of religious awe — suggests that his student should simply refuse all thoughts "unworthy of the gods and incompatible with their peace" (*dis indigna ... alienaque pacis eorum*), so as to "approach their shrines with an untroubled breast" (*delubra deum placido cum pectore adibis*) and "receive in peace and tranquility the images that emanate from their sacred bodies (*de corpore quae sancto simulacra feruntur*) and enter human minds with news of divine beauty" (*divinae nuntia formae*).[44] Contrary to what a modern reader might conclude, Lucretius has not changed his mind, nor can the apparent distance between Books 1 and 6 be counted as evidence for the hypothesis that the *DRN* lacked the *ultima manus*. At the start of his initiation into the truths of Epicurean philosophy, the average Roman student — who has been raised in the cult of the traditional *religio* as well as in the fear of breaking the *pax deorum* — needs to undergo a kind of shock therapy, which presents Epicureanism and Roman religious lore as mutually incompatible. The frightening fantasies (*somnia*) of the seers are the exact opposite of the words of Epicurus, who in Book 1 is portrayed as an imperturbable defeater of religious oppression.[45] In applying his first-aid therapy, Lucretius follows an Epicurean pattern well attested in Philodemus, according to whom the key to the dismissal of "the inner emotions arising from false opinions" (τὰ [δ' ἐν τῆι ψ]υχῆι πάθη διὰ τὴ[ν ἡμ]ετέραν ψευδοδοξ[ία]ν παρακολουθοῦντα) lies in "perceiving their intensity and the mass of evils they contain and bring along with them" (ἐν [τ]ῶι

---

[44] Cf. Lucr. 6.68–79. This and other similar passages incontrovertibly attest that Lucretius understood his gods as real atomic beings, not as innate thought-constructs — i.e., that he endorsed the so-called "realist" interpretation of Epicurean theology, not the "idealist" view. This is acknowledged even by such an assertive supporter of the "idealist" and "innatist" view of the Epicurean gods as Sedley 2011, 50 n. 60. Cf. also Konstan 2011, 55–59.

[45] On Epicurus' imperturbability in his battle against religion, see esp. Lucr. 1.62–71. On Lucretius' depiction of Epicurus as a triumphant general, which echoes the style of Hellenistic and Roman political eulogies, see Buchheit 1971.

θεωρῆσ[αι τ]ὸ μέγεθος καὶ τὸ πλ[ῆθ]ος ὧν ἔχει καὶ συνεπι[σπ]ᾶται κακῶν).[46] Clearly, the pathetic effect produced by Lucretius' anticipation of the student's betrayal forms part of this first-stage psychagogic approach.

At a later stage, however, a milder treatment can be employed, and the student/reader can be provided with more detailed information about the place of the gods in the natural world. Already in Book 2, Lucretius explains that the real danger for his pupil is not to acknowledge the existence of the gods or the need for worship, but to endorse the traditional belief that the cosmos is ruled by divine providence — a belief that was widely shared by both philosophers and poets.[47] Quite significantly, Lucretius maintains that only in due course will he offer further explanations about the nature and the limits of divine agency, as he clearly considers the understanding of the laws of atomic motion to be preliminary to any theological analysis (2.174–183):[48]

> [...]   *quorum omnia causa*
> *constituisse deos cum fingunt, omnibus rebus*
> *magno opere a vera lapsi ratione videntur.*
> *nam quamvis rerum ignorem primordia quae sint,*
> *hoc tamen ex ipsis caeli rationibus ausim*
> *confirmare aliisque ex rebus reddere multis,*
> *nequaquam nobis divinitus esse creatam*
> *naturam mundi: tanta stat praedita culpa.*
> *quae tibi posterius, Memmi, faciemus aperta;*
> *nunc id quod super est de motibus expediemus.*

In supposing that the gods have arranged everything for the benefit of humanity, these thinkers have obviously deviated far from the path of sound judgment in every respect. For even if I had no knowledge of the primary elements of things, I would venture to deduce from the actual behavior of the sky, and from many other facts, evidence and proof that the world was by no means created for us by divine agency: it is marked by such seri-

---

46 Philod. *De ira* col. 6.13–22 Indelli, with the comments of Tsouna 2007, 74–87.
47 Lucr. 2.174–183. It is hard to believe that here and in 5.55–234 Lucretius is not aware of the overwhelming influence of Stoic providentialism on Roman culture, literature, and politics — as has been argued by Furley 1966, 27–30, who makes the speculative claim that Lucretius criticizes a thesis defended by Aristotle "in some of the books, now lost, which he wrote for a wider public". However, it is reasonable to suppose that Lucretius is not attacking *only* the Stoics *qua* "professional" thinkers, for an anthropocentric view of divine agency was deep-rooted in poetic and folkloric wisdom long before the Stoics. See also Lévy 1999.
48 Lucretius' choice makes perfect sense in light of the "realist" interpretation of Epicurean theology, according to which the very idea of the gods arises in human minds when the atomic films (εἴδωλα/*simulacra*) emitted by divine bodies impact on the minds themselves. Cf. Essler 2011 and Konstan 2011.

ous flaws. Later, Memmius, I will make this plain to you; but now I will complete my explanation of the movements of atoms.

Compared to the uncompromising criticism of religion of Book 1, this is a notable restatement of the poet's polemical point, providing new — yet not exhaustive — particulars on the subject of natural theology. However, only in Book 5 will the student be ready to learn the source of the belief in divine providence. At that point, Lucretius will create an emphatic transition to signal that the time has come to throw light on the physical origins of religion. According to the poet, after exploring the earliest phases in the history of humankind — with the invention of society, language, and urbanism[49] — "it is not so difficult to explain with words the reason" (*non ita difficilest rationem reddere verbis*, 5.1168) for the emergence of religious feelings and institutions (5.1161–1168):

> *Nunc quae causa deum per magnas numina gentis*
> *pervulgarit et ararum compleverit urbis*
> *suscipiendaque curarit sollemnia sacra,*
> *quae nunc in magnis florent sacra rebus locisque,*
> *unde etiam nunc est mortalibus insitus horror,*
> *qui delubra deum nova toto suscitat orbi*
> *terrarum et festis cogit celebrare diebus,*
> *non ita difficilest rationem reddere verbis.*
>
> Now it is not so difficult to explain with words what cause has made belief in the gods universal throughout mighty nations and filled cities with altars and prompted the institution of solemn religious rites — rites that now flourish in great states and places. It is not difficult to explain what even now implants in mortals this shuddering fear that all over the earth raises new shrines to the gods and crowds them with congregations on festal days.

Having experienced a gradual conversion to the scientific and moral beliefs of Epicureanism, the student is now able to get a full understanding of the historical and psychological roots of religious worship — which, in turn, will allow him to approach the shrines of the gods with an untroubled breast, as proclaimed in the above-cited passage of Book 6.[50] Lucretius has not changed his mind, and his skilled use of poetic simultaneity and thematic adaptability is anything but a sign of unfinishedness.

Equally interesting is the fact that in cases such as the one we have just considered the rhetorical devices of recursive argumentation and thematic

---

49 Cf. 5.925–1160. On the main features and aims of Lucretius' *Kulturentstehungslehre*, see Furley 1977; Sasso 1979; and Manuwald 1980.
50 Cf. above, n. 44.

adaptability intertwine with each other. In Book 5, when introducing the reader to his more "technical" treatment of the issue of divine agency, Lucretius repeats with minor variations the anti-teleological argument of Book 2 quoted above (5.195–199):

> *Quod <si> iam rerum ignorem primordia quae sint,*
> *hoc tamen ex ipsis caeli rationibus ausim*
> *confirmare aliisque ex rebus reddere multis,*
> *nequaquam nobis divinitus esse paratam*
> *naturam rerum: tanta stat praedita culpa.*

> Even if I had no knowledge of the primary elements of things, I would venture to deduce from the actual behavior of the sky, and from many other facts, evidence and proof that the world was by no means created for us by divine agency: it is marked by such serious flaws.[51]

By recalling his own earlier words, the poet/teacher reawakens the reader's attention, signals that he is revisiting a previously introduced subject, and builds a new chapter of his didactic mission on the psychologically powerful basis of verbal memory. Indeed, in the world of Lucretius and his fellow Epicureans, the gradualness, malleability, and sequentiality of instruction draw on repetition as an effective way of punctuating the progress of the student's consciousness — all such elements being part of the same pedagogical project. Even more notably, as Alessandro Schiesaro points out, the overall narratological structure of *DRN*, with its mixture of progressive patterns and cyclical repetitions, is itself a spur to embark on "a repeated and frequent reading of the poem" — a spur to see the eternal palingenesis of the cosmos reflected in the morally instructive palingenesis of Lucretius' work, which continuously reenacts the circle of birth, development, decay, death, and regeneration.[52] Far from giving us any clue about the poem's *unfinishedness*, the rhetorical and didactic devices discussed in the present paper ultimately generate an opening to material *infinity*. What appears utterly unfinished is *our* hermeneutical inquiry into the textual and intellectual universe of *DRN* — which, very much like the Polynesian *moai*, urges us to dismiss preconceived notions and to face the challenge of cross-cultural interpretation.[53]

---

[51] Cf. 2.177–181.

[52] Schiesaro 1994, 102–104. For further insights about the processes of interiorization implied in the narratological structure of *DRN*, see Gale 2004b and Tutrone 2020.

[53] This paper has greatly benefited from the vivid discussions that took place at the 15th *Trends in Classics* conference. I am sincerely grateful to the three organizers as well as to the partici-

Bibliography

Armstrong, David (1995), "The Impossibility of Metathesis: Philodemus and Lucretius on Form and Content in Poetry", in: D. Obbink (ed.), *Philodemus and Poetry: Poetic Theory and Practice in Lucretius, Philodemus, and Horace*, Oxford, 210–232.

Atherton, Catherine (ed.) (1998), *Form and Content in Didactic Poetry*, Bari.

Bahn, Paul/Flenley, John (2011), *Easter Island, Earth Island: The Enigmas of Rapa Nui*, Lanham MD.

Baker, Eric (2007), "Lucretius in the European Enlightenment", in: Stuart Gillespie/Philip Hardie (eds.), *The Cambridge Companion to Lucretius*, Cambridge, 274–288.

Barthes, Roland (1977), "The Death of the Author", in: Id., *Image Music Text* (trans. Seath), London, 142–148.

Baum, Kelly/Bayer, Andrea/Wagstaff, Sheena (2016), *Unfinished: Thoughts Left Visible*, New York.

Bayer, Andrea (2006), "Renaissance Views of the Unfinished", in: Baum/Bayer/Wagstaff 2016, 18–29.

Bignore, Ettore (1945), *Storia della letteratura latina, Vol. 2*, Florence.

Bomford, David (2015), *Unfinished Paintings: Narratives of the Non Finito*, Edinburgh.

Buchheit, Vinzenz (1971), "Epikurs Triumph des Geistes (Lukrez I, 62–79)", *Hermes* 99, 303–323.

Butterfield, David (2013), *The Early Textual History of Lucretius' De Rerum Natura*, Cambridge/New York.

Canevaro, Lilah Grace/O'Rourke, Donncha (eds.) (2019), *Didactic Poetry of Greece, Rome and Beyond: Knowledge, Power, Tradition*, Swansea/Bristol, CT.

Canfora, Luciano (1993), *Vita di Lucrezio*, Palermo.

Capasso, Mario (1982), *Trattato etico epicureo* (PHerc. 346), Naples.

Capasso, Mario (1987), *Comunità senza rivolta: Quattro saggio sull'epicureismo*, Naples.

Cavallaro, Dani (2016), *The Chivalric Romance and the Essence of Fiction*, Jefferson, NC.

Clay, Diskin (1998), *Paradosis and Survival: Three Chapters in the History of Epicurean Philosophy*, Ann Arbor, MI.

Conte, Gian Biagio (1994), *Genres and Readers: Lucretius, Love Elegy, Pliny's Encyclopedia*, trans. G.W. Most, Baltimore, MD.

Deufert, Marcus (1996), *Pseudo-Lukrezisches im Lukrez: Die unechten Verse in Lukrezens De rerum natura*, Berlin/New York.

Dorigatti, Marco (2018), "Italian Editions: A Bibliographical Survey of Epic and Chivalric Poems", in: Jo Ann Cavallo (ed.), *Teaching the Italian Renaissance Romance Epic*, New York, 19–27.

Erler, Michael (1993), "*Philologia medicans*: wie die Epikureer die Texte ihres Meisters lasen", in: Wolfgang Kullmann/Joachim Althoff (eds.), *Vermittlung und Tradierung von Wissen in der griechischen Kultur*, Tübingen, 281–303.

---

pants and attendees of the conference, among whom I should mention at least Myrto Garani, David Konstan, John Miller, and Giulia Sissa. During my revision of this chapter, I have also benefited from comments and insights of other colleagues such as Michael Hanaghan, Matthew Larsen, Pura Nieto Hernández, Alessandro Schiesaro, and Matthew Watton. As usual, any remaining errors and shortcomings are my responsibility alone.

Essler, Holger (2011), *Glückselig und unsterblich: Epikureische Theologie bei Cicero und Philodem (mit einer Edition von PHerc. 152/157, Kol. 8–10)*, Basel.
Farrell, John (1994), "The Structure of Lucretius' 'Anthropology' (*DRN* 5.771–1457)", *MD* 33, 81–95.
Farrell, J. (2007), "Lucretian Architecture: The Structure and the Argument of *De Rerum Natura*", in: Stuart Gillespie/Philip Hardie (eds.), *The Cambridge Companion to Lucretius*, Cambridge, 76–91.
Farrell, John (2017), *Varieties of Authorial Intention: Literary Theory Beyond the Intentional Fallacy*, Cham.
Foucault, Michel (1986), *The History of Sexuality, 3: The Care of the Self* (trans. R. Hurley), New York.
Foucault, Michel (2005), *The Hermeneutics of the Subject: Lectures at the College de France 1981-1982* (ed. F. Gros; trans. G. Burchell), New York.
Fowler, Harold N. (ed.) (1925), *Plato: Plato in Twelve Volumes*, Vol. 9, Cambridge, MA/London.
Fowler, Don (1995), "From Epos to Cosmos: Lucretius, Ovid, and the Poetics of Segmentation", in: D. Innes/H. Hine/C. Pelling (eds.), *Ethics and Rhetoric: Classical Essays for Donald Russell on his Seventy-Fifth Birthday*, Oxford, 3–18.
Friedländer, Paul (1941), "Pattern of Sound and Atomistic Theory in Lucretius", *American Journal of Philology* 62, 16–34.
Furley, David J. (1966), "Lucretius and the Stoics", *BICS* 17, 55–64.
Furley, David J. (1977), "Lucretius the Epicurean: On the History of Man", in: Olof Gigon (ed.), *Lucrèce*, XXIV Entretiens Hardt sur l'Antiquité Classique, Genève, 1–37.
Gale, Monica (ed.) (2004a), *Latin Epic and Didactic Poetry: Genre, Tradition and Individuality*, Swansea/Oakville, CT.
Gale, Monica (2004b), "The Story of Us: A Narratological Analysis of Lucretius' *De Rerum Natura*", in: Gale 2004a, 49–71.
Gallop, Jane (2011), *The Deaths of the Author: Reading and Writing in Time*, Durham/London.
Garani, Myrto (2007), *Empedocles Redivivus: Poetry and Analogy in Lucretius*, New York/London.
Gigante, Marcello (1983), *Ricerche filodemee*, Naples.
Glad, Clarence E. (1995), *Paul and Philodemus: Adaptability in Epicurean and Early Christian Psychagogy*, Leiden.
Gladman, Kimberley R./Mitsis, Phillip (1997), "Lucretius and the Unconscious", in: Keimpe Algra/Mieke H. Koenen/Piet H. Schrijvers (eds.), *Lucretius and his Intellectual Background*, Amsterdam/New York, 215–224.
Goldhill, Simon (2021), "The Union and Divorce of Classical Philology and Theology", in: Catherine Conybeare/Simon Goldhill (eds.), *Classical Philology and Theology: Entanglement, Disavowal, and the Godlike Scholar*, Cambridge, 33–62.
Gosling, J.C.B. (ed.) (1975), *Plato: Philebus*, Oxford.
Gottlieb, Vera (2000), "Chekhov's One-Act Plays and Full-Length Plays", in: Vera Gottlieb/Paul Allain (eds.), *The Cambridge Companion to Chekhov*, Cambridge, 57–69.
Hadot, Pierre (1995), *Philosophy as a Way of Life: Spiritual Exercises from Socrates to Foucault* (ed. with an introduction by A.I. Davidson; trans. M. Chase), Oxford.
Hadot, Pierre (2002), *What is Ancient Philosophy?*, Cambridge, MA/London.
Hamilton, Andy/Pearson, Lara (eds.) (2021), *The Aesthetics of Imperfection in Music and the Arts: Spontaneity, Flaws and the Unfinished*, London/New York/Dublin.
Hardie, Philip R. (1986), *Virgil's Aeneid: Cosmos and Imperium*, Oxford.
Harte, Verity (2019), "The Dialogue's Finale: *Philebus* 64c-67b", in: Panos Dimas/Russell E. Jones/Gabriel R. Lear (eds.), *Plato's* Philebus: *A Philosophical Discussion*, Oxford, 253–267.

Holford-Strevens, Leofranc (2002), "*Horror Vacui* in Lucretian Biography", *Leeds International Classical Studies* 1, 1–23.

Hunt, Terry/Lipo, Carl (2011), *The Statues That Walked: Unraveling the Mystery of Easter Island*, New York.

Kazantzidis, George (2021), *Lucretius on Disease: The Poetics of Morbidity in* De Rerum Natura, Berlin/Boston.

Konstan, David (2008), *A Life Worthy of the Gods: The Materialist Psychology of Epicurus*, Las Vegas.

Konstan, David (2011), "Epicurus on the Gods", in: Jeffrey Fish/Kirk R. Sanders (eds.), *Epicurus and the Epicurean Tradition*, Cambridge/New York, 53–71.

Kyriakidis, Stratis (2004), "Middles in Lucretius' *DRN*: The Poet and his Work", in: Stratis Kyriakidis/Francesco de Martino (eds.), *Middles in Latin Poetry*, Bari, 27–49.

Kyriakidis, Stratis (2006), "Lucretius' *DRN* 1.926–50 and the Proem to Book 4", *The Classical Quarterly* 56.2, 606–610.

Larsen, Matthew D.C. (2018), *Gospels Before the Book*, Oxford/New York.

Leigh, Fiona (2020), "Kinds of Self-Knowledge in Ancient Thought", in: Ead. (ed.), *Self-Knowledge in Ancient Philosophy*, Oxford, 1–50.

Lévy, Carlos (1999), "Lucrèce et les Stoïciens", in: Remy Poignault (ed.), *Présence de Lucrèce*, Tours, 87–98.

Maleuvre, Didier (2019), *The Legends of the Modern: A Reappraisal of Modernity from Shakespeare to the Age of Duchamp*, London/New York/Dublin.

Manuwald, Bernd (1980), *Der Aufbau der lukrezischen Kulturentstehungslehre* (De rerum natura *5,925–1457)*, Stuttgart.

Masson, John (1884), *The Atomic Theory of Lucretius Contrasted with Modern Doctrines of Atoms and Evolution*, London.

Mitsis, Phillip (1993), "Committing Philosophy to the Reader: Didactic Coercion and Reader Autonomy in *De Rerum Natura*", in: Schiesaro/Mitsis/Clay 1993, 111–128.

Nethercut, Jason S. (2021), Ennius Noster: *Lucretius and the* Annales, Oxford/New York.

Nussbaum, Martha C. (1994), *The Therapy of Desire: Theory and Practice in Hellenistic Ethics*, Princeton.

O'Hara, James J. (2007), *Inconsistency in Roman Epic: Studies in Catullus, Lucretius, Vergil, Ovid and Lucan*, Cambridge/New York.

Palmer, Ada (2014), *Reading Lucretius in the Renaissance*, Cambridge, MA/London.

Porter, James I. (2006), "What is 'Classical' in Classical Antiquity?", in: Id. (ed.), *Classical Pasts: The Classical Traditions of Greece and Rome*, Princeton/Oxford, 1–65.

Rull, Valentí/Stevenson, Christopher (eds.) (2022), *The Prehistory of Rapa Nui (Easter Island): Towards an Integrative Interdisciplinary Framework*, Cham.

Sasso Gennaro (1979), *Il progresso e la morte: Saggio su Lucrezio*, Bologna.

Schiesaro, Alessandro/Mitsis, Phillip/Clay, Jenny Strauss (eds.) (1993), *Mega nepios: il destinatario nell'epos didascalico*, Pisa.

Schiesaro, Alessandro (1994), "The Palingenesis of *De Rerum Natura*", *Proceedings of the Cambridge Philological Society* 40, 81–107.

Sedley, David (1998), *Lucretius and the Transformation of Greek Wisdom*, Cambridge.

Sedley, David (2011), "Epicurus' Theological Innatism", in: Jeffrey Fish/Kirk R. Sanders (eds.), *Epicurus and the Epicurean Tradition*, Cambridge/New York, 29–52.

Smith, Martin Ferguson (ed.) (2001), *Lucretius: On the Nature of Things*, Indianapolis/Cambridge.

Snyder, Jane McIntosh (1980), *Puns and Poetry in Lucretius'* De Rerum Natura, Amsterdam.
Taylor, Barnaby (2020), "Common Ground in Lucretius' *De Rerum Natura*", in: Donncha O'Rourke (ed.), *Approaches to Lucretius: Traditions and Innovations in Reading* De Rerum Natura, Cambridge, 59–79.
Tsouna, Voula (2007), *The Ethics of Philodemus*, Oxford/New York.
Tsouna, Voula (2009), "Epicurean Therapeutic Strategies", in: James Warren (ed.), *The Cambridge Companion to Epicureanism*, Cambridge/New York, 249–265.
Tutrone, Fabio (2020), "Coming to Know Epicurus' Truth: Distributed Cognition in Lucretius' *De Rerum Natura*", in: Donncha O'Rourke (ed.), *Approaches to Lucretius: Traditions and Innovations in Reading* De Rerum Natura, Cambridge, 80–100.
Tutrone, Fabio (2021), "A View from the Garden: Contemplative Isolation and Constructive Sociability in Lucretius and in the Epicurean Tradition", in: Rafal Matuszewski (ed.), *Being Alone in Antiquity: Ancient Ideas and Experiences of Misanthropy, Isolation, and Solitude*, Berlin/Boston, 199–225.
Volk, Katharina (2002), *The Poetics of Latin Didactic: Lucretius, Vergil, Ovid, Manilius*, Oxford/New York.
Yonge, Charles D. (ed.) (1853), *Diogenes Laertius: The Lives and Opinions of Eminent Philosophers*, London.

Sylvie Thorel
The Fragment as a Form: A Reading of *Fragments d'un discours amoureux* by Barthes

Abstract: Despite being presented as fragments in their title, *Fragments d'un discours amoureux* is nothing of the kind. This study aims to explore the ambiguities and paradoxes generated by a contradictory formal device.

In 1977, Roland Barthes published *Fragments d'un discours amoureux*, which was his greatest bookstore success and even earned him a guest appearance on the panel of *Apostrophes*, at the same time as Françoise Sagan. Having apparently abandoned the disguise of an arid semiologist, he was consecrated as a writer and as an expert in sentimental affairs. He was finally an author who was readable by all but who, nevertheless, affirmed the theoretical ambition of his latest work.

1 The choice of the fragment

The book is in fact part of a continuity, for the author had hitherto devoted himself only to brief or broken forms; his entire work is presented as "fragments", here exhibited as such by a title that suggests seeing in them the remains of an inaccessible whole, itself absent and evoked by the lacuna. In its etymological sense, the fragment results from the fracture of a totality. When unique, it can only be traced back to the totality according to the principle of synecdoche; when there are many, as in the present case, it lends itself to the puzzle, complete or, more often, incomplete — the blanks drawn by the missing pieces can then be filled in, i.e. interpreted: continuity is thus re-established by default.

The partitive construction of the syntagm formed by the book's title presents the whole, from which these fragments are extracted, as a love discourse which is supposed to pre-exist them: Barthes would be the enlightened editor of detached pages, in relation to which he would enjoy an overarching position. If, on the other hand, the nature of such discourse is to run underground, unbeknownst to the lover, and to manifest itself exclusively via the sudden occurrence of these incomplete pieces that the reader (the beloved?) could interpret as its remainder, we reach a similar paradox. The title of the volume reveals, on the part of its author, a curious knowledge of the unknowable: it stages the immanent plane of experience, which gives rise to the "fragments", and the transcendent plane of knowledge behind which it is possible to identify the discourse of love. A deceptive device is thus at work: designated by their author as fragments, these texts are of course nothing of the sort. The showcasing of such a quality (or defect) reveals the bias of a form that is paradoxical, because it denies itself as such.

Antiquity has been bequeathed to us, for the most part, through fragments of monuments, statues or texts, which it is up to the archaeologist and hermeneutist to reconnect to the whole by tracking down the marks of their diffraction and by endeavouring to fill in the gaps that separate them. Conversely, the wanderer or the poet (Hubert Robert, Diderot, Chateaubriand) is absorbed in melancholy when he is not frightened, as a moralist, of the power of these blocks and of their current radiance in the abyss they have fallen into. The fragment may therefore appear to be a model, which fed Montaigne's *Essays* as well as La Rochefoucauld's *Maxims*, or even La Bruyère's *Characters*: the intermediate spaces, from one paragraph to another or even from one sentence to another, become sound boxes for statements that resound louder and more lastingly. The publication of Pascal's *Thoughts*, which accidentally emerged from an inaccessible or untraceable *Apology for Religion*, confirmed the power of the fragmentary, henceforth linked to the unfinished: such a work in limbo bears the marks of its impeded elaboration and gives access to the gesture of its author. Confused with his life, it seems to deliver, with the truth that it laconically states, an intimate confidence.

As he reiterated, Barthes' main reference is romantic and German. It results from the examination by the *Athenæum* of the powers of the ancient fragment, of which he makes a figure, i.e. a symbolic form or formal expression relevant to an idea of existence. It is a question, according to Lacoue-Labarthe and Nancy, of "delivering Modernity to itself in the mode in which it receives Antiquity, that is, in the mode of the accomplished loss of the great Individuality."[1] However, the issue differs considerably from one era to the next: while the ancient fragment stems from accidental loss, the modern fragment expresses a denial of what is considered as the lure of transcendence. It does not even fit into the framework of a negative theology, which would equate to the sublimation and divinisation of the absent work, but, while evoking this possibility, it expresses

---

[1] Lacoue-Labarthe/Nancy 1978, 72. Translated from the French. All translations from French are my own.

the will to settle here below, in the time after "the great Individuality" to which Antiquity was linked.

Additionally, since it is based on the refusal of transcendence, Modernity perceives the fragment from a democratic perspective: by analogy, the fragment refers to the individual and its practice agrees with a political ideal of free and equal coexistence of the disconnected parts of the whole, which is expressed through parataxis rather than hypotaxis or subordination. Moreover, when it becomes a form, parataxis tends to govern the "fragment" in its own integrity.

Beyond individuality, intimacy is at stake — this is perhaps Pascal's influence. The use of the fragment suggests that the form is lacking, that the writer is not forced (or has not allowed himself to be forced) by the norm of continuity: the remainder has a value in itself. Since its isolation prevents it from being characterised by the completion of a demonstration or the completeness of a figure, the fragment contains a part of intransitivity that leads us to take particular note of its tone or of what Barthes calls its "timbre".

Within the book, some of Barthes' considerations also allow us to see the fragment as a form that is especially relevant to its object, the discourse of love. This is firstly because it is characterised by its solitude and relegation: a discourse "cut off from power, but also from its mechanisms", "drifting", "deported from all gregariousness" — an abandoned, "forgotten"[2] fragment of the General Discourse. The discourse of love also needs to be fragmentary because the lover's fate is his inability to be fulfilled, or to ever receive the answer that would make him join a whole. This is illustrated by a Platonic myth mentioned by Barthes, that of the original double being, of which each of us is a fragment stubbornly trying to find its other so that the lost unity may be restored. Finally, Barthes underlines the fetishism of the lover towards the beloved whose mere nail or eyebrow, for example, demonstrates the inaccessible wonder of his or her whole person.

It is easy to conceive that the fragment seems to him like an ideal, but its pursuit is fraught with difficulties: how can we even imagine that it can result from an intention? The author of *Fragments d'un discours amoureux* was not unaware of this, since in *Roland Barthes by Roland Barthes* he recognised the rhetorical and symbolic dimension of this form:

> I have the illusion of believing that by breaking up my discourse, I cease to speak imaginatively about myself, I attenuate the risk of transcendence; but since the fragment (the haiku, the maxim, the thought, the scrap of diary) is ultimately a rhetorical genre and

---

2 Barthes 1977a, 7.

since rhetoric is that layer of language which best offers itself to interpretation, in believing that I am dispersing myself, I am only wisely returning to the bed of the imaginary.[3]

This confirms the reader's intuition, given the mere title of *Fragments d'un discours amoureux*: the contradiction is difficult to lessen. The analysis of the device will confirm it: a text designated by its author as fragmentary proclaims its completeness in reverse — the fragment undoubtedly exists only by being ignored and its pursuit, as a form, perhaps leads to being engulfed in the well of endless regressions.

2 An annoying paratext

These fragments fit within a complex paratextual framework that tends to order them as a whole. It all begins with the title, which conflates the two levels of experience and knowledge. After the title, the "*exergue*" underlines the need for a book devoted to this common yet solitary discourse, which Barthes overtly aims to support in spite of its very inactuality. From this we can deduce the importance of a latent theoretical issue; his purpose is to characterise any love discourse.

This is followed by the introduction entitled "How this book is made", in which there is still no question of a work but only of a material object, a set of pages sewn or glued together, as befits a collection of fragments. Barthes claims to have resorted to a "dramatic method" in order to avoid any "metalanguage" by opting instead for a "simulation"[4] — fiction thus becomes the instrument of theory. Instead of describing and analysing a discourse of love, Barthes decides to employ it himself, through the implementation of a structure that reveals the "place of speech" of a lonely lover. From afar, we recognise the model of Ovid's *Heroides* but the use of a form of lyricism is subordinated to the wish to practice a science of the particular (*mathesis singularis*), which in itself constitutes a paradoxical object. Thus, Barthes declares that he will use the first-person pronoun so that all readers can share the experience according to a perspective that excludes narcissism as well as egotism since it is a matter of method. The use of "I" is therefore not personal but theoretical.

This introduction is organised around three objects: *Figures*, *Order* and *References*. Barthes calls "figures" the "breaks in discourse", which he equates

---

3 Barthes 1975, 672.
4 Barthes 1977a, 9.

with "scenes of language"[5] that the reader is meant to recognise. It is a matter of capturing the moments when the lover is caught in a posture, such as one of expectation, jealousy, memory, "I-love-you". Each one is as if detached. It is preceded by its "argument", which appears as a name printed in capital letters, like a dictionary entry, and it is followed by the description or suggestion of a situation that introduces the figure: a kind of fragment within a fragment.

The lover, Barthes continues, cannot integrate these figures into any order, nor submit them to any narrative or reduce them to any meaning. Arranging the figures, putting them into perspective, instead of leaving them to the narrative "Other" or "common opinion" — it is totalitarianism. It is therefore necessary to skilfully disorganise them, relying on the "tempered" arbitrariness of their naming and their alphabetising, instead of relying on "pure chance, which could well have produced logical sequences"[6] — it is of course an implicit recognition of the arbitrariness of the author himself.

Finally, the introduction mentions floating and incomplete "references", not of authority but "of friendship", delivered through the assembly of "pieces of diverse origin": the work would thus be a *centon*, a collection and arrangement of quotations i.e. fragments. This is another area of ambiguity. These references are supposed to belong to the life of the author, who stubbornly refuses any "transcendent" position, only to state that he "lends here to the amorous subject his 'culture'", while the latter "passes on to him the innocence of his imagination":[7] a game of knowledge with the unknown. This innocence is all relative: we are reading a work that is not only learned but misleading. Its fragmentary form does not prevent it from being quite complete in spite of Barthes' refusal of continuity, which he considers dubious for philosophical and political reasons.

There follows, in italics at the bottom of a blank page, the formula of the previously mentioned "simulation": "It is therefore a lover who speaks and says".[8] We are thus engaged, by this pact that we sign with the author when turning the page, in the reading of a long prosopopoeia that we are forbidden to confuse with the testimony of the individual called Roland Barthes. It presupposes the elaboration of a model, that is to say a projection of the subject into another space. The work itself is thus caught between the tweezers of imaginary inverted commas, and the reader is not supposed to identify psychologically

---

5 Barthes 1977a, 10.
6 Barthes 1977a, 14.
7 Barthes 1977a, 16.
8 Barthes 1977a, 17.

with the "I" who is getting ready to speak: the reader just has to take his place within the device. The *Fragments* are presented as an "extended metaphor"[9] in the same way as Barthes described La Bruyère's *Characters*: beyond being observations, its components are also signs that make up the demonstrations hidden within the figures. As soon as the formula is pronounced, it is also clear that the author not only uses the personal pronoun's enallage, but that he writes the text in the present tense, in a nonetheless anti-lyrical perspective. Just as "I" is theoretical, the present tense is here deprived of its temporal value; it is its aspectual value of non-time that comes into play. Almost gnomic, it is the present tense of the type or character. Each component of the whole is therefore significant.

The body of work is presented as a series of eighty fragments preceded by their "*enseigne*" (sign) and their "figure". The "*enseigne*" or sign is typographically given as a title and its function is to present the theme of the fragment, sometimes by means of a quotation. Below the sign is the figure it introduces, followed by the outline of a situation, which is more suggestive than definitive. It is noteworthy that the fragments are arranged in the alphabetical order of figures' names and not in the alphabetical order of the signs that surmount them; an uncertainty ensues.

They are governed by parataxis and consist of situations (I'm waiting for a phone call), anecdotes (we part on a station platform), playlets (the beloved is having fun in the company of others), maxims ("The Feast is what you expect"), complaints ("Sometimes anguish is so strong …"), and exact or approximate quotations, of which there are a considerable number, since the work is almost a cento. These quotations are taken from a limited number of authors, mainly Goethe (*Werther*), Plato (*The Banquet*), Ruysbroeck, Zen, Winnicott, Nietzsche, Schubert. In the margins of the pages are given the names of these authors as well as the initials of friends whose words are reported, while at the bottom are a few notes that are more precise but also incomplete as they were written from memory. Each fragment thus gives a great impression of disjointedness: "Not only is the fragment cut off from its neighbours, but also within each fragment there is parataxis",[10] i.e. it itself consists of a series of fragments, generally numbered. The order of increasing values emphasises the impression of arbitrariness given by the alphabetical order. Often the fragment begins with a reference to *Werther*, mentioned forty-two times, and often there is a reference to Barthes's mother in its last lines.

---

9 Barthes 1964, 486.
10 Barthes 1975, 670.

The book ends with a *Tabula gratulatoria* divided into four numbered parts. The first lists the full names of the friends referred to by their initials in the marginal notes; the second gives the references to the *Werther* edition; the third lists the texts quoted and the fourth includes the titles of musical pieces, paintings and films.

Finally, there is a very detailed table of contents that has the particularity of first giving the name of each figure, followed by the sign (*enseigne*) that precedes it in the pages of the book, and the section titles: these titles do not appear in the fragments themselves. From this there emerges what he calls, in *Roland Barthes by Roland Barthes,* the "relief" of the whole:

> This can be clearly seen when drawing up an index of these little pieces; for each of them, the assembly of referents is heterogeneous; it's like a game of rhyming bits: "Let the words be: fragment, circle, Gide, catch, asyndeton, painting, dissertation, Zen, intermezzo; imagine a discourse that can link them." Well, it will simply be this fragment here. The index of a text is therefore not only an instrument of reference; it is itself a text, a second text which is the "relief" (remainder and asperity) of the first one: what is delirious (interrupted) in the reasoning of sentences.[11]

Parataxis, and the heterogeneity it serves, must favour the avoidance of a demonstration and prevent the meaning from becoming fixed.

Their isomorphism and the limited references they bring together, however, make the fragments communicate with each other, so that a kind of web or network is formed. Moreover, the complexity of the paratext, even when disturbed by the inversion of the names of figures and signs as well as by the vagueness of the references, has the effect of ordering it according to a strict and strong hierarchy and of converting the local play of parataxis into the general regime of hypotaxis: transcendence is therefore not ruled out. Above all, it can be said that the table of contents, readable itself as a fragment that characterises each of the others as fragmentary, establishes the fractal dimension of the totality. It is a way of secretly introducing a form of completeness, or even continuity, where there seemed to be none. The fractality of the device contradicts the concept of the fragment.

Similarly, the alphabetical order seems to overarch the collection in an irrefutable manner. But the authority of this convention, found within dictionaries and encyclopaedias alike, suggests conversely that the whole is achieved, that we have come full circle in the "*discours amoureux*". This order is also malicious, as indicated by the opening observation that its arbitrariness can be

---

11 Barthes 1975, 670.

"tempered". The first fragment deals with a subject "damaged" (*abîmé*) in love. We later understand that this is a consequence of his relentlessness in grasping the beloved in its entirety. It ends on the decision of "not wanting to grasp", of not appropriating the beloved. In parallel, since references to *Werther* are omnipresent, the first fragment opens with a quotation from the beginning of Goethe's novel ("In these thoughts I sink, I succumb, under the power of these magnificent visions"), and "Not-wanting-to-grasp", the last fragment, evokes symmetrically "the very moment when Werther kills himself and when he could have given up trying to grasp Charlotte". This is what constitutes, in what is given to us as a disordered collection, both a beginning and an end – in other words, a direction, a meaning.

3 The temptation of the novel

Barthes' attitude towards the fragment fluctuates. Most often, he understands it as the form we have just described: a form towards which he is compelled, whilst having to resist the temptation of narrative. The narrative form is interpreted as the lure of continuity and the sly expression of a submission to power; above all, the novel is a bourgeois genre and it is so worn out that it is threadbare. But sometimes Barthes also refers to the fragment more as an inadequacy than a formal choice, as he explained to Pierre Boncenne:

> [...] writing is never more than the rather poor and thin remainder of the wonderful things everyone has within themselves. Writing is made up of small, erratic blocks or ruins relating to a complicated and dense whole. And that's the problem with writing: how can I bear the fact that this flow within me produces, in the best of cases, a mere trickle of writing? Personally, I cope better by giving the impression of not constructing a totality and by leaving out several residues. That is the way I justify my fragments.

He continued:

> "This said, I now have the urge to write a great piece of work, a piece which is continuous and not fragmentary". He considered this problem "typically Proustian, since Proust lived half his life producing only fragments and then, all of a sudden, in 1909, began to construct the oceanic expanse that is *La recherche du temps perdu*."[12]

---

12 Barthes 1979, 750.

He made such remarks subsequent to the writing of *Fragments d'un discours amoureux*, and as a consequence of "the decision of April 15, 1978", taken the day after his mother's death and set out in *Vita Nova*: in the absence of descendants, he decided to leave behind a great body of work, which he refers to as "literature as a substitute, as an expansion of love."[13] He thought for a moment of leaving the *Collège de France* to devote himself to writing this novel, but then had another idea: to combine teaching and writing by devoting his new lecture to "the preparation of the novel", subsequent to the course on *Werther* on which the 1977 book was based. We know that this project did not come to fruition. This can be explained, at least in part, by Barthes' resistance against the most elementary constraints of the genre, a resistance of a political nature that had already been developed in *Le Degré zéro de l'écriture*.

As early as 1953, he had developed the idea that the simple past tense is "the algebraic sign of an intention"; "the image of an order, it constitutes one of the many formal pacts established between the writer and society, for the justification of the one and the serenity of the other."[14] In the same way, he added, the third person "provides its consumers with the security of a credible fabulation, yet one that is constantly manifested as false". Pursuing the same thought, he declared much later in *Roland Barthes by Roland Barthes* that the adjective is "on the side of the image, on the side of domination, of death."[15] He comes back to this at the time of *La Préparation du roman*, telling Pierre Boncenne:

> Let's say that, if I wanted to write a novel, I would be a little embarrassed to use *he, she*, the simple past tense and to give proper names to my characters. Why would it embarrass me? Because it is part of a completely obsolete code; if I used these forms, it would mean that I accept this obsolete code. It is not impossible: one could say that one accepts it and agrees to write a novel as they were written before; but this raises many issues. There is a resistance to certain forms. For the adjective, it is self-explanatory. It is not the novel's problem, it is the problem of a life lived, of a life lived at all times with the other. Qualifying a being with an adjective, even if the said adjective is laudatory and beneficial, equates to giving the being a kind of essence or image. Consequently, from a sensitivity viewpoint, the adjective becomes a sort of instrument of aggression.[16]

Early on, in *Sarrasine*, Barthes was able to find the model for a novel that partly excludes gender binarity. He was interested in the ways in which Balzac had circumvented the problem posed by his character's sexual identity in order to

---

13 Barthes 2002, 1009.
14 Barthes 1953, 155–156.
15 Barthes 1975, 623.
16 Barthes 1979, 740.

preserve the illusion that Zambinella is a woman, whilst at the same time ensuring that unveiling her as a man remained a possibility, at the end of a retrospective narrative. Deploring the absence of a neuter gender in the French language, he noted uses, by Balzac, of what he called the "feminine neuter" ("une si charmante créature", "une organisation féminine"), as well as the presence of "fugitive masculine hints" linked to stereotypes ("Je puis être un ami dévoué pour vous").[17] Above all, he argued against the agreement of the past participle:

> As the most artificial form of language, the agreement of the past participle entails a ruthless constraint, and removes any possible preterition; the narrator can play with a certain flow of consciousness and words, but the writer is sent back to the compulsory standards of graphic language; he can only trust a systematic truth, above and beyond any other, which is that, not of the author, but of the writing.[18]

We must assume that the designation of the protagonists in *Fragments d'un discours amoureux* by "l'amoureux" and "l'aimé" has a neutral value, as does that of the heroine of *Werther* by "l'objet aimé (Charlotte)". It is also understandable that he often uses the epicene phrase "l'autre" ("the other") and that he uses inclusive writing as a neutral form: "All the same, he (she) could have … He (she) knows well …"; "What I want, quite simply, is to be 'kept', in the manner of a super prostitute, man or woman"; "The one with whom I want to talk about the beloved is the one who loves him (her) as much as I do".

As for a novel that generally excludes the third person, does not use the past tense, avoids retrospective effects, is epistolary and therefore broken, gathers anecdotes with maxims, paintings and complaints, *Werther* could have provided a model. The course on *Werther* had been the laboratory for the writing of *Fragments d'un discours amoureux*.

4 Roland *versus* Barthes

Although hapaxes like Goethe's novel and like *Sarrasine* are found in the history of the genre, Barthes' statement to Pierre Boncenne is surprising. What does remain of a novel once the simple past tense, the third person, the proper noun, the pronouns *he* and *she*, and the adjective have been removed? One might be

---

17 Barthes 1970a, 1042.
18 Barthes 1970a, 1042–1043.

tempted to reply "nothing", but Barthes does not mean it that way. What remains is "the romanticism",[19] which he believes:

> [...] can produce, in writing, in music, in images, "brief forms" of great brilliance: sentences, aphorisms, stanzas, "anamneses", "epiphanies" as Joyce said, at the very least short stories such as those written by oriental thinkers, but not *a* story, not *a* fate.[20]

It is therefore understandable that the place given to haiku in *La Préparation du roman* is, curiously, very considerable. Striving to think about the possibility of a novel freed from the old constraints that give it its structure, Barthes would retain only the sentimental theme and tone. According to him, contrary to the tradition, the "romanesque" is a marvellous opportunity for an apotheosis of the fragmentary. While the novel is a transcendent form, the "romanesque" seems to him the enviable "type" of immanence.

The project of the great long-awaited novel did not succeed and it was not long after he realised the impossibility of the project that he died from injuries sustained in a road accident. The stakes were high but the contradiction difficult to resolve: on the one hand, choosing the fragment above an easy narrative, which is always suspect; on the other hand, the temptation of a long and continuous form called "novel" but reduced to its mere tonality, the "romanesque", in order to celebrate the epiphany ... of the fragment. However, it could be that, at the time of its "preparation", the "novel" had already been written: *Roland Barthes by Roland Barthes, Fragments d'un discours amoureux* and *La Chambre claire* could make up, in three volumes, the Proustian song of his love for his mother — childhood, sentimental affairs, mourning.

We must go back to the strangeness of the contract between Barthes and his reader at the beginning of the *Fragments*: as we know, it is a matter of accepting the principle of a "simulation", which prohibits interpreting the use of the first-person pronoun as personal, because it is theoretical, just as it forbids interpreting the temporal value of the present tense, in favour of its aspectual and quasi-gnomic value. We have seen that, under such conditions, we are led to understand another peculiarity of the text: if "I" and the present tense are in the service of a "Topic", then the general use of the masculine ("l'amoureux", "l'aimé") is not gendered but generic — the cover of the book does not show, as we might have expected, the hands of a man and a woman but those of Tobias and the Angel by Andrea del Verrochio.

---

[19] The word used by Barthes is "romanesque": a substantival adjective that derives from "roman" (*romance*).
[20] Barthes 1977b, 385.

This reading pact does not prevent the reader from identifying a notable ambiguity within the work. Just like in photography, as evoked in *La Chambre claire*, each fragment is a double object that turns the anecdote into its own sign. For instance, an anecdote tells of "I" suffering from waiting for a phone call but this also theoretically means "this is how any lover behaves". At its level, the fragment articulates inseparably the referent (the anecdote) and its sign (the theory): it belongs to "that class of leafy objects whose two leaves cannot be separated without destroying them: the window and the landscape, and why not: Good and Evil, desire and its object; dualities that can be conceived, but not perceived".[21] The principle of delegation of speech, for example, which is reflected in the idea of a prosopopoeia, makes it possible to create one of these "laminated objects": Barthes' discourse is two-fold, both "pathetic" and theoretical at the same time; it is inscribed in a fractal device that actually allows for immanence of the fragment to turn back into the transcendence of the narrative.

We have read that Barthes lends the lover his own culture, in exchange for which the latter "passes on the innocence"[22] of his gaze. In reality, he does not only lend him his culture but also his friends, designated by their initials in the marginal notes of the book and mentioned by name in the *Tabula gratulatoria*: a game of *recto* and *verso*. It is certainly possible to accept the proposal of interpreting the present tense as aspectual and the use of the first person as theoretical, while allowing oneself to be won over by the impression that the temporal value of the present tense and the deictic meaning of the first-person pronoun are also at play. One can pursue this principle of discarding the theoretical hypothesis, considering that the generic value of the masculine is superimposed on its gendered value, which means that the feminine is both included and excluded – his occasional recourse to "inclusive writing" betrays this, since it is only justified by the omission or voluntary abandonment of the generic value of the masculine.[23] Barthes did not hide the fact that this work was inspired by grief and was aimed in particular at a man, Roland Havas, whom he loved unconditionally and who, himself, did not welcome the text with pleasure. *Fragments d'un discours amoureux* would then be a "squared" simulation, the simulation of a simulation.

This somewhat indiscreet interpretation of *Fragments d'un discours amoureux* does not aim to explain the work through the life of the author, far

---

21 Barthes 1980, 793.
22 Barthes 1977a, 16.
23 Cf. Marty 2021.

from it, and it does not replace the theoretical interpretation; instead, it reveals an ambiguity that is the main stake of the *mathesis singularis*. Thus nourished by the experience of its author, *Fragments d'un discours amoureux* could be understood as an extraordinary autobiographically inspired novel in which Barthes rewrites *Werther* by dismembering it. He achieves a real *tour de force* in avoiding the third person pronoun and the proper noun, the simple past tense, the adjective and even the feminine gender, in favour of an individual and personal story, written at the time and which in fact excludes women. The novel of "Roland" runs below the surface of the theoretical and fragmentary discourse of "Barthes".

Bibliography

Barthes, Roland (1953), *Le Degré zéro de l'écriture*, Éditions du Seuil, Paris; (2002) *Œuvres complètes*, t. II, Éditions du Seuil, Paris.
Barthes, Roland (1964), *Essais critiques*, Éditions du Seuil, Paris; (2002) *Œuvres complètes*, t. II, Éditions du Seuil, Paris.
Barthes, Roland (1970a), "Masculin, féminin, neuter", *Mélanges offerts à Claude Lévi-Strauss*, Mouton, Paris; (2002) *Œuvres complètes*, t. IV, Éditions du Seuil, Paris.
Barthes, Roland (1970b), *S/Z*, Éditions du Seuil, Paris.
Barthes, Roland (1975), *Roland Barthes par Roland Barthes*, Éditions du Seuil, Paris; (2002) *Œuvres complètes*, t. IV, Éditions du Seuil, Paris.
Barthes, Roland (1977a), *Fragments d'un discours amoureux*, "Tel Quel", Éditions du Seuil, Paris; (2020) "Points", Éditions du Seuil, Paris.
Barthes, Roland (1977b), "Texte à deux (parties)", *Wunderblock*, Paris; (2002) *Œuvres complètes*, t. V, Éditions du Seuil, Paris.
Barthes, Roland (1979), "Roland Barthes s'explique", entretien avec Pierre Boncenne, *Lire*, Paris; (2002) *Œuvres complètes*, t. V, Éditions du Seuil, Paris.
Barthes, Roland (1980), *La Chambre claire. Note sur la photographie*, Gallimard/Seuil, Cahiers du cinéma, Paris; (2002) *Œuvres complètes*, t. V, Éditions du Seuil, Paris.
Barthes, Roland (2002), "Transcription de *Vita nova*", *Œuvres complètes*, t. V, Éditions du Seuil, Paris.
Barthes, Roland (2003), *La Préparation du roman*, Seuil-Imec, Paris.
Lacoue-Labarthe, Philippe/Nancy, Jean-Luc (1978), *L'Absolu littéraire*, Éditions du Seuil, Paris.
Marty, Eric (2021), *Le Sexe des Modernes. Pensée du neutre et théorie du genre*, Éditions du Seuil, Paris.

Paolo Felice Sacchi
Arrhythmic Historiography, Lost Letters and Broken Meanings: Fulgentius's *De aetatibus mundi et hominis*

Abstract: Fulgentius's *De aetatibus mundi et hominis* tells a Christian history of the world by elaborating on the traditional parallelism between human and cosmic ages. The work is a lipogrammatic one, meaning that chapter one lacks the letter A, chapter two the letter B, chapter three the letter C and so on. Contrary to what is declared by the author in the prologue, though, the narrative does not exhaust the whole alphabet, stopping suddenly at chapter 14 (letter O). Is this an unfinished piece of literature? This paper investigates the friction between closed and open structures, finite series (alphabet, Christian salvation history, human life) and infinite series (time), and relates Fulgentius's treatment of time to his allegorical technique.

1 Broken rhythms

It has become a critical commonplace when dealing with Fabius Planciades Fulgentius, the probable author of the treatise *De aetatibus mundi et hominis* ("On the Ages of the World and of Man"),[1] to review the creatively offensive judgments that some famous scholars have given on this early 6th century CE writer.[2] Here it does not seem necessary to dwell on this dispute, but suffice it to observe how the *De aetatibus mundi et hominis*, although of not evident attribution at the level of manuscript tradition, shows all the "defects" that would confirm it as Fulgentius's work: awkwardness, inconsistency, baroque but very clumsy Latin etc.

---

[1] Cf. Manca 2003, 33–39, and more in general Hays 2003 on the attribution.
[2] See, for example, Domenico Comparetti's assessment, Comparetti (1997) [1896], 112: "the [allegorical] process of Fulgentius is so violent and incoherent, it disregards every law of common sense in such a patent and well-nigh brutal manner, that it is hard to conceive how any sane man can seriously have undertaken such a work, and harder still to believe that other sane men should have accepted it as an object for serious consideration." Cf. also Whitbread 1971, IX: "[Fulgentius's] purposes and methods [are] muddleheaded and dubious, and [his] displays of learning second hand and suspect"; Relihan 1986, 535: "Fulgentius the Mythographer suffers from an academic contempt that seems to be completely justified."

The opening section of the first chapter, which the old Teubner editor Helm (1898) used to isolate as a "preface", offers the rules of the game of this rather infamous late antique text:[3]

> *His ergo uiginti et tribus elementorum figuris, in quibus uniuersis loquendi cursus colligitur, mundi ipsius hominisque discretis temporibus ordines coæquemus necesse est. In id enim, et homo quod crescit et mundus quod uiuit et numerus elementorum quod colligitur, inuenitur in nostro libro rerum omnium concors digestio [...].*
>
> Praef. 131.14–20

> To these twenty-three figures of the letters, to which the entire development of the language can be traced back, it is necessary to compare the orders of the world itself and of man, distinguishing the letters. Therefore, with regard to the growth of man, to the life of the world, to the sequence of letters, we find in our book an exposition that is always plain [...].

The *De aetatibus* aims at telling universal history by making the epochs of the world and the different ages of human life run in parallel, but also by adding a more remarkable restriction: these multiple stories will be narrated in twenty-three chapters, one for each letter of the Latin alphabet, letters that will be progressively absent from the related chapter itself: letter *a* is missing in the first chapter, *b* in the second one, *c* in the third one and so on.

This treatise is, therefore, a clear example of literature produced according to serial procedures and formal restrictions. It is no coincidence that *ordo* ("order") and *numerus* ("number") are words that emerge as strongly connoted already in the passage above — we shall return to their relevance later on. What is really striking is, rather, that the *De aetatibus*, although constructed by interlacing several teleologically closed and finite series, is nevertheless thought to be an unfinished text. In fact, the manuscript tradition preserves 14 chapters, just over half of the 23 promised by the alphabetic series — and yet, even more strikingly, other scholars believe that the work is accomplished.[4] We shall reflect on the structure of a work in which the excess of constraints that seem to doom it to "closure" ends up producing, instead, an unstable textual object whose boundaries are indistinct.

---

3 Manca 1998 and 2003 prove that what Helm thought to be an autonomous "preface" does actually belong to chapter I, since it leaves out the letter *a*. In what follows, quotations from the *De aetatibus* are sourced from Helm's edition, with the indication of book, page and line. Translations are mine.

4 Cf. Manca 2003, 9–13 for a review of the hypotheses.

In the early 2000s, Massimo Manca, one of the very few to have devoted a complete translation with commentary to the *De aetatibus* (as well as a Digital-Humanities project),[5] found in the manifestos of the OuLiPo (the *Ouvroir de Littérature Potentielle*) the tools for a possible aesthetic redemption of Fulgentius's art: the exasperating late antique fondness for literary *lusus* was reevaluated through the lens of "potential literature" (*littérature potentielle*).[6] Twenty years later, now that post-modernism has been declared dead and resurrected a dozen times, enthusiasm for combinatorial literature has become even more problematic, at least in the form it was expressed by the French group:

> It is easy to hold of no account the exemplary value of clever literary tricks. The mere fact of beating a record in one of these excessive structures can be a sufficient justification of the work: the emotion aroused by the sense of its content constitutes a decidedly secondary merit, far from despicable.[7]

However, there is no need for formalist aesthetics to deal with Fulgentius because the fascination of Fulgentius's literary "clever tricks" is that they appear to be defective, if not a complete failure. The finished series that run across the work do not fit together conveniently: they diverge instead of converging, and make the whole work collapse.

For a start, it is useful to single these diverging strands out. The juxtaposition of "ages of the world" and "ages of man" has a history rooted in ancient Greek, Roman, and Jewish cultures and far beyond, as proven fifty years ago by Paul Archambault in a seminal article.[8] Augustine probably remains the most influential Christian *auctoritas* in such a tradition: in various works, the bishop offered a historical-theological model in which universal history, from the Creation to the advent of Christ, was organized into six epochs, corresponding to the subdivision of human life into infancy (*infantia*), childhood (*pueritia*), adolescence (*adulescentia*), youth (*iuventus*), mature age (*senior aetas*) and old age (*senectus*). In particular, in *De Genesi contra Manichaeos* 1.23, the six eras of the world, assimilated to the six ages of man, are interpreted in the light of the six/seven days of the Creation. In an effort to bring together these three series or, we could otherwise say, hermeneutical codes, Augustine puts into effect "allegorical" strategies that have sometimes offended modern sensibility (Archambault charged Augustine with "a certain literary ingenuity" and "an occasional blind-

---

5 See Manca 2019.
6 Cf. Manca 2003, 16–24.
7 Le Lionnais 1973, 25, my translation. Cf. Manca 2003, 18.
8 Archimbault 1966. See also Berardi/Manca 2019.

ness to history").⁹ For instance, the third age, adolescence (*adulescentia*), is made to correspond to the time between Abraham and David because, as the faculties of procreation mature in adolescence, so in those centuries the seed of Scripture and of the Prophets generated the people of God; and again, just as waters and dry ground were separated on the third day of creation, so the "land" of the people of Abraham was separated from the "sea" of the Gentiles.

Now, the allegorical synopses offered by Fulgentius are often much more "specious" than the Augustinian ones, in line with an allegorical gaze that it would make sense to define as radical and which recalls that used in the three books of the *Mythologiae* or in the *Expositio Virgilianae continentiae*.¹⁰ Even so, we are not interested here in the cogency of Fulgentius's comparisons, but in the intersection of the various finite series.

Fulgentius seems to start precisely from the six-part model popularized by Augustine, but the need immediately emerges to harmonize it with the 23 books required by the Latin alphabet. The strategy he adopts is to introduce a new series based on a five-year period. The passage of the introduction in which the chronological/structural criteria of the treatise are discussed is actually quite confusing. After arguing that by attributing a numerical value to the Latin letters one can reach the number 500, Fulgentius states that:

> *Ergo occurrunt in nostris litteris, si secundum illos numeres usque in postremum Z, D, quo duodecies quingenteni mundi uiuentis indicent tempus; sin uero duodecies duodeni, uitae hominis necesse est monstretur excursus; item dum duodecies uiginti tres collexeris, nouem mensium et sex dierum repperies numerum, certissimum ex utero hominis procedentis egressum, ut unde generis primordium sumitur, illinc quoque mortis ordo signetur. Ergo sicut in homine uiginti et tribus lustris mores ordinesque uertuntur et uiginti tribus elementis totius sermonis ordo colligitur, sic quoque et in mundo XX et tres temporum disponendi sunt motus, quo singulis quibusque, ut dictum est, libris et singulorum litteræ obseruentur et mores uitæque hominum picturentur et mundi ipsius res gestæ lucidius demonstrentur.*
>
> Praef. 132.13–28

Therefore, with our letters we reach, if we count their order up to Z, the number 500, with which they will indicate the duration of the world, amounting to twelve times five hundred years; if, on the other hand, you count twelve times twelve, the course of human life necessarily appears; likewise, if you multiply twelve by twenty-three, you will get the number of nine months and six days, a result that very accurately indicates the time after which the man leaves the uterus formed; so that, starting from the moment that we take as the beginning of existence, we can then calculate the consequent moment of death. There-

---

9 Archambault 1996, 204. On Fulgentius's moral allegory in the *Expositio*, see Wolff 2009 and Fabre-Serris 2022.
10 See *infra* on Fulgentius's *atomistic allegory*.

fore, just as the development of human life is comprised of twenty-three decades, and in twenty-three elements the entire language system is brought back, so also with regard to the world, twenty-three moments of time must be arranged, so that, as has been said, in the individual books the respective letters are considered, the customs and life of men are outlined, and the deeds of the world itself are clearly illustrated.

How is this reflected at the level of textual construction? In the first six chapters, the correspondence between the age of the world, the age of man and the division into chapters is meticulously respected. Each chapter corresponds to an epoch, each epoch to a human age, according to a progression of epochs that develops the Augustinian one: the first age goes from the Creation to Enoch, the second from Enoch to Noah, the third from Babel to Abraham, the fourth from Abraham to Jacob, the fifth from Jacob to Moses, and the sixth from Moses to Samuel.

These chapters are very similar in their internal architecture. They start with a few introductory lines defining the age under scrutiny and remind the readers of the difficulties of the project by noting how hard it is to write omitting some letters. They then move on to the review of the historical facts under discussion (or, actually, to a selection of biblical episodes), following the "allegorical" comparison between the three ages of the world and the age of man. Finally, a few concluding words summarize the main lines of the comparison and refer to the world-epoch to be treated in the next chapter.

It is no coincidence that in this first block of chapters we can observe the maximum concentration of the term *aetas* ("age"),[11] but we also find its (lipogrammatic) equivalent *mundi tempus* ("world epoch", I.133.1), or *temporis cursus* ("course of time"), and references to the *ordo operis* ("order of the work") abound (III.138.10). With an interesting semantic crasis, *ordo* ("order") indicates at the same time both the series of epochs/events ("order of the world", *mundi ordo*, V.144.6) and the structure of the work, the formal constraint that limits the author's action (*arta legis catena*, "the tight chain of the rules", II.134.16–17; *tenaci forcipe*, "restraining pincers", II.134.18–19).

But from now on the *ordo* ("order") is going to be disturbed. While in the Augustinian system the sixth epoch included the advent of Christ, in Fulgentius we have not even reached David. From the seventh chapter onwards, we see a deformation of the order, a mismatch in the coordination of the series. The opening lines *Tricesimus humanae uitae annus obuoluitur librorum nostrorum uolumine disponendus* [...] ("The thirtieth year of human life takes place, to be placed in the volume of our books [...]", VII.150.15–16) introduce the five-year

---

11 Cf. Manca 2003, 29.

based system. This time-frame, which was announced in the introduction, has so far remained inactive. Moreover, the systematic comparison with the ages of man becomes more and more sporadic. In the sixth chapter, explicit reference is made to the fact that the sixth age of the world, in Augustinian terms, will include the advent of Christ:

> *Pone nunc sextam mundi aetatem libri delimationibus terminandam, quae et diuinitatis testimonio declaratur et humanitatis plenitudine pingitur. In hoc enim temporis scemate Christus noster apparere dignatus est [...].*
>
> VI.146.25–28

> Consider that now it is necessary to define the sixth age of the world according to the limits of the book, which is manifested by the testimony of the Divinity and depicted in the fullness of humanity. In this phase of time, our Christ deigned to appear.

Therefore, the *plenissima aetas* ("fullest age") (VI.150.2), the theological culmination of history, makes its appearance at what should be only a little over a quarter of the entire work. From this moment on, it is as if the historical-theological progression remained in abeyance: the *evenemential* history of the world, i.e. the actual historical narrative, keeps moving on, but the history narrated in the text is still chronologically far from the birth of Christ; as a result, the sixth age is slow to take place on a symbolic level. Furthermore, in an almost unnoticed way, what for Augustine was the terminal phase of cosmic evolution — the sixth age conceived of as *senectus* ("old age") and included between the two comings of Christ, in short, the "fullness of time" eschatologically understood — becomes for Fulgentius an "age of fullness" because it is close to the full vigor of the human being (as we have seen, chapter VII would correspond to the five-year period between 30 and 35 years).

Fulgentius's treatise had started out as if the different series (ages of the world, alphabet, etc.) could move at the same speed; on the contrary, now, the rhythmic displacement generated, on the one hand, by the suspension of the progression of the *aetates mundi* ("ages of the world"), on the other, by the changed criterion of the scanning of human life, has an impact also on a thematic level. In chapter VI, the advent of the sixth era brings forth, paradoxically, an idea of closure and death. In the story of Moses there is actually insistence on the "death" of the Egyptian people, which is contrasted with the rebirth of the Jewish people led by Moses:

> *Damnatur in mortis sententiam semina masculina; sed ecce in papirea cistula per crepidinem aluei salus enatabat Hebraici supplementi [...]*
>
> VI.147.8–10

> Male offspring are sentenced to death; but behold, in a small papyrus basket, between the banks of the river swam the salvation of relief for the Jews [...]

The idea of a fulfilment of times will re-emerge explicitly in book XII, in which the narration finally touches on the birth of Christ. Chapters VII–XI had abandoned the internal architecture of the first six chapters, limiting themselves to the narration of events and to their "allegorical" reading in relation to possible events in human life. By contrast, with chapter XII the theme of the world-ages becomes evident again so as to reactivate the historical-theological series:

> *Noua saeculi aetas interuenit nostris libellis desiderabiliter exoptanda, cuius aduentu radiante lustrati, suauia Christi nascentis cerepundia libro currente narrentur necesse est* [...]
> XII.170.9–12
>
> Now comes a new age of the world, truly desirable for our chapters: purified by its radiant advent, we must tell in the current book the sweet-sounding rattles of the rising Christ [...]

The theological suspension initiated in chapter VI is therefore dissolved in chapter XII. Massimo Manca has subtly highlighted the significance of number 12 for the structure of the book, stressing how important it is for the calculations proposed in the introduction (as briefly mentioned before), but also noticing that, on the other hand, it seems to emerge quite out of the blue.[12] And it is here that the hypotheses about the completeness of the work can begin. Could possibly chapter XII, as it is devoted to the figure of Christ, represent the centre of the *De aetatibus* and its pivotal moment in the span of the envisaged 23 chapters? The fact is that in this chapter even the *evenemential* series, seems to collapse. Chapter X had inaugurated "gentile" history (*ergo gentiles adgressurus historias*, "I'm going to deal with gentile history", X.163.20) by providing a very quick summary of the events that happened between the Babylonian captivity and the exploits of Alexander the Great, with particular emphasis given to the latter. Chapter XI, starring Rome, is a juxtaposition of *exempla* taken from Roman history from its origins to Caesar; it is a gloomy portrait, characterized by immorality and violence, following in the wake of Orosius's anti-pagan historiographic model, one of Fulgentius's main sources. The remarkable narrative contraction of these two chapters marks a further change of pace: a more marked tendency to preterition is now added to the arrhythmia produced by the displacement of the series, resulting in an even more allusive and episodic storytelling. Any historical linearity is abandoned. After the chapter on Christ, Ful-

---

[12] Cf. Manca 2003, 30.

gentius feels that he must *force* the *evenemential* series in order not to interrupt the Gospel-series: instead of recounting the empire of Augustus, chapter XIII is dedicated to episodes taken from the Acts of the Apostles, with the obvious pre-eminence of Peter and Paul.

Of special interest are the first lines of chapter XIII:

Oportuerat quidem ut temporum ordo dictabat Caesarum actus uitasque describere; sed quia illos siue Deo siue apostolis turpe fuit praeficere, postremo ergo loco quae praetermisimus postmodum edicemus.

XIII.172.19–22

It would have been appropriate, as prescribed by the order of times, to describe the deeds and lives of the Caesars; but since it would have been shameful to put them before both God and the apostles, we will therefore deal with the facts that we have left out in the final part, later on.

The fracture in the *ordo temporis* ("order of time") is deliberate. The passage, in addition to being essential for understanding the conflict between cultural codes that runs through Fulgentius's text (history of salvation/"pagan" history etc.), includes one of the internal textual clues valued with greater conviction by those who think that *De aetatibus* is a finished work. Indeed, how are we to understand the phrase *postremo loco*? "At the end of the work"? In fact, the following chapter XIV is the last to be handed down by the manuscript tradition. It summarizes the entire Roman imperial history from Augustus to Valentinian (the first?) in fewer printed pages than most of the other chapters.

Helm, the Teubner editor of Fulgentius, thought that this was a sufficient indicator of the finiteness of the work, regardless of the statements made by the author himself in the introduction.[13] Even Pennisi, in his studies dating back to the Sixties, considered the fourteenth chapter as definitive, and saw in the mention of Valentinian as the last emperor a proof for a very early dating of Fulgentius.[14]

Here it is relevant to observe how the extreme conciseness of the narrative has seemed, to some scholars, indicative of an interrupted story: Fulgentius would have accelerated the pace to dedicate the second, lost part of the work, to the narration of his contemporary history. To other readers instead, the rapidity of the discussion suggests that Fulgentius, having finished the history of salvation, had little to say in terms of proper historiography, and therefore decided to

---

[13] See Helm 1897 *ad loc.*
[14] See Pennisi 1963 and criticism in Manca 2003, 53–56.

conclude. Similar allegations also abound with respect to the last line: *Ualentinianus militare cingulum spernit et imperii diadematis munus excipit* (XIV.179.10–11, "Valentinian despises the military uniform and receives the gift of the imperial diadem"). For some, this seems to be too abrupt a close and far from the habitus of the other chapters; for others, it is a deliberate sign of discontinuity, interruption and firm conclusion.[15]

To argue for the completeness or incompleteness of *De aetatibus mundi et hominis* would mean, in the current state of knowledge, to commit an act of hermeneutic violence. I think it is more fruitful to remark how a text theoretically dominated by rigid numerical progressions manages instead to escape from any determinism, to the point of disregarding its own alleged premises. A lipogram of 23 chapters dedicated to universal history and probably composed in the sixth century CE should not stop at Valentinian (fourth century CE) with the fourteenth chapter, yet, as we have seen, it seems to display multiple clues of "closure".

The final result is a text that has often been judged to be "wrong" and "flawed", but whose intrinsic dyscrasia, which I have briefly analyzed, deserves to be explored in depth, especially on a literary-aesthetic level. The arrhythmias of Fulgentius's narrative, his patently contradictory *concors digestio* (we translated it as "plain exposition", but the noun *digestio* suggests variety and divergence through the prefix *dis-*) has to be further connected to his allegorical techniques.

2 Broken meanings

Fulgentius's *Mythologiae* and *Expositio Virgilianae continentiae*, two allegorical treatises on ancient Greek and Roman myths and Virgil's *Aeneid* respectively, are his most popular works and exerted a long-lasting influence on western allegorical practice. Even so, an underlying idea of *textual dissolution* can be easily traced in many critical readings that aim to pin down Fulgentius's allegorical technique. In current critical discourse, to define Fulgentius's allegoresis as peculiarly fragmentary and disjointed seems to constitute a fair strategy for avoiding the traditional charges of exegetical arbitrariness and conceptual

---

[15] Cf. Manca 2003, 10–13; 245. Whitbread 1971, 182 observed that the letter *o*, avoided in this chapter, could stand for the Greek omega, thus marking the end of the work.

inconsistency that have haunted Fulgentius's reception to the modern day.[16] Martina Venuti is right to claim that we still lack a systematic description of Fulgentian allegorical procedures, but the actual question remains whether an analytical *expositio* of Fulgentius's practice would be of any help in understanding his textuality. Be that as it may, Venuti identifies some major analytical strands in the *Mythologiae*: etymology, iconography, quotation, and moral/philosophical reading.[17] When commenting on a *fabula*, Fulgentius sometimes draws on all of these domains, or selects just some of them. Accordingly, a mythological figure is in each instance a name that can be etymologically deconstructed as well as an image that can be parceled out into its visual attributes — and finally, all of these conceal moral/philosophical meanings that can be shown and proved to be true by reference to *auctores*. A full-length example will suffice to provide a quick overview of Fulgentius's allegoresis: we shall take the eighth *fabula* from the second book, the *Fabula Ulixis et Sirenarum*, 48.9–49.2:

> *Sirenae enim Grece tractoriae dicuntur; tribus enim modis amoris inlecebra trahitur, aut cantu aut uisu aut consuetudine, amantur enim quaedam <uocis suauitate, quaedam > specie uenustate, quaedam etiam lenante consuetudine. Quas Ulixis socii obturatis auribus transeunt, ipse uero religatus transit. Ulixes enim Grece quasi oloxenos id est omnium peregrinus dicitur; et quia sapientia ab omnibus mundi rebus peregrina est, ideo astutior Ulixes dictus est. Denique Sirenas, id est delectationum inlecebras, et audiuit et uidit id est agnouit et iudicauit, et tamen transiit. Nihilominus ideo et quia auditae sunt, mortuae sunt; in sensu enim sapientis omnis affectus emoritur; ideo uolatiles, quia amantum mentes celeriter permeant; inde gallinaceos pedes, quia libidinis affectus omnia quae habet spargit; nam denique et Sirenes dictae sunt; sirene enim Grece trahere dicitur.*

The Sirens are named as "those who lure"[18] in Greek, for the allure of love is interpreted in three ways, by song or by sight or by habit: some creatures are loved for [the pleasure of

---

[16] See *supra* note 1. But it should be noted that the *Mythologiae* were very popular in the Middle Ages, and not only as a source of myths. Carolingian authors seem to have admired Fulgentius's style and to have adopted some Fulgentian phrases, cf. Laistner 1957 [1928]. Fulgentius's repertoire of myths remained authoritative at least until Giovanni Boccaccio's *Genealogiae deorum gentilium* and Coluccio Salutati's *De laboribus Herculis*. See Hays 2013, esp. 319–333, who concludes that: "The dismissal of Fulgentius as an eccentric and minor author — 'pretentious, yet essentially trivial' — as Laistner called him — is a comparatively recent phenomenon, and one driven primarily by trends in modern classical scholarship."

[17] See Venuti 2010, 89. Fulgentius's allegorical technique was rooted in tradition; for an analysis of his practice in the *Expositio* against the background of other readings of Virgil, see Fabre-Serris 2022.

[18] Whitbread 1971, 73–74 translates *tractoriae* as "deceivers" and, at the end of the passage, *sirene* as "betray", thus losing the etymological pun. Wolff (Wolff/Dain 2013, 95) maintains it,

their song], some for beauty of appearance, and some for pleasant habits. The companions of Ulysses pass by these with ears stopped up, and he himself goes past tied up. For Ulysses in Greek is for *oloxenos* (ὅλος "all, entire" + ξένος "stranger") that is, stranger to all; and because wisdom is a stranger to all things of this world, so Ulysses is called crafty. Then he both hears and sees, that is, recognizes and sizes up and still passes by the Sirens, that is, the allures of pleasure. And they die just because they are heard, in the sense that all self-indulgent feelings of a wise man die away. Also they are winged creatures, because they may quickly enter the minds of lovers; whereby they have feet like a hen's, because the indulgence of lust dissipates all it possesses. And finally they are called Sirens, because sirene is the Greek for "to lure".

As is often the case, etymology here marks the initial threshold of interpretation: *sirenae* and *Ulixes* are, first and foremost, meaningful names whose etymological reading is supposed to disclose the truth about the *res* ("thing, deed") they refer to. The treatment of *Ulixes* is in many respects emblematic. The fact that a Greek etymology is applied to a Latin name makes it clear to what extent Fulgentius's etymological thinking differs from its post-19th century analogues. Drawing on a set of phonic resemblances, Fulgentius creates a new compound which is designed to shed light on the original, apparently opaque name.[19] *Ulixes* is segmented and reshaped as *oloxenos* (ὅλος "all, entire" + ξένος "stranger"), a new string of characters to which the actual explanation is applied. It could be that the (para)etymological line of reasoning is not entirely explicit, as is the case with *sirenae*: the opening statement *Sirenae enim Grece tractoriae dicuntur* ("The Sirens are named as "those who lure" in Greek"), leaves to the reader the task of filling in the gap and linking *sirenae* to the Greek verb σύρω, "to drag".[20]

Both etymologies are seamlessly followed by a moral/philosophical explanation, which is then interrupted by a sketchy narrative of the myth. The last paragraph (*Nihilominus* ...), set up as a series of equations connecting an iconographic or diegetic component of the *fabula* to its allegorization, displays Fulgentius's inclination towards segmenting mythic totality into signifying units. He isolates and magnifies narrative/visual elements in order to transform them

---

but in his translation, "celles qui entraînent" and "entraîner", what is lost is the implicit meaning of "fascination, attraction".
19 See Amsler 1989, 23 *et passim*, on the principal etymological techniques employed during Antiquity and the early Middle Ages, namely *interpretatio* ("interpretation"), *compositio* ("composition"), *derivatio* ("derivation"), and *expositio* ("explanation"). Amsler himself draws consistently on the classic Klinck 1970.
20 Fulgentius likes to display his familiarity with Greek, whose relatively copious presence in the *Mythologiae* has been taken as the sign of a certain (perhaps even active) mastery of the language. See Venuti 2018, 33, and Wolff 2009, 16–17. For the possible interaction between Fulgentius and Greek mythography, see Cameron 2004, 308–310, and Manca 2011.

into the meaningful elements of a new semantic system, a system embedded in *and* divergent from the "original". The problem present here is the *construction of meaning*, that is, the question of how to choose objects that can be pertinently connected in a signifying constellation.

Emily Albu has compared Fulgentius's hermeneutical procedures to late antique *centones*, texts in which lines are taken up from ancient authors and freely reassembled[21] (they have also provided a common critical metaphor for describing the late antique *pseudomorphosis* of ancient culture),[22] although the comparison falls short of accurately describing the mechanisms of such a transference from one cultural code to another. More pertinently, Jon Whitman speaks of *atomistic allegory* when pointing to Fulgentius's habit of dismembering words and stories while looking for new meanings: the "original" totality is fragmented into disconnected particles whose very existence seems to be independent from the system of origin.[23] Once Fulgentius has discovered the hidden meaning, he draws a series of conceptual inferences that are difficult to harmonize with what could be designated as surface meaning: every hidden meaning is made into a semantic matrix on which a *new* semantic system can be built.

If we follow Gordon Teskey's suggestion that semantic matrices function in allegory like *vanishing points* in traditional perspective,[24] Fulgentius's practice would seem to consist of multiplying the vanishing points — admitting the possibility, say, that every single point in the picture might possibly be a vanishing point towards which everything can be made to converge: if the sirens stand for lust, then their wings recall the quickness of lust in grasping lovers' minds, their hen's feet stand for dissipation, and so on. Fulgentius *dissolves* his objects into a network of signifiers depending on, or pointing to, a series of given semantic matrices. What matters here is not so much the name *Ulixes* in its integrity, but rather the newly formed (and *ad hoc*) compound *olo* + *xenos* (ὅλος "all, entire" + ξένος "stranger") that is subsumed under the idea of *peregrinitas* ("being a stranger"), and it is not so much the emblem of a bird-woman that responds to the unifying concept of *libidinis affectus* ("lust") as the sum of wings + hen's feet. Robert Edwards has assumed that "when they explicate complete texts, most allegorists, including Fulgentius, concentrate on small portions at a time.

---

21 On Latin *centones*, see McGill 2005; Formisano/Sogno 2010; Hinds 2014; Elsner 2017.
22 See Schnapp 1992; Formisano/Sogno 2010; Elsner 2017. The use of the crystallographic metaphor of *pseudomorphosis* to describe the reconfiguration of antique culture in the late antique period goes back to Henri-Irénée Marrou, who borrowed it from Spengler's *Der Untergang des Abendlandes*. Cf. Marrou 1978, 71–72.
23 See Whitman 1987, 104–119.
24 See Teskey 1996, 5–31.

They do not feel the urgency of relating every part directly to a unifying whole."[25] I would slightly adjust his argument by observing that these portions, understood as pieces of allegorical information, are conceptually manageable and semantically loaded only when they are projected against a unifying background — the sirens' feet are isolated because they function as part of a more general discursive structure opposing *amor* ("love")/*libido* ("lust") to *sapientia* ("wisdom")/*virtus* ("virtue").

The tension between the incessant segmentation of the material at hand (words, images, narratives) and the ongoing individuation of wide-ranging semantic matrices through which the material is organized may account for the clash, in Fulgentius's text as well as in the related critical debate, between *fragmentation* and *circularity*. Whereas Edwards has insisted that the entire *Mythologiae* can be seen to thematize the impossibility of constructing meaning as a monolithic object, arguing that it presents itself as a text often interspersed with references to fragmentation, multiplicity and semantic collapse,[26] Venuti is convinced that Fulgentius's analysis produces a hermeneutical *circle*: a vortex that homogenizes everything and makes the myth "sink down under new interpretative layers, under which they are hardly recognizable."[27]

Although fragmentary and fragmenting, Fulgentius's allegoresis seems to be *circulating* from detail to detail, from abstraction to abstraction, returning again and again to a few master ethical-philosophical oppositions (*sapientia* "wisdom"/*ignorantia* "ignorance"; *libido* "lust"/*virtus* "virtue" etc.). The circularity pointed out by Venuti can also be described as a form of argumentative density which makes it difficult to follow the interconnections among the diverse, "atomistic" allegorical explanations — if there are interconnections at all. Fulgentius's text is at once profoundly circular/continuous and deeply disjointed.

---

[25] Edwards 1976, 20.
[26] According to Edwards 1976, the very first *fabula*, *Unde idolum* (15.21–17.8), devoted to the birth of idols as substitutes for dead people, thematizes absence and desire as the origin of signs, and the *Mythologiae* as the investigation of this absence; the multifariousness of knowledge is symbolized by Minerva's *triplex* dress in 38.3; the stress on etymology and language implying that "a semantic order can replace an ontological one", 22.
[27] Venuti 2018, 90: "il mito [...] sprofonda sotto nuovi strati, sotto i quali è perfino difficile riconoscerlo."

3 To conclude (?)

Such a dialectical tension between continuity and rupture, such a tendency to merge disparate conceptual domains, seems to find a counterpart in the arrhythmic temporality of the *De aetatibus*. As we have seen, in the historical treatise divergent chronological schemes are made to converge, but they never completely overlap; far from dissimulating the contradiction, Fulgentius's textuality brings the paradox to the surface. The "continuous disjointedness" of Fulgentius's allegory is reflected by the contradictory structure of a chronological architecture in which the heaping of goals (τέλη) (death, the advent of Christ, the end of the world, the end of the alphabet) results in the problematization of the very ideas of ending and closure, just like the heaping of allegorical meanings dissolved the very idea of μῦθος ("myth, narrative"). In other words, and in a peculiarly late antique way Fulgentius's disturbing craftmanship shows the destabilizing power of restrictions. Both his allegorical compendium and his (in a broad sense) historiographical treatise seem to start from maximalist ambitions: the first one aims to provide allegorical mechanisms universally applicable to the entire corpus of "pagan" myths; the second one tries to establish a system of correspondences between macrocosm, microcosm and writing. As we have seen, Fulgentius's universal allegorical method is overturned into an *atomistic allegory*, just as the temporality of Christian historiography, linear and teleological, dissolves into continuous temporal lags. If the *De aetatibus* had also exhausted the alphabetical series, and had thus reached the promised number of chapters, little would have changed in terms of internal arrhythmia: the work could have been said to be "finished" only under its most outward aspect, while keeping its internal fractures unaltered. The overloaded late antique textuality of Fulgentius, a textuality that has generated so many reproaches from the critics, reveals itself as an extraordinary tool of ideological delegitimization, a subtly corrosive element.

Bibliography

Amsler, Mark (1989), *Etymology and Grammatical Discourse in Late Antiquity and the Early Middle Ages*, Amsterdam/Philadelphia.
Berardi, Elisabetta/Manca, Massimo (eds.) (2019), *Età del mondo e dell'uomo. Nascita, vita e morte fra microcosmo e macrocosmo*, Alessandria.
Cameron, Alan (2004), *Greek Mythography in the Roman World*, New York.
Comparetti, Domenico (1997 [1896]), *Vergil in the Middle Ages*, Princeton.

Edwards, Robert (1976), "Fulgentius and the Collapse of Meaning", *Helios* 4, 17–35.
Elsner, Jaś (2017), "Late Narcissus: Classicism and Culture in a Late Roman Cento", in: J. Elsner/J. Hernández Lobato (eds.), *The Poetics of Late Latin Literature*, New York, 176–204.
Fabre-Serris, Jacqueline (2022), "La pratique de l'allégorie chez Virgile et un de ses commentateurs tardifs (*Fulgence, Expositio Virgilianae continentiae secundum philosophos moralis*)", in: S. Clément-Tarantino/J.-C. Jolivet/D. Vallat (eds.), *Poétiques des commentaires antiques, Actes du colloque international (Université Charles de Gaulle-Lille 3, 17-19 novembre 2016)*, Latomus, Bruxelles, 176–189.
Formisano, Marco/Sogno, Cristiana (2010), "Petite poésie portable: The Latin Cento in its Late Antique Context", in: M. Horster/C. Reitz (eds.), *Condensing Texts-Condensed Texts*, Stuttgart, 375–392.
Hays, Gregory (2003), "The Date and Identity of the Mythographer Fulgentius", *The Journal of Medieval Latin* 13, 163–252.
Hays, Gregory (2013), "Fulgentius the Mythographer?", in: S.M. Trzaskoma/R.S. Smith (eds.), *Writing Myth: Mythography in the Ancient World*, Leuven/Paris/Walpole, 309–333.
Helm, Rudolf (1897), "*De aetatibus mundi*", *Philologus* 56, 253–289.
Helm, Rudolf (1898), Fabii Planciadis Fulgentii V. C. *Opera*. Accedunt Fabii Claudii Gordiani Fulgentii V.C. *De aetatibus mundi et hominis* et S. Fulgentii Episcopi *Super Thebaiden*, Recensuit Rudolfus Helm, Teubner, Lipsiae.
Hinds, Stephen (2014), "The Self-conscious Cento", in: M. Formisano/T. Fuhrer (eds.), *Décadence. "Decline and Fall" or "Other Antiquity"?*, Heidelberg, 171–197.
Klinck, Roswitha (1970), *Die Lateinische Etymologie des Mittelalters*, München.
Laistner, Max L.W. (1957 [1928]), "Fulgentius in the Carolingian Age", in: M.L.W. Laistner, *The Intellectual Heritage of the Early Middle Ages*. Selected Essays edited by Chester D. Starr, Ithaca NY.
Le Lionnais, François (1973), *2ᵉ Manifeste de l'Oulipo*, in R. Compagnoli (ed.), *Oulipiana*, Napoli 1995, 25–27.
Manca, Massimo (1998), "Un prologo di troppo nel *De aetatibus mundi et hominis* di Fulgenzio il Mitografo", *Quaderni del Dipartimento di Filologia, Linguistica e Tradizione Classica* 10, 243–246.
Manca, Massimo (2003), *Fulgenzio. Le età del mondo e dell'uomo*, Torino.
Manca, Massimo (2011), "Testi aperti e contaminazioni inestricabili: il (Tri)cerbero tardoantico fra simbolo e ragione", in: L. Cristante/S. Ravalico (eds.), *Il calamo della memoria. Riuso di testi e mestiere letterario nella tarda antichità* IV, Trieste, 65–76.
Manca, Massimo (2019), "Verso un'edizione elettronica del *De aetatibus mundi et hominis* di Fulgenzio. Un saggio, incluso il nuovo manoscritto *Bruxellensis*", in: E. Berardi/M. Manca (eds.), *Età del mondo e dell'uomo. Nascita, vita e morte fra microcosmo e macrocosmo*, Alessandria, 117–122.
Marrou, Henri-Irénée (1978), *Christiana tempora: mélanges d'histoire, d'archéologie, d'épigraphie et de patristique*, Rome.
McGill, Scott (2005), *Virgil Recomposed: The Mythological and Secular Centos in Antiquity*, Oxford.
Pennisi, Giuseppe (1963), *Fulgenzio e la* Expositio sermonum antiquorum, Firenze.
Relihan, Joel C. (1986), "Satyra in the Prologue of Fulgentius' *Mythologies*", in: C. Deroux (ed.), Studies in Literature and Roman History IV, *Latomus* 196, 537–548.
Schnapp, Jeffrey T. (1992), "Reading Lessons: Augustine, Proba, and the Christian Détournement of Antiquity", *Stanford Literary Review* 9, 99–123.

Teskey, Gordon (1996), *Allegory and Violence*, Ithaca NY/London.
Venuti, Martina (2010), "La materia mitica nelle *Mythologiae* di Fulgenzio: la *Fabula Bellerofontis* (Fulg. Myth. 59.2)", in: M. Gioseffi (ed.), *Uso, riuso e abuso dei testi classici*, Milano, 71–90.
Venuti, Martina (2018), *Il prologus delle* Mythologiae *di Fulgenzio. Introduzione, testo critico, traduzione e commento*, Napoli.
Whitbread, Leslie G. (1971), *Fulgentius the Mythographer*. Translated from the Latin, with introductions, by Leslie George Whitbread, Columbus OH.
Whitman, Jon (1987), *Allegory: The Dynamics of an Ancient and Medieval Technique*, Oxford.
Wolff, Étienne (2009), Fulgence. *Virgile dévoilé*. Traduit, présenté et annoté par Étienne Wolff. Postface de Françoise Graziani, Villeneuve d'Ascq.
Wolff, Étienne/Dain, Philippe (2013), Fulgence. *Mythologies*. Traduit, présenté et annoté par Étienne Wolff et Philippe Dain, Villeneuve d'Ascq.

Marco Formisano
"This City Will Always Pursue You": The Impossible End of Rutilius Namatianus' Return

Abstract: The elegiac poem by Rutilius Namatianus entitled *De reditu suo* should narrate the journey of the poet from Rome towards some unnamed and unspecified "Gallic fields," but the text has been transmitted incomplete: the end of the *iter*, both as journey and text, is missing, so that readers cannot know whether Rutilius arrived at his final destination. In this chapter, I argue that although this incompleteness is not a function of authorial intention, it corresponds to the nature of the poem's very topic. For any return to a homeland, as ancient and modern literary reflections suggest, is always incomplete.

> You said: "I'll go to another country, go to another shore,
> find another city better than this one.
> Whatever I try to do is fated to turn out wrong
> and my heart lies buried like something dead.
> How long can I let my mind moulder in this place?
> Wherever I turn, wherever I look,
> I see the black ruins of my life, here,
> where I've spent so many years, wasted them, destroyed them totally."
>
> You won't find a new country, won't find another shore.
> This city will always pursue you.
> You'll walk the same streets, grow old
> in the same neighborhoods, turn gray in these same houses.
> You'll always end up in this city. Don't hope for things elsewhere:
> there's no ship for you, there's no road.
> Now that you've wasted your life here, in this small corner,
> you've destroyed it everywhere in the world.
>
> Konstatinos Kavafis, *The City* (trans. by E. Keeley)

1 The City, and no return

One of the most intriguing characteristics of the period that we rather awkwardly, *faute de mieux*, still call "late antiquity" is its inherent unfinishedness. Inscribed in the negatively connoted prefix 'late' (*spät, tardif, tardo*) — whatever one might say about its neutral chronological value — is the idea that this is still antiquity, yet *late*. This very term indicates a substantial deferral, which, as I have argued elsewhere, deserves to be taken more seriously than has been the case, so that we can make of belatedness a productive hermeneutic principle.[1] The literature of this ineffable period is generally marked by a constant tension between the ancient past as object of desire, and a consciousness of the novelty of its own forms of expression. This tension emerges and is configured in various ways depending on genres and discourses. In the text at the center of this chapter, the elegiac poem *De reditu suo* by Rutilius Namatianus, this specifically *late* antique characteristic is expressed in terms of delay, deferral, and ultimately erasure of the end. As in the case of Claudian's unfinished epic *De raptu Proserpinae* (briefly discussed in the *Introduction* to this volume), where the lack of an end parallels both Proserpina's tapestry as a *labor imperfectus* and a sustained discourse of fragmentariness and interruption in Claudian's poem, the incomplete status of Rutilius' poem, though materially caused by accidents in its transmission, wonderfully responds to the conceptual impossibility of providing an end to the narrative of return — and not only of Rutilius' specific return to his place of origin, but more broadly of any literary return. In other words, the actual incompleteness of this poem, far from being a mere accident due to biographical reasons or the manuscript transmission, becomes a fundamental hermeneutic criterion which can guide our interpretation of a text that constantly thematizes fragmentariness and interruption both through language and narrative. At the same time, through its very topic, the journey towards a *lost* home, the poem represents per se the impossibility of any completion since the Odyssean paradigm.

The title of this chapter is a quote from one of the best known poems of Konstantinos Kavafis, *The City*. Kavafis' poem illustrates the impossibility of abandoning the place where one is born, in a way that not only reflects the fundamental impossibility of any return but also strangely echoes Rutilius' unconditional love for the City, i.e. Rome. In this late antique poem, the themes of staying and leaving are tightly intertwined, so that the place of birth, the unspecified "Gallic fields" (1.22, *Gallica rura*), are replaced by the lofty presence of *the* City, the object of desire. While Kavafis' poem points to the impossibility of a true departure since "the City will always pursue you", Rutilius shows that return itself is unattainable. On this point, this late antique poet presents an astonishing modernity. Literary treatments and theoretical reflections of the 20th

---

1 Formisano 2020.

and 21st centuries constantly emphasize the elusive nature of return.² A return seems to be always incomplete, not fully accomplished. As pointed out by Michel Serres in *Habiter*, for instance, this is the situation of the *émigré*, who returning to his homeland experiences *le vrai mal du pays*, since "the exile outside becomes already more painful inside."³

2 Rutilius' reasons: an unattainable home

The elegiac poem *De reditu suo* of the Gallo-Roman poet and politician Rutilius Namatianus was presumably written in 417, i.e. just a few years after the sack of Rome in 410, an event which the author directly refers to in his work. About this poem much has been written, and one of the most significant points is the fact that it escapes any clear generic definition.⁴ Part of the content might be described as an *iter* or *Reisesatura*, i.e. a description or narrative of a journey but, as has been observed by many scholars, the poem is much more complex both in themes and structure.⁵

Rutilius presents himself as a prominent Gallic politician who had a splendid career in Rome, at the end of which he was appointed *praefectus urbi* in 414. But these were terrible times: only a few years earlier Rome had been assaulted and sacked by the Visigoths under Alaric. The sack of Rome in 410 was a collective shock, described at length by contemporary writers, both pagan and Christian, of course from different and in some ways opposing perspectives, the ones accusing the others according to their particular beliefs and *Weltanschauungen*.⁶ In 417, as we can infer from the poem (1.135–136),⁷ Rutilius had to abandon Rome in order to return to his homeland in Gaul, where he possessed some lands needing his attention after natural disasters and barbaric raids.

In the past this poem has been read, like so many other late antique texts, primarily as a historical source — in this case, in order to reconstruct Italy "post

---

2 See for instance Gardner/Murnaghan 2014 who discuss the model of the Odyssean *nostos* in modern cultures.
3 Serres 2021, 10.
4 For discussion of genre, see Paschoud 1979; Brocca 2003.
5 See the editions, translations and commentaries by Dodlhofer 1972–1977; Fo 1992; Wolff et al. 2007; and Malamud 2016. Wolff 2020 is a collective volume presenting various approaches to *De reditu suo*.
6 See Harich-Schwarzbauer/Pollmann 2013.
7 See Squillante 2005, 171 for a brief status quaestionis on the date.

410" or as an autobiographical piece describing the real journey of its author.[8] More recently, the poem has been rediscovered as an important and unique piece of poetry. As is typical of a major trend in the study of late antique literature, scholars have been particularly eager to reconstruct various classical influences by means of the usual search for intertextual references, in particular to Ovid's *Tristia* and Vergil's *Aeneid*.[9]

In the poem, we read the poet's departure from Rome and part of his journey along the Italian coast towards Gaul. But the poem has been handed down to us incomplete: we only have the first book, consisting of 644 lines, and the first 68 lines of the second book, as well as some fragments published by Mirella Ferrari in 1973. This incomplete state of the poem today has been attributed to various causes: the hypothetical death of the author either *en route* or after his arrival at his destination in Gaul, the author's decision to leave it incomplete or, more probably, the material loss of the last part. The fragments certainly belong to the last part of the second book, towards the end of the poem, so they allow us to confirm that Rutilius did not die during his journey and that he was able to arrive in Gaul.[10] Hagith Sivan insisted that the passage we conventionally call fragment B describes not Albenga in Liguria, as was previously argued by for instance Francesco Della Corte and others, but rather the Gallic capital Arles, considered as both *origo* and destination of Rutilius' journey.[11]

One of the most significant aspects is that in this poem the representation of *nostos*, with a long history of being positively presented in literature since the *Odyssey*, is colored with sadness: Rutilius is tormented by his choice to leave Rome, which had become his home, and his return to Gaul is presented with the language, style and metrical form (the elegiac couplet) of exile, and more specifically Ovidian exile. Recently, a fundamentally biographical approach to the poem has been relaunched, albeit under different premises, by Robert Bedon in a fascinating discussion worth summarizing here since it is relevant to the argument of this chapter.[12] Bedon notices in Rutilius' poem various factors that suggest that the poet seems to have been forced to leave Rome, yet without offering any particular reason why he is going back to his properties in Gaul. For instance, Bedon observes the inconvenient season for a boat trip, late October, a particularly dangerous moment for undertaking such a journey. Also, the long wait (15 days) in

---

8 For instance Pryor 1989; Bedon 2020.
9 See Tissol 2002; Fielding 2017.
10 See Ferrari 1973; Sivan 1986.
11 Sivan 1986, 529.
12 Bedon 2020.

Portus Ostiensis not far from the City is a rather strange circumstance: why would such a high ranking public figure spend so much time in a rather uncomfortable and humble environment instead of waiting in his presumably luxurious home in Rome? Moreover, the kind of boats Rutilius and his crew use, several small vessels, might indicate on the one hand that he had a large amount of luggage and a vast entourage of servants, on the other that he needed small boats that would allow him and the crew to pause more easily along the coast and even go up the course of a river, if necessary. Bedon notices the relaxed way in which those continuous break and pauses are faced by the poetic persona, who never shows a concern about his journey being delayed. Rather, he takes pleasure in lingering in long breaks, for instance while visiting various friends on the way to his alleged final destination in Gaul. Bedon also discusses a hypothesis previously presented by others,[13] according to which Rutilius embarked on his journey with an official mission. Arguably, this seems to be a rather foggy assumption since the text itself makes not the slightest allusion to such a mission, even though the poetic persona certainly does not refrain from depicting himself as an important actor in Roman politics; why would he not emphasize an official task that would possibly increase both his responsibility and his visibility? All these factors together with the lack of details around the motivation of this "sudden return" (1.1, *velocem reditum*) suggest, according to Bedon, that Rutilius has been condemned to a *relegatio*, an exile imposed by the imperial authority, possibly because of his pagan belief. This would explain on the one hand the lack of interest that the poet shows in reaching his final destination, on the other the recourse to the Ovidian poetics of exile. Bedon's hypothesis, though from a completely different hermeneutic perspective, is complementary to the kind of interpretation I am proposing in this chapter: his article also focusses on the non-said, the various and continuous breaks, and, more importantly, the lack of the poem's end that, in turn, results in the lack of a destination itself. For the poet, as Bedon's argument seems to imply, was not really interested in reaching Gaul.

While Bedon is reading Rutilius' text as a source for reconstructing the author's personal story as well as has his possible motivations to write exilic poetry, other interpreters have pointed to different nuances of its poetic language. For instance, Alessandro Fo observes that the poem is characterized by a diffused "antithetical atmosphere",[14] i.e. a disjunctive quality which consists precisely of these apparent contradictions. In a previous study, I pointed to some antitheses such as Rome *versus* Gaul (a compact and solidly built urban *versus* a

---

13 Wolff 2007, XI–XII and XXIX–XXX; Ratti 2005.
14 Fo 1992, 61: "atmosfera antitetica".

ruined natural landscape), going home *versus* exile, fragmentation *versus* stylistic and thematic cohesiveness, centripetal *versus* centrifugal movement.[15] The tormented and antithetical *Stimmung* of Rutilius' poetics deserves emphasis, since more than any external evidence it gives the reader a clear sense of the impossibility of his very project, of 'going home', as Martha Malamud translates the title. To these conceptual tensions I would like to add the one between the inherent longing for the destination, made explicit in the initial reference to *reditus* (1.1), and the continuous deferral of the Gallic destination. For the term *reditus* itself strongly implies the *conclusion* of the journey, i.e. of the *iter* as a text,[16] which nonetheless is absent, denied by Rutilius' poetic language, ultimately deferred and eventually fully erased. Following the approach proposed in this volume, a productive interpretation of the extant work will not focus on speculation about the actual arrival of the author in his native Gaul or on trying to reconstruct the material or historical reasons for the abrupt interruption of the poem. Rather, the text as it presents itself in its incompleteness, no matter whether the author ever completed his journey or not, far from being only an accident of the author's life, actually seems to perfectly fit the poetics of this specific *nostos*, and perhaps of any other. In other words, what might be an accident of transmission ends up in fact strongly influencing our perception and interpretation of the text.

3 The belated return and fragmentariness

In this section, I explore the question how *De reditu suo* as a whole (though incomplete) actually ends up denying its inherent project, i.e. the return, recurring to a language of belatedness and fragmentariness, representing poetic mechanisms that not only undermine textual unity but fundamentally deny any possible completion.

Right at the beginning, the poet clearly expresses his sadness at leaving Rome in order to return home:

> *Velocem potius reditum mirabere, lector,*
> *   tam cito Romuleis posse carere bonis.*
> *Quid longum toto Romam venerantibus aevo!*
> *   Nil umquam longum est, quod sine fine placet.*
>   1.1–4

---

15 Formisano 2017, 227–233.
16 For *itinera* in (especially late) Latin literature, see Soler 2005. Cf. also Benz 2017.

> "O reader, wonder rather at my swift return,
> that I'm so quick to leave behind Rome's charms.
> For what is 'long' to those who've loved Rome all their lives?
> What always gives us pleasure is not long.[17]

These are for readers the first words, and yet they might not actually have been written as such: *potius* ("rather") seems to indicate a comparison with something that we are missing. Most scholars, following Ernst Doblhofer's monumental commentary, think that at least an initial couplet is missing, one in which the poet might have been asked by an interlocutor why he is delaying his return home, and to this question the poet replies that his interlocutor should "rather" (*potius*) wonder how he is able to leave Rome so quickly. While Fo, Wolff and Malamud in their editions all agree with this conjecture, Marisa Squillante expresses a different opinion: making some comparisons with elegiac poetry, she reads *potius* as deliberately creating the effect of a surprising beginning *ex abrupto*,[18] which pairs well with *velocem* ("swift") and *cito* ("quick"). In this chapter, however, the details of a question which cannot be decisively answered, in view of this text's transmission, are less important than interpreting the text as it has been handed down to us, acknowledging its fundamental incompleteness. And in this sense the word *potius*, symptomatically appearing at the beginning — whether it is the poem's first line or third — marks precisely the disjunctive or "antithetical" quality of this text as emphasized by Fo.

Moreover, as has been noticed by commentators, the "swift return" (*velocem reditum*) is presented in an impersonal manner, whereas the reader, not least because of the elegiac form, might expect a more personal expression. Etienne Wolff comments that this initial strategy serves as an "effacement du je".[19] This avoidance of the first person in fact characterizes the poem in its entirety. *Potius* undermines the swiftness of the voyage undertaken, which turns out to be anything but slow, resulting from a constant fragmentation represented on the one hand by the various stops along the way that continuously interrupt both text and journey as well as the text as *iter*, and on the other by the appearance of ruins and tortured landscapes.

---

[17] In this chapter I use the English translation of *De reditu suo* by Malamud 2016 slightly adapted at times.
[18] Squillante 2005, 189–191. See also Fielding 2017, 74 n. 90 who refers to the possibility that the poem might have begun with a preface in prose or in a different meter.
[19] Wolff 2007, 62 n. 75.

In the first two couplets, the spirit of the entire poem is epitomized in terms of both content and style. The return journey happens too swiftly (*velocem* and *tam cito*) and this is in contrast with the eternity of Rome (*longum toto aevo* and *sine fine*). The repetition of *longum* in 1.3 and 1.4 is noticeable in this opening. The insistence is significant, indicating spatial and temporal extension as well as belatedness. The *velox reditus*, manifestly announced at the opening, is constantly and constitutively belated and eventually undone by its opposite, the *morae*. The poem is actually nothing but a description of a long, seemingly open series of various stages and stops during the journey that is constantly delayed by various factors. Already at the beginning, while still in Portus, the poet and his crew are blocked by bad weather conditions:

> *cunctamur temptare salum portuque sedemus,*
> *nec piget oppositis otia ferre moris*
>
> 1.185–186

> we hesitate to try the sea, and sit in port,
> enjoying the leisure of enforced delays.

Another typical delay is to be found, when a raging northwest wind, (1.463, *rapidus Corus*) compels them to stop (*consistere*) at the house of an absent friend:

> *vix tuti domibus saevos toleravimus imbres:*
> *Albini patuit proxima villa mei.*
>
> 1.465–466

> We barely got inside before the cruel storm:
> my dear Albinus shared his home with me!

Later still, at 1.492 the poet comments in these terms on the whole experience: *tempestas dulcem fecit amara moram* ("The bitter storm made such a sweet delay"). These delays are caused not only by atmospheric factors but also by the poet's own desire to meet some friends and visit certain places, for instance when he decides to see Protadius (1.541–542) and, more extensively, to visit Pisa, to admire the statue of his father Lachanius exposed in the forum (1.559–614).

These and many other delaying scenes render Rutilius' return home virtually *sine fine*, precisely like his *infinite* longing for Rome: *Nil umquam longum est quod sine fine placet* (1.4), where temporality and history are annihilated by the exuberant *jouissance* of what the poet loves above everything else.

4 Centripetal Rome

Both in the opening lines, where Rutilius dwells on the many advantages of living in the City, and above all, in the most famous part of the poem, the so called "hymn to Rome" (1.47–164), no single historical event or figure is clearly addressed or described. Every reason for Rome to be praised is presented as a timeless abstraction, without any specific historical reference or concreteness. Rome is praised for its central position within the universe (1.48, *inter sidereos, Roma, recepta polos*, "O Rome, received among the starry skies") and for the fact that she is a global capital (1.66, *urbem fecisti quod prius orbis erat*, "You have made one city of the world."). In this depiction of Rome, the City erases every difference between cultures and national identities (1.63, *fecisti patriam diversis gentibus unam*, "From many different peoples you have made one nation"), for she incorporates and includes everything in herself: there are no natives and foreigners anymore. Rome is the child of Venus and Mars who are the parents of Aeneas' and Romulus' offspring (1.67–68, *auctores generis Venerem Martemque fatemur / Aeneadum matrem Romulidumque patrem*, "We state that Mars and Venus are parents of our race, / mother of Aeneas' offspring and father of Romulus'"). She is eternal, no other empire has lasted so long (1.83–86), and it would be pointless "to count your lofty monuments and all your trophies" since it would be "a task like numbering the stars" (1.93–94, *percensere labor densis decora alta tropaeis / ut si quis stellas pernumerare velit*). The City is represented as an extra-temporal entity, assimilated to natural elements: time will not diminish Rome "as long as earth and stars and sky remain" (1.138, *dum stabunt terrae, dum polus astra feret*). Time is frozen and Rome becomes a natural entity that does not follow the usual temporal development. She may have an origin, but her end cannot be foreseen: she is eternal and therefore endless.

The end of the hymn reminds us of the unpleasant *return* which Rutilius is facing:

> *Sive datur patriis vitam componere terris,*
>   *sive oculis umquam restituere meis,*
> *fortunatus agam votoque beatior omni,*
>   *semper digneris si meminisse mei.*
>
>   1.161–164

> "Whether it's my lot to end my life at home
> or see you once again with my own eyes,
> I will be happier than I hoped to be,
> and blest, if only you remember me."

By recalling the actual destination of his trip after having unendingly praised Rome (1.4, *sine fine*), the poet here seems to indicate the possibility of *returning* to the City after his *return* to Gaul. The alternative represented by *sive ... sive* leaves open Rutilius' destiny and, for that matter, his *iter* as a poetic project: the true final destination might in fact not be Gaul, but Rome. And while the return to Gaul is colored as the end of life, since it is associated with death (*patriis vitam componere terris*), the return to Rome is marked by a sense of exuberant vividness (*oculis meis*) and restoration to a previous condition (*restituere*). In other words, the poet indicates here two different possible endings to his journey: the first corresponds to the end of his own life (*vitam componere*), the other, on the contrary, brings life and is marked by vividness (*oculis restituere meis*). However, these alternatives are antithetical, the one undoes the other so that their appearance not only leaves open the end of the poet's *iter*, but even erases ending altogether.

Both Rome and the *Gallica rura* to which the poet is heading are marked by absence: he has left Rome but is still very far from the destination. Jesús Hernández Lobato has provided a compelling interpretation of the poem in Lacanian terms as "a poem about 'lacking': the painful verification of an unbearable absence."[20] And as he convincingly writes:

> Rutilius feels compelled to *leave* Rome, the origin and support of all that exists, in order to *return* to his own personal origin, that is, his fatherland in the most literal sense (the land of his father, somewhere in southern Gaul). This is the underlying paradox of *De Reditu Suo*: leaving an origin in search of an origin.[21]

The reader of *De reditu suo* confronts a conceptual short cut: while longing for his *origo*, the poet constantly experiences the impossibility of that very return. Accordingly, the text denies and undoes its own poetic project by erasing the poet's final destination inscribed in its very title. A destination that, by the way, is described only generically as *Gallica rura*, remaining simply — and very surprisingly — unnamed.

---

[20] Hernández Lobato 2022, 329.
[21] Hernández Lobato 2022, 326–327.

5 A journey through ruins and fragments

De reditu suo is perhaps best known for its depictions of ruins, both natural and urban. In the past, these passages titillated readers with the common image of late antiquity as an age of decline and fall. The poet explains the reasons why he feels obliged to go back to his native Gaul.

> at mea dilectis fortuna revellitur oris
> indigenamque suum Gallica rura vocant.
> illa quidem longis nimium deformia bellis,
> sed quam grata minus, tam miseranda magis.
> 1.21–24

> Fate snatches me away from these beloved shores-
> the fields of Gaul are calling for their son.
> Those fields, as lovely once as now they're pitiful,
> are ravaged and deformed by these long wars.

He emphasizes that his properties in Gaul are now disfigured because of long wars, and hence they deserve pity. Rutilius here refers to himself in the third person as *indigenam suum*, an expression that on the one hand contrasts the previous reference to Rome, whose *curia* is open to immigrants (*peregrini*):

> religiosa patet peregrinae curia laudi,
> nec putat externos quos decet esse suos
> 1.13–14

> The sacred Senate opens its doors to immigrants
> whose merit earns them senatorial rank

and on the other thematizes the going back to origins that represents the leitmotif of the poem. The adjective *deformia*, i.e. "without form", is an interesting detail since it recalls an original, primordial age of chaos, perhaps located, in Ovidian manner, before time and history; accordingly, it erases the traces of historical and human development with the effect of zeroing out temporality altogether. Moreover, as noticed by Wolff,[22] only the result of the barbaric incursions is named, not their agent; here, once again, no attention is given to historical details. Rutilius depicts both ends of his poetic *iter*, the colossally built and everlasting Rome on the one hand, and his unnamed ruined birthplace located somewhere in Gaul, depriving them of any historicity so that, although very

---

22 Wolff 2007, 49.

different in their appearance, they both display a refraining from an active participation in history. Rome in her eternity is removed from the passage of time, while the Gallic estates are brought back to their original status.

In what follows the passing of time itself is thematized, again without any reference to historical events:

> *nec fas ulterius longas nescire ruinas*
>   *quas mora suspensae multiplicavit opis*
>
> 1.27–28
>
> Ignoring such disasters further is not right:
> Delaying aid will only make them worse.

These lines perfectly represent Rutilius' conception of temporality and history: the ruins of his homeland are "long", indicating a temporal dimension rather than spatial, as the following remark seems to confirm: the delay 'multiplies' them. Moreover, Rutilius' typically unpersonal way of representation ("unpersönliche Darstellung")[23] — emerges here (*mora suspensae opis*) as was the case with *velox reditus* at 1.1. On this point, it deserves notice that right at the beginning of book 2 *longus* reappears in order to qualify Rutilius' *liber*:

> *Nondum **longus** erat nec multa volumina passus,*
>   *iure suo poterat **longior** esse liber.*
>
> 2.1–2
>
> Not yet long, my scroll has not endured too many turns;
> by rights, it could have been a longer book.

As has been discussed by various commentators, the repetition *longus ... longior* in this opening couplet symmetrically recalls the opening of book 1 (3–4, *quid longum toto Romam venerantibus aevo / nil umquam longum est, quod sine fine placet*). The parallelism between the stay in Rome and the length of the work is illuminating also because it can be read as a trace of allegoresis: what was presented as *longus* in the first book is now a textual quality, to be considered in its materiality, as the phrase *multa volumina* indicates.[24]

---

23 Doblhofer 1977, 32. See also Wolff 2007, 47.
24 See Doblhofer 1977, 262. and discussion in Fo 1992, 121. Fielding 2017, 75 seems to confuse the two instances. He refers to a *reditus longus* (a phrase not found in the poem) and he argues that Rutilius places emphasis "on the poem's length at the beginning of each of the two books."

In other words, the first lines of book 2, which have the function of a "proemio al mezzo" (as Gian Biagio Conte would call it),[25] serve as a commentary and explanation of the first lines of book one, 'unveiling' their meaning by textualizing its essence.[26] And, more importantly, they not only further delay the end but implicitly create a conceptual gap between a return that could actually take place in reality, and the literary representation of this specific *reditus*, which turns out to be unachievable.

Returning to book 1, in the following lines:

iam tempus laceris post saeva incendia fundis
  vel pastorales aedificare casas.
                                1.29–30

Great fires have ravaged proud plantations. Now it's time
to start from scratch, rebuilding humble huts

the poet wishes to build in the ruined landscape at least *pastorales casas*, "shepherd huts", a hint at a pre-civilized and pre-urban atmosphere in which nature prevails over culture and architecture.

This treatment of a return to a natural condition is of course in striking contrast with the hymn to Rome, where the City (1.97–114) is described as having splendid temples and other architectural elements which contain rivers and mountains and woods. And yet, as just noticed, both locations are deprived of historicity.

In the following lines, nature is given human feelings:

ipsi quin etiam fontes si mittere vocem
  ipsaque si possent arbuta nostra loqui,
cessantem iustis poterat urgere querelis
  et desideriis addere vela meis.
                                1.31–34

And if my native springs themselves could utter words,
and if the trees themselves could speak aloud,
they'd pick me up and scold me, fill my sails, and end
my homesickness by sending me back home.

---

25 Conte 1980, 122–136.
26 Likewise, Soler 2005, 274 interprets the first lines of book 2 as a metaliterary statement on the *reditus* itself: as Rutilius presents the second part of his text to the reader, so the reader acknowledges entering the second part of the journey. Text and journey run thus parallel.

Rutilius' final destination, never named, is significantly associated here with a lack of language: it ends up being muted precisely — and paradoxically — through the Virgilian reference. Petra Schierl has pointed to the link with Tityrus in Virgil's first *Bucolic*:[27]

> *Tityrus hinc aberat. ipsae te, Tityre, pinus,*
> *ipsi te fontes, ipsa haec arbusta vocabant.*
>
> 1.38–39

> Tityrus had gone from here. The very pine trees, Tityrus,
> and the springs and these orchards were calling for you.

No matter how the reference to Vergil is interpreted, there is a substantial difference: in Rutilius the *fontes* and the *arbusta* cannot utter any word (note the subjunctive *si possent*). Moreover, Rutilius depicts himself as *cessantem*, the one who is constantly delaying his own return and hence the very end of the poem, which is not attainable. And never attained.

Moreover, the structure of Rutilius' *reditus* is conceived as a series of fragments. The voyage of the protagonist is described in terms of vignettes, containing the different places visited during his *nostos*. Moreover, his journey takes place by sea; water fills the gaps between the individual scenes. As pointed out by Wolff, water is an essential element in Rutilius' poetry. Its ubiquitous presence is, to be sure, justified by the fact that the journey is made on the Tyrrhenian Sea along the Italian coast, but water persistently also characterizes the descriptions both of landscapes and of urban contexts, both in Rome and in other towns (see for example Pisa at 1.565–570 and *Centumcellae* at 1.251–266).[28] At certain points water is associated with the ruinous state of the land and urban centers.

An exemplary passage comes right at the beginning of the journey, where Rutilius explains the reason why he prefers to sail:

> *electum pelagus, quoniam terrena viarum*
> *plana madent fluviis, cautibus alta rigent.*
>
> 1.37–38

> I chose to go by sea, for rivers flood the level
> roads and rocks obstruct the mountain ways.

---

[27] Schierl 2013, 138.
[28] Wolff 2007, XLIV–XLV.

Here water conceptually overcomes land, or rather the text creates the impression that "land and sea have mingled".[29]

The effect of this narrative technique is astonishing: it gives us the possibility of conceptualizing unfinishedness. This text presents itself as a ruin sustained by a fragmentary structure interspersed by water, and as such it continuously delays and denies its own end.

In an earlier discussion of the poem I identified two different textual movements that seem to polarize the progression of the *iter*:

> The textual movement in *De reditu suo* has two directions, which I define as 'centripetal' and 'centrifugal', the centre being represented by Rome. The two kinds of movement have different but complementary characteristics. The centripetal movement indicates the proximity of Rome and is characterized by a language pervaded by multiplication, cohesivity, familial terminology, repetitions, all figures that emphasize centrality and compactness but produce at the same time a sense of saturation. The centrifugal movement indicates the process of separation from Rome and is characterized by dispersion, fragmentation, deformation and a massive presence of water and ruins. Since nearly every line of Rutilius' poem contains language indicating one or the other kind of movement, I would argue that the poem, as a whole, allegorizes displacement as such.[30]

For the purposes of this chapter devoted to the poem's conceptual unfinishedness, it is worth noting that the presence of both a centrifugal and a centripetal movement also has the effect of *avoiding* endings and the final destination of the *iter*, since their interaction makes the poem constitutionally placed between two poles: Rome that has been left and Gaul that must be reached.

In a recent discussion Paola Paolucci brilliantly identifies as a feature of Rutilius' poem the recurrence of the prefix *re-*. While others have observed the pro-gressive and di-gressive character of the text, she reveals its inherent re-gressive quality: "Tutto torna indietro nel poema di Rutilio e la cifra costante del reflusso condiziona anche la narrazione dei mitemi prescelti."[31] Astutely, Paolucci notices the co-presence of two orders of *reditus*: a macro and a micro *reditus*. While the first defines the overarching incomplete narrative, the latter concerns the single vignettes, where individual friends and other people as well as various places are encountered and then left again.[32] Hernández Lobato also pays attention to this stylistic characteristic, going so far as to suggestively note that the poem could bear the title *De re-*, since it is "a poem on the ideas

---

29 Clarke 2015, 96.
30 Formisano 2017, 228–229.
31 Paolucci 2020, 293.
32 Paolucci 2020, 290.

of re-turn, re-production, re-stauration, re-creation and re-presentation". He further describes Rutilius' *reditus* as "a desperate nostos in search of an origin that continuously slips away."[33] The *regressive* quality of this late antique but paradigmatic poem embodies through its peculiar poetic language the impossibility of Rutilius' *reditus*. And, I would argue, of any return.

6 Open coda

Edward Said, pointing to various effects of exile, both negative and positive, emphasized the sharpened vision provided by the set of lenses used by the one who lives in a condition of exile:

> Since almost by definition exile and memory go together, it is what one remembers of the past and how one remembers it that determine how one sees the future (...) *no return to the past is without irony, or without a sense that a full return, or repatriation, is impossible.*[34]

Indeed. By subverting the meaning of a *reditus* to a home that is lost forever, Rutilius describes a journey made of holes, fragments, ruins and water, all factors that unavoidably defer, delay, and erase the destination, and with it the end of his poem, equally lost forever.

Bibliography

Bedon, Robert (2020), "Une hypothèse sur la cause du retour en Gaule de Rutilius Namatianus", in: Étienne Wolff (ed.), *Rutilius Namatianus aristocrate païen en voyage et poète*, Bordeaux, 13–27.
Benz, Maximilian (2017), "Reiseliteratur", *Reallexikon für Antike und Christentum* 28, 951–966.
Brocca, Nicoletta (2003), "A che genere letterario appartiene il 'De reditu' di Rutilio Namaziano?", in: Franca Ela Consolino (ed.), *Forme letterarie nella produzione Latina di IV–V secolo: con uno sguardo a Bisanzio*, Roma, 231–255.
Clarke, Jacqueline (2015), "The Struggle for Control of the Landscape in Book 1 of Rutilius Namatianus", *Arethusa* 47.1, 89–107.
Conte, Gian Biagio (1980), *Virgilio, il genere e i suoi confini*, Milan.
Dodlhofer, Ernst (1972–1977), *Rutilius Claudius Namatianus. De reditu suo sive Iter Gallicum*, Heidelberg.

---

[33] Hernández Lobato 2021, 340.
[34] Said 2002, xxxv (emphasis added).

Ferrari, Mirella (1973), "Frammenti ignoti di Rutilio Namaziano", in: Mirella Ferrari, *Spigolature bobbiesi* (Italia medioevale e umanistica, 16), 1–41.

Fielding, Ian (2017), *Transformations of Ovid in Late Antiquity*, Oxford.

Fo, Alessandro (1992), *Rutilio Namaziano. Il Ritorno*, Turin.

Formisano, Marco (2020), "Il tardo antico come contemporaneo? Identificazione e alterità di un'età non classica", *Classico contemporaneo* 6, 60–66.

Formisano, Marco (2017), "Displacing Tradition: A New-Allegorical Reading of Ausonius, Claudian and Rutilius Namatianus", in: Jaś Elsner/Jesús Hernández Lobato (eds.), *The Poetics of Late Latin Literature*, Oxford, 207–235.

Gardner, Hunter/Murnaghan, Sheila (eds.) (2014), *Odyssean Identities in Modern Cultures. The Journey Home*, Columbus, OH.

Harich-Schwarzbauer, Henriette/Pollmann, Karla (eds.) (2013), *Der Fall Roms und seine Wiederauferstehungen in Antike und Mittelalter*, Berlin/Boston.

Hernández Lobato, Jesús (2022), "In the Name-of-the-Father: Rutilius Namatianus and the Collapse of Classical Logocentrism", *Arethusa* 54.3, 321–359.

Malamud, Martha (2016), *Rutilius Namatianus' Going Home. De reditu suo*, London.

Paolucci, Paola (2020), "Metapoesia del prefisso "re-" in Rutilio Namaziano", in: Étienne Wolff (ed.), *Rutilius Namatianus aristocrate païen en voyage et poète*, Bordeaux, 289–306.

Paschoud, François (1979), "À quel genre littéraire le poème de Rutilius Namatianus appartient-il?", *Revue des études latines* 57, 315–322.

Pryor, J.H. (1989), "The Voyage of Rutilius Namatianus: From Rome to Gaul in 417 C.E.", *Mediterranean Historical Review* 4.2, 271–280.

Ratti, Stéphane (2005), "Le *De reditu suo* de Rutilius Namatianus: un hymne païen à la vie", *Vita Latina* 173, 66–74.

Said, Edward (2002), *Reflections on Exile and Other Essays*, Cambridge, MA.

Schierl, Petra (2013), "Tityrus' Heimkehr. Zur Bukolikrezeption in Rutilius Namatianus, De reditu suo", in: Viktoria Zimmerl-Panagl (ed.), *Dulce melos II. Akten des 5. Symposiums: Lateinische und griechische Dichtung in Spätantike, Mittelalter und Neuzeit*, Pisa, 131–150.

Serres, Michel (2021), *Habiter*, Paris.

Sivan, Hagith (1986), "Rutilius Namatianus, Constantius III and the Return to Gaul in Light of New Evidence", *Medieval Studies* 48, 522–532.

Soler, Joëlle (2005), *Écritures du voyage. Héritages et inventions dans la littérature latine tardive*, Paris.

Squillante, Marisa (2005), *Il viaggio, la memoria, il ritorno. Rutilio Namaziano e le trasformazioni del tema odeporico*, Naples.

Tissol, Gareth (2002), "Ovid and the Exilic Journey of Rutilius Namatianus", *Arethusa* 35, 435–446.

Wolff, Étienne/Lancel, Serge/Soler, Joëlle (2007), *Rutilius Namatianus. Sur son retour*, Paris.

Wolff, Étienne (ed.) (2020), *Rutilius Namatianus aristocrate païen en voyage et poète*, Bordeaux.

Part IV: **Reading Unfinishedness**

David Konstan
Finishing *Iphigenia in Aulis*

Abstract: Euripides' *Iphigenia in Aulis* has been deemed to have been mutilated both by the excision of passages in the original and by their replacement by later interpolations. The surviving text is thus regarded as being simultaneously deficient and overfilled. The play is also notable for the numerous occasions in which characters change their minds. This chapter proposes an alternative reading, in which each new plan is taken to suggest a potential plot line that is cut off by successive obstacles, thus constantly inviting the audience to imagine alternative narrative possibilities. The repression or blocking of alternative narratives is characteristic of ideology, which cannot eliminate all traces of other visions and the scripts that authorize them. Euripides' *Iphigenia in Aulis* thus makes manifest the ideological labor of the text, as it brings to the surface programs that are not allowed to advance, and cannot be seamlessly assimilated to a single unity.

1 Introduction: too little and too much

We regard a work as incomplete when it appears to be missing some essential part. The criteria for determining such an absence are various, as is the nature of the missing bit itself: is it just a word or a few words needed to produce proper syntax? A passage, small or large, lost in transmission, due perhaps to a folio torn out of a manuscript? Or a more subtle lack, such as a faulty conclusion, where generic expectations or the critic's own taste suggest that this cannot be the proper ending? And yet, if poets can decide to begin a work *in medias res*, why not grant them the option of ending it *in mediis rebus*? There is also an obverse side to such imperfection. The same logic that reveals a presumed deficiency in a work may be invoked to show an excess. Instead of being incomplete, the work is deemed overly replete, too full instead of partly empty. Where certain canons of aesthetic unity are assumed, and great artists are deemed to respect them, then such signs of surplus are ascribed to later hands that tampered with the original. The trick then is to identify and excise such interpolations.

Euripides' *Iphigenia in Aulis* has had the fortune to be subject to both such critical procedures. It is the poster piece for studies of interpolation, with critics impugning the authenticity of anywhere between a third to a large majority of the verses in the text as we have it. But once these superfluities are surgically removed, what is left is insufficient to constitute a complete tragedy, for the later intrusions displaced a good deal of the original matter. And so, several of the finest textual scholars, such as James Diggle and David Kovacs, have concluded that Euripides in fact left the play in an unfinished state, and that it was revised for performance after his death by his son (or nephew), and then again later, some time in the fourth century, by yet another, and still less competent, poet.[1] The play that survives gives us simultaneously too little and too much.

How is one to approach such a beast? Pruning away the corrupt parts is no easy task. There is no reason to suppose that even the most refined Sprachgefühl of a modern critic will suffice to distinguish the lexical or metrical features of Euripides' style from those of his son (or nephew), or even of a fourth-century imitator. What is left, then, is the story line. As David Kovacs put it, in seeking to recover what the original audience may have seen and heard, "The chief criterion ... is not whether a passage resembles Euripides in diction or general manner ... but whether a given passage coheres with the plot implied by the most clearly genuine parts of the play".[2] James Diggle, in his OCT edition, invented a set of sigla to distinguish among passages he thought were likely to be Euripidean, those less likely, those scarcely likely, and those undoubtedly not from his pen (note the absence of a sign for passages certainly by Euripides).[3] But for all that this system commended itself as a great advance to Sean Gurd, in his fine book on the history of reconstructions of the *Iphigenia*, since it leaves the transmitted text intact, it only highlights the problem of the play's dubious integrity.[4]

---

1 See, for example, Diggle 1971, 180 = Diggle 1994, 50. Kovacs (2003, 102–103) concludes: "The total of these deletions is 696 lines (or, with 231–302 deleted as well, 768 lines) out of a transmitted 1692, leaving a play of only 996 (or 924) lines. That is clearly too short. But at least 50 lines must have disappeared from the prologue's two scenes when it was revised, and the wholesale revision of the first episode will have resulted in the loss of some 200–300 lines. A play of some 1,250 to 1,350 lines seems reasonable in length." The very last verses, as Martin West has demonstrated, were added in the early Byzantine period; see West 1981, 73–76.
2 Kovacs 2003, 77.
3 Diggle 1981.
4 On the several successive editions of the *IA* as each a new version, see Gurd 2005. More generally, see Tarrant, 1995. Tarrant writes: "instead of seeing manuscripts as embodiments or versions of the text, the classical editor regards them as imperfect carriers of an entity that is wholly independent from them and far superior to them in value" (p. 96). See also Frampton 2019, 22.

2 Dead ends

I would like to suggest a different approach, in line with the theme of the conference. As has often been remarked, the *IA* is notable for being a play in which characters change their minds, to a greater extent than in any other surviving tragedy. Agamemnon, Menelaus, Achilles, and, finally, Iphigenia herself all alter their positions so radically as to call into question the coherence of their characterization, beginning with Aristotle's critique of Iphigenia's about-face in respect to her sacrifice (*Poetics* 15, 1454a31–32). We can, however, regard each new plan as suggesting a potential plot line that is cut off by successive challenges and obstacles. The action seems set to move in one direction, perhaps an unexpected one, but when that one is blocked, it shifts course, promising yet another that in turn proves unfulfilled, a dead end or *cul-de-sac*.[5] The play is thus constantly inviting us to imagine alternative scripts, signaled perhaps in the initial act in which Agamemnon composes, erases, and rewrites a letter, which we might think of as symbolizing the written text of the tragedy itself.[6] The literary device of projecting alternate histories goes under the French name, *uchronie*, and has recently been theorized by critics.[7] Such a work will seem both overstuffed, since it intimates too many story lines, and incomplete, inasmuch as none is carried through to its proper *telos*. Rather than treat anticipated but unexplored avenues as excrescences to be pruned back, they are better regarded as what in William Gibson's science fiction world are called stubs, traces of other timelines.[8]

One such strand is what might have happened if, for example, Agamemnon's letter warning Clytemnestra not to send Iphigenia to Aulis had gotten

---

[5] For a film analogy, see *Cul-de-sac* (1966), directed by Roman Polanski, written by Polanski and Gérard Brach, and starring Donald Pleasence, Françoise Dorléac, Lionel Stander, Jack Mac-Gowran, Iain Quarrier, Geoffrey Sumner, Renée Houston, William Franklyn, Trevor Delaney, and Marie Kean. It also features Jacqueline Bisset (credited as Jackie Bisset) in a small role, in her second film appearance. Polanski's second English-language feature, it follows two injured American gangsters who take refuge in the remote island castle of a young British couple in northern England, spurring a series of mind games and violent altercations.
[6] On letters within a drama representing the act of poetic composition, see Barbiero 2022.
[7] See Grandazzi and Queyrel Bottineau 2018; the volume includes my chapter, "It might have been: *L'Uchronie Tragique*," pp. 167–178. Ted Mason, "Writing Iphigenia" (unpublished paper), observes: "from the beginning of the play through to the end, the characters' words and actions allude to earlier literary traditions and, in doing so, imagine an alternative tradition that cannot, in the end, be realized."
[8] See Gibson 2014; 2020.

through to her, at the cost of disbanding the Greek armada and never sailing to Troy. In such a development, the horror of sacrificing a daughter would have outweighed the claims of honor that drove the Greeks to avenge the elopement of Helen, and history would have taken a different course. Such an outcome is blocked in the play, not just once, as in Sophocles' *Philoctetes*, where the appearance of Heracles *ex machina* sets events on their proper path, but multiple times, yet never quite decisively. For the countervailing pressure of the family bond keeps reasserting itself, as a *leitmotiv* that nevertheless does not achieve a final resolution. It is this, I suggest, that lends the tragedy that pervasive sense of incompleteness, of frustrated progression. By way of illustration, we may examine a few lines in the second part of the prologue as it stands, where the meter shifts from anapestic dimeter to iambic trimeter (both segments are marked as *vix Euripidei* by Diggle, though Kovacs accepts the latter as going back to the first performance).

3 Helen's marriage

Agamemnon recounts to his old retainer that Leda had three daughters, Phoibe, his own wife Clytemnestra, and Helen (49–51); there is no mention of Helen's descent from Zeus, and she is treated simply as mortal.⁹ The most prosperous young men of Greece compete for her, and each utters dire threats should he fail to get her: ὅcτιc μὴ λάβοι τὴν παρθένον ("whoever may not get the maiden," 54). The verb is telling. For when Tyndareus finds himself in a quandary over whether to give his daughter away under these circumstances (δοῦναί τε μὴ δοῦναί τε, 56), he lights upon the device of extracting an oath from her suitors. With regard to whoever's woman (or wife: γυνή, 61) she becomes, should anyone take her (λαβών, 62) from his home and expel the man who has her (τόν τ' ἔχοντ[α], 63) from the bed, the rest will combine to destroy his city. This language is that of possession, not marriage: the verb *gamein* does not occur in this passage (in contrast to the promise to wed Iphigenia to Achilles).¹⁰ But Tyndareus does not let the matter rest here. Further, to avoid bearing responsibility for making a decision, he cleverly tricks the suitors (ὑπῆλθεν αὐτοὺς ... πυκνῇ φρενί, 67) by allowing Helen to choose among them in whichever way the dear

---

9 ἐγένοντο Λήδαι Θεcτιάδι τρεῖc παρθένοι,
  Φοίβη Κλυταιμήcτρα τ', ἐμὴ ξυνάοροc,
  Ἑλένη τε (49–51).
10 For λαμβάνω of "taking" a woman, see the appendix.

breezes of Aphrodite may waft her (ὅποι πνοαὶ φέροιεν Ἀφροδίτης φίλαι, 69). She chooses Menelaus, of course, who, Agamemnon laments, ought never to have taken her (ὅς σφε μήποτ' ὤφελεν λαβεῖν, 70). The audience will have realized at once that this is a recipe for trouble. Tyndareus has abdicated his duty as a father, and effectively treated his daughter as though she were an independent woman, with no *kurios* in charge. The marriage that a woman contracts on such terms, in accord with her predilections and without paternal authority, is one of convenience.[11]

We may compare the scene in Menander's *Perikeiromene*, in which the soldier Polemo proposes attacking the house where his παλλακή (concubine), Glycera, has taken refuge. His friend Pataecus reminds him that the case would be different if Glycera were his γαμετὴν γυναῖκα (lawfully wedded wife, 487), as Polemo pretends (cf. 486).[12] Polemo objects that he considers Glycera to be his wedded wife (489), to which Pataecus replies: "Who, then, is it who gave her to you?" (490). Polemo exclaims: "Who? She herself." "Fine," says Pataecus; "She liked you then, no doubt; now she does not" (490–491). Put simply, if Glycera was free to give herself to Polemo, she is free to leave him when she pleases. Her relationship with Polemo depended on sentiment, not law or custom.[13] Glycera has this autonomy because, as a foundling, she has no status as a citizen, and

---

11 Cf. Brindley 2016, 18: "Greek fathers generally chose husbands for their daughters; by granting Helen choice in this matter, Tyndareus abrogates his responsibilities as a father in an attempt at political compromise. The points of comparison with Agamemnon's situation and actions within the play are considerable; Agamemnon, like Tyndareus, must mediate between public pressures and his role as a father." Also Luschnig 1988, 112–113.

12 Contrast Agamemnon's description of Paris' relation to Helen as γάμος (marriage): αἰαῖ, τὸν Ἑλένης ὥς μ' ἀπώλεσεν γάμον / γήμας ὁ Πριάμου Πάρις, ὃς εἴργασται τάδε (467–468). Note the ironic use of the expression γαμετὴ ἑταίρα (lawfully wedded courtesan) at *Samia* 130; on the behavior of Alcesimarchus in the *Cistellaria*, who, in defiance of his father's prohibition promises marriage to Selenium, see Fantham 1975, 58–59. In a new fragment of the *Misoumenos* (see Turner 1981), Thrasonides, who has given his former slave Crateia her freedom (38–39), announces that he considered her a wife (γυναῖκα νομίσας, 40). A mutilated line (45) seems to contain the words οὐδὲ κυρία, which Turner tentatively translates: "[Even if she were legally her own mistress ...]. Cf. also Goldberg 1980, 50–51; Barigazzi 1985.

13 See Vernant 1980, 46, on κυριεία (proprietary authority) in marriage, and the contrast with the παλλακή (concubine), who "installed herself on her own responsibility." Demosthenes 59.46 indicates that a metic woman with no male relatives might be spoken of as κύριος (being in authority) of herself. See Brown 1990, 56–57 n. 40. The old woman who "gave" (130) Glycera to the soldier was not in a position to contract a binding relationship. Cf. Harrison 1968, 14–15 on the power of a male to give a woman to another male as concubine. Contrast Harrison pp. 19, 21, 108 and 108–109 on the inability of an Athenian woman to enter into a contract or to "engage her own hand in marriage," and cf. Isaeus 10.10 (cit. Harrison, p. 73 n. 3).

so her role is equivalent to that of a ἑταίρα (courtesan). She will only become eligible for marriage when she is discovered to be a citizen after all, and her father, who turns out to be Pataecus, will then officially betroth her to Polemo (1014).

We may cite a further case from the novel *Callirhoe*, by Chariton. At a trial presided over by the king of Persia, Dionysius, the second husband of Callirhoe, defends his claim to her as his wife against her first husband, Chaereas. The ἀντερασταί (rival lovers, 5.8.4) exchange insults with one another, and at a critical moment Chaereas affirms: "Her father gave her to me", to which Dionysius responds: "She gave herself to me." Here again, the reader will have recognized the legitimacy of Chaereas' allegation, who indeed will, after a series of further adventures, regain Callirhoe in the end.[14]

It is thus no surprise that when a handsome and opulently decked out young foreigner turns up at Menelaus' palace, one who, moreover, is reputed, as Agamemnon puts it, to have judged the goddesses (ὁ τὰς θεὰς / κρίνας ὅδ', ὡς ὁ μῦθος ἀνθρώπων ἔχει, 71–72), Helen should surrender to erotic passion, as Paris, equally enamored, carried her off to Troy (ἐρῶν ἐρῶσαν ᾤχετ' ἐξαναρπάσας / Ἑλένην πρὸς Ἴδης βούσταθμ[α], 75–76). In ceding the choice of mate to Helen, Tyndareus has treated her as though she were a ἑταίρα (courtesan), and she follows her whim. Menelaus in turn, driven to frenzy (οἰστρήσας, 77), invokes the suitors' oath and the Greeks prepare for war.

This brief hint of an irregularity in Helen's marriage to Menelaus is echoed implicitly, perhaps, when Menelaus repents of intercepting Agamemnon's letter to Clytemnestra, countermanding his earlier instruction to send Iphigenia to Aulis. Menelaus there declares that he can perfectly well find another marriage, and a distinguished one, if he so desires (εἰ γάμων ἱμείρομαι, 486). Helen, and conceivably the manner in which she was won, are not worth the sacrifice of Iphigenia. Later, to be sure, the chorus prays to be free of excessive *erôs*, of the kind that brought Paris to Argos, where he conferred *erôs* upon the eyes of Helen and was himself excited by *erôs* (ἔρωτά τ' ἔδωκας ἔρωτί τ' αὐτὸς ἐπτοήθης, 585–586), leading in turn to strife (*eris*, 587) between the Greeks and Trojans.[15]

---

[14] Marriage based on reciprocal *erôs* was celebrated in the Greek novels, but is rare in other genres; see Konstan 1994. In Xenophon's *Symposium* (8.3), Nikeratos is said to be in love with his wife and his wife equally in love with him (ἀλλὰ μὴν καὶ ὁ Νικήρατος, ὡς ἐγὼ ἀκούω, ἐρῶν τῆς γυναικὸς ἀντερᾶται).

[15] Another topic that seems undeveloped is the touristic voyeurism of the chorus of married women, who travel alone to see the heroes and the fleet. They recite an ecphrasis of the great warriors at ease, engaged in peaceful pursuits. On the chorus' erotic interest in Achilles, and on their recital of the γάμος (marriage) of Peleus and Thetis, see Weiss 2017, 200, 212.

That immoderate *erôs* could cause trouble, especially in a woman, was commonplace; one need look no further than Euripides' *Hippolytus* for evidence. But there is no reprise here of the theme of paternal irresponsibility, which is the innovative feature in Agamemnon's earlier account. If we think of this detail as a MacGuffin, planted in the prologue so as to trigger a development in the plot, it turns out to be merely a loose end. Thematically, however, it is complemented by Agamemnon's account of how he planned to wed Iphigenia to Achilles: "I wrote in the folded tablet and sent to my wife, [telling her] to send our daughter to be married [ὡc γαμουμένην] to Achilles, and I exalted the worth of the man" (98–101). This is how a marriage is properly arranged, with the girl's father making a suitable choice of husband for his daughter, not leaving such a decision to a fleeting passion. Of course, it is all fake: Iphigenia was being summoned to be sacrificed. We might see here an incipient theme of corrupted marriage, with a father twice over failing to perform his proper role in bestowing a daughter in wedlock. If so, it is again a path not taken, or taken further. It is a false lead, unfinished business.

4 Agamemnon's ambition

We may adduce a further example of a theme that is raised, only to be dropped without further elaboration. In defending his action of intercepting Agamemnon's second letter, Menelaus refers to Agamemnon's desire to be chosen as general of the expedition to Troy. To achieve this, Menelaus alleges, he knocked on every door and sought to ingratiate himself with all, only to become remote and haughty once he had been elected to the office (337–348). This odd equation of a Mycenaean king with a glad-handing politician in a modern democracy (cf. δημοτῶν, 340) serves little purpose and merely casts a shadow on Agamemnon's character and motives for conducting the war. As Kovacs observes, "This argument is obliquely relevant at best: what difference does it make to the present issue that Agamemnon opened his doors before his election and closed them later? Like his change of mind about Iphigenia it is an inconsistency, but the two inconsistencies have nothing to do with one another" (Kovacs 2003, 85). Now, characters who dispute in an ἀγών (contest, trial) avail themselves of all the tricks of rhetoric at their command, and do not necessarily limit themselves to what is strictly relevant to the case. Within the larger trajectory of the play, however, the suspicions cast upon Agamemnon's motives and character, as well as on the basis of Helen's marriage to Menelaus, serve, I think, to undercut Iphigenia's stirring patriotic speech, as she steps up to offer her life for the greater good of Greece and its right to rule barbarians (1378–1401). We the audience know, as she does not, just how tawdry the real reasons for the war are. This is not to say that Kovacs' criticism simply misses the point. Rather, the superimposed story that is retrospectively constructed as justifying Iphigenia's choice overrides and leaves no place for the doubts, tergiversations, and mixed motives that come to light earlier. This new master narrative cuts off the possible elaborations of the themes that are previously adumbrated, leaving them with nowhere to go.[16]

5 The infant Orestes

Among the passages especially vulnerable to excision have been those involving the baby Orestes. The sentimentality bestowed on the infant has been judged to be more characteristic of fourth-century taste than fifth, though on what basis it is hard to say. Iphigenia begs the baby to intercede with her father: "Brother, you are a small aid for your friends, but nevertheless weep with me, supplicate our father that your sister not die" (1241–1243). Later, she exclaims: "My dearest, you aided your dear ones as much as you could" (ὦ φίλτατ', ἐπεκούρησας ὅσον εἶχες φίλοις, 1452). This was clearly not very much, and David Kovacs thought the verse absurd (Kovacs 2003, 98). Guy Brindley, however, has discovered a thematic relevance in Orestes' role: "The theme of brotherly solidarity is perhaps most clearly represented in the play by Iphigenia's infant brother Orestes. Whilst Menelaus and the Dioscuri combine public and familial interests and activities …, Orestes is, as an infant, completely familial in his focus." Despite Orestes' impotence, Brindley notes that "the language used of Orestes by the other characters often implies abilities or even activities far beyond the limits of his age" (Brindley 2016, 21). We may add that the affection bestowed on Orestes may also reinforce awareness of the bond between mothers and their children, for Iphigenia's affection for the infant seems almost maternal; correspondingly, it sets in relief Agamemnon's failures as a father. Nevertheless, one might have expected some further consequence of the infant's

---

16 For the hollowness of Iphigenia's speech, see Siegel 1981. Burgess 2004, 55 sees a further twist in Clytemnestra's skepticism about the final rescue of Iphigenia: "When Clytemnestra expresses her final doubts about the veracity of the tale of Iphigenia's death (1615–18) we see a counter-example to Iphigenia. For the first time in the play we see a character who fully resists the impulse to refuse to see what she sees." But those final verses are almost certainly by a much later hand, as West 1981 demonstrated.

presence, some deeper integration in the plot. Once more, there is an intimation of a possible development that is not followed up. Orestes is introduced, only to drop out of the picture, another signpost leading to a dead end.

6 Conclusion: the textual unconscious

In conclusion, I suggest that the repression of alternative narratives is characteristic of ideology, even if it cannot eliminate all traces of other truths and the scripts that authorize them. The apparent unity of a literary work is, in the words of John Frow, "a labor of transformation carried out on a raw material of ideological values" (Frow 1986, 19). To put it differently, social tensions and contradictions are embedded in a literary text, which inevitably betrays symptoms of the strain required to forge such refractory materials into a unified composition. The fissures or inconsistencies that remain are indices of this effort. As Fredric Jameson has observed: "the deviation of the individual text from some deeper narrative structure directs our attention to those determinate changes in the historical situation which block a full manifestation or replication on the discursive level" (Jameson 1981, 146). The tensions that inhabit a text are manifested also in the construction of characters or dramatic personae, as well as in the detours of the plot. As Mieke Bal observes: "Characters embody contradictions; only if we endure lapses can we take them as existing in a stable and unchanging, if fictive, ontology" (Bal 1987, 107–108). Seen this way, the tergiversations of Agamemnon, Menelaus, Achilles, and Iphigenia are not signs of a lapse in artistry or of interpolation in the text by different hands, but a function of what we may call, adapting a phrase of Fredric Jameson, the textual unconscious, just as much as the deviations in the plot that have puzzled critics. In the words of Pierre Macherey: "What begs to be explained in the work is not that false simplicity which derives from the apparent unity of its meaning, but the presence of a relation, or an opposition, between elements of the exposition or levels of the composition, those disparities which point to a conflict of meaning." Macherey continues: "The book is not the extension of a meaning; it is generated from the incompatibility of several meanings, the strongest bond by which it is attached to reality, in a tense and ever-renewed confrontation."[17]

---

[17] Macherey 1978, 79–80. Cf. Thompson 1984, 25: "The representation of unity in the context of restricted and mutable social relations thus implies the projection of an 'imaginary community' by means of which 'real' distinctions are portrayed as 'natural,' the historical is effaced in the atemporality of essence." For further discussion and bibliography, see Konstan 1995, 5–7 *et passim*.

Euripides' *Iphigenia in Aulis*, more than most other works, makes manifest the ideological labor of the text, as it brings to the surface programs that are not allowed to advance, and cannot be seamlessly assimilated to a single overarching construct. For this very reason, perhaps, it was more susceptible to revision and addition than more tightly woven tragedies such as Sophocles' *Oedipus Tyrannus*, where the contradictions in the text (which are real enough) were less apparent, rendering it harder to insert superfluous material.[18] The exceptional disjointedness of the *Iphigenia in Aulis* may in turn reflect Euripides' response to the extraordinary tensions of the time, as the defeat of Athens in the Peloponnesian War seemed ever more imminent, and the motives of those who prolonged it ever more suspicious. Athenians must have wondered what would have happened had Athens not sent the fleet to Sicily but had respected instead the Peace of Nicias, among other possible paths not taken. The liminal nature of the setting at Aulis, suspended between a past exposed to revision (recalling the fleet) and a future still uncertain, was an ideal locus for such speculation, open as it was both spatially and temporally to alternative possibilities. And so the resulting script, or scripts, of the *Iphigenia in Aulis* seem flawed, overstuffed with extraneous matter and yet incomplete without it. It is the perfect *labor imperfectus*.

Appendix

On λαμβάνειν and Marriage:[19]

> LSJ s.v. λαμβάνω:
> **I.1.b.** *take by violence, carry off as prize or booty*, Il.5.273, 8.191, Hdt.4.130, S.Ph.68 (Pass.), 1431, etc.;
> **II.1.c.** *receive in marriage*, Hdt.1.199, 9.108, E.Fr.953.27, X. HG4.1.14, Isoc.10.39, PEleph.1.2 (iv B. C.), Men.Pk.436;

(1) The Herodotus passage is hardly a good example: Ἐπεὰν δὲ μιχθῇ, ἀποσιωσαμένη τῇ θεῷ ἀπαλλάσσεται ἐς τὰ οἰκία, καὶ τὠπὸ τούτου οὐκ οὕτω μέγα τί οἱ δώσεις ᾧ μιν λάμψεαι ("After their intercourse, having discharged her sacred

---

18 My thanks to Philip Hardie for this suggestion. Also to Fabio Tutrone for his encouraging comments, and to Stavroula Kiritsi for being there.
19 Translations mine unless otherwise indicated.

duty to the goddess, she goes away to her home; and thereafter there is no bribe however great that will get her.")

(2) So too the second Herodotus passage: δοκέων αὐτὴν μᾶλλον λάμψεσθαι ἢν ταῦτα ποιήσῃ ("Xerxes found no other way to accomplish his purpose than that he should make a marriage between his own son Darius and the daughter of this woman and Masistes, for he thought that by doing so he would be most likely to win her," i.e. the wife of his brother).

(3) The Euripides fragment is equally problematic:

> ἢ πῶς δίκαιόν ἐστιν ἢ καλῶς ἔχον
> τῶν μὲν ἀγαθῶν με τὸ μέρος ὧν εἶχεν λαβεῖν,   (25)
> τοῦ συναπορηθῆναι δὲ μὴ λαβεῖν μέρος;
> φέρ' ἢν ὁ νῦν <δὴ> λαμβάνειν μέλλων μ' ἀνήρ,
> ὃ μὴ γένοιτο, Ζεῦ φίλ', οὐδ' ἔσται ποτέ,
> οὐκ οὖν θελούσης οὐδὲ δυναμένης ἐμοῦ, etc.

> How is it just or honorable,
> that I should take my share of the good things he had,
> but he in his poverty take no share at all?
> Now, if the man who is now about to take me...
> But, dear Zeus, may it never happen, nor will it ever,
> not if I am willing or able...

(4) Here is the Xenophon passage:

> Ἐμοὶ μὲν τοίνυν, ἔφη, δοκεῖ, ὁ Ἀγησίλαος, σὲ μέν, ὦ Σπιθριδάτα, τύχῃ ἀγαθῇ διδόναι Ὄτυϊ τὴν θυγατέρα, σὲ δὲ λαμβάνειν.

> "'Well, then,' said Agesilaus, 'I think it best that you, Spithridates, should give your daughter to Otys — and may good fortune attend upon the deed — and that you, Otys, should accept her.'"

(5) The Isocrates passage is from the *Encomium of Helen*: (39)

> Μετὰ γὰρ τὴν Θησέως εἰς Ἅιδου κατάβασιν, ἐπανελθούσης αὐτῆς εἰς Λακεδαίμονα καὶ πρὸς τὸ μνηστεύεσθαι λαβούσης ἡλικίαν, ἅπαντες οἱ τότε βασιλεύοντες καὶ δυναστεύοντες τὴν αὐτὴν γνώμην ἔσχον περὶ αὐτῆς· ἐξὸν γὰρ αὐτοῖς λαμβάνειν ἐν ταῖς αὐτῶν πόλεσι γυναῖκας τὰς πρωτευούσας, ὑπεριδόντες τοὺς οἴκοι γάμους ἦλθον ἐκείνην μνηστεύσοντες. So too in the continuation (40): εἴ τις ἀποστεροίη τὸν ἀξιωθέντα λαβεῖν αὐτήν, νομίζων ἕκαστος τὴν ἐπικουρίαν ταύτην αὐτῷ παρασκευάζειν.

> After the descent of Theseus to Hades, when Helen returned to Lacedaemon, and was now of marriageable age, all the kings and potentates of that time formed of her the same opinion; for although it was possible for them in their own cities to wed women of the first rank, they disdained wedlock at home and went to Sparta to woo Helen. And before it had

yet been decided who was to be her husband and all her suitors still had an equal chance, it was so evident to all that Helen would be the object of armed contention that they met together and exchanged solemn pledges of assistance if anyone should attempt to take her away from him who had been adjudged worthy of winning her; for each thought he was providing this alliance for himself (trans. Norlin 1980).

(6) Finally, the *Perikeiromene* is of a woman taking a lover:

(Δω) κόψω τὴν θύραν· (184)
οὐδεὶς γὰρ αὐτῶν ἐστιν ἔξω. δυστυχής, (185)
ἥτις στρατιώτην ἔλαβεν ἄνδρα. παράνομοι
ἅπαντες, οὐδὲν πιστόν.

(Doris) I'll knock at the door;
for none of them is outside. Unfortunate
is she who takes a soldier as her man. They're lawless,
all of them, totally untrustworthy.

The upshot is that λαμβάνω seems hardly the right term for taking a legitimate wife.

Bibliography

Bal, Mieke (1987), *Lethal Love: Feminist Literary Readings of Biblical Love Stories*, Bloomington.
Barbiero, Emilia (2022), *Letters in Plautus: Reading between the Lines*, Cambridge.
Barigazzi, Adelmo (1985), "Menandro: L'inizio del *Misumenos*", *Prometheus* 11, 97–125.
Brindley, Guy (2016), "Conflicted Fatherhood and Committed Brotherhood in Euripides' *Iphigenia in Aulis*", *Pons Aelius: Newcastle University Postgraduate Forum E-Journal* 13, 13–24.
Brown, Peter G. McC. (1990), "The Bodmer Codex of Menander and the Endings of Terence's *Eunuchus* and other Roman Comedies", in: Eric Handley/Andre Hurst (eds.), *Relire Menandre*, Geneva: Librairie Droz = Recherches et Rencontres 2, 37–61.
Burgess, Dana L. (2004), "Lies and Convictions at Aulis", *Hermes* 132, 37–55.
Diggle, James (1971), "Review of G. Mellert-Hoffmann, *Untersuchungen zur 'Iphigenie in Aulis' des Euripides*", *CR* 21, 180; reprinted in: James Diggle *Euripidea*, Oxford, 1994.
Diggle, James (1981), *Euripidis: Fabulae*, Vol. 2: *Supplices; Electra; Hercules; Troades, Iphigenia in Tauris; Ion*, Oxford.
Fantham, Elaine (1975), "Sex, Status, and Survival in Hellenistic Athens: A Study of Women in New Comedy", *Phoenix* 29, 44–74.
Frampton, Stephanie Ann (2019), *Empire of Letters: Writing in Roman Literature and Thought from Lucretius to Ovid*, Oxford.
Frow, John (1986), *Marxism and Literary History*, Cambridge, MA.
Gibson, William (2014), *The Peripheral*, New York.
Gibson, William (2020), *Agency*, New York.
Goldberg, Sander M. (1980), *The Making of Menander's Comedy*, Berkeley.

Grandazzi, Alexandre/Anne Queyrel-Bottineau (eds.) (2018), *Antiques uchronies: Quand Grecs et Romains imaginent des histoires alternatives*, Dijon.
Gurd, Sean Alexander (2005), *Iphigenia at Aulis: Textual Multiplicity, Radical Philology*, Ithaca.
Harrison, A.R.W. (1968), *The Law of Athens*, Vol. 1, Oxford.
Jameson, Fredric (1981), *The Political Unconscious: Narrative as a Socially Symbolic Act*, Ithaca.
Konstan, David (1994), *Sexual Symmetry: Love in the Ancient Novel and Related Genres*, Princeton.
Konstan, David (1995), *Greek Comedy and Ideology*, New York.
Kovacs, David (2003), "Toward a Reconstruction of *Iphigenia Aulidensis*", *JHS* 123, 77–103.
Luschnig, Celia (1988), *Tragic Aporia: A Study of Euripides'* Iphigenia at Aulis, Berwick.
Norlin, George (1980), trans., *Isocrates*, Cambridge, MA.
Macherey, Pierre (1978), *A Theory of Literary Production*, trans. Geoffrey Wall, London.
Siegel, Herbert (1981), "Agamemnon in Euripides' *Iphigenia at Aulis*", *Hermes* 109, 257–265.
Tarrant, Richard (1995), "Classical Latin Literature", in: D.C. Greetham (ed.), *Scholarly Editing: A Guide to Research*, Modern Language Association of America, New York, 94–148.
Thompson, John B. (1984), *Studies in the Theory of Ideology*, Cambridge.
Turner, E.G. (ed.) (1981), "P. Oxy. 3371 A", *Oxyrinchus Papyri* 48, 1–21.
Vernant, Jean-Pierre (1980), "Marriage", in: Jean-Pierre Vernant, *Myth and Society in Ancient Greece*, trans. Janet Lloyd, Sussex.
Weiss, Naomi (2017), *The Music of Tragedy*, Berkeley.
West, M.L. (1981), "Tragica V", *BICS* 28, 61–78.

Stavros Frangoulidis
Seneca's *Phoenissae*: In Search of an Ending

Abstract: In Seneca's *Phoenissae* the notion of closure undergoes constant redefinition in the evolution of the play's plot. Oedipus wishes to end his life as a form of punishment due to his additional guilt from his vision of his sons' deliberately planning to recommit and surpass his own inadvertent crimes. This prophecy is tantamount to the birth of the *Phoenissae* and leads to Oedipus' reframing of closure as punishment that is no longer his own death but the destruction of his entire family and city. The play's lack of an ending and Oedipus' search for one are thematized as the dramatic deadlock in Thebes parallels the metatheatrical stand-off in the play with a series of debates involving characters with an objective opposed to that of Oedipus and who try to forestall the forward movement of his single vision. This sequence of interrupted trajectories and the conflict of narratives shape our understanding of the scope and stakes of Oedipus' envisioned (but narratively incomplete) closure.

1 Unfinishedness and closure

The extant text of Seneca's *Phoenissae* exhibits several features that have led the majority of scholars to suggest we have an incomplete work, either because Seneca did not finish it or because of losses during textual transmission.[1] These features include the supposed lack of a prologue, the absence of choral lyrics, and, most obviously, the lack of an ending that resolves the play's tensions. But the issue of how to find the right ending is also foregrounded in the text as a metatheatrical problem from the very beginning and the play dramatizes a search for closure and its resignification as the plot unfolds.

The surviving play opens in the countryside outside Thebes with a suicidal Oedipus struggling to find the right narrative ending to his own life to achieve his self-punitive closure. It emerges eventually that he is driven by his vision of

---

The text and translations of Seneca's *Phoenissae* are from the Loeb edition by Fitch 2002. I would like to thank warmly David Konstan and Stephanie Jayne Winder for most thoughtful comments and suggestions on various stages in the preparation of this essay.

[1] For an opposite view, namely that the play is complete and experimental in form see, e.g., Tarrant 1978, 219, 229–230.

his warring sons consciously recommitting his own unwitting crime of spilling family blood and causing damage to Thebes. His vision is tantamount to prophecy, and becomes his plot script, providing a "better" solution for punitive closure that allows him to be persuaded by Antigone not to end his life. The dramatic deadlock in Thebes parallels the metatheatrical stand-off of the play as a series of characters who oppose Oedipus' plot, and hence the movement of the play, try to direct it to their own endings.

The unfinished state of the *Phoenissae* does not allow an audience to see fully how and to what extent Oedipus' authorial narrative is realized. In his extraordinary guilt Oedipus seems to envision an end to the pollution in a future that transcends the probable limits of the dramatic narrative, inasmuch as the current war will not end with the utter ravaging of Thebes — the mythological tradition further includes the future struggles of the Epigonoi before the eventual end of Oedipus' royal line, and hence the end of pollution.

Even though the theme of death at the intra-narrative level has been treated adequately, its connection with the problem of the play's narrative unfinishedness on the one hand and metatheatrical closure on the other has been overlooked. This essay focuses on how Oedipus' debate about the right way to end his life as a punishment sets up a metatheatrical contest between his master narrative of total destruction and the other characters' vain attempts to force him (either in person or symbolically) into a reconciliatory role.

2 Negotiating closure: Oedipus and Antigone

The intersection of plans with opposing objectives for controlling the action structures the play's (extant) beginning in the debate between Antigone and her father. Oedipus seeks initially to free himself from his daughter's guidance so as to implement the narrative of his life's end.[2] However, he does not at first explain the cause of his urgent suicidal desire i.e. his vision of his warring sons that brought a renewed awareness of his criminality. Instead, he drops hints that it is connected with his past crimes as a way to create suspense and draw the audience's attention to the play's central issues.[3] The audience has no guid-

---

[2] Here there may be a trace of an intertextual context between competing versions of what happens to Oedipus after the revelations: Oedipus is in exile as in Sophocles, and unlike Euripides' *Phoenissae* and Statius' *Thebaid*, where he is living in the palace.
[3] Frank 1995a, 75, observes that Seneca exploits suspense to the fullest: he mentions the quarrel of the brothers but does not associate it with Oedipus' death wish (53–58); then alludes

ance from the traditional myth, which represented Oedipus' current blindness as his choice of a punishment worse than death. So what additional crimes could he be seeking punishment for? The suspense this creates for the audience, matched by Antigone's later urgent questioning about the cause, draws attention to its significance for the play.

As narrative creator seeking the right setting for his suicide, he looks to Mt Cithaeron and casts ending his life as the payment of his debt for being saved from death by exposure there, and also as the penalty for his subsequent crimes. He considers in turn possible specific sites that bear the penal symbolism of his mythopoetic (and familial) precedents, such as Actaeon, Pentheus, Dirce and Ino (12–26), before zeroing in on the actual place of his exposure as the right place to pay the sentence ordained in his infancy (27–38). His ensuing vision of Laius' ghost attacking his eyes connects his urge to die with his past crimes, which in turn motivates his warning to Antigone to stay away from him in fear of repeating his incest.[4]

Like the audience, Antigone is in the dark as to the cause of her father's grim raging. She gives the first hint about the brothers' hostilities but only in the context of distinguishing herself in *pietas*. It is as evidence of her *pietas* that she declares herself his everlasting companion, whether he chooses to live or die, even to the point of pledging her willingness to abandon her plot to keep him alive and her determination to end her life along with him in savage terrains if he persists, thus adding to the horrors (66–76). However, Antigone also tries to move forward her non-suicidal narrative when she exhorts her father to change his mind and summon up his old *virtus* in the face of adversities, implying that he can endure his troubles (77): *flecte mentem* ("change your thinking"). Whereas Oedipus framed his death narrative in terms of his paying debts and facing penalties, Antigone tries to recast it in more militaristic terms with Oedipus as the defeated.

As Oedipus sees salvation only in death, he insists on moving forward his death narrative, yet again without disclosing the cause of his wrath, thus intimating its importance for the play. He starts to hint at the reason when he connects the urge to end his life with his realization that his crimes are not yet paid for in full, that is, in blinding himself he only punished the crime involving his

---

to it briefly (108–110), and finally points to the power struggles between the brothers as the cause of Oedipus' desire to die (273–306).

4 Frank 1995a, 93. On Seneca's portrayal of Antigone and the risk of repeating familial incest, see the illuminating discussion of Ginsberg 2015, 199–230. On the reception of Senecan drama in Statius' *Thebaid*, see Augoustakis 2015, 377–392.

mother (92–93) and not the crimes against his father of murder and usurping his throne. His determination to be in control of his own narrative is clear (105):[5] *regnum mei retineo* ("I keep the kingship over myself"). This motivates his ensuing exhortation to his daughter to give up on her efforts to rescue him and yield to his own narrative of savage death as his assistant.[6] His new survey of possible means of dying as well as locations (105–139) includes two rich options for symbolic closure in terms that point to key moments in his criminal biography and identify him as a *monstrum maius*: using the sword infected by Laius' blood, and hurling himself from the crag of the Sphinx.

Antigone's refusal to cooperate is evinced when Oedipus envisages her efforts to cut him off from all external means of death — the sword, falling, the noose and poison.[7] Oedipus assures her that he can overcome her endeavors and his third survey of death options ranges in gruesome detail through the bodily sites where death can be dealt, culminating in the powerful symbolism of asking his father to assist him in thrusting his nails into his eye sockets to reach his brain, so as to bring a proper ending to his story and closure for his crimes.[8]

As Oedipus insists on his initial decision to move forward his death narrative, Antigone in despair assures her father that her only aim is to dissuade him from surrendering to the *dolor* that drives him to death (189). Her metadramatic endeavor is based on her belief that his troubles cannot become worse so as to justify the additional punishment of death, and that he is, in any case, innocent (182–205).[9] Like the audience, Antigone too contemplates the various reasons that could be driving her father to death as punishment but she concludes that he has already paid the penalty by his self-blinding. This explains her urgent desire to know what is goading him on or whom he is trying to escape (205–215). Her insistent focus on learning the cause for the outburst of his suicidal wrath directs attention to its relevance for the play and in Oedipus' plot construction.

---

[5] Oedipus here sounds like Seneca's Stoic *proficiens* as he claims that when he has no control over anything else at least he has control over himself and the manner of his death.

[6] Oedipus' determination to commit suicide as punishment for his crimes despite Antigone's attempt to dissuade him is reminiscent of Hercules being dissuaded from suicide by Amphitryon in the *Hercules Furens*.

[7] Frank 1995a, 120.

[8] In Seneca's *Oedipus*, the chief crime is patricide, or rather regicide. Whereas Sophocles was writing for a democratic city, Seneca was wrestling with what it means to kill the king. On this point, see the excellent discussion in Konstan 1994, 3–23.

[9] On the contrast between innocence and guilt depending on intention, see Frank 1995a, 135–136.

In response, Oedipus begins to disclose the reason for his urge to die, gradually lifting the dissonance arising from his desire to end his life and the concealment of the cause that stirred his wrath anew. He explains that he wishes to escape himself, that is, his own criminal conscience. His emphasis on destroying his ability to hear (224–229) is not only an expression of his desire to avoid hearing words that remind him of his crimes, e.g. 'father', but also a hint that the source of his new rage is something that he has heard (232–233): *aures ingerunt quidquid mihi / donastis* ("my ears force on me all that my eyes have spared me"). The effect of it he sees as tantamount to renewing his crimes (231): *recrudescit nefas* ("the evil ... grows repeatedly").

When Antigone attempts to oppose him, Oedipus orders her to stay away so as to maintain control of his narrative. He surveys all his crimes that cast him as the worst criminal who ever existed (245–277).[10] He thus restates the problem of finding the proper novel ending as a matter of finding the right new punishment to match the crimes (242): *nouamque poenam sceleribus ... parem* ("it is seeking a new punishment to match for my crimes"). His previous focus on his patricide as unpunished now gives way to an emphasis on his incest. In the hierarchy of crimes, Oedipus views this as worse than patricide (*maius scelus*, 269) in that it led to his siring incestuous children (270–271).[11]

It is at this point, with the mention of his sons, that Oedipus finally starts to reveal the cause of his current rage. The new crimes for which he seeks punishment are the present and, more importantly, future ones of his warring sons, which he holds himself responsible for as their father. His culpability is represented by the image of casting away his scepter, which has armed their hands (273–274). His ability to presage the future (*praesagit*, 278) stems from his knowledge that the scepter is stained with familial blood and that this infection is symbolized in the passing of the scepter (274–278). In fact, he acquires the status of a blind *vates*, with the ability to link past, present and future, thus enabling him to have full mastery over the play's plot. He finally discloses the reason for his current wrath and search for closure in the form of a vision, a dire prophecy of the imminent war of his sons for the scepter and the devastation threatening the city (278–287).[12] His prophecy is tantamount to the play's plot.[13]

---

10 Papadopoulou 2008, 111.
11 See Ginsberg 2018, 59.
12 Papadopoulou 2008, 111, defines Oedipus' vision as prophecy.
13 Frank 1995a, 152, points out that Oedipus is exceptional as the only living human character in Senecan tragedy who has this visionary ability.

In begetting sons Oedipus is also the ultimate creator of the tragedy underway.[14] From this poetological vantage point, his earlier survey of all his crimes help cast him as the worst criminal who ever existed, securing the novelty of his composition.

When Antigone learns the cause of her father's rage she alters the objective of her narrative since she tries to persuade her father to carry on with his life in order to act to prevent fratricidal war (288–294). But Oedipus shatters her expectations when he refuses to intervene on the grounds that it is impossible given that his sons have no love for their ruined father and are completely driven by frenzied rage (*ira*, 299) with no moral scruples at all (295–302). Far from being a reason to live, the fraternal strife is identified by Oedipus explicitly as the reason for his own death wish (303–306) and he rushes to end his own narrative before his authorial vision is realized.

The initial tension generated by the intersection of opposing plotlines is eventually resolved in the closing sequence of the debate by a gesture of *pietas*. Antigone falls to her father's knees and Oedipus yields to her supplication. However, her success is partial as she is unable to persuade her father to restore peace between her brothers, because of the inevitability of his prophecy, signaling passion's triumph over reason for the evolution of the tragic plot.[15]

The interaction of characters with opposing objectives is further manifested in the clash between Oedipus and the Nuntius who conveys the plea of the Thebans for him to prevent fraternal war and the ravaging of the city. As a *vates*, not only does Oedipus refuse to mediate, but he even spurs his sons on to prove their criminal lineage (334–339):

> *agite, o propago clara, generosam indolem*
> *probate factis; gloriam ac laudes meas*   335
> *superate, et aliquid facite; propter quod patrem*
> *adhuc iuuet uixisse. facietis, scio:*
> *sic estis orti. scelere defungi haud leui,*
> *haud usitato, tanta nobilitas potest.*

Come on, my glorious issue, prove your noble ancestry by your deeds, surpass my fame and renown, and achieve something to make your father glad that he lived till now! You

---

14 This overtly metapoetic Oedipus differs considerably from the Oedipus of Euripides' *Phoenissae* who only delivers his curse against his sons for mistreating him.

15 Again there is an illuminating parallel with the *Hercules Furens*. Here Antigone's (partial) success is necessary for Oedipus' new plot to begin, whereas in *HF* 1200 ff. Amphitryon's success in persuading Hercules to abandon his resolution to commit suicide and return to reason signals the play's end. See Frank 1995a, 160.

will do it, I know: you were born to it. Such high birth cannot make do with ordinary or trivial crime.

This is the most overtly metatheatrical scene in the play. Oedipus the *vates* here also assumes the role of director of action since he opts to promote the implementation of his prophecy.[16] Overstepping the strict confines of his role as messenger, the Nuntius comes close to developing his own independent agenda when he exhorts Oedipus to discard the authorial role in his destruction narrative and take on that of writer (*auctor*) of a peace narrative for his sons (347–349). What is more, Oedipus takes on the role of inset audience for his envisioned plot when he announces that he will stay in his mountain location to audibly follow the brothers' war (358–362).

At the culmination of his narrative planning, Oedipus now finds closure in a different ending that requires he stay alive, and in so doing he modifies the meaning of the ending he seeks. Cithaeron is transformed from the stage for his suicide play to the auditorium for his Theban destruction play that will include fratricide and matricide, recasting Jocasta's traditional suicide as *matrocinium* in the military context since Jocasta will commit suicide at the sight of her sons' lifeless bodies (354–358).[17] Whereas previously Oedipus' rage at himself for his sons' actions caused his wish to die before experiencing their greater crimes, now, the same rage makes him spur them on to surpass him in criminality by engaging in acts of destruction and sacrilege, involving the burning of crops and the ravaging of Thebes along with the temples.[18] His previous shame at his incest-produced sons is replaced by a grimly sardonic pride in the brothers' warped *pietas*. Now he sees that the right ending, securing self-punishment, is not escape by suicide, but the pain of experiencing the realization of his vision. Thus, in his *furor* he desires (*cupio* 354) the self-punishing pleasure of suffering the death of his family (*dolor*) as closure and the metapoetic enjoyment of his own success as *auctor*.

---

16 This is set in contrast to the Oedipus of the Euripidean *Phoenissae* who is not involved in the action.
17 In prophesying the death of both his sons and Jocasta Oedipus moves away from Euripides' *Phoenissae* in which Jocasta's death does not feature in his curse.
18 On Oedipus' wrath as the driving force for his actions, see Papadopoulou 2008, 112.

3 Closing negotiations: Jocasta, Polynices, and Eteocles

In what amounts to the commencement of Oedipus' master narrative, Jocasta is paralyzed with grief at the news of her sons' upcoming war. Like Oedipus, she sees her worst crime as having produced guilty sons (369): *feci nocentes* ("I have made others guilty"). But the narrative of her distress stresses her contrasting evaluation of incestuous progeny to that of Oedipus: Jocasta grieves for both her sons, whereas Oedipus is lost in grief for himself; Jocasta loves both her sons equally but sees Polynices as having the better cause, whereas Oedipus views both as equally wrong with an equally criminal lust for power.

Both the attendant and Antigone intervene to rouse Jocasta to action: the former urges the mother to restore amity between her sons (401–402) and the latter to break up the fighting or suffer the consequences (403–405). In their advice to Jocasta both the attendant and Antigone recall the Nuntius when he offers to Oedipus the authorial role for a peace narrative (349). Acting on the advice of both, Jocasta devises her plan to prevent the *nefas* or die (406–414). In undertaking action, Jocasta appears in a position similar to Oedipus as plot director. There is a difference, however. Whereas Oedipus refuses to mediate between his sons who are consciously planning to add to his inadvertent crimes (328–332), Jocasta intervenes in the conflict to bring amity to her sons, though eventually disclosing her inability to respond to their need for power in their own terms (408–414).

In the play, there are two plotlines of opposing objectives, one authored by Oedipus and the other by Jocasta. Both are driven on by *furor* (427) and guilt, and both are directed at the *furor* of their sons who have no sense of guilt. The mingling of the two creates irony and enables the plot to advance to its tragic resolution. Jocasta tries to act as a reconciliatory force between her sons but ironically ends up bringing the implementation of Oedipus' master narrative a step closer. Irony is thus built into the fabric of the play, aiming at augmenting audience engagement and advancing the plot.

The unfolding of Oedipus' plotline continues unabated. The critical point at which it directly intersects with that of his mother is the moment when Jocasta takes up position in the middle of the battle lines, the inner stage of Oedipus' master narrative (433–434). Jocasta offers her sons an ultimatum: to kill her as she stands between them or make peace, hoping that their *pietas* would prevent the *nefas* and the outcome Oedipus desires (443–449). Like Oedipus, Jocasta too traces the war back to its origin, i.e. the family's guilt, but she also draws a distinction between the family's past unintentional criminality and the current outrage, committed willfully in full knowledge (451–454). Like Antigone with Oedipus, Jocasta's intervention appears to be at least partially successful; she temporarily suspends the imminent death of warfare (435);[19] but she too will end up advancing Oedipus' objective rather than achieving her own.

The intersection of two plotlines continues in the sequence of action when Jocasta determines to move forward her narrative of entreaties to her sons, so as to lure them away from Oedipus' plotline, and thus thwart the outcome he desires.[20] Her narrative, like that of Antigone earlier, depends on the persuasive power of *pietas* and parental love. This determines her command to Polynices to remove his armor and join her in an embrace.[21] That Polynices is acting as agent in Oedipus' master narrative is evinced when he refuses to lay down his weapons fearing a trap from both his brother and mother (478–480). When she turns to Eteocles to exhort him to disarm first on the grounds that he caused the war by violating the agreement (483–487), he too parallels Polynices in being unwilling to disarm for fear of treachery from his brother. By referencing Oedipus she evokes recognition of the fact that both sons are engaged in *Oedipal* actions in seeking to claim the scepter by familial murder (496–497). The dramatic deadlock in the conflict expresses the metatheatrical stand-off in the play. It is only after assuring them that she will act as the defensive armor for both sides that the brothers disarm, enabling her to set her pleas for her peace narrative in motion.[22]

The parallel plotlines continue to intersect in Jocasta's ensuing pleas to Polynices so as to prevent the ending Oedipus desires. Her narrative is rich in ironic echoes of Oedipus' own words and evocations of the parallelism between the threatened *nefas* and that of Oedipus.[23] In recognition of their joint suffering, Jocasta begins by mourning over Polynices' Oedipus-like exile and mistaken marriage (500–525). As before, the parallelism helps cast Polynices as his father's

---

19 Frank 1995a, 189–190.
20 On the Vergilian resonances in Jocasta's intervention, see Barchiesi 1988, ad Sen. *Phoenissae* 427; also Schuur 2018, 130.
21 Ginsberg 2018, 66–67, offers an excellent analysis of the erotic language and imagery in the scene of embrace as evoking the original incest to suggest that the cycle of civil war continues from generation to generation. See also van der Schuur 2018, 131.
22 On Jocasta using her body as a shield, see Voigt 2015, 2.
23 See Frank 1995a, 5, with further bibliography.

double,[24] a point Jocasta explicitly underlines (513–514): *ne quid e fatis tibi / deesset paternis* ("lest you should lack any part of your father's fate"). This motivates the mother's plea for him to withdraw his forces so as to prevent conscious repetition of the family's inadvertent crimes and hence of Oedipus' master narrative. Pointed irony is discerned when Jocasta views herself as wretched for being so close to witnessing a greater *nefas* than their father (531–532), unaware that Oedipus is waiting eagerly to hear of the greater *nefas* to be perpetrated by his sons and the extinction of his family. The irony is compounded when she later invokes the authority of Oedipus as if he were in support of her pleas (537–538): *per irati sibi / genas parentis* ("by the eyes of your self-castigating father"), and is deepened when she conjures up the presence of Oedipus as judge of punishments (553–555): *occurrat tibi / nunc Oedipus, quo iudice, erroris quoque / poenae petuntur* ("Think now about Oedipus, who judges that punishment is required even for a mistake").

As an indication of the progress of Oedipus' master narrative Jocasta views the greatest part of Polynices' *nefas* as already perpetrated since the cavalry is trampling the meadows and the leaders in chariots are flying around seeking to destroy their homes (542–550). In what serves as a self-referential commentary on the novelty of Oedipus' master narrative, Jocasta views fratricidal war as new kind of crime, unknown even in Thebes renowned for its tragic history of familial crime (548): *facinus ... novum* ("a deed unknown").

The intersection of binary plotlines continues to be seen in Jocasta's ensuing nightmare vision of the ravaging of Thebes, involving a series of entreaties to her son not to engage in acts of destruction and sacrilege, i.e. tearing down his fatherland, the house gods, its crops and its divinely built walls (556–571). Her pleas run counter to Oedipus' parallel vision of the worst imaginable crimes his sons are to carry out when he exhorts them to destroy the crops, tear down the walls and temples and ravage their city (340–347). Jocasta's nightmare vision further includes the humiliating images of his enslaved fellow countrymen, including his mother, as adornments of his triumphal display, culminating with her appeal for a return to *pietas* (571–580).

Instead of luring Polynices away from Oedipus' narrative by bringing him back to *pietas*, Jocasta's pleas have the effect of igniting his wrath further, paralleling Oedipus' increased *furor* after Antigone's and the Nuntius' appeals. As justification of his assault on Thebes, Polynices counters his mother's vision of

---

[24] Ginsberg 2018, 58–74, advances the excellent idea of Polynices as his father's double. She views his assault on Thebes described in erotic terms as surpassing his father's incestuous conquest of Jocasta.

the would-be sufferings of the Thebans with the reality of his own situation, wandering forever in exile, as a result of his brother's actions. His resentment grows on recollection of his life in exile, subservient to his regal bride and his father-in-law.

Perceiving her son's need for power, Jocasta catalogues a number of foreign kingdoms wherein he could wage war, and hence reroute the trajectory of Oedipus' master narrative (599–618). After envisioning the punishment of crime, she ends her narrative of entreaties with a plea to free his *patria* from fear and his parents from grief — a final grim irony given Oedipus' passion for the prospect of Thebes' ravaging and the extinction of his family (641–643):[25] *infaustas age / dimitte pugnas, libera patriam metu, / luctu parentes* ("Come, drop this accursed fight; free your country from fear and your parents from grief").

The dramatic and metatheatrical stand-off now turns to the issue of the punishment of crimes — the very dilemma that opened the play with Oedipus' search for the right penal ending as closure. Acting as agent in Oedipus' master narrative, Polynices furiously seeks to know the price his brother will pay for violating the sacred pact (643–644). Jocasta echoes Oedipus' earlier evaluation of the cursed Theban scepter (274–278) in her assurance that Eteocles will pay a high price for wielding the scepter, like all his royal predecessors starting from Cadmus and continuing on to his descendants (645–651).

Rather than reconciling her sons, Jocasta effectively restarts the conflict in her inability to address their need for power in their own terms and to offer an acceptable alternative closure, ironically precipitating the outcome Oedipus desires. This is evinced in the brothers' ensuing hurling of insults at each other (651–664).[26] As agent in Oedipus' winning narrative, Eteocles dismisses all consideration of consequences with his final stark declaration that the scepter is worth any price (664): *imperia pretio quolibet constant bene* ("power is well purchased at any price"). The extant play ends with this final statement of an unnegotiable principle, the inverse of Oedipus' own realization that no price can pay for the crime, and a confirmation of Oedipus' vision and narrative success.

Oedipus' master narrative breaks off at last in full force, as the text gives out. Based on the mythological tradition, we may reconstruct an ending for the *Phoenissae* in which the brothers kill each other and Jocasta commits suicide,

---

25 On Jocasta borrowing language from both Cicero's *Catilinarian Orations* and Sallust's *Bellum Catilinae*, see the excellent discussion in Ginsberg 2016, 483–494.
26 On the allocation of speakers for these final lines of the play, see Frank 1995a, 251–253.

framed as matricide.[27] But of course a final irony is that, despite his authorial mastery and his extraordinary vatic *furor*, Seneca's Oedipus has generated a vision of satisfactory closure that will elude him since it depends on an extra-dramatic tradition in which future sons, the Epigonoi, must reenact civil war before the envisioned total extinction of Oedipus' royal line.[28]

4 Summing-up: redefinitions of closure

The foregoing analysis shows that the notion of closure undergoes constant redefinition in the evolution of the play's plot. Oedipus wishes to end his life as a form of punishment due to his additional guilt from his vision of his sons' deliberately planning to recommit and surpass his own inadvertent crimes. This prophecy is tantamount to the birth of the *Phoenissae* and leads to Oedipus' reframing of closure as punishment that is no longer his own death but the destruction of his entire family and city. The play's lack of an ending and Oedipus' search for one are thematized as the dramatic deadlock in Thebes parallels the metatheatrical stand-off in the play with a series of debates involving characters with an objective opposed to that of Oedipus and who try to forestall the forward movement of his single vision. This sequence of interrupted trajectories and the conflict of narratives shape our understanding of the scope and stakes of Oedipus' envisioned (but narratively incomplete) closure.

Bibliography

Augoustakis, Antony (2010), *Motherhood and the Other: Fashioning Female Power in Flavian Epic*, Oxford.

Augoustakis, Antony (2015), "Statius and Senecan Drama", in: William J. Dominik/Carole E. Newlands/Kyle Gervais (eds.), *Brill's Companion to Statius*, Leiden, 377–392.

Barchiesi, Alessandro (1988), "L'incesto e il regno", in: Le Fenicie, Venice.

---

[27] This is set in contrast to the Jocasta of Euripides whose unforeseen death causes sorrow to Oedipus.

[28] This of course is due to the enormity of the mythic narrative which is treated separately in the literary tradition e.g. the lost Greek epic *Epigonoi*, Aeschylus' Ἀστυδάμας, Sophocles' Ἐπίγονοι, Accius' *Epigona*, the mythographies of the Epigonoi in Apollodorus and Hyginus, and Pausanias' *ekphrasis* of statues of the Epigonoi at Argos and Delphi (2.20.5, 10.10.4).

Bexley, Erica M. (2022), *Seneca's Characters: Fictional Identities and Implied Human Selves*, Cambridge.
Fantham, Elaine (1983), "*Nihil Iam Iura Naturae Valent*: Incest and Fratricide in Seneca's *Phoenissae*", in: A.J. Boyle (ed.), *Seneca Tragicus: Ramus Essays on Senecan Drama*, Victoria, 61–76.
Fitch, John G. (2002), *Tragedies, Volume I: Hercules; Trojan Women; Phoenician Women; Medea; Phaedra*, Loeb Classical Library, Cambridge, MA.
Frank, Marica (1990), *Seneca's Phoenissae: Introduction and Commentary*, PhD Diss., St. Andrews.
Frank, Marica (1992), "A Note on the Text of Seneca's *Phoenissae*", *Classical Quarterly* 42, 284.
Frank, Marica (1995a), *Seneca's Phoenissae: Introduction and Commentary*, Leiden.
Frank, Marica (1995b), "The Rhetorical Use of Family Terms in Seneca's *Oedipus* and *Phoenissae*", *Phoenix* 49, 121–130.
Frank, Marica (2014), "Phoenissae", in: Gregor Damsen/Andreas Heil (eds.), *Brill's Companion to Seneca: Philosopher and Dramatist*, Leiden, 449–458.
Frangoulidis, Stavros (2020), "From Victor to Victim: Metadrama and Movement of Plot in Seneca's *Hercules Furens*", *EuGeStA* 10, 144–162, https://eugesta-revue.univ-lille.fr/en/issues/issue-10-2020 [accessed on 12/08/2023].
Ginsberg, Lauren (2015), "Don't Stand So Close to Me: Antigone's *Pietas* in Seneca's *Phoenissae*", *TAPA* 145, 199–230.
Ginsberg, Lauren (2016), "Jocasta's Catilinarian Oration (Sen. *Phoen.* 632–43)", *The Classical Journal* 111, 483–494.
Ginsberg, Lauren (2018), "*Ut et hostem amarem*: Jocasta and the Poetics of Civil War in Seneca's *Phoenissae*", *Ramus* 46, 58–74.
Harrison, Stephen J. (2003), "Hot or Strong? A Textual Note on Seneca, *Phoenissae* 254", *Classical Quarterly* 53, 633–634.
Kohn, Thomas D. (2013), *The Dramaturgy of Senecan Tragedy*, Ann Arbor, MI.
Konstan, David (1994), "Oedipus and his Parents: The Biological Family from Sophocles to Dryden", *Scholia* 3, 3–23.
Li Causi, P. (2009), "La paternità dei male. Caos parentale e guerra civile nelle *Phoenissae* di Seneca", *Annali Online di Ferrrara-Teatro* 4, 270–296.
Littlewood Cedric, A.J. (2004), *Self-Representation and Illusion in Senecan Tragedy*, Oxford.
Pratt, Norman T. (1983), *Seneca's Drama*, Chapel Hill.
Schiesaro, Alessandro 1997, "Passion, Reason and Knowledge in Seneca's Tragedy", in: Susanna Morton Braund/Christopher Gill (eds.), *The Passions in Roman Thought and Literature*, Cambridge, 89–111.
Schiesaro, Alessandro (2003), *The Passions in Play: Thyestes and the Dynamics of Senecan Drama*, Cambridge.
Schur, Marco van der (2018), "Civil War on the Horizon: Seneca's *Thyestes* and *Phoenissae* in Statius' *Thebaid* 7", in: Lauren Donovan Ginsberg/Darcy A. Kranse (eds.), *After 69 CE - Writing Civil War in Flavian Rome*, Berlin, 123–142.
Staley, Gregory A. (2014), "Making Oedipus Roman", *Pallas* 96, 111–124.
Tarrant, Richard J. (1978), Senecan Drama and its Antecedents", *HSPh* 82, 213–263.
Trinacty, Christopher V. (2015), *Senecan Tragedy and the Reception of Augustan Poetry*, Oxford.
Voigt, Astrid (2015), "The Intertextual Matrix of Statius' *Thebaid* 11.315–23", *Dictynna* 12, 1–15, https://journals.openedition.org/dictynna/1149 [accessed on 12/08/2023].
Zanobi, Alessandra (2014), *Seneca's Tragedies and the Aesthetics of Pantomime*, London.

Jacqueline Fabre-Serris
How to Read Hyginus' *Fabulae*? Theories and Practices

Abstract: The *Fabulae* of Hyginus results from the editing work of a Renaissance scholar, Micyllus, in 1535, based on a single damaged manuscript, in which an "original text" was/is impossible to identify due to successive interpolations and deletions. Two approaches can be applied to this "unfinished text", depending on the answers given to two questions: What is a mythographer? What is the mythographer's project? The first approach is based on the idea that the mythographer is a compiler who intended to provide a variety of information, deemed useful for a better knowledge of mythology in general. The second approach is based on the idea that "the first author" wrote his text as poets do, that is, by selecting mythological elements from the tradition, organizing them and creating individual versions of the myths. I support this second approach by giving as an example a detailed analysis of *Fabulae* 66–75 focused on the Theban myth.

The first editor of Hyginus' *Fabulae* was Jacob Molsheim, usually referred to by his Latin name, Micyllus, who published the collection under the title "The Book of *Fabulae* by Caius Julius Hyginus, the Freedman of Augustus" in 1535. Unfortunately, the manuscript used by him was lost soon after publication. We do not know if this manuscript gave the full name of the author. The identification of this Hyginus may be due to Micyllus himself because the freedman of Augustus seemed to him the best candidate. According to Suetonius (*De Gram.* 20), Caius Julius Hyginus, who lived in the first centuries BCE and CE, was placed at the head of the Palatine Library. He was a close friend of the poet Ovid and of the consul and historian Clodius Licinus. In the absence of any substantiated argument, this identification is now widely rejected.[1]

What is certain is that the *Fabulae* were not originally written after the end of the second century. We know, in fact, that the work existed before 207 CE under another title. In the preface of a bilingual book, a schoolteacher, now referred to as Pseudo-Dositheus, writes that on September 11 in 207 CE he transcribed "the

---

[1] See Smith 2007, xliv; Fletcher 2013, 136–137. Two exceptions are Guidorizzi 2000, XXXVIII–XL, and Expósito 2003, 276–277. However, the general consensus is that the Hyginus of the *Fabulae* could be the same as the Hyginus of the *Astronomica*.

world-famous *Genealogy* of Hyginus". Although his book suffered damage, the remaining accounts of Prometheus, Philyra, and Ulysses and the Sirens, are close enough to those in the *Fabulae* that the copy of myths used by Pseudo-Dositheus can be said to be a relative of the *Fabulae*.[2] Since the book attributed to Hyginus is presented as well known, it was likely written some time before the late second century CE. As Scott Smith noted,[3] the text of Pseudo-Dositheus contains some lists that are not found in the *Fabulae*, and the text of the *Fabulae* we have today contains material that was added later. Consequently, one can only say that a version of the *Fabulae* was well known in the early third century CE. Since Micyllus did not publish the collection under the title *Genealogy* and did not mention any title for the collection in his introduction, we may assume that he coined the title *Fabulae*,[4] probably chosen because *fabula* was the Latin word employed to transcribe the Greek word *mythos*.

Micyllus used a manuscript from around 900 CE written in Beneventan script that was damaged and difficult to read. Whatever the original form of Hyginus' work, this manuscript provided a text resulting from so numerous modifications — additions, deletions, and reorganizations, all anonymous and difficult to identify — that Alan Cameron speaks of a "miserably abridged, interpolated and debased version of a work published no later than the second century".[5] How are we to read this version of the text as we have it now? I argue that it depends on how one defines what a mythographer is and what a mythographer's project was? As I will try to show, how one examines this unfinished work depends on the answers given to these two questions.

1 The mythographer is defined as a compiler

Greek and Latin myths have been transmitted to us mainly by poets and mythographers. In fact, there is no original word in Greek or Latin to refer to the texts of mythographers, which were never classified as a literary genre. The word "mythographer" is used only from the 17th century in the titles of collections of Roman or Greek myths: *Mythographi latini*,[6] Amsterdam, 1681, then

---

[2] Smith 2007, 193.
[3] Smith 2007, xliii.
[4] Smith 2007, xl
[5] Cameron 2004, 11.
[6] The editor was Thomas Munckert, the collection included C. Jul. Hyginus, Lactantius Placidus, Albricus philosophus.

Mythographi graeci,⁷ Leipzig, 1894. In Greece, the first authors who can be classified in this category date back to the 6th and 5th centuries BCE. They gave themselves the names of λογοποιοί and λογογράφοι, choosing a word, λόγος, used for all sorts of subjects, historical, geographical, ethnological, scientific, and literary. Although not ancient, mythography is a very useful category for examining a set of works and reflections by ancient authors on myths and their interpretations, even if it is not possible to define "mythography" univocally, given the variety of practices and the duration of its development (Antiquity, Middle Ages, Renaissance). The best way to understand what mythography is, is to examine the diverse and complex practices of those who are called *a posteriori* "mythographers".⁸

For some critics, the mythographer is a compiler who brings together various elements found in the works of poets or commentators. Scott Smith, who published in 2007, with Stephen Trzaskoma, a translation of Apollodorus' *Library* and of Hyginus' *Fabulae*, writes in the introduction: "Mythography was a continuous tradition, and we should not assume that *each compiler of myths*⁹ was a *scholar* independently verifying the *truth* of earlier works by consulting the originals — that in fact is a modern notion of scholarship".¹⁰ I have highlighted in italics three words — compiler, scholar and truth — which are not self-evident, but, in any case, are particularly revealing of the way Scott Smith sees the work of a mythographer. In his view, the mythographer is a *scholar* who is supposed to *collect* and exactly *reproduce* some elements found in earlier texts, versus a poet, who changes minor or major components of earlier versions, invents new motifs and creates his own individual narration of a mythological story.¹¹ Unfortunately, the mythographer does not always do his job correctly, because he uses secondary sources and does not always verify the information found in these secondary sources by comparing them with the "originals", i.e., the texts of poets. According to Smith, the result is not "true", if it is not consistent with earlier texts the mythographer should have consulted directly. For example, in his opinion, Hyginus probably did not use Vergil, but his commentator, Servius: "Upon closer examination, however, the Vergilian material might not even come from Vergil's poem, but rather from Servius' commentary on

---

7 The editor was Richard Wagner, the collection included Apollodorus of Athens, Joannes Pediasimus, Antoninus Liberalis, Parthenios of Nicaea, Palaephatus, Erastothenes, Heraclitus of Ephesus.
8 See Zucker/Fabre-Serris/Tilliette/Besson 2016.
9 The italics are mine.
10 Smith 2007, xliii.
11 Guidorizzi (2000, XXIII) develops the same kind of point of view.

Vergil's *Aeneid*, compiled in the fourth century AD".[12] It should be noted that another critic, Kristopher Fletcher, who shares the same vision of the mythographer, lists numerous passages in the *Fabulae* to argue, on the contrary, that Hyginus read Lucretius, Vergil and Ovid, all poets who had a dominant position in Roman education and were familiar to most educated Romans.[13] About the text itself, Fletcher suggests that we are "to think of the *Fabulae* as more like a collection of *scholia* than Vergil's *Aeneid*, to consider them an organic text rather than a fixed text like Livy's *Ab Urbe Condita*".[14] "Organic" versus "fixed". Since the text has evolved over time as a result of successive additions and deletions, Fletcher proposes that it is necessary "to see the *Fabulae* as a living organism, of which the version we have is just a snapshot, one moment of its life frozen in time".[15]

What was the purpose of the mythographer, if he was a compiler? Or, following Fletcher's suggestion, what were the intentions of the different scholars who collected, added or deleted information if the *Fabulae* are a collection of *scholia* evolving over time? If we refer to Smith's definition, the most likely first answer is that the mythographer seeks to provide accurate information about the myths. But why? The second answer is generally summed up in one word: utility. I quote Fletcher: the primary function of this type of mythography is "utility (though for what purpose or whose is debatable)".[16] In a footnote, he specifies: "Scholars have generally assumed that the *Fabulae* have a pedagogic function, e.g. J. Dietze, *Quaestiones Hyginianae* (Diss. Kiel, 1890) 21; J.-Y. Boriaud (ed.), *Hygin. Fables* (Paris, 2003²) xxv; G.M. Expósito, "Caius Iulius Hyginus, Mitógrafo," *Anuario de Estudios Filológicos* 26 (2003) 267–277 at 271. Not everyone, however, agrees: Werth (*De Hygini Fabularum Indole*, 4) suggests that all of the unexplained Greek means that the work could not be intended for students, but is instead meant for people wanting to understand art and literature (43)".[17] Hyginus would have the purpose either of providing knowledge about myths, which was a task assigned to teachers, or of enabling readers (students, interested audience) to understand art and literature.[18] Basically, the usefulness of

---

12 Smith 2007, xlviii.
13 Fletcher 2013, 147–162.
14 Fletcher 2013, 134.
15 Fletcher 2013, 162.
16 Fletcher 2013, 134.
17 Fletcher 2013, 134 n. 5.
18 On the assumption that Hyginus' *Fabulae* focus on utility and that the text is intended to remind readers of the basic details of myths rather than to analyze or interpret those myths, see Fletcher 2022.

the mythographer is indirect and arises from the fact that knowledge of myths was useful to Roman citizens.

How do we examine the work of a compiler that has been further modified by various deletions and additions that we cannot determine? Researchers like H.J. Rose, Antony Breen, Scott Smith and Kristopher Fletcher have sought to deconstruct the work we read today by identifying its various sources. It should be noted that, surprisingly and even paradoxically, although they see the *Fabulae* as a text modified by many anonymous hands, they seem to refer to "Hyginus" as a single author when they examine the existing text and point out its weaknesses, i.e., its non-compliance with the "primary" and "secondary" sources. In order to deconstruct the work of the compiler/s, these researchers in fact compare the narrations of the *Fabulae* to (ideally) all texts dealing with Greek and Roman myths that have been transmitted to us: works of poets, scholia, texts of other mythographers etc. What is the result? They observe that "Hyginus" does not reproduce a single source, or that he seems not to accurately well reproduce the text identified as a possible source text, or also that there are no identifiable sources for one or another detail of his narration. How do these researchers explain such a conclusion? The differences between "Hyginus" and his possible sources are attributed to mistakes made by the mythographer. In this regard, the status of unfinished text is used as a convenient explanation. In any case, since there have been many changes, it is impossible to determine "what" can be attributed to "whom".

Before giving a few examples to illustrate this kind of analysis of Hyginus' narratives, I recall that the *Fabulae* are organized into three sections as follows: a theogony providing a genealogy of gods (41 entries), narrative accounts of various myths (1–220), and a series of lists (221–277), but there also are some lists in the narrative section and some narrative accounts amid the lists. One of the first modern editors, Rose, suggested that Hyginus might have translated a single earlier handbook of mythology, written in Greek (since the *Fabulae* almost exclusively encapsulate Greek myths).[19] This hypothesis of a Greek handbook (lost, of course) has led scholars to search for textual elements that could both imply the use of an earlier original book written in Greek, and betray a poor understanding of Greek language. One of the most cited "translation mistakes"[20] of Hyginus is at the beginning of *Fabula* 186, entitled *Melanippe*: *Melanippen Desmontis filiam, siue Aeoli ut alii poetae dicunt, formosissimam*

---

19 Rose 1963, VII.
20 Werth 1901, 11–12; Smith 2007, 159; Fletcher 2013, 140.

Neptunus compressit, ex qua procreauit filios duos[21] ("Neptune raped Melanippe, Desmontes' daughter, who was exceptionally beautiful (other poets say she was Aeolus' daughter), and fathered two sons by her"). This suggests Hyginus has misunderstood the title of Euripides' play, Μελανίππη Δεσμῶτις, i.e., "Melanippe in Chains (or the Captive)" and he has taken the adjective as a patronymic. Since it is impossible to know whether this error was in Hyginus' original text or is due to a later addition, it is difficult to take it as an argument for the hypothesis of a misunderstood Greek model. As Fletcher rightly observes,[22] more broadly, the approach that consists of attempting to reconstitute a Greek text, supposed to have been mistranslated, is problematic: "coining a new Greek phrase to explain an emended passage is just one of the more extreme examples of how quick people are to assume that Hyginus is somehow 'wrong'". The hypothesis of a Greek handbook that has been (often poorly) translated, is now found not credible. Among the possible sources are the summaries of Euripides' plays, known today as the *Tales from Euripides*, that Hyginus might have used in some *Fabulae* and which conversely are used to reconstruct fragmentary tragedies.[23] In any case, the fact that the myths told in the *Fabulae* are Greek myths does not mean that Hyginus' sources are only Greek sources. From the beginnings of Latin literature Greek myths have been rewritten: re-interpreted and adapted to be integrated into Roman culture, and as a result Roman writers have also provided various intertexts for mythographers.[24]

Scholars who see Hyginus as a compiler often express disappointment at the lack of expected information. For example, about *Fabula* 7, "presumed to be a *Fabula* proper", and *Fabula* 8, "presumed to be a variant ... heavily influenced by the *Tales from Euripides*",[25] Breen regrets that "as a mythographical handbook, the *Fabulae* do not stress the twice-founded aspect of Thebes"[26] (i.e., founded by Cadmus and fortified by Antiope's sons, Amphion and Zethus). Cadmus is indeed described as the first king of Thebes in *Fabula* 76, he is named as the founder of the city in *Fabula* 275 (a list of cities and Their founders), and Amphion is said to have fortified Thebes in *Fabula* 69. Breen concludes that "for a handbook which supposedly emphasizes variants (by juxtaposition), this is *a grave*

---

[21] I use the edition of Marshall 1993.
[22] Fletcher 3013, 141.
[23] Smith 2007, xlvii.
[24] On the emergence of Latin Literature as a result of "translations", as rewritings, of Greek literary texts undertaken by Roman writers, see Feeney's masterful study (2016): *Beyond Greek. The Beginnings of Latin Literature*.
[25] Breen 1991, 112.
[26] Breen 1991, 112.

oversight".²⁷ But is it correct to say that the *Fabulae* were conceived by Hyginus as a mythographical handbook, especially if, when this assumption is applied, the result is not satisfactory? After having noted that "the fortification of Thebes by Amphion and Zethus is the first element in *Niobe* (*Fab.* 9)" and judged this information "of a subordinate nature", since "the entry concentrates on Niobe and her children (and their fate)", Breen makes some hypotheses about the three *fabulae* — the contents of and relationships among 7, 8, 9 — and concludes that "As a result, Hyginus has served up such a salmagundi of loosely connected information that, as is often the case in the collection, it is impossible to discern the intention of the version preserved".²⁸

However, if we change points of view and methods, would it be possible to provide some hypotheses, not on the current version that results from additions and deletions impossible to trace, but on the intentions of the original author? Before going in this direction, I would like to specify that I do not deny any interest in the approach consisting in comparing Hyginus' text to all available documents (texts and visual representations) on the same myths, especially when modern researchers do not merely list probable errors but also try to find an explanation for them.

2 The mythographer is an author who rewrites myths as poets do

2.1 Definition and methods

I will briefly present the views supported in the European network *Polymnia*, focused on "the mythographical tradition in Europe from Greece to the 17th century".²⁹ First point: as Timothy Gantz rightly said,³⁰ myth cannot be defined as

---

27 Breen 1991, 112–113.
28 Breen 1991, 113.
29 Founded in 1999 by Françoise Graziani and me, this European network has developed numerous activities: panels and conferences, a collection *Mythographes* (Presses Universitaires du Septentrion), and an electronic review, also called *Polymnia*.
30 Gantz 1993, XVI. In fact, if the myth has been defined as "something that exists", it is because we have been misled by the perspective used by the mythographers as Gantz has rightly pointed out about Apollodorus' *Library*: "as such (an avowed synthesis), it inevitably promotes the concept of Greek myths as a cultural commodity, the product of a united Greek mind rather

"the product of a united Greek mind". The different versions of mythological stories do not in fact exist "outside" their successive elaborations and reconfigurations by poets, philosophers, historians, artists and ... mythographers. Second point: each version of a myth, whether it is due to a poet, a philosopher, a historian, an artist or a mythographer, must be examined in Greece, in Rome or in Western cultures, in its own cultural, historical and ideological context both as a specific production and as a part of the mythographic tradition. Studying from these perspectives the various practices of mythographers in Greece, Rome, the Middle Ages and the Renaissance highlights that the mythographers cannot be considered as simple mediators and more or less skillful "compilers" (in the narrow sense, as defined above). On the contrary, we can conclude that they were clever analysts, ingenious interpreters and (re)creators of myths, who have raised questions and produced reconfigurations whose relevance is not inferior to those of poets and philosophers. Therefore, reading the mythographers today leads us to reflect on a rich and complex tradition that from the end of 6th and 5th centuries BCE in Greece bears witness to successive efforts of exegesis and attests to constant rewritings which, along with those of poets and artists, have contributed to making Greek and Roman myths a still-living legacy of Antiquity in Western culture.[31]

Hyginus is one of the mythographers who used a new narrative form to produce their own versions of mythological stories that they gather in collections. The specificity of these mythographers was indeed to provide a "summary" of the "whole" mythological story they were telling. This paradox was well highlighted by Parthenius of Nicaea in the preface to his collection of Ἐρωτικὰ Παθήματα (Amorous Passions), addressed to the Roman poet Caius Cornelius Gallus. Parthenius states that he has told each story by itself (αὐτοτελῶς, 1) and in the briefest possible terms (μάλιστ' ἐν βραχυτάτοις, 1), in such a way that Gallus (or the reader) can understand the gist of these stories (κατανοήσεις ἐκ τῶνδε τὰ πλεῖστα, 1). This implies a linear narrative in which acts and situations are briefly described in successive sequences. Parthenius organized his collection thematically: he gathered exemplary stories of Ἐρωτικὰ Παθήματα.[32]

---

than contributions from many different tellers of tales, in many different contexts over a great span of time".

31 For more information on these views, see the introduction of the collective book *Lire les Mythes. Formes, usages et visées des pratiques mythographiques de l'Antiquité à la Renaissance*, edited by Zucker/Fabre-Serris/Tilliette/Besson (2016, 7–23).

32 On the fact that Parthenius uses the same narrative or rhetorical compositional techniques as the authors of literary texts, see Voisin 2008; 2016; and Biraud 2008a; 2008b.

And Hyginus? In two previous papers,[33] I tried to show that some of his *fabulae* are collected in the form of mini-cycles with two organizing principles, one geographical and genealogical (which would correspond to the title *Genealogies*) or chronological, the other thematic. Despite the additions and deletions that have modified the original text, i.e., despite its unfinished aspect, I argued that in these mini-cycles it is possible to reconstruct, in a sufficiently meaningful way, the initial project of the first author by using the methods of structural analysis. This is a way of deconstructing mythological narratives other than the search for their probable sources. It can be justified by the fact that there is a similarity between this modern tool of analysis used by the reader (to deconstruct these narratives) and the ancient technique used by the first author, Hyginus (to construct them), when he wrote his summaries and put them together in a narrative cycle. The application of structural analysis methods to the *Fabulae* reveals that, like Parthenius, Hyginus cuts each of his narratives into successive sequences that are repeated or vary (especially by being reversed) from one *fabula* to another. The combination of these sequences made up of acts or situations allows him to thematically organize geographical and chronological cycles, as I will try to show by summarizing my study on *Fabulae* 66–75 focused on some stories of the Theban myth.

2.2 The example of the Theban cycle in *Fabulae* 66–75

The author has grouped his narratives into three blocks. The first two blocks are geographically and genealogically, and/or chronologically, organized. The first block is made up of three narratives on three Theban heroes genealogically linked, *Laius* (66), *Oedipus* (67), and *Polynices* (68). The second block includes three narratives, chronologically linked, on the two military expeditions against Thebes directed by Adrastus: *Adrastus* (69), *Reges septem Thebas profecti* (70), *Septem Epigoni id est filii* (71). The third block is made up of four narratives, thematically linked, focused (as highlighted by their titles) on women or diviners: *Antigona* (72), *Amphiaraus, Eriphyla et Alcmaeon* (73), *Hypsipyle* (74), *Tiresias* (75).

As in the first approach I have described, the first task is to compare the versions of the *Fabulae* with all those transmitted to us in order, not to criticize the choices made, but to highlight the selected narrative elements and the innovations (or supposed innovations) that can be imputed to the (first) author ac-

---

[33] Fabre-Serris 2017; 2019.

cording to the current state of our sources.[34] This task is facilitated by the great work done by Gantz in *Early Greek Myths*, a book that remains unsurpassed on all the versions of myths transmitted to us, whether through texts or figurative documents. I will not detail this investigation,[35] but I only point out that, if Hyginus is very close to Euripides (in his *Phoenician Women*), some narrative elements seem to be specific to him, even if many assumptions have been made about their potential origins, from lost tragedies, for example.

2.2.1 The key themes in the three blocks

The comparison with the remaining versions of the Theban myth also allows us to see that Hyginus conceived the different narrative sequences in each block thematically by associating certain themes to the three protagonists of these stories, Laius, Creon and Adrastus and to their respective offspring.

The *fabulae* of the first block are structured to emphasize a major theme: the use of violence between members of the royal family (Laius, Oedipus, and his sons) when the exercise of power is at stake. A father (Laius) tries to eliminate his newborn son (Oedipus), presumed to kill him in the future. A son (Oedipus) kills his father without recognizing him, and, unlike his father, without being warned by an oracle. Two brothers (Polynices and Eteocles) voluntarily kill each other because both want to reign over the city. Three details suggest that this use of violence is a familial characteristic. Hyginus relates that Oedipus is called "adopted child" because his character is different from that of Polybus, described as so gentle (*tam clemens*), while Oedipus is considered brazen (*impudens*). His encounter with his real father is described in such a way that their (hidden) kinship is confirmed by their common strong propensity for violence. When Oedipus, ordered by the guards to give way to the king (*uiam regi dari*), refuses, Laius pushes his horses and crushes Oedipus' foot. Angry (*iratus*), Oedipus kills him. This motif is indirectly supported by the fact that twice a third party fails to prevent these family killings. Apollo warns Laius to beware death at the hands of his son. Before leaving the city, Oedipus establishes a rule of rotation on the throne of Thebes (*regnumque filiis suis alternis annis tradidit*) apparently to prevent any rivalry between his sons. Nevertheless, after one year, Eteocles refuses to give up the

---

34 We have alternate versions of *Fabulae* 67–71, recovered in 1820 by B.G. Niebuhr from a palimpsest, dating to the fifth century CE (Guidorizzi 2000, XLII, Smith 2007, li, 107, n. 17), but which does not include different narrative details.
35 See Fabre-Serris 2019, 100–110.

kingdom to Polynices (*cedere noluit*) and the two brothers fight and kill each other. Their dissension persists after death: when funeral rites are held for them in Thebes, even if there is a strong wind, the smoke never turns in one direction, but separates into two different directions (*fumus se numquam in unam partem conuertit, sed alius alio seducitur*). This detail is present in Seneca (known or invented by him) and used, in his *Oedipus*, to allude to the future fight between Polynices and Eteocles. During the sacrifice offered to Laius, Manto, who describes the aspect of the flame to her blind father, Tiresias, sees it change color, become red, then black and finally separate into two parts (*in partes duas / discedit*, 321–322). In the *Thebaid* of Statius (12.429–432), when the corpse of Polynices is placed near that of Eteocles, it is thrown out of the pyre (*busto pellitur*, 430), and the flames spring up, divided at the top (*exundant diuiso uertice flammae*, 431). Regarding the context, Hyginus appears closer to Statius, but he chooses an expression (*numquam in unam partem*) similar to that used by Seneca (*in partes duas*). Consequently, he likely refers to both predecessors.[36]

Since Oedipus is not warned of his fate by an oracle, *de facto*, in Hyginus' account incest is a less important element, as is confirmed by the small role attributed to Jocasta, whose family ties and death are mentioned, but not commented on. While Euripides attributes a major role to Jocasta during the siege of Thebes, Hyginus does not even mention her name. The royal family of Corinth is apparently used as counter-example. While Polybus is described as *tam clemens*, the main role in family relations is given to the adoptive mother, Periboia. She finds the child exposed and she reveals to Oedipus that he has been adopted, when, after Polybus' death, Oedipus feels grief as expected of a son in these circumstances (i.e., *aestimans patrem suum obisse*, "thinking that his father was dead").

---

36 Fletcher (2013, 147–149) has suggested that Hyginus made this kind of double reference in *Fabula* 57 when he tells how Proetus decided to kill Bellerophon by sending him to the Chimaera (a story told by Homer), taking up an expression used by Lucretius, when the latter transcribed Homer. Fetcher observes: "Indeed, if Hyginus *were a poet*, likely he would receive praise from scholars for reinserting Lucretius' translation of Homer's Bellerophon episode, which Lucretius had put into a new context, into the Bellerophon episode, showing that he knows where Lucretius got it in the first place" (148–149). I have underlined in italics this important point: referring to both authors one of whom had previously referred to the other is a usual practice among poets. But instead of drawing the expected conclusion (Hyginus rewrites mythological stories as poets do), Fletcher explains: "This is exactly the kind of game we should expect of a Roman author, and thus there is no reason to delete such lines in Hyginus. This is not to try to claim that we should read Hyginus like we read Ovid or Vergil, but is a reminder that he is to some extent a product of the same educational background" (149). Guidorizzi (2000, XXIV) also thinks that Hyginus drew information directly from literary texts.

In the second block, the dominant theme, associated with Adrastus, the leader of the Seven against Thebes, is, on the contrary, total devotion in family relations, which goes so far as to die on a battlefield. Like Laius, Adrastus has received an oracle from Apollo about his family. He will marry his daughters Argia and Deipyle to a boar and a lion, respectively. Hyginus tells in detail how Adrastus is led to understand this oracle by identifying the boar with Tydeus and the lion with Polynices because the one wears a boar's hide and the other that of a lion. Adrastus agrees to help his son-in-law to take back his kingdom by providing him an army. Hyginus specifies that Adrastus "non only gave him an army but himself went with other six war leaders" (*cui Adrastus non tantum dedit exercitum sed etiam ipse cum (VI) aliis ducibus profectus est*). They fail to take Thebes, and all these leaders perish except himself. Later Adrastus sends their sons to attack Thebes to avenge the wrongs done to their fathers (whose corpses were left unburied). The Epigoni take Thebes. Only one perishes, Adrastus' son, Aegialeus. Hyginus notes that Aegialeus has given up his life in exchange for his father's (*pro patre uicariam uitam dedit*). The three narratives emphasize the implications of family relations by blood or marriage: successive military help, whatever the consequences. It is tempting to identify this familial conduct as Roman, since "good" family relations, especially between fathers and sons, are promoted in the glorious history of the city.

Another motif is associated with Creon, who is present in the first and in the third blocks: the priority given to the fatherland. In *Fabula* 67, Creon, who has become king of Thebes after the death of Laius, proclaims that he will give the kingdom and his sister, Jocasta, in marriage to the man who can solve the riddle of the Sphinx. The word *patria* is not used, but here the priority is clearly to save the city. When Thebes is struck by a shortage of cereals, the diviner Tiresias reveals that, if a descendant of the *Draco* (*ex draconteo genere*) is alive and dies for the fatherland (*pro patria interiisset*), he will deliver it from this plague (*pestilentia liberaturum*). Menoeceus, introduced as the father of Jocasta, throws himself off the city walls. In *Fabula* 68, when the city is assaulted, Tiresias prophesies that the town will be liberated (*liberari*) if a descendant of the Draco dies. Menoeceus, Creon's son, who "saw that he alone could save his fellow citizens" (*se unum ciuium salutem posse redimere*), throws himself off the city walls. This doublet is found only in Hyginus. Even if the first episode seems to be modelled on the second one, which exists in Euripides, it is significant that "someone" has introduced it. It should be noted that Hyginus did not take up a choice of Euripides (his main model) that was not consistent with his own choice to describe Creon as an ardent defender of the fatherland. In the *Phoenician Women*, when Creon learns that he must sacrifice his son to save Thebes, his paternal love conflicts with his love for the homeland, and Creon tries to convince his son to leave Thebes secretly. Menoeceus pretends to follow his advice but throws himself off the ramparts. The verb *liberare* is used in the two episodes. Fighting for *libertas* and *patria* is a central theme in Roman military ideology. In the third block (*Fab.* 72), after the victory, Creon issues a decree stipulating that no one should bury Polynices or those who accompanied him, "because they have come to attack the fatherland" (*quod patriam oppugnatum uenerint*). When his fiancée, Antigone, is arrested, Haemon is ordered by his father to kill her, but caught by love (*amore captus*), he lies to his father (*ementitusque est*). Haemon entrusts Antigone to some shepherds and pretends to have killed her. Creon refuses to forgive Haemon when he later discovers the truth because of a clue that recalls the two previous episodes of suicide. Antigone was pregnant and gave birth to a son. When this son goes to Thebes to participate in an athletic competition, he is recognized by his grand-father "from the birthmark that all the descendants of the dragon have on their body" (*quod ex draconteo genere omnes in corpore insigne habebant cognouit*). Haemon kills himself and Antigone. In the current state of the text, Hyginus notes that Creon gives his daughter Megara in marriage to Hercules and that she gives birth to two sons. He does not specify that thus Creon rewards Hercules for having saved Thebes and that later, having gone mad, Hercules will kill the two boys. In Roman ideology, total dedication to the fatherland is a major value, which is praised as much in its positive aspect, when in wartime every citizen must fight for the fatherland and freedom, as in its negative aspects, when a father punishes his own son to death for having disobeyed his orders, as illustrated by the famous *exemplum* of the consul Titus Manlius Torquatus. The latter condemned his son to death, although he had returned victorious after having engaged the enemy contrary to orders.[37] To conclude, Hyginus has conceived his portraits of Adrastus and Creon emphasizing their *pietas*, i.e., the parameter used in Roman ideology to evaluate family and civic behavior.

2.2.2 Narrative structure and major themes in the third block

Why did Hyginus, unlike Apollodorus, take some episodes out of the chronological/linear axis chosen for the two first blocks? Leaving aside the fact that the protagonists are women or diviners, what main themes are selected to structure these narratives?

---

[37] See Sall. *Cat.* 52.30; Liv. 8.7.1.

In the two first blocks, a first series of elements alludes to the foundation of Thebes by Cadmus and particularly to two episodes of this foundation. I summarize Ovid's version because Hyginus probably refers to this version of the Theban myth, previously referred to by Seneca in his *Oedipus*. The first episode is the killing by Cadmus of a serpent/dragon on the site of the future city. Cadmus is ordered by Apollo to follow a heifer to the site planned by the gods for the foundation of Thebes. When he needs water to sacrifice the animal, he sends his companions to find a spring. They are killed by the custodian of the spring, a dragon, whom later Cadmus fights and kills. The second episode is the birth of armed men, called Spartoi ("Sown") for having been created by the earth after Cadmus was ordered by the goddess Athena to sow the dragon's teeth. These armed men immediately fight and kill each other, except for five of them, who help Cadmus to found his city. The reader finds a first allusion to the birth of the Spartoi from the dragon's teeth in the *fabulae* in which are mentioned the voluntary sacrifices of the father or of the son of Creon, both called Menoeceus, who commit suicide to save the city. In these episodes where the first seems to have been modelled on the second, the man who must perish to save Thebes is designated by an analogous expression: *si quis ex draconteo genere superesset et pro patria interiisset* (67); *si ex dracontea progenie aliquis interiisset* (68). Both these Menoecei are indeed descendants of the Spartoi. According to a scholium to Euripides' *Phoenician Women*,[38] Menoeceus, father of Jocasta and Creon, is son of Oclasos, son of Pentheus, himself son of Agave and Echion, one of the Spartoi.

Since in the third block the reader finds several passages about the "Theban dragon" or other serpents in similar contexts (death, killing, expiation), this block seems to have been conceived by the first author to shed light in retrospect on the foundation of the city and its consequences for the royal line, linked by marriage to some *Spartoi*. In *Fabula* 72 (*Antigona*), Creon understands that Haemon has spared Antigone by seeing a boy who bears on his body a mark typical of the descendants from Spartoi (*quod ex draconteo genere omnes in corpore insigne habebant*). He refuses to forgive his son for having disobeyed him, although Hercules appeals to him on Haemon's behalf. In *Fabula* 74 (*Hypsipyle*), the reader finds a story that seems to reshuffle the cards of the first episode of the foundation of Thebes. When someone (Hypsipyle) is asked by the Seven Argive Chiefs to find water for them and draws from a spring, a snake, which was guarding the spring (*draco fontis custos*), appears and kills (devours) a child, the son of king Lycurgus, whom Hypsipyle had placed in a tall patch of

---

38 Σ. *Phoen.* 942.

parsley. The motif of expiation is also present in this story, but shifted. The woman who drew from the spring protected by the snake, is about to be punished, not for this act, but for not having taken proper care of the child. She was warned by an oracle not to put the boy down on the ground before he could walk. She has not put the child down on the ground, but on a plant that has grown very high, next to the spring, but the boy perishes. Moreover, she is spared because Adrastus and his companions, after killing the serpent, successfully appeal (unlike Hercules in *Fabula* 72) to the king Lycurgus, father of the boy, on Hypsipyle's behalf.[39] Another story including snakes, violence against them and a "negative" effect, is told in *Fabula* 75, a story about how Tiresias became the best seer among mortals. Tiresias, who was shepherd, is said to have struck (*baculo percussisse*) or stepped on (*calcasse*[40]) two snakes while they were copulating (*dracones uenerantes*) on Mount Cyllene. Following this act (potentially a fault) committed in a sexual context, Tiresias changes sex (*ob id in mulieris figuram conuersus est*). Later, advised by an oracle[41] (*monitus a sortibus*), a detail that we find in Phlegon (257F26),[42] when he sees snakes in the same place again, Tiresias steps on them and resumes his previous form. Changing sex is not presented as a punishment, but Tiresias clearly prefers to be a man (otherwise he would continue to live as a woman). It can be noted that Tiresias is also a descendant of the Spartoi: he is the grand-son of Udaeus, one of the Spartoi. In my opinion, the choice made by Hyginus in *Fabulae* 74 and 75 to associate a punishment with the killing of a snake, which is not immediate but occurs afterwards and is shifted, may be taken as a way of referring to the initial episode of the Theban myth. It follows that the reader is implicitly invited to compare the stories of Hypsipyle and of Tiresias with those of some descendants of the Spartoi. Should we see in their tragic fates the price to be paid for expiating Cadmus' (sacrilegious) act (i.e., having sown the dragon's teeth after killing it), even if Cadmus was obeying divine orders? This is the point of view developed by Ovid in the *Metamorphoses*, where the violent deaths of Cadmus' descendants and his final metamorphosis into a serpent are explicitly linked to the killing of the snake and the sowing of its teeth into the earth (*Met.* 4.570–

---

39 In Marshall's edition, the name of the king is Lycus. Smith, who prints the name Lycurgus, specifies that he has "restored Lycurgus for Lycus in the belief that that is an error of transcription, and not a mistake on the part of Hyginus" (2007, 189).
40 According to Rose 1963, *ad loc.*, this second version is only found in Hyginus, who would have misunderstood a Greek source.
41 This detail does not exist in Ovid and Apollodorus.
42 See Gantz 1993, 529.

580).⁴³ In Seneca's *Oedipus*, the third chorus, excluding Cadmus from any responsibility, explains the great present dangers (*tantis ... periclis*, 709), by referring to the ancient anger of the gods (*ueteres / deum irae*, 711–112). He incriminates the earth for having produced, at the time of the coming of Cadmus, "new monsters" (*noua monstra*, 725), that is, the snake and the Spartoi, qualified as *impio partu* ("impious children", 731) because of their incestuous origin (the snake is the son of the earth). The Spartoi kill each other in a combat described as a civil war (*ciuile nefas*, 748). The chorus express the wish that Thebes know only these fraternal combats (*fraterna proelia*, 750), which immediately makes the spectators think of the future duel between Eteocles and Polynices. Since he never mentions Cadmus, Hyginus appears closer to Seneca than to Ovid, but also close to Statius. In the *Thebaid*, whose main model is Euripides, Tiresias reveals that a final sacrifice (*extrema litamina*, 10.610) is demanded by the gods, specifying that "the snake, son of Mars" (*Martius ... anguis*, 10.612) requires (*efflagitat*, 10.612) as a victim the last descendant of the Spartoi (*generis quicumque nouissimus exstat / uiperei*, "Whoever he is, the last descendant of the race of the serpent", 10.613–614).

The way in which Hyginus has grouped in his third narrative block stories echoing the major themes of the first two blocks concerns not only the series of variations on snakes, sexual faults and expiation, but also the question of the oracles. In the first block, Laius receives a prophecy (*responsum*) from Apollo, which warns him of a mortal danger. Laius more or less heeds this warning: he has a son but tries to eliminate him. When ominous signs warn him that his death at his son's hands is near, he leaves for Delphi, but he is killed on the way. In the second block, Adrastus also receives an oracle (*responsum*) from Apollo about the marriage of his daughters. He follows this oracle and gives his daughter, Argia, in marriage to Polynices, but later, during the war against Thebes, his own son is killed. Both Menoecei (Creon's father and son) take into account the prophecy made by the diviner Tiresias, commit suicide, and save the city. In the third block, the reader finds again the theme of oracles in the two *fabulae* centered on the diviners Amphiaraus and Tiresias, but also in the *fabula* on Hypsipyle. In *Fabula* 73, Amphiaraus knows, as a diviner (*augur*), that if he comes to attack Thebes, he will not return. He tries in vain to escape this fate by hiding, but he is betrayed by his wife. In *Fabula* 75, on the advice of an oracle, Tiresias steps on some snakes again and is transformed into a man. In *Fabula* 74, Hypsipyle tries to follow Apollo's oracle that warns her not to put the boy she was nursing on the ground before he can walk. Although she places him on

---

43 About the Theban myth in the *Metamorphoses*, see Fabre-Serris 2011.

a very high plant (*apium altissimum*, the adjective suggests that the boy is posed far from the ground), he is killed by the snake.

What can we conclude from this emphasis on oracles in the third block? In my opinion, by giving other examples on this major topic in the Theban myth, the first author Hyginus intended to raise questions in the mind of readers, about what to do with the oracles: should/could they be followed or not? Men's reactions are different, but, if the readers compare the results, it is striking that none is more relevant than the other. Men follow (Adrastus, both Menoecei, Tiresias), neglect (Laius), or fail to follow some warnings (Laius, Amphiaraus, Hypsipyle), with consequences either positive (for Tiresias and to a lesser extent for Creon's father and son who save the city but die), or limited (for Hypsipyle, who is not punished) or negative (for Laius, Amphiaraus and Adrastus whose every companion and his own son perish). As it appears difficult to make a moral judgment on the reactions of the different characters given the different outcomes of their stories, what did the author expect but that his readers realize how difficult it was to do so? In my opinion, reading *Fabulae* 66–75 indeed makes the readers aware both of the uncertainty of the future and that a reversal of any situation is still possible.[44]

3 Conclusion

The text of Hyginus "as we have it" results from the editing work of a Renaissance scholar, based on a single damaged manuscript, in which an "original text" was/is impossible to identify due to successive interpolations and deletions. Two approaches can be applied to this "unfinished text", depending on the answers given to two questions: What is a mythographer? What is a mythographer's project?

The first approach consists of comparing the current text to all the texts and figurative documents transmitted to us in order to try to identify its sources. Since scholars who use this approach define the mythographers (i.e., both the first author and those who made further deletions or additions) as compilers, their investigation leads them to list various inconsistencies (with the presumed sources), mistakes and misunderstandings, instead of evaluating the selections made and appreciating the innovations introduced, as is customary for a poet or

---

[44] On the importance of oracles in the *Thebaid*, a poem chronologically close to Hyginus, see Fabre-Serris 2019, 122.

an artist, praised for creating his own versions of myths. It is impossible to know whether the *Fabulae* ever circulated in the present form (but it is unlikely under the circumstances of Micyllus' editing work), as well as to identify and date its successive forms over time. As a result, this approach only enables the scholars who use it to conclude that the various compilers probably intended to provide a variety of information deemed useful for a better knowledge of mythology in general.

The second approach consists of taking into account the new narrative form (a summary, broken down and divided into sequences) used in the *Fabulae* as in other texts by ancient mythographers. Examining the *Fabulae*, successively and in detail, from this perspective, highlights, in spite of additions and deletions, the narrative construction of certain accounts, particularly when they are grouped in genealogical and thematic mini-cycles. This second approach — which includes the first but as a preliminary step to appreciating what the mythographer has selected from the mythological tradition and what he has changed or invented — is based on the idea that "the first author" wrote his text as poets do and thus that deconstructing his narrative allows us to recover and understand both his intentions and what he expected from readers.

In my opinion, the version of Theban stories, which I have tried to highlight in *Fabulae* 66–75 through this second approach, i.e, from the structural analysis of the remaining sequences, must be seen as part of the long poetic tradition formed by all the receptions of the Theban myth in Rome from the Republican period. In a paper in which she emphasizes the central place that Thebes occupied in the Roman literary imagination, Susanna Braund lists a series of theater plays: the *Antiope* and *Pentheus* by Pacuvius, the *Amphitryo, Bacchae, Thebais, Eriphyla, Phoenissae, Antigona,* and *Epigoni* by Accius;[45] a Theban epic by Ponticus alluded to by Propertius (in elegies 1.7 and 1.9.10), who, in elegy 2.34, refers to another friend, Lynceus, in a way that may imply that Lynceus is contemplating composing a Theban epic.[46] Braund also points to the popularity of the *Phoenissae* of Euripides, attested by the quotations by Cicero (*Att.* 2.25.1 and 7.11.1).[47] The Theban myth is included in the list of epic themes rejected by Propertius in elegy 2.1.31, or neglected by Ovid in *Tristia* 2.318–319. However, book 3 of the *Metamorphoses* entirely focuses upon various Theban episodes, from the foundation of the city by Cadmus until his second exile and his metamorphosis into a serpent. Three of Seneca's tragedies also focus on Theban and

---

45 Braund 2006, 264.
46 Braund 2006, 264–265.
47 Braund 2006, 266.

Argive material: *Hercules Furens*, *Oedipus* and the *Phoenissae*. Statius writes a *Thebaid*. To explain this strong interest in the Theban myth in Rome, Braund suggests that, in addition to Troy and Athens, "Thebes too was important for the Romans in thinking about themselves".[48] Like the foundation of Rome, the foundation of Thebes results from a divine decision, but is preceded by a fraternal fight (Romulus and Remus/Spartoi). Later the two cities experience fratricidal wars (attack of the Seven against Thebes, duel between Eteocles and Polynices/civil wars in the first century BCE), both seen as the repetition of the original fraternal fights.[49] Braund claims that Thebes offered "a rich material in terms of 'same' and 'other' for understanding Roman ideology, with fluctuations dictated by changing political contexts at Rome".[50] If Thebes provided a mirror for Rome to contemplate an image of its origins, several episodes could also be seen as a warning about a disastrous fate to be avoided. It is in this rich and complex literary context that Hyginus positions himself when he creates and combines narrative sequences using Roman reading grids such as the respect (or not) for the *pietas* in familial and military contexts, the priority given (or not) to the *patria*, and the taking into account (or not) of the oracles. In this mini-cycle, Hyginus highlights the destructive effects of violence in a royal family when power is at stake, a motif that can allude to past and/or recent events in the ruling dynasties in the Roman Empire. He also gives his own interpretation of the negative impact of Thebes' founding on the rest of its history, suggesting, through stories dealing with similar motifs, that the results could have been/could be not so tragic. In doing so, Hyginus appears to have proceeded no differently from poets and philosophers, who used Greek and Italo-roman myths as analytical tools to contribute to the moral, politic and intellectual debates of their time.[51]

To conclude, judging by the respective results of the two approaches and methods described, if we consider that the mythographers were clever scholars, subtle interpreters[52] and inventive creators of myths, we arrive at a more interesting and fruitful reading of an unfinished text like Hyginus' *Fabulae*.

---

48 Braund 2006, 259.
49 See Horace, *Ep.* 7.17–20.
50 Braund 2006, 259.
51 See Fabre-Serris 1998.
52 On the "interpretation" of myths as a fundamental objective of mythographic practice, see Graziani (forthcoming).

Bibliography

Biraud, Michele (2008a), "Complexité narrative et structuration du recueil des *Erotika Pathémata* de Parthénios de Nicée", in: Arnaud Zucker (ed.), *Littérature et érotisme ans les* Passions d'amour *de Parthénios de Nicée*, Grenoble, 67–82.

Biraud, Michele (2008b), "Comptes syllabiques et clausules accentuelles: des principes de composition rythmiques dans certains récits des *Erotika Pathémata* de Parthenios de Nicée", in: Arnaud Zucker (ed.), *Littérature et érotisme dans les* Passions d'amour *de Parthénios de Nicée*, Grenoble, 83–123.

Boriaut, Jean-Yves (ed.) (1997), *Hygin. Fables*, Paris.

Braund, Susanna (2006), "A Tale of Two Cities: Statius, Thebes and Rome", *Phoenix* 60, 259–273.

Breen, Anthony (1991), *The Fabulae Hygini Reappraised: A Reconsideration of the Content and Compilation of the Work*, Diss. Urbana-Champaign, IL.

Cameron, Alan (2004), *Greek Mythography in the Roman World*, Oxford/New York.

Expósito, Guadalupe (2003), "Caius Iulius Hyginus, Mitógrafo", *Anuario de Estudios Filológicos* 26, 267–277.

Fabre-Serris, Jacqueline (1998), *Mythologie et littérature à Rome. La réécriture des mythes aux 1ers siècles avant et après J.-C.*, Lausanne.

Fabre-Serris, Jacqueline (2011), "Le cycle thébain des *Métamorphoses*: un exemple de mythographie genrée?", *Eugesta* 1, 99–120.

Fabre-Serris, Jacqueline (2017), "Un exemple de sélection, ordre et traitement mythographique chez Hygin: les fables 1–27", *Polymnia* 3, 26–50.

Fabre-Serris, Jacqueline (2019), "le mythe thébain à Rome. Les fables 66–75 d'Hygin. l'interprétation d'un mythographe", *Polymnia* 4, 97–124.

Feeney, Denis (2016), *Beyond Greek. The Beginnings of Latin Literature*, Cambridge, MA/London.

Fletcher, F.K.B. (2013), "Hyginus' *Fabulae*: toward a Roman Mythography", in: Scott Smith/Stephen Trzaskoma (eds.), *Writing Myth. Mythography in the Ancient World*, Leuven, 133–164.

Fletcher, F.K.B. (2022), "Hyginus, *Fabulae*", in: Scott Smith/Stephen Trzaskoma (eds.), *The Oxford Handbook of Greek and Latin Mythography*, Oxford.

Gantz, Timothy (1993), *Early Greek Myth. A Guide to Literary and Artistic Sources*, Baltimore.

Graziani, Françoise (forthcoming), "Fonction herméneutique de la tradition mythographique: les *Opuscula mythologica physica et ethica* de Thomas Gale (1688)", in: Minerva Alganza Roldán/Álvaro Ibáñez Chacón (eds.), Mythographica and Paramythographica Graeca: *La Transmisión de los textos*, Universidad de Granada.

Guidorizzi, Giulio (ed.) (2000), *Igini*, Milano.

Hoyo Calleja, Javier del y García, José Miguel (2009), *Fábulas, Higino*, Madrid.

Marshall, Peter K. (ed.) (1993), *Hygini Fabulae*, Leipzig.

Rose, H.J. (1936), *Modern methods in Classical Mythology*, St Andrews.

Rose, H.J. (rep. 1963), *Hygini Fabulae*, Lugduni Batavorum.

Smith, Scott/Trzaskoma, Stephen (eds.) (2007), Apollodorus' *Library and* Hyginus' *Fabulae. Two Handbooks of Greek Mythology*, Indianapolis.

Voisin, Dominique (2008), "*Dispositio* et stratégies littéraires dans les *Erotika Pathémata* de Parthénios", in: Arnaud Zucker (ed.), *Littérature et érotisme dans les* Passions d'amour *de Parthénios de Nicée*, Grenoble, 40–55.

Voisin, Dominique (2016), "Décomposition et recomposition des motifs mythologiques dans les *Passions d'amour* de Parthenios de Nicée", in: Arnaud Zucker/Jacqueline Fabre-Serris/Jean-Yves Tilliette/Gisèle Besson, (eds.), *Lire les mythes. Formes, Usages et visées des pratiques mythographiques de l'Antiquité à la Renaissance*, Lille, 67–83.

Werth, Albertus (1901), *De Hygini Fabularum Indole*, Leipzig.

Zucker, Arnaud/Fabre-Serris, Jacqueline/Tilliette, Jean-Yves/Besson, Gisèle (eds.) (2016), *Lire les mythes. Formes, Usages et visées des pratiques mythographiques de l'Antiquité à la Renaissance*, Lille.

Giulia Sissa
The Rest was not Perfected: Platonic Endings and their Modern Echoes

Abstract: Plato's *Critias*, whose Latin title is *Atlanticus*, is famously a *labor imperfectus*. Francis Bacon's *New Atlantis* (1626) ends, or fails to end, or even refuses to end with the equally famous, maddening, bracketed sentence: "[the rest was not perfected]". I argue that, if we want to understand the significance of this double textual "imperfection" — ancient (in the *Critias*) and modern (in the *New Atlantis*) —, we must concentrate on three moments in Bacon's "worke unfinished": the identification of Plato's Atlantis as Great Atlantis, namely America; the replacement of an earthquake with a deluge, so that New Atlantis is not engulfed in an ocean of mud; and the experimental re-writing of Plato's allegory of the cave in the *Republic*. Deceptive grottos are relevant in Bacon's reception/elaboration of the Platonic cave in the *Novum Organum*. But cavernous spaces and subterranean holes play a startlingly novel role in the *New Atlantis*. A truly epoch-making question is at stake. What do these modern variations mean? In this paper, I try to answer this question.

Francis Bacon's *New Atlantis* offers a model of *labor* deliberately, and literally, left *imperfectus*. Probably written in 1612, it was published posthumously in 1626, under the curatorial responsibility of Bacon's literary executor, William Rawley, the Chaplain of Lord Verulan himself as well as of King James I. This canonical piece of utopian thought bears an eloquent subtitle: *A Worke Unfinished*.[1] It also ends with a few enigmatic words: "The rest was not perfected". The text comes across as an abruptly, ostensibly, emphatically interrupted piece of narrative thinking. Not only does it break off, but it announces this fact not once, but twice — as if it deserved the reader's full attention. Such a textual feature, I will argue, conveys two ideas.

The first is that *New Atlantis* mimics its ancient model, namely Plato's *Critias*, the notoriously incomplete dialogue in which a divinely-crafted island, called Atlantis, is described. The second idea is that the unfinished state of Bacon's own *worke* may well be an authorial direction or an editorial whim, or even a coquettish erudite device, but it could not be more appropriate to the

---
[1] On the date, see Bacon 2000, 16. In this article I cite from Francis Bacon, *New Atlantis*, edited by Gerard Wegemer, CTMS Publishers at the University of Dallas, 2020, 16.

theoretical content of the book.² Textual unfinishedness adds a metaliterary, final touch to the epistemic and colonial utopia encapsulated in the work itself.

Bensalem, the island portrayed in *New Atlantis*, is a possible world in which an ambitious, relentless, progressive endeavour drives the entire society: knowledge, experimentation, research.³ It is an enlightenment project. Innovative by definition, such a project must continue on its trajectory of investigational, forward-looking, new inquiries. As an exemplary world, Bensalem is open to the future. As a book, *New Atlantis* embodies that open-endedness. While the frontispiece of the 1628 edition shows a naked woman cheerfully emerging from a dark hollow, while a motto frames the image: "*tempore patet occulta veritas*" ("hidden truth becomes apparent over time"), the last sentence appended to the first edition confirms that the travel from obscurity to light is not over.⁴ Enlightenment must go on. "The rest is not perfected", I will argue, is not merely an allusion to some missing pages; it is rather a nod to the quest that, in the possible world of Bensalem, remains to be continued. Knowledge is never done once and forever; it is always imperfect and indefinitely perfectible. The thought of having reached a satisfactory degree of accomplishment would compromise an aspiration that *must* be asymptotic. Perfection is the enemy of perfectionism. This is, after all, the essence of the experimental method for which Francis Bacon is considered a canonical thinker.

The two ideas conveyed by textual unfinishedness — the Platonic sub-text and the paratextual corroboration of open-endedness — are intricately connected. Plato's memory, I will argue, is indeed present in the *New Atlantis*: the famous cave, depicted in the *Republic* as a place of perceptual illusion, is reinvented here, in Bacon's travelogue, as a research laboratory buried deep down under the surface of the earth.⁵ In Bensalem there are caves. And in these caves,

---

2 For a discussion on the multiple interpretations of the unfinished status of the text, see Hurd Hale 2013.
3 Lucas 2018, 120 emphasizes the radical innovation: "Bacon, by contrast, is introducing something genuinely new, and his view of progress is implicit throughout the New Atlantis. The task of Salomon's House is not to recapitulate and preserve ancient wisdom but to forge ahead into an exhilarating future, cutting the ties that bind knowledge to ancient metaphysics and Athenian ideals ... The New Atlantis should not be read then, as the contemporary fascination with the Atlantis myth might lead us to read it, as the history of a storehouse of ancient wisdom which has been lost in the mists of time. Bacon's Atlantis, like Plato's Atlantis, is the enemy of Athens. It represents an independent (though Christian) tradition dedicated to a new type of learning." On the epistemic ambition, see Grafton 2001.
4 The engraving appears on the title page of *New Atlantis* in the second edition of Bacon 1628.
5 Pl. *Resp.* 7, 514 a–515 a.

perceptions are actively put to the test. Plato's allegorical environment of shadows, trompe-l'oeil and make-believe becomes a space of inquisitive experiments. What was a tenebrous trap, to be left behind in an arduous ascent toward the light of the sun, becomes a place where, on the contrary, the quest for clarity can flourish. Light itself becomes an object of manipulation, tweaking and trials. An ironic, subtle interplay of reception and reinterpretation of Plato's narratives emphasizes Francis Bacon's conviction that something new is not merely happening in European culture. Rather, the very purpose of Bensalem must be pursued there, in the old world. To this allegorical reading of *New Atlantis*, I hope to add a nuanced discussion of both the Platonic inter-text and the epistemological significance of an editorial strategy. "The rest was not perfected" means that the unknown remains to be discovered.

1 Plato's sub-text

To reach this open-ended conclusion, let us start from the beginning. In the *Novum Organum*, which includes a first book of "Aphorisms", Bacon argues that Nature is "subtle" (1, X). So much so that the kind of knowledge human beings have been able to produce over the centuries, in ancient Greece and, collaterally, in other societies, falls short of capturing the fine, intricate, elusive complexity of the world. When Francis Bacon deploys his expurgation of science and philosophy — ancient and modern —, we learn a new language. Hopefully, from now on, we will be able to make true discoveries. Human understanding will be furthered, bettered, deepened. For, also according to Bacon, what have we accomplished so far? Nothing but "specious meditations, speculations, and theories of mankind", which "are but a kind of insanity" (1, X).[6] Science as we know it is useless "for the discovery of effects". And "logic is useless for the discovery of the sciences" (1, XI). Since the dawn of time, Bacon laments, the will to knowledge has generated nothing but epistemological obstacles.

A Greek philosopher, Aristotle, is the major culprit, for the masterpiece of his logic, the syllogism, "rather assists in confirming and rendering inveterate the errors founded on vulgar notions than in searching after truth and is therefore more hurtful than useful" (1, XII). In creating an illusion of logical necessity and of conclusive reasoning, the syllogism is especially persuasive, therefore pernicious. "Very unequal to the subtlety of nature ... It forces assent, therefore,

---

[6] See also Bacon 2017, 31 and ff.

and not things" (1, XIII). This is because syllogisms are all made up of words, mere "signs of notions" that might be "confused and carelessly abstracted from things ... Our only hope, then, is in genuine induction" (1, XIV). In sum: both in logic and physics, notions such as matter, form, substance, quality, moisture, dryness, generation, corruption, attraction, repulsion, are all "fantastical" and "ill-defined" (1, XV). A completely new epistemic equipment must be invented, in order for us to think properly and to offer new findings. This, and only this, will do justice to the subtlety of Nature.

Are the Ancients only a bunch of old fools? Aristotle is definitely hopeless. But Plato's case is more nuanced. Plato deserves to be classified among those who mix up philosophy with "superstition and theology". At first sight, these thinkers are treacherous because the "impressions of fancy" fascinate people and threaten human understanding, no less than "vulgar notions".

> The disputatious and sophistic school entraps the understanding, while the fanciful, bombastic, and, as it were, poetical school, rather flatters it. There is a clear example of this among the Greeks, especially in Pythagoras, where, however, the superstition is coarse and overcharged, but it is more dangerous and refined in Plato and his school. (1, XLV)

"Abstracted forms", "fantastical philosophy", "the absurd mixture of matters divine and human" and, more generally, this kind of "worship of folly" are "the apotheosis of error". And this is "the greatest evil of all" (1, LXV). Fanciful, fantastical, bombastic, poetical, flattering for human understanding and, to make it worse, highly "refined", Plato is literally "dangerous". And yet, Plato's thought lurks and is incessantly present in Bacon's own language.

In the *Novum Organum*, to classify the errors of the past, Bacon introduces four vivid — shall we say fanciful, or perhaps even poetical? — images. These are what he calls "idols": the idols of the tribe, the idols of the den, the idols of the marketplace, the idols of the theatre.

> Four species of idols beset the human mind, to which (for distinction's sake) we have assigned names, calling the first Idols of the Tribe, the second Idols of the Den, the third Idols of the Market, the fourth Idols of the Theatre. (1, XXXIX)

The "Den" is actually a cavern. It is the world in which we live, plunged in fancies and, most important, fastened to our inveterate habits of knowledge.

> The idols of the Den derive their origin from the peculiar nature of each individual's mind and body, and also from education, habit, and accident; and although they be various and manifold, yet we will treat of some that require the greatest caution and exert the greatest power in polluting the understanding. (1, LIII)

Let such, therefore, be our precautions in contemplation, that we may ward off and expel the idols of the den, which mostly owe their birth either to some predominant pursuit, or, secondly, to an excess in synthesis and analysis, or, thirdly, to a party zeal in favor of certain ages, or, fourthly, to the extent or narrowness of the subject. (1, LVIII)

Investigation helps us emerge from the Den. This language, not unlike the engraving on the frontispiece of *New Atlantis*, echoes Plato's allegory of the cave in the *Republic*. Socrates asks Glaucon to imagine

> people as it were in an underground dwelling like a cave with a long wide entrance facing the light along the whole length of the cave. They have been there since childhood shackled by the legs and the neck, so that they remain in the same spot facing only forward, unable to turn their heads right round because of the chains. There is light from a fire burning from above a long way behind them, and between the fire and the prisoners there is a path leading upward across which you should imagine there is a low wall built, just as puppeteers have a screen in front of the audience above which they present their entertainments.
> I can see it, he said.
> Now imagine people carrying props of all kinds along this wall above the top of it and statues and other creatures made of wood and stone and fashioned in all kinds of ways. Some of those carrying these objects speak, others are silent as you would expect.[7]

The theatrical, even cinematographic, cave where we grow up to enjoy the spectacle of the silhouettes of puppets, projected from behind onto a wall, is a deeply buried, penumbral place from which we must exit, Socrates claims, in order to leave behind dolls and shadows in a chiaroscuro atmosphere — the *simulacra* we take for real things — and, finally, walk into the light of the day. As a precocious student at Trinity College, Cambridge, Francis Bacon had been superbly trained as a classical scholar. We can be confident that the "idols of the Den"

---

[7] Pl. *Resp.* 7, 514 a–515 a: ἰδὲ γὰρ ἀνθρώπους οἷον ἐν καταγείῳ οἰκήσει σπηλαιώδει, ἀναπεπταμένην πρὸς τὸ φῶς τὴν εἴσοδον ἐχούσῃ μακρὰν παρὰ πᾶν τὸ | σπήλαιον, ἐν ταύτῃ ἐκ παίδων ὄντας ἐν δεσμοῖς καὶ τὰ σκέλη καὶ τοὺς αὐχένας, ὥστε μένειν τε αὐτοῦ εἴς τε τὸ πρόσθεν μόνον ὁρᾶν, κύκλῳ δὲ τὰς κεφαλὰς ὑπὸ τοῦ δεσμοῦ ἀδυνάτους περιάγειν, φῶς δὲ αὐτοῖς πυρὸς ἄνωθεν καὶ πόρρωθεν καόμενον ὄπισθεν αὐτῶν, μεταξὺ δὲ τοῦ πυρὸς καὶ | τῶν δεσμωτῶν ἐπάνω ὁδόν, παρ' ἣν ἰδὲ τειχίον παρῳκοδομημένον, ὥσπερ τοῖς θαυματοποιοῖς πρὸ τῶν ἀνθρώπων πρόκειται τὰ παραφράγματα, ὑπὲρ ὧν τὰ θαύματα δεικνύασιν.
Ὁρῶ, ἔφη.
Ὅρα τοίνυν παρὰ τοῦτο τὸ τειχίον φέροντας ἀνθρώπους σκεύη τε παντοδαπὰ ὑπερέχοντα τοῦ τειχίου καὶ ἀνδριάντας καὶ ἄλλα ζῷα λίθινά τε καὶ ξύλινα καὶ παντοῖα εἰργασμένα, οἷον εἰκὸς τοὺς μὲν φθεγγομένους, τοὺς δὲ σιγῶντας τῶν παραφερόντων.
Ἄτοπον, ἔφη, λέγεις εἰκόνα καὶ δεσμώτας ἀτόπους (Text and translation from The Loeb Classical Library).

are, indeed, an allusive reception of the *Republic*. But there is more. Bacon engages with Plato, and he does so programmatically.

In the *New Atlantis*, we are told the story of a group of European sailors who, surviving famine "in the midst of the greatest wilderness of waters in the world", wash ashore on an unknown island, called Bensalem.[8] The Bensalemites, more precisely the Governor of the House of Strangers, welcome the starving and mostly sick navigators, allowing them to discover a marvelous society in which learning, inquiry and experimentation are practiced in a myriad ingenious fashions. This is an epistemic utopia/eutopia, generally acknowledged as the prefiguration of "The Royal Society of London for Improving Natural Knowledge", founded in 1660. While recounting the history of this happy land to his European visitors, the Governor alludes to a "great man with you" — whom we cannot fail to recognize. It is Plato.[9] It is, more to the point, Plato as the author of *Critias*, the unfinished dialogue about an island designed by the mighty sea-god, Poseidon, beyond the Pillars of Heracles, namely the straits of Gibraltar. It is Atlantis. We know from the *Timaeus* that Atlantis was wonderfully landscaped, prosperous, and well governed, but also aggressive: once upon a time, the Atlantans had waged war against Egypt as well as archaic Athens, at a moment when Athens was a truly marvelous, optimal (ἀρίστη) city. They ended badly, however, because a cataclysmic earthquake made their land crumble and sink beneath the sea. This caused the water to thicken, so that, beyond the boundaries of the Mediterranean, there now lies an ocean of mud, compact to the point of unnavigability. Nobody can venture there. Plato places this narration in the mouth of an Egyptian priest, addressing a Greek statesman and philosopher, Solon:

> So this power (Atlantis), being all gathered together, made an attempt one time to enslave by one single onslaught both your country (Greece) and ours (Egypt) and the whole of the territory within the Straits (the Mediterranean). And then it was, Solon, that the manhood of your State (Athens) showed itself conspicuous for valour and might in the sight of all the world. For it (Athens) stood pre-eminent above all in gallantry and all warlike arts, and acting partly as leader of the Greeks, and partly standing alone by itself when deserted by all others, after encountering the deadliest perils, it defeated the invaders and reared a trophy; whereby it saved from slavery such as were not as yet enslaved, and all the rest of us who dwell within the bounds of Heracles (the Mediterranean) it ungrudgingly set free. But at a later time there occurred portentous earthquakes and floods, and one grievous day and night befell them, when the whole body of your warriors was swallowed up by the earth, and the island of Atlantis in like manner was swallowed up by the sea and vanished; wherefore also the ocean at

---

[8] Bacon 2020, 1.
[9] Bacon 2020, 16–17; Pl. *Ti.* 25 b-d (Text and translation The Loeb Classical Library).

that spot has now become impassable and unsearchable, being blocked up by the shoal mud which the island created as it settled down.¹⁰

αὕτη δὴ πᾶσα ξυναθροισθεῖσα εἰς ἓν ἡ δύναμις τόν τε παρ' ὑμῖν καὶ τὸν παρ' ἡμῖν καὶ τὸν ἐντὸς τοῦ στόματος πάντα τόπον μιᾷ ποτ' ἐπεχείρησεν ὁρμῇ δουλοῦσθαι. τότε οὖν ὑμῶν, ὦ Σόλων, τῆς πόλεως ἡ δύναμις εἰς ἅπαντας ἀνθρώπους διαφανὴς ἀρετῇ τε καὶ ῥώμῃ ἐγένετο· πάντων γὰρ προστᾶσα εὐψυχίᾳ καὶ τέχναις ὅσαι κατὰ πόλεμον, τὰ μὲν τῶν Ἑλλήνων ἡγουμένη, τὰ δ' αὐτὴ μονωθεῖσα ἐξ ἀνάγκης τῶν ἄλλων ἀποστάντων, ἐπὶ τοὺς ἐσχάτους ἀφικομένη κινδύνους, κρατήσασα μὲν τῶν ἐπιόντων τρόπαια ἔστησε, τοὺς δὲ μήπω δεδουλωμένους διεκώλυσε δουλωθῆναι, τοὺς δ' ἄλλους, ὅσοι κατοικοῦμεν ἐντὸς ὅρων Ἡρακλείων, ἀφθόνως ἅπαντας ἠλευθέρωσεν. ὑστέρῳ δὲ χρόνῳ σεισμῶν ἐξαισίων καὶ κατακλυσμῶν γενομένων, μιᾶς ἡμέρας καὶ νυκτὸς χαλεπῆς ἐλθούσης, τό τε παρ' ὑμῶν μάχιμον πᾶν ἀθρόον ἔδυ κατὰ γῆς, ἥ τε Ἀτλαντὶς νῆσος ὡσαύτως κατὰ τῆς θαλάττης δῦσα ἠφανίσθη· διὸ καὶ νῦν ἄπορον καὶ ἀδιερεύνητον γέγονε τὸ ἐκεῖ πέλαγος, πηλοῦ καταβραχέος ἐμποδὼν ὄντος, ὃν ἡ νῆσος ἱζομένη παρέσχετο.

In *New Atlantis*, Francis Bacon echoes this passage of the *Timaeus* together with the geographical and urbanistic overview of Atlantis in the *Critias*. The Governor of the House of Strangers recounts:

At the same time, and an age after, or more, the inhabitants of the great Atlantis did flourish. For though the narration and description which is made by a great man with you, that the descendants of Neptune planted there, and of the magnificent temple, palace, city, and hill; and the manifold streams of goodly navigable rivers (which, as so many chains, environed the same site and temple); and the several degrees of ascent whereby men did climb up to the same, as if it had been a *scala coeli*; be all poetical and fabulous: yet so much is true, that the said country of Atlantis, as well that of Peru, called Coya, as that of Mexico, then named Tyrambel, were mighty and proud kingdoms, in arms, shipping, and riches; so mighty, as at one time (or at least within the space of ten years) they both made two great expeditions; they of Tyrambel through the Atlantic to the Mediterranean Sea; and they of Coya, through the South Sea upon this our island. And for the former of these (sc. Tyrambel=Mexico), which was into Europe, the same author amongst you (as it seemeth) had some relation from the Egyptian priest whom he citeth (Pl. *Ti.* 21a ff; *Criti.* 110a f.). For assuredly such a thing there was. But whether it were the ancient Athenians that had the glory of the repulse and resistance of those forces, I can say nothing; but certain it is there never came back either ship or man from that voyage. Neither had the other voyage of those of Coya upon us had better fortune, if they had not met with enemies of greater clemency.¹¹

Francis Bacon offers a modern, colonial interpretation of the history and geography of *Timaeus* and *Critias*. Although "poetical and fabulous", Plato's story is

---

10 Pl. *Ti.* 25 b-d. Hartmann 2015.
11 Bacon 2020, 17–18.

presented as being true precisely about Atlantis' vicissitudes and wars. But the Bensalemite adds his own knowledge: firstly, the Atlantis envisioned by Plato can now be identified as a region belonging to a larger landmass, aptly called *Great* Atlantis. This is Mexico. Secondly, Plato's story must be amended on an all-important detail, the alleged irreversibility of the natural catastrophe that befell Atlantis. If Atlantis is America, then it is still there in the Atlantic Ocean and we are not meant to infer that it was "swallowed up by the sea and vanished". The ocean itself has not become an "impassable and unsearchable" mass of mud. Quite the opposite. It is by sailing through the Atlantic that navigators such as Christopher Columbus have (re)discovered Atlantis.

Let me expand on the first of the Governor's revelations. Since Plato is indeed "the same author amongst you", who learned from an Egyptian priest about the attack of old Atlantis on the Mediterranean Sea, and since Bacon redescribes this imperialistic move as the Tyrambelian/Mexican attempt to conquer the entire Mediterranean world (including Greece and Egypt), it means that Bacon conceives Plato's relatively small Atlantis as part of Great Atlantis, and more precisely as Mexico. This implies, furthermore, that in his own fabulous manner Plato must have prefigured the discovery of the American continent. Now, after Columbus (of whom there is a statue in Bensalem), both the Europeans and the Bensalemites have become aware of the existence of America. But only the Bensalemites know that America is indeed what the Ancients had imagined as Atlantis. The Governor reveals to his guests the dramatic history of "the great Atlantis (that you call America)".[12] Plato helps them understand the antiquity of the New World. The New World, *vice versa*, helps them understand Plato's seemingly fanciful narration. Furthermore, the Bensalemite offers a sequel to the ancient history of Atlantis: miles away from the exiguous, crowded Mediterranean Sea, in the middle of the immense, wild South Sea, Bensalem itself suffered an analogous invasion from the other people who inhabit Great Atlantis, namely Coya/Peru. Like the Athenians, the Bensalemites, too, have resisted.

This alignment of Athens and Bensalem, as victims respectively of Tyrambel/Mexico and Coya/Peru, means that Bensalem itself cannot be the "New Atlantis" of the title. And here we come to the second eye-opener. In Bacon's tale, once again, "New Atlantis" is not an alternative name for Bensalem, as it might be assumed. Instead, what the text refers to as "Great Atlantis" is a completely different land, once powerful, expansionist and rich, but subsequently flooded, impoverished, and depopulated. Plato's Atlantis literally ceases to exist, leaving behind an impenetrable mass of mud that seals the Mediterranean within the

---

[12] Bacon 2020, 16.

Pillars of Heracles. But the Bensalemite historian sets the record straight: America, alias Great Atlantis "was utterly lost and destroyed: not by a great earthquake, as your man saith, but by a particular deluge or inundation".[13] This seemingly trivial detail makes a significant difference. When a massive downpour falls on Great Atlantis, most people perish but some survive; buildings, cities and material goods are submerged but the landmass itself does not collapse into the water, thereby vanishing forever. Crucially, the ocean remains navigable.[14] Even more water falls from the sky and flows into the Atlantic. Indeed, the inhabitants of America/Atlantis lose their "letters, arts, and civility", but some individuals take refuge on the highest mountains. And later, a few "wild" survivors come down, live scattered, destitute and naked, except for the feathers they have learned to pluck from flying birds. These new Atlantans, whom the narrator explicitly calls "Americans", are now isolated from the rest of the world. "So, you see", the Bensalemite narrator tells his visitors, "by this main accident of time, we lost our traffic with the Americans, with whom of all others, in regard they lay nearest to us, we had most commerce."[15]

2 New Atlantis

This is *New* Atlantis. Its novelty can only be understood through the intertextual play with antiquity. Once a maritime super-power, the Atlantans / Americans nowadays have become a diminished population, ignorant of any technology, especially sailing and shipping, lacking an army, a prosperous economy and a

---

[13] Bacon 2020, 17.
[14] Bacon 2020, 18: "For the poor remnant of human seed which remained in their mountains peopled the country again slowly, by little and little, and being simple and a savage people (not like Noah and his sons, which was the chief family of the earth), they were not able to leave letters, arts, and civility to their posterity; and having likewise in their mountainous habitations been used (in respect of the extreme cold of those regions), to clothe themselves with the skins of tigers, bears, and great hairy goats, that they have in those parts; when after they came down into the valley, and found the intolerable heats which are there, and knew no means of lighter apparel, they were forced to begin the custom of going naked, which continueth at this day. Only they take great pride and delight in the feathers of birds, and this also they took from those their ancestors of the mountains, who were invited unto it by the infinite flight of birds that came up to the high grounds, while the waters stood below. So you see, by this main accident of time, we lost our traffic with the Americans, with whom of all others, in regard they lay nearest to us, we had most commerce."
[15] Bacon 2020, 18.

political structure. The flood has transformed Great Atlantis into what we could call a "newly reborn" Atlantis, a rejuvenated Atlantis, which is also, from the author's standpoint and for his contemporary readers, a "New World" in the sense of a recently discovered continent. Francis Bacon replaces Plato's fictional Atlantis — an island nowhere to be found, having been engulfed by a sea which is now reduced to a mass of solid sludge — with America, which is indeed there, depopulated, decivilized, cut off from commerce with the rest of the world but still potentially reachable. Traffic has indeed resumed. Let me insist on this crucial point.

The narrator describes America as early-modern travelers/ethnographers used to do: a space of wilderness, "new" in the sense of "young". In an additional intertextual twist, Bacon applies to America the vicissitudes that, in the *Timaeus*, Plato (via the Egyptian priest [who speaks to Solon]) attributes to Greece itself, and more precisely to Athens. The new Atlantans/Americans are as new/young (νέοι) as the Greeks. "When ... the flood from heaven comes sweeping down afresh upon your people", says the Egyptian priest, "it leaves none of you but the unlettered and uncultured, so that you become young all over again (ὥστε πάλιν ἐξ ἀρχῆς οἷον νέοι γίγνεσθε)".[16] Likewise, the Governor of the House of

---

16 Pl. *Ti.* 22d-e: "And when, on the other hand, the Gods purge the earth with a flood of waters, all the herdsmen and shepherds that are in the mountains are saved, but those in the cities of your land are swept into the sea by the streams; 23 a-c: "when, after the usual interval of years, like a plague, the flood from heaven comes sweeping down afresh upon your people, it leaves none of you but the unlettered and uncultured, so that you become young as ever, with no knowledge of all that happened in old times in this land or in your own. Certainly the genealogies which you related just now, Solon, concerning the people of your country, are little better than children's tales; for, in the first place, you remember but one deluge, though many had occurred previously; and next, you are ignorant of the fact that the noblest and most perfect race amongst men were born in the land where you now dwell, and from them both you yourself are sprung and the whole of your existing city, out of some little seed that chanced to be left over; but this has escaped your notice because for many generations the survivors died with no power to express themselves in writing. For verily at one time, Solon, before the greatest destruction by water, what is now the Athenian State was the bravest in war and supremely well-organized also in all other respects. It is said that it possessed the most splendid works of art and the noblest polity of any nation under heaven of which we have heard tell."

καὶ πάλιν δι' εἰωθότων ἐτῶν ὥσπερ νόσημα ἥκει φερόμενον αὐτοῖς ῥεῦμα οὐράνιον καὶ τοὺς ἀγραμμάτους τε καὶ ἀμούσους ἔλιπεν ὑμῶν, ὥστε πάλιν ἐξ ἀρχῆς οἷον νέοι γίγνεσθε, οὐδὲν εἰδότες οὔτε τῶν τῇδε οὔτε τῶν παρ' ὑμῖν ὅσα ἦν ἐν τοῖς παλαιοῖς χρόνοις. τὰ γοῦν νῦν δὴ γενεαλογηθέντα, ὦ Σόλων, περὶ τῶν παρ' ὑμῖν ἃ διῆλθες, παίδων βραχύ τι διαφέρει μύθων, οἳ πρῶτον μὲν ἕνα γῆς κατακλυσμὸν μέμνησθε πολλῶν ἔμπροσθεν γεγονότων, ἔτι δὲ τὸ κάλλιστον καὶ ἄριστον γένος ἐπ' ἀνθρώπους ἐν τῇ χώρᾳ τῇ παρ' ὑμῖν οὐκ ἴστε γεγονός, ἐξ ὧν σύ τε καὶ πᾶσα ἡ πόλις ἔστι τὰ νῦν ὑμῶν περιλειφθέντος ποτὲ σπέρματος βραχέος, ἀλλ' ὑμᾶς λέληθε διὰ τὸ τοὺς περιγενομένους ἐπὶ

Strangers reveals something similar to his European guests: "For you must account your inhabitants of America as a young people, younger a thousand years at the least than the rest of the world".[17]

The identification of Atlantis as America emerges from a close reading of Bacon's text. Harold J. Cook offers an illuminating background by writing that, after the publication of Francisco Lopez de Gomara's *Historia general de las Indias* in 1552, the idea "that the New World appeared as Atlantis in the histories of the ancients, was quickly adopted by many other authors". Built on the early-modern reception of Plato, such an idea "finds one of its last expressions in 1626, when Francis Bacon's *New Atlantis* advised its readers that three thousand years earlier there had been a golden age of navigation in which the Americans had participated under the more ancient name of Atlanteans".[18] The Europeans discovered the Atlantans/Americans in their new state of nature, after the flood. No less attentive to the text, Jacqueline Cowan writes that "the title of Bacon's Utopian text does not refer to the e/utopian land that its Old-World mariners

---

πολλὰς γενεὰς γράμμασι τελευτᾶν ἀφώνους. ἦν γὰρ δή ποτε, ὦ Σόλων, ὑπὲρ τὴν μεγίστην φθορὰν ὕδασιν ἡ νῦν Ἀθηναίων οὖσα πόλις ἀρίστη πρός τε τὸν πόλεμον καὶ κατὰ πάντα εὐνομωτάτη διαφερόντως· ᾗ κάλλιστα ἔργα καὶ πολιτεῖαι γενέσθαι λέγονται κάλλισται πασῶν, ὁπόσων νῦν ὑπὸ τὸν οὐρανὸν ἡμεῖς ἀκοὴν παρεδεξάμεθα.
Cf. Pl. *Leg.* 677 a-e.

17 Bacon 2020, 17–18. See also *Novum Organum*, 1, 71: "Nor must we omit the opinion, or rather prophecy, of an Egyptian priest with regard to the Greeks, that they would forever remain children, without any antiquity of knowledge or knowledge of antiquity; for they certainly have this in common with children, that they are prone to talking, and incapable of generation, their wisdom being loquacious and unproductive of effects. Hence the external signs derived from the origin and birthplace of our present philosophy are not favorable".

18 Cook 1978, 25–26: "In 1552, Francisco Lopez de Gomara finished writing his *Historia general de las Indias*, in which he remarked that Plato knew the Indies under the name Atlantis. This idea, that the New World appeared as Atlantis in the histories of the ancients, was quickly adopted by many other authors. It finds one of its last expressions in 1626, when Francis Bacon's *New Atlantis* advised its readers that three thousand years earlier there had been a golden age of navigation in which the Americans had participated under the more ancient name of Atlanteans. Bacon, like Gomara, stressed the basic truth of Plato's story and added that the Atlantean civilization had been destroyed in a great flood, from which its descendants, the Americans, were only just recovering when they were discovered by the Europeans. By Bacon's time most writers on the New World had ceased to connect it with Atlantis, but during the half century following the publication of Gomara's work many historians, geographers, and cosmographers did accept the connection. In fact, according to Lee E. Huddleston's recent survey, during the third quarter of the sixteenth century the theory that the Americans were once Atlanteans was the most popular explanation for the origin of the American Indians". This close reading of the text unfortunately goes against a number of authoritative studies on *New Atlantis*. See Hurd Hale 2013.

encounter, but to the New World. Bacon maps the Atlantis mythologised in Plato's *Timaeus* and *Critias* onto America: 'the great Atlantis ... [is] that you call America'".[19] Indeed, if America rather than Bensalem is a New Atlantis, the title of Bacon's travelogue can only perplex the reader.[20] Along this line, Tobin Craig has argued that such a title is meant to echo the destiny of Plato's own narrative (in *Timaeus* and *Critias*) about a state called Atlantis.[21] The title *New Atlantis*, Craig goes on to say, designates not a place, but a text; not the island called Bensalem, but the whole *history* of Bensalem. *New Atlantis*, therefore, is a modern re-writing of the vicissitudes of "Atlantis" told by Plato in *Timaeus* and *Critias*.

I agree, also on account of Bacon's very interesting claim that

> probable conjectures, or obscure traditions, many times turn themselves into prophecies; while the nature of man, which coveteth divination, thinks it no peril to foretell that which indeed they do but collect, as that of Seneca's verse; for so much was then subject to demonstration, that the globe of the earth had great parts beyond the Atlantic, which might be probably conceived not to be all sea; and adding thereto the tradition in Plato's *Timæus*, and his *Atlanticus*, it might encourage one to turn it to a prediction.[22]

If, for Bacon, Plato's *Critias* is entitled *Atlanticus* then Bacon's own work is a "New *Atlanticus*". An "obscure tradition" by a fanciful philosopher, joined to a probable conjecture "that the globe of the earth had great parts beyond the Atlantic", has turned into a prediction. Now, we know that there is a land beyond the Atlantic Ocean. *New Atlantis* retells its story, from the standpoint of yet another newly found place in the Pacific Ocean, Bensalem.

New Atlantis is indeed the re-make of a text, but I would argue that geography matters. In the text itself, as I mentioned, Great Atlantis is the American continent (including Coya/Peru and Tyrambel/Mexico), and *that* vast Atlantis has become "new" by reverting to a renewed primitive state, after the flood. *New Atlantis* makes for a much more interesting title than "Bensalem", because it draws attention to Bensalem's history, so intertwined with that of Coya/Peru. It brings to the fore Bensalem's past triumph over the Peruvian/Atlantic invaders. It also connects with the first sentence of the narration: "We sailed from Peru". I would also add that Bensalem is, indeed, a utopia. Archaic Athens has been, indeed, a utopia. But neither version of Atlantis — ancient or modern — was meant to be so: both super-powers behaved badly and ended badly. I would

---

19 Cowan 2011, 417.
20 Cowan 2011, 409–410.
21 Craig 2010.
22 Francis Bacon, *Wisdom of the Ancients*, 35.

also argue that the context of colonization is crucial. As a Chancellor of the Crown, Francis Bacon was mentioned in the "Charter of the London and Bristol Company" (1610) and he was actively involved in the creation of a Company for the colonization of a large territory in North America, aptly called "Newfoundland". He also advocated for an English conquest of Mexico and Peru, to replace the Spanish empire.[23] As Samuel Zeitlin argues,

> It is a fact universally acknowledged that Francis Bacon's *New Atlantis* opens with a sailor's narration to the effect that "We sailed from Peru." Yet, it is less noted in scholarship and writing on Bacon that the former Lord Chancellor had openly advocated the British invasion and colonial seizure of Peru, at the time a Spanish colony, in the years in which he is thought to have composed his *New Atlantis*.[24]

Travelling from Peru, the European visitors leave behind a Spanish colony that Bacon considered to be as imperialist as it was vulnerable, much weaker than what people might have thought. Or is it rather the case that, in *New Atlantis*, Peru has already become an English colony, from where those English visitors sail towards China and Japan? This is how we have flourished, the Governor of the House of Strangers recounts, notwithstanding the invasion by the powerful people who dwelled in Great Atlantis, a land now reduced to a condition of new wilderness — a land ready to be explored, populated, and planted anew.

3 Atlantis, ancient and modern

I have emphasized Francis Bacon's strategies of allusion and reception vis-à-vis Plato's *Timaeus* and *Critias* for a reason. Both *Critias* (the *Atlanticus* in Latin translation) and *New Atlantis* are works left unfinished. But their unperfected finales as texts are compatible with two different temporal perspectives. On the one end, by identifying Atlantis as Great Atlantis, *scilicet* America, Francis Ba-

---

23 On the crucial importance of Bacon's practical and theoretical involvement in colonization, see Zeitlin 2021; for the relevance of Bacon's justifications of colonization for the understanding of *New Atlantis*, see Zeitlin 2023.
24 Zeitlin 2023, 1015. See also footnote 42 in which Zeitlin quotes Francis Bacon's *Considerations touching a War with Spain*: "Against the third, touching the treasure of the Indies, and especially the West Indies, there are three expedients. 1. The destroying the shipping of Spain upon the Spanish Coast before they set sail, as Drake did twice. 2. The intercepting the fleet in its course about the islands, or elsewhere. 3. The invasion of Peru or Mexico (for Brazil methinks is a poor thing)."

con focuses on a narrative that, in both versions, ends with a catastrophe. The unhappy ending is the culmination of the story told by the Egyptian priest in the *Timaeus* as well as by the Governor of the House of Strangers in Bensalem. But, on the other hand, by replacing the Platonic earthquake with a deluge, Bacon creates the premises of a stark contrast: the crumbling of a telluric mass *versus* a flood of water. This variation of the meteorological storyline has certain consequences. Firstly, Great Atlantis has not been completely destroyed by a terrestrial upheaval, as Plato claimed about his own Atlantis, so that now, we also learn, Great Atlantis is still there. Although fatal for a sophisticated and flourishing social life, a flood is less lethal than a seismic catastrophe. After the inundation, the mighty Atlantic civilizations have simply reverted to a state of nature. A similar thing happened to Greece, hence its "youthfulness" in comparison with Egypt. Secondly, the liquid cataclysm that has befallen America has not solidified the oceans, Atlantic and Pacific. Quite the opposite: there is even more water available, vacant, accessible to "traffic". The seafarers who wash ashore in Bensalem set sail precisely from Peru. The coast is clear.

While reading Bacon's reading of Plato, we have two parallel tales, one ancient and one modern. In Plato's Greek past, Atlantis was the aggressive *enemy* of an optimal *polis*, primordial Athens. Then, one day, as Plato claims, an earthquake made Atlantis disintegrate into an ocean that, *ipso facto*, became an impenetrable mass of mud, a thick sludge in which navigation was utterly impossible. To quote Plato again: "The island of Atlantis in like manner was swallowed up by the sea and vanished; wherefore also the ocean at that spot has now become impassable and unsearchable, being blocked up by the shoal mud which the island created as it settled down."[25] Once the maritime space beyond the Pillars of Heracles became inaccessible, the Mediterranean was forever sealed. No travel, no commerce, no discovery, no research. In Bacon's global past, by contrast, Atlantis (more precisely Peru) is once again the aggressive foe of an optimal state, Bensalem, and, like its Platonic paradigm, Atlantis suffers a natural disaster. But this is not an annihilating earthquake. It is rather a half-devastating deluge that causes a brutal arrest of the busy life of a developed society, and even a regression to the simplicity of nature, but keeps the future open-ended. Atlantis does not vanish, and the Oceans remain still open to navigation. There are still a few people over there. We can sail and visit again. It is a world to re-discover and to reconquer.

The openness of the world matches the openness of the text. To advance my argument, I must now direct our attention to Bensalem itself. How can we situate

---

25 Pl. *Ti.* 25 d.

Bensalem in this elaborate intertextual play? As we have seen, Bensalem cannot possibly be a modern version of the Atlantis depicted in Plato's *Critias*. The text says otherwise. If we juxtapose the ancient and the modern plots, Bensalem rather matches isotopically an idealized, pre-democratic Athens. Atlantis/Peru has invaded the island in the South Sea, as Atlantis/Mexico has invaded Athens. Both states have resiliently reconstructed themselves. But the analogy stops there. For Bacon, Athens is ancient; Bensalem is modern. The radical novelty imbued in the latter compels us to object to the hypothesis that Bensalem mimics Plato's Egypt.[26] "So far from being the 'New Atlantis' of the title", Tobin Craig writes, "Bacon's Bensalem is the equivalent to or stand-in for Plato's Egypt".[27] To this ingenious argument I would like to reply as follows. True, Bensalem hardly looks like any Platonic political fantasy — be it archaic Athens, Kallipolis, Magnesia, or Atlantis itself. Not merely because Bacon's heterotopia is committed to perpetual peace, uninterested in the trade of material goods, and devoted to only one pursuit and to the import of one commodity, knowledge. Bensalem is, indeed, the opposite of the warlike, commercial, imperialistic powers that both the antique (Platonic) and the modern (Baconian) Atlantis used to be. But Bensalem is novel, first and foremost, on account of how the Bensalemites live their life. These are industrious, hard-working, novelty-seeking, forward-looking *researchers*. Their experience of time is radically oriented toward the future. They care for what is not yet known and must be not merely discovered, but attempted, invented, devised. True, Bensalem cannot possibly be Atlantis resurrected. But ancient Egypt? I am not sure either.

To understand what Bensalem is, we must keep in focus its paradoxical position in the New World. Whereas mighty Atlantis has backslided to a rude lifestyle, tiny Bensalem is pushing the boundaries of innovation. The comparison yields a contrast: retrogression versus progression. A progress that not even Athens could achieve. Remember: the Greeks too are "new", in the sense of youthful children. Only the Bensalemites are true innovators. "The end of our foundation is the knowledge of causes, and secret motions of things", claims the Father of the House of Salomon. Even more ambitiously, their goal is "the

---

26 Craig 2010, 233: "In the *Critias* Plato's only unfinished, or apparently unfinished dialogue, we are offered a continuation of this account [that of the story of Atlantis, found in the *Timaeus*], one that features a much more extensive description of Atlantis. In that account the magnificence and splendor of Atlantis is contrasted with the rustic and moderate simplicity of old Athens. Atlantis itself is said to be of 'great elevation' (118a) and characterized by magnificent opulence. What, then, do we learn from Plato's account of Atlantis that can help us to make sense of Bacon's title?"
27 Craig 2010, 234.

enlarging of the bounds of human empire, to the effecting of all things possible".[28] Their sense of unbound possibility presupposes their awareness of being at the forefront of an unlimited process of modernization. Such awareness emerges precisely in the confrontation with an ancient world, stuck in time and mired in an impervious space. No way out of the Mediterranean! No expansive empire in view!

To understand the different temporalities at work in *New Atlantis*, we have emphasized the significance of the earthquake *versus* the deluge affecting, respectively, Plato's and Bacon's Atlantis. The former is doomed, while the Atlantic Ocean becomes a colossal mass of quicksand, unmanageable in any form of travel, on foot, on horseback, on wheels or by boat. The latter, on the contrary, has a future because America is already being colonized, developed, and reconnected to the globe, thanks to the bustling circulation on the Atlantic and the South Sea. In Bensalem itself, there may well be vestiges of the Platonic past, but the project of technological perfectibility is unstoppable. The rest is *never* perfected.

4 Caves and labs

Now, to conclude our argument, we must go back to the cave.

In the *Novum Organum*, the "Idols of the Den" must be avoided, Bacon argues, because the den/cavern is a place of bad perceptual habits. These are "contemplations", "preconceived fancies", "shadows of resemblance" to which people have become "attached" and "habituated" over the years, on account of their "predominant pursuits".[29] This echoes the habit to watching shadows on a wall, which the prisoners of Plato's cave have acquired — a habit impossible to change, except by force. And we have seen that these idols also resonate with the qualities attributed to Plato's own philosophy — which is especially fanciful, bombastic, poetical, fantastical. On the one hand, Plato is the inventor of the exemplary cave, the allegory of a full immersion in the realm of perception to be abandoned by ascending towards the light (philosophy is the remedy). On the other, according to Francis Bacon, it is Plato's cave that becomes an allegory of Plato's own philosophy — a philosophy in itself emblematic of the "idols of the Den". Beware of the cave!

---

28 Bacon 2020, 32.
29 Francis Bacon, *Novum Organum*, 1, LIII-LVII.

But there are caves in Bensalem. The venerable Father of Salomon's House reveals the purpose of the very foundation of their Houses, the "preparations and instruments", "the several employments and functions" their fellows are assigned, "the ordinances and rites which [they] observe".

> The preparations and instruments are these: We have large and deep caves of several depths: the deepest are sunk 600 fathoms; and some of them are digged and made under great hills and mountains: so that if you reckon together the depth of the hill and the depth of the cave, they are (some of them) above three miles deep. For we find that the depth of a hill, and the depth of a cave from the flat, is the same thing; both remote alike from the sun and heaven's beams, and from the open air. These caves we call the Lower Region. And we use them for all coagulations, indurations, refrigerations, and conservations of bodies. We use them likewise for the imitation of natural mines and the producing also of new artificial metals, by compositions and materials which we use, and lay there for many years. We use them also sometimes (which may seem strange) for curing of some diseases, and for prolongation of life in some hermits that choose to live there, well accommodated of all things necessary, and indeed live very long; by whom also we learn many things.[30]

Plato's cave becomes a laboratory.[31] Replace contemplation (and words) with all this clever fiddling with the states of matter — coagulations, indurations, refrigerations, and other attempts to find a way of conserving bodies. Put "imitation" to work to produce not poems, but "new artificial metals". Bury people alive, deep down in those cavernous spaces, where they will live and work much longer than at the surface. All this investigational busyness will do nothing less than "enlarging the bounds of human empire, to the effecting of all things possible".

The experimental caves are similar to the perspective-houses, in which light is observed, tested, produced, transformed, multiplied, moved, colored. The telescope and the magnifier help the alteration of natural eyesight. Illusion itself is mastered as methodical creativity. "We represent also ... all delusions and deceits of the sight, in figures, magnitudes, motions, colors; all demonstrations of shadows ... We make artificial rainbows, halos, and circles about light. We also represent all manner of reflections, refractions, and multiplications of visual beams of objects".[32] Plato's misleading trompe-l'oeil becomes what we call "optics", namely "a science that deals with the genesis and propagation of

---

30 Bacon 2020, 32–33.
31 This has nothing to do with the epistemic power of caves, argued for in Ustinova 2009.
32 Bacon 2020, 38.

light, the changes that it undergoes and produces".[33] Light has a behavior. And that behavior is observed, studied, tried, modified, manufactured, and controlled.

Such a project — effecting the possible, all of it — is interminable. And so it must be. How long will it take to exhaust the subtlety of nature? How many more experiments await the researchers, intent on mining its treasures? They dwell in caves where a bustling, restless curiosity yields more and more new phenomena. The time to be spent underground, in Bensalem's caves, is purely and simply unrestricted. No need to climb out of it! Breakthroughs happen down there. Nobody could set a limit to the progress of knowledge. This is why the inconclusiveness of Plato's *Atlanticus* may well be a textual accident — but it creates a challenging suggestion. Francis Bacon takes up Plato's challenge, with a radically modern twist: he resuscitates Atlantis, gets rid of the sludge, fluidifies the ocean, makes the famous *antrum platonicum* depicted in the *Republic* into a research facility. Finally, in one of the most momentous moves in the history of intertextuality, he (or his admiring literary executor) writes those *last* words: "the rest was not perfected".[34] "Not perfected" means perfectible. It is true of the text. It is true of the world. Perfectibility, as far as the eye can see. The enlightenment, together with the adventurous settlement in Newfoundland, is on the horizon.

---

33 This is the current definition in the Merriam Webster Dictionary.

34 The connection between the unfinished status of the text and the perspective of progress has been noticed by Faulkner 1993, 230–234. See also Killacky 2018, 13: "Thus, supposing that the *New Atlantis*'s unfinished and enigmatic state is calculated to serve a function, I propose that this unfinished design is a literary device that demonstrates the unfinished status of natural philosophy". Killacky rightly emphasizes the language of mining, digging and extracting in Bacon's epistemology. Unfinishedness, I have tried to demonstrate in this paper, concerns everything: writing, science, philosophy and the world. For Bacon's misgivings about progress, Rossi 1995; Studer 1998. For controversial views among contemporary scholars on Bacon's ideas about progress, see Vickers 1992. Letter from Francis Bacon to Tobie Matthew, "from Gray's Inn, Feb. 27, 1610": "My great work goes forward; and after my manner, I alter ever when I add. So that nothing is finished till all is finished".

Fig. 6: Plato's allegory of the cave by Jan Saenredam, according to Cornelis van Haarlem, 1604, Albertina, Vienna.

Bibliography

Bacon, Francis (2000), *New Atlantis*, edited by Gerard Wegemer, CTMS Publishers at the University of Dallas.
Bacon, Francis (2017), *New Atlantis* and *The Great Instauration*, edited by Jerry Weinberger, Malden/Oxford/Chichester.
Bacon, Francis (1620), *Novum Organum*, London.
Bacon, Francis (1628), *Sylva sylvarum: Or, A Natural History in Ten Centuries*, London. Printed by J.H. for William Lee at the Turks Head in Fleet-street, next to the Miter.
Cook, Harold (1978), "Ancient Wisdom, the Golden Age, and Atlantis: The New World in Sixteenth-Century Cosmography", *Terrae Incognitae* 10.1, 25–43.
Cowan, Jacqueline (2011), "Francis Bacon's 'New Atlantis' and the Alterity of the New World", *Literature and Theology* 25.4, 407–421.
Craig, Tobin (2010), "On the Significance of the Literary Character of Francis Bacon's 'New Atlantis' for an Understanding of His Political Thought", *The Review of Politics* 72.2, 213–239.
Faulkner, Robert (1993), *Francis Bacon and the Project of Progress*, Lanham.

Grafton, Anthony (2001), "Where Was Salomon's House? Ecclesiastical History and the Intellectual Origins of Bacon's *New Atlantis*", in: Herbert Jaumann (ed.), *Die europäische Gelehrtenrepublik im Zeitalter des Konfessionalismus*, Wiesbaden, 21–38.

Hartmann, Anna-Maria (2015), "The Strange Antiquity of Francis Bacon's *New Atlantis*", *Renaissance Studies* 29, No. 3 (June), 375–393.

Hurd Hale, Kimberly (2013), *Francis Bacon's "New Atlantis" in the Foundation of Modern Political Thought*, New York.

Killacky, M.S. (2018), *Sir Francis Bacon's New Atlantis as a Literary Representation of the Perpetually Unfinished Status of Natural Philosophy as Articulated in his Philosophical Text*, The Advancement of Learning ("Thesis submitted in partial fulfilment of the requirements for the Degree of Bachelor of Arts with Honours in English at Acadia University").

Lucas, Peter (2018), "Bacon's New Atlantis and the Fictional Origins of Organised Science", *Open Cultural Studies* 2, 114–121.

Rossi, Paolo (1995), *Naufragi senza spettatore: l'idea di progresso*, Bologna.

Studer, H. (1998). "Francis Bacon on the Political Dangers of Scientific Progress", *Canadian Journal of Political Science/Revue Canadienne De Science Politique* 31.2, 219–234.

Ustinova, Yulia (2009), *Caves and the Ancient Greek Mind: Descending Underground in the Search for Ultimate Truth*, Oxford.

Vickers, Brian (1992), "Francis Bacon and the Progress of Knowledge Author", *Journal of the History of Ideas* 53.3, 495–518.

Zeitlin, Samuel Garrett (2021), "Francis Bacon on Imperial and Colonial Warfare", *The Review of Politics* 83.2, 196–218.

Zeitlin, Samuel Garrett (2023), "Eutopia of Empire: Francis Bacon's *Short View* and the Imperial and Colonial Background to the *New Atlantis*", *Political Research Quarterly* 76.2, 1012–1023.

Francesca Cadel
War as a Permanent Civil War: The "Unfinished" History in Pasolini's *Petrolio*

Abstract: The essay considers *Petrolio* as one of the most important Italian literary documents of the 1970s, a testimony of the unfolding of neocapitalism in postwar Italy portraying the multinational space of capital's expansion, its ubiquitous relations with politics and power. The political manipulations of an explosive and divisive context such as the postwar Italian one are described by Pasolini as they were happening. *Petrolio* represented this sprawling colonial politics of development ("la politica dello sviluppo"), and denounced its connections with a structural violence against Italian civilians perpetrated within the new Italian State Power to eliminate any residual resistance opposing the expansion of neocapitalism and Anglo-American hegemony in the Mediterranean after the end of the Second World War.

1 Introduction: the fragmentary nature of *Petrolio*

Being "unfinished" and "incomplete" can be considered the driving tension characterizing Italian postwar history, from the 1940s to the 1970s, as this tension is contemplated and represented in the pages of Pier Paolo Pasolini's posthumous novel *Petrolio*, first published in 1992.[1] *Petrolio* describes the multinational space of capital's expansion, its ubiquitous relations with politics and power, like no other Italian novel written in the 1970s. It can be considered one of the most important literary documents portraying the unfolding of neocapitalism in postwar Italy. The political manipulations of an explosive and divisive context such as the postwar Italian one are represented by Pasolini as they were happening, and as they could (and will) continue to happen outside of his novel in the future. Through his creative narrative, abstractions and allegories, Pasolini intended to share the *summa* of his knowledge with his readers – an intellectual and biopolitical legacy – in the form of a contemporary text, inclusive of many different genres (from autobiography to the essay) and media (from film documentary to radio and tv interviews). The fragmentary character of the

---

[1] Pasolini 1992.

whole book is immediately declared by its author in his project note, dated Spring 1973:

> All of *Petrolio* (from the second draft) should be presented as a critical edition of an unpublished text (considered a monumental work, a modern Satyricon). Four of five versions of that text survive ... Hence this edition makes use not only of a comparison between the various surviving manuscripts ... but also of the contribution of other materials ... an enormous quantity of historical documents that have some bearing on the events of the book will be used, *especially regarding politics and, in particular, the history of ENI*[2] ... The author of the critical edition will therefore summarize, on the basis of these documents — in a flat, objective, colorless, etc. style — long passages of general history to link the "fragments" of the reconstructed work ... *The fragmentary character of the whole book ensures that, for example, certain "narrative pieces" are in themselves complete, but we can't be certain, for example, whether they are real events, dreams, or conjectures made by one of the characters* (ix–x, *my italics*).[3]

Petrolio is therefore considered by its author an "unpublished text", a "monumental work", a "modern *Satyricon*", that is to say it is intentionally characterized by its "fragmentary character", as is the case of the Menippean satire, the *Satyricon liber* or *Satyrica*, whose surviving sections (or chapters) came to be understood by nineteenth and twentieth century readers as a Roman novel, dated with uncertainty between the 1st century BCE and the 3rd century CE and attributed to Gaius Petronius Arbiter.[4]

---

[2] Pasolini 1997, see *Translator's note*, p. ix: "ENI, or Ente Nazionale Idrocarburi, is the Italian state oil-and-gas company".

[3] All quotes in English are from the American edition of the novel, translated from the first Italian edition (1992). All quotes in Italian are from the last 2022 edition. Here, Pasolini 2022, 675–676: "Tutto 'PETROLIO' (dalla seconda stesura) dovrà presentarsi sotto forma di edizione critica di un testo inedito (considerato opera monumentale, un Satyricon moderno). Di tale testo sopravvivono quattro o cinque Manoscritti ... La ricostruzione si vale dunque del confronto dei vari manoscritti conservati ... ma anche dell'apporto di altri materiali ... verrà adoperato un enorme quantitativo di documenti storici che hanno attinenza coi fatti del libro: specialmente per quel che riguarda la politica, e, ancor più, la storia dell'ENI ... L'autore dell'edizione critica 'riassumerà' quindi, sulla base di tali documenti — in uno stile piano, oggettivo, grigio ecc. — lunghi brani di storia generale, per legare fra loro i "frammenti" dell'opera ricostruita ... Il carattere frammentario dell'insieme del libro, fa sì per esempio che certi "pezzi narrativi" siano in sé perfetti, ma non si possa capire, per esempio, se si tratta di fatti reali, di sogni o di congetture fatte da qualche personaggio."

[4] Harrison 1999, xvi.

2 A satire of the national political situation: chaos as a structure and a strategy

In this sense, *Petrolio* Note 97, entitled *The Narrators*, is extremely important for Pasolini's political satire addressed to Italian post-fascist statesmen, businessmen and major entrepreneurs. Note 97 (*The Narrators*) ends with the proclamation of the death of the narrative art: "'The narrative art, as you well know,' began this narrator, 'is dead ...'".[5] Pasolini ironically apostrophizes the "average reader", minimizing the relevance of his "very diligent" report (*referto*) and inviting the reader to skip these pages, if not provided either of a deep civic sentiment or particularly malicious:

> As this point, I must in all honesty* warn the average reader that if he wants to, he can skip, so to speak, over all these pages and go on to the next Note. Although this report on one of the many hot spots of humble Italy is very diligent, it's not essential to our Allegory; it can be of interest only to a reader who is either endowed with a deep civic sentiment or particularly malicious.
>
> * One should be suspicious of this honesty, precisely because it is sincere.[6] (348)

These pages are devoted entirely to the *Festa della Repubblica*, the national festivity celebrating Italian Republic Day on June 2nd, a commemoration of the referendum that chose to abolish the Monarchy by universal suffrage on June 2, 1946 thereby inaugurating the post-fascist years of Italian government. In Pasolini's point of view they imply a specific narrative of power, represented by *caos* (chaos) and *brulichio* (milling/swarm), as the proximity to power was perceived by Carlo Valletti, Pasolini's protagonist, on June 2, 1972 (that year the President of the Republic was Giovanni Leone, not Giuseppe Saragat as indicated in the text), while he entered the salon of the Quirinale, the Presidential Palace in Rome: "Meanwhile, as soon as he entered, pure chaos surrounded him. The

---

5 "'The narrative art, as you well know,' began this narrator, 'is dead. We are in mourning. Therefore, dear listeners, in the absence of wine you must content yourselves with ciceone'" (Pasolini 1992, 353).
6 A questo punto, per onestà, (*) devo avvertire il lettore medio che, se vuole, può saltare, come si dice, a piè pari tutte queste pagine e passare all'appunto seguente. Questo referto, peraltro assai diligente, su uno dei tanti bullicami dell'umile Italia, non è essenziale alla nostra Allegoria: può presentare qualche interesse solo a un lettore dotato di un profondo sentimento civico, oppure particolarmente maligno. (*) Si diffidi di questa onestà, e proprio perché è sincera" (Pasolini 2022, 477).

frenetic milling of the 'nobodies', those who lead exposed lives, the usual ... Here Carlo Valletti has to pay the price of democracy" (345).[7] The "nobodies" live exposed lives, while the secrecy of power is active within "pure chaos", and these are also the characteristics of Pasolini's novel and his open-ended, digressive, nonlinear narrative: "Mine is a /novel/ not 'on a spit' but 'in a swarm', and so it's understandable if the reader remains a little < ... > disoriented" (82).[8]

This chaos surrounding Carlo Valletti inside the Quirinale implies the intertwining of national and international politics: Italy's oil policies in the Middle East, with its many contrasting interests, and the specificity of divisive internal Italian politics, which will lead only three years after the assassination of Pier Paolo Pasolini to Aldo Moro's kidnapping and murder by the Red Brigades in 1978, and to other crimes and massacres of civilians, often characterized by secrecy and impunity:

> There was Cottafavi, the former chief of staff of the Honorable Moro, just named the new ambassador from Italy to Tehran. He is "rather combative" toward the Arab-favoring politics of ENI. As a result he is tied to Attilio Monti instead, and to the oil interests of BP ... And there among them, too, is a certain Angelo Berti — who is part of the leadership of the Mario Fani Clubs, a political-religious organization established some years ago by Gedda. Berti is charged with maintaining contact between Professor Luigi Gedda and the industrialist Attilio Monti, who since September I has been paying a million lire a month to the National Civic Committee. (I insist on reminding the reader that we are in 1972.)
>
> Note 97, *The Narrators*, 351[9]

---

[7] "Intorno a lui c'era, frattanto, appena entrato, il puro caos. Il brulichio frenetico dei 'nessuno', quelli che vivono una vita scoperta, la solita ... Qui Carlo Valletti doveva pagare lo scotto della democrazia" (*idem*, 474).

[8] Note 22 A, *The so-called empire of the Troyas: the branches closest to the mother company*, 81–84, see translator's note, p. 82: "'On a spit' and 'in a swarm' are literal translations of *a schidionata* and *a brulichio*. By 'novel on a spit' Pasolini seems to mean a narrative form that follows a conventional, progressive cause-and-effect logic, as represented by the *schidione*, or long metal spit on which meat is roasted. By contrast, the 'novel in a swarm' seems to mean an open-ended, digressive, nonlinear narrative, as represented by the word *brulichio*, which generally refers to the swarming, teeming activity of ants".

[9] In Pasolini 2022, Appunto 97, *I narratori* (p. 474), is introduced by footnote (a) "*segue l'annotazione*: Tutto visto con 'la lucidità della malinconia mortale' di Carlo 'mutato in altro'", see Pasolini 2022, 480: "Ecco là Cottafavi, ex capo di gabinetto dell'on. Moro, appena nominato nuovo ambasciatore d'Italia a Teheran. Egli è 'piuttosto polemico' verso la politica filo-araba dell'ENI. Risulta piuttosto legato ad Attilio Monti e agli interessi petroliferi della BP ... Ed ecco anche, tra loro, un certo Angelo Berti — che fa parte del direttivo dei circoli 'Mario Fani', un'organizzazione politico-religiosa costituita qualche anno fa da Gedda. Il Berti è appunto incaricato di mantenere in contatto il prof. Luigi Gedda e l'industriale Attilio Monti, il quale

This passage continues by referring to industrialist Attilio Monti's implication in financing the fascist extremist Pino Rauti and "the progress of the judicial inquiries involving Rauti 'regarding the attacks of the extreme right' and the accusations that had been made against Monti of having financed Pino Rauti's extremist movement" (352).

Italy's polarized, divided post-fascist society — "Reds" versus "Blacks" (Left versus Right) since the 1940s — is represented realistically in Pasolini's *Petrolio* and is characterized by the same perduring state of civil war that had been lyrically evoked in his 1964 poem *Vittoria*.[10]

When North American students look online for a plot summary, they find useful syntheses such as this blurb, promoting the first US edition of *Petrolio*, translated by Ann Goldstein:

> Pasolini's unfinished novel, found in his desk shortly after his murder in 1975, explores the psychological workings of fascism in postwar Italy by mapping connections among the Fascist Party, the Mafia, the CIA and even the Communist Party. The novel depicts, in loosely connected fragments of stories and allegorical tales, the dual personality of a man named Carlo, his rise to power and his eventual complicity with the Fascists and the Mafia. Carlo 1 is a liberal thinking Catholic from an upper-middle-class family, an executive in an oil company; Carlo 2 explores and acts on his sexual urges by dominating (raping his mother) and being dominated (paying 20 boys to sexually abuse him). The narration, objective and cold and without even the slightest hint of sentimentality, is similar to the unflinching camera's eye of Pasolini's films.[11]

If students ask for clarification, I start by telling them that, despite its cold and objective narration, a sympathy for all discussion, or better a shared empathy, is at the core of *Petrolio*, since the novel's ambition is inclusive and emphasizes a rich orality. Until his last years, Pasolini was committed to fighting the calamity of misology and faithful to the Socratic and Platonic heritage he had embraced from the very beginning of his career as a poet in Italian and Friulian, as well as in his film theory, since he used this quote from Plato's *Phaedrus* in opening *The Written Language of Reality* (1966), his essay on cinema:

> 'It doesn't matter', Socrates used to say, 'however first of all, we must be careful that an unpleasant event doesn't befall us ... to become misologists, that is, that an aversion and

---

versava mensilmente dal I settembre un milione di lire al Comitato Civico Nazionale. (Insisto nel ricordare al lettore che siamo nel 1972)."

10 Pasolini 1964.
11 https://www.publishersweekly.com/9780679429906 [accessed on 08/07/2023].

antipathy to all discussion rises in us ... Oh! Truly there is no greater calamity than this antipathy for all discussion'.[12]

3 The unsolved political tensions in Pasolini's novel: *Petrolio* as "labor imperfectus"

Pasolini started thinking about his novel around 1972 when he first isolated the lexeme *Petrolio* as a possible title, from which a plot was then schemed in less than an hour (!), as he recalled:

Spring or summer 1972

My eyes fell by chance on the word "Petrolio" in an article in, I think, L'Unità, and the mere thought of the word "Petrolio" as the title of a book spurred me on to think of the plot of that book. In less than an hour this sketch was conceived and written.[13] (xvii)

Petrolio is a *labor imperfectus* by definition: it does not begin, as stated in Note 1: "This novel does not begin" (3),[14] and it is unfinished, left incomplete because of Pasolini's murder.

Angelo Guglielmi (1929–2022), an important Italian literary critic and intellectual, a former member of *Gruppo 63*, stated in a 2010 interview that among all Pasolini's novels he would only save *Petrolio*, precisely because of its being characterized by the unfinished: "I would save only *Petrolio*, because it is characterized by the unfinished".[15] Ten years later, in another interview he would refer to *Petrolio* as a "world-novel" destined to project Pasolini into the future:

"*Petrolio* is his great world-novel destined to project him into the future. In his late years Pasolini realizes that reality is not something concluded that one can isolate within

---

12 See Pasolini 2005, 197–222.
13 "Primavera o Estate 1972. Mi sono caduti per caso gli occhi nella parola 'petrolio' in un articoletto credo dell'Unità, e solo per aver pensato la parola 'Petrolio' come il titolo di un libro mi ha spinto poi a pensare alla trama di tale libro. In nemmeno un'ora questa 'trama' era pensata e scritta" (Pasolini 2022, 668).
14 "Questo romanzo non comicia", Appunto 1 (19).
15 Antonio Gnoli 2010: "Salverei solo *Petrolio* per il suo carattere inconcluso".

predesigned borders, it is instead an uninterrupted flux of events. And he [Pasolini] pours this chaos into his most important literary text".[16] (my translation)

A chaotic *labor imperfectus* were also the questions left like open wounds by the Italian Civil War of 1943–1945 whose conflicts were still infecting the immediate post-fascist years. These unsolved historical issues had consequences whose violent effects were still unfolding in the 1960s and 1970s. Pasolini had directly experienced the trauma of such a divisive history since he had joined the Italian Communist Party (PCI) after his brother Guido had fallen in a 1945 ambush aiming to annex the Northeastern Italian territories to the former Yugoslavia. Guido and his group of 17 partisans were killed by Italian communist fighters under the command of the Slovenian IX Corpus in the so-called Porzûs massacre.[17] In 1949, Pasolini was finally expelled from PCI because of his homosexuality. In *Vittoria*, a poem dated 1964, Pasolini described the two different souls animating postwar Italy, and the radical divisions between Reds and Blacks. It is a ubiquitous, unfinished history, with all its casualties and murders: his brother's death is listed among the "assassinii degli Anni Amari". In *Vittoria*, Pasolini apostrophized the partisans who had fought against Nazi-Fascism in the name of Italian democracy, his brother Guido among them, and asked them to acknowledge that all politics is Realpolitik, and that history is as ambiguous as human nature. He invited them (and his readers) to contemplate and comprehend the two different souls of the socio-political conflict, and the compromises necessary to any form of ruling power: "'All politics is Realpolitik,' warring / soul, with your delicate anger! / You do not recognize a soul other than this one … you do not recognize the heart / that becomes slave to its enemy, / and goes / where the enemy goes, led by a history / that is the history of both …'".[18]

---

16 Interview with Simonetta Fiori, "Il critico. 'Ho imparato ad amarlo'", *Robinson* (*la Repubblica*), February 2, 2022: "*Petrolio* è il suo grande romanzo-mondo destinato a proiettarlo nel futuro. Negli ultimi anni Pasolini si rende conto che la realtà non è qualcosa di finito che si possa chiudere entro confini predisegnati, ma è un flusso continuo di accadimenti. E riversa questo caos nella sua opera letteraria più importante."
17 See Petacco 2020, 76–78.
18 Pasolini, *Vittoria*:

"Ogni politica è una realpolitica", anima
guerriera, con la tua delicata rabbia!
Non riconosci un'altra anima, eh? Questa
dove c'è tutta la prosa dell'uomo abile,
del rivoluzionario attaccato all'onesta
media dell'uomo (anche la complicità
con gli assassinii degli Anni Amari s'innesta

From *Petrolio* to the last poem he wrote in Friulian, *Saluto e augurio* (*Goodbye and Best Wishes*),[19] and his late theoretical essays, articles, and public debates on Italy's cultural and socio-economic development (*sviluppo*), Pasolini is willing to discuss the unsolved political tensions stemming from the past. Moreover, in the 1970s, Pasolini started accusing the postwar state apparatus — the police, the army and the secret services — of supporting young fascists extremists. His accusations would be repeated in many articles, published on the front page of the Milan based *Corriere della Sera*, until the day he was murdered in 1975. In an article published on June 24th 1974, and entitled *Il Potere senza volto* ("The Faceless Power"), he reinforced what he had already stated in a previous article, that indeed the so-called *stragismo* was a state business: "The real people in charge of the massacres in Milan and Brescia are the government

---

nel classicismo protettore, che fa
il comunista perbene): non riconosci il cuore
che diventa schiavo del suo nemico, e va
dove il nemico va, condotto dalla storia
ch'è storia di tutti due, e li fa, nel profondo,
stranamente fratelli ...

In English, see Pasolini, *Victory*, cf. Hirshman 2010, 212–213:

"All politics is Realpolitik," warring
soul, with your delicate anger!
You do not recognize a soul other than this one
which has all the prose of the clever man,
of the revolutionary devoted to the honest
common man (even the complicity
with the assassins of the Bitter Years grafted
onto protector classicism, which makes
the communist respectable): you do not recognize the heart
that becomes slave to its enemy, and goes
where the enemy goes, led by a history
that is the history of both, and makes them, deep down,
perversely, brothers ...

19 See Pasolini May 1975; in English *Cf.* Sartarelli 2014, 440–446: "This will almost certainly be my last poem in Friulian; / I want to speak to a Fascist before I, or he, get too far away. / He's a young Fascist ... / "Come here, come here, Phaedrus. / Listen. I want to tell you something / that will sound like a testament. / But remember, I have no illusions / about you. I know, know all too well, / that your heart is not free, nor do you / wish it to be, and you cannot be sincere; / but I will speak to you, even if you are dead."

and the Italian police: because if the government and the police had only wanted it, those massacres would have never happened".[20] (my translation)

4 "The light of history needs a calendar": unfolding the mystery in Pasolini's novel

In 1972, the term "globalization" was not commonly used by economists,[21] yet the new President of the Italian state oil-and-gas company ENI (Ente Nazionale Idrocarburi) Eugenio Cefis (1921–2004), Enrico Mattei's (1906–1962) powerful successor, isolated the numbers of *la politica dello sviluppo* and its expansive capitalism in a global perspective, from the 1950s to the 1970s:

> In 1950 the amount of the global import-export trade (except for Eastern European countries) reached 153 billion dollars. Twenty years later, in 1970, the amount of import-export trade, in the same area, surpassed 573 billion (constant-value) dollars. Therefore, in twenty years the amount of the global import-export trade almost quadrupled.[22] (my translation)

Petrolio represented this sprawling colonial politics of development (*la politica dello sviluppo*), and denounced its connection with the structural violence against Italian civilians that was perpetrated within the new Italian State Power to eliminate any residual resistance to the expansion of neocapitalism and Anglo-American hegemony in the Mediterranean after the end of the Second World War. Using an intentionally uncanny strategy of estrangement, Pasolini's act of accusation, a veritable *J'Accuse*, depicted real historical facts, including

---

20 Pasolini *Il Potere senza volto*, *Corriere della Sera*, June 24th 1974, then in *id. Scritti corsari*, Garzanti, November 1975, 2005: 45–50, 48, "I responsabili reali delle stragi di Milano e di Brescia sono il governo e la polizia italiana: perché se governo e polizia avessero voluto tali stragi non ci sarebbero state".
21 "As a term "globalization" was used as early as 1944 but economists began applying it around 1981. Theodore Levitt is usually credited with its coining through the article he wrote in 1983 for the *Harvard Business Review* entitled *Globalization of markets*, https://www.cs.mcgill.ca/~rwest/wikispeedia/wpcd/wp/g/Globalization.htm [accessed on 12/08/2023].
22 Eugenio Cefis, *La mia patria si chiama multinazionale*. Discorso di Eugenio Cefis all'Accademia Militare di Modena Modena, 23 febbraio 1972, included in the 2022 Italian edition of *Petrolio*, see Documenti, 699–716: "Nel 1950 il volume dell'interscambio mondiale (ad eccezione dei paesi dell'est europeo) raggiunse i 153 miliardi di dollari. Vent'anni più tardi, nel 1970, il volume dell'interscambio ha toccato, per la stessa area, i 573 miliardi di dollari (a valore costante). In vent'anni, quindi, il volume dell'interscambio si è quasi quadruplicato" (703).

massacres and murders perpetrated for political reasons, as retroactively collocated in an historical chronology, a calendar:

> The light of history needs a calendar: upset the chronological sequence of events just a little — perhaps breaking them down into their elements — and look, the light of history goes out and no longer explains anything.
>
> Placing a series of (realistic) crimes after a Vision — a placement that mocks the logic of Machiavellianism or of political realism, making it extremely antiquated — is, moreover, still (let it be clear) an accusation. Because political men, besides not being assassins, must be able to have Visions.[23] (404)

Pasolini's intentional displacement of real facts and abstract fictional tales confuses his readers, as in a baffling mystery. His novel is structured as a *brulichio* or "vortex": "swarm, or vortex, / which is the / structural part of my tale" (Note 22A, 82–83); the reader needs to engage in its contradictions as in a *divertissement*, Pasolini specifies. In *Petrolio*, the entire *Mattei affair* (1962) is initially dated to the end of the 1950s, then moved forward chronologically to the late 1960s. Introducing the character of Troya — Eugenio Cefis in the novel — Pasolini wrote:

> Troja, who emigrated to Milan in 1943 … took part in the Resistance (this, as we'll see, constitutes the *scandal*). There was a mixed group of De Gasperians and Republicans (the *mixture* started immediately, as we'll see), who fought in the mountains of the Brianza. The head of that partisan group was the current president of ENI, Ernesto Bonocore [Enrico Mattei] … What I would like to underline is the following: in the partisan group Troya was the *second in command* … As the "second" (second in command or vice president), he could more fully realize his ascetic tendency to "produce" … He did not advance, he accumulated. It would take too long and would be impossible for me, besides, to follow the whole slow story (two decades) of this accumulation and this expansion.[24] (81–82)

---

23 "La luce della storia ha bisogno di un calendario: sconvolgi appena un po' il seguito cronologico degli avvenimenti — magari scomponendoli nei loro elementi — ed ecco che la luce della storia si spegne, e non spiega più niente. La posposizione di una serie di delitti (realistici) a una Visione — posposizione che irride la logica del machiavellismo o del realismo politico, rendendola spaventosamente antiquata — è però tuttavia — sia chiaro — un atto di accusa. Perché gli uomini politici, oltre che non essere assassini, devono anche essere in grado di avere delle Visioni." (Pasolini 2022, Appunto 103b, 550).

24 Troya emigrato a Milano nel 1943 … Partecipò … alla Resistenza (questo, come vedremo, costituisce lo *scandalo*). C'era una formazione mista degasperiana e repubblicana (il *misto* cominciò subito, come si vede), che lottava sui monti della Brianza. Il capo di questa formazione partigiana era l'attuale presidente dell'Eni, Ernesto Bonocore … La cosa che vorrei sottolineare è la seguente: Troya nella formazione partigiana era *secondo* … In qualità di "secondo" (vicecomandante o vicepresidente) la sua tendenza ascetica a "realizzare" si attuava molto meglio … Egli non avanzava, accumulava. Non saliva, si espandeva. Sarebbe troppo lungo, e

As revealed at the end of *Petrolio* by the author, only one narrator — whose fictional source is a CIA agent — is telling the truth, in the manner of a classic detective story, a story of true facts. This is also the thesis and scheme of the book, as is made explicit by Pasolini:

> * All the inserted stories are the concrete and living representations of facts or characters that in the text are the product of pure abstract distortion.
> 1) E.g., the first group of stories "represents" the political types who in the Text <?>—abstractly—the politics of development and the two groups of political massacres— Only one of the narrators—at the end—tells a true story—He omits names—but gives the concrete facts, that is, of the massacres he committed, in their historical setting (he pretends that a CIA agent on the point of death confided everything to him)—*This is also the thesis of my book (do not say this explicitly but let it be understood, saying that this is also the outline of my book).[25] (463)

5 Italy's "orientalism": ENI's role in the global post-fascist political scene

The *Mattei affair* is an *exemplum* through which Pasolini elaborated his representation of the mutational process taking place in Italy's 1960s and early 1970s. Cefis was Mattei's powerful successor and finally moved ENI towards a new multinational identity. In 1971, he became president of a new company, called *Montedison*, progressively extending his financial powers up to the point of controlling national media and secret services. Between 1971 and 1974, a *strategia della tensione* ("a strategy of tension") between Italy's Red and Black entities was dividing Italian politics and society, while the effects of the first energy crisis of the postwar era, the oil crisis and austerity policies, manifested themselves in

---

per me, poi, impossibile, seguire tutta la lenta storia (due decenni) di questa accumulazione e di questa espansione ..." (Pasolini 2022, Appunto 22A, 125–126).

25 *Tutti i racconti inseriti sono la rappresentazione concreta e vivente di fatti o personaggi che nel testo sono frutto di pura deformazione astratta. 1) Per es. il primo gruppo di racconti "rappresenta" i personaggi politici che nel testo compiono – astrattamente – la politica dello sviluppo e i due gruppi di stragi politiche – Solo uno dei narratori – alla fine – racconta un racconto vero – Omette i nomi – ma racconta in concreto i fatti, appunto, delle sue stragi nella loro sistemazione storica (finge che un agente della CIA gli abbia confidato tutto in punto di morte) – * Questa è anche la tesi del mio libro (non dire questo esplicitamente, ma lasciandolo intendere dicendo che questo è anche lo schema del mio libro)" *idem*, 657.

1973.²⁶ Beginning with Note 22 — *Troya's so called empire: Troya himself* — Troya/Cefis is carefully described by Pasolini, both physically and psychologically, as a character defined by the mixed elements of his nature and politics: *il misto* (the mixed). He is a figure without any weakness, but the reader knows from the first lines of his portrait that he is guilty: "The first thing that strikes one about him is the smile ... it is definitely a guilty smile" (79). Troya/Cefis is treated as the key character (*guilty*) in a classic detective story, and Pasolini is explicit about this point: "Business was the language in which he expressed himself, and so to interpret him I ought to be a businessman as well as a detective. I have done the best I can, and you'll see what I found out" (81). An interesting aspect of Troya/Cefis' biography is his Friulian roots (he was born in that region in 1921) and also his participation in the anti-fascist resistance, in a mixed group (not communist) linked to De Gasperi and the Republicans who were active in Lombardia from 1943 to 1945. These are interesting pages, where Troya's biography is used in a twisted direction and produces an effect of estrangement in the reader. This is true specifically with regards to the theme of resistance and its connection to Pasolini's own traumatic memories: the death of his brother Guido (who had joined the Osoppo Brigade), killed in the Friulian Alps, at Porzûs, in what is still considered the bloodiest page of the internal conflict that arose in Northern Italy among the Garibaldi Brigade (communist) and the Osoppo Brigade (linked to De Gasperi and the Republicans).

The character of Troya/Cefis is imagined to be a member of the same group of partisans in which Mattei/Bonocore was the leader: both Mattei and Cefis were in fact Christian Democrats with a history in the anti-Fascist resistance. Troya/Cefis, the key character of the detective story unfolding in *Petrolio* is the architect of Mattei/Bonocore's elimination. He is described by Pasolini as an invincible pragmatist, a successful example of accumulation and expansion, with no real ambition other than to represent by his actions the championship of a specific — and mixed — post-fascist reality. These pages clarify the mixed nature of the events Pasolini is discussing in *Petrolio*, and the deeply traumatic origins of the First Italian Republic (1948–1994). A character such as Troya/Cefis helps the readers understand the reasons for development, that same *sviluppo senza progresso* ("development without progress") Pasolini was addressing as the major failure of the anti-Fascist resistance. This has nothing to do with any nostalgia for the past, but rather it is the admission of a bitter disillusionment about the present. In one of his articles, originally published in *Corriere della*

---

26 See "La prima crisi energetica del dopoguerra", *Il* Post, March 17, 2022 https://www.ilpost.it/2022/03/17/austerity-1973 [accessed on 12/08/2023]; see also Moro 1993, 119–124.

Sera on February 1st, 1975, with the title *Il vuoto di potere in Italia*, the infamous *articolo delle lucciole* ("article of the fireflies"), Pasolini wrote: "If my opinion were of any interest to the reader, I would give away the entire Montedison, even multinational, for a firefly".[27] (my translation)

The fragmentary character of *Petrolio* is an element that finds a pivotal source of new energy in Pasolini's representation of the 1960s. This decade functions as a vortex accelerating the chronotopes and narratives represented in the novel, and its idea of an "unfinished" and "incomplete" history. The protagonist, Carlo, ascended to power among the hierarchies of the Italian state oil-and-gas company ENI in these years. His success was made possible by his shift towards "that technological vanguard", the corporate new reality that ENI had become after Enrico Mattei's death. Carlo finally became an insider and an accomplice to political crimes committed within that secret "space" where real power is found. A new phase began in the 1960s, which allowed a faster movement of capital and relocated Italian geopolitics and major interests within a new set of alliances and lobbies:

> When the sixties arrived, he [Carlo] was ready. In fact, that was his moment. That was the moment in which he became/a Catholic of the left/, and this enabled him on the one hand to differentiate himself, to stand out, from those in power and, at the same time, through his particular, specialized work in that technological vanguard which was ENI after the death of Mattei, to insert himself boldly (and never ostentatiously) into the "space" where real power is found.[28] (24)

The 1960s ended abruptly with the state massacre in the Piazza Fontana at Banca Nazionale dell'Agricoltura in Milan, on December 12, 1969. After the false accusations against the Italian anarchists, the death of a first suspect, Giuseppe Pinelli, during a police interrogation, and the arrest and judicial persecution of a second suspect, the dancer Pietro Valpreda, a new wave of state repression began. In 1969 Pasolini devoted a long poem to this moment in Italian history, entitled *Patmos*. Despite Pasolini's 1968 contentious accusations against students

---

27 Pasolini 1999, 411: "Ad ogni modo, quanto a me (se ciò ha qualche interesse per il lettore) sia chiaro: io, ancorché multinazionale, darei l'intera Montedison per una lucciola".
28 "Quando arrivarono gli Anni Sessanta, egli era pronto a viverli. Era anzi quello il suo momento. Fu quello il momento in cui divenne un cattolico di sinistra: e questo gli consentì da una parte di differenziarsi o distinguersi dal potere, e, nel tempo stesso, attraverso il suo lavoro specifico e specialistico in quella punta tecnicamente avanzata che era l'ENI anche dopo la morte di Mattei, di inserirsi quasi con spavalderia (mai ostentata) nello 'spazio' dove si trova il potere reale" Pasolini 2022, 46. See also "Poesie mondane", in *Poesia in forma di rosa* (1964): *23 aprile 1962*.

(of being *bourgeois* and therefore representing their fathers' privileges), after the Piazza Fontana state massacre in 1969 Pasolini publicly engaged in support of the youth movements. In his poem *Patmos* he accused state power, represented by the then President of the Italian Republic, the socialist Giuseppe Saragat, declaring his solidarity with the extra-parliamentary groups of the radical left, *Potere Operaio* among them.[29] Moreover, between 1970 and 1972, Pasolini supported and financed the radical left group *Lotta Continua*, and created the documentary *12 dicembre*, filmed between December 12th 1970 and June 1971 and co-directed with Giovanni Bonfanti and Goffredo Fofi.

6 Towards a conclusion: the death of Giangiacomo Feltrinelli as a climax

I would like to conclude by referring to Note 60, and the death of Giangiacomo Feltrinelli (1926–1972) as it is represented by Pasolini in *Petrolio*:

> Italy appeared to be in reality the Arab East. It was only the sixteenth or seventeenth of March 1972, but the spring was so advanced that it already seemed midsummer. The hills <...> of the Syrian desert or the bare Lebanese slopes looked like the pale backdrop of an almost Nordic landscape, familiar to French or German crusaders, compared with the savage light that invaded Italy; and in fact central Italy, not just Naples or Sicily. Carlo had landed in Milan and had traveled to Rome by car. In Milan, it's true, the weather was gray, although in the car it was hot enough to sweat. But here the 'East' assumed other forms; a few days before, there had been a battle between extraparliamentary groups and the police (while the Fascists had calmly held their meeting, I believe, with Birindelli and Almirante). The extraparliamentary groups had organized what would later be considered the first real clash of 'urban guerrilla warfare' in Italy; everything that had preceded it was casual and dilettantish. The youths of Communist Struggle were well armed and organized, almost like a little army, etc. Milan still showed the signs of that clash; and the smoke of the tear-gas bombs, of the bombs, did not yet seem to have dissipated. Then there had been the news of the death of Feltrinelli: the image of the pylon at the foot of which Feltrinelli had died overwhelmed whatever other real images the continuation of life immediately began to offer as a comforting alternative (succeeding / and it would succeed / in the end). But on the day of Carlo's return from / Syria / none of the details of Feltrinelli's death were known yet; it was known only that the dead man was he. And there had been the hasty statement signed by a group of intellectuals declaring that he had been assassinated by the Fascists — or rather, probably, by an organization that was

---

29 Pasolini, *Patmos*, first published in *Nuovi argomenti* no. 16, October–December 1969, then in Pasolini 1971.

not Italian; that is, the CIA — in order to create a climate favorable to the right in the coming elections ... Thus it was the death of Feltrinelli that gave Italy an Oriental, almost Palestinian look, in actions, things, bodies, aspects of life, the air; but at the same time threw on it a new and crazy light: a newness that Carlo at once felt unable to resist, was overcome by.[30] (196–197)

In his reading of the novel, Antonio Negri considered Note 60 as the pivotal link to contemporary times and the years in which Pasolini was writing. With Feltrinelli's death, the events narrated accelerate the beginning of another era, and the 1970s become the topic of *Petrolio*:

> Thus, we get to the contemporary ... we get to March 16–17, '72. Milan. It is the first true urban guerrilla clash, following the death of Feltrinelli under the big pylon of electrical light. And it is this access to the 1970s that from now on begins to characterize the rest of the tale.[31] (my translation)

---

30 L'Oriente arabo pareva in realtà essere l'Italia. Non era che il sedici o diciassette marzo 1972, ma la primavera era così avanzata che pareva già piena estate. Le gobbe V del deserto siriano o le spelacchiate collinette libanesi, parevano pallidi fondali di un paesaggio quasi nordico, famigliari a crociati francesi o tedeschi, in confronto alla luce pazzesca che invadeva l'Italia; e l'Italia centrale, poi, neanche Napoli o la Sicilia. Carlo era disceso a Milano, e aveva raggiunto Roma in macchina. A Milano, è vero, il tempo era grigio, per quanto caldo, da sudare dentro la macchina. Ma lì l'"oriente" aveva altre forme; pochi giorni prima c'era stata battaglia tra i gruppi extraparlamentari e la polizia (mentre i fascisti avevano tranquillamente tenuto il loro comizio, credo, con Birindelli e Almirante). I gruppi extraparlamentari avevano organizzato quello che sarebbe stato poi considerato il primo vero e proprio scontro di 'guerriglia urbana' in Italia: tutto ciò che l'aveva preceduto era casuale e dilettantesco. I giovani di 'Lotta Comunista' erano tecnicamente armati e organizzati quasi come un piccolo esercito ecc. Milano conservava ancora i segni di quello scontro; e il fumo delle bombe lacrimogene, dei candelotti pareva non essersi ancora diradato. Poi c'era stata la notizia della morte di Feltrinelli: l'immagine del traliccio ai piedi del quale Feltrinelli era morto divorava qualsiasi altra immagine reale che il continuare della vita cominciava subito a offrire come alternativa consolatoria (e ci sarebbe riuscito, a alla fine). Ma il giorno del ritorno di Carlo dalla /Siria/, ancora non si sapeva nulla dei particolari della morte di Feltrinelli: si sapeva solo che il morto era lui. E c'era stato il precipitoso comunicato firmato da un gruppo di intellettuali in cui si dichiarava che egli era stato assassinato dai fascisti — o meglio, probabilmente, da un'organizzazione non italiana, cioè la CIA — per creare un ambiente favorevole alla destra nelle imminenti elezioni ... Dunque era la morte di Feltrinelli che dava all'Italia un'aria orientale, quasi palestinese, nei fatti, nelle cose, nei corpi, negli aspetti della vita, nell'aria; ma nel tempo stesso vi gettava una luce di pazzesca novità: novità a cui Carlo sentì subito di non poter resistere, di essere sconfitto" (Pasolini 2022, Appunto 60, 279–280).

31 Antonio Negri, 2011. Full lecture available at: http://ici.berlin/events/antonio-negri, Lecture II, 2.40–5.34 [accessed on 12/08/2023]: "E così si giunge alla contemporaneità ... si giunge al 16-17 marzo '72. Milano. Il primo vero e proprio scontro di guerriglia urbana, si accompagna alla morte

The death of Feltrinelli is the climax representing a final shift into a new phase in the history of Italian workers' struggles and their repression as represented in *Petrolio*: "a new and crazy light: a newness that Carlo at once felt unable to resist, was overcome by" (197).

In the early 1970s, Feltrinelli and his Gruppi d'Azione Partigiana (GAP) guerrilla fighters feared a neo-fascist coup after Piazza Fontana, and they were directly calling for a new Italian armed Resistance since the Civil War of 1943–1945 was considered incomplete, as Max Henninger writes:

> One of the insurrectionary organizations that emerged after Piazza Fontana, the Gruppi d'Azione Partigiana (GAP), lost its leader, Gian Giacomo Feltrinelli, that spring. Feltrinelli's mangled body was found on 15 March 1972; he had died while assembling explosives in the countryside. Feltrinelli had been an outspoken advocate of "lotta armata." Founder of an archive on the Italian labor movement and one of the country's most acclaimed publishers, he had been personally familiar not only with Fidel Castro and internationally known theorists of guerrilla warfare such as Regis Debray, but also with a number of German and Italian militants, including members of the Red Army Faction and Red Brigades cofounders Curcio and Franceschini. Unlike the Red Brigades, the GAP operated on the assumption that a right-wing coup was imminent, and that the appropriate strategy for combating the state was that of a rural (rather than an urban) guerrilla. The name of Feltrinelli's group was intended to evoke what he perceived to have been the "guerra rivoluzionaria" of the partisans. The GAP dissolved following Feltrinelli's death.[32]

In *Petrolio*, Carlo's reaction to the news of the death of Feltrinelli is indicative of his conformism and pragmatism and can be related to the final implications of the end of an era: an historic cycle had been interrupted, the crisis of Humanism will inaugurate the beginning of Postmodernism:[33]

> Carlo's own immediate interpretation was that Feltrinelli had been murdered alone, playing the guerrilla; that if he had been poor or simply some petit bourgeois, he would already have been in a clinic, or even an asylum, for some years; that, in short, he was a

---

di Feltrinelli sotto il grande traliccio della luce elettrica. Ed è questo ingresso negli anni '70 che comincia a caratterizzare di qui il resto del racconto".

32 Max Henninger 2006, 629–648, 633. On Gian Giacomo Feltrinelli, and the immediate consequences of his death, see the opening sequences of the 1972 movie *Slap the Monster on Page One* (*Sbatti il mostro in prima pagina*), by Marco Bellocchio. Blending newly shot sequences with footage of real demonstrations in Milan, vindicating Feltrinelli (protesters were screaming "Compagno Feltrinelli sarai vendicato!"), the film opens with a bang as a right-wing newspaper's headquarters are attacked by anarchists.

33 See Vattimo 1985, 39–56: "La crisi dell'umanesimo ... si risolve probabilmente in una 'cura di dimagrimento' del soggetto ... che dissolve la sua presenza-assenza nei reticoli di una società trasformata sempre di più in un sensibilissimo organismo di comunicazione" (55).

madman who had met the end of an idiot; there was no contempt in this interpretation; in fact, there was a certain compassion — certainly there was no pity.[34] (197)

7 To conclude: *Petrolio*, salvific mockery and "the preamble to a testament"

The final note in all editions of *Petrolio* is the last of the incomplete novel: Note 133, *Mockery (from the "Plan")*. Here, a quote from Guido Gozzano's poem *Un'altra risorta*[35] has the uncanny effect of eliminating the very idea of the past and all possible regrets. By quoting these lines, Pasolini is reaffirming a narrative pattern that exalts the possibility of using salvific mockery as the freest and most liberating act of hermeneutics and mystical comprehension of reality:

> I am happy. My life is so much
> the same as my dream: a dream that doesn't vary:
> to live in a villa, solitary,
> without the past, without regret:
> to belong, to meditate ... I sing
> of exile, of renunciation that is voluntary.[36] (648)

---

34 "Carlo aveva interpretato subito in cuor suo che Feltrinelli si era ammazzato da solo, facendo il guerrigliero; che se egli fosse stato povero, o semplicemente un piccolo borghese qualunque sarebbe finito in una clinica, o addirittura in un manicomio già da qualche anno, e che in definitiva era un matto che aveva fatto la fine di un idiota; non c'era disprezzo, in questa sua interpretazione, c'era anzi una certa compassione — ma non c'era certamente pietà" (Pasolini 2022, 280).

35 On Guido Gozzano's presence and relevance in *Petrolio*, see Liszka-Drążkiewicz 2017, 209–218, 213: "L'ultima citazione si trova nell'ultimo Appunto 133, intitolato *L'irrisione* e costituisce un tipo di chiusura di questo romanzo che altrimenti non finisce. Si tratta dei versi di *Un'altra risorta*: ... Le ultime parole dell'Appunto 133 sembrano pronunciate insieme dal poeta-Gozzano, dal protagonista di *Petrolio* e dal poeta-Pasolini ...".

36 Guido Gozzano's poem *Un'altra risorta*, quoted in Appunto 133, *L'irrisione (Dal "Progetto")*:

> Sono felice. La mia vita è tanto
> Pari al mio sogno: il sogno che non varia:
> vivere in una villa solitaria,
> senza passato più, senza rimpianto:
> appartenersi, meditare ... Canto
> l'esilio e la rinuncia volontaria. (648)

As Pasolini wrote in a letter to Alberto Moravia (1907–1990) asking him to read his manuscript and provide some advice on the novel, the early 1970s were for him the years of detachment and disillusion, and yet *Petrolio* is defined here as a testimony, "the preamble to a testament":

> I'm sending you this manuscript so that you can give me some advice ... This novel is not very useful anymore in my life (as are the novels or poems that were written in youth), it is not an announcement, hey, men! I exist, but the preamble to a testament, testimony of the little knowledge that one has accumulated, and is completely different from what one expected \imagined\![37]

In the end, after all the true historical facts, abstract allegories and fictional tales narrated and represented in *Petrolio*, Pasolini isolated "o beata solitudo, o sola beatitudo"[38] — exile, solitude, meditation, and renunciation — as the only possible dimension available to Carlo, his protagonist, to finally grasp the lessons of his previous personal involvement in "the management of this world" (462). Meanwhile, as the Italians would say, *bontà sua*: with Angelo Guglielmi's approval, *Petrolio* is Pasolini's "great world-novel destined to project him into the future", a complex fragmentary literary text that belongs to unfinished history and its uninterrupted flux of events.

Bibliography

Biscione, Francesco Maria (ed.) (1993), *Il memoriale di Aldo Moro rinvenuto in Via Monte Nevoso a Milano*, Roma.
Gnoli, Antonio (May 5th, 2010), "Angelo Guglielmi: 'L'errore del gruppo 63? Elogiare solo i libri illeggibili'", *La Repubblica*.
Harrison, S.J. (1999), *Oxford Readings in the Roman Novel*, Oxford.
Henninger, Max (2006), "The Postponed Revolution: Reading Italian Insurrectionary Leftism as Generational Conflict", *Italica* 83, 3/4.

---

[37] See Pier Paolo Pasolini's letter to Alberto Moravia, in Pasolini 2022, 8–9: "Caro Alberto, ti mando questo manoscritto perché tu mi dia un consiglio ... Questo romanzo non serve più molto alla mia vita (come sono i romanzi o le poesie che si scrivono da giovani) ... ma il preambolo di un testamento, la testimonianza di quel poco di sapere che uno ha accumulato, ed è completamente diverso da quello che uno si immaginava". See also Walter Siti's *Postfazione*, ibid, 778: "Il finale di *Petrolio* si può leggere come controcanto nichilista alle richieste del 'processo alla DC' che Pasolini stesso invocava dagli editoriali del 'Corriere della Sera'".
[38] The Latin expression attributed to Saint Bernard, see https://www.treccani.it/vocabolario/ricerca/solitudo [accessed on 12/08/2023].

Liszka-Drążkiewicz, Agnieszka (2017), "Il poeta del *pastiche*. Echi gozzaniani in *Petrolio* di Pier Paolo Pasolini", *Annales Universitatis Paedagogicae Cracoviensis* 9.3, 209–218.
Moro, Aldo (1993), "La DC nel periodo della strategia della tensione", in: Francesco Maria Biscione, 119–124.
Negri, Antonio (2011), "Su *Petrolio* di Pier Paolo Pasolini", ICI Berlin, http://ici.berlin/events/antonio-negri [accessed on 12/08/2023].
Pasolini, Pier Paolo (1964), "Vittoria", in: *Poesie in forma di rosa*, Milano.
Pasolini, Pier Paolo (1964), Poesie mondane, in: *Poesie in forma di rosa*, Milano.
Pasolini, Pier Paolo (1971), *Trasumanar e organizzar*, Milano.
Pasolini, Pier Paolo (November 1975), *Scritti corsari*, Milano.
Pasolini, Pier Paolo (May 1975), "Saluto e augurio", in: *La nuova gioventù*, Torino.
Pasolini, Pier Paolo/Careri, Maria Grazia/Chiarcossi, Graziella/Roncaglia, Aurelio (eds.) (1992), *Petrolio*, Torino.
Pasolini, Pier Paolo (1993), "Patmos", in: Graziella Chiarcossi/Walter Siti (eds.), *Bestemmia: Tutte le poesie*, Milano.
Pasolini, Pier Paolo (1997), *Petrolio*, translated by Ann Goldstein, New York.
Pasolini, Pier Paolo (1999), *Saggi sulla politica e sulla società*, Milano.
Pasolini, Pier Paolo (2005), "The Written Language of Reality", in: Luise K. Barnett (ed.), *Heretical Empiricism*, Washington, DC.
Pasolini, Pier Paolo (2010), "Victory", in: Jack Hirshman (ed., transl.), *Danger: A Pasolini Anthology*, San Francisco.
Pasolini, Pier Paolo/Siti, Maria Careri/Siti, Walter (eds.) (2022), *Petrolio*, Milano.
Pasolini, Pier Paolo, (2014), "Saluto e augurio / Goodbye and Best Wishes", in: Stephen Sartarelli (ed.), *The Selected Poetry of Pier Paolo Pasolini: A Bilingual Edition*, Chicago.
Petacco, Arrigo (2020), *A Tragedy Revealed: The Story of Italians from Istria, Dalmatia, and Venezia Giulia, 1943–1956*, Toronto.
Sartarelli, Stephen (2014) (ed.), *Pasolini, Pier Paolo. The Selected Poetry of Pier Paolo Pasolini: A Bilingual Edition*, Chicago.
Vattimo, Gianni (1985), *La fine della modernità*, Milano.

Part V: **Searching for Completion**

Andrew Zissos
The Missing Conclusion to Valerius Flaccus' *Argonautica*

Abstract: This paper surveys the development of critical thinking on the missing conclusion to the *Argonautica* of Valerius Flaccus. The question of how the completed poem might have concluded is broken down into three separate but related questions: (i) how much of the poem is missing? (ii) at what point in the myth of Jason and Medea would it have concluded? (iii) what additional episodes would have been included? The paper evaluates the full spectrum of scholarly theories, as well as charting their evolution from the sixteenth century to the present day; it also establishes a set of analytical principles that offer guidance in assessing the plausibility of the various critical positions.

1 Introduction

The *Argonautica* of Valerius Flaccus breaks off in tantalizing fashion after line 467 of its eighth book. The narrative situation is complex and shot through with tension. Stuck on the island of Peuce in the Danube delta, and with a hostile Colchian armada blocking their path upstream, the Argonauts have been secretly urging Jason to surrender Medea to avoid coming to blows with a numerically superior foe (8.385–399). Although he and Medea have just enacted a wedding ceremony, Jason is inclined to do as his comrades suggest (8.400–407). But Medea, ever acute in moments of peril, has got wind of this scheme and bitterly confronts her new spouse over his faithlessness (8.415–444). In these fraught circumstances, Jason begins to respond to Medea's reproaches (8.463a–467):

> *Maestus at ille minis et mota Colchidos ira*
> *haeret et hinc praesens pudor, hinc decreta suorum*
> *dura premunt. utcumque tamen mulcere gementem*
> *temptat et ipse gemens et †temperat† dictis:*
> *'mene aliquid meruisse putas, me talia velle?*

Perturbed by the threats and passionate anger of the Colchian, he hesitates; on this side burning shame, on that the stern counsels of his men press upon him. Yet he tries, howsoever he can, to soothe the groaning woman, groaning himself all the while, and calms her anger with his words: 'Do you think that I have merited anything like this, that such is my wish?'

This is evidently not where Valerius' poem was meant to end. From the time of the rediscovery of Valerius' text in the early fifteenth century through to the present day, critics have been drawn to speculate on how it might have concluded. Sustained, text-driven analyses emerge with Peters and Summers at the end of the nineteenth century and have continued through to the present day.[1]

The most widely accepted explanation for the poem's incompleteness is that the poet died before completing it. Both internal and external evidence make this more likely than the alternative, namely, that the poem was completed but lost its conclusion at some stage of its transmission. I have addressed this issue elsewhere, and need not relitigate it, as it is inessential to the matter at hand.[2] What I am concerned with here is how the completed poem would have concluded. This can be broken down into three separate but related questions: (i) how much of the poem is missing? (ii) at what point in the myth of Jason and Medea would it have concluded? (iii) what additional episodes would have been included? In what follows I undertake a systematic examination of these questions, which have continued to vex and fascinate readers of Valerius' epic over a span of centuries. My purpose is to survey and evaluate the full spectrum of scholarly theories, as well as chart their development; I also want to establish a set of analytical principles that will provide guidance in assessing the plausibility of the various critical positions.

2 Analytical foundations

Scholars choosing to speculate on Valerius' missing conclusion find themselves in an unusually strong position: the principal events of the mythic narrative were well established long before the Flavian Age, and Valerius' self-conscious poetics often involve him signaling his mediating role as a selector of variants within a rich literary tradition.[3] What has sometimes been lacking in critical discussions is methodological clarity; it will thus be helpful to begin with the explicit identification of a set of analytical principles that can be appealed to in critical speculation on Valerius' missing conclusion.

---

[1] Peters 1890, 33–39; Summers 1894, 2–7.
[2] Zissos 2008, xxvi–xxvii.
[3] Zissos 1999.

2.1 Intended length and narrative terminus

All else being equal, we should expect intended length and narrative terminus to be in a roughly proportional relationship. The rule of thumb will be: the later the posited narrative terminus, the greater the number of books needed to reach it. To establish an initial orientation, let us consider the three main theories of length: eight, ten and twelve books (§ 3) in relation to the most 'natural' and intertextually authorized of the possible narrative termini (§ 4), the Argonauts' *nostos* (homecoming). We would expect an eight-book total to align more readily with a pre-*nostos* termination; whereas a ten- or twelve-book total would align more readily with a *nostos* or post-*nostos* termination.

A helpful point of reference is provided by the sixteenth-century editor Giovan Battista Pio, who wrote a two-book conclusion to Valerius' incomplete epic in Latin hexameters, which he appended to his Bolognese edition of 1519. Whatever its flaws, this 'continuation' amounts to the first major theoretical intervention regarding the poem's missing conclusion. After extending Valerius' unfinished eighth book from 467 to 580 lines, Pio added a ninth and a tenth of 520 and 790 lines respectively. Pio's supplementary text draws heavily — and at times incongruously — upon Apollonius Rhodius' *Argonautica*, of which it is often little more than a Latin translation, and concludes at precisely the same point, with the Argonauts making landfall in Greece.[4]

The expectation of proportionality is not, of course, a hard-and-fast law: we are dealing with probabilities rather than certainties. The intrinsically episodic nature of a travel narrative would have afforded scope to add or subtract episodes, as well as to dilate or abridge them. So, for example, narrative streamlining could be employed to have an eight-book total see the Argonauts home, but this would have required a *tour de force* of compression.[5] At the other end of the spectrum, advocates of a twelve-book total will need to posit an elaborate and extended homeward journey if they also advocate a pre-*nostos* or even a *nostos* termination.

---

[4] On Pio's supplement and its incompatibility with aspects of Valerius' storyline, see Zissos 2014. Its considerable influence derives in part from its inclusion in many subsequent editions of Valerius Flaccus through the nineteenth century; the most recent critic to adduce it as evidence for Valerius' missing conclusion is Soubiran 2002, 33.

[5] As proposed by Shey 1968, 236–249: see § 5.3.

2.2 Foreshadowing and anticipation

Valerius' poem contains an extraordinary number of anticipations of future events (prolepses), particularly regarding the careers of Jason and Medea.[6] All these anticipations accord with the mainstream literary tradition. In broad terms, Valerius might be said to anticipate a cataclysmic 'Euripidean' finale for the ill-starred couple, including Medea's infanticide in Corinth and her airborne escape from that city.[7] It does not necessarily follow, of course, that Valerius meant to narrate these post-Argonautic developments in the missing portion of his epic. As Moore pointed out more than a century ago, a key methodological difficulty is distinguishing between internal and external prolepses in an unfinished work.[8] In this regard the completed *Argonautica* of Apollonius Rhodius, Valerius' chief narrative model (§ 2.3), provides helpful guidance. That the Hellenistic poet likewise anticipated the tragic fallout in Corinth but concluded his narrative with the much earlier completion of the Argonauts' homebound voyage suggests that such anticipations in Valerius' narrative were likewise meant to be external prolepses; but we cannot be certain, and some scholars have proposed the infanticide at Corinth as the intended narrative terminus of Valerius' epic (§ 4.2). Another key instance of foreshadowing in the Flavian *Argonautica* is the anticipation of the death of Medea's brother Absyrtus: narrative developments towards the end of Valerius' text and the fact that the death was a central episode in Apollonius Rhodius' final book make it virtually certain that Valerius meant this to be an instance of internal prolepsis. Trying to glean how Absyrtus' death would have played out in Valerius' narrative is a fundamental issue around which debate over the missing conclusion continues to swirl (§ 6.1).

2.3 Influence of Apollonius Rhodius

It has long been recognized that Valerius' chief narrative model is Apollonius Rhodius' *Argonautica*. Critics have habitually tagged the earlier epic with designa-

---

[6] Cf. Moore 1921, 162: "Valerius cannot resist the temptation to introduce prophecies as to the fate of individual heroes."
[7] These anticipations begin at 1.224–226 and extend to the unpropitious wedding omens interpreted by Mopsus at 8.247–251; they are especially prominent in the poem's second half: see Zissos 2008, xxx–xxxi.
[8] Moore 1921, 163; cf. Hershkowitz 1998, 24.

tions like 'the Greek original' or 'the Greek exemplar'.[9] It is certainly true that, on the level of plot, the Flavian epic is systematically indebted to its Hellenistic predecessor: the basic storyline includes most of Apollonius' material and follows the same order of events.[10] That said, the Flavian poet sometimes opts to depart from his Hellenistic exemplar in significant ways.[11] There are several noteworthy additions to and excisions from Apollonius' storyline.[12] Conspicuous among Valerius' early innovations vis-à-vis Apollonius are the compelled suicide of Jason's parents Aeson and Alcimede (1.730–851) and the rescue of Hesione by Hercules during a stopover at Troy (2.451–578); in the later books, the Colchian civil war, in which Jason and his companions fight on Aeetes' side (6.1–426, 507–760), has no precedent in Apollonius. On the other side of the ledger, the Apollonian episode of the Stymphalian Birds (Ap. Rhod. 2.1030–1089) is omitted by Valerius. An overarching thematic difference is that Valerius adheres to the Roman poetic tradition in making Argo the world's first ship, whereas Apollonius merely makes the vessel an exceptional embodiment of existing technology.[13]

Valerius' tendency systematically to reproduce Apollonius' storyline in the poem as extant needs to be taken into account in any speculation on the missing conclusion. The default assumption should be that Valerius intended to follow the plot of the Hellenistic *Argonautica*, but critics must remain alert to signs in the extant text of potential divergences in the missing conclusion. It has, moreover, long been recognized by scholars that the second half as a whole shows a pattern of increasing divergence from Apollonius' version. This is particularly true for what we have of Valerius' eighth book: there is a noteworthy acceleration of events (§ 4.3), along with indications of narrative compression,

---

9 'Original': Summers 1894; 'exemplar': Vessey 1982; as Peters 1890, 33 succinctly observes, "*satis notum est Valerium carminis sui materiam hausisse ex Apollonii Rhodii Argonauticon poemate.*"
10 Zissos 2008, xxv.
11 Moore 1921, 160.
12 A number of Valerius' more significant alterations to Apollonius' storyline draw upon the version of Dionysius Scytobrachion's *Argonautae*, preserved at Diod. 4.40–55 (= *FGrHist* 32F14): see conveniently Zissos 2008, xxv–xxvi.
13 Among the various knock-on effects, this obligates the elimination of the Argonauts' rescue of the Greece-bound sons of Phrixus, who had been shipwrecked *en route* (Ap. Rhod. 2.1090–1237). Elsewhere the tension between Apollonius' storyline and the first-ship tradition sometimes gives rise to narrative incongruities, as with the sudden materialization of a sizeable Colchian fleet that gives pursuit to the Argonauts on the return voyage (8.259–263), which Valerius explains and 'justifies' with an arch rhetorical question at 8.287–290.

after the Argonauts depart from Colchis.[14] This trend of increasing independence from Apollonius is obviously pertinent to any assessment of how the Flavian epic might have ended.

2.4 'Episodic foreclosure' and 'preemptive reallocation'

Given the formative influence of the Hellenistic *Argonautica* upon Valerius' storyline, a key analytical objective must be to identify in Valerius' text indications of potential deviation in the missing portion of his poem. What I am calling 'episodic foreclosure' is an intertextual knock-on effect arising from plot alterations made by Valerius in the extant text that render implausible the inclusion of a later episode from the Hellenistic exemplar. For the most part this principle relies upon narrative logic; it may also appeal to notions of poetic or narrative economy, that is, a guiding compositional aesthetic that seeks to avoid repetition on the macro level.

A noteworthy example of episodic foreclosure concerns Valerius' inclusion of a 'surrogate Circe' episode at 7.210–406, in which the goddess Venus assumes the form of Medea's aunt Circe and pays her 'niece' a visit in Colchis with the aim of stoking her erotic passion for Jason. This inventive textual sequence, which corresponds to nothing in the Hellenistic *Argonautica*, almost certainly rules out Valerius' later inclusion, in the missing portion of his epic, of the Apollonian episode in which Jason and Medea visit Circe on her island off the coast of Italy (Ap. Rhod. 4.659–752) — which, as various critics have pointed out, would generate discursive mismatches and thematic redundancy.[15] The principle of episodic foreclosure can also be applied negatively, as when Valerius omits the Apollonian sequence in which the Colchian fleet dispatched in pursuit of the Argonauts breaks into two contingents which follow different paths (Ap. Rhod. 4.303–306). The fact that the Valerian account entirely omits Apollonius' second contingent, which catches up with the Argonauts and confronts them on Phaeacia, is a strong indication that the Flavian poet meant to omit Apollonius' Phaeacian episode in its entirety.[16]

A second intertextual phenomenon, 'preemptive reallocation', involves a more subtle and less definitive exclusionary effect, touching on secondary or

---

[14] Jachman 1935, 239–240; Hershkowitz 1998, 207–208; cf. Pellucci 2012, v: "man mano che il racconto procede, la divergenza tra i due testi si fa sempre più accentuata."
[15] Peters 1890, 36–37; Summers 1894, 5; Shey 1968, 243–244; Nesselrath 1998, 350–351. See § 6.2 for further discussion of this instance of episodic foreclosure.
[16] Nesselrath 1998, 350–351.

non-essential features of an Apollonian episode that bear high poetic or mythographic value. In cases of episodic elision and other significant divergences from Apollonius Rhodius' storyline, Valerius tends to reallocate iconic elements from the eliminated Apollonian episode or rejected variant to a different narrative setting. The presence in Valerius' *Argonautica* of Apollonian elements estranged from their original narrative context will thus often signal a departure from the Hellenistic model. In cases where the original narrative context is subsequent to the break-off point of Valerius' narrative, this will constitute important evidence for the missing conclusion.

A suggestive example of this phenomenon is constructed around a cloak that Hypsipyle gives to Jason during the Argonauts' sojourn on Lemnos.[17] In the Hellenistic model, this lavish garment, memorably described in a racy ecphrasis, is the principal object used by Medea to lure Absyrtus to his doom (Ap. Rhod. 4.421–434). Valerius twice mentions such a cloak, with the first of the two passages accompanied by an ecphrasis; each passage occurs much earlier in the narrative than its Apollonian counterpart. In the second of the two passages, which unfolds in the aftermath of the deadly calamity on Cyzicus, Jason places the cloak given to him by Hypsipyle on the king's funeral pyre (Val. Fl. 3.340–342). All this amounts to a highly sophisticated instance of preemptive redeployment: in Valerius' account, Hypsipyle's cloak has been redeployed to an earlier point in the narrative; it will, moreover, not be available for the episode of Absyrtus' death because it no longer exists in the storyworld of the Flavian *Argonautica*, having been consumed on a funeral pyre several books earlier. That of course does not make something like Apollonius' version of Absyrtus' death impossible, but the redeployment of such an iconic element from that version is very likely to constitute a metaliterary marker, an indication that Valerius meant to deviate from his Greek model in treating the death of Absyrtus.

2.5 Sources of deviation from Apollonius

Where Valerius departs from Apollonius' storyline, there are three principal possibilities: (i) the innovation has no definitive intertextual basis, but is driven by aesthetic, cultural or scientific factors; (ii) the poet has drawn on a different account of the Argonautic legend; (iii) the poet has drawn on and adapted

---

17 What follows is a *précis* of one of the arguments in Zissos 2017.

material from a non-Argonautic text. Here we are chiefly concerned with the last category.[18]

Valerius' most important *poetic* model is Virgil's *Aeneid*.[19] While broadly following Apollonius' storyline, the Flavian poet might be said to have grafted onto the narrative body of the Greek *Argonautica* the poetic language and thematic concerns of the *Aeneid*. Hershkowitz instructively overstates the case in characterizing Valerius' poem as "an epic trying to be an *Aeneid* but dissimulating as an *Argonautica*."[20] This neat, if somewhat reductive, formulation captures very well the prevailing scholarly view of Valerius' epic, a view that sees it as oscillating between two poles — Apollonian and Virgilian — and constantly negotiating the tensions that arise from these contrasting modes of literary indebtedness.[21] It is thus probable that, as with the existing portion, components of the missing conclusion to Valerius' epic would have been inflected along Virgilian lines — or, to use a popular critical term, would have undergone 'Aeneidization'.

That Homeric epic is a second poetic model of immense importance for Valerius Flaccus is well-established in scholarship, though it remains somewhat undervalued.[22] Homeric influence operates both directly and indirectly through its reception in Apollonius Rhodius' *Argonautica* and Virgil's *Aeneid*. As with the *Aeneid*, Valerius treats both the *Iliad* and the *Odyssey* as vast reservoirs of archetypal scenes and episodes to be reappropriated according to the aesthetic or thematic exigencies of the narrative moment.[23] Such intertextual strategies were already employed, albeit to a lesser degree, in the *Argonautica* of Apollonius Rhodius, which frequently draws upon the *Odyssey*. The most noteworthy feature of Valerius' Homeric program is not that he follows the example of his Hellenistic predecessor in drawing upon the *Odyssey*, but that he adopts a bold and counter-intuitive appropriation of scenes and motifs from the *Iliad*. In terms of the *Argonautica* tradition, indeed, Valerius enacts what might be called a

---

[18] With respect to the first category, it must be borne in mind that Valerius was a poet embedded in a Roman socio-cultural context, writing in Latin for a Roman audience roughly three centuries after his Hellenistic predecessor. Such differences bear heavily, for example, on the vexed question of the return route (§ 5.1). The second category is well represented by the elements of Dionysius Scytobrachion's version of the myth that have found their way into Valerius' account (note 12).
[19] See conveniently Zissos 2008, xxxiv–xxxvi.
[20] Hershkowitz 1998, 271; resistance to the formulation at Zissos 2002, 69–71.
[21] Cf. e.g. Liberman 1997, xlvii–xlix, Nesselrath 1998, 353.
[22] For detailed discussion, see Zissos 2002, 79–96.
[23] Zissos 2002, 87.

'Homeric paradigm shift' in making the *Iliad*, not the *Odyssey*, his chief Homeric model and intertext.

3 Theories of intended length

I turn now to the three issues raised in the Introduction. The question of intended length, expressed as a total number of books, is at present the least controversial of the triad, as a critical consensus has emerged over the last several decades. Three principal hypotheses have been advanced: eight, ten, and twelve books; these will be discussed in the chronological order of their development.

3.1 Ten books

The theory of ten books, first advanced by Giovan Battista Pio in the sixteenth century, has never won widespread and unequivocal support, though it has always found advocates.[24] Supporters of this theory are often consciously or unconsciously indebted to Pio's *supplementum* of Valerius' *Argonautica*, which followed Apollonius' storyline closely, and ran to ten books (§ 2.1). The most recent case for a ten-book total has been made by Soubiran.[25] A predictable relationship to Apollonius' *Argonautica*, Valerius' chief narrative model, underpins his argument, which rests upon the observation that Valerius tends to expansion in his reworking of episodes inherited from the Hellenistic *Argonautica*. He measures a 'coefficient de dilatation' of 20–29.5% in the first seven books of the poem, and so feels justified in assuming a figure of 25% for what remained of the poem. The moment at which Valerius' narrative breaks off corresponds to Ap. Rhod. 4.395; the Hellenistic epic concludes at 4.1781: the missing portion of Valerius' account thus corresponds to 1386 Apollonian verses. Applying the prescribed 'coefficient de dilatation' yields a projected total of 1731 missing verses for Valerius. The average verse total in the completed books is 732: assigning that total to Books 9 and 10 would leave 267 to round out Book 8. Soubiran's arithmetic, then, aligns perfectly with a ten-book total. One difficulty with this analysis is that it depends on the unexamined assumption that Valerius' intended

---

[24] A number of critics, including e.g. Schenkl 1871, iii and Peters 1890, 39 follow Heinsius (note 26) in equivocating between ten and twelve books; the unspecific reference in Hull 1979, 407 to "the remaining books" likewise seems intended to hedge.
[25] Soubiran 1997, 119–123 and 2002, 32–34.

terminus was to have been the same as Apollonius', which is unlikely (§ 4.1). Moreover, if, as seems probable, Valerius meant to continue the trend of *increasing* independence from Apollonius (§ 2.3) then such a 'coefficient de dilatation' would have less pertinence for the missing portion of the poem than for the part we have.

3.2 Twelve books

Heinsius' suggestion of a twelve-book epic, matching the total of the *Aeneid*, and calling to mind Statius' explicit Virgilian affiliation (*Theb.* 12.810–819) held sway until well into the twentieth century.[26] This would sit well with Valerius' tendency toward 'Aeneidization' on the level of episodic composition. A twelve-book total would almost certainly call for significant supplementation of Apollonius' narrative.[27] Hershkowitz is the most recent scholar to advocate provisionally for twelve books, viewing it as a plausible alternative to the scholarly consensus that has emerged in favor of eight.[28]

3.3 Eight books

The critical tide began to turn in 1959, when Schetter extended the principle of Virgilian influence from individual episodes to overall structure in making the case for an eight-book total.[29] In what proved to be a watershed moment in Valerian scholarship, Schetter suggested that the Flavian poet had organized his

---

[26] Heinsius 1680, x actually equivocated slightly, specifying "*duodenis aut, ut minimum, decem*", and others followed his example (note 24). Bährens 1875, iv more unhesitatingly stipulated twelve books; this occasioned a thoughtful critique from Peters 1890, 33–36. An influential English-language advocate of the twelve-book theory was Summers 1894, 6–7, who went on to speculate that Valerius would have devoted most of the concluding four-and-one-half books to the return voyage, and that "the poet meant to bring his heroes into connection with Italy". Twentieth-century advocates of a twelve-book total include Butler 1909, 121; Dimsdale 1915, 447; Moore 1921, 166; and, more guardedly in the wake of Schetter 1959 (discussed below), Vessey 1982, 580.

[27] Cf. Summers 1894, 6: "a mere reproduction of Apollonius' episodes could not, I feel confident, have occupied four books".

[28] Hershkowitz 1998, 9–10.

[29] Endorsements of Schetter's eight-book theory include Frank 1967; Adamietz 1976, 108–113; Shreeves 1978, 52–53; Scaffai 1986, 2374–2375; Liberman 1997, xlvii; Nesselrath 1998, 138; Zissos 2008, xxvii–xxviii.

epic into halves, along Virgilian lines, with the medial proem at 5.217–221 marking the beginning of the second half, corresponding to *Aen.* 7.37–40. At the same time, the eight-book total would signal an affiliation to Apollonius' *Argonautica* in that each pair of books in the Flavian poem would correspond to one in its Hellenistic predecessor. Since Book 8 breaks off at line 467 and none of the earlier books exceeds 850 odd lines, it would follow that fewer than 400 additional verses would likely have completed the opus.[30] This represents a considerable reduction vis-à-vis Apollonius Rhodius, who by one reckoning requires nearly 1400 verses to conclude his epic from the corresponding point in his narrative (§ 3.1).

Though a critical consensus has emerged in favor of Schetter's groundbreaking analysis, it is by no means the case that all critics have been persuaded: Soubiran for one, rejects it out of hand;[31] others have expressed lingering doubts.[32] Hershkowitz cautions that, the prevailing scholarly consensus notwithstanding, the eight-book total remains conjectural, and that many of the structural arguments adduced by Schetter and subsequent scholars could be accommodated by a "false Apollonian closure" at the end of Book 8 followed by a "genuine Virgilian closure" at the end of Book 12.[33]

4 Theories of the intended terminus

The difficulty of identifying an appropriate end point for Valerius' storyline prompted one baffled scholar to speculate that the unfinished state of the *Argonautica* was not due to the poet's untimely death (as discussed above), but because "the problem of how to finish the epic proved too much for the poet."[34] But Valerius' control of his subject matter can hardly be called into question.[35] It will be more fruitful to acknowledge at the outset that the genre of mythological epic manifests a certain equivocation over closure because when it comes to

---

30 Cf. Liberman 1997, xlvii reckoning 250–400 verses; Nesselrath 1998, 138 venturing an upper limit of 400–500 verses.
31 Soubiran 2002, 32, dismissing Schetter's thesis as "inacceptable".
32 Cf. Shreeves 1978, 50–51.
33 Hershkowitz 1998, 9–13; cf. Summers 1894, 6–7, quoted below, note 39.
34 Mendell 1967, 136.
35 See the rich discussion of Feeney 1991, 315–320.

mythic cycles there is always a sequel, always another story to be told.[36] With respect to Valerius' intended terminus, I shall again proceed chronologically following the historical development of scholarship. In broad terms that development manifests a gradual shift in emphasis from the influence of Apollonius' *Argonautica*, Valerius' primary narrative model, to Virgil's *Aeneid*, his principal poetic model.

4.1 *Nostos* completion

That Valerius would have concluded his epic with the homecoming of the Argonauts, that is, with their safe return to Iolcus, was the implicit and unexamined assumption of the overwhelming majority of scholars from the early sixteenth to the late twentieth centuries.[37] It is easy to understand why this should be so. In concluding at this point, Valerius would be keeping faith with his Hellenistic model, whose epic concluded with the Argonauts making landfall in Greece, reported within an *envoi* addressed to the heroes themselves (Ap. Rhod. 4.1778–1781):

> ... ἀλλὰ ἕκηλοι
> γαῖαν Κεκροπίην παρά τ' Αὐλίδα μετρήσαντες
> Εὐβοίης ἔντοσθεν Ὀπούντιά τ' ἄστεα Λοκρῶν
> ἀσπασίως ἀκτὰς Παγασηίδας εἰσαπέβητε.

> ... after calmly passing by the Cecropian land and Aulis within Euboea and the Opuntian town of the Locrians *you gladly set foot on the shores of Pagasae*. (tr. Race, my emphasis)

Apollonius combines two closural themes: the successful completion of the heroic quest, entailing not merely the winning of the Golden Fleece, but also its repatriation to Greece; and the *nostos* or homecoming, which has strong epic resonance and intrinsic closural force. It took some time for scholars to recognize that *nostos* completion would not have brought the same satisfying close to Valerius' storyline: on making landfall in Thessaly, Jason will face the shocking revelation that his family has been exterminated — his parents by compelled suicide, his younger brother by execution — at the behest of the tyrant Pelias. That murderous textual sequence, one of Valerius' more significant early departures from

---

36 Valerius applies this principle through a recurring emphasis on the 'genetic' relationship between the Argonauts' expedition and the Trojan War, in which many sons of Argonauts will participate; see Zissos 2002, 80–84.
37 Its survival into the early twenty-first century is evident in Soubiran 2002.

Apollonius' storyline, occurs at the end of the opening book (1.719–830). By rupturing the emotional 'containment' of Apollonius' centripetal *nostos* plot this interpolated episode all but rules out the possibility that Valerius meant to replicate his predecessor's narrative terminus.

4.2 A point subsequent to *nostos* completion

A terminus subsequent to completion of the voyage, thereby exceeding the narrative span of Apollonius' *Argonautica*, is clearly a more plausible alternative. A frequently suggested possibility, which follows naturally from the previous section, is the death of Jason's malignant uncle Pelias. This would be a fitting conclusion since, in addition to the just-mentioned atrocities, Pelias had initially devised the quest for the Golden Fleece as an indirect death sentence for Jason.[38] The Thessalian tyrant's death is twice anticipated in the poem (1.803–814, 2.4–5), both times with an implication of Jason's involvement. Summers opines that "this [conclusion] alone would justify the introduction of the suicide episode at the end of the first book."[39] This view is seconded by Butler in the early twentieth century and has continued to find supporters, including Hull, who points out that such a finale would have well-suited Valerius' strong thematic interest in tyranny.[40] It is perhaps worth adding that the thematic pattern of *nostos* followed by domestic conflict would give the conclusion an 'Odyssean' shape.

The frequent anticipations of Medea's infanticide at Corinth, the final chapter in the story of her relationship with Jason, point to another possible terminus that has found numerous advocates, reaching back to Maserius in the early sixteenth century and extending into the twentieth.[41] This theory has receded in popularity as the critical support for Schetter's arguments in favor of an eight-

---

38 Val. Fl. 1.31–32 with Zissos 2008, 101–102 *ad loc.*
39 Summers 1894, 6–7, further speculating, in a precocious theory of 'Aeneidization' (§ 2.5) that "Apollodorus says that Medea performed the murder in revenge for Pelias' ill-treatment of her lover's parents, and Valerius may well have wished to close his poem, as Virgil closed his, with an act of retributive justice, in which Jason may have echoed with but slight alteration the words *Pallas te hoc volnere, Pallas / immolate et poenam scelerato ex sanguine sumit.*"
40 Butler 1909, 121; Hull 1979, 407, noting that "Valerius' preoccupation with the power of tyrants and with tragic conceptions of retribution is obvious and he would have perhaps seen [the death of Pelias] as a fitting conclusion to his work."
41 Maserius 1509 ad 1.218–226; Moore 1921, 166; the objection of Adamietz 1976, 110 n. 8 that such anticipations are a standard feature of ancient epic underplays their peculiar intensity in Valerius.

book total has increased (§ 3.3): it is difficult to imagine Valerius reaching such a late point in the myth in anything less than ten books, with twelve favored by most advocates of this termination.[42]

4.3 A point prior to *nostos* completion

In 1998 an important new thesis emerged. In a striking synchronism, two scholars, Hershkowitz and Nesselrath, independently raised in the same year the possibility that, far from extending his narrative to the Argonauts' homecoming or beyond, Valerius' intention might have been to make the imminent death of Absyrtus the final episode of the poem.[43] This was, as far as I am aware, the first time that any scholars had advanced arguments for the possibility that Valerius meant to conclude the poem *before* the Argonauts' completion of the return journey. Whereas a post-*nostos* terminus was proposed no later than the early sixteenth century, an earlier terminus was virtually inconceivable before the later twentieth century, since an important foundation for it was the appearance of Schetter's structural arguments in favor of an eight-book total. For critics accepting the eight-book theory, two obvious possibilities would arise vis-à-vis Apollonius' narrative: (i) compression: extending the narrative at least to completion of the homeward voyage, but streamlining the account, perhaps foregoing episodic elaboration altogether; and (ii) truncation: ending the narrative at some point prior to completion of the homeward journey. The importance of the Hershkowitz/Nesselrath thesis is the conceptual advance from the idea of narrative compression to outright narrative truncation.[44] What they specifically proposed was

---

[42] Moore 1921, 166. But even nineteenth-century critics expressed doubts: see the skeptical assessment of Peters 1890, 35 and n., endorsed by Summers 1894, 7. As Peters rightly points out, the infanticide is not the latest point in Medea's turbulent biography anticipated in the poem; the underlying issue, as already noted, is the difficulty — often the impossibility — of distinguishing between internal and external prolepses in an incomplete work (§ 2.2).
[43] Hershkowitz 1998, 9; Nesselrath 1998.
[44] Pindar provides an example of *both* compression and truncation: as Jason is about to face the dragon guarding the Golden Fleece, the poet rather mischievously states μακρά μοι νεῖσθαι κατ' ἀμαξιτόν· ὥρα / γὰρ συνάπτει καί τινα / οἶμον ἴσαμι βραχύν ('It is too long a way for me to go by the beaten track; for time presses, and I know a shortcut', *Pyth.* 4.246–248) and quickly deals with the acquisition of the Golden Fleece and the return journey, the account of which terminates in Lemnos rather than Thessaly. The closest precursors for the Hershkowitz/Nesselrath truncation thesis are Shey 1968, 236–249, Adamietz 1976, 112 and Liberman 1997, xlix: these critics accommodate the eight-book total by arguing that the remaining narrative would have been skimmed over with little to no additional episodic elaboration. Shey proposed

the 'Turnus-like' death of Absyrtus as the poem's *finale*.⁴⁵ This could mean a scenario in which Jason and Absyrtus heroically engage in single combat to resolve the narrative impasse, with the former ultimately emerging victorious.

A crucial piece of evidence for the Hershkowitz/Nesselrath truncation thesis is Valerius' reordering and acceleration of the two key events in the return journey, namely, the death of Absyrtus and the marriage of Jason and Medea.⁴⁶ The grim future awaiting Jason and Medea, famously recounted in the tragedies of Euripides and Seneca, is predicated on the fact that they marry. Their wedding is a "shared moment of transgression" that sets the stage for their later tragic separation, a traumatic event that is repeatedly anticipated in the Flavian *Argonautica*.⁴⁷ The wedding is, in effect, the one mythological event that Valerius is obliged to report before the narrative ends.⁴⁸ In Apollonius' *Argonautica* Jason and Medea become husband and wife on Phaeacia (Ap. Rhod. 4.1111–1169), long after Absyrtus' murder in the Brygian Islands. In Valerius' reordering, the wedding takes place on the island of Peuce in the Danube delta, with Absyrtus arriving in the vicinity just in time to witness the ceremony from afar (Val. Fl. 8.225–258).⁴⁹ This adjustment in relative chronology is highly suggestive: Valerius has at the very least made it possible for his narrative to conclude with the death of Absyrtus without leaving any mythographic 'loose ends'.

The cumulative evidence for the truncation thesis – and more specifically for the 'Turnus-like' death of Absyrtus bringing the Valerian epic to a Virgilian close – is quite strong. On the level of poetics, it would fit Valerius' broad agenda of raising the epic level of Apollonian content through a specifically Virgilian (and Iliadic) intertextual agenda (§ 2.5). Add to this the degraded closural effect of an Apollonian *nostos*-termination in Valerius' altered storyline (§ 4.1) and the cogent structural arguments in favor of eight books, now the critical consensus

---

that Valerius' Argonauts would have changed course soon after the text breaks off, ultimately repeating the outbound route (§ 5.3) in reverse.
45 Hershkowitz 1998, 9, characterizes it as the "Turnus-like murder of Absyrtus at the hands of Jason (and Medea?)".
46 Cf. Shey 1968, 242 who, though making a somewhat different point, observes that "Valerius is clearly compressing his narrative in order to include an important event which could have been reported in a more leisurely manner" if he were planning to continue by following Apollonius' return itinerary.
47 Scott 2012, 10–11.
48 Cf. Shey 1968, 241–242.
49 The tradition offered a variety of locations for the marriage ceremony between Jason and Medea. These included the banks of the Phasis prior to the return journey, Drepane during the journey, and Greece after the journey. As Pellucchi 2012, xi observes, Valerius' choice of Peuce is otherwise unattested, and may well be an innovation on his part.

(§ 3.3), which would mean that the poem is missing less than 400 additional verses. Be that as it may, it should be recalled that, in contrast to Nesselrath, Hershkowitz does not commit herself to the eight-book total or even to her own truncation thesis; she goes on to entertain the scenario of a twelve-book epic culminating, after a "false Apollonian closure" at the end of Book 8, in a "genuine Virgilian closure" at the end of Book 12.[50] Hershkowitz' ambivalence has no doubt played a role in the muted critical response to the truncation thesis.[51]

5 Theories of the return itinerary

The question of the Argonauts' return journey cannot be left unaddressed, as it bears on both the length and content of Valerius' missing conclusion. If Valerius intended to chronicle the Argonauts' return to Greece in some manner, the literary tradition had bequeathed a broad range of options. The chief possibilities will be examined below.[52]

5.1 Apollonius' return route

As always, we begin with the default theory that Valerius would have faithfully followed his Hellenistic exemplar with respect to the return itinerary. Apollonius concludes his epic with an extended account of the Argonauts' torturous return voyage, an itinerary shaped in large part by divine anger over the deceitful murder of Absyrtus (§ 6.2). In this account the Greek heroes traverse the Black Sea to the Danube delta and then sail up the Danube to the Adriatic, from which they pass to the Po, then the Rhone, and then enter the Mediterranean to the west of Italy. After a visit to Circe's island, where Medea and Jason are ritually purified for the murder of Absyrtus, a storm drives Argo southward to the Syrtes, where the vessel finds itself grounded after the storm waters recede. The Argonauts then hoist the vessel onto their shoulders and carry it overland to the Tritonian Lake, whence Triton directs them to the sea and they resume their

---

50 As discussed above, § 3.3.
51 Pelluchi 2012, xvii voices agreement with the Hershkowitz/Nesselrath thesis; Fucecchi 2014, 131–133 (quoted below, note 70) declares Valerius' pending narrative developments unforeseeable, without referring to either Hershkowitz or Nesselrath.
52 Soubiran 2002, 32–36 provides a more comprehensive overview, including his own preference for a Danube-Rhine return route.

homeward journey. After a brief stopover on Crete, where Medea slays the bronze giant Talos, the Argonauts finally reach the Greek mainland, and the narrative concludes with a hymnic *envoi* as they make landfall (§ 4.1).

Apollonius' homeward route was an innovation within the tradition: it added interest while facilitating a series of 'Odyssean' replays. It is unsurprising that scholars long assumed that Valerius would have followed his Hellenistic exemplar as to the return itinerary, for his Argonauts, after traversing the Black Sea, commit themselves to the second leg of the Apollonian route. It is the helmsman Erginus who initially advocates making for the Danube delta (8.185–191):

> *haud procul hinc ingens Scythici ruit exitus Histri,*
>
> ...
>
> *illius adversi nunc ora petamus et undam*
> *quae latus in laevum Ponti cadit, inde sequemur*
> *ipsius amnis iter donec nos flumine certo*
> *perferat inque aliud reddat mare.*
>
> Not far from here is the vast outlet of Scythian Hister ... Let us seek its mouth, entering the stream that empties into the left side of Pontus; then we shall follow the river's course, while it bears us onwards in its steady flow-until it delivers us to another sea.

Valerius' intention appears straightforward enough, all the more so given that the text breaks off with the Argonauts at the mouth of the Danube (Hister). But as critics have long recognized, the next leg of Apollonius' itinerary would have placed the Flavian poet in a position of geographical embarrassment. The problem, simply put, is that this route is impossible: the Danube could not deliver the Argonauts unto *aliud mare* (8.191), which is to say the Adriatic Sea. The misconception that the Danube possessed such a branch may have been prevalent among Hellenistic geographers;[53] it could scarcely have passed muster in Valerius' day. In the centuries that separate the two poets this cartographic misapprehension had been rectified — and even debunked within the specific context of the Argonautic myth by Diodorus Siculus (4.56.7–8).[54] Peters was among the earliest modern critics to voice doubts as to whether a Roman audience of Valerius' day could have accepted the geographically impossible route reported by Apollonius; a number of subsequent critics have concurred.[55] Others, though, have cited Valerius' contemporary Pliny the Elder who, while dismissing the possibility that the Argo had come down any river into the Adriatic,

---

[53] Preston 1803, 261.
[54] The geographer Strabo likewise rejected this route (1.3.15).
[55] Peters 1890, 37–39; echoed by e.g. Shey 1968, 236; Neseelrath 1998, 351.

reconciled that tradition with the current state of geographical knowledge by proposing that the Argonauts had in fact carried the vessel over the Alps (*HN* 3.127–128).⁵⁶ It is not inconceivable that Valerius would have adopted the ingenious 'solution' of his renowned contemporary, particularly as there was a precedent for an Argonautic portage in Apollonius, whose heroes carried the vessel in Libya to deliver from the Syrtes to Lake Triton (Ap. Rhod. 4.1381–1392).⁵⁷

If instead of adopting Pliny's solution, Valerius meant to avoid Apollonius' problematic geography altogether, two revisionary possibilities would have been open to him: adjusting the incipient route (§ 5.2) or abandoning it altogether (§ 5.3). Both possibilities are facilitated by Valerius' relocation of the wedding of Jason and Medea, which in Apollonius takes place much later on at Phaeacia, to Peuce (§ 4.3), while very probably opting to have Absyrtus perish in the same place (§ 6.1), thereby dispatching the two essential events in his predecessor's later narrative well ahead of schedule.

5.2 Return via the Don and the North Sea

If Valerius meant to emend Apollonius' route, an exotic solution was ready to hand. This was to have the Argonauts follow the Don (Tanais) to the Baltic, then sail southward along the European coast through the North Sea past Britain and Gaul and finally reenter the Mediterranean via the Pillars of Hercules. Ample scope for additional episodes would thereby be afforded; at the same time, once the Argonauts had reentered the Mediterranean, Valerius would be in a position to include any or all of Apollonius' corresponding return-voyage episodes, while adding new episodes as he saw fit.⁵⁸ There was even a precedent for this exotic route: Diodorus Siculus (4.56.3–4) credits it to the third-century BCE historian Timaeus of Tauromenion; it would also be the chosen return itinerary of the later *Orphic Argonautica*. Summers was the first to point out the advantages this route would have offered Valerius, and his arguments have won the approval of

---

56 Summers 1894, 5; Shreeves 1978, 55; Soubiran 2002, 34.
57 If Valerius' intention were to exclude his predecessor's Libyan digression (§ 6.4), such a redeployment of the portage motif would constitute a noteworthy instance of 'preemptive reallocation'.
58 Soubiran 2002, 35 provides a list of Apollonius' episodes that he deems Valerius more or less likely to have been minded to include once the Argonauts re-entered the Mediterranean.

a number of subsequent scholars.⁵⁹ In essence, Valerius would manage to avoid Apollonius' errant geography, while at the same time significantly expanding the return journey in such a way as to afford scope for all of Apollonius' episodes and many more besides.⁶⁰

5.3 Retracing the outbound route

One additional possibility is worth mentioning. Shey has argued that Valerius might have been minded to have the Argonauts retrace in reverse their outbound route, thereby allowing a heavily abridged account of the journey devoid of major incidents.⁶¹ Since the Argonauts have already reached the Danube delta when the text breaks off, this would require a punctual 'course correction': they would have to sail back down the Black Sea, pass through the now immobilized Clashing Rocks and enter the Mediterranean via the Bosporus. Shey points out that retracing the outbound route was the original intention of Valerius' Argonauts (8.178–182); they subsequently changed course to avoid facing the perils of the Clashing Rocks once again. He conjectures that at a subsequent point in the narrative the Argonauts would have realized that the Clashing Rocks had in fact been immobilized and no longer constituted a danger. This realization would then prompt them to revert to their original itinerary.⁶² This is not impossible, but there is scant evidence for any of it in Valerius' text.⁶³ Working in the

---

59 Summers 1894, 7; Butler 1909, 121, reckoning the conjectured route to have some "some probability, slight as is the evidence on which it rests"; Feeney 1991, 335 n. 76; cf. Soubiran 2002, 35.
60 Less certain is the effect that would be achieved by bringing the Argonauts' route into contact with the proemic praise of the emperor Vespasian at 1.7–9, who is rather speciously credited with achieving greater fame (*maior ... fama*) than the Argonauts for himself sailing the North Sea as part of Claudius' invasion of Britain. Summers 1894, 7 and Butler 1909, 121, both see the overlap as reinforcing the initial praise to Vespasian, but it would surely risk undermining the tenuous imperial compliment to have the Argonauts sail the same waters many centuries earlier as a tiny fraction of a more extended and groundbreaking voyage.
61 Shey 1968, 236–249; Duplicating the outbound itinerary was the solution employed by the Greek tragedians (Eur. *Med.* 431–435) and Dionysius Scytobrachion (Diod. 4.49); likewise Ov. *Am.* 2.2.4; Sen. *Med.* 454–456. Other return routes were known, including returning via the Orient and the Red Sea, which was Pindar's choice (*Pyth.* 4.251), with the Lemnian sojourn taking place on the return voyage (*Pyth.* 4.252–256).
62 This realization could arise from recollection of Phineus' words at 4.581–584, which affirmed a divinely sanctioned synchrony between his deliverance from the Harpies and the immobilization of the Clashing Rocks.
63 See the detailed critique by Shreeves 1978, 52–56.

wake of Schetter, whose arguments he had taken on board, the problem Shey confronted was to conceive of a return narrative that could be accommodated in what remained of the eighth book. Having the Argonauts revert to the outbound itinerary after events on Peuce would have allowed Valerius to recount the rest of the homeward journey in a highly abbreviated form. Shey's thesis would be recapitulated by Adamietz, but has otherwise gained little traction among critics; it is arguably more important as a conceptual precursor to the Hershkowitz/Nesselrath truncation thesis (§ 4.3).[64]

5.4 An unspecified return route

Valerius clearly regarded it as a foregone conclusion that the Argonauts did make it back to Greece (§ 2.2). But the theory of a pre-*nostos* terminus (§ 4.3) raises the possibility that this section is premised on the wrong question: perhaps we ought not ask *how* Valerius would have seen the Argonauts home but *whether* he would have troubled to do so. The problematic geography of the second leg of Apollonius' itinerary (§ 5.1) might have been conceived by the Flavian poet in intertextual terms as something like a narrative *cul-de-sac*, authorizing him to end the narrative at an earlier stage of the return voyage. As we have seen, there are difficulties associated with each of the other proposed routes, lending further credence to the theory that Valerius did not intend to narrate the homeward journey in its entirety.[65]

Subtle intertextual support for this theory can be found in the manner whereby the Flavian poet has altered the supernatural framing of the homeward journey vis-à-vis his Hellenistic exemplar. In Apollonius the prophet Phineus informs the Argonauts well in advance that they are not destined to return home via their outbound route but must take a different route home (Ap. Rhod. 2.421–422 ἐπεὶ δαίμων ἕτερον πλόον ἡγεμονεύσει | ἐξ Αἴης, "… for a god will lead you by a different route from Aea" [tr. Race]). This indication, recalled by Jason at 4.253–255, prepares and 'authorizes' Apollonius' innovative homeward route. It is, moreover, noteworthy that Phineus attributes the return itinerary to divine oversight — an aspect that will feature prominently in the return narrative

---

[64] Shey's analysis is recapitulated by Adamietz 1976, 112–113, with the refinement that the confrontation between Jason and Absyrtus would have been the culminating scene of the missing portion, with anything subsequent being anticlimatic. Nesselrath 1998, 351 credits Adamietz' analysis as leading him to posit a pre-*nostos* termination.
[65] Nesselrath 1998, 353.

itself.⁶⁶ It is thus significant that in crafting Phineus' corresponding utterance in the Roman *Argonautica*, Valerius omits any such statement.⁶⁷ By this omission the Flavian poet subtly avoids committing himself to the return itinerary of his Hellenistic model. Rather than making for the Danube delta after recalling Phineus' indication of a divine agenda, Valerius' Argonauts do so by overlooking or failing to recall the prophet's indication that the Clashing Rocks had been immobilized (Val. Fl. 8.195–196; cf. 4.707–710). Authorizing prophecy and divine oversight in Apollonius give way to forgetfulness and geographic ineptitude: this is clearly fertile intertextual terrain for truncating the account of the homeward journey.

Finally, let us recall that one of Valerius' most profound departures from Apollonius' account was to make Argo the first ship (§ 2.3). For the Roman poet the invention of navigation is the transcendent event of his narrative, making the outbound journey vastly more consequential that the return. Though he was making a very different point, Spaltenstein's remarks can be usefully applied to the issue at hand: after noting that the theme of navigation disappears from the narrative at the beginning of Book 5 and remains suppressed until well into Book 8, Spaltenstein concludes "la navigation de retour n'a aucune importance en tant que telle."⁶⁸

6 Apollonius' remaining episodes

As a culminating analytical endeavor, I want briefly to consider four major episodes in Apollonius' account of the return-journey, episodes that correspond, in terms of narrative chronology, to the missing portion of Valerius' text. These are: the confrontation with Absyrtus, the visit to Circe's island, the Phaeacian sojourn, and the Argonauts' Libyan wanderings. In each case we will consider the plausibility of the episode's inclusion in the missing portion of Valerius' text. By identifying Valerius' resort to the devices of 'episodic foreclosure' and 'preemptive reallocation' (§ 2.4), it will be shown that none but the first of these episodes could be readily accommodated in the missing portion of his narrative.

---

66 Zeus: Ap. Rhod. 4.557–561; Argo's Dodonian oak: 4.580–588; Hera: 4.640–644.
67 The omission is adduced by Shey 1968, 237 in support of a slightly different argument.
68 Spaltenstein 1991, 96.

6.1 Confrontation with Absyrtus (Ap. Rhod. 4.323–521)

As noted earlier, the Argonauts and Medea are encamped on the island of Peuce when Valerius' narrative breaks off.[69] A storm generated by Juno is protecting the Greek heroes from their Colchian pursuers for the moment, but the precise manner in which this narrative crisis will be permanently resolved is not altogether clear.[70] There is, nonetheless, a broad critical consensus that, as in the Hellenistic model, the resolution will involve the slaying of Absyrtus, an event that seems to be looming on the narrative horizon as the text draws to its premature close.[71] Absyrtus' death has been carefully foreshadowed, beginning with the very moment he entered the narrative in the fifth book (Val. Fl. 5.457–458):[72]

> *filius hunc iuxta primis Absyrtus in annis,*
> *dignus avo quemque insontem meliora manerent.*

> "Next to him [sc. Aeetes] was his son Absyrtus, in his first years, worthy of his grandfather and *for whom, blameless as he was, better things should have been waiting.*"

In Apollonius' account the murder of Absyrtus takes place later in the narrative and in a different location, but in similar circumstances to those facing Valerius' Argonauts on Peuce. In the Hellenistic poem, Jason and Medea resolve their predicament by hatching a deceitful plot to ambush and kill Absyrtus, correctly judging that the loss of their commander will confuse the Colchian forces and weaken their resolve. The murderous scheme is set in motion by Medea contacting her

---

[69] Apollonius mentions Peuce *en passant*, as it were, at 4.309–313, reporting that the Argonauts and their pursuers pass by it on opposite sides — neither group actually makes landfall on the island — thereby accounting for how the Colchians get ahead of the Greek heroes in the Hellenistic epic.

[70] Cf. Fucecchi 2014, 133: "In fact we cannot really tell what will follow. To resolve the narrative impasse, the intervention of Juno is needed, whom we have seen at work throughout the whole text, as the internal master of the plot. The tempest she raises manages temporarily to prevent war from breaking out, but now everybody — the poet included, it seems — is waiting for a possible solution from the great goddess (*expediant donec Iunonia sese / consilia atque aliquem bello ferat anxia finem*, 'til Juno's schemes work themselves out and her anxious care set some ending to the war' 8.383–4." This assessment holds true for the immediate situation but seems overly pessimistic with respect to the broader contours of the upcoming narrative.

[71] Cf. Peters 1890, 36: "*constat Valerium in octavo libro descripturum fuisse mortem Absyrti*"; similarly e.g. Summers 1894, 5; Hull 1979, 407; Nesselrath 1998, 348.

[72] Absyrtus' death is likewise anticipated at 8.136, where he is referred to as (Medea's) "ill-starred brother" (*infelix frater*); it may be ironically anticipated at additional points: see Hershkowitz 1998, 15, discussing 7.339–340; 8.106–108.

brother on the pretense of arranging a secret meeting between the two of them, with Jason playing the role of assassin when Absyrtus appears at the rendezvous. Critics have often identified the murder of Absyrtus in the Hellenistic *Argonautica* as "the central crisis of the voyage of the Argo".[73] As a murder achieved by treachery and stealth it constitutes a gross violation of heroic norms.

The episode as narrated by Apollonius would surely have been unthinkable for Valerius. Although readers are afforded glimpses of problems with Jason's character in the second half of the poem, there is nothing to suggest the drastic collapse of epic level and heroic standards found in the Hellenistic exemplar.[74] As discussed earlier, the 'preemptive reallocation' of Hypsipyle's cloak, the iconic 'regifted' garment used by Medea to entice her brother to his doom in the Hellenistic model, is a strong indication of thematic divergence (§ 2.4). Apollonius' episode is, moreover, premised on the willingness of Greeks and Colchians to enter into negotiation, with a view to adjudicating the status of Medea in particular. It is true that Valerius' Argonauts, like their Apollonian counterparts, are minded to surrender Medea to the Colchians in exchange for free passage (Val. Fl. 8.385–399). In the earlier epic, though, there have already been contacts between the two sides, and an adjudication has been set in motion (Ap. Rhod. 4.339–349). The situation in the Flavian poem could hardly be more inverted: not only has there been no contact between the two sides, but Absyrtus has already declared that the return of Medea would not satisfy him (*nec te | accipio, germana, datam*, Val. Fl. 8.270–271) and that he will consider no pact whatsoever with the Argonauts (*nec foederis ulla | spes erit, aut irae quisquam modus*, "there will be no treaty, nor will I set a limit to my wrath", 8.271–272).[75] This declaration operates on the metaliterary level as an indication of 'episodic foreclosure', a punctual rejection of Apollonius' version.

There is, then, little scope in Valerius' narrative for a naïve and forgiving Absyrtus to be murdered through a deceitful stratagem, as he was in the Hellenistic *Argonautica*. How, then, might he have met his end in a completed version of the Flavian poem? The speculation of Hull that Valerius might have "devised

---

[73] Mori 2008, 187–188.
[74] The evidence for Medea is somewhat more equivocal; cf. the objections raised by Summers 1894, 5 to the arguments made by Peters 1890, 86; Hull 1979, 406 is nonetheless right to observe that Valerius is at pains to emphasize her affection for her brother.
[75] Absyrtus goes on to declare that his unshakable purpose is the invasion of Greece itself (8.275–276). As Shey 1968, 254–255 well notes, "Jupiter's vision of history in Book 1 and his concept of the discord between East and West is now coming true"; but Absyrtus' bellicose ambitions are intolerably precocious for the fated scheme, and again seem to call for his elimination.

some less shameful way of fending off the pursuing Colchians than the one chosen by Apollonius" is surely to the point, and stands as an important, if vague, precursor to the solution of Hershkowitz and Nesselrath.[76] Absyrtus' own bellicose declarations strongly suggest that he will die fighting. As a full-scale battle is ruled out by the numerical superiority of the Colchians, some manner of winner-take-all duel between Jason and Absyrtus, the two commanders, is a plausible solution to resolve the narrative impasse, and one with a lofty epic pedigree in the death of Turnus at the end of the *Aeneid*.[77] This kind of forthright, properly 'epic' version of Absyrtus' demise would amount to a culminating act of 'Aeneidization' of the inherited Apollonian narrative. Earlier scholars had surmised that Absyrtus' death must be drawing nigh as Valerius' text breaks off, and had also recognized that his version of that death would have differed profoundly from its Apollonian exemplar. The innovation of Hershkowitz and Nesselrath consists in (i) giving that demise a specifically Virgilian form, and (ii) proposing it as the intended narrative terminus.[78]

6.2 Visit to Circe's island (Ap. Rhod. 4.659–752)

In Apollonius the treacherous murder of Absyrtus by Jason and Medea has profound narrative consequences that punctually register when Zeus condemns the Argonauts to wander and suffer for a lengthy term before reaching home (Ap. Rhod. 4.557–561).

> αὐτόν που μεγαλωστὶ δεδουπότος Ἀψύρτοιο
> Ζῆνα, θεῶν βασιλῆα, χόλος λάβεν, οἷον ἔρεξαν.
> Αἰαίης δ' ὀλοὸν τεκμήρατο δήνεσι Κίρκης
> αἷμ' ἀπονιψαμένους, πρό τε μυρία πημανθέντας,
> νοστήσειν.

When Absyrtus was brutally cut down, anger seized Zeus himself, king of the gods, at what they [sc. Jason and Medea] had done, and he determined that they should cleanse

---

[76] Hull 1979, 407.
[77] Shey 1968, 242–243 less plausibly suggests that Absyrtus' death might have been achieved more impersonally via the sea storm raised by Juno to protect the Argonauts, which had already put an end to Styrus, Medea's suitor (8.356–368). Such a repetition would run obvious compositional risks, anticlimax not least among them.
[78] Hershkowitz 1998, 9 sums up the congruent effect well: "With this ending, the structural influence of Virgil's text, which was at work at the center-point of the *Argonautica*, would also be operational at the conclusion, once again bringing to the foreground the intertextual tension between Apollonius' *Argonautica* and the *Aeneid* which runs throughout the epic."

themselves from the murderous blood through Aeaean Circe's instruction and suffer countless woes before returning home. (tr. Race, slightly modified)

This passage, whose terms are promptly reiterated at Ap. Rhod. 4.580–588, holds far-reaching implications for Valerius' reworking of his model. For if in the Flavian epic Jason were to have killed Absyrtus in a more forthright and heroic manner, this would obviate any such punitive intervention by the supreme god, and in one fell swoop eliminate the *raison d'être* for many of the remaining episodes in Apollonius' final book.[79] This holds true for the visit to Circe in particular, the only episode with a direct causal connection to Absyrtus' murder and to the Argonauts' homecoming, and the only narrative action explicitly stipulated in Zeus' punitive pronouncement. Independently of this line of analysis, Valerius' text offers decisive corroborative evidence of the episode's exclusion via 'episodic foreclosure' and 'preemptive reallocation'.

The most obvious difficulty with Medea visiting Circe on the Italian coast in the missing portion of Valerius' epic is that it would be nearly impossible to square with the Book 7 episode in which a false Circe (Venus in disguise) visits Medea in Colchis. As discussed earlier (§ 2.4), the scene in Colchis, an ingenious invention on Valerius' part, constitutes an instance of 'episodic foreclosure', all but ruling out the later visitation reported by Apollonius. Critics have also pointed out that Valerius has included in Book 3 a lengthy scene of ritual purification following the Argonauts' inadvertent slaying of their hosts at Cyzicus (3.362–458), so that "the repetition of such a ceremony in Book 8 would be tedious at best."[80] In other words, the Book 3 passage looks very much like a case of preemptive redeployment, reallocating an esteemed narrative element from an excluded Apollonian episode.

6.3 Phaeacian sojourn (Ap. Rhod. 4.981–1222)

In the Hellenistic *Argonautica* the wedding of Jason and Medea takes place on Phaeacia, long after the murder of Absyrtus, with the Argonauts disputing

---

[79] This argument appears to originate with Peters 1890, 36–37; it is reiterated by many subsequent critics, including Shey 1968, 243–244; Shreeves 1978, 51–52; Nesselrath 1998, 350.
[80] Shey 1968, 244; similarly Nesselrath 1998, 350–351; the argument goes back to Peters 1890, 36–37 and Summers 1894, 5. The elimination of the Apollonian purification episode does not necessarily mean, as Shey goes on to argue, that Valerius "would not have made Jason and Medea responsible for Absyrtus' death", merely that they would not have been ethically compromised by the manner of it.

Medea's status with a second Colchian contingent at the royal court of Alcinous. As critics have long recognized, Valerius' geographic and chronological repositioning of the wedding almost certainly constitutes an instance of episodic foreclosure: that is, it "probably meant the total omission of the visit to Phaiacia" by eliminating any mythographic motivation for the Argonauts to land there.[81]

There is moreover, a second strong indication of episodic foreclosure arising at an earlier stage of the narrative. In Apollonius' account, after the Argonauts gain possession of the Golden Fleece and take to the waves, the Colchians assemble a massive fleet to pursue them. Part of this force sails through the Bosporus into the Mediterranean, while a second contingent under the command of Absyrtus makes for the Danube (Ap. Rhod. 4.303–306). It was the first-mentioned group that Apollonius' Argonauts would later encounter in Phaeacia. As noted earlier (§ 2.4), the fact that Valerius does not follow his Hellenistic exemplar in breaking the Colchian pursuers into two contingents makes a second confrontation between the Argonauts and Colchians — on Phaeacia or anywhere else — extremely unlikely.

6.4 Libyan wanderings (Ap. Rhod. 4.1432–1619)

Apollonius' lengthy Libya sequence requires more detailed consideration, as it involves a number of distinct episodes, including the paired deaths of Canthus and Mopsus (4.1485–1536), and, just before that, the Argonauts' near-encounter with their erstwhile comrade Hercules, who removes the Apples of the Hesperides from the eponymous Garden the day before the Argonauts' arrival in the same place (4.1432–1449). A plausible case can be made for Valerius' intention to exclude this entire textual sequence.[82]

Apollonius has Hercules gain the Apples of the Hesperides, one of his canonical Labors, after being separated from the Argonauts in Mysia, in an arch and sometimes humorous episode that is alien to Valerius' stylistic norms and incompatible with his altered chronology of Hercules' career. Instead of this Labor, the Flavian poet opts to have the mighty hero liberate Prometheus from his Caucasian confinement as his chosen Herculean synchrony — an apt alteration, given the Flavian poet's emphasis on technological innovation (§ 2.3). Just

---

[81] Summers 1894, 6; similarly Adamietz 1976, 111; Shreeves 1978, 51; Pelluchi 2012, x.
[82] So Peters 1890, 86–87; cf. *contra* Soubiran 2002, 35, arguing that Valerius would likely have retained this Apollonian episode, on the grounds that it would have afforded the Flavian poet an opportunity to measure himself against one of Lucan's most notorious passages (*BC* 9.363–510).

before reaching Colchis, the Argonauts in both epics sail by the region of Prometheus' captivity. Valerius departs from his Hellenistic exemplar in making this the precise moment of the Titan's long-awaited liberation, so that it is here that the Argonauts and Hercules come close to crossing paths (4.154–176). That Hercules would thereafter proceed from the Caucasus to Libya is intrinsically unlikely, not least because it is strongly implied that his heroic agenda will next take him back to Troy (4.78).

The foregoing amounts to an instance of 'episodic foreclosure' that calls into doubt the inclusion of Apollonius' extended Libyan sequence. Additional evidence for its exclusion can be found in Valerius' handling of the death of Canthus, which is markedly accelerated vis-à-vis the Apollonian account.[83] In the Flavian epic Canthus dies not in Libya nor even on the return voyage, but during the Colchian civil war, an extended 'Iliadic' interpolation that features the Argonauts as prominent combatants. His death and the subsequent struggle for his corpse (6.317–372), which is modelled on the struggle for the corpse of Patroclus in *Iliad* 17, constitute a central sequence.[84] The preemptive redeployment of Canthus' death thus offers additional evidence for Valerius intending to dispense with the Apollonian Libyan episode in its entirety.[85]

7 Conclusion

Scholarly speculation on Valerius' missing conclusion, which began in markedly 'Apollonian' terms with the publication of Giovan Battista Pio's *supplementum* in 1519 (§ 2.1), has made progress only with difficulty and at a seemingly glacial pace. As a rule, advances have depended on an analytical recalibration that allows greater scope for the creative influence of the *Aeneid* as against close adherence to Apollonius' storyline. The last two centuries have seen significant forward progress, a phase ushered in by Peters, who proposed and carefully

---

83 So classified rather than 'narrative foreclosure' because Canthus' death does not seem essential to the Libyan episode.
84 The importance of this textual sequence is underscored by its anticipation in the catalogue of the Argonauts at 1.450–456, and its recollection at 7.422.
85 Cf. Peters 1890, 39, concluding from the preemptive repositioning of the death of Canthus alone that Valerius meant to eliminate the Libya episode. But that episode is still conceivable in the wake of Canthus' death, not least because it includes a second important death, that of Mopsus (Ap. Rhod. 4.1502–1536), which does not occur in an accelerated position in Valerius' text.

supported the thesis that Valerius' missing conclusion would have deviated significantly from Apollonius' storyline. He thereby bequeathed a crucial — if rarely acknowledged — legacy to scholars of the twentieth and twenty-first centuries.[86] The second half of the twentieth century saw two further noteworthy developments: in 1959 Schetter published persuasive structural arguments for an intended length of eight books (§ 3.3); and in 1998 Hershkowitz and Nesselrath both proposed that Valerius might have intended to conclude his narrative at a point prior to the Argonauts' return to Greece (§ 4.3). While a scholarly consensus has emerged in favor of Schetter's thesis, there has to date been scant critical response to the Hershkowitz/Nesselrath 'truncation thesis'.

I want to close by briefly considering what might be deemed the maximal case, namely, that Peters, Schetter and Hershkowitz/Nesselrath are all correct. This would mean that the eighth was to be Valerius' final book, that less than 400 verses remained to complete the poem, and that it would have concluded with the death of Absyrtus on or near the island of Peuce. What would the Flavian poet have had to sacrifice or forego vis-à-vis his Hellenistic model if that were all true? In terms of intertextual poetics, the obvious answer is Apollonius' Odyssean replay, a textual sequence extending from the Circe visit to the Phaeacian episode (Ap. Rhod. 4.659–1222). The omission of such a sequence would undoubtedly have involved difficult tradeoffs, but the 'Homeric paradigm shift', which is to say Valerius' reweighting of Homeric intertextuality towards the *Iliad* (§ 2.5), makes it more plausible than it might otherwise seem.[87] With respect to cultural poetics, one lost opportunity towers above the rest: that of bringing the Argonauts into contact with Italy.[88] On the face of it, this forfeiture would constitute a significant sacrifice for a Roman *Argonautica*, and one that would require some manner of explanation if it were not to cast a shadow over

---

86 Peters 1890, 33–34; cf. Summers 1894, 5–6, acknowledging Peters' primacy and offering qualified agreement: "Although [Peters' arguments] seem to me insufficient, there are other considerations which lead me to the same conclusion that what remained of the work would have diverged somewhat widely from the Greek original."

87 In addition to the exclusion of the Circe episode (§ 6.2) and the Phaeacian episode (§ 6.3), Summers 1894, 6 makes a subtle case for the intended exclusion of the Wandering Rocks/ Scylla and Charybdis sequence (Ap. Rhod. 4.920–967). Perhaps the most appealing of Apollonius' Odyssean episodes would have been the Argonauts' encounter with the Sirens (4.900–920), regarding which Valerius has left no anticipatory signals that I have noticed. Of the non-Odyssean episodes, the most memorable is arguably the brief Cretan stopover, prior to which Medea slays the bronze giant Talus (4.1635–1693). Among *nostos*-termination advocates, Soubiran 2002, 35 deems it likely that Valerius would have included this episode.

88 For the argument in Summers 1894, 6–7 that Valerius intended to bring the Argonauts in contact with Italy, see note 26.

the truncation theory. There are, I believe, plausible grounds for supposing that Valerius did not care to bring his Greek heroes into direct contact with Italy: but, as this paper has already exceeded reasonable limits of space and time, that argument will have to wait for another occasion.[89]

Bibliography

Adamietz, J. (1976), *Zur Komposition der Argonautika des Valerius Flaccus*, Munich.
Bährens, A. (ed.) (1875), *C. Valerii Flacci Setini Balbi Argonauticon Libri Octo*, Leipzig.
Butler, H.E. (1909), *Post-Augustan Poetry: From Seneca to Juvenal*, Oxford.
Delage, E. (1930), *La géographie dans les Argonautiques d'Apollonios de Rhodes*, Paris.
Dimsdale, M.S. (1915), *A History of Latin Literature*, London.
Feeney, D.C. (1991), *The Gods in Epic*, Oxford.
Frank, E. (1967), "The Structure of Valerius Flaccus' *Argonautica*", *CB* 43, 38–39.
Fucecchi, M. (2014), "War and Love in Valerius Flaccus' *Argonautica*", in: M. Heerink/G. Manuwald (eds.), *Brill's Companion to Valerius Flaccus*, Leiden, 115–135.
Hershkowitz, D. (1998), *Valerus Flaccus' Argonautica: Abbreviated Voyages in Silver Latin Epic*, Oxford.
Hull, K.W.D. (1979), "The Hero Concept in Valerius Flaccus", in: C. Deroux (ed.), *Studies in Latin Literature and Roman History* 1, Brussels, 379–409.
Jachman, G. (1935), "Eine Elegie des Properz", *RhM* 84, 192–237.
Liberman, G. (ed., tr.) (1997), *Valerius Flaccus, Argonautiques. Tome 1: Chants I-IV*, Paris.
Mendell, C.W. (1967), *Latin Poetry: The Age of Rhetoric and Satire*, London.
Moore, C.H. (1921), "Prophecy in the Ancient Epic", *HSCP* 32, 99–175.
Nesselrath, H.-G. (1998), "Jason und Absyrtus: Überlegungen zum Ende von Valerius Flaccus' *Argonautica*", in: U. Eigler/E. Lefèvre (eds.), *Ratis omnia vincet II: Neue Untersuchungen zu den* Argonautica *des Valerius Flaccus*, Munich, 347–354.
Pellucci, T. (2012), *Commento al libro VIII delle Argonautiche di Valerio Flacco*, Hildesheim.
Peters, J. (1890), *De C. Valerii Flacci Vita et Carmine*, Diss. Königsberg.
Preston, W. (1803), *The Argonautica of Apollonius Rhodius*, vol. 3, Dublin.
Scaffai, M. (1986), "Rassegna di Studi su Valerio Flacco (1938–1982)", *ANRW* 2.32.4, 2359–2447.
Schetter, W. (1959), "Die Buchzahl der *Argonautica* des Valerius Flaccus", *Philologus* 103, 297–308.
Scott, B. (2012), *Aspects of Transgression in Valerius Flaccus' Argonautica*, Diss. University of Liverpool.
Shey, H.J. (1968), *A Critical Study of the Argonautica of Valerius Flaccus*, Diss. University of Iowa.
Shreeves, C.E. (1978), *Landscape, Topography and Geographical Notation in the Argonautica of Valerius Flaccus*, Diss. University of North Carolina at Chapel Hill.

---

[89] I wish to express my deepest gratitude to the volume editors for their more-than-human patience in sticking with me as I belatedly expanded this paper from a much more narrowly framed initial version.

Soubiran, J. (1997), "Deux Notes sur Valerius Flaccus", *RPh* 77, 119–132.
Soubiran, J. (ed., tr.) (2002), *Valerius Flaccus. Argonautiques*, Louvain.
Spaltenstein, F. (1991), "Continuité Imaginative et Structure dans les *Argonautiques*", in: M. Korn/H.J. Tschiedel (eds.), *Ratis omnia vincet: Untersuchungen zu den* Argonautica *des Valerius Flaccus*, Munich, 89–100.
Summers, W.C. (1894), *A Study of the Argonautica of Valerius Flaccus*, Cambridge.
Vessey, D.W.T.C. (1982), "Flavian Epic", in: E.J. Kenney (ed.), *The Cambridge History of Classical Literature, Volume II: Latin Literature*, Cambridge, 558–596.
Zissos, A. (1999), "Allusion and Narrative Possibility in the *Argonautica* of Valerius Flaccus", *CP* 94, 289–301.
Zissos, A. (2002), "Reading Models and the Homeric Program in Valerius Flaccus' *Argonautica*", *Helios* 29, 69–96.
Zissos, A. (2008), *Valerius Flaccus' Argonautica Book 1. Edited with Introduction, Text, Translation and Commentary*, Oxford.
Zissos, A. (2014), "*Interpres operis alieni*? Giovan Battista Pio's continuation of Valerius Flaccus' *Argonautica*", in: M. Heerink/G. Manuwald (eds.), *Brill's Companion to Valerius Flaccus*, Leiden, 361–380.
Zissos, A. (2017), "Generic Attire: Hypsipyle's Cloaks in Valerius Flaccus and Apollonius Rhodius", in: F. Bessone/M. Fucecchi (eds.), *The Literary Genres in the Flavian Age: Canons, Transformations, Reception*, Berlin, 201–228.

Bettina Reitz-Joosse
Speaking Silences: The Incompleteness of Tacitus' *Annals* and Gustav Freytag's *Die verlorene Handschrift*

Abstract: This chapter approaches the incomplete transmission of Tacitus' *Annals* through the lens of a 19th-century German novel by Gustav Freytag entitled *Die verlorene Handschrift* ("The Lost Manuscript"), which deals with a Latin professor's hunt for a lost manuscript of Tacitus' historical works. First, I argue that the characters in Freytag's novel model a range of different responses to Tacitean incompleteness, challenging readers to question the characters' — and their own — motives for wishing to fill Tacitus' gaps. Second, I suggest that the novel in its entirety proposes a different way of responding to the incompleteness of the Tacitean works: to understand and embrace *silence*, including the silence produced by the lost sections, as an essential characteristic and as an integral and meaningful feature of Tacitus' work. Freytag's novel performs a constructive response to Tacitus' silences: it treats them as the inviting pauses of an interlocutor who falls silent to allow his readers to speak.

1 Introduction

The incompleteness of Tacitus' historical works, the *Annals* and the *Histories*, has sparked the imagination of his readers for centuries. Two circumstances are chiefly responsible for this. The first is the extremely precarious transmission of the surviving parts of the *Annals* and *Histories*. Famously, only two manuscripts — the so-called First and Second Medicean, dating to the mid-9th and the 11th century respectively — stand between us and the total loss of the historical works of Tacitus. In the words of Denis Feeney, "[w]e are two rolls of the dice away from

---

I would like to thank the editors for the invitation to contribute to a stimulating conversation about 'incompleteness', the audiences in Thessaloniki and Berlin for their helpful questions, and my friend Kelly Shannon-Henderson for her many insightful suggestions on Freytag and Tacitus. This chapter was completed during an Alexander-von-Humboldt fellowship at the Humboldt-University of Berlin.

having nothing at all left of the greatest of Latin histories".[1] Furthermore, significant parts of Tacitus' work have not survived this transmission, and its lost parts have long exercised a strong fascination on the minds of his readers. In the case of the *Annals*, which this chapter focuses on, the lost sections appear to have been dramatic highpoints of the narrative: the stand-off between Sejanus and Tiberius, the entire reign of the notorious Caligula, Nero's death.

In this chapter, I consider the incompleteness of Tacitus' *Annals* in light of the experience of his readers. What can incompleteness do *to* and *for* Tacitus' readers? I propose to reflect on this question through the lens of a 19th-century German novel by Gustav Freytag entitled *Die verlorene Handschrift* ("The Lost Manuscript"), which deals with a Latin professor's hunt for a lost manuscript of Tacitus' historical works. I approach Tacitus' incompleteness through Freytag's novel for two reasons. First, its characters model a range of different responses to Tacitean incompleteness. *Die verlorene Handschrift* challenges us to reflect on these responses and to question the characters' — and our own — motives for wishing to fill Tacitus' gaps. Second, I argue that the novel in its entirety proposes a different way of responding to the incompleteness of the Tacitean works: to understand and embrace *silence*, including the silence produced by the lost sections, as an essential characteristic and as an integral and meaningful feature of Tacitus' work. Freytag's novel itself performs a constructive response to Tacitus' silences: it treats them as the inviting pauses of an interlocutor who falls silent to allow us to speak.

2 *Die verlorene Handschrift*

Gustav Freytag (Kluczbork/Kreuzburg 1816 — Wiesbaden 1895) was both a writer and a politically active public intellectual. As a 'liberal nationalist', he was critical of 'Kleinstaaterei' and of the particularism of the ruling German aristocracies, energetically supported the interests of the German Protestant bourgeoisie, and was strongly in favour of the unification of what he saw as one German 'Volk' under Prussia's rule, in a parliamentarian and constitutional monarchy.[2] He was also one of the most-read German authors of the second half of the 19th century. Today, he is outshone by more famous contemporaries such as Theodor

---

[1] Feeney 2019. On the manuscript traditions of Tacitus, see e.g. the introductions by Martin 2010 and Tarrant in Reynolds 1983², 406–409.
[2] On Freytag's politics and their reflection in his literary output, see Schofield 2012 and Ping 2006.

Fontane, but among his contemporaries, Freytag's novels and plays were extremely popular. His most successful novel, *Soll und Haben* (1855), went through a phenomenal sixty-three print runs in the first fifty years since its publication and also enjoyed great success in translation, especially in English.[3] While *Die verlorene Handschrift* could not quite match the enormous success of *Soll und Haben*, it was also widely read and appreciated.[4]

Die verlorene Handschrift was first published in 1864. It consists of five books of an imposing total length of more than twelve hundred pages. The novel's hero, Felix Werner, is a professor of classical philology in an unnamed German university town. According to Freytag, his hero is partly modelled on his friend Moriz Haupt, a philologist of Latin and German, who had succeeded to Karl Lachmann's chair in Berlin in 1853.[5] In the novel, Werner comes across clues to the existence of a manuscript which appears to contain the entire *Annals* and *Histories*. In an inventory of the treasures of the (fictional) defunct monastery of Rossau, Werner discovers this entry (Freytag 1955, 8):[6]

"Das alt ungehür puoch vonußfart des swigers" ... Eine spätere Hand hat in lateinischer Sprache dazugeschrieben: "Dies Buch ist latein, fast unlesbar, fängt an mit den Worten: *lacrimas et signa* und endet mit den Worten: Hier schließt der Geschichten — *actorum* — dreißigstes Buch."

---

[3] On the sales success of *Soll und Haben*, see Ping 2006, 65–66, who calls it "the preeminent 'best seller' of the century" (65). Sommer 1905 writes that, through *Soll und Haben*, Freytag became "einer der populärsten Dichter seines Volkes". Today, *Soll und Haben* is widely viewed as a highly problematic construction of German "Volksgeist" through the use of anti-semitic clichés (s.v. *Gustav Freytag* in *KLL* 5.730–731).
[4] According to Ping 2006, 162, the novel went through sixteen German editions by 1890, and was released in English translation in the United States and Great Britain. Sommer 1905, 14 estimates that "der Roman fand aber nur etwa halb soviel Verehrer wie 'Soll und Haben'". On contemporary critical reception, which seems to have focused on the (lack of) realism of the final parts, see Sommer 1905, 14–15.
[5] According to Freytag's later autobiography, a beer-fuelled conversation with Haupt about the existence of some lost books of Livy provided the initial inspiration for the novel (Ping 2006, 160–161, see also Sommer 1905, 10–11). Haupt himself ironically acknowledged his close relationship with the novel when he called himself "Magister Knips" in the announcements of his lectures about Ammianus (Sommer 1905, 11; Baisch/Lüdeke 2000, 225). Freytag himself was well-versed in the world of German universities, having begun his career with a Privatdozentur at the University of Breslau (Wrocław), which lasted until 1847. On the somewhat humiliating ending of this university career, see Ping 2006, 151–153.
[6] There is no critical edition of Freytag's work. I cite *Die verlorene Handschrift* according to the 1955 edition of Droemersche Verlagsanstalt. The translations are my own, sometimes inspired by Giorgiana Malcolm's translation, published in London by Chapman and Hall (Freytag 1865).

"The old extraordinary book of the travels of the silent one" ... A later hand has added in Latin: "This book is Latin, almost illegible; it begins with the words *lacrimas et signa* and ends with the words: here concludes the thirtieth book of the histories (*actorum*)."

Professor Werner immediately realises that the phrase *lacrimas et signa* ("tears and signs") occurs at *Annals* 1.5.[7] He surmises that the text opens with these words because one folio of a manuscript may have been lost, and that this item in the inventory is actually a complete manuscript of the thirty books of the *Annals* and *Histories* together.[8] Taking into account the work's ancient title *Ab Excessu Divi Augusti* ("Following the Death of the Deified Augustus"),[9] the strange German title is easily explained as a mistranslation of a shortened title of the manuscript: *Ab Excessu Taciti* becomes "von ußfart des swigers" or "of the travels of the silent one".

From a further remark in the inventory, Werner and his younger friend and colleague, Fritz Hahn, deduce that the last monk of his order hid all the treasures of his monastery in an unknown location to protect them from the approaching Swedes during the Thirty Years' War. Together they follow the traces of the manuscript to a rural castle in Rossau, where they do not (yet) find the manuscript. Werner does, however, meet a young woman called Ilse, whom he marries.

The reigning sovereign of the area (the otherwise unnamed "Fürst") then lures the professor to his palace with the promise of providing him with every kind of support in his search for the manuscript; in reality, however, he is pursuing Felix's wife Ilse. The farmer's daughter Ilse is uncomfortable in these courtly circles and unable to avoid the persistent attentions of the sovereign. Felix Werner, engrossed in his search for the manuscript, fails to notice her distress. He believes that he has found new leads and ignores Ilse's request to remove her from the vicinity of the palace. A forgery, skilfully orchestrated by the Fürst, lures Werner onto a false trail and away from Ilse, who is dramatically rescued from the Fürst's persecutions at the last minute by a friend, a hat-maker from the city. Meanwhile, the Fürst, who has gradually been descending into total paranoia, comes close to killing Werner with a hunting rifle. Eventually,

---

[7] *Ann.* 1.5.1: ... *multas illic utrimque lacrimas et signa caritatis spemque ex eo fore ut iuvenis penatibus avi redderetur.* — "(It was said) that there had been many tears and signs of love on both sides, and as a result there was hope that the young man might be returned to the hearth of his grandfather."

[8] We are indebted to Jerome for the knowledge that the total number of the books of *Annals* and *Histories* was thirty (*Comm. ad Zach.* 3,14,1–2): see Martin 2010, 241–242.

[9] On the title, see Oliver 1951 and Goodyear 1972, 85–87.

and with the help of Fritz Hahn, the full extent of the forgery is unmasked and the forgery revealed to be the work of a certain Magister Knips. In the final chapter of the novel, the remains of the hidden treasure, including the manuscript, are after all discovered in a cave close to Ilse's home. However, only the covers of the precious manuscript remain — the text itself has been thrown away and lost forever.

3 The lure of the *lacuna*

The basic premise of the novel's plot is the possibility of discovering a third manuscript of the historical works of Tacitus. The current incompleteness of the Tacitean works and the opportunity to rediscover its missing sections motivates many of the characters of the novel for the whole of its substantial length. The absent manuscript is even itself a character in the novel: Freytag has it appear as a ghost or phantom at several points of the narrative, as in this passage:[10] "Wieder stieg die alte unheimliche Handschrift vor den Freunden aus dem Boden, deutlich sichtbar, mit den Händen zu greifen" ("Again, the old, uncanny manuscript rose out of the ground in front of the friends, clearly visible, within reach of their hands").[11] Freytag's characters respond in different ways to the tantalizing absence and imagined existence of the manuscript. Their responses reveal much about their respective personalities and about their deepest desires and longings, which all of them are hoping to satisfy by the discovery of the manuscript. For each of them, the lost manuscript would fill a different kind of 'Leerstelle'.

3.1 Fritz Hahn

Dr. Fritz Hahn is Professor Felix Werner's younger colleague and collaborator. When the possibility of discovery first beckons, Hahn is especially excited by

---

[10] Freytag 1955, 28.
[11] Another example is Freytag 1955, 424, where Werner describes how the ghost of the manuscript pursues him by day and by night ("das Gespenst verfolgt mich bei Tag und Nacht"), and the princess wonders whether spells and the help of Hecate may help to tame it.

the many new historical facts which this discovery would unlock.¹² He is particularly interested in the "älteste Geschichte [der] Germanen",¹³ and when it seems, at one point, as though the colleagues will not be able to recover the manuscript, he exclaims "… und niemals werden wir erfahren, was römische Kaiser an Thusnelda und Thumelicus gefrevelt haben …" ("… and never shall we learn what outrages Roman emperors committed against Thusnelda and Thumelicus …").¹⁴ This bewilderingly specific regret should be understood in light of the political situation of the time: as the unification of the German states was finally about to become a reality, the discovery — or construction — of a shared and credentialed German heritage seemed not only a scholarly but also a political necessity. To Hahn, precise knowledge of the fate of the wife and son of the archetypical Germanic hero Arminius/Hermann seems of momentous importance. In fact, Thusnelda, the daughter of Segestes and wife of Arminius, already features in the preserved part of the *Annals*, although she is not named (*Annals* 1.55–59). In this passage, Tacitus also announces that he will treat the sorry fate of her son Thumelicus at a later point of the narrative. Since he does not do so in the extant books of the *Annals*, it seems possible (but not certain) that he kept his promise in the lost books on Caligula's reign.¹⁵ In any case, Hahn's desire to recover the manuscript is fuelled by his interest in very specific historical information regarding the fate of two relatively marginal figures in the *Annals*, one of whom the historian does not even bother to name.

Hahn's narrow-mindedly 'nationalist' approach to the lost parts of Tacitus also manifests in another way. When Werner ponders the wisdom of publishing a note about the possible existence of the manuscript immediately, Hahn cautions against this course of action, because this might allow a foreigner to discover the manuscript, which, according to Hahn, would lead to the treasure being lost to Werner, to their country, and to the whole academic community.¹⁶

---

12 "'Unschätzbar', bestätigte der Doktor, 'für unsere Kenntnis der Sprache, für hundert Einzelheiten römischer Geschichte'." ("'Inestimable', the doctor confirmed, 'for our knowledge of the language, for a hundred details of Roman history'.")
13 Freytag 1955, 12.
14 Freytag 1955, 13.
15 Tacitus, *Annals* 1.55–59 treats Segestes and Thusnelda; see 1.58.6 for the announcement regarding Thumelicus. It is surprising that Tacitus' highly influential *Germania* is not mentioned at all (see however McNamara 2021 on the near-complete absence of historiographical narrative in the *Germania*, which may account for its absence in this context).
16 Freytag 1955, 29: "[W]er steht dir dafür, dass nicht die behende Tätigkeit eines Antiquars oder eines Ausländers allen weiteren Nachforschungen zuvorkommt? In solchem Falle mag der Schatz, selbst wenn er gefunden wird, nicht nur für dich, auch für unser Land, ja für die Wis-

And although Werner virtuously claims that he will only let the intellectual importance of this discovery weigh with him, he does not publish such a note, but instead enters upon the hunt himself, together with Hahn.

3.2 Struvelius

In the second chapter of the second volume, we encounter several of Werner's university colleagues, among them a somewhat haughty professor by the name of Struvelius. One day, he appears at Werner and Ilse's house and asks Werner to lend him his materials about the textual transmission of Tacitus. Only a short time later, Struvelius publishes a small fragment of an unknown manuscript which appears to contain a hitherto lost section of Tacitus' *Annals*. While Werner is at first hopeful that this fragment may be further proof of the existence of the lost manuscript, he soon comes to suspect that Struvelius has been duped and that the fragment is a forgery. A bitter academic dispute between Werner and Struvelius ensues, in which Struvelius reveals himself as unable to admit his mistake. Even in the face of compelling evidence to the contrary, he refuses to relinquish the claim to the discovery of a lost bit of Tacitus and to the academic glory this would bring. Although the quarrel is eventually made up, Struvelius' academic integrity and reputation have suffered. The lure of the lacuna has brought Struvelius close to his academic downfall.

3.3 Felix Werner

Werner Freytag's hero is driven neither by a desire for personal glory, like Struvelius, nor by a yearning for specific historical facts, like Hahn. Discussing the lost manuscript with Hahn, he stresses: "Aber es sind doch nicht Einzelheiten, welche uns den größten Gewinn brächten, ... und nicht, daß wir diese missen, macht uns den Verlust der Handschrift empfindlich. Denn für die Hauptsachen versagen andere Quellen nicht." ("But it is not details that would bring us the greatest gain, ... and it is not that we lack these that makes the loss of the manuscript painful. Regarding the main facts, other sources do not fail us.").[17] For him, the value of a complete Tacitus would rather reside in a better understanding of

---

senschaft verloren gehen." "[W]ho can guarantee that the nimble activity of an antiquary or a foreigner will not prevent all further investigation? In that case, the treasure, even if found, may be lost not only to you, but also to our country and to scholarship."
17 Freytag 1955, 13.

Tacitus *as a person*. Werner yearns, as he says, to gaze into Tacitus' face, and to understand his mind — he wants "einen sichern Blick in die tiefsten Falten eines römischen Gemütes" ("a reliable view into the deepest recesses of a Roman mind"),[18] because "was uns am meisten fördert, ist doch nicht die Summe des Wissens, die wir einem großen Manne verdanken, sondern seine eigene Persönlichkeit, die durch das, was er für uns geschaffen, ein Teil unseres eigenen Wesens wird" ("what helps us most is not, after all, the sum of knowledge we owe to a great man, but his own personality, which becomes a part of our own being through what he created for us.").[19] This burning desire to intimately know and understand Tacitus' personality appears no more realistic than Hahn's hope for precise information on Germanic tribes. If we did possess the ending of the *Annals*, for example, would we feel that we really *knew* Tacitus as a person, in a way that we now do not because of the missing books? As we shall see, Freytag's novel suggests an answer to this question, which I will return to in the second half of the chapter.

Freytag stresses that Werner is also not initially motivated by a desire for personal glory. However, as the novel proceeds, the idea of the manuscript begins to have a destructive influence on him. His yearning for the discovery reduces him to an unpleasant single-mindedness, bordering on an obsession that in the end renders him just as vulnerable to a forgery as his colleague Struvelius whom he had despised in the first part of the novel. Freytag suggests that Werner's obsession also distorts his moral priorities and obscures his sense of duty. Throughout the novel, Freytag shows how Werner's wife on the one hand and the lost manuscript on the other pull Werner in different directions. It is only when Werner finally masters his obsession with the manuscript and returns to Ilse's side that the author has him discover, almost by accident, the treasure he has sought for so long.

3.4 Magister Knips

Finally, there is the tragic figure of Magister Knips, a 'Privatgelehrter' of humble origins and meagre income, who exists at the margins of the academic community. Knips is led the furthest astray by the temptations that the incompleteness of Tacitus presents. He is the forger of the fragment that dupes Struvelius, and later on, at the behest of the Fürst, of the pages that briefly succeed in duping

---

[18] Freytag 1955, 13–14.
[19] Freytag 1955, 14.

Werner. Although financial gain is part of his objective, he commits these forgeries mainly in order to be revenged on the professors who have exploited him, and to experience a brief moment of superiority and power: "Zuerst kam der Einfall, auch über solche zu lachen, die mich benutzen und verachten, ich dachte, wenn ich will, kann ich euch in meiner Hand haben, ihr Herren Gelehrten" ("First came the idea of mocking those who exploit and despise me; I thought, if I want, I can have you in my power, you learned gentlemen").[20] Knips recognises, and mercilessly exploits, the weakness of his more privileged colleagues, namely their extreme, even obsessive desire to find the missing parts of Tacitus. And yet Knips, just like his colleagues, dreams of finding the manuscript himself — again motivated by his hurt pride and his desire for revenge. He phantasizes about discovering the codex,[21] and imagines that he will ask Werner to serve as his assistant in editing it. Ultimately, Knips's existence is destroyed by the lure of the Tacitean lacunae. When his forgery is uncovered, he is forever disgraced in the eyes of the scholarly community. He almost commits suicide, but in the end decides to escape to America.[22]

Through these four characters, Hahn, Werner, Struvelius and Knips, Freytag shows us the range of temptations that Tacitean incompleteness can present, and its intoxicating and destructive power.[23] He also shows us that all those tempted by the manuscript are really searching for something beyond it, something that the discovery of the manuscript would not, in fact, be able to provide: a reliable history of the earliest history of Germany, an intimate understanding of Tacitus' personality, or an escape from feelings of one's own inferiority — either as a scholar (Struvelius) or as a result of social marginalisation (Knips).

In the second part of this chapter, I argue that the plot of *Die verlorene Handschrift* proposes an alternative way of responding to Tacitean incompleteness.

---

20 Freytag 1955, 529.
21 Freytag 1955, 411: "'Ich selbst finde den Kodex', fuhr er zuversichtlicher fort. 'Jacobi Knipsii sollertia inventum ...'", "'I myself will discover the codex', he continued more optimistically, 'Jacobi Knipsii sollertia inventum ...'".
22 The story of Knips is inspired by the real case of a forger who briefly succeeded in duping famous scholars as well as the Berliner Akademie der Wissenschaften, and whose case Freytag covered during his time as a journalist. See Sommer 1905, 12–13. Freytag's original article appeared in *Grenzboten* 1870, Nr. 15 (Freytag 1870).
23 The idea of intoxication occurs several times: for example, Werner says that the idea of the potential discovery has the same effect on a man as Roman wine (Freytag 1955, 12). Freytag 1955, 469–470, describes in detail the bodily symptoms of Werner's intoxication and addiction to the idea of the manuscript's discovery.

Not only individual characters *in* the novel, but the novel *as a whole* is driven by this incompleteness — and Freytag proposes and performs a constructive response to it.

4 Talking with the silent one

Die verlorene Handschrift first introduces us to Tacitus not by his actual Latin name but by a literal German translation of it as "Schweiger", "the silent one". Thereafter, silence is foregrounded in connection with Tacitus throughout the novel, and returned to most explicitly at its conclusion. When it becomes clear that only the covers of the manuscript, but not the text between them has survived, Freytag writes:[24]

> Er hielt die Deckel an das Licht, auf der innern Seite des einen waren unter Staub und Moder in alter Mönchschrift die Worte zu lesen: "Von Ausfahrt des Schweigenden." Jetzt fuhr der Schweigende aus seiner Höhle, aber er schwieg, sein Mund blieb stumm für immer.
>
> He held the book covers into the light. On the inside of one of them, under dust and mould, one could read in an old monastic script the words: "Of the travels of a silent man". Now the silent man left his cave, but he was silent, his mouth remained forever mute.

Much more lies behind this passage than a wordplay on Tacitus' name.[25] Readers of Tacitus have long recognised the crucial importance of silence in his preserved oeuvre. In the historical works, the silence of Tacitus' characters in certain situations is often a yardstick by which readers can assess their personality and the political situation in which they find themselves. I argue that Freytag systematically highlights this quality of the historian's work, portraying Tacitus as an author whose silences are particularly eloquent.

For example, Strocchio has argued that being silent is a regular characteristic of Tacitus' "bad" emperors, especially in the case of Tiberius, whose silence is a feature of the *dissimulatio* ("dissembling") that is so fundamental to his (ab)use of power.[26] The spotlights which Freytag shines on Tacitus' *Annals* foreground this role of silence in the work. For example, in chapter IV.8, the Fürst picks up a volume of Tacitus, opens it by chance in the middle of the sixth book

---

24 Freytag 1955, 569–570.
25 This kind of play, and the suggestion of a relationship between Tacitus' name and the nature of his writings, is already found in Humanist texts (Römer 2012 and Dotzler 2011, 244).
26 Strocchio 1992, 15–25.

of the *Annals*, and reads the following passage (one of very few marked quotations of Tacitus' work in *Die verlorene Handschrift*):[27]

> Er las mit halblauter Stimme eine Stelle: "So schreibt der römische Kaiser seinem Senat: Die Götter und Göttinnen sollen mich ärger strafen, als ich mich täglich gestraft fühle, wenn ich weiß, was ich euch, versammelte Väter, schreiben soll, oder wie ich es schreiben soll, oder was ich euch in diesem Augenblicke durchaus nicht schreiben darf." Er schlug auf das Buch. "Der hat's gefühlt. Den Brief könnte noch mancher andere schreiben und er könnte weinen, daß er so schreiben muß."
>
> He read a passage in a low voice: "Thus writes the Roman emperor to his senate: Let the gods and goddesses punish me more severely than I feel myself punished every day if I know what I should write to you, assembled fathers, or how I should write it, or what I am absolutely not allowed to write to you at this time". He slapped the book: "He felt it. Many a man could write this letter and cry about having to write in that way."

The passage cited by the Fürst occurs at *Annals* 6.6.1. Tacitus there introduces and cites the opening of a Tiberian letter to the senate:[28]

> *Insigne visum est earum Caesaris litterarum initium; nam his verbis exorsum est: "quid scribam vobis, patres conscripti, aut quo modo scribam aut quid omnino non scribam hoc tempore, di me deaeque peius perdant quam perire me cotidie sentio, si scio."*
>
> The start of that letter of Caesar's was regarded as distinctive, for he opened with these words: "If I know what to write to you, conscript fathers, or how to write or what not to write at all at this time, may the gods and goddesses destroy me worse than the daily death I feel."[29]

Tacitus presents this opening sentence as emblematic (*insigne*) of Tiberius' personality: the secretive, unhappy and paranoid emperor explicitly puts his 'wordlessness' into words. The sentence is the culmination of many episodes in which Tiberius has chosen silence over speaking, or partial silence over open and comprehensive communication, and has thereby created an atmosphere of fear and insecurity among the Roman aristocracy.[30] Here, the emperor seems to be so tortured by his inability to communicate openly that he admits this to the senate. Freytag's choice to have the Fürst read this particular passage from the *Annals* serves to alert his readers to the importance of characters' silences in

---

27 Freytag 1955, 453.
28 This same sentence is also cited by Suetonius, with only small differences: Suetonius, *Tiberius* 67.1.
29 Translation: Woodman 2004.
30 On Tacitus' Tiberius as a silent *princeps*, see Bruno 2022, 39–52; Strocchio 1992, 7 and 17–22.

Tacitean characterisation. Furthermore, for the knowledgeable reader of Tacitus, the Fürst's translation demonstrates how rich and multi-interpretable silences can be: he renders Tacitus' crucial phrase *quid omnino non scribam hoc tempore* as "what I am absolutely not *allowed* to write to you at this time", sharpening and interpreting Tiberius' more open phrasing and ascribing to him a feeling of being hemmed in by the senate and prevented from speaking his mind freely.

Readers of Tacitus can come to understand the character of tyrants through their 'speaking silences', but no less meaningful are the silences of political opponents or victims of the emperor. Their absence of speech can signify fear and cowed submission, but silence can also serve as a mode of resistance, a pointedly unspoken testimony to the lack of *libertas* and the tyrannical traits of the emperor.[31] Silence in Tacitus, as Strocchio well shows, should always be weighed as a meaningful political act. This charged quality of silence in an environment of limited freedom of speech is of existential importance to Tacitus himself, as a politician and an author. His first work, the *Agricola*, opens with a reflection on the silences forced on him and his fellow Romans by the regime of the tyrannical Domitian, including the famous phrase *memoriam quoque ipsam cum voce perdidissemus, si tam in nostra potestate esset oblivisci quam tacere* ("We would have lost memory itself as well as voice, had we been able to forget as easily as to be silent.") (*Agricola* 2.3).[32] Although the *Agricola*, standing at the beginning of Tacitus' career as an author, seems to suggest that a new era of free speech has now dawned, Tacitus' silences are all but a thing of the past. The theme of silence and its alternatives under an oppressive regime lies at the very heart of the debate depicted in the *Dialogus de Oratoribus*,[33] and in regard to his historiographical works, scholars have noted just how frequently Tacitus' own deliberately self-imposed silences are as productive of meaning as speech.[34] Tacitus' very style has been called "lo stile lacunoso" to describe how his idiosyncratic prose communicates as much by *not* saying things as by making them explicit.[35] When Tacitus explicitly points to omissions or silences (a rhetorical

---

[31] Strocchio 1992, 25–37.
[32] On the role of forgetting and its relation to silence in Tacitus see Schulz 2022. The *Agricola* is frequently in the background of Freytag's narrative: Kelly Shannon-Henderson kindly alerted me to several allusions to the *Agricola* throughout the novel.
[33] See e.g. Winter 2021 on "speaking silences" in the *Dialogus de Oratoribus*.
[34] Cf. also Henderson 1989, 195 n. 4. Tacitus is of course not alone in this: a recent volume (Jouanno 2019) investigates the use of silence as an "ideological tool", a strategic choice in the strongly rhetorical genre of Greco-Roman historiography.
[35] Gardini 2014, 83–85.

technique known as *reticentia* or ἀποσιώπησις), he often attributes these to avoiding the dangers of *taedium* or *satietas* ("weariness" or "satiety"); as Galtier has recently argued, however, these instances paradoxically highlight the historian's determination *not* to be silenced regarding the moral conditions under which he is writing.[36]

Tacitus' own silences in the face of injustice and tyranny, too, are foregrounded by Freytag at several points in the narrative. For example, when Felix Werner first attempts to characterize Tacitus to Ilse in the early phase of their acquaintance, he describes his personality as follows (alluding to the famous prologue of the *Histories*):[37]

> "Es ist ergreifend, wie der besonnene Mann zweifelt, ob dies furchtbare Schicksal von Millionen eine Strafe der Gottheit ist, oder die Folge davon, daß kein Gott sich um das Los der Sterblichen kümmert. Ahnungsvoll und ironisch betrachtet er die Geschicke der einzelnen, die beste Weisheit ist ihm, das Unvermeidliche schweigend und duldend zu ertragen."

> "It is heart-breaking how this sensible man wonders whether this terrible fate of millions is a divine punishment, or the consequence of no god caring for the lot of mortals. With foreboding and irony he contemplates the destinies of individuals; the highest wisdom for him is to bear the inevitable silently and patiently."

The Fürst, too, recognises judicious silence as a quality of Tacitus the historian and politician, but unlike Werner, these silences fill him with nothing but scorn. As the very cause of Roman emperors' descent into madness he points to the weakness and servility of the likes of Tacitus and his senatorial colleagues, who, he claims, adopted as their policy that of the Obersthofmeister, "to bear all with a silent obeisance": a dangerous misinterpretation, as will soon become apparent.[38]

We may conclude, then, that Freytag, a sensitive reader of Tacitus, systematically foregrounds a key characteristic of the historian's works: the many ways in which the silences of both his characters and the authorial voice itself are productive of meaning. For Freytag, Tacitus' speaking silences are the most defining characteristic of this eternally elusive author, and this, as I shall argue next, has important implications also for the reader's response to Tacitean silences produced not by the author's pen but by the history of transmission.

---

36 Galtier 2019, independently of Strocchio 1992.
37 Freytag 1955, 108, alluding to *Histories* 1.3.
38 Freytag 1955, 452: "... seine beste Politik ist die des alten Obersthofmeisters, mit stummer Verbeugung zu ertragen". On the Fürst's misguided interpretation of his Obersthofmeister's silence, see below, p. 399–400.

5 *Die verlorene Handschrift* as the lost manuscript

At the key moment of the novel at which the irrevocability of the manuscript's loss becomes apparent, Freytag writes about the silent man/Tacitus: "er schwieg, sein Mund blieb stumm für immer".[39] This phrase makes explicit what Freytag has been hinting at throughout his novel: that readers are to understand the losses of transmission, too, as authorial silences. And unlike Freytag's characters, who are caught up in unproductive attempts to force Tacitus to *speak* after all, the novel itself demonstrates how Tacitus' incompleteness can be productive and "generative".[40] The title *Die verlorene Handschrift* confidently sets up the novel itself as a substitute, as filling the void left by the lost manuscript and by Tacitus' incompleteness.[41]

There is one core episode in particular in which Freytag performs the generative potential of incomplete or fragmentary transmission in miniature.[42] In chapter IV.11, Werner briefly believes that he has discovered a fragment of the lost manuscript (which however is soon revealed as another forgery, designed to distract him so that the Fürst can approach Ilse). The fragment contains the first part of an episode in the sixth book of the *Annals* (6.21), in which the astrologer Thrasyllus is brought to Tiberius during his exile in Rhodes. Werner recounts:

> "Am Schluss stand noch eine Anekdote aus dem Privatleben des Tiberius. Der verstörte Geist des Fürsten klammert sich an die Astrologie; er ruft Sterndeuter zu sich und läßt in das Meer schleudern, die er in Verdacht eines Betruges hat. Auch der kluge Thrasyllus wird über den verhängnisvollen Felsenpfad zu ihm geführt, er verkündet die verborgenen Geheimnisse des kaiserlichen Lebens. Da forscht Tiberius lauernd, ob er auch wisse, was ihm selbst der gegenwärtige Tag bringen werde. Der Philosoph fragt die Gestirne und ruft zitternd aus: 'Bedenklich ist meine Lage, ich sehe mich in Todesgefahr.' An dieser Stelle

---

39 Full passage cited above, p. 392.
40 On the "generative" force of absences in Latin literature, see Geue/Giusti 2021, 3.
41 On *Die verlorene Handschrift* as substitution, see Dotzler 2011, 244: "So ist es auch unter diesem Aspekt kein Zufall, daß ausgerechnet Tacitus als Autor der verlorenen Handschrift fungiert - Tacitus, der per se Figuren der Rekursion induziert, und die nur lückenhafte Überlieferung seiner Werke, die erstens den Fund einer bislang unbekannten Handschrift so verlockend erscheinen läßt und zweitens, da der Fund ausbleibt, der *Verlorenen Handschrift* die Stelle bezeichnet, an der sie selber auf-, weil eintreten kann." On the "supplementary drive at the heart of reception" in general, see Geue/Giusti 2021, 6 and 11.
42 For a discussion of this episode from a different perspective, see Baisch/Lüdeke 2000, 231–232.

bricht unser Bruchstück ab. Der Vorfall mag sich wiederholt haben, dieselbe Anekdote haftet auf mehr als einem Fürstenleben."[43]

"At the end stood an anecdote from the private life of Tiberius. The troubled mind of the prince clings to astrology; he calls astrologers to him and has those of them he suspects of fraud hurled into the sea. The clever Thrasyllus, too, is led up to him by the fateful rock path; he proclaims the hidden secrets of the emperor's life. Then Tiberius inquires slyly whether he also knows what the present day will bring him. The philosopher consults the stars and exclaims with trepidation: 'My situation is critical, I see myself in mortal danger.' At this point our fragment breaks off. The incident may have repeated itself, the same anecdote attaches to more than one ruler's life."

The (forged) fragment breaks off at this point, initially depriving Freytag's readers (especially those unfamiliar with this Tacitean episode) of the outcome of the situation. However, in the very next scene, the episode is continued and transformed in Freytag's own narrative. While the Tacitean Tiberius takes this astrologer's answer as evidence of his reliability and does not have him killed but rather embraces him as a friend, the Fürst's paranoia drives him to attempt to assassinate Werner with his hunting rifle:[44]

Der Gelehrte sah den Fürsten an, aus den Augen sprühte tödlicher Haß und der glitzernde Schein des bösen Blickes, er sah die Mündung des Gewehres gegen seine Brust gerichtet und daß der gehobene Fuß des Fürsten um den Drücker fuhr. Der Wetterstrahl zuckte, kein Raum zur Flucht, keine Zeit zur Neigung; der Gedanke des letzten Augenblicks fuhr ihm durch das Haupt. Er erblickte vor sich das verzerrte Antlitz des Kaisers Tiberius und er sagte leise: "Ich stehe auf dem Pfad des Todes."

The scholar looked at the Fürst, from whose eyes deadly hatred and the glittering gleam of the evil eye flashed, he saw the muzzle of the rifle pointed against his chest and that the lifted foot of the prince went towards the trigger. Lightning flashed, no room to flee, no time to duck; the thought of the last moment flashed through his head. He beheld before him the distorted countenance of the emperor Tiberius, and he said softly, "I stand on the path of death."

The Thrasyllus episode, which Freytag artificially turns into an incomplete episode interrupted by transmission, receives a new ending in the dramatic

---

43 The Fürst earlier also refers to this episode and his conscious re-enactment of the Tiberian trial (Freytag 1955, 506): "Reicht dein Witz aus, Philosoph, dein Schicksal vorauszusehen, wie jenem alten Sterndeuter gelang, den dein Tiberius nach der eigenen Zukunft frug? Laß uns versuchen, wie weise du bist." ("Is your wisdom sufficient, philosopher, to foresee your destiny, as that old astrologer succeeded in doing, whom your Tiberius asked about his own future? Let us try how wise you are.").
44 Freytag 1955, 510.

near-assassination of Werner at the hands of the modern-day tyrant. Through this episode, Freytag performs in miniature the openness and the generative force which incomplete textual transmission creates — and which, on a much larger scale, underpins his entire novel. Freytag's plot is inspired yet unconstrained by his model precisely because Tacitus' work is so deeply characterized by its generative silences.

By contrast, in 1859, years before the publication of *Die verlorene Handschrift*, Freytag completed a play entitled "Die Fabier", an allegorical representation of contemporary class conflict in the guise of a historical episode about patrician-plebeian confrontations during the Roman Republic. The historical inspiration is Livy's account of events surrounding the fate of the *gens Fabia* at the battle of Cremera (477 BCE, recounted at *Ab Urbe Condita* 2.49–50). Freytag's correspondence from the period of composition tells us that he struggled with the play.[45] In its first version, his play's plot more or less followed the Livian narrative (although Freytag adds a dramatic conspiracy and a love story). However, both Freytag and his friend Eduard Devrient, to whom he showed the finished play, found the initial ending to the story unsatisfactory, both dramatically and in terms of the desired contemporary political message. On the advice of Devrient, Freytag subsequently altered the play's ending (resulting in a second version, published in 1861 and in the *Gesammelte Werke*). This version, unlike the first, concluded with the wholesale legalization of inter-class marriage between patricians and plebeians, presented as a means to promote the plebeian (i.e. bourgeois) cause. This change rendered the play a more readily comprehensible and more optimistic "political allegory of social change".[46] However, this new ending involves a considerable departure from Livy's account, in which the explicit legalization of inter-class marriage in the form of the lex Canuleia occurs several decades later (in 445 BCE, recounted at *Ab Urbe Condita* 4.3–6) and is therefore entirely divorced from the events surrounding the Fabii and the battle of Cremera. While Freytag ultimately felt that the changes and the new conclusion improved the play from a dramaturgical point of view, he initially seems to have had serious scruples about deviating from his historical source.[47]

I believe that this episode can help us understand why Freytag embraces the silences and incompleteness of Tacitus' *Annals*. In *Die Fabier*, Freytag had already acknowledged the suitability of the Roman past as a means for promoting

---

[45] On this episode and Freytag's correspondence surrounding it, see Schofield 2012, 111–118.
[46] Schofield 2012, 118.
[47] Schofield 2012, 113, 118.

political change in the present. However, he had also found the particulars of his historical source something of a hindrance in expressing his contemporary vision of social change. In contrast, the very incompleteness of the Tacitean text offers the author a means of escape from the restrictions of the source.

As the narrative unfolds, Freytag's characters sometimes show an awareness of the fact that their experiences bear a striking resemblance to Tacitus' *Annals*, and in particular to the Tiberian books. They note similarities and differences between their own situation and that of Tacitean characters and events, and they variously submit to or attempt to resist these moulds. For example, in chapter IV.6, fittingly entitled "A chapter from the lost manuscript" ("Ein Kapitel aus der verlorenen Handschrift"), Werner attempts — apparently without guile — to entertain the Fürst by discoursing at length about Tacitus' psychopathology of power. In the grip of scholarly fervour and lost to his surroundings, Werner informs his audience that all rulers who enjoy absolute and unlimited power eventually go mad, and praises the clear-sighted analysis of this phenomenon which he finds in Tacitus. The Fürst, rather understandably, projects this analysis onto himself, and it is precisely this self-recognition that precipitates his own descent into madness.[48] He consciously attempts to resist the parallel, telling himself that he is far removed from the homicidal mania of the Tacitean emperors,[49] but in vain, as his failed assassination attempt on Werner will soon prove.[50]

At other points, however, Freytag particularly stresses the extent to which his characters can — and should — break free from reperforming Tacitean models, and stresses the openness of potential historical parallels. For example, as mentioned above, the Fürst attributes the cause of the Roman emperors' madness to the weakness and servility of the likes of Tacitus and his senatorial colleagues, who, he claims, adopted as their policy "die des alten Obersthofmeisters, mit

---

48 For example, directly after Werner's lecture, he and the Obersthofmeister are disturbed by a strange animalistic sound in the castle, which is suggested to have been produced by the Fürst: "Als sie auf der Treppe waren, klang ein heiserer Mißton aus der Ferne ... Der Professor lauschte, alles war still. 'Das war wie der Schrei eines wilden Tieres', sagte er." (Freytag 1955, 436) — "When they were on the stairs, a hoarse, ugly sound came from afar ... The professor listened, everything was silent. 'It was like the cry of a wild animal,' he said."
49 "Du lügst, Professor, wenn du mich deinen alten Kaisern vergleichst. Mir graut bei dem Gedanken an Dinge, die jene lachend taten, und mein Hirn weigert sich zu denken, was einst ein kurzer Wink der Hand befahl." (Freytag 1955, 506) — "You lie, Professor, when you compare me to your ancient emperors. I shudder at the thought of things they did laughingly, and my brain refuses to think what once a brief wave of the hand commanded."
50 See above, p. 397.

stummer Verbeugung zu ertragen" ("that of the old High Steward, to bear all with a silent obeisance").[51] However, this scornful comparison misses more than the fact that senatorial silence, as argued above, rarely conveys only cowed submission. More importantly, the Fürst's casting of his own Oberhofmeister in the role of a silent and inactive senator turns out to be entirely inaccurate. In chapter V.2, this old courtier, far from remaining silent, bravely confronts his sovereign. He threatens to make public the Fürst's deranged mind, as evidenced by his assassination attempt on Werner, "denn ich bin nicht gewohnt, halbe Wahrheit für Wahrheit zu achten" ("for I am not used to consider a half-truth the truth").[52] Unblinkingly accepting the Fürst's incontinent rage and his dismissal, he continues to threaten public exposure unless the Fürst immediately abdicates.

Despite having described, in the final third of his novel, a "Tacitean" dysfunctional court and an autocratic ruler descending into paranoia, Freytag peoples it with characters who are free to change the world in which they live, and is thus able to conclude his own narrative optimistically: the reign of the despot ends, the young crown prince promises political modernisations in his state, and a stronger and more influential position for the morally upright *Bürgertum* seems assured.

Freytag also marshals the incompleteness and resulting openness of his model as a call to action for his readers. He implies that his readers, too — like the characters in his novel — are called to write their own history. Tacitus' work may be able to teach us about the dangers of unconstrained absolutism, but where Tacitus breaks off, modern citizens are able to continue the narrative, and thereby to transform their own society. Through the voice of his hero Werner, Freytag reminds his readers that they, too, face a choice: it lies in their power to prevent "daß die Zustände des alten Roms in unserer Nation gespenstisch aufleben" ("a ghostly revival of the conditions of ancient Rome in our time").[53] They can reinvigorate the nation and its leaders, because "wir sind nicht Römer, sondern warmherzige und dauerhafte Germanen" ("we are not Romans, but warm-hearted and steady Germans").[54]

---

51 See above, p. 395.
52 Freytag 1955, 541.
53 Freytag 1955, 539.
54 Freytag 1955, 515.

6 Conclusion

While the title *Die verlorene Handschrift* stakes out the novel's ambition to stand as a supplement to Tacitus' work, the experience of reading it is utterly unlike reading the *Annals* or the *Histories*. While Tacitus challenges his readers with his dense and oblique prose, Freytag's own style is expansive and often painstakingly explicit in matters of description.[55] While a bitingly ironic undercurrent is one of the *Annals'* most distinctive qualities, Freytag's novel deliberately assumes a lightly humorous tone, featuring extended passages about the everyday arguments between two neighbouring families (which can strike modern readers as somewhat ponderous).[56] And yet, reading Freytag's novel can offer us a fresh look at Tacitus' characteristic 'speaking silences'. Werner's idea that Tacitus will fully reveal himself to him if only he discovers the manuscript is misguided: Tacitus, Freytag suggests, reveals his very essence through his silences, and therefore also through his incompleteness. In the introduction to their 2021 volume on *Absence in Latin Literature and its Reception*, Geue and Giusti remind Classical scholars that "much can be said by and about the [ancient] texts themselves once we start reading their *lacunae* as active producers of meaning rather than empty vessels waiting to be filled by speculation."[57] I read Freytag's novel as a narrative substantiation of just such an approach. To become wrapped up in finding out what exactly Tacitus might have said in the absent parts of his work is not only unproductive, but dangerous, as his Werner, Hahn, Struvelius and Knips all find out to their cost. On the other hand, to embrace Tacitus' silences as the very essence of this author opens them up as productive of meaning, inviting readers to respond, to converse with the author across two millennia, and to rewrite not only the past, but also the present.

Abbreviations

KLL: Arnold, Heinz Ludwig (2009), *Kindlers Literatur-Lexikon: KLL*, Springer Nature Switzerland, https://doi.org/10.1007/978-3-476-05728-0.

---

[55] Ping 2006, 175: "Freytag certainly understood Tacitus's ideas but the spare and direct qualities of Tacitus's writing were clearly beyond the reach of his ever-wordy writing style."
[56] For a frank aesthetic judgement and some illuminating contemporary responses to the novel's literary quality, see Ping 2006, 161–163.
[57] Geue/Giusti 2021, 3.

Bibliography

Baisch, Martin/Lüdeke, Roger (2000), "Das Alte ist das Neue. Zum Status des historisch-kritischen Wissens in G. Freytags *Die verlorene Handschrift* und A. S. Byatts *Possession*", in: Christiane Henkes/Harald Saller (eds.), *Text und Autor: Beiträge aus dem Venedig-Symposium 1998 des Graduiertenkollegs »Textkritik« (München)*, Berlin/Boston, 223–251.

Barnes, T.D. (1977), "The Fragments of Tacitus' *Histories*", *Classical Philology* 72.3, 224–231.

Bruno, Nicoletta (2022), "Unspoken Messages: Tiberius and the Power of Silence in Tacitus' *Annals*", in: Giulia Dovico/Olivia Montepaone/Marco Pelucchi (eds.), *The Limits of Exactitude in Greek, Roman, and Byzantine Literature and Textual Transmission*, Trends in Classics – Supplementary Volumes 137, Berlin/Boston, 37–58.

Dörr, Volker C. (2001), "Idealistische Wissenschaft. Der (bürgerliche) Realismus und Gustav Freytags Roman 'Die verlorene Handschrift'", in: Norbert Oellers/Hartmut Steinecke (eds.), *'Realismus'? Zur deutschen Prosa-Literatur des 19. Jahrhunderts*, Zeitschrift für deutsche Philologie, Sonderheft, Berlin, 3–33.

Dotzler, Bernhard J. (2011), "*Litterarum secreta — fraus litteraria*: Über Gustav Freytag: die verlorene Handschrift", in: H. Kircher/M. Kłańska (eds.), *Literatur und Politik in der Heine-Zeit: Die 48er Revolution in Texten zwischen Vormärz und Nachmärz*, Köhn/Weimar, 235–250.

Feeney, Denis (2019), "Lacking Any Exception: The Best Book of Tacitus", *TLS, Times Literary Supplement* 6068 (July), 32–33.

Freytag, Gustav (1865), *The Lost Manuscript*, Translated by Giorgiana Malcolm, 3 vols., London.

Freytag, Gustav (1870), "Die Handschriften von Arborea", *Grenzboten* 1870, 15. Cited according to https://www.gustav-freytag.info/index.php/originaltexte/30–die-handschriften-von-arborea

Freytag, Gustav (1955), *Die verlorene Handschrift*, München.

Galtier, Fabrice (2019), "Le silence et la mémoire dans les *Annales* de Tacite", in: Corinne Jouanno (ed.), *Les silences de l'historien: oublis, omissions, effets de censure dans l'historiographie antique et médiévale*, Giornale Italiano di Filologia - Bibliotheca 20, Turnhout, 135–154.

Gardini, Nicola (2014), *Lacuna: saggio sul non detto*, Saggistica letteraria e linguistica 627, Torino.

Geue, Tom/Giusti, Elena (2021), "Introduction", in: Tom Geue/Elena Giusti (eds.), *Unspoken Rome*, Cambridge, 1–16.

Goodyear, Francis Richard David (1972), *The Annals of Tacitus: Books 1–6, Volume 1, Annals 1.1–54*, Cambridge Classical Texts and Commentaries 15, Cambridge.

Henderson, John (1989), "Tacitus/The World in Pieces", *Ramus* 18.1–2, 167–210.

Jouanno, Corinne (ed.) (2019), *Les silences de l'historien: oublis, omissions, effets de censure dans l'historiographie antique et médiévale*, Giornale Italiano di Filologia - Bibliotheca 20, Turnhout.

Martin, R.H. (2010), "From Manuscript to Print", in: A.J. Woodman (ed.), *The Cambridge Companion to Tacitus*, Cambridge, 241–252.

McNamara, James (2021), "Lost in *Germania*: The Absence of History in Tacitus' Ethnography", in: Tom Geue/Elena Giusti (eds.), *Unspoken Rome*, Cambridge, 201–218.

O'Gorman, Ellen (2021), "Conspicuous Absence: Tacitus' *De Re Publica*", in: Tom Geue/Elena Giusti (eds.), *Unspoken Rome*, Cambridge, 219–236.

Oliver, Revilo P. (1951), "The First Medicean MS of Tacitus and the Titulature of Ancient Books", *Transactions and Proceedings of the American Philological Association* 82, 232–261.
Ping, Larry L. (2006), *Gustav Freytag and the Prussian Gospel: Novels, Liberalism, and History*, Oxford.
Reynolds, L.D./Marshall, Peter K. (1983)² (eds.), *Texts and Transmission: A Survey of the Latin Classics*, Oxford.
Römer, Franz (2012), "Sprache und Stil des 'Schweigsamen Historikers' als Anreiz für neulateinische Deutungen", in: Astrid Steiner-Weber/Karl A.E. Enenkel (eds.), *Acta Conventus Neo-Latini Monasteriensis: Proceedings of the Fifteenth International Congress of Neo-Latin Studies*, Münster, 430–439.
Schofield, Benedict (2012), *Private Lives and Collective Destinies: Class, Nation and the Folk in the Works of Gustav Freytag (1816–1895)*, Bithell Series of Dissertations, Institute of Germanic and Romance Studies 37, London.
Schulz, Verena (2022), "Formen des Vergessens bei Tacitus", *Millennium* 19.1, 131–144.
Sommer, Paul (1905), *Erläuterungen zu Gustav Freytags Die verlorene Handschrift*, Dr. Wilhelm Königs Erläuterungen zu den Klassikern 112/113, Leipzig.
Strocchio, Roberta (1992), *I significati del silenzio nell'opera di Tacito*, Memorie dell'Accademia delle scienze di Torino, Classe di scienze morali, storiche e filologiche, Ser. 5, Vol. 16, fasc. 1–4, Torino.
Winter, Kathrin (2021), "Speaking Silence in Cicero's *Brutus* and Tacitus' *Dialogus de Oratoribus*", in: Tom Geue/Elena Giusti (eds.), *Unspoken Rome*, Cambridge, 125–141.
Woodman, Anthony John (2004), *Tacitus, The Annals. Translated with Introduction and Notes*, Indianapolis-Cambridge.

Stéphanie Dord-Crouslé
Putting an Unfinished Novel Back into Motion: A Digital Tool to Create Possible "Second Volumes" of *Bouvard et Pécuchet*

Abstract: As Flaubert feared, death interrupted the writing process of *Bouvard et Pécuchet*. But does this incompletion express the structural impossibility of completing an encyclopedic novel that was to include, in its unwritten second volume, something like the totality of the world's discourses? Without denying the interest that regards this novel as the precursor of our modernity, the Bouvard project (https://www.dossiers-flaubert.fr) wanted to consider its incompletion as essentially undergone and situational. By using digital media, it started again from the documentary materials gathered by Flaubert — these papers constitute only a work in progress that was brutally immobilized by the author's death — and gave new life to the specific composition process of the second volume, which is based on an arrangement of textual fragments. There can then emerge a plurality of possible "second volumes", which, far from remedying the effective incompleteness of the work, takes account of it and makes the mobility of its fragments a constitutive dimension of this unfinished work.

Flaubert was concerned with perfection. He was a writer who polished his sentences at length and constructed his works with the precision of an architect. But the time required to satisfy this irrepressible aspiration came into conflict with the novelist's often expressed desire to finish each novel promptly. For him, the tension was always extreme between the infinite work necessary to achieve the ideal ("That's what's diabolical about prose — it's never finished")[1] and the immediate desire to finish the work in progress (Flaubert was always "in a hurry to finish [his] damned book").[2]

It was no different for his final novel, *Bouvard et Pécuchet*. This "encyclopedia of modern foolishness"[3] tells the story of two copyists who leave Paris for a

---

[1] Flaubert 2017. Letter from Flaubert to Louise Colet, June 28, 1853. (All translations are mine.) This article has received financial support from the Maison des Sciences de l'Homme Lyon Saint-Étienne.
[2] Flaubert 2017. Letter from Flaubert to Olympe Bonenfant, November 28, 1855.
[3] Flaubert 2017. Letter from Flaubert to Adèle Perrot, October 17, 1872.

house in Normandy "on a stupid plateau between Caen and Falaise",[4] where they will put to the test all the branches of knowledge of their time (agriculture as well as calisthenics and philosophy) before finally returning, disappointed, to their original activity as copyists, but this time applied to the works they have previously read.

However, this "kind of critical encyclopedia in farce"[5] has two specificities. The first is that the work was never finished because Flaubert literally died on the job; the second is that several critical readings of the novel assert that this incompleteness is a defining characteristic of the work. In order to examine this singular situation, we must first consider to what extent the novel was unfinished and the reasons why it could be argued that it was unfinishable — that Flaubert's unexpected death was paradoxically the only conceivable way out. Then, without denying the interest in considering this novel a precursor of modernism, we will explain why those of us working on the Bouvard project have chosen to consider this incompletion as essentially imposed and accidental, not to provide an "end" to the novel, but on the contrary to take a dynamic approach to a fragmentary work and allow for the emergence of an infinite number of possible "second volumes," rediscovering in another way the novel's element of incompleteness.

1 *Bouvard et Pécuchet*: an unfinished novel

1.1 The novel as testament

Flaubert never found writing easy. As a young man (when he was working on *Madame Bovary*), he felt the "*torments* of art" so acutely that they made him "want to die".[6] As his health deteriorated, he was concerned that his writing anxiety would make him unable to complete his works. A month before his death, he wrote to Tourgueneff:

---

4 Flaubert 2017. Letter from Flaubert to Caroline Commanville, June 24, 1874.
5 Flaubert 2017. Letter from Flaubert to Edma Roger des Genettes, August 19, 1872.
6 Flaubert 2017. Letter from Flaubert to Louise Colet, January 12, 1853.

> When Pradier [the sculptor of Napoleon's tomb] was working at the Invalides in 1848, he used to keep saying: "The Emperor's tomb will be mine," so tired was he of his work. As for me, I can say: "It is time for the end of my book, otherwise it will be my own end."[7]

The development of *Bouvard et Pécuchet* was like a race against time to determine which would be finished first: the writer or the novel. In 1879, Flaubert, under pressure to publish, exclaimed:

> *My two gentlemen* [i.e. Bouvard and Pécuchet] *are nowhere near being finished!* The first volume will be done this summer, but when? & the second will take me another six months, if I haven't been finished off myself before the book![8]

Yet the writer hoped to see his novel through to the end: "I would like to visit the dark shores only after *I have vomited the bile that is suffocating me*: that is to say, not before I have written the book I am preparing",[9] he stated in 1873. For he saw this novel as a sort of a testament, as he confided to George Sand: "The difficulties of such a book frighten me. And yet I would not like to die before I have accomplished it, for in the end, it is my testament".[10] It was inconceivable for the novelist not to complete a text intended to contain the ultimate expression of his thought, indeed the presentation of the essential principles of his art.

1.2 A structure planned, but unfinished

But that is what happened on May 8, 1880, the ill-fated day when Flaubert suddenly died, leaving his last novel unfinished. It is certain that the work was to have two volumes. The first — which Flaubert wrote almost entirely — consists of ten chapters organized around the various subjects that Bouvard and Pécuchet successively study once they have left Paris and their job as copyists: agriculture, science, history, etc. The only thing missing is the final scene of the tenth chapter. However, the second volume, although Flaubert stated in January 1880 that it was "three-quarters done",[11] exists only as an outline and as a collection of gathered documents. It should have included two chapters. The

---

7 Flaubert 2017. Letter from Flaubert to Ivan Tourgueneff, April 7, 1880.
8 Flaubert 2017. Letter from Flaubert to Juliette Adam, December 2, 1879.
9 Flaubert 2017. Letter from Flaubert to Edma Roger des Genettes, February 22, 1873.
10 Flaubert 2017. Letter from Flaubert to George Sand, February 18, 1876. Auguste Sabatier also reported that Flaubert confided to him: "This philosophical novel [...] is my testament, the summary of my experiences and my judgment on man and man's works" (Flaubert 2011, 457).
11 Flaubert 2017. Letter from Flaubert to Edma Roger des Genettes, January 24, 1880.

first (the eleventh chapter) was planned to be highly developed and would have presented the "copy" that the two characters had written, sometimes referred to as their *sottisier* (a collection of foolish comments), i.e. a catalogue categorized by headings of all the nonsense they found during the readings done for the experiments they conducted in the first volume. Finally, a twelfth and last chapter would have been the novel's "conclusion in three or four pages".[12]

Flaubert's death halted the work on the second volume. The unfinished work was then posthumously published by the writer's niece only a few months after his death. She herself prepared the text for the first ten chapters and had to resign herself to leaving out the material for the second volume after Maupassant's unwillingness to provide a publishable version. Flaubert's "disciple" chose to "recognize the impossibility of completing what [he had] undertaken:"

> I have just spent three months compiling and trying to arrange the notes of our poor dead man, in order to extract from them the book he wanted to produce, and I now believe the task is unachievable.[13]

Yet Maupassant's work was not in vain since successive editions of the novel soon included an appendix with an overview of the material that this mysterious "second volume" would have contained. From the 1950s onwards, a few editions even attempted extensive speculative reconstructions of this *sottisier*.

1.3 A providential incompletion?

Maupassant was right to be worried about the lack of understanding that would inevitably arise from "this heap of documents in the midst of which his own [Flaubert's] thought would no longer shed any light." But the "disciple" was absolutely convinced that the project conceived by the hermit of Croisset would ultimately have been finished and would have been a success. Many critics did not share this opinion, Émile Faguet among them:

> It was not unwise of Flaubert to die before the publication of *Bouvard*, first as the work gained success because the author was dead; second because, published during his lifetime, the book would have flopped; and third because Flaubert himself, whose eyes were

---

12 Flaubert 2017. Letter from Flaubert to Edma Roger des Genettes, April 7, 1879.
13 Flaubert/Maupassant 1993, 261–262. Letter from Maupassant to Caroline Commanville, July 30, 1881.

opened to his works when they were printed, would have found it below his expectations and would have suffered, given the enormous effort he had put into it.[14]

So was death a happy accident for a tired, worn-out writer whose work would have missed its target if the author had been able to finish it? Other critics go even further, claiming that the author's unexpected death was a blessing for the work, which at its core was impossible to complete, as maintained by Claudine Gothot-Mersch:

> One cannot help but think that fate settled things even better than the author could have done; that Flaubert's death before the completion of his work was in accordance with the logic of the project, and that this was a providential event for *Bouvard*, definitively and radically removing the question of the ending of this novel, which I have tried to show was by its very nature interminable.[15]

But why would the unfinished novel *Bouvard et Pécuchet* have been "by its very nature" unfinishable?

2 *Bouvard et Pécuchet*: an unfinishable novel?

2.1 Structural incompleteness: circularity

First of all, there are thematic causes: the encyclopedic research of the two characters is in essence infinite, and the stupidity they reveal is bottomless. But we won't dwell on this here as there is, above all, a structural basis for the novel's unfinished character. In fact, it is based on a "remarkable formal circularity: the story keeps repeating the same path, it keeps going back over its own tracks".[16] In the first chapter, when the two characters meet in Paris, they discuss their interests and comment on what is happening in front of them, already making an initial round of the knowledge they will later experiment with in

---

14 Faguet 1899, 137. This critic also wrote: "*Bouvard et Pécuchet* should not be judged too severely, since it is a posthumous and unfinished work, and one may believe, given Flaubert's obstinacy in correcting himself, that he would have profoundly reworked it" (127). The same severe judgement can be found in Albert Thibaudet: "*Bouvard et Pécuchet* is the very report card, the sanction of this old age, this decadence, this dissolution; it is the base level, the zero altitude that the river reaches at the moment when it is going to disappear" (Thibaudet 1935, 177–178).
15 Gothot-Mersch 1981, 22.
16 Gothot-Mersch 1981, 9.

chapters two to nine, the second time around. Then chapter ten, which deals with pedagogy, brings back to the foreground much of the knowledge that must be taught to Victor and Victorine, the children taken in by Bouvard and Pécuchet. According to the plans left by Flaubert, the next chapter was meant to be the two men's "copy", consisting of extracts from the previously read works (fourth round), presented as an anthology. Finally, the novelist seemed to have envisaged "two last turns of the spiral",[17] which would have consisted first of Bouvard and Pécuchet's discovery of a letter from the doctor at Chavignolles placing them in the category of harmless lunatics, which would have "had to be the reader's critique of the novel"[18] (fifth round) and then, in the final round, the insertion of "the copy *in extenso* crowning the whole."[19] The novel's diegetic mainspring thus approaches eternal recommencement; as Claudine Gothot-Mersch remarks, "it seems [that Flaubert] never resigns himself to putting the finishing touches on his novel".[20]

2.2 Aesthetic incompleteness: modernism

This structural circularity, certainly intended by Flaubert but whose effect is muddied by the unexpected interruption of the work, has paved the way for the famous analyses that have made *Bouvard et Pécuchet* one of the works at the source of modernism, given that incompleteness, according to Barthes, is one of the four constituent traits of the concept.[21] We need only recall a few lines from Michel Foucault's inspired interpretation, who, when asked what the two characters are copying at the end of the novel, offers this fascinating answer:

> Books, their books, all books, and this book, no doubt, which is *Bouvard et Pécuchet*: for to copy is to do nothing; it is to be the books that are copied, it is to be this infinitesimal distension of language that redoubles itself, it is to be the fold of discourse on itself, it is to be this invisible existence that transforms the passing word into the infinity of rumor.

And then concludes:

---

17 Gothot-Mersch 1981, 22.
18 Flaubert 2013. Ms. gg 10, folio 67.
19 Gothot-Mersch 1981, 22. This hypothesis, put forward by Demorest and supported by Claudine Gothot-Mersch, seems, however, unlikely. In our view, chapter eleven would have presented the copy and chapter twelve the conclusion "in three or four pages."
20 Gothot-Mersch 1981, 22.
21 See Barthes, 1976.

> Bouvard and Pécuchet triumph over all that is foreign to the book and resist it, by becoming themselves the continuous movement of the Book. The book opened by Saint Anthony and from which all temptations have flown away, the two men will prolong it without term, without illusion, without greed, without sin, without desire. [22]

Clearly, it is the distinctive nature of the second volume that allows the emergence and development of these reflections and gives them their speculative and suggestive scope. Flaubert's last scenario ends with this gloss on the copy the characters are engaged in: "The page must be filled, everything is equal: the good and the evil, the beautiful and the ugly, the farcical and the sublime, the insignificant and the characteristic. There are only phenomena".[23] The text no longer seems to have a defined boundary or limit — the inside and the outside blend indistinctly.[24]

This levelling of everything might seem to be in line with Flaubert's vehement denunciation of conclusions that has often been considered his trademark: "*Ineptitude consists of the desire to conclude*",[25] he asserted as early as 1850. He went on to stress in 1863: "The urge to want to conclude is one of the most fatal and fruitless manias of humanity".[26] Would writing the impossibility of its completion into the text itself be the magic formula, the ultimate solution, preventing it from being subjected to the idiocy of concluding? Did Flaubert deliberately forge a "fundamentally and systematically unfinishable work"?[27] We argue that this conception in fact reflects an incomplete and biased understanding of the novelist's refusal of the conclusion that he so often expressed.

2.3 Textual incompleteness: the "non finito"

The conclusion that Flaubert rejected is not to be found at the end of a novel. It is found in the patient work that produces each sentence, gradually building up the impossibility for the reader to settle on the meaning of the work and thus the disappearance of any conclusive character. The author does not avoid this by refraining from writing the end of a novel. Nothing is more complete than *L'Éducation sentimentale*, a novel that has in fact two successive concluding

---

[22] Foucault 1983, 122.
[23] Flaubert 2011, 401.
[24] See Mouchard/Neefs 1980, 171–217.
[25] Flaubert 2017. Letter from Flaubert to Louis Bouilhet, September 4, 1850.
[26] Flaubert 2017. Letter from Flaubert to Marie-Sophie Leroyer de Chantepie, October 23, 1863.
[27] De Biasi 1986, 45.

chapters, and which Flaubert loudly rejoiced at having finished on "Sunday morning," May 16, 1869, at "exactly 4:56": "Finished, my friend! Yes, my book is finished!"[28] And yet there is nothing less conclusive than this novel whose meaning endlessly eludes us because the novelist has worked to make it indeterminable ... Flaubert achieves this effect by pushing to the extreme a concerted aesthetic approach that leaves gaps in the textual process, preventing the meaning from being arrested. The effect is "non finito", the paradoxical result of neither renunciation nor abandonment, but conversely of "an obsession with mastered form, [with] the definitive, [with] completion and perfection".[29] In this way, the incompletion that is integral to Flaubert's writing process aims to preclude any conclusion regarding the meaning while at the same time perfecting the form.

This poetics of the non finito does not only concern *Bouvard et Pécuchet* — it is not specific to this unfinished work. The mechanics on which it is based were built up progressively and their effects are visible in all the novelist's works. Flaubert's refusal to conclude is not equivalent to the impossibility of bringing a text to an end, as is evident in the writer's correspondence, the essentially classic novelistic aesthetics of his last novel, and his outline. While the effect of eternal recommencement due to the structure of the work is obviously deliberate and the poetics of the novel are the bearer of this singular and characteristic non finito, the fact remains that the incompletion of *Bouvard et Pécuchet* is fundamentally imposed and accidental, caused by the unforeseen death of the author. It is this incompletion that we can try to remedy — not, of course, by writing the continuation and the end of the adventures of the two copyists in Flaubert's place, but by trying to understand what configurations (with an emphasis on the plural) might have been adopted in the second and final volume the writer planned for his novel.

---

28 Flaubert 2017. Letter from Flaubert to Jules Duplan, May 16, 1869.
29 De Biasi 1986, 48.

3 "Finishing" *Bouvard et Pécuchet*: creating a plurality of possible "second volumes"

3.1 Unfinished business: a frozen corpus of manuscripts

Imagining the potential content of the second volume of *Bouvard et Pécuchet* would require a review of all the preparatory manuscripts collected by the novelist to write his last novel; these were preserved after his death, and are found today mainly in Rouen's municipal library. But our purpose here is not to provide an exhaustive inventory,[30] rather to explain why the printed editions proposing speculative reconstructions, based on the archives in Rouen, are unsatisfactory, leading us to develop an alternative editorial project: the Bouvard project. This takes advantage of the digital medium, allowing a different, reformulated response to the problems raised by the novel's incompleteness.

Although the printed editions of the "second volume" have considerable merit, they suffer from unavoidable bias insofar as they have to make selections and classification choices from the documentary materials gathered by Flaubert, while at the time of the author's death, these materials were only a work in progress. By establishing a list of closed categories and dividing the citations present in the known files between these categories, these printed editions artificially freeze a work in progress in which certain items are missing (some, kept in private collections, are still unknown) and, above all, in which the copying process had not yet been completed. Flaubert worked by successively copying the same textual fragments onto different types of documents: reading notes, summary pages and finally pages he was preparing for the second volume.[31] Each text had to pass through all these successive stages before it could appear in the second volume. But the novelist did not have enough time to copy many of them, although they were marked "for copying" in the margin of the reading notes. And even those that were, Flaubert may have decided not to include in the end. Thus, in any editorial reconstruction of the work, everything should remain fluid.

Moreover, the annotations made by the writer, which indicate the probable place of each citation's classification, are often multiple. Even in the case of the

---

[30] For an inventory, see Dord-Crouslé 2014, 25–46; for regular updates of this inventory and more on the Bouvard project, see Dord-Crouslé 2008.
[31] See Dord-Crouslé/Morlock-Gerstenkorn/Tournoy 2011, 123–145, Dord-Crouslé 2012; and 2016, 115–137.

citations that seem most in keeping with what Flaubert may have been aiming for, the categories of classification intended by the writer for his "second volume" prove to be unstable. For example, in folio 14, volume 7, the top fragment is linked to three classification categories. One is crossed out ("Medical style"), but the other two ("Rococo" and "The dangers of chocolate") coexist without any clear distinction.[32] This fundamental instability compels us to preserve a mobility for the textual fragments that is necessarily defeated by the fixity of a printed edition. Taking advantage of the possibilities offered by digital technology, the ongoing Bouvard project, which received funding from the French National Research Agency (ANR) from 2008 to 2012, seeks to correct this bias and restore the mobility of the corpus by allowing the production of "second volumes" on demand.

3.2 The methodological conditions for reworking the corpus

The Bouvard project has two intrinsically linked goals: one is to make a complex corpus accessible in the form of an online edition; the other is to allow any Internet user to produce configurations of citations extracted from the corpus. These textual arrangements are possible "second volumes" based on various hypotheses regarding the selection and classification of the textual fragments. The link between the two parts of the project is based on the use of XML-TEI as a pivot format: the integral encoding of the corpus allows for both visualizing and cutting the textual fragments, and then organizing them via a computer tool (named the "Arranger") developed during the project to permit the production of "second volumes." This tool allows the textual fragments constituting the corpus to be ordered following different hypotheses to give rise to an infinite number of possible "second volumes".[33]

A methodological clarification is nevertheless necessary. We should emphasize that we do not in any way presume that any production resulting from the Arranger and available in the website files of *Bouvard et Pécuchet* can legitimately claim the title — even the cautious title — of "conjectural reconstitution of the second volume of *Bouvard et Pécuchet*". Flaubert himself points out to us, his future academic editors, the limits that should not be crossed by drawing attention to a quotation from Claude de Loynes d'Autroche, who translated the

---

32 Flaubert 2012. Ms g226 (7), folio 14. See https://www.dossiers-flaubert.fr/cote-g226_7_f_014__r ____-trd [accessed on 08/08/2023].
33 A video available online shows how the tool works. See Dord-Crouslé/Dury 2016.

Aeneid into French verse in 1804. An extract from the preface that this obscure literary scholar wrote for his work is quoted in the entry devoted to him in a supplement to Michaud's famous *Biographie universelle*, a biography of notable individuals:

> "Besides the translation of the *Aeneid* as it exists, I would have proposed," he says in his preface, "a new edition such as I suppose Virgil might have composed if a longer life had allowed him to put the finishing touches to his work. *I would therefore have removed the weak or useless things* ... and, preserving all that was beautiful, I would have tried *to add that which he would have included* WITH CERTAINTY".[34]

Flaubert took note of part of this quotation,[35] which serves as a repellent. He stored the recopied fragment in a file entitled "Corrected classics" that includes editorial practices that he clearly felt were the height of folly!

Naturally, the primary ambition of our editorial enterprise was not to incur Flaubert's posthumous wrath. Our intention was not to make "weak or useless things" disappear or add "beautiful things" of our own, but to make all the existing documentary material available in order to generate dynamic, nonconclusive, open, potential second volumes of the unfinished novel.

3.3 The Arranger, a tool for dynamic incompletion

The Arranger is a computer tool that allows the fragments of the corpus to be organized. It can be compared to a kaleidoscope in that it is made up of a finite number of elements contained in a space that is itself finite, but allows an indefinite number of combinations of its elements. A kaleidoscope has the characteristic of creating something new simply by rearranging what already exists. A finite number of elements can thus produce an infinite number of different patterns. The totality is not the elements themselves, but the form that they take when combined. Like a kaleidoscope, the Arranger allows us to experience that the whole is more than the sum of its parts. While the Arranger is a reading tool and a distribution tool for a work published in digital format, it is also a tool for composing and structuring that work. As a result, it extends the field of critical editing to fragmentary textual content.[36]

---

34 Villenave 1834, 583. Italics and small caps are in the source text.
35 Flaubert 2012. Ms g226 (2), folio 17. See https://www.dossiers-flaubert.fr/cote-g226_ 2_f_017__r____-trn [accessed on 08/08/2023].
36 See Dord-Crouslé/Morlock-Gerstenkorn 2011, 169–183.

By making it possible to create as many second volumes of *Bouvard et Pécuchet* as desired, the Arranger allows all conceivable hypotheses to be tested, while considering each work a conjecture, with none taking precedence over the others, even if some necessarily have more verisimilitude and relevance than others. These reconstructions make sense both through the particular arrangement that each provides and through the co-presence of all the arrangements that they generate. An illustration of this principle can be found in an article where we proposed an experimentation of the digital tool on a small but very interesting part of the "second volume", the one that was to appear in the category entitled "Agricultural style". The different reconstructions proposed and allowed by the Arranger are presented.[37]

The editorial undertaking carried out in the framework of the Bouvard project is at the origin of a perennial and valuable destabilization of the second volume of *Bouvard et Pécuchet*: it clearly demonstrates the unfinished status of this novel, whereas all the conjectural reconstitutions in print freeze a chimerical state of the text and, quite simply, wrongly constitute it as "a text". In contrast, the digital interface for arranging the citations places each reader at the center of the process by allowing him/her to engage in the logic that may have guided Flaubert. By appropriating the compositional process to a greater or lesser extent, the reader becomes aware of its complexities and plunges into the forever-interrupted making of this second volume. He/she is put in a context that allows first-hand experience of the strengths and weaknesses of editorial mechanisms; he/she can grasp the automatisms that pace the novel's development (the serialization of phenomena; a repetitive genetic pattern: reading notes / summary pages / pages prepared for the second volume; etc.), he/she even has the opportunity to discern the failures that lurk in the enterprise, the gaps through which the errors or even the bad faith of the novelist can be guessed at, and the bias these result in.

The Arranger computer tool thus allows a recomposition of the work as fundamentally a "non-work", which the reader can experiment with on the project website. By varying the potential second volumes, by reorganizing fixed resources, the reader experiences from the inside the plastic virtuality of the arrangements he/she produces. He/she puts the critical power of the novelist's project to the test, while appreciating the irreducible distance that separates him/her forever from the completion of the enterprise.

---

[37] See Dord-Crouslé 2019.

Bibliography

Barthes, Roland (1976), "Flaubert. La crise de la vérité", *Magazine littéraire* 108.
De Biasi, Pierre-Marc (1986), "Flaubert et la poétique du non-finito", in: Louis Hay (ed.), *Le manuscrit inachevé. Écriture, création, communication*, Textes et manuscrits, Paris, 45–73.
Dord-Crouslé, Stéphanie (2008 …), *Le Projet Bouvard & ses suites*, blog, https://flaubert.hypotheses.org [accessed on 12/08/2023].
Dord-Crouslé, Stéphanie (2012), "Notes de lecture et édition du second volume de *Bouvard et Pécuchet*: configurations complexes de l'inachèvement", *Flaubert. Revue critique et génétique* 7, https://journals.openedition.org/flaubert/1808 [accessed on 12/08/2023].
Dord-Crouslé, Stéphanie (2014), "La 'BP-sphère'. Inventaire raisonné des pièces du dossier de genèse de *Bouvard et Pécuchet*", in: Anne Herschberg Pierrot/Jacques Neefs (eds.), *Bouvard et Pécuchet: archives et interprétation*, Nantes, 25–46.
Dord-Crouslé, Stéphanie (2016), "Les seconds volumes possibles de *Bouvard et Pécuchet*: l'avènement d'un lecteur auteur?", in: Dominique Pety (ed.), *Patrimoine littéraire en ligne: la renaissance du lecteur?*, Corpus, Chambéry, 115–137.
Dord-Crouslé, Stéphanie (2019), "Le sottisier agricole de *Bouvard et Pécuchet*", *Revue Flaubert* 18, https://shs.hal.science/halshs-02275613 [accessed on 12/08/2023].
Dord-Crouslé, Stéphanie / Dury, Christian (2016), "Les dossiers de *Bouvard et Pécuchet*", online video slideshow, https://25images.msh-lse.fr/portails/bouvard-pecuchet [accessed on 12/08/2023].
Dord-Crouslé, Stéphanie/Morlock-Gerstenkorn, Emmanuelle (2011), "Sur le modèle du kaléidoscope: concevoir l'édition électronique du second volume de *Bouvard et Pécuchet*", *Nouveaux Cahiers François Mauriac* 19, 169–183.
Dord-Crouslé, Stéphanie/Morlock-Gerstenkorn, Emmanuelle/Tournoy, Raphaël (2011), "Nouveaux objets éditoriaux. Le site d'édition des dossiers documentaires de *Bouvard et Pécuchet* (Flaubert)", *Les Cahiers du Numérique* 3–4, 123–145.
Faguet, Émile (1899), *Flaubert*, Hachette, Les grands écrivains français, Paris.
Flaubert, Gustave/Maupassant, Guy de (1993), *Correspondance*, édition d'Yvan Leclerc, Paris.
Flaubert, Gustave (2011), *Bouvard et Pécuchet, avec des fragments du "second volume" dont le Dictionnaire des idées reçues*, édition de Stéphanie Dord-Crouslé, GF, Paris.
Flaubert, Gustave (2012-…), *Les dossiers documentaires de Bouvard et Pécuchet*, Édition intégrale balisée en XML-TEI des documents conservés à la bibliothèque municipale de Rouen, accompagnée d'un outil de production de "seconds volumes" possibles, sous la dir. de Stéphanie Dord-Crouslé, https://www.dossiers-flaubert.fr [accessed on 12/08/2023].
Flaubert, Gustave (2013), *Édition électronique du manuscrit intégral de Bouvard et Pécuchet, premier volume*, Centre Flaubert, université de Rouen Normandie, https://flaubert-v1.univ-rouen.fr/bouvard_et_pecuchet/ [accessed on 12/08/2023].
Flaubert, Gustave (2017), *Édition électronique de la correspondance de Flaubert*, par Yvan Leclerc et Danielle Girard, université de Rouen Normandie, https://flaubert-v1.univ-rouen.fr/correspondance/edition/index.php [accessed on 12/08/2023].
Foucault, Michel (1983), "La bibliothèque fantastique", in: *Travail de Flaubert*, Paris.
Gothot-Mersch, Claudine (1981), "Le roman interminable: un aspect de la structure de *Bouvard et Pécuchet*", in: *Nouvelles recherches sur "Bouvard et Pécuchet"*, Paris, 9–22.

Mouchard, Claude/Neefs, Jacques (1980), "Vers le second volume", in: *Flaubert à l'œuvre*, Textes et manuscrits, Paris, 171–217.
Thibaudet, Albert (1935), *Gustave Flaubert*, Paris.
Villenave (1834), "Autroche (Claude de Loynes d')", in: *Biographie universelle*, Paris, Michaud, supplément 56, 582–584.

List of Contributors

Francesca Cadel teaches Italian and Film Studies at the University of Calgary, in Canada, after teaching in the U.S. She has a PhD in Comparative Literature from the CUNY Graduate Center, and a doctorat in Italian from the University of Sorbonne-Paris IV. She has published *La langue de la poésie. Langue et dialecte chez Pier Paolo Pasolini (1922–1975) et Andrea Zanzotto* (Presses Universitaires du Septentrion 2001), *La lingua dei desideri. Il dialetto secondo Pier Paolo Pasolini* (with Davide Rondoni) (Manni 2002), *Poeti con nome di donna* (Rizzoli-BUR 2008), articles on Pasolini, Zanzotto, Pound, Morante, interviews (with Andrea Zanzotto, Pina Kalc, Nico Naldini, Antonio Negri among others) and translations: Franco Berardi Bifo, *The Soul at Work* (MIT 2009) (from Italian into English), Clemente Martini, *Il commediante* (Mimesis 2020) (from English into Italian). With Paola Nastri she edited Carlo Collodi's masterpiece, *Pinocchio. Storia di un burattino* (Farinelli 2013). Her current book project is entitled *Dai Quaranta ai Settanta. Un percorso di "Scorciatoie": da Umberto Saba al "Moro" di Pietro Di Donato* (Mimesis *forthcoming*).

Stéphanie Dord-Crouslé is a researcher at the Centre national de la recherche scientifique (CNRS) within the Institut d'histoire des représentations et des idées dans les modernités (Lyon, UMR 5317). A Flaubert specialist, she analyzes the genesis of this writer's novels and is working on their publication in print and digital formats. She has contributed to the new edition of his *Complete Works* in the Bibliothèque de la Pléiade and she is coordinating the digital edition of Flaubert's documentary files for *Bouvard et Pécuchet* (https://www.dossiers-flaubert.fr).

Jacqueline Fabre-Serris is Professor of Latin Literature at the University of Lille. She is the author of *Mythe et Poésie dans les Métamorphoses d'Ovide* (1995), *Mythologie et littérature à Rome* (1998), *Rome, l'Arcadie et la mer des Argonautes. Essai sur la naissance d'une mythologie des origines en Occident* (2008), and co-editor of *Women and War in Antiquity* (2015), *Lire les mythes: Formes, usages et visées des pratiques mythographiques de l'Antiquité à la Renaissance* (2016), and *Identities, Ethnicities and Gender in Antiquity* (2021). She has published many articles on Augustan poetry, mythology and mythography, and gender studies. She is co-director of the electronic reviews *Dictynna*, *Eugesta*, and *Polymnia*, and of the series *Mythographes* (Presses du Septentrion). She is currently writing a book on Sulpicia and Ovid.

Marco Formisano is Professor of Latin literature at Ghent University. He has published extensively on late antique literature, early Christian martyr acts, Greek and Latin technical and scientific texts, Ovid's *Metamorphoses* and its reception. He is the editor of the series "*sera tela*. Studies in Late Antique Literature and its Reception" (Bloomsbury, London) and of "The Library of the Other Antiquity" (Winter, Heidelberg). Currently he is the principal investigator of the research project "Coming After. Late Antique Ecopoetics", funded by FWO (Research Foundation, Flanders), and the creator of "Titubanti Testi. Binomio di lettura", a series of online meetings aiming at putting classicists and non-classicists in dialogue around ancient Greek and Latin texts.

Stavros Frangoulidis is Professor of Latin at the Aristotle University of Thessaloniki. He is the author of articles and book chapters on Roman comedy, Senecan tragedy and the Latin novel. He is co-editor of several volumes on Greek and Latin prose and poetry for the series *Ancient Narrative* and *Trends in Classics*. His monographs include: *Handlung und Nebenhandlung: Theater, Metatheater und Gattungsbewusstein in der römischen Komödie* (1997); *Roles and Performances in Apuleius' Metamorphoses* (2001); and *Witches, Isis and Narrative: Approaches to Magic in Apuleius' Metamorphoses* (2008).

Myrto Garani is Associate Professor of Latin Literature at the National and Kapodistrian University of Athens, Greece. She is the author of *Empedocles Redivivus: Poetry and Analogy in Lucretius* (2007), co-editor with D. Konstan of *The Philosophizing Muse: The Influence of Greek Philosophy on Roman Poetry* (2014), co-editor with A.N. Michalopoulos and S. Papaioannou of *Intertextuality in Seneca's Philosophical Writings* (2020) and co-editor with D. Konstan and G. Reydams-Schils of the *Oxford Handbook of Roman Philosophy* (2023). She is currently working on a monograph on Seneca's *Naturales quaestiones* Book 3 (for the Pierides series) and a commentary on Lucretius's *De rerum natura* 6 (for the Fondazione Lorenzo Valla series).

Philip Hardie is a Fellow of Trinity College, Cambridge, and Emeritus Honorary Professor of Latin in the University of Cambridge. His most recent book is *Celestial Aspirations: Classical Impulses in British Poetry and Art* (Princeton and Oxford 2022).

Richard Hunter is Regius Professor of Greek Emeritus at the University of Cambridge and a Fellow of Trinity College, Cambridge. His most recent books are *The Measure of Homer* (2018), (with R. Laemmle) *Euripides, Cyclops* (2020), *The Layers of the Text. Collected Papers on Classical Literature 2008–2021* (2021) and *Greek Epitaphic Poetry. A Selection* (2022).

Laura Jansen is Associate Professor (Reader) in Classics and Comparative Literature at the University of Bristol. She is the author of *Borges' Classics: Global Encounters with the Graeco-Roman World* (CUP 2018), editor of *Susan Sontag's Tangential Classics* (OUP 2024), *Anne Carson's Euripides* (UCP 2023), *Anne Carson/Antiquity* (Bloomsbury 2021), and *The Roman Paratext: Frame, Texts, Readers* (CUP 2014). She is General Editor of the monograph series *Classical Receptions in Twentieth-Century Writing* (Bloomsbury). Forthcoming is her monograph on *Indisciplinary Classics: Anne Carson's Writings on Antiquity* (CUP).

David Konstan is Professor of Classics at New York University. He has written on classical comedy and the novel, as well as on the emotions and value concepts of ancient Greece and Rome. Among his publications are books on friendship, pity, forgiveness, beauty, and love. He has translated several ancient Greek commentaries on Aristotle, as well as Seneca's two tragedies about Hercules. His most recent book is *The Origin of Sin: Greece and Rome, Early Judaism and Christianity*. He is a past President of the American Philological Association (now the Society for Classical Studies) and is a fellow of the American Academy of Arts and Sciences and Honorary Fellow of the Australian Academy of the Humanities.

Rosa Rita Marchese is Associate Professor of Latin Literature ("Lingua e letteratura Latina") at the University of Palermo. Her interests focus on the intersection of literature and culture at Rome, including research themes such as ethical models, gift and reciprocity, identity and change, love and honour, competition and respect, growth and development, and most recently vulnerability. Among her books are *La morale e il singolo. Individualismo, modelli etici e poesia romana* (Palumbo 1998), *Figli benefattori, figli straordinari. Rappresentazioni senecane dell'"essere figlio'* (Palumbo 2005), Mutat terra vices. *Identità, cambiamento e memoria culturale nell'ultimo Orazio* (Palumbo 2010), *Morir d'amore. Il nesso Amore/Morte nella poesia di Properzio* (Palumbo 2012), *Uno sguardo che vede. L'idea di rispetto in Cicerone e in Seneca* (Palumbo 2016). She is author of "Cicerone, *Bruto*. Introduzione, traduzione e commento" (Carocci 2011), and co-author (with Giusto Picone) of "Cicerone, *De officiis*. Quel che è giusto fare" (Einaudi 2019^2). She is also co-editor of the book series "GenerAzioni. Letteratura e altri saperi", Palermo University Press.

John F. Miller is Arthur F. and Marian W. Stocker Professor of Classics at the University of Virginia. He works chiefly in Latin poetry, its religious backgrounds, and Renaissance receptions. His many publications include *Apollo, Augustus, and the Poets*, and *Ovid's Elegiac Festivals: Studies in the Fasti*.

Bettina Reitz-Joosse is Associate Professor of Latin Language and Literature at the University of Groningen in the Netherlands. Her research focuses on Latin literature of the late republic and early empire, specifically on textual representations of architecture and landscape. She is the author of *Building in Words: The Process of Construction in Latin Literature* (OUP 2021) and co-editor of *Landscapes of War in Greek and Roman Literature* (Bloomsbury 2021). She also works on political uses of the Latin language in the 20th and 21st century; together with Han Lamers she is the author of *The Codex fori Mussolini: A Latin Text of Italian Fascism* (Bloomsbury 2016) and the editor of a digital collection of Fascist Latin texts.

Paolo Felice Sacchi received his PhD from Ghent University in 2020 with a thesis on Late Latin epitomes. His research interests include late Latin poetry, literary theory and comparative literature. He co-edited with Marco Formisano *Epitomic Writing in Late Antiquity and Beyond. Forms of Unabridged Writing* (Bloomsbury 2023).

Giulia Sissa is Distinguished Professor in the Departments of Political Science, Classics and Comparative Literature at UCLA. While anchoring her research to the societies and cultures of the Greek and Roman world, Giulia connects the study of the past to moments of reception, modern recontextualizations and significant resonances in the contemporary world. Her publications include *Greek Virginity* (Harvard UP, 1900); *The Daily Life of the Greek Gods*, with M. Detienne, (Stanford UP, 2000); *Le Plaisir et le Mal. Philosophie de la drogue* (Paris, Odile Jacob, 1997); *L'âme est un corps de femme* (Paris, Odile Jacob, 2000); *Sex and Sensuality in the Ancient World* (Yale UP, 2008); *Utopia 1516-2016: More's Eccentric Essay and Its Activist Aftermath*, co-edited with Han van Ruler (Amsterdam UP, 2017); *Jealousy: A Forbidden Passion* (Polity Press, 2017); *Le Pouvoir des femmes. Un défi pour la démocratie* (Paris, Odile Jacob, 2021); *A Cultural History of Ideas in Classical Antiquity*, co-edited with Clifford Ando (Bloomsbury, 2023); *Ovid and the Environmental Imagination*, co-edited with Francesca Martelli (Bloomsbury, 2023).

Evina Sistakou is Professor of Greek Literature at the Aristotle University of Thessaloniki. She is the author of *The Geography of Callimachus and Hellenistic Avant-Garde Poetry* (Athens 2005, in Modern Greek), *Reconstructing the Epic. Cross-Readings of the Trojan Myth in Hellen-*

istic Poetry (Leuven 2008), *The Aesthetics of Darkness. A Study of Hellenistic Romanticism in Apollonius, Lycophron and Nicander* (Leuven 2012) and *Tragic Failures. Alexandrian Responses to Tragedy and the Tragic* (Berlin/Boston 2016). She has published articles on Apollonius, Callimachus, Lycophron, Euphorion, Greek epigram and Hellenistic aesthetics.

Sylvie Thorel is Emerita Professor of French Literature at the University of Lille. Her work focuses primarily on issues of representation and prose in the 19th and 20th centuries. She recently published *Le Thyrse de la prose. La fiction d'après Poe, Baudelaire et Mallarmé* (Champion 2022) and *Duras et les fantômes d'Anne-Marie Stretter* (Presses universitaires de Rennes 2023).

Fabio Tutrone is Assistant Professor of Classical Philology at the University of Palermo. He has held visiting positions in the United States, Switzerland, and Germany. His research focuses on the history of Latin literature, science, and philosophy, with special regard to Lucretius, Seneca, and the Roman reception of Greek thought. His publications include *Filosofi e animali in Roma antica: Modelli di animalità e umanità in Lucrezio e Seneca* (Pisa, ETS 2012), and *Healing Grief: A Commentary on Seneca's* Consolatio ad Marciam (Berlin/Boston, De Gruyter 'Cicero' Series, 2023).

Craig Williams is Professor of Classics at the University of Illinois Urbana-Champaign. His books include *Roman Homosexuality* (Oxford University Press 1999, rev. ed. 2010), a commentary on Book 2 of Martial's epigrams (Oxford University Press 2004), and *Reading Roman Friendship* (Cambridge University Press 2012). He is currently writing a book on Native American writers' receptions of Greco-Roman antiquity.

Andrew Zissos is Professor of Classics and Director of the Global Cultures program at the University of California, Irvine. He has published widely on Roman epic of the early imperial period, including a commentary on the first book of Valerius Flaccus' *Argonautica* (Oxford, 2008) and numerous articles on the same poem.

General Index

absence
- generative 396, 398
- Hellenic 152–154

Achilles 128–142
adaptability, thematic 192, 199, 205–206
allegory/allegoresis 231, 233–237
America 319, 326, 327, 328, 329, 330, 331, 332, 334
analogy/analogical (image)/analogically 41, 46, 49–51
analysis, structural 297, 306
ancient 319, 320, 321, 322, 325, 326, 329, 330, 331, 333, 334
anthology 410
Ara Pacis 119–120, 124–125
Argo 357, 368–373
Argonauts 353, 355, 364–365, 368–373, 375–381
argumentation, recursive 192–193, 195–196, 205
Aristarchus 89–113
aristocracy 384, 393
Aristonicus 99
Aristophanes of Byzantium 89–113
Aristotle 95–99
arrangement
- of fragments/episodes 22, 27, 29–30, 32, 34, 35, 37
arrhythmia 231–233, 238
Augustus 115–116, 119–123

Barthes, Roland 23, 38
Bensalem 318, 320, 321, 324, 327, 330, 332, 334, 335, 336
biographism 191–193, 199
bladder, image of 51–52, 54
body, fragmented 34, 37

calendar 115–125
Callimachus
- *Aetia* 25–31
- *Hecale* 32–38
Calvino, exactitude 173
causation, divine 54

cave 319, 320, 322, 323, 334, 335, 336
Chariton
- *Callirhoe* 104–105, 266
choice, epistemological 168, 170–171
Choniates, Michael 21–22
cinaedus 71–80
civil war
- as mythic theme 357, 379
- state of 337, 344–347
classification 413
closure
- and open-endedness 115–125
- false 363
- coinciding with death 366–368
- coinciding with *nostos* 364–365
- negotiations of 276–281
- provisional 131–137
- redefinitions of 275–286
- within mythic cycle 363–364
colonial 320, 325, 331, 338
community, interpretive 31, 38
compiler(s) 289–294, 296, 305–306
conclusion 408, 410–412
conflicting plotlines/narratives
- Oedipus and Antigone 276–280
- Oedipus and Jocasta 282–286
- Oedipus and the Nuntius 280–281
crimes, political 338–341
Cul-de-sac (film) 263 n. 5

De officiis
- editorial question 165–166
Demetrius of Phaleron 102
Demodocus 103, 105–106, 107–110
didacticism 190–192, 195–199, 201–203, 206
Dionysius of Halicarnassus 99
doxography/doxographical 44, 47

ecphrasis 359
encyclopedia 405–406, 409
epic
- Roman 128–142
Epicureanism 192–200, 202–206

Epigonoi 276, 286
Euripides
– *Iphigenia in Aulis* 262–270
Eustathius 92, 93, 94, 95 n. 26, 96, 97 n. 3, 98, 102–103, 106
excursus, theological
– in Lucretius 54–55
– in Theophrastus 45, 53
experiment 319, 320, 324, 335, 336

first person 220–222
Flora 120–121
foreshadowing 356, 358–359, 373–379
forgery 386, 387, 389–391, 396–397
formula 168, 180–181, 183, 184
fragment(s)
– modern 211–214
– textual 413–415
fragmentariness/fragmentary style 31, 38–39, 246–248
Freytag, Gustav
– *Die Fabier* 398–399
– *Die verlorene Handschrift* 383–403
– *Soll und Haben* 385
Fulgentius
– Latin writer of late antiquity 225–238
– *De aetatibus mundi et hominis* 225–233, 238
Fulvius Nobilior 117

gender 219–222
geography 369–373
Gorgias
– *Palamedes* 96

Hercules
– Labors of 378–379
Hercules Musarum
– temple of 116–117
historiography 225–233
Hollis, Adrian 32–33, 35–36
Homer
– *Odyssey* 89–113
– papyri of 100–101
Hyginus 289–306
Hypsipyle 359

imperfect (readers/reading) 159–160
imperfection, aesthetic 191, 195, 198
incompleteness
– aesthetic 406, 410–411
– structural 406–410
– textual 406–407, 411–412
incompletion 406, 408–409, 411–412, 415–416
intention
– authorial 23, 27, 36
– editorial 24, 32
interpolation 261, 269
intertextuality
– across mythic traditions 359–361, 362–363, 365 n. 39, 367–368, 369, 376, 380
– between ancients and moderns 327, 328, 333, 336
– within a mythic tradition 356–359, 372–373
Isaac Porphyrogenitus
– *Praefatio in Homerum* 103
Italy
– post-fascist 342–343
– post-war history 331, 335, 337–339, 341–344
iter/journey 243–248

Janus 121
Jason 353, 357, 358–359, 364–365, 367, 372, 374–378
jigsaw puzzle 27–28

lacuna(e) 63–71, 73–76, 79–80, 387–392, 401
landscape 251–256
linearity 35–37
lipogram 225–226
Longinus
– *On the Sublime* 90–91, 97
Lucian 101

Mars 116, 118–119
masculinity 62–63, 66–80
Medea 353, 358, 359, 365 n. 39, 367, 368–369, 374–378

memory
- and forgetfulness 152–154
- and loss 151, 153
Menander
- *Perikeiromene* 265–266
Metarsiologica (Μεταρσιολογικά) 41, 43, 45, 47, 49, 55
meteorology/meteorological 41–46, 49, 51, 54–55
mobility 414
mockery, salvific 347
modern 319, 328, 330, 332, 334, 336
mora 140–142
Morisot, Claude-Barthélemy 116
myth
- late antique interpretation of 233–237
- Theban 297–298, 302–303, 304 n. 43, 305–306
mythographer(s) 289–296, 305–306

narration
- elegiac 25–26, 28–30
- epic 35, 37
navigation/sailing 373
neocapitalism 331, 339
networks 144–146
new 321, 322, 327, 328, 329, 330, 331, 333, 335, 336
non-finito 189–191, 411–412
nostos/homecoming/return 241–250, 355, 364–365
not-perfected 319, 320, 334, 336
novel
- in hollow 218–223
- posthumous 408–409, 415
- unfinishable 406, 409–413
- unfinished 406–409, 412–414, 416

Odysseus 89–113
old 318, 320, 321, 322, 328, 329
open-ended 320, 321, 332
opposition, political 394–395
Ovid
- the poet 115–125
- exile 115–117, 123–124

paratext 27–28, 35, 214–218
Pasolini, Pier Paolo
- *Petrolio* 331–333, 335–336, 347–348
Pelias 364–365
Penelope 89–113
perfectible 319, 320, 334, 336
perfection 405, 412
Petronius
- *Satyricon* 332
Pfeiffer, Rudolf 22, 25–29, 32–33, 35–36
pietas 277, 280, 281, 282, 283, 284
Plato
- *Critias* 319, 324, 325, 330, 331, 333
- *Phaedrus* 96
Timaeus 324, 325, 328, 330, 331, 332
poet(s) 289–296, 299 n. 36, 305–307
poetry book 22
prester (πρηστήρ) 47–48
proem, medial 362–363
progress 320, 333, 336
Prometheus 378–379
prophecy 275, 276, 279 n. 12, 280, 281, 286

reader response 23–25, 27–31, 36–39
reconstitution, conjectural 414, 416
regifugium 118, 124
relativity, cultural 190–192
repetition 194–198, 206
ring-composition 137–140
Roman culture/ideology 294, 301, 307
ruins 251–252
Rutilius Namatianus 241–256

sexuality 62–63, 66–80
silence 383–403
Statius 128–142
strategia della tensione (strategy of tension) 343–344
summary/-ies 294, 296–297, 306
supplementum/continuation 355, 361, 379

Tacitus 383–403
technology/technological advance 373
teleological (ideas, principle) 53
teleology 238

temporality 228–233, 238
tense, present 220–222
testament 406–407
Theophrastus 41–55
Thrasyllus 396–398
Tiberius 384, 392–394, 396–397
tool, digital 414–416
tradition 291, 295–296, 306
transcendence 212–213
translation(s)
– modern 73–78
– fragmentary Syriac-Arabic 41, 44, 46, 48
– mistranslation 46
transmission
– of Callimachus' *Aitia* and *Hecale* 22–23, 25–27
– of Tacitus' *Annals* 383–384, 389, 395, 396–398
Tubilustria 124–125
tyrant(s)/tyranny 365, 394, 398

uchronie 263
unknown, the 143, 147, 152

vates 279, 280–281
Vesta 120–121, 123
Virgil 107–110

water 254–255

Index of Passages

The list of passages includes both ancient and modern sources (e.g. Euripides, Flaubert). Fragmentary texts are cited by the number and name of modern editor only. The relevant editions of both sources and fragmentary texts are to be found in the bibliography accompanying each article. Abbreviations for ancient works are as per *OCD*.

Anaxagoras (DK 59)
A68 (D60 Laks & Most =
Aristotle *Ph*. 4.6.213a22–27)   52

Apollonius of Rhodes
Argon.
2.421–422   372–373
4.253–255   372
4.421–434   359
4.557–561   376–377
4.1184–1185   109
4.1778–1781   364–365
4.1781   100

Archelaus (DK 60)
A16 (D16 Laks & Most = Aëtius 3.3.5)   50

Aristaenetus
Ep.
1.12.24–26 Mazal   106–107

Aristides Quintilianus
Mus.
2.9   105–106, 109

Aristophanes
Nub.
398–402   53–54
403–407   51–52

Aristotle
Mete.
1.1.338a26   42
1.1.338b20–22   43
3.1.371a15–18   47
Ph.
4.6.213a22–27 (=Anaxagoras D60 Laks &
Most < DK59 A68)   52

Poet.
8.1451a15–29   95
15.1454a31–32   263
17.1455b16–23   97–98
Rh.
3.1415a21–3   99
3.1417a13–14   94 n. 20

Augustine
Genes. Manich.
1.23   227

Aulus Gellius
3.5   76

Barthes, Roland
"Flaubert. La crise de la vérité"   410

Callimachus
Aet.
fr. 1.3–6 Pf./H.   30–31
fr. 54–60j H.   25
fr. 75 Pf./H.   25
fr. 110–110f Pf./H.   26
fr. 112.9 Pf./H.   22
Hec.
fr. 12–15 H.   36
fr. 230–231 Pf. = 1–2 H.   35
fr. 232 Pf. = 3–7 H.   36

Chariton
Call.
5.8.4   266
8.1.17   104–105, 106

Cicero
Att.
2.21.4   176 n. 32

Brut.
71	176 n. 32

Fam.
1.9.15	176 n. 32
16.17.1	54 n. 31

Fin.
3.22	170

Off.
1.2	166 n. 3, 167
1.4	170
1.7	168
1.8	169
1.20–22	181, 182 n. 42
1.30	181 n. 41
1.46	170
1.93	171
1.94	172 n. 24
1.95–96	172
3.7–8	173–174
3.9–10	175
3.11	178
3.13	178
3.14–15	178
3.16	179 n. 36
3.18	180
3.19	180
3.20	181
3.21	181
3.27	182
3.28	181 n. 40
3.33–34	182–183
3.34	173 n. 27

Orat.
73	176 n. 32

CIL 4.2319b with add p. 216	76

Diogenes of Oenoanda
fr. 2.5.14 Smith	192 n. 10
fr. 72.3.13 Smith	192 n. 10
fr. 116.6–8 Smith	192 n. 10

Dionysius of Halicarnassus
Pomp.
3.3	99

Epicurus
Ep. Hdt.
36	194 n. 16
83	197 n. 26

Ep. Men.
124	193 n. 14
135	194 n. 15

Ep. Pyth.
84–85	194 n. 18
104	48

Euripides
IA
49–70	264–265
71–77	266
337–348	267
1241–1252	268–269
1378–1401	267–268

Flaubert, Gustave
Bouvard et Pécuchet (drafts and documentary material)   410–411, 414–415
Correspondance   405–408, 411

Foucault, Michel
"La bibliothèque fantastique"   411

Fulgentius
Aet. Mund.
Praef. 131.14–20	226
Praef. 132.13–28	228
1.133.1	229
2.134.16–17	229
2.134.18–19	229
3.138.10	229
5.144.6	229
6.146.25–28	230
6.147.8–10	230
6.150.2	230
7.150.15–16	229
10.163.20	231
12.170.9–12	231
13.172.19–22	232
14.179.10–11	233

Myth.
15.21–17.8	237 n. 26
48.9–49.2	234

'Heraclitus'
Quaest. Hom.
1.7   99–100

Hieronymus/Jerome
Chron.
1923 = Ol. 171.3 = 94 BC   191 n. 6
Comm. Zach.
3.14.1–2   386 n. 8

Homer
Il.
24.804   101
Od.
2.174–176   97 n. 31
8.266–366   105–106, 107–110
9.391–393   50
13.87–92   94, 95
23.248–250   89
23.266–270   89
23.290–294   110
23.296   89–113
23.302–305   94
23.306–307   94, 95, 96
23.310–343   93, 94–95, 96
24.1–204   93
24.196–198   102–103
24.413–416   98, 108

Hyginus
Fab.
67   298–300, 302
68   299, 300, 302
69   300, 304
71   300
72   301–302
73   304
74   302, 305
75   303
186   293–294

Livy
2.49–50   398

Longinus
Subl.
9.11–15   89–90, 98 n. 33

Lucilius
fr. 291 Marx   51 n. 25
fr. 1058 Marx   76

Lucretius
1.62–71   203 n. 45
1.62–83   196
1.102–106   202
1.112–135   195
1.136–145   195
1.146–148 = 2.59–61 = 3.91–93 = 6.39–41
                               196
1.398–409   201 n. 37
1.921–925   198
1.926–950 = 4.1–25   198
1.950   198
2.37–54   197
2.55–58 = 3.87–90 = 6.35–38   197
2.174–183   204
2.177–181   198 n. 28, 206 n. 51
2.581–585   194
3.32–86   197
5.55–234   204 n. 47
5.155   192, 199
5.195–199   198 n. 28, 206
5.925–1160   205 n. 49
5.1161–1168   205
5.1161–1240   203
5.1168   205
6.1–34   196
6.24–25   196
6.68–79   203 n. 44
6.121–131   52 n. 27
6.145–149   50–51
6.387–422   54
6.423–435   47–49
6.424   48
6.426–427   48
6.527–534   201 n. 37

Martial
7.67   80

Maupassant, Gustave de
Correspondance   408

Menander
Pk.
486–491	265–266

Ovid
Fast.
1.1–2	122
1.13–14	119
1.317–318	124
1.709–724	119–120, 125
1.721–722	121
1.724–725	119, 122
2.685	124
2.685–852	118
2.857–864	118–119
3.57–58	116
3.199–200	116
3.849–850	124 n. 23
3.879–882	122
3.883–884	122–123
4.939–942	124 n. 22
4.943–954	120–121
5.147–148	116
5.721–734	122–125
6.797–812	116–117

Met.
12.542–548	140

Tr.
2.249–252	115–116, 123
2.550	115, 119

Parthenius
Amat. narr.
Praef. 1	296

Petronius
Sat.
7–8	67–73
9–10	62, 67–70
12–15	67–70
16–26	73–80
80	62
138	78

Philodemus
De elect.
11.7–20 Indelli/Tsouna-McKirahan	194 n. 16

De ira
col. 6.13–22 Indelli	204 n. 46

De lib. dic.
fr. 4.9 Olivieri	192 n. 10
fr. 34.5 Olivieri	192 n. 10
fr. 36.1–2 Olivieri	192 n. 10
fr. 40.8 Olivieri	192 n. 10
fr. 78.6–7 Olivieri	192 n. 10
col. 6b.10–11 Olivieri	192 n. 10

Hom.
col. 20.33–34 Dorandi	104

PHerc. 346 ("Trattato etico epicureo")
fr. 3 IVb.7 Capasso	192 n. 10
fr. 3 IV.24–28 Capasso	192 n. 10
fr. 3 VII.24 Capasso	192 n. 10
PHerc. 1676	198 n. 27

Plato
Phlb.
67b	200 n. 34

Pliny the Elder
HN
2.112	51 n. 25
26.96	60
28.119	60
35.92	177 n. 34
35.145	176, 191 n. 4

Plutarch
De tuend. san.
126A	76

Quaest. conv.
705E	76

Quaest. Graec.
292C	43

[Plutarch]
Hom.
1.7	97 n. 31
2.185	103

POxy 3010	63

Index of Passages

Quintilian
10.1.93–95	60

Rutilius Namatianus
Red.
1.1–4	246–247, 248
1.13–14	251
1.21–24	251
1.22	242
1.27–28	252
1.29–30	253
1.31–34	253
1.37–38	254
1.47–164	249
1.48	249
1.63	249
1.66	249
1.67–68	249
1.93–94	249
1.138	249
1.161–164	249
1.185–186	248
1.465–466	248
1.492	248
1.541–542	248
2.1–2	252

Sch. in Call. *Hymn*.
2.106	34–35

Sch. in Hom. *Od*.
23.296	89–113
23.310–343	94, 95

Sch. in Soph. *Aj*.
492	106

Seneca
Ep.
95.21	80

Oed.
321–322	299
709	304
711–712	304
725	304
731	304
748	304
750	304

Phoen.
77	277
105	278
231	279
232–233	279
242	279
269	279
278	279
299	280
334–339	280–281
354	281
513–514	284
537–538	284
548	284
553–555	284
664	285

QNat.
2.27	52 n. 25

Statius
Achil.
1.866–874	141
1.912–916	141
2.1–11	137–138
2.166–167	132–135

Silv.
4.7.21–24	139

Theb.
9.788–800	136–137
10.610	304
10.612	304
10.613–614	304
12.430–431	299

Strato
fr. 73 Wehrli	47 n. 16

Suetonius
Tib.
67.1	393 n. 28

Tacitus
Agr.
2	394

Ann.
1.5.1	386 n. 7
1.55–59	388
6.6.1	393
6.21	396–398
16.17–19	60

Hist.
1.3	395

Theophrastus
frs. (ed. Fortenbaugh/Huby/Sharples/Gutas):
159	43
186A	43 n. 4
186B	43 n. 4
187	43 n. 4
188	43 n. 4
689A	54–55 n. 31
689B	55 n. 31
690	55 n. 31
707	50 n. 23, 54 n. 31

Ign.
1.4–11	47 n. 17
1.8–9	47

Metars. (ed. Daiber)
1.9–11	49
2.6	46 n. 14
2.10–12	49
6.29–41	52
6.63–67	52
6.67–81	52–53
6.81	46
6.86–91	46
7.3	46
13.37–38	49
13.43–44	47
14.14–29	53
14.17	46
14.28–29	46

Vent.
53	47 n. 17

Valerius Flaccus
Argon.
1.730–851	357
3.340–342	359
4.154–176	379
5.217–221	362–363
5.457–458	374
7.210–406	358
8.185–191	369–370
8.270–272	375
8.463a–467	353–354

Virgil
Ecl.
1.38–39	254

Aen.
1.342	183 n. 46
4.165–174	107–110
7.37–40	363

www.ingramcontent.com/pod-product-compliance
Lightning Source LLC
Chambersburg PA
CBHW031749220426
43662CB00007B/330